FASCISM WITHOUT BORDERS

FASCISM WITHOUT BORDERS

Transnational Connections and Cooperation between
Movements and Regimes in Europe from 1918 to 1945

Edited by Arnd Bauerkämper and
Grzegorz Rossoliński-Liebe

berghahn
NEW YORK · OXFORD
www.berghahnbooks.com

Published in 2017 by
Berghahn Books
www.berghahnbooks.com

© 2017, 2019 Arnd Bauerkämper and Grzegorz Rossoliński-Liebe
First paperback edition published in 2019

Library of Congress Cataloging-in-Publication Data
Names: Bauerkèamper, Arnd, editor. | Rossolinski, Grzegorz, editor.
Title: Fascism without borders: transnational connections and cooperation
   between movements and regimes in Europe from 1918 to 1945 / edited by
   Arnd Bauerkèamper and Grzegorz Rossoliânski-Liebe.
Description: New York: Berghahn Books, 2017. | Includes bibliographical
   references and index.
Identifiers: LCCN 2016054892 (print) | LCCN 2017007755 (ebook) | ISBN
   9781785334689 (hardback : alk. paper) | ISBN 9781785334696 (ebook)
Subjects: LCSH: Fascism--Europe--History--20th century. | Europe--Politics
   and government--1918-1945.
Classification: LCC D726.5 .F3717 2017 (print) | LCC D726.5 (ebook) | DDC
   320.53/309409041--dc23
LC record available at https://lccn.loc.gov/2016054892

British Library Cataloguing in Publication Data
A catalogue record for this book is available from the British Library

ISBN 978-1-78533-468-9 hardback
ISBN 978-1-78920-058-4 paperback
ISBN 978-1-78533-469-6 ebook

ᴄᴴ Contents

List of Abbreviations   vii

Introduction   Fascism without Borders: Transnational Connections
and Cooperation between Movements and Regimes
in Europe, 1918–1945   1
Arnd Bauerkämper and Grzegorz Rossoliński-Liebe

Chapter 1   Transnational Fascism: The Fascist New Order,
Violence, and Creative Destruction   39
Artistotle Kallis

Chapter 2   Corporatist Connections: The Transnational Rise
of the Fascist Model in Interwar Europe   65
Matteo Pasetti

Chapter 3   Organizing Leisure: Extension of Propaganda
into New Realms by the Italian and British Fascist
Movements   94
Anna Lena Kocks

Chapter 4   "The Brotherhood of Youth": A Case Study
of the Ustaša and Hlinka Youth Connections
and Exchanges   119
Goran Miljan

Chapter 5   The Estado Novo and Portuguese–German Relations
in the Age of Fascism   142
Cláudia Ninhos

Chapter 6   Inter-Fascist Conflicts in East Central Europe: The
Nazis, the "Austrofascists," the Iron Guard, and the
Organization of Ukrainian Nationalists   168
Grzegorz Rossoliński-Liebe

Chapter 7   Fascist Poetry for Europe: Transnational Fascism
and the Case of Robert Brasillach   192
Marleen Rensen

Chapter 8   Native Fascists, Transnational Anti-Semites:
The International Activity of Legionary Leader
Ion I. Moța   216
Raul Cârstocea

Chapter 9   Italian Fascism from a Transnational Perspective:
The Debate on the New European Order
(1930–1945)   243
Monica Fioravanzo

Chapter 10   The Nazi "New Europe": Transnational Concepts
of a Fascist and Völkisch Order for the Continent   264
Johannes Dafinger

Chapter 11   Communist Antifascism and Transnational Fascism:
Comparisons, Transfers, Entanglements   288
Kasper Braskén

Chapter 12   Antifascism in Europe: Networks, Exchanges, and
Influences. The Case of Silvio Trentin in Toulouse
and in the Resistenza in Veneto (1926–1944)   312
Silvia Madotto

Chapter 13   German and Italian Democratic Socialists in Exile:
Interpretations of Fascism and Transnational
Aspects of Resistance in the Sopade and
Giustizia e Libertà   336
Francesco Di Palma

Afterword   Between Cooperation and Conflict: Perspectives of
Historical Research on Transnational Fascism   355
Arnd Bauerkämper

    Index   365

Abbreviations

AA	Auswärtiges Amt (German Ministry of Foreign Affairs)
AEV	Acção Escolar Vanguarda (School Action Vanguard)
AIZ	*Arbeiter-Illustrierte-Zeitung* (The Workers Pictorial Newspaper)
AO	Auslandsorganisation der NSDAP (Foreign Relations Organization of the NSDAP)
AR	Acţiunea Românească (Romanian Action)
BF	British Fascists
BUF	British Union of Fascists
CAUR	Comitati d'Azione per l'Universalità di Roma (Action Committees for the Universality of Rome)
CLNRV	Resistance Central Committee in Veneto (Comitato di liberazione nazionale regione veneto)
Comintern	Communist International
CP	Communist Party
CS or CSP	Christlichsoziale Partei (Christian Socialist Party)
DAAD	Deutscher Akademischer Austauschdienst (German Academic Exchange Service)
DAF	Deutsche Arbeitsfront (German Work Service)
DAP	Deutsche Arbeiterpartei (German Workers' Party)
DNSA	Deutsche Nationalsozialistische Arbeiterpartei (Austrian German Nationalist Workers' Party)
DPG	Deutsch–Portugiesische Gesellschaft (German–Portuguese Society)
EKNL	Egyesült Kereszteny Nemzeti Liga (United Christian National League)
ESV	Europäische Schriftsteller-Vereinigung (European Writers' Union)
FNAT	Fundação Nacional para a Alegria no Trabalho (National Foundation for Joy at Work)
FRN	Frontul Renaşterii Naţionale (Front of National Rebirth)
GIL	Gioventù Italiana del Littorio (National Youth Organization in Fascist Italy since 1937)
GL	Giustizia e Libertà (Justice and Freedom)
GUF	Gruppi Universitari Fascisti (Fascist University Groups)

HDN	Nezavisna Država Hrvatska (Independent State of Croatia)
HJ	Hitlerjugend (Hitler Youth)
HM	Hlinkova mládež (Hlinka Youth)
HSLS	Hlinkova slovenská l'udová strana (Hlinka's Slovak People's Party)
HSP	Hrvatska stranka prava (Croatian Party of Rights)
HSS	Hrvatska Seljačka Stranka (Croatian Peasant Party)
IAC	Instituto para a Alta Cultura (Institute for High Culture)
IAH	Internationale Arbeiterhilfe (International Workers' Relief)
ILO	International Labour Organization
ISK	Internationaler Sozialistischer Kampfbund (International Socialist Association)
JEN	Junta de Educação Nacional (National Education Board)
KdF	Kraft durch Freude (Strength through Joy)
KPD	Kommunistische Partei Deutschlands (German Communist Party)
LAF	Lietuvos aktyvistų frontas (Lithuanian Activist Front)
LANC	Liga Apărării Naţional-Creştine (League of National-Christian Defense)
LP	Legião Portuguesa (Portuguese Legion)
LSI	Labour and Socialist International
MNE	Ministério dos Negócios Estrangeiros (Portuguese Ministry of Foreign Affairs)
MOPR	Meschdunarodnaja organisazija pomoschtschi borzam rewoljuzii (International Red Aid)
MP	Mocidade Portuguesa (Portuguese Youth Organization)
NDH	Nezavisna Država Hrvatska (Independent State of Croatia)
NEO	New European Order
NSB	Nationaal Socialistische Beweging (National Socialist Movement)
NSDAP	Nationalsozialistische Deutsche Arbeiterpartei (National Socialist German Workers' Party)
NSV	Nationalsozialistische Volkswohlfahrt (National Socialist People's Welfare Organization)
ONB	Opera Nazionale Balilla (National Youth Organization in Fascist Italy)

ONC	Organización Nacional Corporativa (National Corporatist Organization)
OND	Opera Nazionale Dopolavoro (National After-Work Institution in Fascist Italy)
OUN	Orhanizatsia Ukraïns'kykh Natsionalistiv (Organization of Ukrainian Nationalists)
OVRA	Organizzazione di Vigilanza e Repressione dell'Antifascismo (Organization for Vigilance and the Repression of Anti-Fascism)
PAAA	Politisches Archiv des Auswärtigen Amtes (Archives of the German Foreign Office)
PCF	Parti Communiste Français (French Communist Party)
PCI	Partito comunista italiano (Italian Communist Party)
PN	Partidul Națiunii (Party of the Nation)
PNF	Partito Nazionale Fascista (Italian National Fascist Party)
PSI	Partito socialista italiano (Italian Socialist Party)
PVDE	Polícia de Vigilância e de Defesa do Estado (State Defence and Surveillance Police)
RAD	Reichsarbeitsdienst (State Labor Service)
RCP(B)	Russian Communist Party (Bolsheviks)
RGASPI	Russian State Archives of Social and Political History (Russian State Archive of Socio-Political History)
RSHA	Reichssicherheitshauptamt (Reich Security Main Office)
RSI	Repubblica Sociale Italiana (Italian Social Republic)
SAPMO	Stiftung Archiv der Parteien und Massenorganisationen der DDR (Foundation Archives of Parties and Mass Organisations of the GDR in the Federal Archives)
SD	Sicherheitsdienst (Security Service)
SOE	Special Operations Executive
Sopade	Sozialdemokratische Partei Deutschlands (Social Democratic Party of Germany in exile)
SPD	Sozialdemokratische Partei Deutschlands (German Social Democratic Party)
SPN	Secretariado de Propaganda Nacional (National Propaganda Secretariat)
SR	Slovenská republika (Slovak Republic)
UM	Ustaška mladež (Ustaša Youth)
UN	Uniao Nacional (National Union)
UNK	Ukraïns'kyi Natsional'nyi Komitet (Ukrainian National Committee)

UPA	Ukraïns'ka Povstans'ka Armiia (Ukrainian Insurgent Army)
USSR	Union of Soviet Socialist Republics
UTsK	Ukraïns'kyi Tsentral'nyi Komitet (Ukrainian Central Committee)
UVO	Ukraïns'ka Viis'kova Orhanizatsiia (Ukrainian Military Organization)
VNV	Vlaams Nationaal Verbond (Flemish National Union)

⳯ Introduction

FASCISM WITHOUT BORDERS
Transnational Connections and Cooperation between
Movements and Regimes in Europe, 1918–1945

Arnd Bauerkämper and Grzegorz Rossoliński-Liebe

Fascist movements and regimes have usually been conceived as and presented themselves as national political forces. In fact, contemporaries as well as scholars have highlighted hyper-nationalism as one of the most important features of fascism which separated fascist movements and regimes from each other. Not accidentally, all attempts to forge a "Fascist International" foundered between the two world wars. Many historians have therefore dismissed or failed to recognize cross-border cooperations between fascists. In fact, the hyper-nationalism of fascist movements and their social Darwinist doctrines, as well as the expansionist and racist policies of the Third Reich and Fascist Italy, have led most experts to argue that fascist internationalism or international fascism was merely a camouflage and a sham.[1] The interpretation that "international fascism is unthinkable, a contradiction in terms" has received broad support from most historians.[2] As a corollary, fascism has largely been investigated in the framework of national history.[3] Beyond volumes that have collected national case studies, few systematic comparative studies have been published.[4] In particular, cross-border interactions between fascist movements and regimes have largely been dismissed in historical scholarship.[5]

The considerable obstacles and barriers to transnational cooperation between fascists must not be ignored. Yet despite the failure of attempts to establish institutional cooperation, especially through the Comitati d'Azione per l'Universalità di Roma (CAUR) in the mid-1930s, the transnational communications, exchanges, interactions, and transfers between fascists merit serious analysis.[6] They offer new perspectives on the subject, as this volume demonstrates. Its chapters show that European fascism between 1918 and 1945 was a complex and heterogeneous phenomenon. Research has largely disregarded studies of various aspects of fascism such as small movements, youth organizations, thinkers, writers, and poets in eastern, southeastern, southern, and northern Europe. These publications have evidenced that fascism was both a national and transnational phenomenon, as it transcended national borders but was rooted in national communities. Although its centers were in Rome and Berlin, fascism in interwar Europe was clearly transnational. Its reduction to Italy and Germany simplifies or even distorts the history of fascism. Taking recent historiographical debates on comparison, transfers, and entanglements in modern history as a starting point, we will therefore trace and explain communications and interactions between European fascists. They occurred at specific points in the trajectory of fascist movements and regime. Studies of transnational perceptions and interactions therefore shed light on the dynamics of fascism that was a contingent and contested phenomenon. Moreover, they highlight selective borrowings, misunderstandings and wishful thinking as crucial dimensions of mutual perceptions, exchange and transfers.[7]

In conceptual terms, at least three dimensions of "transnational fascism" are to be distinguished. First, fascism was a transnational movement. It spread across borders, but specific national manifestations are conspicuous. Second, fascism was perceived as a transnational phenomenon, both by its adherents and its foes. Third, fascism can be analyzed from a transnational perspective. It includes comparative studies as well as investigations of transfers, exchanges, and even entanglements. Leaders as well as minor functionaries and members from different European states or movements met on innumerable occasions and different levels, not only to exchange views on ideological questions and policies, but also to communicate on political styles and representations. Not least, fascists of different nation-states repeatedly agreed on common initiatives. Thus, despite its undisputedly strong and inherent ultranationalism, fascism needs to be understood as a transnational political and social practice, inspired by a set of similar national convictions. Ideas were therefore interlinked with, rather than subordinated to, performative practices.[8]

Clearly, fascists entertained mutual relations and accentuated their bonds. After the "March on Rome" in late October 1922, by which Mussolini came to power, the Italian capital galvanized fascists throughout Europe. "Fascism" became both the name of the Italian Fascists and a political value or ideal to which many other similar movements felt closely related, even if they did not use the word "fascist" in their names (e.g., the German National Socialists, the

Croatian Ustaša, and the Organization of Ukrainian Nationalists). Italian Fascism seemed to demonstrate that the detested parliamentary rule and social conflict that were held responsible for all the problems in postwar Europe could be overcome. Although its influence declined in the late 1930s, Mussolini's Fascist regime continued to attract Europeans well into World War II. Even though he shared his generals' disappointment about the military failures of his Italian alliance partners who had suffered humiliating defeats in Greece and Africa as early as 1940–41, Adolf Hitler cherished Benito Mussolini as an ally and a friend as late as April 1945, when Nazi Germany lay in ruins.[9]

Transfers between fascists, their movements and regimes cannot be reduced to mere mimesis. Instead of a one-way emulation or opportunistic takeover, fascists selectively appropriated foreign elements, molding them into their particular (national) contexts. Rejecting democracy, liberalism, communism, and socialism as well as the politics of compromise and negotiation, fascist parties and groups undoubtedly shared a common point of departure. Interchange and communication between fascists in Europe not only related to overtly political issues such as propaganda, labor relations, violence, and mutual assistance in war, but also to the seemingly non-political fields of cultural and aesthetic representations. Many fascists were aware of their affinity, as reflected in fascist political staging, especially its symbolism and rituals. For instance, they not only wore uniforms in order to impress and intimidate their opponents in domestic politics but also to demonstrate their claim to represent a transnational movement of warriors united by the hostility to common enemies, including the communists, democrats, conservatives, and liberals. The Soviet Union, in particular, was as strongly repulsed and despised as the Jews. Several fascist movements equated the latter with communists, as the belief in a "Judeo-Bolshevik" conspiracy demonstrates. Moreover, fascists shared a commitment to action (instead of discussion).[10]

Interwar Europe was home not only to fascist movements and regimes but also to various authoritarian dictatorships. The latter were transnational, too, and they sometimes borrowed from fascism or fascistized themselves when it promised political gains. In the long term, however, dictatorships such as Francisco Franco's Spain and Antonio de Oliveira Salazar's Portugal were not fascist, but authoritarian in the first instance. They lacked the idea of a permanent and national revolution, which propelled fascist movements and regimes, and they clung to the past or the present. Horthy's regime in Hungary, Antanas Smetona's rule in Lithuania, and Józef Piłsudski's regime in Poland, were also primarily authoritarian. Some of them even fought fascists in their states. Unlike fascist movements and regimes, not all authoritarian dictatorships placed racism and ultranationalism center stage in their programs. Piłsudski was even an adherent of socialism. The Communist International (Comintern) labelled him "fascist," because he betrayed communism in their eyes.[11]

Mutual perceptions, relations, and exchange among fascist movements and regimes were unequal. In the 1920s, Mussolini's regime galvanized Europeans across national and political boundaries. In fact, the Fascist dictatorship continued to attract attention in the early 1930s, as demonstrated by the visits of European fascists who came to Italy in order to see the Exposition of the Fascist Revolution opened, exactly ten years after the "March on Rome". For instance, twelve young French fascists bicycled from Paris to Rome in order to inspect what was claimed to be the radiating center of European fascism. As Hitler's National Socialists rose in the early 1930s, Italy's Fascists were increasingly confronted with a mighty and increasingly superior rival. They responded to the new threat by temporarily vying for French support, not least by highlighting the common heritage of Latin culture (*latinité*). The Fascist leaders also supported the Austrian sovereignty that was threatened by the German and Austrian National Socialists. Yet Italy's attack of Abyssinia deprived Mussolini (*Il Duce*, the leader) of this option to counter Hitler's growing influence after his seizure of power. In World War II, the Duce had to adjust to an inferior position, although the remaining Italian Fascists emphasized Italy's leading role as a cultural power. In 1944–45, Mussolini finally became Hitler's lackey. Smaller fascist movements that never managed to seize power, or at least to exert sizable political influence in their countries, remained subordinate to or even dependent on the two major fascist regimes throughout the years from 1922 to 1945. Not least, even the relationship between minor fascist parties like Jacques Doriot's Parti populaire français and Léon Degrelle's Belgian Rexists was frequently asymmetrical.[12]

Moreover, the trajectories of fascist parties and groups differed according to specific political and cultural contexts, and also due to the nature of transnational influences. Thus, understandings and features of fascism changed in the process of transfers. Ideas, institutions, political styles and policies were continuously de-contextualized and re-contextualized. Fascist movements and regimes represented hybrids of indigenous traditions and external influences, not only in border regions such as Alsace or Ukraine.[13] More generally, fascism underwent multiple permutations and cannot be grasped according to a typological taxonomy. Instead of clinging to static concepts like "pre-fascism" or "para-fascism," scholars should investigate processes of "fascistization." It primarily affected authoritarian elites who were prone to selectively adopt fascist "innovations." They seemed to comply with their overriding aim to secure stability, the status quo, and their power in interwar Europe. However, the rise of fascism also impressed outright political opponents, who closely studied the "fascist" recipe. All in all, fascism assumed specific meanings to different groups, both fascists and non-fascists. Moreover, views and interpretations of individual fascist movements and regimes changed over time. As fascism was a moving target rather than a static entity, it was adapted or rejected according to a wide scope of reasons and for a large variety of (sometimes even contradictory) purposes. They need to be distinguished as much as "positive" interaction (especially processes of exchange, transfer, appropriation and even learning) and "negative" interaction (rejection and blockage).[14]

By no means accidentally, the adversaries of fascist movements and regimes emphasized the cross-border interchange between and the universal claims of fascist leaders, members, and supporters in the 1920s and 1930s. As George Orwell stated in 1937: "Fascism is now an international movement, which means not only that the Fascist nations can combine for purposes of loot, but that they are groping, perhaps only half-consciously as yet, towards a world system."[15] In the same year, political scientist and jurist Karl Loewenstein, who had been forced to emigrate from Germany to the United States in 1933, observed the "missionary efforts of the fascist International in carrying political propaganda into other nations."[16]

Theoretical and Methodological Paths toward a Transnational History of Fascism

The dominance of the "national paradigm" has been a persistent feature in the writing of history in the modern period. In political history as well as in social historical writing, the nation-state has been routinely employed as the prevalent analytical framework. Yet more recent approaches to comparative history have superseded the national paradigm. Although Belgian historian Henry Pirenne, as well as scholars of the French "Annales" school like Marc Bloch and Lucien Febvre, had called for the application of comparative approaches to European history as early as the late 1920s, it was mostly after 1945 that the predominant focus on national history was gradually complemented by regional or continental comparative perspectives. In fascist studies, connections between Mussolini's and Hitler's dictatorships were explored as early as the 1940s, and systematic comparisons of regimes as well as movements started in the 1960s.[17]

The more recent debate on investigations of cross-border transfers, exchanges, and entanglements has promoted transnational history since the 1990s, not least due to the impact of globalization.[18] Historians have proposed studies of transfers and entanglements that are explicitly devoted to the interrelations and mutual influences. The concept of "entanglements" highlights "a relational perspective which foregrounds processes of interaction and intermixture in the entangled histories of uneven modernities."[19] This research perspective underscores the fact that, since in historical reality most units of historical comparison cannot be neatly separated, the world should be better viewed as a web of interactions, encounters, and exchanges.[20]

We assert that comparative history and transfer studies are complementary rather than incompatible approaches in fascist studies. On the one hand, far from being obsolete, historical comparisons remain an indispensable method in the historian's toolkit. Efforts to identify and explain similarities and differences among units of research cannot be fully supplanted by the studies of transfers and entanglements between those units. In general, however, historical comparisons need to be combined with investigations of transfers in order to grasp interrelations among intertwined historical phenomena.[21]

Yet transnational studies of fascism are a new and unexplored field. Historians have investigated cross-border connections, interactions, and exchange between fascist movements and regimes only in the last few years. Most commonly, scholars are increasingly devoting attention to mutual perceptions and discourses, even in bilateral or multilateral relations between fascist states or between them and other countries.[22] Some publications have concentrated on specific fascist movements, especially the Italian Fascists and German National Socialists,[23] or on certain regions.[24] Fascists promoted or espoused particular concepts of European unification that served to justify their "crusade" against the Soviet Union and bolshevism in the units of the Waffen-SS during World War II. These pan-European concepts were directed against liberal visions of a united Europe as well as against Communist internationalism. Foreign supporters like poet Ezra Pound, British fascist James Strachey Barnes, and Irish writer James Vincent Murphy also endorsed and propagated the cross-border claims of Italian Fascism and German National Socialism.[25]

Beyond the national historical straightjacket, fascism has primarily been investigated in comparative studies. By contrast, studies of mutual perceptions, relations, transfers, and entanglements between fascists have received less attention. Few scholars have analyzed contacts and collaboration between European fascists and similar-minded followers and adherents in the non-European world. The cross-border attraction of Nazi Germany and Fascist Italy, and the relations between the leaders and supporters of the two regimes, are an exception to the rule. Some overviews of the history of fascism have highlighted specific networks, too.[26] Historical studies have also reconstructed the intrusion of fascists into the League of Nations, especially its International Labour Organization, and the International Criminal Police Commission that was founded in 1923. Moreover, the cross-border activities of organizations such as the Deutsche Kongreß-Zentrale (set up in the Third Reich) are notable.[27] Fellow-travelers of German Nazism and Italian Fascism in the Near East and in India have received particular attention. Yet the responses of Arabs and Muslims to Hitler's and Mussolini's dictatorships cannot be reduced to collaboration. In fact, most of them rejected both these regimes, and colonial rule by the Western powers. Some Arabs and Muslims even saved Jews from persecution.[28] By contrast, scholarship has neglected the interrelationship between fascism and non-communist antifascism, although contemporaries observed mutual perceptions, partial exchange, and selective transfers between the two camps, notwithstanding their political antagonism. More generally, most publications on fascism still mention transfers and entanglements between the movements and regimes only passingly.[29]

Mutual Perceptions, Exchanges, Transfers, and Adaptions: Transnational Relations between Fascists in Europe

After Mussolini had been sworn in as prime minister of Italy in Rome on 31 October 1922 and successfully set up a full-fledged dictatorship in 1925, the Duce found an increasing number of admirers in European states as different as Britain, France, Germany, Croatia, and Ukraine. Thus, Rotha Lintorn Orman established the British Fascisti in 1923, and Pierre Taittinger set up his Jeunesses Patriotes in France two years later. In the early 1920s, the spiritual leader of Ukrainian ultranationalist youth, Dmytro Dontsov, was both mesmerized and shocked by the intrinsic similarities between the Italian Fascists and the Ukrainian nationalists.[30] Most importantly, Hitler admired Mussolini as a strong leader. By the mid-1920s, the Duce had become "the very model of a modern tyrant."[31]

These individuals, groups, and their leaders were attracted by Mussolini's promise to overcome the perennial party strife by strong leadership, ban class conflicts in favor of cooperation between the employers and workers, and eliminate ceaseless economic competition by protectionist policies. The vision of a "new era" and the ideal of the "new man" seemed to compare favorably to the performance of democratic governments. Appalled by the contradictions and frictions of liberal and capitalist modernity, the fascist leaders strove for a comprehensive renewal, which was to be achieved by instilling heroic vitality, imposing military order, promoting racism, and subordinating individuals to the community and state. Fascists were also impressed by the cult of the *Romanità*, as Mussolini and his followers celebrated the political and cultural legacy of ancient Rome through exhibitions, urban reconstructions, and excavations in Italy and North Africa. Relating the past to the present and visions of the future, the Duce's dictatorship seemed to combine "revolution and eternity." Although these concepts of regeneration and rejuvenation ultimately sought to justify dictatorship, suppression and foreign conquest, even conservative intellectuals and politicians like Winston Churchill and St. Leo Strachey (editor of the *Spectator*) showed themselves favorably impressed by Mussolini's apparently strong performance as Italy's new leader in the mid-1920s. Yet their interest was usually restricted to certain points in the trajectory of Italian Fascism, and they contrasted their indigenous problems with the seemingly irresistible advance of Mussolini's regime. This admiration and adulation, in turn, nourished the Fascists' sense of superiority. These synergies between fascists and conservatives need to be investigated.[32]

Although Mussolini and his lieutenants initially emphasized the national character of Italian Fascism, their political ambitions clearly transcended the borders of Italy as early as the 1920s. They busily propagated the model of a new transnational European Fascist civilization purportedly embodied by their dictatorship. The Duce, therefore, encouraged Italian Fascists living in different European states to support the new regime. Thus, organizations like the Fasci Italiani all'Estero, which had been set up by the prominent Fascist Giuseppe Bastianini as early as 1923, not only integrated Italians living in foreign states into Italian Fascism but also represented and spread the regime's claim of a renewal of civilization. The central office of the ancillary organization in Rome was to promote Fascism in Europe, Asia, and Africa, as well as in North and South America. Although they refrained from direct intervention into the politics of their host countries, the *Fasci* unequivocally espoused Mussolini's regime and propagated it as a model.[33]

The ascendency of the National Socialists in Germany revitalized Mussolini's transnational initiatives. Even before the Duce had openly committed himself to a "political and spiritual renewal of the world"[34] in 1932, Italian Blackshirts were delegated to foreign countries in order to mobilize support for the Fascist regime. In China, 400 out of the 430 Italian residents belonged to the branch of the Fasci Italiani all'Estero in Beijing. In Paris and New York, the activities of this organization were mainly pursued by blue-collar workers in the mid-1920s. Italian Fascists in foreign countries not only worked together to support Mussolini's dictatorship and thereby closed their ranks against the liberals and democrats, but also attempted to appeal to the indigenous populations. Despite the new competition, Hitler's seizure of power seemed to evidence the success of Mussolini's regime and thus strengthened the "magnetic field" of Italian Fascism.[35]

It had struck a particularly strong chord among German nationalist conservatives and *völkisch* groups that hoped to bring about antiparliamentarian authoritarian rule in a strong state. Before 1932, most German visitors to Mussolini were conservative and Catholic politicians and journalists who looked for an authoritarian alternative to the despised Weimar Republic. Although he had criticized German expansionism in World War I, the Duce established strong relations to veterans' organizations like the Stahlhelm, especially through his liaison officer Giuseppe Renzetti. However, the Führer's movement only aroused considerable attention among leading Italian Fascists after it had won 36.9 percent of the vote in the Reichstag elections of 31 July 1932.[36] Conversely, the Italian Fascists had become heroes for many National Socialists as early as the 1920s. Thus, members of the Nationalsozialistische Deutsche Arbeiterpartei (National Socialist German Workers' Party, NSDAP) who were asked to name great personalities of history in an opinion poll in 1929 placed Mussolini third, behind Bismarck and Hitler. Although the Nazis' adversaries attempted to stigmatize and discredit the Führer in the last few years of the Weimar Republic, they proved unable to halt Hitler's political rise.[37]

As he felt challenged by the ascending rival movement, the Duce openly committed himself to intensified cross-border propaganda for the Italian model in 1932. To buttress his claim to political leadership in Europe, Mussolini started to subsidize fascists in foreign countries. In 1933–34, for instance, the Italian ambassador, Dino Grandi, passed considerable funds to the British Union of Fascists (BUF). It had been officially founded by former Conservative and Labour politician Sir Oswald Mosley in October 1932, following his encounter with Mussolini in Rome. The Duce also subsidized some other Fascist groups and parties in Europe like the Austrian Heimwehr and the Belgian Rexists of Léon Degrelle. Moreover, the Croatian Ustasha and the OUN were both trained at the same camps on Sicily in the early 1930s. It was the assassination of the Polish interior minister Bronisław Pieracki in Warsaw on 15 June 1934, as well as the murder of King Alexander I of Yugoslavia and the French foreign minister Louis Barthou in Marseilles on 9 October 1934 that drew international attention to Mussolini's support for these fascist "liberation movements." The unwelcome attention forced him to proceed more carefully. Nevertheless, the Duce continued to fund fascist groups throughout Europe.[38]

As these examples show, Italian Fascism was not exclusively perceived as a national movement, but as a transnational pan-European force of renewal that both inspired and supported some other European movements. Yet cooperation between the Fascists and the National Socialists continuously went hand in hand with rivalry and competition as well as mutual reservations and recriminations.[39] Mussolini's doubts grew when Nazi Germany increasingly outflanked Fascist Italy from 1933 onwards. Despite their initial reservations about the expansionist program espoused by the National Socialists, many European fascists had enthusiastically applauded Hitler's seizure of power. The leaders of the fascist movements of France and the Netherlands, in particular, did not hesitate to approach the new rulers of Germany in 1933. Dontsov, the main ideologist of Ukrainian nationalists, perceived Hitler as a model of a fascist leader, and many ordinary members of the OUN, too, admired the German Führer for his inflexible anti-Semitism and anti-Bolshevism.[40] After they had rapidly established their undisputed dictatorship in 1933–34, the Nazis managed to increase their influence among European fascists. The seemingly unbeatable Third Reich assumed the status of the dominant model, increasingly surpassing Italian Fascism. The Nazis attempted to take advantage of their growing international clout. Directed by Ernst Wilhelm Bohle, the Foreign Organization (Auslandsorganisation, AO) of the NSDAP nourished, and controlled the activities of its branches in many foreign countries.[41]

The turn of the BUF to the Nazi rulers was particularly conspicuous. The fascist organization was renamed the "British Union of Fascists and National Socialists" in 1936. Mosley's party had openly adopted anti-Semitism and increasingly abandoned the ideal of the corporate state that the British Fascists had initially espoused. In the summer of 1936, the party was granted a subvention of ten thousand pounds by Hitler, who was also involved in Mosley's secret marriage to Diana Mosley in Berlin in October 1936. The Belgian Rexists of Leon Dégrelle, who had initially been supported by Mussolini, received German subventions in the mid-1930s, too.[42] One of the most important sources of income of the Ukrainian Military Organization and its follow-up, the OUN, was the German Abwehr (military intelligence).[43]

The adoption of anti-Semitism and racism was largely due to the growing attractiveness of National Socialism to the radical Right throughout Europe. In the Netherlands, for instance, Anton Mussert's Nationaal Socialistische Beweging (National Socialist Movement, NSB), which had initially been inspired by Italian Fascism, launched a propaganda campaign against the Jews in 1935. Anti-Semitism was particularly promoted among Dutch Fascists by Rost van Tonningen, who was received by Hitler in Berlin in August 1936. In Britain, openly pro-Nazi groups like the "Link" and the "Right Club" attempted to surpass the BUF in their hatred of Jews in the late 1930s. In Eastern Europe, OUN ideologist Volodymer Martynets adjusted the Nuremberg Laws to the Ukrainian context in his brochure "The Jewish Problem in Ukraine," which was published in 1938 in London. He argued that the Jews who live among Ukrainians are a race that should be completely isolated from the Ukrainian people.[44]

Altogether, personal contacts, financial subventions, and visits to Germany, as well as cultural events organized by friendship societies like the Anglo-German Fellowship, and bilateral associations like the German–French Society and the German–Dutch Society, tied European fascists ever more firmly to the Third Reich. The increasing rivalry between the Fascist and Nazi regimes by no means excluded pragmatic cooperation. In fact, close interaction between the two nations continued in a number of policy fields. Not coincidentally, the German propaganda minister, Joseph Goebbels, complained about the flurry of visits of high-ranking Fascists and National Socialists between Italy and Germany in 1937. Apparently, he felt excluded by the exchange, and reacted with envy and scorn to the increasing number of meetings between high-ranking leaders and members of the state parties that ruled the two countries.[45] Ukrainians studying in Rome joined the Italian student fascist organization Gruppi universitari fascisti, which assembled young fascists from many other European countries and showed themselves concerned about the future of their continent.[46]

The impact of the "successful" fascist movements on the smaller groups in Europe was ambiguous. On the one hand, both Italy's Fascist regime and the Nazi dictatorship had clearly demonstrated that fascists were able to seize power. They thereby encouraged smaller parties such as Norway's Nasjonal Samling and the British Union of Fascists, which even received funds from the German Nazis and the Italian Fascists, if only temporarily. Not least, the second-wave fascists of the 1930s could borrow ideas and institutions that had been successful in Italy and Germany. On the other hand, this selective appropriation of proven and settled "models" robbed the minor fascist parties of the flexibility, adaptability, and fluidity that had been crucial to the success of Fascism and Nazism. The fascist parties that were founded in the 1930s did not manage to gain an independent status. On the contrary, many of them were riven by conflicts between national conservatives and radicals, as well as between the supporters of Italian Fascism and German National Socialism. Together, the two regimes and the successful fascist movements played a constitutive role in the formation and development of the minor groups, which were transnationally oriented from their very foundation onward.[47]

As World War II approached, fascist calls for European "unity" and "peace" (according to the terms of Nazi Germany and Fascist Italy) became more numerous and urgent. Yet the cracks in the "Axis" alliance that had been established between Italy and Germany in October 1936 in the wake of Mussolini's diplomatic isolation after the attack on Abyssinia one year before became apparent in 1938 when Italy had to abandon its protection of Austria's independence to Nazi Germany's demand for forced accession (*Anschluss*). Moreover, Mussolini and his foreign secretary, Count Galeazzo Ciano, refused to enter the war that Germany initiated by attacking Poland on 1 September 1939.[48]

Following the German occupation of Norway, the Netherlands, Belgium, and France, and Italy's entry into the war, high-level exchange between Fascists was gradually reduced to military cooperation and open support for the collaboration. Exchange between the indigenous fascists and the German or Italian occupiers increasingly bordered on national treason, because the National Socialists preferred to cooperate with stable authoritarian regimes than ideologically akin fanatics. Nevertheless, in March 1939 the Hlinka Party proclaimed a Slovak fascist state, and in April 1941 the Ustasha founded a Croatian one. Both were established because Nazi Germany needed the support of those fascist movements. After the German attack on the Soviet Union on 22 June 1941, however, Hitler did not approve of states proclaimed by radical right-wing or fascist movements in the territories released from the Soviet occupation. After the proclamation of the Ukrainian state on 30 June 1941 in Lviv, the leaders of the OUN were detained. The same had happened a week earlier to the elite of the Lithuanian Activist Front (Lietuvos aktyvistų frontas, LAF) when they proclaimed a Ukrainian state in Kaunas. The OUN leaders remained detained in German concentration camps as special political prisoners (*Ehrenhäftlinge* or

Sonderhäftlinge) until fall 1944, together with the Romanian fascists of the "Iron Guard."[49]

Under the strong impact of the occupation of Norway and France in spring 1940, scares of subversion led to the internment of fascists in states like Britain. Whereas fears of high-ranking "traitors" were mostly unfounded, volunteers were recruited to the German Army and to the armed SS in various European states, and many Fascists consented to defend the European "fortress" against "Bolshevism." As early as 1941–42, forty-three thousand foreign volunteers joined German military forces in their fight against the Soviet Union. Even from non-belligerent, and then neutral, Spain, a "Blue Division" of volunteers flocked to the German army in order to support its soldiers in their military crusade against the Soviet troops. By late 1944, 763,000 soldiers had been recruited in the territories annexed by Germany alone. Policemen in numerous East European countries outnumbered their German superiors and were deeply involved in the annihilation of the Jews in their respective countries.[50] Clearly, pan-Europeanism was not only espoused by liberals and democrats but also exploited by the Fascists and National Socialists. They proved capable of mobilizing hundreds of thousands of men and women in order to kill millions of civilians.[51]

Yet the vision of a fascist Europe proved to be a chimera. Fascists clearly espoused different versions of European unity. Thus, the Nazis aimed at German hegemony. Moreover, fissures between the Third Reich and Fascist Italy grew in the early 1940s. Due to his country's weakness as an industrial nation, Mussolini had to succumb to Nazi Germany's claims of superiority. As the Italian war efforts virtually collapsed in 1942–43, the Duce increasingly rejected the racist ideology and annihilation policies of the Nazis. He attempted to regain status by claiming that Italian civilization would ultimately prevail over brute German power. Many foreign volunteers in the armed SS, too, were not prepared to abandon their demands for independence. Nevertheless, the vision of a fascist Europe was still influential at the end of the war, primarily due to the menace of bolshevism.[52]

Dimensions of Transnational Fascism

New research on fascist movements and regimes has uncovered and highlighted multiple connections between leaders and followers, both in party organizations and regimes. It has demonstrated that fascism was both a national and transnational phenomenon. In contrast to our knowledge about some, although not all, national cases, the transnational dimensions of European fascism are still under-researched. One important reason for this state of affairs is that studies of fascism require the knowledge of several languages and national histories; another has been the lack of an appropriate methodology with which to compare particular national cases and show how transnationalism shaped the numerous national forms of fascism. Thus, a comprehensive "history of fascist entanglement" has been proposed in order to assess the relative importance and significance of exchanges.[53]

A promising approach to the transnational nature of fascism is the investigation of cross-border networks and interactions between specific actors in fields such as propaganda, party organization, and public representation. As recent research on the history of fascism has demonstrated, a "productive transnational method begins with the socially and culturally constructed realities of protagonists, with purposive action that takes place through the use of solidarities of various scales from personal networks and local solidarities through the national to the transnational."[54] Beyond leaders and activists, fascist actors included students, politicians, poets, artists, emigrants, and youths. Ordinary members as well as luminaries of small organizations, huge movements, and regimes interacted on various levels.[55] Despite their strong nationalist convictions, fascists felt related to each other and performed transnational exchange on a regular basis, regarding it as a part of their everyday life. The multifarious interactions resulted from diverse motivations such as common beliefs and interests, the hostility to communism, liberalism, and democracy, as well as the perceived need to discuss and agree on the future shape of their countries or of their continent. Mutual perceptions frequently led to exchange and even learning. Yet they also highlighted differences, reinforced tensions, and exacerbated national antagonisms. As the chapters of this book demonstrate, studies of transnational fascism have to take the full scale of these interrelations into account.

Fascists lived in different states and stateless communities. They were primarily concerned about their national organizations, but they shared values and points of views with fascists in foreign countries. Even though there was no coherent ideology, and compromises shaped their political agenda and social practice, fascist movements and regimes embraced a similar set of political ideas, and they shared a militaristic style. Not only the Nazis and the Italian Fascists, but also the Iron Guard and the Ustasha, developed new concepts of presenting themselves in public, manipulating public opinion, or eliminating enemies. Preoccupied by their expansionist ideas, fascists were dedicated to the aggrandizement of their own country, and they strove for conquest in order to expand their particular nation-state. Yet they sought inspiration from like-minded groups across national borders, and they initially regarded Fascist Italy as their model before they turned to the Third Reich.

Transnational discourse between fascists proceeded on various levels. Texts by Hitler, Mussolini, and many other politicians and ideologists were translated into almost all European languages, frequently by their admirers in the particular states. Discourse on anti-Semitism, racism, and eugenics played an especially important role among European fascists. Similarly, fascist aesthetics, including the style of uniforms, symbols on (national) flags, words, and the tunes of marching songs were clearly shaped by influences across national borders, although we should not disregard national specifics such as the role of folkloristic costumes in the movements of East and Southeast European fascists, nor the extensive fascination with racist symbolism in National Socialism and several movements in East-Central Europe.

In order to further knowledge about fascism in Europe between 1918 and 1945, the editors have decided to focus on some of the most important dimensions and levels of transnationalism. The scope of the volume is not restricted to cross-border interactions between representatives of fascist states, which would be more typical of an international than a transnational approach to the subject. Nevertheless, official politics, ideology, and policies are obviously an important dimension of studying fascism from a cross-border perspective. They also serve as a starting point for a more thorough and comprehensive exploration of the nature of fascist transnationalism. Besides highlighting interaction between high-ranking politicians, the volume engages with other actors who were involved in transnational fascist activism, such as intellectuals, scientists, proponents of the concept of a fascist Europe, and youth organizations.

Propaganda and representations are important fields of exploring transnational interactions, too, as some chapters of this volume demonstrate. The cross-border flows of symbols, meanings, and aesthetics, in particular, merit close scholarly attention. Similarly, fund-raising, the financial organization of societies, and the vexed issues of nationalism, anti-Semitism, and racism were important issues in the cross-border exchange between fascists throughout Europe. No less important were discourses on mass violence, expansionism, and the role of religion in fascist movements. In addition to these most essential and obvious levels and dimensions of interactions and cooperation, transnationalism also occurred through conflicts among individuals, groups, movements, and regimes. Contrary to transfers, controversies and bloody conflicts related fascists to each other in a negative way.

The transnational nature of fascism was both a source and a subject of discourses on a fascist international in Europe and the very idea of a fascist Europe. Moreover, fascist transnationalism was interrelated to cross-border antifascism, as it triggered multiple reactions and responses by intellectual and political opponents. As early as the 1930s, contemporaries recognized the interrelationship between the transnational cooperation of the fascists on the one hand, and the cross-border collaboration between antifascists on the other. Like the fascists, their opponents perceived fascism as a transnational political alternative to democracy, the important differences between Italian Fascism and German National Socialism, as well as between the minor fascist parties, notwithstanding. For instance, Carlo Rosselli, the leading luminary of the liberal group Giustizia e Libertà, envisaged an "antifascist Europe" as a response to fascist transnationalism.[56]

Similarly, Karl Loewenstein highlighted the interrelationship between the fascist onslaught and "militant democracy" as early as 1937. In general, the fascist threat activated, mobilized, and radicalized the antifascists, not only in the confines of the various nation-states, but also beyond their borders. As scholars such as Dan Stone have emphasized, however, antifascism cannot be reduced to its communist variant.[57] In fact, liberal and conservative intellectuals contributed significantly to defining and implementing resistance against fascism, as Silvia Madotto and Francesco Di Palma demonstrate in this volume. Altogether, antifascist conceptualizations and understandings of fascism enabled its opponents to clarify and expose the fascist threat, and thus helped to defeat it. Conversely, communist antifascist internationalism encouraged fascists to cooperate most strongly. In a similar vein, transnational cooperation between fascists, as well as collaboration between the communists, were interrelated in attempts to forge a "Catholic International," especially by the Vatican's "Secretariat on Atheism" in the 1930s. All in all, the boundary between right-wing politics and antifascism was fluid in interwar Europe. In Italy, for instance, some nationalist supporters of an intervention of the country in the early part of World War I (1914–15) strongly opposed Mussolini's dictatorship in the 1920s and 1930s. Nevertheless, they still shared a commitment to political violence with the Italian Fascists. Similarly, the Vatican asserted a rejection of fascism, or at least independence from it, while its "Secretariat on Atheism" partially endorsed fascist anticommunism. In the late 1930s, it even collaborated with fascists and Nazis in on-the-ground campaigns against communism.[58]

State authorities, too, identified an interrelationship between fascism and antifascism. In Britain, for instance, the Security Service was concerned that the British Union of Fascists boosted and radicalized the antifascist movement, especially the efforts of the Communist International.[59] Some intellectuals, such as Orwell, even wondered immediately after the defeat of the Third Reich "how much of the present slide towards Fascist ways of thought is traceable to the 'anti-Fascism' of the past ten years and the unscrupulousness it has entailed?"[60] Altogether, some contemporary observers emphasized the interrelationship between transnational fascism and antifascism.

Addressing these issues and analytical dimensions, the authors highlight the role that transnationalism played between European fascist movements and regimes. They also demonstrate how transnational fascism in Europe actually evolved from the early 1920s until the end of World War II. The aim of this approach is to open a broad perspective and to promote a new research vista that recognizes fascism as an ensemble of manifold but closely intertwined movements. This will hopefully pave the way to more comprehensive studies that will help to specify and understand the nature of fascist transnationalism.

Although the volume is largely restricted to Europe, fascism undoubtedly mobilized support beyond the confines of the continent. In some states, like Japan and Argentina, radical nationalists were inspired by the successful models of Fascist Italy and Nazi Germany. The military and authoritarian regimes of Tōjō Hideki (1941–44) and Juan Perón (1946–55), respectively, borrowed specific mechanisms of rule (for instance propaganda and techniques of representation), as well as certain policies such as corporate economic organization, from fascism. Yet the settings and contexts differed markedly from those prevalent in Europe after 1918. As Robert Paxton has rightly emphasized, "the similarities seem matters of tools or instruments, borrowed during fascism's apogee, while the differences concern more basic matters of structure, function, and relation to society."[61] Moreover, European fascist movements like the Dutch NSB clearly clung to the imperial rule by their respective nation-states as late as World War II. Yet these schemes clashed with Nazi policies, which aimed at a "New Order" in Europe.[62]

Similarly, the book confines itself to the time between 1918 and 1945. The catastrophic failure of Italian Fascism, and particularly German Nazism and its numerous associates, was a significant obstacle for the multiple neo-fascist and neo-Nazi movements after World War II. Even more importantly, the Holocaust and other atrocities committed during the war have profoundly transformed memory cultures of fascism, National Socialism, and of World War II itself, all over the world, at least since the 1970s. They have largely delegitimized any open racist violence, too. After 1945, leaders and members of right-wing and neo-fascist groups had to relate themselves to Nazism, Hitler, and the Holocaust. Looking backward rather than forward, they largely remained on the political fringe. Altogether, despite the "generic similarities among movements of the modern secular Right, which include both classic fascism and the present radical Right in Western Europe, critical changes in the historical context set these two phenomena apart in essential ways."[63] For pragmatic reasons, too, a certain geographical limitation can therefore be justified. "If you spread your net too wide the fish may get through, and early attempts to give fascism a global status as an example of 'developmental dictatorship' made its contours still more infinite."[64]

The Chapters of the Volume

Exploring various aspects of transnational fascism, the volume is composed of thirteen chapters. The texts address the major levels of transnational fascism as well as negative reactions to fascism, known as antifascism. The first section is devoted to theories and methodology (Aristotle Kallis and Matteo Pasetti), followed in the second by chapters on propaganda, leisure, and representations (Anna Lena Kocks, Goran Miljan, and Cláudia Ninhos). The third section of the volume deals with actors, conflicts, and religion (Grzegorz Rossoliński-Liebe, Raul Cârstocea, and Marleen Rensen) and the fourth with fascist concepts of Europe (Monica Fioravanzo and Johannes Dafinger). The fifth section investigates the interrelations and transnational exchange between fascists, and cross-border interaction between their opponents (Kasper Braskén, Silvia Madotto, and Francesco Di Palma).

Following this introduction, Aristotle Kallis explains why fascism cannot be understood in national terms. In fact, he identifies its transnationality in its generic and contradictory nature. Fascism manifested itself in a number of similar movements in Europe and beyond. This was neither a coincidence nor a by-product of other political movements or ideologies. Scholars of fascism have tried to approach this problem in divergent theoretical and empirical studies that, however, frequently restricted themselves to governmental internationalism or bi- or trinational comparisons. As Kallis evidences, however, violence and anti-Semitism are central to transnational fascism. Destruction correlated to visions such as a "new order." These two dimensions constituted transnational fascism as a highly dynamic phenomenon. Its complexity is demonstrated in the following chapters.

Matteo Pasetti analyzes the dissemination of corporatist ideas in Europe. This shows an important dimension of fascist transnationalism, paying special attention to theoretical concepts of cross-border diffusion and flow of ideas and ideologies. Pasetti explains how an economic system, deeply rooted in Italian culture and policies, found, thanks to Mussolini, adherents in many European fascist and non-fascist states, and was adapted to various economic and political circumstances outside Italy. Corporatism was intended to become a third way, different from socialism and capitalism, and an integral element of an authoritarian state. It was central to the political appeal and inclusiveness of fascism in Italy and beyond.

Anna Lena Kocks compares the organization of leisure in two unequal fascist communities: the Italian Fascists and the British Union of Fascists. She shows the flow of transnational ideas and concepts between them, and points out the leading role of Italy in the discourse on fascist self-representation. Despite different premises, Italian and English fascists used propaganda in similar ways to prepare their members for leisure, and used it as propaganda. However, we find also dissimilarities and political differences, such as the role of women in the concept of leisure in Italy and the BUF.

Goran Miljan analyzes the youth organizations of the Croatian Ustasha and the Slovak Hlinka Party. These two similar and equal organizations, which both understood themselves as "liberation movements," operated in the interwar period in similar political circumstances, and established collaborationist states under the aegis of Nazi Germany as the Germans began to remodel the map of Europe. The youth organizations of these movements fulfilled similar roles in the Slovak and Croatian societies, and felt spiritually related to each other. During joint summer camps they discussed the roles of their states in the New Europe, and exercised their bodies to the glory of their leaders. The transnational activism was strengthened by the similarity of languages and the idea of belonging to very closely related people, both racially and spiritually.

Cláudia Ninhos explores the German–Portuguese relationship in the context of science, knowledge, and power. She concentrates on the worker and youth organizations, scientists, and diplomats, and investigates the impact of German *Kulturpropaganda* on Portugal. Ninhos highlights the complexity of the relationships between these two nations, and unveils their channels of fascist transnationalism, as well as the meaning of colonialism and the role of the extermination of the Jews in the German–Portuguese discourse.

Grzegorz Rossoliński-Liebe opens fascist studies to a new subject of conflicts. Using the example of the relationships between the National Socialists, and the Austrian, Romanian, and Ukrainian fascists, he shows what caused the conflicts between fascists, and why the National Socialists sometimes preferred not to cooperate with ideologically closely related movements. Paying attention to National Socialists' geopolitical interests, and their wish to secure resources for the war against the Soviet Union and the extermination of European Jews, Rossoliński-Liebe demonstrates how the National Socialists persecuted or detained fascists from Austria, Romania, and Ukraine, and preferred to cooperate with other forces in these countries.

Marleen Rensen presents the French intellectual Robert Brasillach, who turned to fascism while watching a rally in Nuremberg in 1937. Analyzing his worldview and exploring his life, she highlights the role of ultranationalism and fascism in writings of this journalist, and film critic. Rensen demonstrates how Brasillach adapted National Socialist proposals to the French circumstances, became a collaborationist, and developed the concept of a new European order where Franco-German relations would have played a central role.

Another scholar who explains the transnational nature of fascism on the basis of one personality is Raul Cârstocea. Concentrating on the leading member of the Iron Guard, Ion I. Moța, he demonstrates that the organization wanted to ally with other fascist movements in order to combat their common enemies, especially the communists and the Jews. In 1934, at the meeting of European fascists in Montreaux, Moța supported the idea of a fascist international, despite the ambivalent attitude of other fascist movements to religion—the most important part of the identity of every Romanian legionary. It was the anti-Semitism and racism that convinced him to be ideologically closely related to other European fascists, even those who did not cherish religion, mysticism, or folklore like the Iron Guard did.

Monica Fioravanzo analyzes the Italian fascist visions of Europe. Unsurprisingly the cultural and political center of Europe in this concept was Rome. Italy was intended to spread fascist culture in the entire continent, which would create a common European fascist identity. Other parts of Europe would subordinate themselves to Italy and consider themselves to be the colonies of the true European fascist center—the truly Italian Rome. At the same time, Mussolini had to react to domestic quests and demands for renewal, especially in the early 1930s. For these reasons Mussolini first created the Fasci Italiani all'Estero, and in 1933 the CAUR. Italian intellectuals, journalists, and politicians who spread these "universalist" ideas across Europe ignited a vivid debate between representatives of different European fascist movements, and challenged the National Socialist hegemonic plans.

The Nazi concepts of Europe are explained by Johannes Dafinger, who emphasizes the importance of *völkisch* elements in a fascist Europe dominated by the Germans. Because of their unlimited racism, and the obsession with eugenics and the Slavic and Jewish contamination of the Aryan race, the German fascists defined *völkisch* as the component that would both purify and join the European races into a continent united by fascism. Given the anti-universalist nature of racism, uniting Europe around *völkisch* culture was truly challenging; many racist German thinkers began with anti-European ideas but ended as supporters of European models. Like nationalism, racism and *völkisch* ideology were excluding concepts, but they neatly corresponded to fascism. They were next to nationalism and obsession with violence the most intrinsic and thus transnational element of European fascism. Yet the Nazi "New Order" did not prevent the emergence and dissemination of competing cultural influences.[65]

To what extent and in which sense antifascism became transnational is explained by Kasper Braskén, Silvia Madotto, and Francesco Di Palma. Braskén emphasizes the correlation between transnational fascism and antifascism. Concentrating on communist groups, he demonstrates how transnational antifascism affected the dynamics of fascism, which in turn impacted on antifascism. Indeed, the history of transnational fascism cannot be properly understood without paying attention to the activities of antifascist groups, movements, and parties. This broad perspective embeds the final two chapters. Silvia Madotto's investigation deals with a particular case—the antifascist resistance at the European universities—and concentrates on the crucial role of the University of Padua and the activities of an influential networker, Silvio Trentin. Besides popularizing fascism and racism, universities were the centers of antifascism activism. However, many students and professors did not understand fascism and antifascism as contradictory, but rather changed and adjusted their behavior according to the political circumstances. All in all, the interrelationship between fascism and antifascism was a constitutive element of their transnationality. Francesco Di Palma, on the other hand, analyzes the antifascist activities of the German Social Democratic Party in exile and the Giustizia e Libertà, an Italian resistance group. Investigating their contacts with other antifascist groups and their reactions to fascism, Di Palma exposes the channels of transnationalism among antifascists in exile.

An afterword by Arnd Bauerkämper concludes this volume. Taking up some crucial findings and insights from the contributions to this book, he elaborates on perspectives of historical research on transnational fascism.

This book would not have been published without the generous support from the Fritz Thyssen Foundation for our project. We are grateful to Chris Chappell of Berghahn Books, not only for his meticulous editorial work, but also for his helpful advice. Moreover, the volume could not have been published without Nigel Smith's and Caroline Kuhtz's careful corrections of the English texts. Aylin Herker and Felicitas Remer provided indispensable editorial assistance.

ARND BAUERKÄMPER is professor of Modern European History at the Freie Universität Berlin. He studied History and English at the universities of Bielefeld, Oxford, and Göttingen. Selected publications: Der *Faschismus in Europa 1918–1945* (Stuttgart, 2006); *Das umstrittene Gedächtnis. Die Erinnerung an Nationalsozialismus, Faschismus und Krieg in Europa seit 1945* (Paderborn, 2012); "Transnational Fascism: Cross-Border Relations between Regimes and Movements in Europe, 1922–1939." *East Central Europe* 37 (2010): 214–46.

GRZEGORZ ROSSOLIŃSKI-LIEBE, researcher and lecturer at the Freie Universität Berlin, studied History and Cultural Studies at the Viadrina European University. Selected publications: *Stepan Bandera: The Life and Afterlife of a Ukrainian Nationalist: Fascism, Genocide, and Cult* (Stuttgart, 2014); "The Fascist Kernel of Ukrainian Genocidal Nationalism," *The Carl Beck Papers in Russian and East European Studies* 2402 (May 2015); *Alma mater antisemitica: Akademisches Milieu, Juden und Antisemitismus an den Universitäten Europas zwischen 1918 und 1939* (Vienna, 2016).

Notes

1. Throughout this volume, "Fascism" (capitalized) refers to the Italian variant, whereas "fascism" denotes the generic concept.
2. Walter Laqueur, *Fascism: Past, Present, Future* (New York, 1996), 218. For similar interpretations, see Wolfgang Schieder, "Einleitung," in *Faschistische Diktaturen:. Studien zu Italien und Deutschland*, ed. idem (Göttingen, 2008), 16; Jerzy W. Borejsza, "Die Rivalität zwischen Faschismus und Nationalsozialismus in Ostmitteleuropa," *Vierteljahrshefte für Zeitgeschichte* 29 (1981): 579–614, esp. 607; Radu Ioanid, *The Sword of the Archangel: Fascist Ideology in Romania* (Boulder, 1990), 190; Constantin Iordachi, "God's Chosen Warriors: Romantic Palingenesis, Militarism and Fascism in

Modern Romania," in *Comparative Fascist Studies: New Perspectives*, ed. idem (London, 2010), 353; Hans Woller, *Rom, 28. Oktober 1922: Die faschistische Herausforderung* (Munich, 1999), 172–73; Jerzy W. Borejsza, *Schulen des Hasses:. Faschistische Systeme in Europa* (Frankfurt/Main, 1999), 267; Philip Morgan, *Fascism in Europe, 1919–1945* (London, 2003), 159.

3. For research reports, see especially: Stanley G. Payne, "George L. Mosse and Walter Laqueur on the History of Fascism," *Journal of Contemporary History* 50 (2015): 750–67; António Costa Pinto, "Back to European Fascism," *Contemporary European History* 15 (2006): 103–15.

4. For an overview, cf. Constantin Iordachi, "Comparative Fascist Studies: An Introduction," in *Comparative Fascist Studies: New Perspectives*, ed. idem (London, 2010), 1–50.

5. For exceptions, see notes 22, 23, and 24.

6. The CAUR had been initiated by Fascist functionary Asvero Gravelli, who edited the journal *Ottobre*. Gravelli spearheaded a group of Fascist leaders who aspired to redefine Italian Fascism as a youthful movement that was to mobilize support throughout Europe. Directed against the new National Socialist regime, the CAUR was to spread Fascist Italy's claim to represent a universal force of cultural renewal. Yet a conference of fascist leaders (including Vidkun Quisling, Oswald Mosley, General Eion O'Duffy, and Marcel Bucard) in Montreux in December 1934 failed to achieve unity, largely due to different views on the importance of anti-Semitism. Neither did another meeting of fascist leaders in Amsterdam in April 1935 arrive at binding decisions. On the CAUR, see Michael A. Ledeen, *Universal Fascism: The Theory and Practice of the Fascist International, 1928–1936* (New York, 1972), esp. 104–32; idem, "Italian Fascism and Youth," *Journal of Contemporary History* 4 (1969): 137–54.

7. David D. Roberts, *Fascist Interactions: Proposals for a New Approach to Fascism and Its Era, 1919–1945* (New York, 2016), 129. For instructive deliberations, also see António Costa Pinto and Aristotle Kallis, "Introduction," in *Rethinking Fascism and Dictatorship in Europe*, ed. António Costa Pinto and Aristotle Kallis (New York, 2014), 2–3; idem, "Conclusion: Embracing Complexity and Transnational Dynamics. The Diffusion of Fascism and the Hybridization of Dictatorships in Inter-War Europe," in ibid., 274; Susanne Hohler, "Russian Fascism in Exile: A Historical and Phenomenological Perspective on Transnational Fascism," *Fascism* 2, no. 2 (2013): 125, 140. For recent studies on relations between Italian Fascism and German National Socialism, see Christian Goeschel, "*Italia docet?* The Relationship between Italian Fascism and Nazism Revisited," *European History Quarterly* 42 (2012): 480–92.

8. David D. Roberts, "Fascism and the Framework for Interactive Political Innovation during the Era of the Two World Wars," in *Rethinking Fascism*, 44, 48, 53; Hohler, "Russian Fascism," 121, 124, 140. The role of ideas in Italian Fascism has been downplayed by Wolfgang Schieder, *Der italienische Faschismus 1919–1945* (Munich, 2010), 59–60; idem, *Benito Mussolini* (Munich, 2014), 18–22.

9. Davide Rodogno, *Fascism's European Empire: Italian Occupation during the Second World War* (Cambridge, 2006), 30.

10. See, for instance, Oswald Mosley, *Fascism in Britain* (Westminster, 1935), 11: "We have had enough talk; we will act!"

11. Grzegorz Rossoliński-Liebe, *Stepan Bandera. The Life and Afterlife of a Ukrainian Nationalist: Fascism, Genocide, and Cult* (Stuttgart, 2014), 22, 25, 27, 33.

12. Arnd Bauerkämper, "Ambiguities of Transnationalism: Fascism in Europe between Pan-Europeanism and Ultra-Nationalism, 1919–39," *German Historical Institute Bulletin* 29, no. 2 (2007): 43–67. For the various dimensions of *latinité*, cf. Catherine Fraixe, Christophe Poupault, and Luca Piccioni, eds, *Vers une Europe latine: Acteurs et enjeux des échanges culturels entre la France et l'Italie fasciste* (Paris, 2014). On the French fascist cyclists, cf. Marla Stone, "Staging Fascism: The Exhibition of the Fascist Revolution," *Journal of Contemporary History* 28 (1993): 238.

13. Hohler, "Russian Fascism," 126. On fascism in Alsace, see Samuel Huston Goodfellow, "Fascism as a Transnational Movement: The Case of Inter-War Alsace," *Contemporary European History* 22 (2013): 97–106; Anne Kwaschik, "An der Grenze der Nationen: Europa-Konzepte und regionale Selbstverortung im Elsass," *Zeithistorische Forschungen / Studies in Contemporary History* 9 (2012): 387–408.

14. Roberts, *Interactions*, 127; Stein U. Larsen, "Decomposition and Recomposition of Theories: How to Arrive at Useful Ideas Explaining Fascism," in *Rethinking the Nature of Fascism: Comparative Perspectives*, ed. António Costa Pinto (Basingstoke, 2011), 16, 29, 40, 43; Aristotle Kallis, "The 'Fascist Effect': On the Dynamics of Political Hybridization in Inter-War Europe," in *Rethinking Fascism*, 16–17, 21, 36; idem, "'Fascism', 'Para-fascism' and 'Fascistization': On the Similarities of Three Conceptual Categories," *European History Quarterly* 33 (2003): 219–50, esp. 220–21, 226–27, 233; Arnd Bauerkämper, "Der 'Große Krieg' als Beginn: Das Verhältnis zwischen traditionalen Ordnungskonzepten, Faschismus und Autoritarismus," *Totalitarismus und Demokratie* 12 (2015): 73–96; Roberts, "Fascism," 57, 61; Pinto and Kallis, "Conclusion," 278–80; Pinto and Kallis, "Introduction," 2–5.

15. George Orwell, *The Road to Wigan Pier* (London, [1937] 2001), 200. Also see Dietrich Orlow, "Fascists among Themselves: Some Observations on West European Politics in the 1930s," *European Review* 11 (2003): 245, 247, 250; Hohler, "Russian Fascism," 125.

16. Karl Loewenstein, "Militant Democracy and Fundamental Rights," *American Political Science Review* 31 (1937): 655.

17. Goeschel, "*Italia docet?*" 483, 489. For more details, see Aristotle Kallis's chapter in this volume.

18. For the meanings and concepts of "transnational," see Pierre-Yves Saunier, "Transnational," in *The Palgrave Dictionary of Transnational History*, ed. Akira Iriye and Pierre-Yves Saunier (Houndmills, 2009), 1047–54.

19. Shalini Randeria, "Entangled Histories of Uneven Modernities: Civil Society, Caste Solidarities and Legal Pluralism in Post-Colonial India," in *Unraveling Ties: From Social Cohesion to New Practices of Connectedness*, ed. Yehuda Elkana et al. (Frankfurt/Main, 2002), 287. Also see the contributions to Wolf Lepenies, ed., *Entangled Histories and Negotiated Universals: Centers and Peripheries in a Changing World* (Frankfurt/Main, 2003).

20. Marc Bloch, "Für eine vergleichende Geschichtsbetrachtung der europäischen Gesellschaften," in *Alles Gewordene hat Geschichte: Die Schule der Annales in ihren Texten 1929–1992*, ed. Matthias Middell and Steffen Sammler (Leipzig, 1994), 123, 125, 130. Also see Alette Olin and Boyd H. Hill, "Marc Bloch and Comparative History," *American Historical Review* 85 (1980): 828–46.

21. Deborah Cohen and Maura O'Connor, "Introduction: Comparative History, Cross-National History, Transnational History—Definitions," in *Comparison and History: Europe in Cross-National Perspective*, ed. Deborah Cohen and Maura O'Connor (New York, 2004), XVIII, XIX, XXII. With regard to studies of fascism, cf. Goeschel, *"Italia docet?"* 486.

22. Roberts, *Interactions*; Arnd Bauerkämper, "Interwar Fascism in Europe and Beyond: Toward a Transnational Radical Right," in *New Perspectives on the Transnational Right*, ed. Martin Durham and Margaret Power (Houndmills, 2010), 39–66; idem, "Transnational Fascism: Cross-Border Relations between Regimes and Movements in Europe, 1922–1939," *East Central Europe* 37 (2010): 214–46; Roger Griffin, ed., *International Fascism: Theories, Causes and the New Consensus* (London, 1998); Kiran Klaus Patel, "In Search of a Transnational Historicization: National Socialism and its Place in History," in *Conflicted Memories: Europeanizing Contemporary History*, ed. Konrad H. Jarausch and Thomas Lindenberger (New York, 2007), 96–116; idem, "Der Nationalsozialismus in transnationaler Perspektive," *Blätter für deutsche und internationale Politik* 9 (2004): 1122–34; Glenda Sluga, "Fascism and Anti-Fascism," in *The Palgrave Dictionary of Transnational History*, 381–83; Stefan Ihrig, "The History of European Fascism—Origins, Foreign Relations and (Dis)Entangled Histories," *European History Quarterly* 41 (2011): 278–90; Karsten Linne, "Sozialpropaganda—Die Auslandspublizistik der Deutschen Arbeitsfront 1936–1944," *Zeitschrift für Geschichtswissenschaft* 57 (2009): 237–54; Ricky W. Law, "Knowledge is Power: The Interwar German and Japanese Mass Media in the Making of the Axis," *Bulletin of the German Historical Institute* 54 (2014): 27–47.

23. Armin Nolzen and Sven Reichardt, eds., *Faschismus in Deutschland und Italien: Studien zu Transfer und Vergleich* (Göttingen, 2005); Dietrich Orlow, *The Lure of Fascism in Western Europe: German Nazis, Dutch and French Fascists, 1933–1939* (New York, 2009); idem, "Fascists among Themselves"; Wolfgang Schieder, *Mythos Mussolini: Deutsche in Audienz beim Duce* (Munich, 2012); idem, "Faschismus im politischen Transfer: Giuseppe Renzetti als faschistischer Propagandist und Geheimagent in Berlin 1922–1941," in *Faschismus in Italien und Deutschland: Studien zu Transfer und Vergleich*, ed. Sven Reichardt and Armin Nolzen (Göttingen, 2005), 28–58; idem, "Das italienische Experiment: Der Faschismus als Vorbild in der Krise der Weimarer Republik," *Historische Zeitschrift* 262 (1996): 73–125; Beate Scholz, *Italienischer Faschismus als „Export"-Artikel (1927–1935)* (Trier, 2001); Thies Schulze, "Die Zukunft der Diktaturen: Der Niedergang der Diktatur Miguel Primo de Riveras aus der Perspektive des Mussolini-Regimes," *Zeitschrift für Geschichtswissenschaft* 57 (2009): 134–56.

24. Goodfellow, "Fascism as a Transnational Movement"; Kwaschik, "An der Grenze."

25. Mark Mazower, *Hitler's Empire: Nazi Rule in Occupied Europe* (London, 2008); Dieter Gosewinkel (ed.), *Anti-liberal Europe: A Neglected Story of Europeanization* (New York, 2015); Robert Grunert, *Der Europagedanke westeuropäischer faschistischer Bewegungen 1940–1945* (Paderborn, 2012); Alastair Hamilton, *The Appeal of Fascism: A Study of Intellectuals and Fascism 1919–1945* (London, 1971), esp. 257–90; James J. Barnes and Patience P. Barnes, *James Vincent Murphy: Translator and Interpreter of Fascist Europe, 1880–1946* (Lanham, MD, 1987), 157–92; Roger Griffin, "Europe for the Europeans: Fascist Myths of the European Order 1922–1992," in *A Fascist Century: Essays by Roger Griffin*, ed. Matthew Feldman (New York, 2008), 132–80; Peter Schöttler, "Dreierlei Kollaboration: Europa-Konzepte und deutsch-französische Verständigung—am Beispiel der Karriere von SS-Brigadeführer Gustav Krukenberg," *Zeithistorische Forschungen* 9 (2012): 365–86; Lorna L. Waddington, *Hitler's Crusade: Bolshevism and the Myth of the International Jewish Conspiracy* (London, 2007); idem, "The Anti-Komintern and Nazi Anti-Bolshevik Propaganda in the 1930s," *Journal of Contemporary History* 42 (2007): 573–94; Jan C. Behrends, "Back from the USSR: The Anti-Comintern's Publications on Soviet Russia in Nazi Germany (1935–41)," *Kritika: Explorations in Russian and Eurasian History* 10, no. 3 (2009): 527–56; Monica Fioravanzo, "Die Europakonzeptionen von Faschismus und Nationalsozialismus (1939–1943)," *Vierteljahrshefte für Zeitgeschichte* 58 (2010): 509–41.

26. Cf. Arnd Bauerkämper, *Der Faschismus in Europa, 1918–1945* (Stuttgart, 2006), 13–46; Morgan, *Fascism*, 117–18; Woller, *Rom*, 59–60, 97, 153, 172–75, 193–94. On the role of Nazi Germany and Fascist Italy as models, see António Costa Pinto, *The Nature of Fascism Revisited* (New York, 2012), 26, 89; Martin Blinkhorn, *Fascism and the Right in Europe, 1919–1945* (Harlow, 2000), 42. For an overview of recent research, see Thomas Schlemmer and Hans Woller, "Politischer Deutungskampf und wissenschaftliche Deutungsmacht: Konjunkturen der Faschismusforschung," in *Der Faschismus in Europa: Wege der Forschung*, ed. Thomas Schlemmer and Hans Woller (Munich, 2014), 7–15.

27. Madelaine Herren, "'Outwardly an Innocuous Conference Authority': National Socialism and the Logistics of International Information Management," *German History* 20 (2002): 67–92; Patrick Bernhard, "Konzertierte Gegnerbekämpfung im Achsenbündnis: Die Polizei im Dritten Reich und im faschistischen Italien 1933 bis 1943," *Vierteljahrshefte für Zeitgeschichte* 59 (2011): 229–62; Mathieu Deflem, "International Police Cooperation, History of", in *Encyclopedia of Criminology*, vol. 2, ed. Richard A. Wright and J. Mitchell Miller (New York, 2005), 795–98; idem, *Policing World Society: Historical Foundations of International Police Cooperation* (Oxford, 2002), 174–95.

28. Jeffrey Herf, *The Jewish Enemy: Nazi Propaganda during World War II and the Holocaust* (London, 2006); idem, *Nazi Propaganda for the Arab World* (New Haven, CT, 2009); idem, "Nazi Germany's Propaganda Aimed at Arabs and Muslims during World War II and the Holocaust: Old Times, New Archival Findings," *Central European History* 42 (2009): 707–36. For different interpretations, see Sugata Bose, *His Majesty's Opponent: Subhas Chandra*

Bose and India's Struggle against Empire (Cambridge, MA, 2011); Marc David Baer, "Muslim Encounters with Nazism and the Holocaust: The Ahmadi of Berlin and Jewish Convert to Islam Hugo Marcus," *American Historical Review* 120 (2015): 140–71, esp. 145, 169–70; David Motadel, *Islam and Nazi Germany's War* (Cambridge, MA, 2014); Ulrike Freitag and Israel Gershoni, eds., *Arab Encounters with Fascist Propaganda 1933–1945* (Göttingen, 2011); Nir Arielli, *Fascist Italy and the Middle East, 1933–40* (Basingstoke, 2013); Federico Finchelstein, *Transatlantic Fascism: Ideology, Violence and the Sacred in Argentina and Italy, 1919–1945* (Durham, NC, 2010).

29. Ihrig, "History," 285. For an exception, see Francesco Di Palma, *Liberaler Sozialismus in Deutschland und Italien im Vergleich: Das Beispiel Sopade und Giustizia & Libertà* (Berlin, 2010).

30. "Chy my fashysty?," *Zahrava* 1, no. 7 (1923): 97–102. See also Grzegorz Rossoliński-Liebe, "The Fascist Kernel of Ukrainian Genocidal Nationalism," *The Carl Beck Papers in Russian and East European Studies* 2402 (2015): 9–11.

31. Richard J.B. Bosworth, "Dictators Strong or Weak? The Model of Benito Mussolini," in *The Oxford Handbook of Fascism*, ed. idem (New York, 2009), 274.

32. Fernando Esposito and Sven Reichardt, "Revolution and Eternity: Introductory Remarks on Fascist Temporalities," *Journal of Modern European History* 14 (2015): 24–43. Also see Joshua Arthurs, "The Excavatory Intervention: Archaeology and the Chronopolitics of Roman Antiquity in Fascist Italy," *Journal of Modern European History* 13 (2015): 44–58; Claudio Fogu, "The Fascist Stylisation of Time," *Journal of Modern European History* 13 (2015): 98–114; Roberts, *Interactions*, 61-124, 181; Reynolds, *The Long Shadow*, 71, 73; Griffin, *Modernism and Fascism*, esp. 215–16; Eatwell, *Fascism*, 5, 11; Schieder, "Die Geburt", 159–79; idem, *Der italienische Faschismus*, 65.

33. Luca de Caprariis, "'Fascism for Export'? The Rise and Eclipse of the Fasci Italiani all'Estero," *Journal of Contemporary History* 35, no. 2 (2000): 152–54, 159–60, 177. For a case study, see Claudia Baldoli, *Exporting Fascism: Italian Fascists and Britain's Italians in the 1930s* (Oxford, 2003), 9, 25, 27, 187; idem, "Anglo-Italian Fascist Solidarity? The Shift from Italophilia to Naziphilia in the BUF," in *The Culture of Fascism: Visions of the Far Right in Britain*, ed. Julie V. Gottlieb and Thomas P. Lineham (London, 2004), 148.

34. Roger Griffin, ed., *Fascism* (New York, 1995), 73.

35. Kallis, "Fascist Effect," 20 (quotation), 26.

36. Schieder, "Faschismus im politischen Transfer," esp. 37–53; idem, *Mythos*, 58–70; idem, *Benito Mussolini*, 71–72. On Mussolini's hostility to Germany in World War I, see Klaus Heitmann, "Delenda Germania! Deutschland aus der Sicht des jungen Mussolini," *Quellen und Forschungen aus italienischen Archiven und Bibliotheken* 90 (2010): 311–45.

37. See Matthias Damm, *Die Rezeption des italienischen Faschismus in der Weimarer Republik* (Baden-Baden, 2013); Hans Woller, "Machtpolitisches Kalkül oder ideologische Affinität? Zur Frage des Verhältnisses zwischen Mussolini und Hitler vor 1933," in *Der Nationalsozialismus. Studien zur Ideologie und Herrschaft*, ed. Wolfgang Benz, Hans Buchheim, and Hans Mommsen (Frankfurt/Main, 1993), 42–63; Manfred Wichmann, "Die Gesellschaft zum Studium des Faschismus: Ein antidemokratisches

Netzwerk zwischen Rechtskonservativismus und Nationalsozialismus," *Bulletin für Faschismus- und Weltkriegsforschung* 31/32 (2008): 72–104; Josef Schröder, "Die Italienreise einer brandenburgisch-pommerschen Stahlhelm-Gruppe im November 1930: Fallbeispiel für Renzettis ungeahntes Tätigsein in Deutschland," in *Hitler und Mussolini: Aspekte der deutsch-italienischen Beziehungen, 1930–1945. Festgabe für Josef Schröder zum 70. Geburtstag*, ed. Carl August Lückerath and Michael Salewski (Zurich, 2009), 1–82; Schieder, "Das italienische Experiment," 84.

38. Richard J.B. Bosworth, *Italy and the Wider World 1860–1960* (London, 1996), 156. On Italian support for the BUF, cf. Martin Pugh, *"Hurrah for the Blackshirts!" Fascists and Fascism between the Wars* (London, 2005); Karen Bayer, *"How Dead is Hitler?" Der britische Starreporter Sefton Delmer und die Deutschen* (Mainz, 2008), 46–47, 51, 61–62, 285–86. On the OUN, Ustasha, and Mussolini, see Rossoliński-Liebe, *Stepan Bandera*, 75–76.

39. Wenke Nitz, *Führer und Duce: Politische Machtinszenierung im nationalsozialistischen Deutschland und im faschistischen Italien* (Cologne, 2013), 65, 111, 119, 124, 131, 142–43, 323–25, 385–86.

40. Rossoliński-Liebe, *Stepan Bandera*, 79.

41. On Bohle's AO, cf. Hans-Jürgen Döscher, *Das Auswärtige Amt im Dritten Reich: Diplomatie im Schatten der "Endlösung"* (Berlin, 1987), 166–74. Bob Moore, "Nazism and German Nationals in the Netherlands, 1933–40," *Journal of Contemporary History* 22 (1987): 45–70. Also see John Perkins, "The Swastika Down Under: Nazi Activities in Australia, 1933–39," *Journal of Contemporary History* 26 (1991): 111–29; Jürgen Müller, *Nationalsozialismus in Lateinamerika: Die Auslandsorganisation der NSDAP in Argentinien, Brasilien, Chile und Mexiko* (Stuttgart, 1997), esp. 210–80, 399–496.

42. Elke Fröhlich, ed., *Die Tagebücher von Joseph Goebbels. Sämtliche Fragmente I: Aufzeichnungen 1924–1941, Bd. 2: 1.1.1931–31.12.1936* (Munich, 1987), 629–30, 632, 649; Richard Griffiths, *Fellow Travellers of the Right: British Enthusiasts for Nazi Germany 1933–39* (London, 1980), 104–7, 173; Arnd Bauerkämper, *Die „radikale Rechte" in Großbritannien* (Göttingen, 1991), 232. On the change in the programmatic orientation of the BUF, see Baldoli, "Anglo-Italian Fascist Solidarity?" 147–61.

43. See Rossoliński-Liebe, *Stepan Bandera*, 73–74.

44. Rossoliński-Liebe, *Stepan Bandera*, 80–81. On the strongly pro-German "Link" in 1939 and 1940, cf. Richard Griffiths, *Patriotism Perverted: Captain Ramsay, the Right Club and British Anti-Semitism 1939–40* (London, 1998), 170–71, 219–24; Richard Thurlow, *Fascism in Britain: A History 1918–85* (Oxford, 1987), 179–83. On the NSB, see H. van der Wusten and R.E. Smit, "Dynamics of the Dutch National Socialist Movement (the NSB), 1931–35," in *Who Were the Fascists? Social Roots of European Fascism*, ed. Stein U. Larsen, Bernt Hagtvet, and Jan P. Myklebust (Bergen, 1980), 524–41; Blinkhorn, *Fascism*, 62.

45. Woller, *Rom*, 192–93; Waltraud Sennebogen, "Propaganda als Populärkultur? Werbestrategien und Werbepraxis im faschistischen Italien und in NS-Deutschland," in *Faschismus*, ed. Nolzen and Reichardt, 119–47, esp. 127–30, 144, 146.

46. Rossoliński-Liebe, *Stepan Bandera*, 76.

47. Salvatore Garau, *Fascism and Ideology: Italy, Britain, and Norway* (New York, 2015), 130, 216, 230; idem, "The Internationalisation of Italian Fascism in the Face of German National Socialism, and its Impact on the British Union of Fascists," *Politics, Religion & Ideology* 15 (2014): 45–63.

48. Brian R. Sullivan, "From Little Brother to Senior Partner: Fascist Italian Perceptions of the Nazis and of Hitler's Regime, 1930–1936," in *Knowing Your Friends: Intelligence inside Alliances and Coalitions from 1914 to the Cold War*, ed. Martin Alexander (London, 1998), 85–108, esp. 103–4.

49. Rossoliński-Liebe, *Stepan Bandera*, 180, 197–98, 234–35, 251–52. For Romania, see Gerhard Köpernik, *Faschisten im KZ: Rumäniens Eiserne Garde und das Dritte Reich* (Berlin, 2014), esp. 249–50.

50. For the role of police in the Holocaust in Eastern Europe, cf. Christoph Dieckmann, Babette Quinkert, and Tatjana Tönsmeyer, eds., *Kooperation und Verbrechen: Formen der "Kollaboration" im östlichen Europa 1939–1945* (Göttingen, 2003).

51. Rolf-Dieter Müller, *An der Seite der Wehrmacht: Hitlers ausländische Helfer beim "Kreuzzug gegen den Bolschewismus" 1941–1945* (Berlin, 2007), 243–44. Also see Max Bonacker, "'Europa den Europäern!' Europapropaganda im NS-Rundfunk (1941–1944)," *Rundfunk und Geschichte: Mitteilungen des Studienkreises Rundfunk und Geschichte* 28 (2001): 121–27. On the "Blue Division," see Xosé-Manoel Núñez, "Als die spanischen Faschisten (Ost) Europa entdeckten—Zur Russlanderfahrung der 'Blauen Division' (1941–1944)," *Totalitarismus und Demokratie* 3 (2006): 323–44.

52. Sandrine Kott, "Internationalism in Wartime: Introduction," *Journal of Modern European History* 12 (2014): 321; Fioravanzo, "Europakonzeptionen," 515, 522, 525; Sullivan, "Brother," 106; Bosworth, *Italy*, 157.

53. Goeschel, "*Italia docet?*" 490.

54. Kevin Passmore, "Introduction: Political Violence and Democracy in Western Europe, 1918–1940," *Political Violence and Democracy in Western Europe, 1918–1940*, ed. Kevin Passmore and Chris Millington (Basingstoke, 2015), 5.

55. See, for example, the contributions to Julie V. Gottlieb and Thomas P. Lineham, eds., *The Culture of Fascism: Visions of the Far Right in Britain* (London, 2004); Fraixe, Poupault, and Piccioni, *Vers une Europe latine*.

56. Hugo García, Mercedes Yusta, Xavier Tabet, and Cristina Clímaco, ed. *Rethinking Antifascism. History, Memory and Politics, 1922 to the Present* (Oxford and New York, 2016); Stéfanie Prezioso, "Antifascism and Anti-totalitarianism: The Italian Debate," *Journal of Contemporary History* 43 (2008): 555–72. Also see Daniel Tilles, "Narratives of Violence: Fascists and Jews in 1930s Britain," in *Political Violence and Democracy in Western Europe, 1918–1940*, ed. Kevin Passmore and Chris Millington (Basingstoke, 2015), 192; Pinto and Kallis, "Conclusion," 274; Pinto and Kallis, "Introduction," 2–3; Kallis, "Fascist Effect," 36.

57. Dan Stone, "Anti-Fascist Europe Comes to Britain: Theorizing Fascism as a Contribution to Defeating It," in *Varieties of Anti-Fascism: Britain in the Inter-War Period*, ed. Nigel Copsey and Andrzej Olechnowicz (Houndmills, 2010), 183–201, esp. 183, 196–97.

58. Nigel Copsey, *Anti-Fascism in Britain* (Basingstoke, 2000), 5, 189; Andrzej Olechnowicz, "Introduction: Historians and the Study of Anti-Fascism in Britain," in *Varieties of Anti-Fascism: Britain in the Interwar Period*, ed. Andrzej Olechnowicz and Nigel Copsey (Houndmills, 2010), 3; Giuliana Chamedes, "The Vatican, Nazi-Fascism, and the Making of Transnational Anti-communism in the 1930s," *Journal of Contemporary History* 51 (2016): 261–90, esp. 261–62, 271–72, 279–81, 289; Stéfanie Prezioso, "Fighting Fascism with Its Own Weapons: A Common Dark Side?" in *Political Violence and Democracy in Western Europe, 1918–1940*, ed. Kevin Passmore and Chris Millington (Basingstoke, 2015), 31–47, esp. 31, 34, 37; Loewenstein, "Militant Democracy," 655–57.
59. Richard Thurlow, "Passive and Active Anti-Fascism: The State and National Security, 1923–45," in *Varieties of Anti-Fascism*, 168.
60. George Orwell, "Appendix I. Orwell's Proposed Preface to *Animal Farm*," in *Animal Farm* (London, 2000), 105.
61. Robert Paxton, *The Anatomy of Fascism* (New York, 2004), 197.
62. Jennifer L. Foray, "An Old Empire and a New Order: The Global Designs of the Dutch Nazi Party, 1931–1942," *European History Quarterly* 43, no. 1 (2013): 27–52, esp. 29, 41.
63. Diethelm Prowe, "Fascism, Neo-fascism, New Radical Right?" in *International Fascism: Theories, Causes and the New Consensus*, ed. Roger Griffin (London, 1998), 320. Also see Richard Griffiths, "Anti-Fascism and the Post-War British Establishment," in *Varieties of Anti-Fascism: Britain in the Interwar Period*, ed. Andrzej Olechnowicz and Nigel Copsey (Houndmills, 2010), 260.
64. Adrian Lyttelton, "Concluding Remarks," in *Rethinking the Nature of Fascism: Comparative Perspectives*, ed. António Costa Pinto (London, 2011), 271.
65. David Stephen Frey, "The Paradox of Hungarian Cultural Imperialism in Nazi New Order Europe, 1939–42," *Journal of Contemporary History* 51 (2016): 577–605.

Bibliography

Arielli, Nir. *Fascist Italy and the Middle East, 1933–40*. Basingstoke, 2013.

Arthurs, Joshua. "The Excavatory Intervention: Archaeology and the Chronopolitics of Roman Antiquity in Fascist Italy." *Journal of Modern European History* 13 (2015): 44–58.

Baer, Marc David. "Muslim Encounters with Nazism and the Holocaust: The Ahmadi of Berlin and Jewish Convert to Islam Hugo Marcus." *American Historical Review* 120 (2015): 140–71.

Baldoli, Claudia. *Exporting Fascism: Italian Fascists and Britain's Italians in the 1930s*. Oxford, 2003.

———. "Anglo-Italian Fascist Solidarity? The Shift from Italophilia to Naziphilia in the BUF." In *The Culture of Fascism: Visions of the Far Right in Britain*, ed. Julie V. Gottlieb and Thomas P. Lineham, 147–61. London, 2004.

Barnes, James J. and Patience P. Barnes, *James Vincent Murphy: Translator and Interpreter of Fascist Europe, 1880–1946*. Lanham, MD, 1987.

Bauerkämper, Arnd. *Die „radikale Rechte" in Großbritannien*. Göttingen, 1991.

———. *Der Faschismus in Europa, 1918–1945*. Stuttgart, 2006.

———. "Ambiguities of Transnationalism: Fascism in Europe between Pan-Europeanism and Ultra-Nationalism, 1919–39." *German Historical Institute Bulletin* 29, no. 2 (2007): 43–67.

———. "Interwar Fascism in Europe and Beyond: Toward a Transnational Radical Right." In *New Perspectives on the Transnational Right*, ed. Martin Durham and Margaret Power, 39–66. Houndmills, 2010.

———. "Transnational Fascism: Cross-Border Relations between Regimes and Movements in Europe, 1922–1939." *East Central Europe* 37 (2010): 214–46.

———. "Der 'Große Krieg' als Beginn: Das Verhältnis zwischen traditionalen Ordnungskonzepten, Faschismus und Autoritarismus." *Totalitarismus und Demokratie* 12 (2015): 73–96.

Bayer, Karen. *"How Dead is Hitler?" Der britische Starreporter Sefton Delmer und die Deutschen*. Mainz, 2008.

Behrends, Jan C. "Back from the USSR: The Anti-Comintern's Publications on Soviet Russia in Nazi Germany (1935–41)." *Kritika: Explorations in Russian and Eurasian History* 10, no. 3 (2009): 527–56.

Bernhard, Patrick. "Konzertierte Gegnerbekämpfung im Achsenbündnis: Die Polizei im Dritten Reich und im faschistischen Italien 1933 bis 1943." *Vierteljahrshefte für Zeitgeschichte* 59 (2011): 229–62.

Blinkhorn, Martin. *Fascism and the Right in Europe, 1919–1945*. Harlow, 2000.

Bloch, Marc. "Für eine vergleichende Geschichtsbetrachtung der europäischen Gesellschaften." In *Alles Gewordene hat Geschichte: Die Schule der Annales in ihren Texten 1929–1992*, ed. Matthias Middell und Steffen Sammler, 121–67. Leipzig, 1994.

Bonacker, Max. "'Europa den Europäern!' Europapropaganda im NS-Rundfunk (1941–1944)." *Rundfunk und Geschichte: Mitteilungen des Studienkreises Rundfunk und Geschichte* 28 (2001): 121–27.

Borejsza, Jerzy W. "Die Rivalität zwischen Faschismus und Nationalsozialismus in Ostmitteleuropa." *Vierteljahrshefte für Zeitgeschichte* 29 (1981): 579–614.

———. *Schulen des Hasses. Faschistische Systeme in Europa*. Frankfurt/Main, 1999.

Bose, Sugata. *His Majesty's Opponent: Subhas Chandra Bose and India's Struggle against Empire*. Cambridge, MA, 2011.

Bosworth, Richard J.B. *Italy and the Wider World 1860–1960*. London, 1996.

———. "Dictators Strong or Weak? The Model of Benito Mussolini." In *The Oxford Handbook of Fascism*, ed. Richard Bosworth, 259–75. New York, 2009.

Chamedes, Giuliana. "The Vatican, Nazi-Fascism, and the Making of Transnational Anti-communism in the 1930s." *Journal of Contemporary History* 51 (2016): 261–90.

"Chy my fashysty?" *Zahrava* 1, no. 7 (1923): 97–102.

Cohen, Deborah, and Maura O'Connor. "Introduction: Comparative History, Cross-National History, Transnational History—Definitions." In *Comparison and History: Europe in Cross-National Perspective*, ed. Deborah Cohen and Maura O'Connor, IX–XXIV. New York, 2004.

Copsey, Nigel. *Anti-Fascism in Britain*. Basingstoke 2000.

Damm, Matthias. *Die Rezeption des italienischen Faschismus in der Weimarer Republik*. Baden-Baden, 2013.

De Caprariis, Luca. "'Fascism for Export?' The Rise and Eclipse of the Fasci Italiani all'Estero." *Journal of Contemporary History* 35 (2000): 151–83.

Deflem, Mathieu. *Policing World Society: Historical Foundations of International Police Cooperation*. Oxford, 2002.

———. "International Police Cooperation, History of." In *Encyclopedia of Criminology*, vol. 2, ed. Richard A. Wright and J. Mitchell Miller, 795–98. New York, 2005.

Dieckmann, Christoph, Babette Quinkert, and Tatjana Tönsmeyer, eds. *Kooperation und Verbrechen: Formen der "Kollaboration" im östlichen Europa 1939–1945*. Göttingen, 2003.

Di Palma, Francesco. *Liberaler Sozialismus in Deutschland und Italien im Vergleich: Das Beispiel Sopade und Giustizia & Libertà*. Berlin, 2010.

Döscher, Hans-Jürgen. *Das Auswärtige Amt im Dritten Reich. Diplomatie im Schatten der "Endlösung"*. Berlin, 1987.

Eatwell, Roger. *Fascism: A History*. London, 1995.

Esposito, Fernando, and Sven Reichardt, "Revolution and Eternity: Introductory Remarks on Fascist Temporalities." *Journal of Modern European History* 14 (2015): 24–43.

Finchelstein, Federico. *Transatlantic Fascism: Ideology, Violence and the Sacred in Argentina and Italy, 1919–1945*. Durham, 2010.

Fioravanzo, Monica. "Die Europakonzeptionen von Faschismus und Nationalsozialismus (1939–1943)." *Vierteljahrshefte für Zeitgeschichte* 58 (2010): 509–41.

Fogu, Claudio, "The Fascist Stylisation of Time." *Journal of Modern European History* 13 (2015): 98–114.

Foray, Jennifer L. "An Old Empire and a New Order: The Global Designs of the Dutch Nazi Party, 1931–1942." *European History Quarterly* 43, no. 1 (2013): 27–52.

Fraixe, Catherine, Christophe Poupault, and Luca Piccioni, eds. *Vers une Europe latine: Acteurs et enjeux des échanges culturels entre la France et l'Italoe fasciste*. Brussels, 2014.

Freitag, Ulrike, and Israel Gershoni, eds. *Arab Encounters with Fascist Propaganda 1933–1945*. Göttingen, 2011.

Fröhlich, Elke, ed. *Die Tagebücher von Joseph Goebbels. Sämtliche Fragmente I: Aufzeichnungen 1924–1941, Bd. 2: 1.1.1931–31.12.1936*. Munich, 1987.

Garau, Salvatore. "The Internationalisation of Italian Fascism in the Face of German National Socialism, and its Impact on the British Union of Fascists." *Politics, Religion & Ideology* 15 (2014): 45–63.

———. *Fascism and Ideology: Italy, Britain, and Norway*. New York, 2015.

García, Hugo, Mercedes Yusta, Xavier Tabet, and Cristina Clímaco, eds. *Rethinking Antifascism. History, Memory and Politics, 1922 to the Present*. Oxford and New York, 2016.

Goeschel, Christian. "*Italia docet*? The Relationship between Italian Fascism and Nazism Revisited." *European History Quarterly* 42 (2012): 480–92.

Goodfellow, Samuel Huston. "Fascism as a Transnational Movement: The Case of Inter-War Alsace." *Contemporary European History* 22 (2013): 97–106.

Gosewinkel, Dieter, ed. *Anti-liberal Europe: A Neglected Story of Europeanization.* New York, 2015.

Gottlieb, Julie V., and Thomas P. Lineham, eds. *The Culture of Fascism: Visions of the Far Right in Britain.* London, 2004.

Griffin, Roger, ed. *Fascism.* New York, 1995.

———. *Modernism and Fascism: The Sense of a Beginning under Mussolini and Hitler.* Houndmills, 2007.

———. "Europe for the Europeans: Fascist Myths of the European Order 1922–1992." In *A Fascist Century. Essays by Roger Griffin*, ed. Matthew Feldman, 132–80. New York, 2008.

Griffiths, Richard. *Fellow Travellers of the Right: British Enthusiasts for Nazi Germany 1933–39.* London, 1980.

———. *Patriotism Perverted: Captain Ramsay, the Right Club and British Anti-Semitism 1939–40.* London, 1998.

———. "Anti-Fascism and the Post-War British Establishment." In *Varieties of Anti-Fascism: Britain in the Interwar Period*, ed. Andrzej Olechnowicz and Nigel Copsey, 247–64. Houndmills, Palgrave Macmillan, 2010.

Grunert, Robert. *Der Europagedanke westeuropäischer faschistischer Bewegungen 1940–1945.* Paderborn, 2012.

Hamilton, Alastair. *The Appeal of Fascism: A Study of Intellectuals and Fascism 1919–1945.* London, 1971.

Heitmann, Klaus. "Delenda Germania! Deutschland aus der Sicht des jungen Mussolini." *Quellen und Forschungen aus italienischen Archiven und Bibliotheken* 90 (2010): 311–45.

Herf, Jeffrey. *The Jewish Enemy: Nazi Propaganda during World War II and the Holocaust.* London, 2006.

———. *Nazi Propaganda for the Arab World.* New Haven, 2009.

———. "Nazi Germany's Propaganda Aimed at Arabs and Muslims during World War II and the Holocaust: Old Times, New Archival Findings." *Central European History* 42 (2009): 707–36.

Herren, Madelaine. "'Outwardly an Innocuous Conference Authority': National Socialism and the Logistics of International Information Management." *German History* 20 (2002): 67–92.

Hohler, Susanne. "Russian Fascism in Exile: A Historical and Phenomenological Perspective on Transnational Fascism." *Fascism* 2, no. 2 (2013): 121–40.

Iggers, Georg G. "Nationalism and Historiography, 1789–1996, the German Example in Historical Perspective." In *Writing National Histories: Western Europe since 1800*, ed. Stefan Berger, Mark Donovan, and Kevin Passmore, 15–29. London, 1999.

Ihrig, Stefan. "The History of European Fascism—Origins, Foreign Relations and (Dis)Entangled Histories." *European History Quarterly* 41 (2011): 278–90.

Ioanid, Radu. *The Sword of the Archangel: Fascist Ideology in Romania.* Boulder, 1990.

Iordachi, Constantin. "Comparative Fascist Studies: An Introduction." In *Comparative Fascist Studies: New Perspectives*, ed. C. Iordachi, 1–50. London, 2010.

———. "God's Chosen Warriors: Romantic Palingenesis, Militarism and Fascism in Modern Romania." In *Comparative Fascist Studies: New Perspectives*, ed. C. Iordachi, 316–57. London, 2010.

Kallis, Aristotle. "'Fascism', 'Para-fascism' and 'Fascistization': On the Similarities of Three Conceptual Categories." *European History Quarterly* 33 (2003): 219–50.

———. "The 'Fascist Effect': On the Dynamics of Political Hybridization in Inter-War Europe." In *Rethinking Fascism and Dictatorship in Europe*, ed. António Costa Pinto and Aristotle Kallis, 13–41. New York, 2014.

Köpernik, Gerhard. *Faschisten im KZ: Rumänins Eiserne Garde und das Dritte Reich*. Berlin, 2014.

Kott, Sandrine. "Internationalism in Wartime: Introduction." *Journal of Modern European History* 12 (2014): 317–22.

Kwaschik, Anne. "An der Grenze der Nationen: Europa-Konzepte und regionale Selbstverortung im Elsass." *Zeithistorische Forschungen / Studies in Contemporary History* 9 (2012): 387–408.

Laqueur, Walter. *Fascism: Past, Present, Future*. New York, 1996.

Larsen, Stein U. "Decomposition and Recomposition of Theories: How to Arrive at Useful Ideas Explaining Fascism." In *Rethinking the Nature of Fascism: Comparative Perspectives*, ed. António Costa Pinto, 13–52. Basingstoke, 2011.

Law, Ricky W. "Knowledge is Power: The Interwar German and Japanese Mass Media in the Making of the Axis." *Bulletin of the German Historical Institute* 54 (2014): 27–47.

Ledeen, Michael A. "Italian Fascism and Youth." *Journal of Contemporary History* 4 (1969): 137–54.

———. *Universal Fascism: The Theory and Practice of the Fascist International, 1928–1936*. New York, 1972.

Lepenies, Wolf, ed. *Entangled Histories and Negotiated Universals: Centers and Peripheries in a Changing World*. Frankfurt/Main, 2003.

Linne, Karsten. "Sozialpropaganda—Die Auslandspublizistik der Deutschen Arbeitsfront 1936–1944." *Zeitschrift für Geschichtswissenschaft* 57 (2009): 237–54.

Loewenstein, Karl. "Militant Democracy and Fundamental Rights." *American Political Science Review* 31 (1937): 638–58.

Lyttelton, Adrian. "Concluding Remarks." In *Rethinking the Nature of Fascism: Comparative Perspectives*, ed. António Costa Pinto, 271–78. Basingstoke, 2011.

Mazower, Mark. *Hitler's Empire: Nazi Rule in Occupied Europe*. London, 2008.

Moore, Bob. "Nazism and German Nationals in the Netherlands, 1933–40." *Journal of Contemporary History* 22 (1987): 45–70.

Morgan, Philip. *Fascism in Europe, 1919–1945*. London, 2003.

Mosley, Oswald. *Fascism in Britain*. Westminster, 1935.

Motadel, David. *Islam and Nazi Germany's War*. Cambridge, MA, 2014.

Müller, Jürgen. *Nationalsozialismus in Lateinamerika: Die Auslandsorganisation der NSDAP in Argentinien, Brasilien, Chile und Mexiko*. Stuttgart, 1997.

Müller, Rolf-Dieter. *An der Seite der Wehrmacht: Hitlers ausländische Helfer beim "Kreuzzug gegen den Bolschewismus" 1941–1945.* Berlin, 2007.

Nitz, Wenke, *Führer und Duce: Politische Machtinszenierung im national-sozialistischen Deutschland und im faschistischen Italien.* Cologne, 2013.

Nolzen, Armin, and Sven Reichardt, eds. *Faschismus in Deutschland und Italien: Studien zu Transfer und Vergleich.* Göttingen, 2005.

Núñez, Xosé-Manoel. "Als die spanischen Faschisten (Ost)Europa entdeckten— Zur Russlanderfahrung der 'Blauen Division' (1941–1944)." *Totalitarismus und Demokratie* 3 (2006): 323–44.

Olechnowicz, Andrzej. "Introduction: Historians and the Study of Anti-Fascism in Britain." In *Varieties of Anti-Fascism: Britain in the Interwar Period,* ed. Andrzej Olechnowicz and Nigel Copsey, 1-27. Houndmills, 2010.

Olin, Alette, and Boyd H. Hill. "Marc Bloch and Comparative History." *American Historical Review* 85 (1980): 828–46.

Orlow, Dietrich. "Fascists among Themselves: Some Observations on West European Politics in the 1930s." *European Review* 11 (2003): 245–66.

———. *The Lure of Fascism in Western Europe: German Nazis, Dutch and French Fascists, 1933–1939.* New York, 2009.

Orwell, George. *The Road to Wigan Pier.* London, (1937) 2001.

———. *Animal Farm.* London, 2000.

Passmore, Kevin. "Introduction: Political Violence and Democracy in Western Europe, 1918–1940." In *Political Violence and Democracy in Western Europe, 1918–1940,* ed. Kevin Passmore and Chris Millington, 1–13. Basingstoke, 2015.

Patel, Kiran Klaus. "Der Nationalsozialismus in transnationaler Perspektive." *Blätter für deutsche und internationale Politik* 9 (2004): 1122–34.

———. "In Search of a Transnational Historicization: National Socialism and its Place in History." In *Conflicted Memories: Europeanizing Contemporary History,* ed. Konrad H. Jarausch and Thomas Lindenberger, 96–116. New York, 2007.

Paxton, Robert. *The Anatomy of Fascism.* New York, 2004.

Payne, Stanley G. "George L. Mosse and Walter Laqueur on the History of Fascism." *Journal of Contemporary History* 50 (2015): 750–67.

Perkins, John. "The Swastika Down Under: Nazi Activities in Australia, 1933–39." *Journal of Contemporary History* 26 (1991): 111–29.

Pinto, António Costa. *The Nature of Fascism Revisited.* New York, 2012.

Pinto, António Costa, and Aristotle Kallis. "Back to European Fascism." *Contemporary European History* 15 (2006): 103–15.

———. "Conclusion: Embracing Complexity and Transnational Dynamics. The Diffusion of Fascism and the Hybridization of Dictatorships in Inter-War Europe." In *Rethinking Fascism and Dictatorship in Europe.* Ed. António Costa Pinto and Aristotle Kallis, 272–82. New York, 2014.

———. "Introduction." In *Rethinking Fascism and Dictatorship in Europe.* Ed. António Costa Pinto and Aristotle Kallis, 1–10. New York, 2014.

Prezioso, Stéfanie. "Antifascism and Anti-totalitarianism: The Italian Debate." *Journal of Contemporary History* 43 (2008): 555–72.

————. "Fighting Fascism with Its Own Weapons: A Common Dark Side?" In *Political Violence and Democracy in Western Europe, 1918–1940*, ed. Kevin Passmore and Chris Millington, 341–47. Basingstoke, 2015.

Prowe, Diethelm. "Fascism, Neo-fascism, New Radical Right?" In *International Fascism: Theories, Causes and the New Consensus*, ed. Roger Griffin, 305–24. London, 1998.

Pugh, Martin. *"Hurrah for the Blackshirts!" Fascists and Fascism between the Wars.* London, 2005.

Randeria, Shalini. "Entangled Histories of Uneven Modernities: Civil Society, Caste Solidarities and Legal Pluralism in Post-Colonial India." In *Unraveling Ties: From Social Cohesion to New Practices of* Connectedness, ed. Yehuda Elkana, Ivan Krastev, Elisio Macamo, and Shalini Raneria, 284–311. Frankfurt/Main, 2002.

Reynolds, David. *The Long Shadow: The Great War and the Twentieth Century.* London, 2013.

Roberts, David D. *Fascist Interactions: Proposals for a New Approach to Fascism and Its Era, 1919-1945.* New York, 2016.

————. "Fascism and the Framework for Interactive Political Innovation during the Era of the Two World Wars." In *Rethinking Fascism and Dictatorship in Europe*, ed. António Costa Pinto and Aristotle Kallis, 42–66. New York, 2014.

Rodogno, Davide. *Fascism's European Empire: Italian Occupation during the Second World War.* Cambridge, 2006.

Rossoliński-Liebe, Grzegorz. *Stepan Bandera. The Life and Afterlife of a Ukrainian Nationalist: Fascism, Genocide, and Cult.* Stuttgart, 2014.

————. "The Fascist Kernel of the Ukrainian Genocidal Nationalism." *The Carl Back Papers in Russian and East European Studies* 2402 (2015): 1–65.

Saunier, Pierre-Yves. "Transnational." In *The Palgrave Dictionary of Transnational History*, ed. Akira Iriye and Pierre-Yves Saunier, 1047–54. Houndmills, 2009.

Schieder, Wolfgang. "Das italienische Experiment: Der Faschismus als Vorbild in der Krise der Weimarer Republik." *Historische Zeitschrift* 262 (1996): 73–125.

————. "Die Geburt des Faschismus aus der Krise der Moderne." In *Deutschland und Italien 1860–1960: Politische und kulturelle Aspekte im Vergleich*, ed. Christof Dipper, 159–79. Munich, 2005.

————. "Faschismus im politischen Transfer: Giuseppe Renzetti als faschistischer Propagandist und Geheimagent in Berlin 1922–1941." In *Faschismus in Italien und Deutschland: Studien zu Transfer und Vergleich*, ed. Sven Reichardt and Armin Nolzen, 28–58. Göttingen, 2005.

————. *Faschistische Diktaturen. Studien zu Italien und Deutschland.* Göttingen, 2008.

————. *Der italienische Faschismus 1919–1945.* Munich, 2010.

————. *Mythos Mussolini: Deutsche in Audienz beim Duce.* Munich, 2012.

————. *Benito Mussolini.* Munich, 2014.

Schlemmer, Thomas, and Hans Woller. "Politischer Deutungskampf und wissenschaftliche Deutungsmacht: Konjunkturen der Faschismusforschung." In *Der Faschismus in Europa: Wege der Forschung*, ed. Thomas Schlemmer and Hans Woller, 7–15. Munich, 2014.

Scholz, Beate. *Italienischer Faschismus als „Export"-Artikel (1927–1935)*. Ph.D. diss., University of Trier, 2001.

Schöttler, Peter. "Dreierlei Kollaboration: Europa-Konzepte und deutsch-französische Verständigung—am Beispiel der Karriere von SS-Brigadeführer Gustav Krukenberg." *Zeithistorische Forschungen* 9 (2012): 365–86.

Schröder, Josef. "Die Italienreise einer brandenburgisch-pommerschen Stahlhelm-Gruppe im November 1930. Fallbeispiel für Renzettis ungeahntes Tätigsein in Deutschland." In *Hitler und Mussolini. Aspekte der deutsch-italienischen Beziehungen, 1930–1945. Festgabe für Josef Schröder zum 70. Geburtstag*, ed. Carl August Lückerath and Michael Salewski, 1–82. Zurich, 2009.

Schulze, Thies. "Die Zukunft der Diktaturen: Der Niedergang der Diktatur Miguel Primo de Riveras aus der Perspektive des Mussolini-Regimes." *Zeitschrift für Geschichtswissenschaft* 57 (2009): 134–56.

Sennebogen, Waltraud. "Propaganda als Populärkultur? Werbestrategien und Werbepraxis im faschistischen Italien und in NS-Deutschland." In *Faschismus in Deutschland und Italien: Studien zu Transfer und Vergleich*, ed. Armin Nolzen and Sven Reichardt, 119–47. Göttingen, 2005.

Sluga, Glenda. "Fascism and Anti-Fascism." In *The Palgrave Dictionary of Transnational History*, ed. Akira Iriye and Pierre-Yves Saunier, 381–83. Houndmills, 2009.

Stone, Dan. "Anti-Fascist Europe Comes to Britain: Theorizing Fascism as a Contribution to Defeating It." In *Varieties of Anti-Fascism: Britain in the Inter-War Period*, ed. Nigel Copsey and Andrzej Olechnowicz, 183–201. Houndmills, 2010.

Stone, Marla. "Staging Fascism: The Exhibition of the Fascist Revolution." *Journal of Contemporary History* 28 (1993): 215–43.

Sullivan, Brian R. "From Little Brother to Senior Partner: Fascist Italian Perceptions of the Nazis and of Hitler's Regime, 1930–1936." In *Knowing Your Friends: Intelligence inside Alliances and Coalitions from 1914 to the Cold War*, ed. Martin Alexander, 85–108. London, 1998.

Thurlow, Richard. *Fascism in Britain: A History 1918–85*. Oxford, 1987.

———. "Passive and Active Anti-Fascism: The State and National Security, 1923–45." In *Varieties of Anti-Fascism: Britain in the Inter-War Period*, ed. Nigel Copsey and Andrzej Olechnowicz, 162–180. Houndmills, 2010.

Tilles, Daniel. "Narratives of Violence: Fascists and Jews in 1930s Britain." In *Political Violence and Democracy in Western Europe, 1918–1940*, ed. Kevin Passmore and Chris Millington, 173–99. Basingstoke, 2015.

Van der Wusten, H., and R.E. Smit. "Dynamics of the Dutch National Socialist Movement (the NSB): 1931–35." In *Who Were the Fascists? Social Roots of European Fascism*, ed. Stein U. Larsen, Bernt Hagtvet, and Jan P. Myklebust, 524–41. Bergen, 1980.

Waddington, Lorna L. *Hitler's Crusade: Bolshevism and the Myth of the International Jewish Conspiracy*. London, 2007.

———. "The Anti-Komintern and Nazi Anti-Bolshevik Propaganda in the 1930s." *Journal of Contemporary History* 42 (2007): 573–94.

Wichmann, Manfred. "Die Gesellschaft zum Studium des Faschismus: Ein antidemokratisches Netzwerk zwischen Rechtskonservativismus und

Nationalsozialismus." *Bulletin für Faschismus- und Weltkriegsforschung* 31/32 (2008): 72–104.

Woller, Hans. "Machtpolitisches Kalkül oder ideologische Affinität? Zur Frage des Verhältnisses zwischen Mussolini und Hitler vor 1933." In *Der Nationalsozialismus. Studien zur Ideologie und Herrschaft*, ed. Wolfgang Benz, Hans Buchheim, and Hans Mommsen, 42–63. Frankfurt/Main, 1993.

———. *Rom, 28. Oktober 1922. Die faschistische Herausforderung.* Munich, 1999.

⚜ 1

Transnational Fascism
The Fascist New Order, Violence, and Creative Destruction

Aristotle Kallis

In his fascinating study of fascist ideology in Argentina and Italy, Federico Finchelstein describes interwar fascism as a "traveling political universe."[1] To reconstruct its story of spectacular—if short-lived in most cases—political success in so many countries, he argues, the historian would be best served by a perspective that extends beyond nations and states, beyond conventional geographic boundaries of regions and continents, and even beyond traditional patterns of interaction between specific actors with clearly defined ideological and political profiles. The chosen title for his monograph—*Transatlantic Fascism*—deliberately cuts across long-established barriers, both geographic and historiographical, that have severed the history of right-wing radicalism and dictatorship in Latin America from the fascinating parabola of interwar fascism in Europe. The mere suggestion that an intellectual and political phenomenon so deeply rooted in hyper-nationalism could have, or could develop, its own distinct transnational dynamic, with fascinating patterns of cross-border influence that extend across regions and even continents, is perhaps counterintuitive in itself. But Finchelstein's intention is not simply contextual to the study of interwar fascism; instead, in weaving together the history of Italian Fascism with that of Argentina's interwar radical movements, he raises a broader methodological point about the merits of approaching history as a dynamic process of circulation, unpredictable interaction and intersection, multiple transfer, and hybrid, ever-mutating outcomes.

A transnational understanding of interwar fascism is located firmly within the historiographical landscape of generic fascism. Generations of scholars have convincingly argued that "fascism" needs to be liberated from inside the containers of national historiography. It should be understood instead as a political phenomenon with a distinct intellectual core and diverse national roots, but also crucially an international history.[2] Other scholars have attempted to deconstruct the myths of national singularity, be that of the "archetypal" Italian Fascism or the "unique" German National Socialism or indeed the "paradigmatic" nature of the two Axis regimes for the history of generic fascism. They too have converged on an understanding of fascism as a generic ideological label for a multifaceted historical experience. Although it has been seen as different in its permutations in time and place, scholars have emphasized a number of shared ideological characteristics that set this fascism apart from other existing ideologies and movements of its time.[3]

For Ernst Nolte, it was the historical expression of an acute collective desire to resist transcendence—the modern desire to uproot both the individual and society as a whole from their sense of belonging, "from the familiar and beloved," all in the name of transformation, reform, and progress.[4] As George L. Mosse argued, fascism represented the product of an ideological synthesis that was distinct in its specific outcomes but not in terms of the sources or components of the synthesis itself.[5] Two decades later, Roger Griffin postulated a more sophisticated, yet versatile basis for a fascist "ideological minimum" (his "palingenetic populist ultranationalism"). His definition allowed taxonomies of fascist movements and regimes to accommodate variations or even disagreements on key issues such as anti-Semitism or religion without losing sight of other, truly fundamental similarities between them.[6] Roger Eatwell also suggested a refinement that linked more effectively abstract ideology with the kaleidoscope of historical experiences: by proposing a more flexible "fascist matrix" he accounted for the fascinating variations in how different actors understood even the narrow set of key concepts associated with "generic fascism," such as nationalism, national regeneration, and even the notion of a "new man."[7]

Between fascism as a generic ideological force, on the one hand, and fascism as the unwieldy umbrella term for diverse, hybrid ideological and political phenomena across Europe and beyond in the interwar years, lay a fascinating story of circulation, translation, and hybridization in both space and time. This was a story of wide, yet very often unpredictable circulation of ideas along both established and new networks, of many unlikely intersections and influences, as well as of selective appropriations and reflexive translations. This story was somewhat ignored or lost amidst the frenzy of conceptually sophisticated definitions and classifications that had dominated the fray of fascism studies until recently. But this is precisely the story that a transnational approach to the study of fascism has sought to bring into relief. In this chapter, I seek to demonstrate how a transnational perspective may help re-dimension the concept of fascism in a way that encompasses fruitfully not only intentions and outcomes of the various contemporary actors but also the dynamics of interaction and intersection involving a wider gamut of critical agencies over space and time. In other words, I argue that what we typically referred to as interwar (so-called "classic")[8] fascism is better analyzed and understood through a transnational perspective because it was co-produced as a prismatic historical experience over the 1920s, 1930s, and early 1940s by trans- and inter-national agencies. I explore a central facet of fascism's transnational history—the shared belief in a "history-making" project of bringing about a new "European" and global order.[9] This was a Janus-faced venture. On the one hand, it pointed to fascism as a utopian "third-way" alternative to either liberalism or socialism—an alternative that encompassed economics, politics, and culture, but also envisaged the production of a "new man" and a new kind of organic society under the aegis of an all-encompassing, regenerated national state.[10] On the other hand, fascists came to believe that the "new order" they evangelized could only be realized through a fundamental, if need be violent, rupture with the recent past that they perceived as decadent.[11]

This explains why the vision of a fascist new order came to be identified with the idea of *creative destruction*—the need to destroy the perceived forces of "decadence," to shatter the vestiges of the old world, to cleanse and purify society and in many cases the "national community," before embarking on the construction of the new order itself.[12] Violence, I argue, was at the heart of the fascist history-making project. It was destructive of the status quo and generative of a "new order," the perceived nemesis of one kind of transcendence (internationalism-socialism) and the necessary vehicle for counter-transcendence. Fascist ideology invested violence with a critical redemptive function—in the short term deployed against the perceived agents of "decadence" that fascism was fighting against, and in the long term as the vehicle for creative destruction that would pave the way for a new domestic and eventually global order.

Still, it was the rise of National Socialist Germany that transformed the project of a new order into a joint European and increasingly global history-making undertaking. Hitler's regime sought to initiate, and then embarked on an uncompromising campaign of forcing such a "new order," ultimately choosing the path of an all-out war against its perceived enemies as its historical vehicle. National Socialist Germany injected urgency, bold political momentum, and cold-blooded brutality to this project, first within its own territory and, from 1938 onwards, in the territories that it annexed or occupied. But it also inspired or motivated others beyond its borders to think of themselves as agents in a joint undertaking of serving and advancing this new order. It was the Nazi war against the Jews that came to epitomize the devastating potential of fascism's transnational dynamics in interwar and wartime Europe. Active collaboration but also reflexive (and selective) political learning from the Nazi paradigm, fanatical pursuit of the anti-Jewish campaign but also divergence of opinion on a number of matters of substance and execution, appropriations but also sometimes arbitrary translations of precedents—all ensured both the centrality of National Socialist Germany in this undertaking and the crucial inputs of the transnational networks of fascists and their allies.

The focus on the dynamics of diffusion of anti-Semitism in interwar and especially wartime Europe is perhaps the most challenging premise for a transnational perspective on fascism. There is no doubt that, when compared to contemporary fascist movements and regimes, National Socialist ideology and political praxis became linked in a very particular—and in so many respects peerless—way to the fanatical, extreme pursuit of large-scale territorial imperialism, racialism, anti-Semitism, and mass violence.[13] Indeed attitudes to violence and anti-Semitism divided the burgeoning family of interwar fascists/ authoritarians, since not all forces of the "new" radical right embraced violence in similar ways, to the same degree, or with comparable ferocity to the Nazi regime; and certainly not all of them subscribed to the Nazi Final Solution to the so-called "Jewish Question." However, in exploring the empowering effect of the Nazi radical precedent on those ideologically kindred regimes and movements that actively joined in the violent undertaking, I do not simply illustrate how the Nazi project of violent creative destruction was central to the vision (shared by many inter- and transnational agents at the time) of a fascist "new order." I also draw attention to the variety of reflexive translations, recontextualizations, and reformulations of the then unfolding Nazi violent anti-Jewish paradigm by actors in other countries. These ranged from willing collaboration, to translations refracted through distinct national prisms, to volatile attitudes that changed dramatically over time, to refusal to succumb to any Nazi-derived pressure or adopt them altogether. Here then was a complex plane, inhabited by fanatical disciples of the fascist new order as well as rational sympathizers and pragmatic—even cynically calculating—outliers; where ideas and empowering precedents traveled far and fast because they met willing or interested transnational audiences and agents; where diverse actors joined in to adopt, adapt, and reject; where transnational agencies shaped, crucially facilitated, and often inflected the violent undertakings as contributions to the advancement of the fascist new order.

Towards a "Relational" Approach to the Study of Fascism

The transnational approach to fascism was born out of an accumulation of historiographical frustrations. There was the initial postwar over-extension and inflation of the concept of "fascism" to include anything predicated on an authoritarian view of the world. Then there was the early "totalitarian" conflation of fascism with communism as regime models, in joint opposition to liberal democracy. A different kind of over-extension was offered by many Marxist interpretations in the 1960s, conflating fascism with capitalism and overstating the primacy of economics over politics.[14] Gradually, from the excesses of over-extension, the historiography of fascism passed to a phase of intensifying methodological individualism.[15] A group of historians suggested that the rise of National Socialism in Germany was the long-term outcome of a German "special path."[16] Others chose to identify fascism with the movement founded by, and the regime headed by, Mussolini, emphatically excluding National Socialism as something different.[17] Ironically too, the increasing sophistication of definitions of generic fascism resulted unwittingly in higher classificatory benchmarks, which restricted the pool of "fascist" cases while creating new residual categories of fascist "underachievers."[18] Historians now expended considerable effort debating whether a movement was "fascist" or something else, if regimes constituted a useful guide for understanding what fascism really was or whether a comparative approach was methodologically more justified and fruitful than either survey accounts or single case studies. Some would embrace comparison even while otherwise rejecting the notion of fascism as a generic concept.[19]

It was arguably the unfulfilled potential of comparative approaches to fascism that provided the most significant impetus for the transnational alternative. While comparison promoted the suggestion that there was added analytical value for the historian in directing the gaze beyond a single national case study and historical context, comparative studies have ultimately never truly challenged the preponderance of national or state units, often (even unintentionally) reinforcing the notion of national difference if not uniqueness.[20] Furthermore, comparison of particular case studies revolved around a specific set of fields (e.g., modern Italy and Germany as "latecomer" nation-states)[21] that can rarely be generalized beyond a small field of research. In addressing questions about the emergence, popularity, political "success," and indeed geographic diffusion of radical nationalist ideas in the interwar period, it was increasingly felt that explanations cut across national experiences and standard comparative subsets. They also very often involved networks (whether already established or newly formed) of contact, interaction, and competition that traversed a series of established state, ideological, or political boundaries. In many cases, transnational networks functioned as alternative outlets to the more restrictive (and often oppressive) reality of national or state processes.[22] In other instances, they involved national and/or state actors but in pursuit of a radically different kind of global order. Often the lines of influence, transfer, and exchange followed trajectories that defied our own analytical and taxonomical categories—of fascism versus authoritarianism, of old versus new Right, of fascist movements versus established dictatorial regimes.

The definitional approach to the study of interwar "generic" fascism has been particularly unkind to regimes, privileging the ostensibly purer expression of political intention on the level of ideas rather than policies. It was Michel Dobry's sophisticated critique of the definitional rigidity of generic fascism that offered further heuristic nuance to the transnational approach. Dobry championed the relational perspective, embracing the irksome fluidity in the history of fascism, even if it takes us uncomfortably away from any definitional core or classificatory orthodoxy. Dobry is particularly scathing when it comes to the standard designation of German National Socialism and/or Italian Fascism as "archetypal" or "authentic" fascism. For him, the emphasis should shift toward the multitude of processes and series of decisions and events that produced a kaleidoscope of difficult-to-categorize historical outcomes rather than on the outcomes themselves.[23] Dobry also invited scholars of fascism to expand their field of comparison to cases that fall outside the narrow sample of full-fledged or "successful" fascism, focusing instead on entanglements and struggles within the broader, yet overcrowded, constituency of the authoritarian and antiliberal European right for competitive advantage.[24]

Nevertheless, Dobry's critique of the centrality of Italian Fascism and/or German National Socialism in definitions of "generic fascism," however justified, should not distract from a different measure of de facto centrality that is to be reserved for the two movements and later regimes. The "success" of Fascist Italy and National Socialist Germany (real success, in the sense of the two regimes' political consolidation and radicalization; perceived, in the sense of pushing through new, radical "solutions" to taboo "problems") exercised a critical influence over a field that spanned conventional categories. This was a field much broader geographically, more diverse politically and socially, and more crowded than ever previously assumed. It was a hybrid political space where fringe radicals and fervent hyper-nationalists, even in a way revolutionaries of the populist nationalist right,[25] encountered dissident rightists and old-fashioned authoritarians, critics of liberalism and fierce opponents of international socialism. This was a space that also defied classifications as well as rigid distinctions between "old" (authoritarian) and "new" (fascist) Right in interwar Europe.[26] The radical paths trodden by Fascist Italy and National Socialist Germany may have differed from one another in many significant ways, and they certainly appeared starkly different to contemporary observers. Yet a large and constantly growing number of political actors in interwar Europe recognized in the two regimes a single "successful" and increasingly desirable political alternative to both liberalism and socialism in the 1930s. Long before Mussolini spoke of his Fascism as a universal concept, and before he and Hitler embarked on an ever-closer political relationship that formalized the impression of a single front, something that we nowadays broadly identify with fascism was recognized by its contemporaries as a historical force with a self-awarded mission to bring about a new order.

Fascism: From Italian to Transnational Phenomenon

It is ironic that the history of the transnational understanding of fascism began on the revolutionary Left of the political spectrum almost concurrently with its moment of political triumph in Italy in 1922. The dramatic events of the so-called March on Rome in late October that culminated in the appointment of Mussolini as prime minister unfolded a few weeks before the fourth Comintern congress. The rapid rise of Mussolini to power took the Communist delegates, including those from Italy, almost entirely by surprise. Nevertheless, in its final resolution, the Comintern congress noted that "international fascism attempt[ed] through social demagogy to achieve a base among the masses—in the peasantry, the petty bourgeoisie, and even sectors of the working class."[27] By the time of the 1933 meeting of its Executive Committee, Comintern had come to the conclusion that the rise of fascism represented the final throw of the dice by international finance against the proletariat.[28]

From the perspective of the communist Left, a sense of ominous "fascist wind"[29] was now blowing across the continent. For a large number of disoriented and disaffected radicals, on the other hand, this same wind held a fascinating promise of a counter-transcendence to that offered by revolutionary socialism,[30] and the intoxicating sensation of living on the cusp of a new heroic time.[31] New movements with a radical hyper-nationalist ideological profile appeared spontaneously in a growing number of countries. In many ways, these new radical movements responded to similar challenges—a sense of national humiliation or betrayal, socioeconomic dislocation, cultural insecurity, the financial downturn with its debilitating social consequences, and so on.[32] But they also expressed and celebrated a common belief in what they saw as a unique, history-making opportunity for both national regeneration and the total crushing of what they perceived as the most lethal forces of "decadence," domestic and trans- or inter-national.[33]

While fiercely nationalist and rooted in local traditions, these new movements operated as an informal, genuinely transnational "charismatic" community, recognizing Mussolini as the figurehead of a history-making initiative with global relevance. The young Romanian founder of the fascist Legion of the Archangel Michael (Iron Guard), Corneliu Zelea Codreanu, spoke afterwards about the sense of exaltation he experienced upon hearing the news of Mussolini's appointment as Italian prime minister in October 1922. He wrote about the "kinship of sympathy among those who serve the people as there is such a kinship among those who labor for the destruction of people."[34] A few years later, the renegade British politician Oswald Mosley (who had been a most promising parliamentarian) became increasingly fascinated with Mussolini's political experiments to the point that he decided to organize a "study" trip to Rome in January 1932. It was during his stay in the Italian capital that he met with Mussolini. He returned full of praise for the Duce and his regime, founding his own British Union of Fascists (BUF) on 28 October 1932—symbolically, the tenth anniversary of the "March on Rome". He did make further visits to Rome between 1933 and 1935 as leader of the BUF, and described the city as "the birthplace of fascism."[35]

With the advent of Hitler to power in Germany on 30 January 1933, this dynamic interchange intensified—but it also started to shift palpably northwards. The rapid consolidation of the National Socialist regime in 1933–34 appeared to confirm the validity of the alternative radical "third way" that many at the time recognized in both Italian Fascism and German National Socialism. On the one hand, the formal breakdown of democracy in Germany was followed by an authoritarian wave that swept away parliamentary systems in Austria, Latvia, Estonia, and Bulgaria, with even more countries joining this seismic authoritarian "departure" by the end of the 1930s.[36] On the other hand, the international constituency of fascist sympathizers continued to grow, both in geographic reach and political boldness. Whether they named their movement "fascist" or not, they perceived themselves in a dual capacity, both as harbingers of national regeneration within their respective countries and as loyal agents of a pan-European and universal project of rebirth in opposition to established ideologies and political forces.

By the time of the outbreak of the Spanish Civil War in 1936, the geopolitical and ideological centre of gravity of this radical transnational bloc had already shifted from Italy to Germany, and from Fascism to National Socialism.[37] The growing dynamism and appeal of the Nazi regime in Germany not only eclipsed Fascist Italy but also exerted a powerful magnetism over a growing field populated by radical start-ups in a number of European countries. With its declared promise of remaking the world and spearheading a history-making project of regeneration, the Third Reich quickly occupied a position of de-facto authority among the international bloc of hyper-nationalist, antiliberal, and vehemently antisocialist forces across the continent. It inspired awe, admiration, fear, fascination, and a sense of "history-making" enthusiasm to constituencies of radicals across the continent, who came to perceive themselves as national "vanguards" of an emerging international new order.

From the very early days of the movement, a taboo-shattering kind of violence became an integral part of National Socialism's assault on "decadence." It was justified and praised by the regime as a necessary process of destroying enemies and a crucial step toward the production of a new world. The Nazis were not alone in constructing self-images of history-making missionaries and soldiers of a European or even global "new order"; but they were instrumental in actively constructing their perceived enemies as transnational and indeed global "others." Whether they targeted corrupt liberals or internationalists of the Left, or indeed the putative Jewish worldwide "conspiracies," they justified not just their aggressive response but the transnational horizon thereof as a response to the scale of the perceived threat. Uncompromising violence against this grotesque caricature of "the Jew"—not only as a minority within Germany but also as the alleged mastermind of a worldwide conspiracy and as a biological race—became what Zygmunt Bauman has described as an exercise in "creative destruction; conceived as a surgical operation, necessary to health and perpetrated on the way to a perfect … society."[38]

It was precisely at this point that National Socialism, with its obsession with racial anti-Semitism, intersected with local, national, and regional histories of Jew-hatred in other regions of Europe. What started as a "Jewish problem" turned into a chilling Nazi vision of a Germany free from Jews, before moving swiftly into a murderous dystopia of a Europe without Jews, then a Jew-free world.[39] But, even more strikingly, what started as a National Socialist brutal obsession and uncompromising initiative within the borders of Germany radicalized attitudes and decisions on the treatment of Jews in many more parts of the continent during the second half of the 1930s, even without any evidence of Nazi compulsion or even incitement.

In the overwhelming majority of cases it was fascist movements and regimes—or at least ones with growing fascist trappings and leanings—that played a pivotal role in this process, even if they had previously shown little interest in the "Jewish question," whether out of political calculation or because they considered the issue of secondary significance. Leaving aside countries where virulent anti-Semitism had proceeded from the first moment in tandem with the growth of domestic fascism (as happened in 1920s Romania, where the radicalization of anti-Semitic discourses had preceded the rise of the Iron Guard and met far broader support than the fringe constituency of radical nationalists),[40] anti-Semitism did become noticeably more prominent and aggressive in the discourses of fascist movements in the course of the 1930s. The Dutch National Socialist Movement (NSB), founded in 1931 as a hyper-nationalist group with clear fascist sympathies, had always perceived its role as a fighting force for a broader campaign of regeneration led by Mussolini's Fascist Italy. Nevertheless, with the exception of a small *völkisch* party wing, anti-Semitism had played no role in its ideological development until 1936–38. The rise of the more radical (and decidedly pro-Nazi and anti-Semite) Meinoud Rost van Tonningen inside the ranks of the NSB presented the generally more pragmatic leader, Anton Adriaan Mussert, with a direct challenge to his overall authority, and led to escalating in-fighting about the ideological profile of the movement. As a result, from 1936 onward, the NSB's position started to shift on matters of race and anti-Jewish policy in a radical direction influenced by Germany.[41] Eventually, Mussert too succumbed to what he had come to perceive as the history-making dynamism of National Socialist Germany and its project of forcing a "new order" over Europe and beyond. Like Mosley after his pilgrimage to Rome a few years earlier, Mussert returned mesmerized from a visit to Berlin in 1936. As a consequence, the NSB established closer ties with the NS regime and its party organizations.[42] In Belgium, attitudes to the country's Jewish communities had already divided the radical national constituency, with the Verdinaso being openly anti-

Semitic from the beginning, whilst both the Walloon and Catholic Rex and the Flemish National Union (Vlaams Nationaal Verbond, VNV) gradually embraced a radical anti-Semitism from 1935 onward, as part of a wider realignment with National Socialist Germany.[43] In Britain, the BUF began its political life with a rather restrained attitude to anti-Semitism, with Mosley paying particular attention to distance his movement from the NSDAP until 1932–33. Original BUF members, like Richard Bellamy, noted how "the roots of British fascism were Italian and not German," underlining Mosley's affinity for Rome and Mussolini, in combination with his early disparagement of the Nazi ideas as "Teutonic fantasies."[44] Mosley gradually came to see both the Italian and the German regimes as variants of a single historical force, with the BUF offering a distinct and original British variant—that is, not mimetic of either model. However, from 1934 and especially after 1935–36, the movement's rhetoric shifted toward more aggressive positions, betraying a stronger influence of the Nazi anti-Jewish discourse and having a growing affinity with the Third Reich in geopolitical terms.[45] The change in its official name in April 1936—with the addition of the words "and National Socialists" to the existing BUF title—was a symbolic gesture that underlined an already ongoing ideological mutation.[46]

For those and other similar fringe radical national start-ups, it was the combination of a priori ideological fascination with the radical vision of a fascist or Nazi new order and a sense of awe at the spectacle of action-oriented, norm-defying political dynamism unfolding in front of their eyes that proved attractive. There was a deepening impression that National Socialism had already started to force the pace of history toward a final confrontation with "the Jew." It had legitimized the most extreme prescriptions of a brutal campaign of "cleansing." In this quasi-apocalyptic expectation of a fundamentally new beginning over the ashes of the old world, fascists felt that the fate of the Jews in the entire continent, and possibly the world, had already been decided, and an alternative goal had been prescribed by a new, dynamic revolutionary force spearheaded (both symbolically and politically) by the National Socialist regime. In this sense, an ideological and political link between transnational fascism and anti-Semitism, almost absent in the 1920s when the radical agenda was set by Italian Fascism, was firmly established in the 1930s, with the radical component of one reinforcing the dynamism of the other.

Beyond the transnational circle of fascists, however, the political dynamism of the National Socialist regime exerted a strong influence on unlikely political constituencies that spanned the supposed boundary between fascism and the authoritarian Right. As a taboo-breaking radical initiative, it tapped into deep layers of anti-Jewish prejudice and resentment across the continent. But it also provided what sympathetic observers in other countries were only too keen to interpret as an empowering precedent to follow with impunity.[47] In September 1935, the Nazi regime's anti-Jewish policy had entered a new, more radical phase. While until that point discriminatory legislation aimed to "cleanse" the professional, economic, cultural, and social spheres from Jewish presence, the introduction of the "Law for the Protection of German Blood and German Honor" and the Reich Citizenship Law— together referred to as "Nuremberg Laws"—marked the beginning of the biological death of Germany's Jewish community.

To be sure, National Socialist Germany was not the first interwar European regime to introduce discriminatory measures against Jewish minorities; the dubious distinction for this goes to the Hungarian *numerus clausus* law that was introduced in 1920. Even if subsequent Hungarian governments proved less eager to enforce the law (and by 1926 it had lapsed), it was praised and invoked by anti-Semites in other countries throughout the 1920s and early 1930s.[48] But it is clear in hindsight that the particular approach of the Nuremberg model—using racial criteria to redefine legal citizenship and on that basis to actively discriminate against the majority of the country's Jews—influenced similar initiatives in a wide range of other countries, both before and during World War II. The impact ranged from the two Hungarian racial laws of 1938–39 to the Romanian citizenship law of 1938 and the 1940 *Statut des Juifs* in Vichy France, the Jewish Codex in wartime Slovakia, and the anti-Jewish legislation introduced in Ustasha-led Croatia in the summer of 1941.

Imitation, Transfer, or Re-contextualization?

This kind of influence has been repeatedly described as a one-way, asymmetrical transfer of ideas and empowering practices from major fascist regimes and movements to minor groups, as well as from a putative "fascist" center to an "authoritarian" periphery of largely passive receivers. Such a radial circulation of "fascist trappings" across Europe and indeed further afield has been analyzed in terms of imitation, either blindly naive, opportunistic, or misunderstood. It has allegedly lacked a revolutionary intention and was eventually destined to underachievement and failure when judged against a "fascist" ideological gold standard. In this view of diffusion and passive imitation, individual actors beyond the paradigmatic fascist regimes were denied any substantial sense of ideological or political agency beyond borrowing, emulating, and reproducing foreign prototypes.

The "transfer" historical perspective—as a process with a fixed source and passive receivers—would at first sight be compatible with the notion of a transnational network of loyalty and commitment to a new fascist order, in which the authoritative position of Fascist Italy and (later) National Socialist Germany was overwhelmingly recognized by local, national, and regional fascist actors. But a shift of focus from the source of inspiration to the dynamic process of circulation over time reveals a fascinatingly granular reality of multiple intentions, understandings, and multidirectional transfers that could generate new meaning and empowerment for others.[49]

As the methodological and theoretical literature on transnational history has emphasized, influential ideas and empowering precedents circulate across place and time by being constantly transformed, adapted, and fused with other existing, context-specific elements along the way. The processes of circulation and intersection are essentially generative of new meanings and unintended hybrid outcomes that take a life of their own in different historical contexts. This is a dynamic and highly unpredictable process that can be described as recontextualization. Essentially a reframing of an object (for instance an idea) in more contextually aware ways that generate new understandings and applications, recontextualization involves a series of active processes of adaptation, consciously and unconsciously applied to the source of influence. These may involve filtering and selection, whereby some aspects are appropriated while others are ignored or even rejected. Moreover, substitutions have to be taken into consideration: original attributes are translated into the different context in ways that make more sense or have more impact on the actual reality they refer to. They may finally involve additions, whether of new elements or new processes, that may even have a radicalizing effect on the original idea or practice. But in all these cases, the transnational actors are active nodes not passive imitators on the receiving end of a "transfer."[50]

When one looks at the diffusion of the racial anti-Jewish paradigm in 1930s Europe as legal and political practice, it becomes obvious that the model pioneered by the Nazi regime with the 1935 Nuremberg Laws broke taboos and set a new radical precedent. In so doing, it also appealed to and activated pre-existing, yet latent or partly suppressed, anti-Jewish sociopolitical demand in other countries. This contributed critically to its adoption, adaptation, and reproduction in other European countries during 1936–41. The Nazi Nuremberg model served both as an empowering, legitimizing precedent and as a "successful," scalable bold model for "solving" the so-called Jewish Problem outside Germany, especially in East European countries with Jewish communities larger than in Nazi Germany, such as Poland, Ukraine, and Hungary. In addition, by becoming recontextualized according to particular national and regional realities or traditions, it served as a basis for extending violent persecution and elimination to further groups of particular national "others." Recontextualization was capable of transforming the original idea into new meanings that were more congruent in a specific local or national context. In this way, those at the receiving end of the transfer could present the appropriation as rooted in tradition, not as foreign import.[51]

The diverse recontextualizations of the Nazi Nuremberg paradigm in a number of European countries divulge as much about the strength of the "fascist" (in this case, National Socialist) attraction at the time as about the domestic roots and dynamics of anti-Semitism in receiving societies—not as a simple imitation or reproduction of the German laws but crucially redefined and actively recontextualized. In wartime Slovakia, governed by the clerical Slovak People's Party, for instance, the 1941 Jewish Codex was based on a very restrictive legal definition of Slovak citizenship, and contained more than three hundred specifically anti-Jewish regulations. The initiative was driven by a radical faction within the government that supported a closer ideological and political alignment with Nazi Germany, emboldened by the perceived "success," dynamism, and impending victory of the Axis forces. But the Slovak law also introduced religious principles that were more in line with the clerical roots of the governing Slovak People's Party. In so doing, the Slovak definition of 1941 outdid the Nuremberg one, including not only more "half-Jews" (largely unaffected by the 1935 German law) but also those with only one Jewish grandparent, so long as they had continued to practice the Jewish religion until April 1939.[52]

1941 was also marked by the introduction of a racially based anti-Jewish law in Hungary by the Horthy regime. It was in fact the third revised version of legislation that had first been introduced in 1938 and was then reframed in a more restrictive direction in 1939 before reaching its 1941 predominantly racial, Nuremberg-inspired iteration. A reflexive recontextualization had ensured that the first two laws introduced distinctions meaningful to their Hungarian context (allowances for those who had converted or moved to Hungary before a specific date). By contrast, the 1941 law divulged the empowering and radicalizing effect of Nazi taboo-shattering precedent in this domain. Yet it also continued to underline the significance of reflexive adaptation, with some regulations exceeding in harshness the Nuremberg mold or following a different restrictive recipe (e.g., the revival of the 1920 principle of *numerus clausus*), while other stipulations accounted for mitigating factors (religion, residence) that made sense in the Hungarian context alone.[53]

But it was in wartime Croatia that the two violent transnational visions of a "fascist epoch" and the Nazi "new order" produced the most brutal example of how local and national violent agency intersected with history-making creative destruction. The so-called Independent State of Croatia (Nezavisna Država Hrvatska, HND) was forged from the ashes of the occupied and destroyed Yugoslavia in the spring of 1941. The National Socialist leadership eventually chose the leader of the radical nationalist group Ustaša to head the new state. Ante Pavelić had founded his movement in 1929 but had spent most of the 1930s in exile from Yugoslavia (mainly in Italy). Like most of its kindred contemporaries, the movement had come to perceive its role in dual, history-making terms: first, as the harbinger of a long-awaited national self-fulfillment and regeneration of the Croat nation in its own (independent) country; and, second, as part of the vanguard of a new radical international cause that would transform the course of European and human history. While operating under the auspices of Fascist Italy and then growing increasingly closer to the National Socialist regime, the Ustaša movement was nevertheless consumed by its very particular goal of independent, homogeneous nation statehood and its escalating retributive anti-Serb outlook.

When their moment came in the spring of 1941, rather unexpectedly and dramatically, Pavelic and his Ustaše cadre did not waste the opportunity. Far from being passive imitators, the HND leadership appropriated numerous, but selective, fascist ideas and practices in order to recontextualize them, in a deliberately adapted form, and thus advance the Ustaša regime's particular priorities in direct relevance to the movement's national setting and circumstances.[54] "Cleansing" operations, particularly in areas with sizable Serb communities, had been reported only days after the founding proclamation of the HND. These were followed by a series of legislative arrangements and local measures that set the tone of the regime's aggressively ethno-exclusive future policies with regard to Serbs and Jews. Measures restricting access to public spaces for Jews were put in place within days of the proclamation of the new state. In many areas, Serbs were obliged to wear a blue band with the letter "P", similar to the yellow equivalent (with the letter "Z") for the Jews ("Židov" in Croatian).[55] Meanwhile, a "racial" definition for ("Aryan") Croats, as well as for Jews and Roma, came into effect in late April 1941 with the decrees "on Racial Affiliation" and "for the Protection of the Aryan Blood and Honour of the Croatian People."[56] The combined effect of the two decrees was more far-reaching than the stipulations of the 1935 Nuremberg Laws in Nazi Germany, making substantial inroads into the categories of "half-Jews," illegitimate children, offspring of unmarried Jewish women, and spouses of "Jews," regardless of their own "racial" makeup. This definition enabled a full assault on the rights of the Jewish population: regulation of marriage and sexual relations between Jews and Croats; removal of the former from any profession; and confiscation of their assets. Other measures introduced swiftly included confiscation of Serb and Jewish property, marriage regulations following a mixture of religious, ethnic, and racial ideas, and restrictions in movement and freedom of worship.[57] But it was the overwhelmingly unruly, wanton Ustaša mass violence, seemingly uncontrollable in scale and very often ritualistic in execution, that proved to be the defining feature of Ustaša rule in the NDH. With its performative, culturally symbolic excesses, which appeared to have shocked even the authorities of the German army in Yugoslavia, the extreme character of Ustaše eliminationist violence offered another glimpse of recontextualization. While Jews were handed over to the Nazi authorities for deportation in the killing camps of Poland, the HND reserved its most brutal treatment for the country's Serb minority, with a kind of violent conduct that was rooted in Balkan traditions of banditry and ritualized revenge, with little respect for authority and impervious to any form of bureaucratic regulation.[58]

A Co-produced History of Transnational Fascism?

The Nazi murderous dystopia of a world free from Jews intersected with an already well-established and deep-rooted transnational dynamic of aggressive nationalism, racism, and anti-Semitism, driving not just willing collaboration during World War II but also a depressing register of so many more violent initiatives—against Jews as well as against other "enemies," specific to and meaningful in particular national or regional contexts. Fascists from across the continent seized the violent Nazi precedent as an empowering initiative for similar radical steps within their own countries. Many of them volunteered to fight alongside the German army and SS forces during the invasion of the Soviet Union in 1941. Others provided voluntary logistical support and fanatical momentum for Nazi "cleansing" operations and massacres.[59] A significant section of them stayed loyal to the fading vision of a "fascist new order" until the very end, joining Waffen-SS divisions and carrying out with undiminished dedication the deportation of Jews from their lands.[60] But beyond these devoted fascist transnational "soldiers of international fascism"[61] there were many more unlikely sympathetic observers who saw in fascism a versatile and adaptable "third-way" alternative project, capable of shattering the internationalist Left and superseding liberalism once and for all. What they saw in the unfolding experiments of Fascist Italy and later Nazi Germany was what each of them wanted to see—a selective and reflexive reading, capable of rejecting, tempering, accentuating and generally adapting in ways that made sense within their respective national, cultural, and political contexts. The diffusion of the Nazi "Nuremberg model" of legal eliminationism in very different European countries highlighted how a transnational history of fascism did not involve just those devoted adherents of a "fascist new order" but included the entangled aspirations and agencies of many further constituencies of the interwar European Right. When Nazi Germany decided to take the leap into mass murder, the undertaking was, as Dan Stone has pointed out, a supremely transnational one, with some of the most willing participants on all levels (from planning and coordination to practical execution and volunteer initiative) recruited across the continent from among fascists and radical nationalists.[62]

The transnational history of fascism was in itself shaped dynamically by the crisscrossing of numerous parallel transnational dynamics—of an angry pan-European revolt against "decadence," of antiliberalism and antisocialism, of the long history of anti-Semitism and the more recent one of exclusive racial nationalism, of a resurgence of aggressive nativism and the ensuing demonization of "others." In this chapter, I have sought to demonstrate how the multiple visions of a radical, history-making "new order" that were held by various fascist actors in the interwar period shared the belief in a violent destruction of the established order as a precondition for a fascist victory. The constructive elements ("new order," "century of fascism," etc.) and the destructive ones (violence against "enemies" and "others"; the vision of a redemptive and cleansing violent campaign) were inextricably linked in conceptual terms. But they also become entangled in the process of a history of transfers and intersections, where one taboo-breaking violent initiative liberated similar or even more radical demand in another part of Europe. In this respect alone, the role of National Socialist Germany, as both the purveyor of a unique chiliastic vision of a "new order" and the fanatical, uncompromising agent of creative destruction as an integral part thereof, must continue to be highlighted.

However, the history of the violent pursuit of the fascist "new order" in the late 1930s and during World War II is neither a Nazi nor a German nor even an exclusively "fascist" narrative. It is not a case of transmission and one-way transfer from seemingly successful fascisms to failed outliers, from the core to the periphery. Those who came to identify themselves with a fascist "new order" (as they understood it at any given time or place; whether they called or perceived themselves as "fascists" or not; whether they subscribed to the vision itself or saw it as useful in defeating collective "enemies") facilitated the circulation and radicalization of ideas of redemptive violence within their respective countries. They did so with a strong awareness of a transnational and indeed global undertaking but in a highly active, selective, and reflexive way, taking stock, interpreting, filtering, deducing, and essentially "recontextualizing" ideas and practices. In this fractal flow of ideas and practices, transnational agents not only reproduced but also co-produced in the process new hybrid ideas and practices. Even if these hybrids—as well as the processes through which they were produced—appear bewildering and unwieldy from within the definitional lens of "generic fascism," they nevertheless form a critical part of a fascinating "relational" history of fascism.

ARISTOTLE KALLIS is professor of Modern and Contemporary History at Keele University, UK. His current research interests are in the field of generic and transnational fascism, right-wing radicalism in contemporary Europe, and the transnational history of twentieth-century modernism. His most recent publications include *The Third Rome 1922–43: The Making of the Fascist Capital*; and (together with Antonio Costa Pinto) the edited volume *Rethinking Fascism and Dictatorship* (both 2014).

Notes

1. Federico Finchelstein, *Transatlantic Fascism: Ideology, Violence, and the Sacred in Argentina and Italy, 1919–1945* (Durham, NC, 2010), 6.
2. Federico Finchelstein, "Fascism and the Holocaust," in *The Holocaust and Historical Methodology*, ed. Dan Stone (New York and Oxford, 2012), 255–57.
3. Arnd Bauerkämper, "Transnational Fascism: Cross-Border Relations between Regimes and Movements in Europe, 1922–1939," *East Central Europe* 37, no. 2–3 (2010): 214–46.
4. Ernst Nolte, *The Three Faces of Fascism* (London, 1965), 529, 538.

5. George L Mosse, *Masses and Man: Nationalist and Fascist Perceptions of Reality* (New York, 1980), 183, 195.
6. Roger Griffin, *The Nature of Fascism* (London and New York, 1991), 38–44.
7. Roger Eatwell, "The Nature of 'Generic Fascism': The 'Fascist Minimum' and the 'Fascist Matrix,'" in *Rechtsextreme Ideologien in Geschichte und Gegenwart*, ed. Uwe Backes (Cologne, 2003), 93–137.
8. David D. Roberts, *Fascist Interactions: Proposals for a New Approach to Fascism and Its Era* (Oxford and New York, 1994), 6; Diethelm Prowe, "'Classic Fascism' and the New Radical Right in Western Europe: Comparisons and Contrasts," *Contemporary European History* 3, no. 3 (1994): 289–313.
9. David D. Roberts, *The Totalitarian Experiment in Twentieth-Century Europe: Understanding the Poverty of Great Politics* (New York and London, 2005), esp. 68–92.
10. Tamil Bar-On, *Rethinking the French New Right: Alternatives to Modernity* (Abingdon and New York, 2013), 81–83.
11. Robert Soucy, *French Fascism: The Second Wave, 1933–1939* (New Haven, CT and London, 1997), 280–82; Griffin, *Nature of Fascism*, 141.
12. Stanley G. Payne, *A History of Fascism, 1914–1945* (London, 1996), 8–9; cf. Roger Griffin, *Modernism and Fascism: The Sense of Beginning under Mussolini and Hitler* (Basingstoke, 2007).
13. Panikos Panayi, *Weimar and Nazi Germany: Continuities and Discontinuities* (Abingdon and New York, 2014), 3–31.
14. For an overview of Marxist interpretations of fascism, see David Renton, *Fascism: Theory and Practice* (London, 1999), 44–63; cf. Daniel Woodley, *Fascism and Political Theory: Critical Perspectives on Fascist Ideology* (London and New York, 2009).
15. Aristotle Kallis, "El concepto de fascismo en la historia anglófona comparada," in *El fascismo clásico, 1919–1945 y sus epígonos*, ed. Joan Antón Mellón (Madrid, 2012), 15–68; and idem, ed., "Introduction," in *The Fascism Reader* (London, 2003), 1–41.
16. Fritz Fischer, *From Kaiserreich to Third Reich: Elements of Continuity in German History, 1871–1945* (London and Boston, 1986); Hans-Ulrich Wehler, *The German Empire, 1871–1918* (Leamington Spa and Dover, NH, 1985). See also Ian Kershaw, "Hitler and the Uniqueness of Nazism," *Journal of Contemporary History* 39, no. 2 (2004): 239–545.
17. Zeev Sternhell, *The Birth of Fascist Ideology* (Princeton, NJ, 1995), 1–6; Renzo De Felice, *Interpretations of Fascism* (Cambridge, MA, 1977).
18. Antonio Costa Pinto and Aristotle Kallis, "Introduction," in *Rethinking Fascism and Dictatorship*, ed. idem (Basingstoke, 2014), 1–11.
19. Macgregor Knox, *Common Destiny: Dictatorship, Foreign Policy, and War in Fascist Italy and Nazi Germany* (Cambridge, 2000), 56.
20. Hartmut Kaelbe, "Between Comparison and Transfer—and What Now? A French–German Debate," in *Comparative and Transnational History: Central European Approaches and New Perspectives*, ed. Heinz-Gerhard Haupt and Jürgen Kocka (New York and Oxford, 2009), 33–38.
21. Knox, *Common Destiny*, 21.
22. Markku Ruotsila, "International Anti-Communism before the Cold War: Success and Failure in the Building of a Transnational Right," in *New*

Perspectives on the Transnational Right, ed. Martin Durham and Margaret Power (Basingstoke, 2010), 32.

23. Michel Dobry, "Desperately Seeking a 'Generic Fascism': Some Discordant Thoughts on the Academic Recycling of Indigenous Categories," in *Rethinking the Nature of Fascism: Comparative Perspectives*, ed. Antonio Costa Pinto (Basingstoke, 2011), 78.

24. Paul Mazgaj, *Imagining Fascism: The Cultural Politics of the French Young Right, 1930–1945* (Newark, 2007), 31.

25. Roger Griffin, "Revolution from the Right: Fascism," in *Revolutions and the Revolutionary Tradition in the West, 1560–1991*, ed. David Parker (London, 2000), 185–200.

26. Hans Rogger and Eugen Weber, eds., *European Right: A Historical Profile* (Berkeley, 1965); Arnd Bauerkämper, "Interwar Fascism in Europe and Beyond: Toward a Transnational Radical Right," in *New Perspectives on the Transnational Right*, ed. Martin Durham and Margaret Power (Basingstoke, 2010), 39–66.

27. John Riddell, ed., *Toward the United Front: Proceedings of the Fourth Congress of the Communist International, 1922* (Amsterdam, 2012), esp. 13–20.

28. Ian Kershaw, "The Essence of Nazism: Form of Fascism, Brand of Totalitarianism or Unique Phenomenon?" in *Fascism: Critical Concepts in Political Science. vol. IV: The "Fascist Epoch,"* ed. Roger Griffin and Matthew Feldman (London and New York, 2004), 53–54; Kevin Passmore, *Fascism: A Very Short Introduction* (Oxford, 2002), 7–8. Also see Kasper Braskén's chapter in this volume.

29. Andrea Mammone, *Transnational Neofascism in France and Italy* (Cambridge, 2015), 15–16.

30. As Charles Maier noted, one that "could answer Marxism in its own terms … a counter-revolution that relied upon democracy to defeat democracy." See Charles S. Maier, *The Unmasterable Past: History, Holocaust, and German National Identity* (Cambridge, MA, 2009), 27.

31. Geoff Eley, *Nazism as Fascism: Violence, Ideology, and the Ground of Consent in Germany* (London and New York, 2013), 210–12; Griffin, *Nature of Fascism*, 186–95; Griffin, *Modernism and Fascism*, 22–48.

32. Causal links between the so-called 'interwar crisis' and the rise of fascist movements in the 1920s and 1930s have been identified by a range of works on the period. See, for example, Richard J. Overy, *The Interwar Crisis 1919-1939*, New York, 2007.

33. Maier, *The Unmasterable Past*, 26–28.

34. Corneliu Zelea Codreanu, *Pentru Legionari* (Sibiu, 1936); English online translation by G. van der Heide at https://ia700501.us.archive.org/10/items/ForMyLegionariesTheIronGuard/ForMyLegionaries.pdf.

35. Claudia Baldoli, *Exporting Fascism: Italian Fascists and Britain's Italians in the 1930s* (London, 2003), 44.

36. Michael Mann, *Fascists* (Cambridge, 2004), 24, 31–93.

37. Ibid., 38–43.

38. Zygmunt Bauman, "The Camps: Eastern, Western, Modern," in *The Fate of the European Jews, 1939–1945: Continuity or Contingency?* ed. Jonathan Frankel (New York and Oxford, 1997), 33–34.

39. Alon Confino, *A World Without Jews: The Nazi Imagination from Persecution to Genocide* (New Haven, CT and London, 2014), esp. 233–45.
40. William Brustein, *Roots of Hate: Anti-Semitism in Europe before the Holocaust* (Cambridge, 2003), 153–62.
41. Kristen R. Monroe, *Ethics in an Age of Terror and Genocide: Identity and Moral Choice* (New Haven, CT, 2012), 138–85.
42. Dietrich Orlow, "Relations between the Nazis and the French and Dutch Fascists, January 1933–August 1934," in *The Impact of Nazism: New Perspectives on the Third Reich and Its Legacy*, ed. Alan E. Steinweis and Daniel E. Rogers (Lincoln, NE and London, 2003), 39–67; Michael Wildt, *Hitler's Volksgemeinschaft and the Dynamics of Racial Exclusion: Violence against Jews in Provincial Germany, 1919–1939* (New York, 2012), 247–48.
43. Luc Schepens, "Fascists and Nationalists in Belgium, 1919–1940," in *Who Were the Fascists? Social Roots of European Fascism*, ed. Stein Ugelvik Larsen, Bernt Hagtvet, and Jan Petter Myklebust (Bergen, Oslo, and Tromso, 1980), 501–16.
44. Claudia Baldoli, "Anglo-Italian Fascist Solidarity? The Shift from Italophilia to Naziphilia in the BUF," in *The Culture of Fascism: Visions of the Far Right in Britain*, ed. Julie V. Gottlieb and Thomas P. Linehan (London, 2004), 153.
45. Daniel Tilles, *British Fascist Antisemitism and Jewish Responses, 1932–40* (London, 2015), esp. 33–56.
46. David Stephen Lewis, *Illusions of Grandeur: Mosley, Fascism, and British Society, 1931–81* (Manchester, 1987), 195–96.
47. Aristotle Kallis, "The 'Fascist Effect': On the Dynamics of Political Hybridisation in Interwar Europe," in *Rethinking Fascism and Dictatorship*, ed. Antonio Costa Pinto and Aristotle Kallis (Basingstoke, 2014), 13–41.
48. Mária M. Kovács, *Liberal Professions and Illiberal Politics: Hungary from the Habsburgs to the Holocaust* (New York, 1994), 49, 54–62. On the *numerous clausus* discussions in interwar Europe in general, see Regina Fritz, Béla Rásky, and Grzegorz Rossoliński-Liebe, *Alma mater antisemitica: Akademisches Milieu, Juden und Antisemitismus an den europäischen Universitäten zwischen 1918 und 1939* (Vienna, 2016).
49. Michael Werner and Bénédicte Zimmermann, "Beyond Comparison: *Histoire croisée* and the Challenge of Reflexivity," *History and Theory* 45, no. 1 (2006): 32–34.
50. Andrea Mayr, *Language and Power: An Introduction to Institutional Discourse* (London and New York, 2008), 101–2.
51. Bauerkämper, "Transnational Fascism."
52. Eduard Nižnanský, "Expropriation and Deportation of Jews in Slovakia," in *Facing the NS Genocide: Non-Jews and Jews in Europe*, ed. Beate Kosmala and Feliks Tych (Berlin, 2004), 205–30; cf. Aristotle Kallis, *Genocide and Fascism* (London and New York, 2009), 244–50.
53. Maria M. Kovács, "The Problem of Continuity between the 1920 numerus clausus and Post-1938 Anti-Jewish Legislation in Hungary," *East European Jewish Affairs* 35, no. 1 (2005): 23–32; Jason Wittenberg, "External Influences on the Evolution of Hungarian Authoritarianism," in *Rethinking Fascism*

and Dictatorship, ed. Antonio Costa Pinto and Aristotle Kallis (Basingstoke, 2014), 226–27.

54. Rory Yeomans, *Visions of Annihilation: The Ustasha Regime and the Cultural Politics of Fascism, 1941–1945* (Pittsburgh, 2013), 363–64.
55. Marco Aurelio Rivelli, *La Génocide Occulté* (Paris, 1998), 38.
56. Sabrina Ramet, *The Independent State of Croatia, 1941–1945* (New York, 2007), 71; Paul Mojzes, *Balkan Genocides: Holocaust and Ethnic Cleansing in the Twentieth Century* (Lanham, MD, 2011), 54–55.
57. Rivelli, *Génocide Occulté*, 45; Jonathan Steinberg, "Types of Genocide? Croatians, Serbs and Jews, 1941–45," in *The Final Solution: Origins and Implementation*, ed. David Cesarani (London and New York, 1996), 179.
58. Cathie Carmichael, *Ethnic Cleansing in the Balkans: Nationalism and the Destruction of Tradition* (New York, 2002), 5. See also Alexander Korb, "A Multipronged Attack: Ustasa Persecution of Serbs, Jews, and Roma in Wartime Croatia," in *Eradicating Differences: The Treatment of Minorities in Nazi-Dominated Europe*, ed. Anton Weiss Wendt (Newcastle, 2010), 145–63.
59. For example, Krisztián Bene, *La collaboration militaire française dans la Seconde guerre mondiale* (Paris: Codex, 2012), 69–141; Martin Dean, *Collaboration in the Holocaust: Crimes of the Local Police in Belorussia and Ukraine, 1941–44* (New York, 2003); Roni Stauber, ed., *Collaboration with the Nazis: Public Discourse after the Holocaust* (London and New York, 2011).
60. Jean-Luc Leleu, "From the Nazi Party's Shock Troop to the 'European' Mass Army: The Waffen-SS Volunteers," in *War Volunteering in Modern Times: From the French Revolution to the Second World War*, ed. Christine G. Krüger and Sonja Levsen (London, 2011), 231–47.
61. Bertram M. Gordon, "Un soldat du fascisme: l'évolution politique de Joseph Darnand," *Revue d'Histoire de la Deuxième Guerre Mondiale* 27, no. 1 (1977): 43–70.
62. Dan Stone, *The Holocaust, Fascism and Memory: Essays in the History of Ideas* (Basingstoke, 2013), 23.

Bibliography

Baldoli, Claudia. *Exporting Fascism: Italian Fascists and Britain's Italians in the 1930s*. London, 2003.
———. "Anglo-Italian Fascist Solidarity? The Shift from Italophilia to Naziphilia in the BUF." In *The Culture of Fascism: Visions of the Far Right in Britain*, ed. Julie V. Gottlieb and Thomas P. Linehan, 147–61. London, 2004.
Bar-On, Tamil. *Rethinking the French New Right: Alternatives to Modernity*. Abingdon and New York, 2013.
Bauerkämper, Arnd. "Interwar Fascism in Europe and Beyond: Toward a Transnational Radical Right." In *New Perspectives on the Transnational Right*, ed. Martin Durham and Margaret Power, 39–66. Basingstoke, 2010.
———. "Transnational Fascism: Cross-Border Relations between Regimes and Movements in Europe, 1922–1939". *East Central Europe* 37, no. 2–3 (2010): 214–46.

Bauman, Zygmunt. "The Camps: Eastern, Western, Modern." In *The Fate of the European Jews, 1939–1945: Continuity or Contingency?*, ed. Jonathan Frankel. New York and Oxford, 1997.

Bene, Krisztián. *La collaboration militaire française dans la Seconde guerre mondiale.* Paris, 2012.

Brustein, William. *Roots of Hate: Anti-Semitism in Europe before the Holocaust.* Cambridge, 2003.

Carmichael, Cathie. *Ethnic Cleansing in the Balkans: Nationalism and the Destruction of Tradition.* New York, 2002.

Confino, Alon. *A World Without Jews: The Nazi Imagination from Persecution to Genocide.* New Haven, CT and London, 2014.

Dean, Martin. *Collaboration in the Holocaust: Crimes of the Local Police in Belorussia and Ukraine, 1941–44.* New York, 2003.

De Felice, Renzo. *Interpretations of Fascism.* Cambridge, MA, 1977.

Dobry, Michel. "Desperately Seeking a 'Generic Fascism': Some Discordant Thoughts on the Academic Recycling of Indigenous Categories." In *Rethinking the Nature of Fascism: Comparative Perspectives*, ed. Antonio Costa Pinto, 53–84. Basingstoke, 2011.

Eatwell, Roger. "The Nature of 'Generic Fascism': The 'Fascist Minimum' and the 'Fascist Matrix'". In *Rechtsextreme Ideologien in Geschichte und Gegenwart*, ed. Uwe Backes, 93–137. Cologne, 2003.

Eley, Geoff. *Nazism as Fascism: Violence, Ideology, and the Ground of Consent in Germany.* London and New York, 2013.

Finchelstein, Federico. *Transatlantic Fascism: Ideology, Violence, and the Sacred in Argentina and Italy, 1919–1945.* Durham, NC, 2010.

———. "Fascism and the Holocaust." In *The Holocaust and Historical Methodology*, ed. Dan Stone. New York and Oxford, 2012.

Fischer, Fritz. *From Kaiserreich to Third Reich: Elements of Continuity in German History, 1871–1945.* London and Boston, 1986.

Fritz, Regina, Béla Rásky, and Grzegorz Rossoliński-Liebe. *Alma mater antisemitica: Akademisches Milieu, Juden und Antisemitismus an den europäischen Universitäten zwischen 1918 und 1939.* Vienna 2016.

Gordon, Bertram M. "Un soldat du fascisme: l'évolution politique de Joseph Darnand." *Revue d'Histoire de la Deuxième Guerre Mondiale* 27, no. 1 (1977): 43–70.

Griffin, Roger. *The Nature of Fascism.* London and New York, 1991.

———. "Revolution from the Right: Fascism." In *Revolutions and the Revolutionary Tradition in the West 1560–1991*, ed. David Parker, 185–200. London, 2000.

———. *Modernism and Fascism: The Sense of Beginning under Mussolini and Hitler.* Basingstoke, 2007.

Kaelbe, Hartmut. "Between Comparison and Transfer—and What Now? A French–German Debate." In *Comparative and Transnational History: Central European Approaches and New Perspectives*, ed. Heinz-Gerhard Haupt and Jürgen Kocka, 33–38. New York and Oxford, 2009.

Kallis, Aristotle, ed. *The Fascism Reader.* London, 2003.

———. *Genocide and Fascism.* London and New York, 2009.

―――. "El concepto de fascismo en la historia anglófona comparada." In *El fascismo clásico, 1919–1945 y sus epígonos,* ed. Joan Antón Mellón, 15–68. Madrid, 2012.

―――. "The 'Fascist Effect': On the Dynamics of Political Hybridisation in Interwar Europe." In *Rethinking Fascism and Dictatorship,* ed. Antonio Costa Pinto and Aristotle Kallis, 13–41. Basingstoke, 2014.

Kershaw, Ian. "Hitler and the Uniqueness of Nazism." *Journal of Contemporary History* 39, no. 2 (2004): 239–545.

―――. "The Essence of Nazism: Form of Fascism, Brand of Totalitarianism or Unique Phenomenon?" In *Fascism: Critical Concepts in Political Science. vol. IV: The "Fascist Epoch,"* ed. Roger Griffin and Matthew Feldman, 53–54. London and New York, 2004.

Knox, MacGregor. *Common Destiny: Dictatorship, Foreign Policy, and War in Fascist Italy and Nazi Germany.* Cambridge, 2000.

Korb, Alexander. "A Multipronged Attack: Ustasa Persecution of Serbs, Jews, and Roma in Wartime Croatia." In *Eradicating Differences: The Treatment of Minorities in Nazi-Dominated Europe,* ed. Anton Weiss Wendt, 145–63. Newcastle, 2010.

Kovács, Mária M. *Liberal Professions and Illiberal Politics: Hungary from the Habsburgs to the Holocaust.* New York, 1994.

―――. "The Problem of Continuity between the 1920 numerus clausus and Post-1938 Anti-Jewish Legislation in Hungary." *East European Jewish Affairs* 35, no. 1 (2005): 23–32.

Leleu, Jean-Luc. "From the Nazi Party's Shock Troop to the 'European' Mass Army: The Waffen-SS Volunteers." In *War Volunteering in Modern Times: From the French Revolution to the Second World War,* ed. Christine G. Krüger and Sonja Levsen, 231–47. London, 2011.

Lewis, David Stephen. *Illusions of Grandeur: Mosley, Fascism, and British Society, 1931–81.* Manchester 1987.

Maier, Charles S. *The Unmasterable Past: History, Holocaust, and German National Identity.* Cambridge, MA, 2009.

Mammone, Andrea. *Transnational Neofascism in France and Italy.* Cambridge, 2015.

Mann, Michael. *Fascists.* Cambridge, 2004.

Mayr, Andrea. *Language and Power: An Introduction to Institutional Discourse.* London and New York, 2008.

Mazgaj, Paul. *Imagining Fascism: The Cultural Politics of the French Young Right, 1930–1945.* Newark, 2007.

Mojzes, Paul. *Balkan Genocides: Holocaust and Ethnic Cleansing in the Twentieth Century.* Lanham, MD, 2011.

Monroe, Kristen R. *Ethics in an Age of Terror and Genocide: Identity and Moral Choice.* New Haven, CT, 2012.

Mosse, George L. *Masses and Man: Nationalist and Fascist Perceptions of Reality.* New York, 1980.

Nižnanský, Eduard. "Expropriation and Deportation of Jews in Slovakia." In *Facing the NS Genocide: Non-Jews and Jews in Europe,* ed. Beate Kosmala and Feliks Tych, 205–30. Berlin, 2004.

Nolte, Ernst. *The Three Faces of Fascism*. London, 1965.

Orlow, Dietrich. "Relations between the Nazis and the French and Dutch Fascists, January 1933–August 1934." In *The Impact of Nazism: New Perspectives on the Third Reich and Its Legacy*, ed. Alan E. Steinweis and Daniel E. Rogers, 39–67. Lincoln, NE and London, 2003.

Overy, Richard J. *The Interwar Crisis 1919–1939*. New York, 2007

Panayi, Panikos. *Weimar and Nazi Germany: Continuities and Discontinuities*. Abingdon and New York, 2014.

Passmore, Kevin. *Fascism: A Very Short Introduction*. Oxford, 2002.

Payne, Stanley G. *A History of Fascism, 1914–1945*. London, 1996.

Pinto, Antonio Costa, and Aristotle Kallis, eds. *Rethinking Fascism and Dictatorship*. Basingstoke, 2014.

Prowe, Diethelm. "'Classic Fascism' and the New Radical Right in Western Europe: Comparisons and Contrasts," *Contemporary European History* 3, no. 3 (1994): 289–313.

Ramet, Sabrina. *The Independent State of Croatia, 1941–1945*. New York, 2007.

Renton, David. *Fascism: Theory and Practice*. London, 1999.

Riddell, John, ed. *Toward the United Front: Proceedings of the Fourth Congress of the Communist International, 1922*. Amsterdam, 2012.

Rivelli, Marco Aurelio. *La Génocide Occulté*. Paris, 1998.

Roberts, David D. *Fascist Interactions: Proposals for a New Approach to Fascism and Its Era*. Oxford and New York, 1994.

Roberts, David D. *The Totalitarian Experiment in Twentieth-Century Europe: Understanding the Poverty of Great Politics*. New York and London, 2005.

Rogger, Hans, and Eugen Weber, eds. *European Right: A Historical Profile*. Berkeley, 1965.

Ruotsila, Markku. "International Anti-Communism before the Cold War: Success and Failure in the Building of a Transnational Right." In *New Perspectives on the Transnational Right*, ed. Martin Durham and Margaret Power, 11–37. Basingstoke, 2010.

Schepens, Luc. "Fascists and Nationalists in Belgium, 1919–1940." In *Who Were the Fascists? Social Roots of European Fascism*, ed. Stein Ugelvik Larsen, Bernt Hagtvet, and Jan Petter Myklebust, 501–16. Bergen, Oslo, and Tromso, 1980.

Soucy, Robert. *French Fascism: The Second Wave, 1933–1939*. New Haven, CT and London, 1997.

Stauber, Roni, ed. *Collaboration with the Nazis: Public Discourse after the Holocaust*. London and New York, 2011.

Steinberg, Jonathan. "Types of Genocide? Croatians, Serbs and Jews, 1941–45." In *The Final Solution: Origins and Implementation*, ed. David Cesarani. London and New York, 1996.

Sternhell, Zeev. *The Birth of Fascist Ideology*. Princeton, NJ, 1995.

Stone, Dan. *The Holocaust, Fascism and Memory: Essays in the History of Ideas*. Basingstoke, 2013.

Tilles, Daniel. *British Fascist Antisemitism and Jewish Responses, 1932–40*. London, 2015.

Wehler, Hans-Ulrich. *The German Empire, 1871–1918*. Leamington Spa and Dover, NH, 1985.

Werner, Michael, and Bénédicte Zimmermann. "Beyond Comparison: *Histoire croisée* and the Challenge of Reflexivity." *History and Theory* 45, no. 1 (2006): 32-4.

Wildt, Michael. *Hitler's Volksgemeinschaft and the Dynamics of Racial Exclusion: Violence against Jews in Provincial Germany, 1919–1939*. New York, 2012.

Wittenberg, Jason. "External Influences on the Evolution of Hungarian Authoritarianism." In *Rethinking Fascism and Dictatorship*, ed. Antonio Costa Pinto and Aristotle Kallis, 226–27. Basingstoke, 2014.

Woodley, Daniel. *Fascism and Political Theory: Critical Perspectives on Fascist Ideology*. London and New York, 2009.

Yeomans, Rory. *Visions of Annihilation: The Ustasha Regime and the Cultural Politics of Fascism, 1941–1945*. Pittsburgh, 2013.

❧ 2

CORPORATIST CONNECTIONS
The Transnational Rise of the Fascist Model in Interwar Europe

Matteo Pasetti

In the foreword to *Under the Axe of Fascism*—his famous book on Mussolini's dictatorship, published in 1936 in both New York and London—Gaetano Salvemini emphasized the extraordinary popularity of Fascist corporatism:

> The Fascist "Corporative State" has awakened curiosity, hope, and even enthusiasm. Italy has become the Mecca of political scientists, economists, and sociologists, who flock there to see with their own eyes the organization and working of the Fascist Corporative State. Daily papers, magazines, and learned periodicals, departments of political science, economics, and sociology in great and small universities, flood the world with articles, essays, pamphlets, and books, which already form a good-sized library, on the Fascist Corporative State, its institutions, its political aspects, its economic policies, and its social implications. No details are omitted, no problem concerning its origins and sources is left unexplored, no connection or comparison with philosophical and economic systems is overlooked.[1]

Afterwards, the Italian historian used all the following pages of his book to reveal this collective illusion, to show that "the Fascist corporations existed only on paper," to prove that the corporatist policy was a total failure, or better, a "great humbug." Indeed—according to Salvemini—the worldwide success of the Fascist corporative state was the result of a "wonderfully organized propaganda," which had led people to believe in the birth of a new system of regulation of the relations between capital and labor, whereas "all the categories of the traditional economic system remain[ed] intact: profit, interest, and wages." In practice, Fascist corporatism was nothing more than an ideological smokescreen. The ineffective corporations neither

protected workers nor damaged capitalists in any way. If anything—
in Salvemini's conclusion—big business had to only be afraid of "the
expansion of bureaucratic control" that the Fascist state was extending
over the economy.[2]

This judgment is well known and often quoted, but is a good place
to start from in order to focus on three basic lines of thought. First, the
transnational history of fascism is closely linked with the transnational
development of antifascism.[3] The diaspora of Italian antifascists caused by
the regime's oppression hindered the expansion of fascism as a universal
movement. Unlike Italy, where dissent was almost totally silenced from
1926 onward, any attempt to spread fascism encountered antifascist
counterpropaganda in many countries. Opposing transnational
networks of fascists and antifascists grew in parallel. This had some
important implications for the dissemination of corporatist projects, as
well as for other issues relating to the fascistization of the political arena
in the interwar period.

Second, Salvemini's analysis—like those of many other antifascist
scholars, and even of some critical Fascists such as Camillo Pellizzi—
highlights the weaknesses of the Fascist corporative system, and,
above all, the gap between the magniloquence of the project and
the modesty of its practice.[4] The idea that Fascist corporatism was a
bluff has a long history. In fact, it has become the prevalent opinion
in the historiographical debate from the first postwar years onward.[5]
Certainly, there was some truth in this assessment, but the working of
the system was not such a dismal failure as was thought. New studies
have shown that, despite the undeniable disparity between their stated
objectives and actual results, the policies inspired by corporatism
produced effects that cannot be overlooked, mainly because they
induced profound transformations in the relations between various
socioeconomic interests and the state.[6]

Third, approaching the matter from a transnational perspective, the
interpretation of Fascist corporatism as a bluff tends to overshadow
or even underestimate its historical function in the interwar period
(especially if what is meant by corporatism is both an ideological
discourse and a set of more or less developed, but concrete, policies).
And this may also provide an explanation for the frequent lack of
attention toward this topic in the scholarship on fascism as a global or
generic phenomenon, which often does not recognize the importance
of corporatism as a key factor.[7] Instead, as Salvemini himself
acknowledged in the foreword to his book, the Fascist message was
spreading throughout Europe and across the Atlantic. Propaganda
probably played a crucial role in this popularity but, at the same time,

another crucial precondition was the existence of a true interest in an experiment that dealt with common problems of economic, social, and political order.[8] Since the 1920s, such attentiveness generated a transnational circulation of ideas, knowledge, competences and experiences, working to legitimize the Fascist "solution" to the perceived profound crisis on an international scale.

Within the ongoing debate on the European dimension of fascism, this transnational perspective can reveal not only interconnections between fascist movements, but also their links with the wider political space of interwar Europe. This dynamic and multifaceted space was crowded by actors who interacted with the unfolding fascism, often regarding it with esteem or at least without negative preconceptions. They held divergent perceptions of fascist evolution and borrowed from it different political "lessons."[9] In such a historical perspective, corporatist policy represents a key issue, because it highlights the "traveling potential" of Italian Fascism toward various political areas, even beyond the specifically fascist movements and regimes. In fact, though for different reasons and with variable intensity, Fascism corporatism drew the attention of the nationalist and radical Right, of Catholic and conservative forces, and even of some socialists and democrats. At least for some years (from about the mid-1920s to the early 1930s), corporatism worked as a *passe partout* on behalf of Fascism, opening national and political borders.

This chapter will outline the main implications of Fascist corporatism in European political life of the interwar period, focusing on specific issues such as the exchange of ideas across national borders, the importance of Fascist propaganda abroad, and the influence of the Italian experience on other corporatist experiments.[10] For this purpose, the text is divided into three sections proposing the following periodization: (1) the revival of corporatist cultures after World War I; (2) the rise of the new Fascist model in the second half of the 1920s; and (3) the appearance of corporatist "avatars" in the 1930s.

The Revival: The Recovery of Corporatist Projects in the Aftermath of World War I (1918–1925)

Contrary to common belief, the popularity of corporatism was not an outcome of the Great Depression of 1929. In fact, corporatist leanings were widespread in various countries before that, in particular from the end of World War I onward. Sometimes these leanings updated some old corporatist traditions from the nineteenth century with new ideas. Even though the manifold formulations of the theory do not lend themselves to being classified into a taxonomic scheme, three main political currents present in the corporatist revival in the aftermath of the war can be identified.

The first and oldest one was that of social Catholicism. This was the corporatist current, which showed strong continuity with the past: thinkers such as France's Frédéric Le Play, René de La Tour du Pin, and Albert de Mun, the German Wilhelm Emmanuel von Ketteler, the Austrian Karl Freiherr von Vogelsang, the Italian Giuseppe Toniolo, and, above all, Pope Leo XIII with his encyclical letter, *Rerum Novarum* (1891), were still important in Catholic social thought.[11] This movement was characterized not only by religious inspiration, but also by concern for the social instability that the process of industrialization, as well as the postrevolutionary abolition of medieval guilds and the demise of the feudal order, had caused. Rejecting the liberal world because of the individualistic disintegration of society, the Catholic corporatists mourned the prerevolutionary past, seen as an idyllic golden age during which the old guild organization had ensured the functioning of the production system, respect for social hierarchy, and a form of communitarian protectionism: in two words, order and harmony. Therefore, the Catholic demand for the reconstruction of an organic society foresaw the restoration of legally recognized professional bodies as a cornerstone of a socioeconomic regime in which collective interests would prevail over individual interests, and in which antagonism between capital and labor would be resolved through a non-conflictual approach according to the spirit of Christian solidarity. It was, moreover, a "consensual-licenced" project of corporatism, because it supposed the autonomous collaboration between all social classes, without subordinating the corporatist system to the state.[12] After the Great War, this corporatist tradition permeated the programs of Catholic political parties and trade unions, which were rooted in much of the continent between the Iberian Peninsula and the Balkans[13]. One of the most significant examples may be the Austrian Christian Social Party (Christlichsoziale Partei, CSP), whose leader, the prelate Ignaz Seipel, became the spokesman of a corporatist design for the new republican constitution. However, although he served as federal chancellor twice during the 1920s, his corporatist projects were never implemented.[14]

The second corporatist current, which at times shared much with Catholicism, was that of the "new" nationalism, which acquired a particular ideological shape in the first two decades of the twentieth century. A prototype was the Action Française movement. During this period, the league of Charles Maurras experienced a generational renewal of its leadership, diversifying its own ideological platform away from that of the religious forces. As regards the corporatist doctrine, the most important contribution came from a former anarcho-syndicalist, disciple of Proudhon and Sorel, then royalist from 1906: Georges Valois.[15] Like the Catholic theorists, he outlined a corporatist system that was not subordinate to the state, despite the need to entrust to the latter a control function on the working of the system itself, in order to safeguard the national "common good." The linchpin of his project, however, was the idea of corporatist councils, intended as centers of mediation between union representatives of workers and employers; so the trade union organizations remained the basis of the system.[16] Valois assumed, therefore, a "syndical corporatism"—that is to say a model which in those years had supporters in other countries too, especially in Italy, where it found expression as a result of the ideological convergence between certain nationalists (such as Enrico Corradini) and revolutionary syndicalists (such as Alceste de Ambris, Sergio Panunzio, and Edmondo Rossoni). Hence, the evolution of this current was characterized by this process of ideological hybridization in the name of antiliberalism and antisocialism: the unions had to be included in a corporatist system for the purpose of integrating the nation's labor force, suppressing the class struggle, and nationalizing the workers.[17]

The wing of revolutionary syndicalism that, especially in France and Italy, had approached nationalism was not the only group of the Left to participate in the revival of corporatist theories. In the aftermath of World War I, indeed, corporatist perspectives crossed other socialist groups, as well as that which had its nerve center in London and was known as guild socialism. This is the third current, whose roots, too, dated back to the prewar period, starting from the publication of Arthur Penty's book *The Restoration of the Gild System* (1906), and Alfred Orage's weekly magazine *The New Age* (London, 1907–22). Also in this case, moreover, the war boosted support for the theory, which found its most complete formulation in the writings of G.D.H. Cole.[18] His guild socialism hinged on the concept of social "function," outlining a kind of "industrial democracy" in which every worker would contribute responsibly to the smooth functioning of the economic system, and would see his group interests represented by certain institutional bodies. Unlike other corporatist theorists, Cole was not chasing the myth of an organic community, which moreover often held a certain nostalgia for a distant past, but he defended an idea of pluralism and individual freedom: all citizens should have the right to express their social plurality, because they shared different interests, some of which were tied to ideological beliefs or territorial issues, and others determined rather by the individual citizen's "function" in the production system.[19] Despite not having a real impact on the European Left, guild socialism found supporters across the continent, appearing as an attractive alternative to both collectivism and syndicalism.[20]

These various corporatist leanings proved that the criticism aimed at the parliamentary institutions and the design of a new system of representation of socioeconomic interests did not entail the emergence of authoritarian tendencies. A common perspective involved, instead, the assertion of some autonomy of the corporatist organization regarding state power. Moreover, corporatist ideas permeated different political arenas, as well as crossing national borders (for example, *Rerum Novarum* was a reference text in every Catholic country; Action Française greatly influenced the Portuguese nationalist movement called Integralismo Lusitano; and Cole's theories were well known outside British socialism).

Overall, the corporatist revival in the postwar period was genetically related to the perception of the crisis of the liberal state, which was identified by certain law studies from the beginning of the twentieth century. This was aggravated by the experience of the war economy, a factor common to almost all European states.[21] During World War I, in fact, the dynamics of total mobilization had shown the inefficiency and the futility of the parliaments. Governments had used the skills of the social bodies (namely, their professional, technical, and management capabilities) to reorganize production to achieve the war targets, expanding public intervention above all in the fields of price fixing and labor control. At the same time, governments had sought trade union collaboration in order to ensure a well-functioning production system. This had brought about a partial suspension of the liberal order and parliamentary practices, creating a type of state capitalism, organized according to corporatist rules.[22] Although differing from state to state, the war economy model helped to revive the idea of corporatism as the most effective solution to overcome the weaknesses of the parliamentary system and to achieve social peace.

By the end of the war, the principle of corporatism had inspired manifold reform projects that, regardless of their political source, moved in two directions. On the one hand, corporatism seemed the best way to change the system of labor relations. Establishing institutional bodies capable of reconciling disputes between workers and employers, it was able to promote a kind of self-government of the production system in order to regulate labor relations and eliminate social conflict. The aim was to develop collaboration between all the components of the production system, bring an end to class struggle, and build a harmonious society. On the other hand, corporatism seemed the best solution to provide the political representation of economic interests. By replacing the classic parliamentary system of the liberal state, based on a form of popular representation of ideological or territorial type, with a system founded on direct representation of the social bodies, it could give voice to economic actors in the legislative assembly. The goal was the inclusion of organized interests in the political institutions, with the power to manage both economic policy and the whole economy itself, protecting it from the anarchy of the free market.[23]

However, in the aftermath of the war and in the early 1920s, all attempts to proceed in one direction or another failed. As for the political representation of economic interests, only two new constitutions tried to introduce a parliamentary assembly of a corporatist kind: one in Portugal with constitutional reform implemented in 1918 under the regime of Sidónio Pais; and the other, two years later, in the Italian Regency of Carnaro, with the charter written by Alceste De Ambris and Gabriele D'Annunzio. In both cases, the new constitution established that one of the two parliamentary chambers (or only a portion, in the Portuguese instance) was elected directly by a certain number of corporations, thus giving a degree of legislative power to the representatives of economic interests. Nevertheless, both experiences were too short-lived to provide a significant test of the corporatist project.

With regard to the regulation of labor relations, a great number of experiments, from 1919 onward, could be mentioned: among others, the Whitley Council created in Great Britain; the local joint committees set up in Spain; the national industrial boards established in Belgium by the socialist labor minister Joseph Wauters; the two complex structures assembled in Germany, namely the Zentralarbeitsgemeinschaft (Central Labor Committee), following the agreement between Hugo Stinnes and Carl Legien, and the Reichswirtschaftsrat (Economic Council of the German Reich), established by the Weimar Constitution; and finally, the Conseil National Économique (National Economic Council), inaugurated in France after a difficult genesis in 1925. However, with the partial exception of the latter, which was at least able to serve as an arena for debate between social groups, none of these experiments lived up to expectations.[24] None of them, indeed, provided an institutional tool to resolve labor conflicts or manage the production system through formal collaboration between the organized interests, because these experiments only worked—at best—as advisory councils, without any effective decision-making powers.

The development of Fascist corporatism, and then its transnational prestige, can therefore be understood when considered within this framework. In the European political culture of the twentieth century, Fascist corporatist ideology was an example of syncretism, or better, a mix of heterogeneous elements that were not well blended and derived from revolutionary syndicalism, organic nationalism, technocratic reformism, and economic productivism.[25]

Within the Italian regime, these currents remained separate, devising corporatist systems which differed in several aspects (institutional organization, role of trade unions, duties of the corporations, and so on).[26] Although the authoritarian and nationalistic scheme prevailed over the others, this genetic heterogeneity of Fascist corporatism had important implications. On the one hand, the actual outcomes of corporatist policies led to disappointments and tensions inside the regime; on the other hand, the plurality of the corporatist languages made it easier for many observers to see what they wanted in the Italian experience. These arbitrary interpretations facilitated transnational processes of selective reception and appropriation. As a consequence, the Fascist project had no difficulty finding an audience in different milieus, in Italy and abroad. Furthermore, beyond the ideological empathy that the corporatist theories were able to arouse, all European countries were moving toward greater institutionalization of economic, political, and social relations, with a shift of decision-making power away from parliaments, but without the creation of real procedural rules.[27] From this perspective, the initial stages of Fascist policy put into practice a new system for the political governance of organized interests, which diverged from other corporatist projects due to two essential differences: its effectiveness in labor conflict suppression, and its authoritarian and state-centric brand.

The New Model: The Rise of Fascist Corporatism (1926–1932)

As acknowledged by many observers from several countries, the turning point in the development of corporatism was 1926. According to a Spanish book of that period, for instance, "in the contemporary era, corporations reappeared nominally, for the first time, with the Charter of Carnaro, … but complete legislation was made in Italy on 3 April 1926, through the law for the legal regulation of labor, which laid its foundations through official state recognition of the associations."[28] The author of this book was Eduardo Aunós Pérez, a Catalan jurist who had been appointed labor minister under the dictatorship of General Miguel Primo de Rivera. He had played a paradigmatic role in understanding the transnational circulation of the Fascist model.

From the beginning, Mussolini's seizure of power resonated considerably around the world, but further attention was drawn toward the Italian regime with the inauguration of corporatist policy in April 1926, when the Italian parliament approved the new legal order for collective labor relations.[29] Written by Justice Minister Alfredo Rocco and supplemented in July with two royal decrees outlining its implementation, this law must be considered a cornerstone of the Fascist state. Its provisions defined three cardinal rules of corporatist policy: first, the authoritarian regulation of labor conflict, through the abolition of the right to strike and lockout, and the creation of the Labor Courts (Magistratura del Lavoro); second, the Fascist monopoly on negotiating representation through the legal recognition of a sole employer association and a single labor union for every sector; and third, the creation of the first corporatist bodies through the constitution of the Ministry of Corporations and the National Council of Corporations (Consiglio Nazionale delle Corporazioni, which became operative only in 1930).[30] These elements created a new model of corporatism, without predecessors for its authoritarian structure and its strict subordination to the state. Whereas previously other corporatist projects had contemplated the protection of society from the interference of politics, or the entry of organized interests in the decision-making proceedings, the Fascist experiment attempted a passive integration of the masses into the state. In 1927, the Labor Charter (Carta del Lavoro) provided this model with ideological legitimacy, establishing in its first article that "the Italian nation is an organism having ends, life, and means that are superior, for potency and duration, to those of the individuals or groups of which it is composed. It is a moral, political, and economic unity, realized wholly in the Fascist state."[31] At the same time, Rocco's law only modified the system of labor relations and not the forms of political representation. The corporatist reform of the legislative assembly was postponed, leaving the parliament under the control of the National Fascist Party (Partito Nazionale Fascista, PNF).

Despite its authoritarian hallmark, this Italian legislation immediately attracted considerable interest. It was generally appreciated by the European press (especially in law reviews and trade unionist journals) for one reason in particular: it seemed to solve a common problem, the labor conflict, and to ensure social peace. It did so not by returning to the past through the elimination of trade unions, but by ushering in a new mode of subordination to the state. This opinion was shared by people of varying political persuasions and not only by those who swelled the fascist ranks: for instance, by representatives of nationalist paramilitary movements such as the Heimwehr and the Stahlhelm, Catholic fundamentalism (Herman de Vries de Heekelingen), conservative milieux (Harold E. Goad), and even leftist groups (Juan Chabás).[32] Moreover, at the end of the 1920s, the Italian corporatist state became a case study for a generation of young jurists of the European academies, describing the fascist legislation as "the supreme experience of collaboration between the classes."[33] Obviously, opinion was not always favorable, as demonstrated by the protests against the Italian Fascist delegation during the conferences of the International Labour Organization (ILO). Yet even within the ILO, some statements in favor of the Labor Charter came directly from the director general, Albert Thomas.[34]

Altogether, the Italian legislative experience in syndical matters crossed national boundaries and became a reference case from 1926 through the entire interwar period. For its authoritarian and state-centric imprint, this new model differed from the earlier corporatist projects, but it prefigured some developing directives which looked universally valid because they appeared to have been implemented with a certain effectiveness by the Italian regime. In other words, unlike the ephemeral experiments of the early 1920s, the Fascist "solution" seemed to demonstrate the technical feasibility of labor control by a corporatist policy. This was seen as proof of "the power of precedent," an expression that some scholars have used to explain the influence of Italian Fascism abroad. What had started as a national policy in order to reform the syndicalist system in Italy soon became a transnational pattern for a universal solution. At the same time, national societies did not dissolve. Their specificities shaped the reception and evolution of corporatism emanating from the Italian "dictatorial laboratory" and more generally of the whole fascist experience. As an object of observation, perception and interpretation, Italian Fascism in general and its corporatism in particular were trajectories rather than static "models."[35]

The first country that followed in the footsteps of the Italian model was Spain under Primo de Rivera's dictatorship. From November 1926 to May 1928, Labor Minister Aunós Pérez was the main architect of the National Corporatist Organization (Organización Nacional Corporativa, ONC), a system based on the institution of Comités Paritarios (Joint Committees). They were joint committees of delegates elected in equal numbers by workers and employers from every professional sector.[36] Although it is incorrect to label Primo de Rivera and Aunós Pérez as "fascists," mainly because they were not advocates of a single-party state, both were strongly attracted by Mussolini's regime. Close diplomatic relations were immediately established between the two dictatorships. As is well known, Primo de Rivera went with King Alfonso XIII to Rome in order to meet the Duce on his first official visit abroad in November 1923.[37] Corporatism was one of the most important elements of this attraction. As a matter of fact, Aunós Pérez did not discover corporatist theory through Fascism, but by means of previous ideological training shaped by three political traditions: Catalan nationalism, social Catholicism, and *krausism*—a cultural movement for the regeneration of liberal society, which was rooted especially in nineteenth-century Spain. However, as he himself admitted in his writings, Fascist legislation influenced him greatly. In fact, as labor minister, he followed this policy in the making during a visit to Italy in April 1926. He came into contact with Giuseppe Bottai, the leading spokesman for Fascist corporatism, and he studied carefully the Italian laboratory. Here, as he stated, "a full-fledged social-political experiment" was in progress, aiming to close the "individualistic era."[38]

This is not to say that the ONC was copied from the Italian model. As Aunós Pérez himself, and later numerous scholars, revealed, the Spanish system was different in some key aspects: some degree of trade union freedom, the maintenance of the right to strike, collaboration with a part of the Socialist movement instead of its banning, and greater attention to the defense of workers' interests in the working of the Comités Paritarios.[39] At the same time, as in the Fascist model, the state gained control over labor relations because the joint committees were placed in a pyramidal system subordinated to the Labor Ministry. The state, therefore, had the power to impose decisions on all workers and employers, irrespective of whether they were or were not represented in the joint committees.[40] In other words, the ONC, too, was a centralized and state-led system—"a totalitarian corporatist structure," according to the definition of its creator.[41] Meanwhile, as in a game of mirrors, Italian Fascists paid similar attention to the evolution of Spanish legislation. In particular, Bottai described it in detail, emphasizing the influence of the Fascist model and above all its superiority. As he wrote in March 1927: "The Italian organization is the premise of a new conception of the state, while the Spanish one appears, at least for now, of much more modest scope."[42]

In short, if a comparative analysis can stress similarities and differences between the Spanish and Italian systems, a transnational approach can bring to light connections between these two experiences, like the contacts between key actors, the mutual attention, the exchange of knowledge, and also the enhancement of their own diversity. However, comparative reviews and transnational perspectives are complementary, and not mutually exclusive. Quoting Jürgen Kocka, "*histoire comparée* and *histoire croisée* can be compatible and need each other."[43] While comparative history cannot think of nations as watertight compartments, a transnational approach cannot shirk comparison, because it needs to understand the historical peculiarities of national or local environments. Furthermore, transnational history is a topic of study more than a tool for historical research; equally, comparison might not only be a method but also a source—as a means used in the past for political purposes.[44] For example, regarding the case of corporatism in interwar European dictatorships, Aunós Pérez and Bottai had already proposed comparative analysis of their mutual experiences in order to emphasize convergences and divergences between them. Such reciprocal visions were a factor of the transnational development of corporatist debate.

Moreover, the attraction towards Fascist corporatism was pragmatically motivated, even before being ideological. It was the concrete policy put into practice by Mussolini's regime more than the theoretical debate that aroused interest in Spain, as well as in many other countries. Attention concentrated on the legislation and its benefits for social control. So the Fascist regime became aware that corporatism was offering a powerful tool for self-legitimation in the international field—as noted, for example, in a journal published by the Ministry of Corporations in 1928:

> The corporatist concept of state, corporatist law, the making of corporatist legislation and practice arouse interest and curiosity abroad. Some study and discuss it, some praise it. … The contact that Italian corporatism gained abroad, through the International Labour Organization, … or through the correspondence with foreign civil services and scholars, or through the press, it shows itself to be an expansive force. We don't want to say that the universe will readily take it as an example; but, undoubtedly, we can look at this [corporatist policy] as an attempt at creating a majestic and attractive invention.[45]

Whereas propaganda had a role of secondary importance in spreading corporatism before 1928, Fascism began to use this keyword in its promotional campaign abroad in the following years, given that the label presented the social and modern side of the regime. So, from the late 1920s onward, Bottai—appointed Minister of Corporations in November 1929—became the leading figure in "marketing" corporatism abroad. He collaborated with a group of partners in order to apply the fascist label to the "corporatist solution" and to promote it as a "third way" between liberalism and socialism. This activity consisted of a series of initiatives in all European countries, such as academic conferences and diplomatic meetings, translations of texts and publications of reviews, and exhibitions promoting corporatist policy like the one set up at the International Exposition of Barcelona in 1929.[46]

In this way, a network of Italian politicians, public servants, and intellectuals was established between the end of the 1920s and the early 1930s. They spread the corporatist message to various countries, in particular France, Spain, and Portugal, but also Great Britain, Germany, Austria, Switzerland, Greece, and Eastern Europe. The main centers of this network grew in all cities where there were Italian enclaves, such as communities of migrants, branches of the Fasci Italiani all'Estero (Fascist Foreign Relations Organization), cultural associations, and diplomatic corps. They established contacts with local fascist movements as well as with local governments, academic scholars, technocrats, syndicalists, employers, and anyone interested in the debate on the crisis of the state, which was due to the weakness of parliamentary institutions in governing social conflicts and representing economic interests.

Furthermore, through these corporatist connections, the fascist message crossed not only national boundaries, but also political borders. In fact, the Italian model reached a large part of the European political spectrum, from the right-wing to the left-wing. The idea of the corporatist representation of economic interests, capable of overcoming class divisions and restoring social peace for the good of the entire national community, found supporters in the arena of the extreme nationalism, among conservative circles, among Catholics, and in some socialist groups. In the latter case, the two most notorious instances were those of Henri De Man's "planism" and of the French "neo-socialism," although their "corporatist temptation" was at least partially due to the purpose of weakening the fascist message by exploiting its ideas.[47] But also beyond the Atlantic, inside New Deal's group of reformists, part of the talk of economic planning was inspired by experiments in Mussolini's regime. According to Daniel Rodgers, "corporatism's reputation was still in its high tide in the early 1930s, even among those repelled by the thuggish side of Italian Fascism."[48] Yet "corporatism" was a buzzword, allowing different—and occasionally even opposing—interpretations, and a wide range of adaptations.

To summarize, in a political background permeated by corporatist leanings, the new syndicalist legislation, the Labor Charter, and propaganda abroad raised the Fascist experience to the rank of universal model. In the early 1930s, the impact of the Great Depression increased the popularity of this model, partly because in the eyes of the world Italy seemed less affected by the economic crisis than other states.[49] Indeed, the crisis was perceived as the final phase in the collapse of capitalism and of its political-institutional framework (that is, the liberal-democratic system). This view reinforced the opinion that the Italian corporatist experiment was the only solution at hand, because it was the real alternative both to the decline of liberal capitalism and to the rise of Soviet communism. Intellectuals from all over Europe consecrated Fascist corporatism as the "doctrine of the century."[50] But probably the most significant praise came from the endorsement by Pius XI. In the wake of the convergence between the Italian regime and the Catholic Church, in encyclical letter *Quadragesimo Anno* (1931) the Pope declared his appreciation for the Fascist corporatist state, which was realizing "the peaceful collaboration of classes, the repression of socialist organizations and their retchings, the moderating action of a special court."[51] Undoubtedly, the position of the Pope was in some respects ambiguous, expressing fear of the excessive state intervention. However, notwithstanding the anathema against the sacralization of politics that appeared inherent in the "religious" dimension of Fascism, the Italian corporatist state seemed to represent the only real answer to the ills of capitalism and to the dangers of socialism.[52] The theoretical differences between the Catholic tradition and the Fascist state-centric perspective were to be ignored, at least temporarily.

The "Avatars": The Coming of Other Corporatist Regimes (1933–1939)

In the following years, while Mussolini's regime completed its social corporatist system with the opening of twenty-two corporations in 1934, the term "corporatism" became a buzzword in Europe and beyond. It was often used with different meanings, but was usually associated with Fascism for propagandistic reasons. The fascist network continued to take its corporatist message abroad through conferences and publications. The number of translated texts from Italian into various languages increased significantly, with some intermediate civil servants of the regime carving out a leading role. This applied, for example, to Bruno Biagi, a dull ministerial official who became a spokesman for the corporatist experience throughout Europe.[53] In addition to these transnational exchanges, moreover, fascism tried to give itself an international dimension in that period.[54] In fact, some attempts were made to organize a real international movement, although this effort did not go beyond the organization of a league lacking in strength, called Action Committees for the Universality of Rome (Comitati d'Azione per l'Universalità di Roma, CAUR), and a few events such as the French–Italian meeting of corporatist studies held in Rome in May 1935.[55] However, with regard to the transnational circulation of corporatist projects, a new phase was beginning in the 1930s. It was characterized by two changes.

In the first instance, starting from 1933, the Fascist model was joined by other corporatist systems, which were developed in Salazar's Portugal, Dollfuss's Austria, Pilsudski's Poland, Metaxas's Greece, Tiso's Slovakia, in the authoritarian regimes of Baltic countries, and under the royal dictatorships of Bulgaria and Romania. As well as the Spanish case in the 1920s, each of these was in part influenced by the Italian predecessor, but was also based on local features. These regimes were authoritarian dictatorships with certain elements of fascist hybridization, which "tended to create political institutions in which the function of corporatism was to give legitimation to organic representation and to ensure the co-optation and control of sections of the elite and organized interests."[56] At the same time, it was to ensure the repression of labor movements. Compared with the 1920s, the main innovation concerned the attempts to introduce a parliamentary chamber of a corporatist kind within the political systems. This was achieved in Portugal in 1933, in Austria in 1934, in Estonia and Romania in 1938, and then in Italy in 1939, although everywhere power within the legislative process was modest.

The emergence of new corporatist regimes awarded the Fascist model the honor of being the forerunner of an epoch-making solution for the institutional renewal of political life. But at the same time, the Italian variant was no longer the only reference experience. This rendered more complicated the identification of corporatism with Fascism, because each of these corporatist "avatars" generated new points of reference for other experiments, within the wider transnational dynamics of the interwar "authoritarian turn."[57]

An emblematic example can be drawn from the Portuguese experience, considered by Mussolini in an interview with António Ferro to be "one of the most intelligent in Europe"—along with the Italian one, of course.[58] The creation of the Estado Novo (New State) was formalized in 1933 by a new constitution that laid the foundation for a corporatist republic. As for the political system, the reform approved by Salazar established a single legislative chamber—the Assembleia Nacional. Its deputies were elected from a single list. But the regime also encompassed a consultative corporatist chamber representing local autonomy and social interests. As regards the regulation of labor relations, the foundation stone of the corporatist system was the National Labor Statute (Estatuto do Trabalho Nacional) of September 1933. It decreed a long series of intermediate unions of workers and employers that would lead to the creation of the corporations.[59] The influence of the Fascist model on the genesis of this statute was quite clear, since the first article was an exact copy of the initial regulation of the Labor Charter. This was openly acknowledged even by Marcelo Caetano, one of the architects of the Portuguese corporatist state:

> The Italian school has undeniably influenced the making of Portuguese corporatist policy, as seen in the constitution of Estado Novo and in the Estatuto do Trabalho Nacional. The latter, in its structure and its purposes, corresponds exactly to the Italian Carta del lavoro, from which certain doctrinal formulas and organizational principles have been translated. Just like Fascist corporatism, Portuguese corporatism does not allow syndical liberty; in every district it gives the functions of representation and of professional discipline to the authorized unions, namely the national unions.[60]

However, as Caetano himself admitted on the same pages, the Portuguese experience did not stem only from Italian Fascism. According to him and other scholars, it was indeed the result of a mix of ingredients: transfer from Fascism, but also domestic currents of thought (especially the *Integralismo Lusitano* [Lusitanian Integralism] and the Catholic corporatist doctrine, which had a long tradition in Portugal), as well as some other foreign theories such as the works of Othmar Spann and Mihail Manoilescu.[61] Furthermore, as scholarship has demonstrated, Francisco Rolão Preto's National Syndicalism— namely, the main Portuguese fascist movement—did not provide an actual contribution to the making of this corporatist system.[62] On the one hand, the Italian prototype was more influential on the Catholic background of Salazar than on the Camisas Azuis (Blue Shirts); on the other hand, Salazar also used his corporatist project in order to deprive the national syndicalists of an attractive idea.

Ultimately, this corporatist system, like the others, was the outcome of the hybridization of different corporatist traditions and experiences.[63] This occurred within a transnational network of political exchanges, of which Italian Fascism was one of the main protagonists, but not the only one. The Fascist model exercised a broad influence, but it was not replicated in any one place. All "avatars" sought to emphasize their own differences from the Italian forerunner, in order to avoid the charge of copying foreign models and to show their nationalist credentials. As stressed by the methodological debate on transnational history, putting in relevance transfers and interconnections across national borders does not mean denying the historical importance of nations and nationalisms.[64] Paradoxically, while corporatism seemed to prevail in much of Europe, and Fascist propaganda proudly announced the triumph of the "third way," the Italian model was beginning to lose its centrality.

In the same years, furthermore, the rise of another fascist "avatar," namely the National Socialist dictatorship in Germany, introduced a different transnational model that gave less importance to the corporatist project. In fact, although the Italian laboratory gained prominence in various political sectors of the Weimar Republic, including a wing of the Nazi Party, corporatism played a secondary role in the institutionalization of Hitler's regime. Despite certain similarities between the Deutsche Arbeitsfront (German Labor Front, DAF) and the Fascist corporatist organization, the Nazis distanced themselves from the Italian experience in the field of social and economic policy, rejecting the Fascist representation of organized interests (which included workers, although weakly) as inferior to its strongly hierarchical and racially homogenous idea of *Volksgemeinschaft* (people's community).[65] It was not founded on the chimera of the collaboration between the classes, but on the unconditional acceptance of the cult of the "leader," not least in labor relations. In the ambiguous relationship between Hitler's Germany and Mussolini's Italy, swinging from rivalry to cooperation, corporatism marked a divergence between two ways to envisage the fascistization of Europe.

In the second instance, a wave of disapproval rose up against Fascist corporatism from the antifascist forces in the 1930s. This was to obstruct the development of that transnational myth, which was legitimizing the Italian regime as a universal model. Opposition, likewise transnational, aimed to demonstrate both the inconsistency of Fascist corporatist policy and its repressive, coercive, and authoritarian hallmark. Composed of intellectuals and antifascists from all over the world, this other transnational network of political exchanges put into practice—not without difficulty—an ideological operation to discredit Fascist corporatism. It also aimed to rethink democracy and to reform the state. Unlike the authoritarian corporatism influenced by the Fascist regime, which had banned labor conflicts through a repressive policy and abolished social pluralism through a compulsory representation of the organized interests, the antifascist alternative outlined a new democracy, based on welfare policy and mass parties. It aimed to change the shape of citizenship and political participation.[66] From 1933/34 onward, the evolution of this transnational antifascist discourse meddled in the transnational dissemination of the Fascist corporatist model and curbed its popularity.

Summary

Overall, even if the implemented institutions did not affect policy making as much as expected or claimed, scholarship should not underestimate the epochal importance of corporatism as a tool. It was used by Italian Fascism in order to legitimize itself inside the European political framework. In the interwar period, indeed, the corporatist experience (both as ideology and as policy) carried Fascism to the center of political debate, in particular between the second half of the 1920s and early 1930s. Corporatism created connections between Italian Fascists and interlocutors all over the continent. First of all, corporatism worked as one of the elements of mutual recognition between fascist movements, although not all fascist parties gave it identical importance. For example, it was a minor ideological component not only for the German Nazi Party, but also for Mosley's British Union of Fascists and Codreanu's Iron Guard. Moreover, corporatism worked as a point of contact between fascism and certain Catholic circles (among others, the Salazarist milieu in Portugal and the CSP in Austria), although different opinions on the kind of system persisted. Finally, corporatism worked as a "temptation" for a part of democratic and socialist culture. Not only did it attract De Man and the "neo-socialists," but also some figures within the ILO or near to Roosevelt's administration in the United States. These socialist and democratic variants had influenced the debate on the crisis of the liberal state in the aftermath of the World War I, but they had also been nourished by the appropriation of the corporatist option by Italian Fascism in the late 1920s and early 1930s.

MATTEO PASETTI is research fellow at the Università di Bologna. He is a member of the Istituto per la storia e le memorie del '900 Parri–Emilia Romagna (Institute for the History and Memories of the Twentieth Century Parri–Emilia Romagna) and of the editorial boards of the journals *Storicamente* and *E-Review*. Selected publications: *Tra classe e nazione. Rappresentazioni e organizzazione del movimento nazional-sindacalista, 1918–1922* (Rome, 2008); *Storia dei fascismi in Europa* (Bologna, 2009); *L'Europa corporativa. Una storia transnazionale tra le due guerre mondiali* (Bologna, 2016).

Notes

1. Gaetano Salvemini, *Under the Axe of Fascism* (New York and London, 1936), 10.
2. Salvemini, *Axe of Fascism*, 11, 164, 429.
3. See Glenda Sluga, "Fascism and Anti-Fascism," in *The Palgrave Dictionary of Transnational History*, ed. Akira Iriye and Pierre-Yves Saunier (Houndmills, 2009), 381–83.
4. Camillo Pellizzi, *Una rivoluzione mancata* (Milan, 1949; new ed. Bologna, 2009).
5. A classic instance of this historical scholarship is Alberto Aquarone, *L'organizzazione dello Stato totalitario* (Turin, 1965).
6. See, in particular, Alessio Gagliardi, *Il corporativismo fascista* (Rome, 2010).
7. Among the exceptions, see the definition of fascism proposed by Emilio Gentile, *Fascismo. Storia e interpretazione* (Rome, 2002), 71–73.
8. See Gianpasquale Santomassimo, *La terza via fascista: Il mito del corporativismo* (Rome, 2006), 17–31, 181–83.
9. See Aristotle Kallis, "The 'Fascist Effect': On the Dynamics of Political Hybridization in Inter-War Europe," in *Rethinking Fascism and Dictatorship in Europe*, ed. António Costa Pinto and Aristotle Kallis (Basingstoke, 2014), 13–41.
10. I have dealt with these themes in greater depth in Matteo Pasetti, *L'Europa corporativa. Una storia transnazionale tra le due guerre mondiali* (Bologna, 2016).
11. For an overview of the Catholic social theory during the "long" nineteenth century, see Paul Misner, *Social Catholicism in Europe: From the Onset of Industrialization to the First World War* (New York, 1991).
12. For a sociological distinction between "consensual-licenced" and "authoritarian-licenced" corporatism, see Peter J. Williamson, *Varieties of Corporatism: A Conceptual Discussion* (Cambridge, 1985), esp. 20–22 on the Catholic thought.
13. On the corporatist trend in the growth of Catholic trade unionism, see Patrick Pasture, *Histoire du syndicalisme chrétien international: La difficile recherche d'une troisième voie* (Paris, 1999), 17–24. For an investigation based on three case studies, see William Patch, "Fascism, Catholic Corporatism, and the Christian Trade Unions of Germany, Austria, and France," in *Between Cross and Class: Comparative Histories of Christian Labour in Europe 1840–2000*, ed. Lex Heerma van Voss, Patrick Pasture, and Jan De Maeyer (Bern, 2005), 173–201.
14. See Alfred Diamant, *Austrian Catholics and the First Republic: Democracy, Capitalism and the Social Order 1918–1934* (Princeton, NJ, 1960); Klemens von Klemperer, *Ignaz Seipel: Christian Statesman in a Time of Crisis* (Princeton, NJ, 1972); Helmut Wohnout, "Middle-Class Governmental Party and Secular Arm of the Catholic Church: The Christian Socials in Austria," in *Political Catholicism in Europe 1918–45*, ed. Wolfram Kaiser and Helmut Wohnout (London and New York, 2004), 172–94.

15. On the evolution of Action française, see the classic Eugen Weber, *Action française: Royalism and Reaction in Twentieth-Century France* (Stanford, CA, 1962). For some recent studies on Valois' political route, see Olivier Dard, ed., *Georges Valois, itinéraire et réceptions* (Bern, 2011).

16. See, for example, Georges Valois, *L'économie nouvelle* (Paris, 1919), 209–15.

17. Beyond the sharply criticized Zeev Sternhell's trilogy—*La droite révolutionnaire, 1885–1914. Les origines françaises du fascisme* (Paris, 1978); *Ni droite, ni gauche: L'idéologie fasciste en France* (Paris, 1983); *Naissance de l'idéologie fasciste* (Paris, 1989)—scholarship investigated thoroughly this convergence between nationalism and revolutionary syndicalism, demonstrating ultimately that this was not the only true ideological origin of fascism, contrary to the claim of Sternhell. Regarding the Italian case, see also Maddalena Carli, *Nazione e rivoluzione. Il "socialismo nazionale" in Italia: mitologia di un discorso rivoluzionario* (Milan, 2001); and Matteo Pasetti, *Tra classe e nazione: Rappresentazioni e organizzazione del movimento nazional-sindacalista (1918–1922)* (Rome, 2008).

18. For a recent introduction to the guild socialist movement, see Marc Stears, "Guild Socialism," in *Modern Pluralism: Anglo-American Debates since 1880*, ed. Mark Bevir (Cambridge, 2012), 40–59. For a biography of Cole, a classic reference is Arthur W. Wright, *G.D.H. Cole and Socialist Democracy* (Oxford, 1979).

19. See, for example, G.D.H. Cole, *Guild Socialism Re-stated* (London, 1920).

20. See, among others, some of Karl Polanyi's writings of the early 1920s: Karl Polanyi, "A gildszocializmus (Eszmék és emberek)," *Bécsi Magyar Újság*, 18 June 1922; idem, "Gild és állam," *Bécsi Magyar Újság*, 29 March 1923. I used the translation into Italian, in Karl Polanyi, *La libertà in una società complessa*, ed. Alfredo Salsano (Turin, 1987), 3–9.

21. On the postwar crisis of liberal democracy, see in particular Mark Mazower, *Dark Continent: Europe's Twentieth Century* (London, 1998); Jan-Werner Müller, *Contesting Democracy: Political Ideas in Twentieth-Century Europe* (New Haven, CT, 2011).

22. For a comparative view on several national cases, see Stephen Broadberry and Mark Harrison, eds., *The Economics of World War I* (Cambridge, 2005).

23. Although with various meanings, the distinction between "social corporatism" and "political corporatism" is present in much of the literature on this topic. For a recent definition, see António Costa Pinto, *The Nature of Fascism Revisited* (New York, 2012), 122.

24. On the birth and the working of the Conseil national économique, see Alain Chatriot, *La démocratie sociale à la française: L'expérience du Conseil national économique 1924–1940* (Paris, 2002).

25. On the origins of Fascist corporatism, see Matteo Pasetti, "Alle origini del corporativismo fascista: sulla circolazione di idee corporative nel primo dopoguerra", in *Progetti corporativi tra le due guerre mondiali*, ed. idem (Rome, 2006), 11–27.

26. On the coexistence of different theories within Fascist corporatism, see Gagliardi, *Il corporativismo fascista*, 12–25.

27. Here the classic reference is Charles S. Maier, *Recasting Bourgeois Europe: Stabilization in France, Germany and Italy in the Decade after World War I* (Princeton, NJ, 1975).

28. Eduardo Aunós Pérez, *Las corporaciones del trabajo en el estado moderno* (Madrid, 1928), 35 (my translation).

29. On the resonance of Mussolini's seizure of power, see, among others, Arnd Bauerkämper, "Transnational Fascism: Cross-Border Relations between Regimes and Movements in Europe, 1922–1939," *East Central Europe* 37, no. 2–3 (2010), 214–46, esp. 218–25. Generally, the impact of syndical legislation of 1926 has received insufficient attention in scholarship.

30. For an analysis of the reactions to the Rocco law and its importance in the building of the Fascist dictatorship, see Matteo Pasetti, "Neither Bluff nor Revolution: The Corporations and the Consolidation of the Fascist Regime (1925–1926)," in *In the Society of Fascists: Acclamation, Acquiescence, and Agency in Mussolini's Italy*, ed. Giulia Albanese and Roberta Pergher (New York, 2012), 87–107.

31. *La Carta del Lavoro. Illustrata da Giuseppe Bottai* (Rome, 1927), 136 (my translation).

32. See Francis L. Carsten, *Fascist Movements in Austria from Schönerer to Hitler* (London, 1977), 171; Alessandro Salvador, *La guerra in tempo di pace: Gli ex combattenti e la politica nella Repubblica di Weimar* (Trento, 2013), 161–62; on Catholic fundamentalism, see Herman de Vries de Heekelingen, *Le fascisme et ses résultats* (Brussels, 1927), 72–95; on conservative milieu, see Harold E. Goad, *The Making of the Corporate State* (London, 1932), 86–87; on leftist groups, see Juan Chabás, *Italia fascista (política y cultura)* (Barcelona, 1928), 116–18.

33. Edmond Fucile, *Le Mouvement Syndical et la réalisation de l'État Corporatif en Italie* (Paris, 1929), 11.

34. See *Report of the Director-General. International Labour Conference. Tenth Session* (Geneva, 1927), vol. 2, p. 6. On the relations between the ILO and Italian Fascism, see Stefano Gallo, "Dictatorship and International Organizations: The ILO as a 'Test Ground' for Fascism," in *Globalizing Social Rights: The International Labour Organizations and Beyond*, ed. Sandrine Kott and Joëlle Droux (Basingstoke, 2013), 153–71.

35. On "the power of precedent" and the importance of national contexts, see especially Aristotle Kallis, "Studying Inter-War Fascism in Epochal and Diacronic Terms: Ideological Production, Political Experience and the Quest for 'Consensus,'" *European History Quarterly* 34, no. 1 (2004): 9–42, esp. 22–32. In the literature on transnational history, the persistence of the nations has often been emphasized; see, for a recent viewpoint, George Steinmetz, "Comparative History and Its Critics: A Genealogy and a Possible Solution," in *A Companion to Global Historical Thought*, ed. Prasenjit Duara, Viren Murthy, and Andrew Sartori (Chichester, 2014), 427: "the rise of global and transnational approaches should not lead historians to ignore the continuing importance of nation-states and national boundaries."

36. The making of Spanish corporatist organization started from the decree of 26 November 1926, regarding only the industrial sector, and was

completed by the decree of 12 May 1928, which extended legislation to the agricultural sector. To set this corporatist policy in the dictatorial framework, in addition to the classic Shlomo Ben-Ami, *Fascism from Above: The Dictatorship of Primo de Rivera in Spain 1923–1930* (New York, 1983), see Eduardo González Calleja, *La España de Primo de Rivera: La modernización autoritaria 1923–1930* (Madrid, 2005), esp. 153–63.

37. See Javier Tusell Gómez and Ismael Saz Campos, "Mussolini y Primo de Rivera, las relaciones políticas y diplomáticas de dos dictaduras mediterráneas", *Boletín de la Real Academia de la Historia* 179, no. 3 (1982): 413–83. On Spanish admiration for Mussolini, see also Giulia Albanese, "Alla scuola del fascismo: la Spagna dei primi anni venti e la marcia su Roma," in *Pensare la nazione: Silvio Lanaro e l'Italia contemporanea*, ed. Mario Isnenghi (Rome, 2012), 111–22.

38. Pérez, *Las corporaciones del trabajo*, 172–74 (my translation). Among his main writings, see also Aunós Pérez, *La organización corporativa y su posible desenvolvimiento* (Madrid, 1929); idem, *Estudios de derecho corporativo* (Madrid, 1930); idem, *La reforma corporativa del estado* (Madrid, 1935). For a biographical and ideological sketch of Aunós Pérez, see Sergio Fernández Riquelme, "Política, Autoridad y Trabajo. Eduardo Aunós y Estado corporativo en España," *Razón Histórica*, no. 10 (2010): 17–31.

39. In addition to Pérez, *Las corporaciones del trabajo*, 35–46, see, for example, Anselmo Anselmi, *L'organizzazione corporativa spagnuola dell'agricoltura* (Rome, 1928). For a summary of historiographical debate on this issue, see Marc Prat and Oscar Molina, "State Corporatism and Democratic Industrial Relations in Spain 1926–1935: A Reappraisal," *Labor History* 55, no. 2 (2014), 208–27, esp. 211–14.

40. See, in particular, Miguel Ángel Perfecto, "Regeneracionismo y corporativismo en la dictadura de Primo de Rivera," in *Las derechas en la España contemporánea*, ed. Javier Tusell, Feliciano Montero, and José María Marín (Barcelona, 1997), 177–96; idem, "El corporativismo en España: desde los orígenes a la década de 1930," *Pasado y Memoría*, no. 5 (2006): 185–218, esp. 210–17.

41. Pérez, *La reforma corporativa*, 136 (my translation).

42. Giuseppe Bottai, "L'ordinamento corporativo spagnolo," *Gerarchia*, 3 March 1927, 172 (my translation).

43. Jürgen Kocka, "Comparison and Beyond," *History and Theory* 42, no. 1 (2003): 39–44, quotation p. 39.

44. For a recent focus on the transnational perspective in historical studies, see Pierre-Yves Saunier, *Transnational History* (New York, 2013), esp. 10–13 about the relationship with the comparative approach.

45. "Nota della quindicina," *Informazioni corporative*, 10 July 1928, p. 1 (my translation).

46. For an overview, see Gaetano Napolitano, *La propaganda corporativa nella rivoluzione fascista* (Naples, 1932). In recent Italian scholarship, the topic of Fascist propaganda abroad has received growing attention: see, among others, Benedetta Garzarelli, *"Parleremo al mondo intero." La propaganda del fascismo all'estero* (Alessandria, 2004); Stefano Santoro, *L'Italia e l'Europa orientale: Diplomazia culturale e propaganda 1918–1943* (Milan, 2005); Mario

Ivani, *Esportare il fascismo: Collaborazione di polizia e diplomazia culturale tra Italia fascista e Portogallo di Salazar (1928–1945)* (Bologna, 2008); Francesca Cavarocchi, *Avanguardie dello spirito: Il fascismo e la propaganda culturale all'estero* (Rome, 2010).

47. On De Man and his plan, see, among others, Sternhell, *Ni droite, ni gauche*, ch. 6; Alfredo Salsano, *Ingegneri e politici: Dalla razionalizzazione alla "rivoluzione manageriale"* (Turin, 1987), 24–46; Gerd-Rainer Horn, *European Socialists Respond to Fascism: Ideology, Activism and Contingency in the 1930s* (New York, 1996), 74–95. On French "neo-socialism," see in particular Philippe Burrin, *La dérive fasciste: Doriot, Déat, Bergery, 1933–1945* (Paris, 1986). On the "corporatist temptation" among the ranks of European socialism, see also Emanuel Rota, "La tentazione corporativa: corporativismo e propaganda fascista nelle file del socialismo europeo," in *Progetti corporativi tra le due guerre mondiali*, ed. Matteo Pasetti (Rome, 2006), 85–98.

48. Daniel T. Rodgers, *Atlantic Crossings: Social Politics in a Progressive Age* (Cambridge, 1998), 420.

49. In fact, the historical research has amply demonstrated that even Fascist Italy suffered an important economic slump. For a recent summary, see Paolo Frascani, *Le crisi economiche in Italia: Dall'Ottocento a oggi* (Rome, 2012), 101–19.

50. See, for example, the international conference held in Rome to celebrate the tenth anniversary of Mussolini's regime in November 1932: *Convegno di scienze morali e storiche. 14–20 novembre 1932-XI. Tema: l'Europa* (Rome, 1933). Among the speakers who praised the Italian system were Romanian professor Mihail Manoilescu, Spanish writer Ernesto Gimenez Caballero, the Italian ambassador in Paris Camillo Romano Avezzana, Italian-German sociologist Robert Michels, the Greek delegate to the League of Nations Nikolas Politis, and the German economist Werner Sombart.

51. Pius XI, "Quadragesimo Anno" (1931), in *Tutte le encicliche dei sommi pontefici* (Milan, 1940), 1132.

52. On Fascism as a political religion, see Emilio Gentile, *The Sacralization of Politics in Fascist Italy* (Cambridge, 1996). On the ambiguous relationships between Christianity and Fascism, see, for an overview, Emilio Gentile, *Contro Cesare: Cristianesimo e totalitarismo nell'epoca dei fascismi* (Milan, 2010); and for some case studies, see Jan Nelis, Anne Morelli, and Danny Praet, eds., *Catholicism and Fascism in Europe 1918–1945* (Hildesheim, Zurich, and New York, 2015).

53. Among the several translated writings of Biagi, see, for example, Bruno Biagi, *L'État corporatif* (Paris, 1935); idem, *Desarrollos actuales y futuros del corporativismo* (Madrid, 1938). The practice of translation always performed an important function in transnational cultural interactions, and not surprisingly the fascist regimes sought to exert a pervasive political control on this activity too. For some case studies, see Christopher Rundle and Kate Sturge, eds., *Translation Under Fascism* (New York, 2010).

54. For a conceptual distinction between "transnationalism" and "internationalism," see, among others, Patricia Clavin, "Defining Trans-nationalism," *Contemporary European History* 14, no. 4 (2005): 421–39, who

specifies that in many historical cases "the practices of internationalism, transnationalism and multinationalism coexisted" (p. 425).

55. On this meeting, see Giuseppe Parlato, *Il Convegno italo-francese di studi corporativi (1935)* (Rome, 1990). On the attempt to organize a "Fascist International" through the foundation of CAUR in July 1933, see also Michael A. Ledeen, *Universal Fascism* (New York, 1972); Marco Cuzzi, *L'Internazionale delle camicie nere: I Caur, Comitati d'azione per l'universalità di Roma 1933–1939* (Milan, 2005).

56. Costa Pinto, *Nature of Fascism Revisited*, 126, and 129–45 for a comparative overview on these experiences.

57. See Kallis, "Fascist Effect," 20–23.

58. António Ferro, *Homens e multidões* (Lisbon, 1934), 183 (my translation).

59. Among the wide literature on the Portuguese corporatism, for focusing its role in the long Salazarist dictatorship, see Fernando Rosas, *Salazar e o poder: A arte de saber durar* (Lisbon, 2012), 281–317.

60. Marcelo Caetano, *O sistema corporativo* (Lisbon, 1938), 28 (my translation).

61. See Caetano, *O sistema corporativo*, 25–30. On the ideological hybridization of the Portuguese corporatism, see also Daniele Serapiglia, *La via portoghese al corporativismo* (Rome, 2011), 174–81; Luís Reis Torgal, "Os corporativismos e as 'Terceiras Vias,'" in *Corporativismo Fascismos Estado Novo*, ed. Fernando Rosas and Álvaro Garrido (Coimbra, 2012), 49–79.

62. See António Costa Pinto, *Os Camisas Azuis: Ideologia, Elites e Movimentos Fascistas em Portugal, 1914–1945* (Lisbon, 1994).

63. Like in the whole literature on transfers and entanglements in history, "hybridization" has become a key concept in the most recent studies on transnational fascism. See in particular Aristotle Kallis and António Costa Pinto, "Conclusion: Embracing Complexity and Transnational Dynamics: The Diffusion of Fascism and the Hybridization of Dictatorships in Inter-War Europe," in *Rethinking Fascism and Dictatorship in Europe*, ed. António Costa Pinto and Aristotle Kallis (Basingstoke, 2014), 272–82.

64. See, among others, Clavin, "Defining Transnationalism," 423.

65. In addition to the classic work of Timothy W. Mason, *Sozialpolitik im Dritten Reich. Arbeiterklasse und Volksgemeinschaft* (Opladen, 1977), esp. ch. 5, see Daniela Liebscher, *Freude und Arbeit: Zur internationalen Freizeit- und Sozialpolitik das faschistischen Italien und des NS-Regimes* (Cologne, 2009). On the "myth of the corporatist state" in Germany, see also Franz Neumann, *Behemoth: The Structure and Practice of National Socialism* (New York, 1942).

66. See Alberto De Bernardi, *Discorso sull'antifascismo*, ed. Andrea Rapini (Milan, 2007), 119–29.

Bibliography

Convegno di scienze morali e storiche. 14–20 novembre 1932-XI. Tema: l'Europa. Rome, 1933.

La Carta del Lavoro. Illustrata da Giuseppe Bottai. Rome, 1927.

"Nota della quindicina." *Informazioni corporative*, 10 July 1928.

Report of the Director-General. International Labour Conference. Tenth Session. Geneva, 1927.
Tutte le encicliche dei sommi pontefici. Milan, 1940.

Albanese, Giulia. "Alla scuola del fascismo: la Spagna dei primi anni venti e la marcia su Roma." In *Pensare la nazione: Silvio Lanaro e l'Italia contemporanea,* ed. Mario Isnenghi, 111–22. Rome, 2012.
Albanese, Giulia, and Roberta Pergher, eds. *In the Society of Fascists: Acclamation, Acquiescence, and Agency in Mussolini's Italy.* New York, 2012.
Anselmi, Anselmo. *L'organizzazione corporativa spagnuola dell'agricoltura.* Rome, 1928.
Aquarone, Alberto. *L'organizzazione dello Stato totalitario.* Turin, 1965.
Aunós Pérez, Eduardo. *Las corporaciones del trabajo en el estado moderno.* Madrid, 1928.
———. *La organización corporativa y su posible desenvolvimiento.* Madrid, 1929.
———. *Estudios de derecho corporativo.* Madrid, 1930.
———. *La reforma corporativa del estado.* Madrid, 1935.
Bauerkämper, Arnd. "Transnational Fascism: Cross-Border Relations between Regimes and Movements in Europe, 1922–1939." *East Central Europe* 37, no. 2–3 (2010): 214–46.
Ben-Ami, Shlomo. *Fascism from Above: The Dictatorship of Primo de Rivera in Spain 1923–1930.* New York, 1983.
Bevir, Mark, ed. *Modern Pluralism: Anglo-American Debates since 1880.* Cambridge, 2012.
Biagi, Bruno. *L'État corporatif.* Paris, 1935.
———. *Desarrollos actuales y futuros del corporativismo.* Madrid, 1938.
Boothby, Robert, et al. *Industry and the State: A Conservative View.* London, 1927.
Bottai, Giuseppe. "L'ordinamento corporativo spagnolo." *Gerarchia,* 3 March 1927: 166–72.
Broadberry, Stephen, and Mark Harrison, ed. *The Economics of World War I.* Cambridge, 2005.
Burrin, Philippe. *La dérive fasciste: Doriot, Déat, Bergery, 1933–1945.* Paris, 1986.
Caetano, Marcelo. *O sistema corporativo.* Lisbon, 1938.
Carli, Maddalena. *Nazione e rivoluzione: Il "socialismo nazionale" in Italia: mitologia di un discorso rivoluzionario.* Milan, 2001.
Carsten, Francis L. *Fascist Movements in Austria from Schönerer to Hitler.* London, 1977.
Cavarocchi, Francesca. *Avanguardie dello spirito: Il fascismo e la propaganda culturale all'estero.* Rome, 2010.
Chabás, Juan. *Italia fascista (política y cultura).* Barcelona, 1928.
Chatriot, Alain. *La démocratie sociale à la française: L'expérience du Conseil national économique 1924–1940.* Paris, 2002.
Clavin, Patricia. "Defining Transnationalism." *Contemporary European History* 14, no. 4 (2005): 421–39.
Cole, G.D.H. *Guild Socialism Re-stated.* London, 1920.
Costa Pinto, António. *Os Camisas Azuis: Ideologia, Elites e Movimentos Fascistas em Portugal, 1914–1945.* Lisbon, 1994.
———. *The Nature of Fascism Revisited.* New York, 2012.

Costa Pinto, António, and Aristotle Kallis, eds. *Rethinking Fascism and Dictatorship in Europe*. Basingstoke, 2014.

Cuzzi, Marco. *L'Internazionale delle camicie nere: I Caur, Comitati d'azione per l'universalità di Roma 1933–1939*. Milan, 2005.

Dard, Olivier, ed. *Georges Valois, itinéraire et réceptions*. Bern, 2011.

De Bernardi, Alberto. *Discorso sull'antifascismo*, ed. Andrea Rapini. Milan,2007.

de Vries de Heekelingen, Herman. *Le fascisme et ses résultats*. Brussels, 1927.

Diamant, Alfred. *Austrian Catholics and the First Republic: Democracy, Capitalism and the Social Order 1918–1934*. Princeton, NJ, 1960.

Duara, Prasenjit, Viren Murthy, and Andrew Sartori, eds. *A Companion to Global Historical Thought*. Chichester, 2014.

Fernández Riquelme, Sergio. "Política, Autoridad y Trabajo: Eduardo Aunós y Estado corporativo en España." *Razón Histórica*, no. 10 (2010): 17–31.

Ferro, António. *Homens e multidões*. Lisbon, 1934.

Frascani, Paolo. *Le crisi economiche in Italia: Dall'Ottocento a oggi*. Rome and Bari, 2012.

Fucile, Edmond. *Le Mouvement Syndical et la réalisation de l'État Corporatif en Italie*. Paris, 1929.

Gagliardi, Alessio. *Il corporativismo fascista*. Rome and Bari, 2010.

Gallo, Stefano. "Dictatorship and International Organizations: The ILO as a 'Test Ground' for Fascism." In *Globalizing Social Rights: The International Labour Organizations and Beyond*, ed. Sandrine Kott and Joëlle Droux, 153–71. Basingstoke, 2013.

Garzarelli, Benedetta. *"Parleremo al mondo intero": La propaganda del fascismo all'estero*. Alessandria, 2004.

Gentile, Emilio. *The Sacralization of Politics in Fascist Italy*. Cambridge, 1996.

———. *Fascismo: Storia e interpretazione*. Rome and Bari, 2002.

———. *Contro Cesare: Cristianesimo e totalitarismo nell'epoca dei fascismi*. Milan, 2010.

Goad, Harold E. *The Making of the Corporate State*. London, 1932.

González Calleja, Eduardo. *La España de Primo de Rivera: La modernización autoritaria 1923–1930*. Madrid, 2005.

Heerma van Voss, Lex, Patrick Pasture, and Jan De Maeyer, eds. *Between Cross and Class. Comparative Histories of Christian Labour in Europe 1840–2000*. Bern, 2005.

Horn, Gerd-Rainer. *European Socialists Respond to Fascism: Ideology, Activism and Contingency in the 1930s*. New York, 1996.

Iriye, Akira, and Pierre-Yves Saunier, eds. *The Palgrave Dictionary of Transnational History*. Houndmills, 2009.

Isnenghi, Mario, ed. *Pensare la nazione: Silvio Lanaro e l'Italia contemporanea*. Rome, 2012.

Ivani, Mario. *Esportare il fascismo: Collaborazione di polizia e diplomazia culturale tra Italia fascista e Portogallo di Salazar (1928–1945)*. Bologna, 2008.

Kaiser, Wolfram, and Helmut Wohnout, eds. *Political Catholicism in Europe 1918–45*. London and New York, 2004.

Kallis, Aristotle. "Studying Inter-War Fascism in Epochal and Diacronic Terms: Ideological Production, Political Experience and the Quest for 'Consensus.'" *European History Quarterly* 34, no. 1 (2004): 9–42.

———. "The 'Fascist Effect': On the Dynamics of Political Hybridization in Inter-War Europe." In *Rethinking Fascism and Dictatorship in Europe*, ed. António Costa Pinto and Aristotle Kallis, 13–41. Basingstoke, 2014.

Kallis, Aristotle, and António Costa Pinto. "Conclusion: Embracing Complexity and Transnational Dynamics: The Diffusion of Fascism and the Hybridization of Dictatorships in Inter-War Europe." In *Rethinking Fascism and Dictatorship in Europe*, ed. António Costa Pinto and Aristotle Kallis, 272–82. Basingstoke, 2014.

Kocka, Jürgen. "Comparison and Beyond." *History and Theory* 42, no. 1 (2003): 39–44.

Kott, Sandrine, and Joëlle Droux, eds. *Globalizing Social Rights: The International Labour Organizations and Beyond*. Basingstoke, 2013.

Ledeen, Michael A. *Universal Fascism*. New York, 1972.

Liebscher, Daniela. *Freude und Arbeit: Zur internationalen Freizeit- und Sozialpolitik das faschistischen Italien und des NS-Regimes*. Cologne, 2009.

Maier, Charles S. *Recasting Bourgeois Europe: Stabilization in France, Germany and Italy in the Decade after World War I*. Princeton, NJ, 1975.

Mason, Timothy W. *Sozialpolitik im Dritten Reich: Arbeiterklasse und Volksgemeinschaft*. Opladen, 1977.

Mazower, Mark. *Dark Continent: Europe's Twentieth Century*. London, 1998.

Misner, Paul. *Social Catholicism in Europe: From the Onset of Industrialization to the First World War*. New York, 1991.

Müller, Jan-Werner. *Contesting Democracy: Political Ideas in Twentieth-Century Europe*. New Haven, CT, 2011.

Napolitano, Gaetano. *La propaganda corporativa nella rivoluzione fascista*. Naples, 1932.

Nelis, Jan, Anne Morelli, and Danny Praet, eds. *Catholicism and Fascism in Europe 1918–1945*. Hildesheim, Zurich, and New York, 2015.

Neumann, Franz. *Behemoth: The Structure and Practice of National Socialism*. New York, 1942.

Parlato, Giuseppe. *Il Convegno italo-francese di studi corporativi (1935)*. Rome, 1990.

Pasetti, Matteo. "Alle origini del corporativismo fascista: sulla circolazione di idee corporative nel primo dopoguerra". In *Progetti corporativi tra le due guerre mondiali*, ed. idem, 11–27. Rome, 2006.

———. *Tra classe e nazione: Rappresentazioni e organizzazione del movimento nazional-sindacalista (1918–1922)*. Rome, 2008.

———. "Neither Bluff nor Revolution: The Corporations and the Consolidation of the Fascist Regime (1925–1926)." In *In the Society of Fascists: Acclamation, Acquiescence, and Agency in Mussolini's Italy*, ed. Giulia Albanese and Roberta Pergher, 87–107. New York, 2012.

———. *L'Europa corporativa: Una storia transnazionale tra le due guerre mondiali*. Bologna, 2016.

————. ed. *Progetti corporativi tra le due guerre mondiali.* Rome, 2006.

Pasture, Patrick. *Histoire du syndicalisme chrétien international: La difficile recherche d'une troisième voie.* Paris, 1999.

Patch, William. "Fascism, Catholic Corporatism, and the Christian Trade Unions of Germany, Austria, and France." In *Between Cross and Class: Comparative Histories of Christian Labour in Europe 1840–2000,* ed. Lex Heerma van Voss, Patrick Pasture, and Jan De Maeyer, 173–201. Bern, 2005.

Pellizzi, Camillo. *Una rivoluzione mancata.* Milan, 1949. 2nd ed. Bologna, 2009.

Perfecto, Miguel Ángel. "Regeneracionismo y corporativismo en la dictadura de Primo de Rivera." In *Las derechas en la España contemporánea,* ed. Javier Tusell, Feliciano Montero, and José María Marín, 177–96. Barcelona, 1997.

————. "El corporativismo en España: desde los orígines a la década de 1930." *Pasado y Memoría,* no. 5 (2006): 185–218.

Polanyi, Karl. *La libertà in una società complessa.* Turin, 1987.

Prat, Marc, and Oscar Molina. "State Corporatism and Democratic Industrial Relations in Spain 1926–1935: A Reappraisal." *Labor History* 55, no. 2 (2014): 208–27.

Rodgers, Daniel T. *Atlantic Crossings: Social Politics in a Progressive Age.* Cambridge, 1998.

Rosas, Fernando. *Salazar e o poder: A arte de saber durar.* Lisbon, 2012.

Rosas, Fernando, and Álvaro Garrido, eds. *Corporativismo Fascismos Estado Novo.* Coimbra, 2012.

Rota, Emanuel. "La tentazione corporativa: corporativismo e propaganda fascista nelle file del socialismo europeo." In *Progetti corporativi tra le due guerre mondiali,* ed. Matteo Pasetti, 85–98. Rome, 2006.

Rundle, Christopher, and Kate Sturge, eds. *Translation Under Fascism.* New York, 2010.

Salsano, Alfredo. *Ingegneri e politici: Dalla razionalizzazione alla «rivoluzione manageriale».* Turin, 1987.

Salvador, Alessandro. *La guerra in tempo di pace: Gli ex combattenti e la politica nella Repubblica di Weimar.* Trento, Università degli Studi di Trento—Dipartimento di Lettere e Filosofia, 2013.

Salvemini, Gaetano. *Under the Axe of Fascism.* New York and London, 1936.

Santomassimo, Gianpasquale. *La terza via fascista: Il mito del corporativismo.* Rome, 2006.

Santoro, Stefano. *L'Italia e l'Europa orientale: Diplomazia culturale e propaganda 1918–1943.* Milan, 2005.

Saunier, Pierre-Yves. *Transnational History.* New York, 2013.

Serapiglia, Daniele. *La via portoghese al corporativismo.* Rome, 2011.

Sluga, Glenda. "Fascism and Anti-Fascism." In *The Palgrave Dictionary of Transnational History,* ed. Akira Iriye and Pierre-Yves Saunier, 381–83. Houndmills, 2009.

Stears, Marc. "Guild Socialism." In *Modern Pluralism: Anglo-American Debates since 1880,* ed. Mark Bevir, 40–59. Cambridge, 2012.

Steinmetz, George. "Comparative History and Its Critics: A Genealogy and a Possible Solution." In *A Companion to Global Historical Thought,* ed. Prasenjit Duara, Viren Murthy, and Andrew Sartori, 412–36. Chichester, 2014.

Sternhell, Zeev. *La droite révolutionnaire, 1885–1914: Les origines françaises du fascisme*. Paris, 1978.

———. *Ni droite, ni gauche: L'idéologie fasciste en France*. Paris, 1983.

———. *Naissance de l'idéologie fasciste*. Paris, 1989.

Torgal, Luís Reis. "Os corporativismos e as 'Terceiras Vias.'" In *Corporativismo Fascismos Estado Novo*, ed. Fernando Rosas and Álvaro Garrido, 49–79. Coimbra, 2012.

Tusell Gómez, Javier, and Ismael Saz Campos. "Mussolini y Primo de Rivera, las relaciones políticas y diplomáticas de dos dictaduras mediterráneas." *Boletín de la Real Academia de la Historia* 179, no. 3 (1982): 413–83.

Tusell, Javier, Feliciano Montero, and José María Marín, eds. *Las derechas en la España contemporánea*. Barcelona, 1997.

Valois, Georges. *L'économie nouvelle*. Paris, 1919.

von Klemperer, Klemens. *Ignaz Seipel: Christian Statesman in a Time of Crisis*. Princeton, NJ, 1972.

Weber, Eugen. *Action française: Royalism and Reaction in Twentieth-Century France*. Stanford, CA, 1962.

Williamson, Peter J. *Varieties of Corporatism: A Conceptual Discussion*. Cambridge, 1985.

Wohnout, Helmut. "Middle-Class Governmental Party and Secular Arm of the Catholic Church: The Christian Socials in Austria." In *Political Catholicism in Europe 1918–45*, ed. Wolfram Kaiser and Helmut Wohnout, 172–94. London and New York, 2004.

Wright, Arthur W. *G.D.H. Cole and Socialist Democracy*. Oxford, 1979.

ᴥᴘ 3

ORGANIZING LEISURE
Extension of Propaganda into New Realms by the Italian and British Fascist Movements

Anna Lena Kocks

Introduction

From the mid-nineteenth century onward, the conception of leisure as an integral part of civil liberty became an important political issue in Europe's industrialized nations. A growing working class, living under poor conditions in densely populated, urban, industrialized centers, was seen as a potential threat due to alienation, apathy, and "degeneration." Faced with these developments, philanthropic societies, social reformers, socialist and social democratic parties as well as labor movements regarded the reform of working-class leisure habits as vital, and so established their own welfare organizations. Commercialized leisure was considered to be inadequate or even counterproductive. Liberal and conservative parties feared the emergence of extreme political movements in the socialist strongholds of industrialized centers. After World War I, demands for political solutions and national programs grew. High unemployment, food shortages, wage cuts, and the nations' fears of a general demoralization among the demobilized men lent additional urgency to social reform. Male leisure was regarded as the most pressing problem, but female leisure also gained importance in the context of women's suffrage and representation.

Already at an early stage of their formation, fascist movements in Europe recognized the opportunity to engage in this realm. They seized the initiative to act as suppliers of leisure activities, which were presented as a service to a higher cause. They thereby responded to a growing demand from all levels of society, which was often connected to a search for a deeper meaning in life.

Against the backdrop of these trends, this chapter adopts a comparative and transnational approach to analyze the significance of leisure in Italian and British fascism. Both fascist movements bore close similarities with regard to concepts of supposedly appropriate leisure activities in sports, culture, and excursionism. They both emphasized the importance of fostering an esprit de corps and aimed at the politicization of the only seemingly apolitical realm of leisure. In both cases, dynamism, athleticism, obedience, team spirit, competition, and the educational function of cultural events were essential topics in discourses on the creation of a fascist society. The analysis focuses on the organization of leisure as well as on its propagandistic value for the Italian Fascist regime and the British Union of Fascists (BUF). It investigates the ways in which fascists initiated or took over, staged and ritualized leisure activities to gain approval, and as a means of indoctrination and mobilization.

Here, inspiration is drawn from the "Most Different Systems Design" applied in comparative political science where the chosen units of research are as different as possible on a systemic level with regard to extraneous variables, while the central dependent variable bears strong similarities in both cases.[1] The fascist movements that are analyzed in this chapter are characterized by asymmetry with regard to the respective size of each movement, the sphere of influence, the degree of authority and, as a result of these factors, the financial and infrastructural prerequisites for the implementation of their concepts of fascist leisure. On the one hand, this asymmetry provides a wider perspective on the considerable similarities in political objectives and in the ideology of two fascist movements, which formed in markedly different cultural, political, and social contexts, and differed significantly in their chances to seize power. Here, fascist concepts of the politicization of leisure constitute the dependent variable on a sub-systemic level. On the other hand, the asymmetric comparison makes it possible to reconstruct and to examine the difficulties of implementing fascist sociopolitical objectives from two different points of view. In the case of Italian Fascism, concepts of administered leisure had to be suited to attracting a mass following and capable of securing a majority in order to prevent social unrest; furthermore, they had to incorporate evolving international trends in the fields of culture and leisure. In the British case, the BUF with its leisure activities constituted a subculture in a highly competitive market. What they offered in terms of sports, recreation, and cultural events had to be attractive to the masses but at the same time markedly different from the established leisure and youth culture.

Despite their different historical, political, economic, and cultural contexts, both movements compiled disparate elements that were partly paradoxical. These paradoxes remained unsolved. With regard to leisure, both fascist parties took up contemporary trends and discourses but, at the same time, claimed uniqueness. They simultaneously presented themselves as innovators with the ability to overcome their nations' supposed decadence, as well as being deeply rooted in their nations' "Golden Ages."[2] In doing so, they incorporated areas of tension such as modernity and tradition, inclusion and exclusion, mass movement and elitism.

From the mid-1920s onward, Fascist Italy claimed a leading role in workers' leisure and welfare, measures for offering healthy pastimes, raising the population's fitness, and establishing educational schemes for workers.[3] In 1933, Achille Starace, secretary of the Partito Nazionale Fascista (PNF) from 1931 to 1939, declared Fascist Italy to be the vanguard among all civilized countries, as it offered a recreational program for the majority of the population for the first time.[4]

The recreational program that helped create this impression was conceived by the Italian Fascists, not least to gain consent, to mediate the sharp class conflicts or rather to camouflage them, to propagate Fascist visions of virility and femininity, and to militarize and mobilize young Italians and Italian expatriates.

When the national leisure time agency Opera Nazionale Dopolavoro, OND (National Afterwork Organization) was founded and enacted on 1 May 1925, it was subordinated to the Ministry of National Economy. Thus, Mussolini's regime presented it as an Italian state organization instead of one that was supervised by the Fascist Party.[5] This increased its international appeal. American and British press coverage of the Italian *dopolavoro* (afterwork) program in the 1920s and early 1930s generally acclaimed the institution.

When the British Union of Fascists was founded in October 1932, its self-proclaimed leader, Sir Oswald Mosley, had already established connections to Italian Fascists and publicly praised Italian Fascism. In January 1932, Mosley had met Benito Mussolini in Rome, and he had asked the Duce (Leader) for his advice on organizing a fascist movement in Britain.[6] In an article published in the *Daily Mail*, Mosley referred to the *dopolavoro* club system as "one of the most spectacular achievements of the Fascist regime."[7] In the following years, the movement's weekly and monthly papers contained a large number of propaganda articles on the Italian Fascist party, which transferred considerable funds to the BUF. Especially in the first four years of its eight-year history, the BUF strongly resembled Italian Fascism in terms of ideology, party organization, and political style. Concepts of leisure conceived by the BUF showed a strong resemblance to the Italian role model, but there were also conceptual differences, as the investigation points out.

The Case of Italy: Opera Nazionale Dopolavoro—Reinventing Leisure?

By which means did the Italian Fascists politicize leisure and indoctrinate Italians? And what role did the umbrella organization OND play in this effort? By the time the OND was founded, hundreds of *dopolavoro* circles had been established all over Italy. A high percentage of these were not originally Fascist circles of recreation but they had either existed as socialist working-class clubs, as bourgeois societies, or as rural meeting places. In 1920/21, Fascist squads had systematically attacked socialist circles. From 1922 onward, competing leisure organizations had been dissolved.[8] As a substitute, *dopolavoro* clubs were established at a local level and as part of larger factories and business corporations. These *dopolavoro aziendali* (Company Afterwork Sections) thus remained partly under the control of employers who had often regulated and organized workers' spare time in a paternalistic manner. With the *dopolavoro aziendali* circles installed, sporting and recreational facilities were built in close vicinity to the companies.[9] Fascist ideals and propaganda themes were now integrated into companies' sporting and cultural activities, and welfare clubs.

The OND was conceived not only as an institution which was to provide recreational programs offering physical education, excursions, games, and healthy pastimes but also as a means of educating workers, clerks, and civil servants according to Fascist visions. Furthermore, the institution was concerned with the improvement of working conditions and social welfare. Not least, the OND was to regulate members' consumption and expenditure. The structure of the *dopolavoro* program was highly hierarchical. Provincial boards supervised and controlled the local clubs, which numbered twenty-three thousand in 1939.[10]

By 1929, the OND had reached a membership of 1.6 million, which rose to 4.5 million by 1939.[11] About 40 percent of all industrial workers were members, and almost all civil servants and employees of private enterprises.[12] In 1933, Achille Starace claimed that the OND had succeeded in extending its influence to the remotest villages.[13] However, the establishment of the *dopolavoro* program turned out to be difficult. In northern Italy it generally developed at a quicker pace and reached a higher level of support than in the rural areas of the

Mezzogiorno (Southern Italy), where the scheme proved less appealing to agricultural workers. Here, the traditional ruling elite provided competition for the regime's attempts to control the population.

Despite these difficulties in remote regions, the *dopolavoro* circles generally gained considerable popularity. They provided recreation and entertainment, and access to sports grounds, theaters, and dances. They enabled young people to meet their peers without parental supervision, which proved especially appealing to young women who were otherwise traditionally subjected to rigid constraints. The wide range of activities seemed to remedy the monotony and isolation, as well as the perceived vices of modernity.

Popular culture and knowledge were now defined by Fascist ideologues and conveyed via the *dopolavoro* circles. These also set the tone for politically favored sports and recreational activities, such as excursions. The *dopolavoro* program allowed Italian Fascists to portray themselves as being concerned with people's well-being and promoting the participation of the individual in a common cause. Accordingly, Corrado Puccetti, the director general of the OND, stated in 1938:

> The Fascist Party, through the National Dopolavoro Organization, faithfully puts into practice the desire expressed by the DUCE: "to go towards the people." ... [The OND aims at] making everyone realize, without distinction of age, class, or profession, the supreme duty of keeping healthy and of accustoming their bodies to the hard work which they are called upon to perform by modern life, not least the duty of military service.[14]

The foundation of the OND in 1925 marked the beginning of the regime's extensive publication of propaganda material, such as magazines, yearbooks, and pseudo-scientific works, which depicted and praised the activities of the circles and their members. In these publications the educational aspect of the *dopolavoro* activities was emphasized. They described leisure as a gauge of a nation's progress, stressed Italy's self-proclaimed vanguard role, and argued that the *dopolavoro* activities served a higher goal.[15] In contrast to the claimed originality of establishing educational schemes for workers that aimed at increasing punctuality, abstinence, physical fitness, and offering cultural means of recreation, the official agenda strongly resembled paternalistic concepts dating back to the mid-nineteenth century.

The most popular activities organized by the circles were sports, such as gymnastics, cycling, fencing, volleyball, *bocce* (bowls), hiking, and skiing, which were to be practiced in *formazione di masse* (mass formation).[16] Correspondingly, sports were regularly organized as group activities by the local *dopolavoro* circles and on a larger scale as integral components of regional or national events. Leisure activities thus became part of concerted public manifestations and of the regime's propaganda. The numerous public presentations of the circles' activities served not only as mass spectacles, enforcing a common identity among the participants and visibly excluding non-members, but also pitted the circles against each other. These events were heavily laden with the full range of Fascist symbols. Portraits of the Duce and messages in his praise were as omnipresent as were flags bearing the letters OND. At mass spectacles, *dopolavoristi* wore uniforms that identified them as members of a specific circle. The Fascist salute was given simultaneously. These mass spectacles, for example the Concorso Ginnico Atletico (National Gymnastic-Athletic Competition), had been thoroughly prepared for months to ensure a high degree of synchronicity.[17] Publications had been sent by the OND to all participating *dopolavoro* circles giving precise directions. What aims did the staging of simultaneity of conformism and rivalry have? In the OND's publications the extraordinary role of its members in Italian society is a leitmotif. The discourses placed emphasis on the community spirit of a special elite, which, paradoxically, was not perceived as homogenous but as hierarchical and competitive. The concurrence of synchronicity and competition was not a coincidence but an essential feature of Fascist leisure politics. In order to attract the nation's young and to strengthen members' motivation, the impression of Fascism as an elite phenomenon had to be maintained and defended.

The OND's mass spectacles were staged like theatrical performances, with excessively decorated scenery; they had a high symbolic value as they demonstrated the population's fitness and unity that had seemingly been achieved by Fascism, as well as active and voluntary involvement, the blurring of entrenched boundaries between the public and private spheres, and thus the regime's totalitarian claim. The Fascist dictatorship utilized sporting events to conjure up and portray an image of widespread approval by employing its leadership cult, praise for the Duce, Fascist and imperialist rhetoric, and strict hierarchical principles. By organizing competitions between the participants and staging prizegiving ceremonies, the regime claimed the role of the supreme authority, even in this field. The highly ritualized ceremonies established a link between prizewinning, general respectability, and achievements in the Fascist cause. Thus, they functioned as a kind of consecration.

The *dopolavoro* circles regularly arranged journeys for members and their families. Apart from trips to the seaside or the mountain regions, the OND organized visits to Mussolini's birthplace in Predappio and excursions to the regime's supposed signature projects. By offering these outings, often at reduced fares, the OND aimed at the "organization of consent"[18] and simultaneously at strengthening patriotic feelings among members.

These tours became an important propaganda tool and had a transnational impact. Other fascist movements drew inspiration from the OND's practice of organizing vacations. The BUF followed the Italian example and ran holiday camps, which were heavily advertised in the party's publications, and which strongly imitated the Italian Fascist ones. At the BUF's seaside camps, the full range of fascist symbols were displayed together with the British Union Jack; members wore uniforms and Oswald Mosley inspected the camps. Excursions also served to foster transnational contacts as fascist movements in Europe organized them in order to enable members to meet adherents of foreign fascist groups.

In Italy, amateur dramatic societies, bands and orchestras, dance groups and writing competitions were established by the *dopolavoro* circles, as were lending libraries. The Carro di Tespi groups (Traveling Theatrical Companies) and the so-called theatrical Saturday became highly popular. The performing arts spectacles, concerts, movies, and radio broadcasting events turned former cultural deserts into regions with a varied cultural life.

Fascist propaganda was extended excessively into these realms. Via cultural programs, Fascist visions, economic aims, and imperialist, expansionist ambitions were presented to the public. The circles served as grounds for the mobilization and militarization of the public. According to Victoria de Grazia, the network of *dopolavoro* sections and other Fascist mass organizations "was entrenched enough to be seen as a primary means of rallying the population for the war effort"[19] by late 1935, when the Fascist regime attacked Ethiopia. Measures taken by the companies and their *dopolavoro* circles, which aimed at Italy's autarchy, are a common feature of the 1938 compilation *I Dopolavoro Aziendali in Italia*.

Contradictory Perceptions of Women's and Men's Leisure in Italian Fascism

The range of activities available in the *dopolavoro* sections resembled the regime's ambivalent ideals of femininity and virility. With regard to women's role, Fascist Italy was characterized by reactionary ideas. "Mussolini's regime stood for returning women to home and hearth, restoring patriarchal authority, and confining female destiny to bearing babies."[20] Fascist discourses on femininity, female leisure and appropriate sports largely reflected this perception. However, the actual programs dealt with female leisure in a contradictory manner: they offered, first and foremost, activities for women who were young, dynamic, athletic, and self-confident.

As in other contemporary Western societies, women in Italy had gained influence during World War I. From the late nineteenth century onward, Italian feminist movements had been founded by socialist working-class women, by Catholic women's groups, and in urban lower-middle-class constituencies. They shared common goals such as civil rights and education for women, but differed strongly in their tactics.[21] In comparison with the British suffragette movement, up until the war, Italian feminists had been heavily criticized, politically ignored, and regarded as an alien phenomenon. The realm of upper- and middle-class women had remained largely confined to the family and church-related voluntary work. Although urban and rural working-class women were actually a visible part of the public sphere, they were denied recognition as such.

World War I marked a turning point to some degree. Not only were women expected to maintain morale, and were therefore addressed in an unprecedented way by patriotic, nationalist propaganda; they also became actively involved, as their labor and voluntary work proved important in stabilizing the home front. "By 1916–17, the government had begun to call attention to women's sacrifices."[22] A propagandistic notion of women "as guardians of the nation"[23] was coined, and especially middle-class women acted as "politically active female patriots."[24] Thus, women became more visible in the public sphere, received attention from the Liberal government and the male dominated society, and gained self-confidence.

After the war, feminists' hopes for female suffrage were soon frustrated. Still dominated by Catholic and patriarchal views on family life and the role of women, postwar Italian society was marked by strong tendencies to return to the prewar status quo.

Although the Fascists' program of 1919 included demands for full voting rights for women aged over twenty-one, few women joined the movement. Those who did and formed the early *fasci femminili* (Fascist women's groups) were marginalized and ignored by the movement's leadership. According to Paul Ginsborg, they were regarded as "hysterical and unreliable" by the early Fascists.[25] By reinforcing traditional notions of family, motherhood, and paternal authority, Italian Fascism defined and regarded the role of women from a reproductive point of view. Propagandistically this was accompanied by a strong appeal to patriotic, nationalist, and imperialist sentiments.

The preservation of *Italianità* (Italianness) and of the Italian race was declared to be women's duty. By contrast, postwar feminism and the impact of modern mass culture on young women were condemned. Women's influence was largely confined to the private sphere. At the same time, women depicted in Fascist visual culture differed strikingly from the propagated ideal of the woman. Apart from the glorified concept of the Italian mother, Fascism presented young, pretty, athletic women as advertising characters, "the girls' fresh bodies being stylish ornaments attesting to Fascism's modernity."[26] Allison Scardino Belzer has highlighted Mussolini's paradoxical approach:

> [It] attempted to reassert traditional roles for women while simultaneously trying to reinvent femininity through public participation in gymnastics and organizing female youth groups. He idealized peasant women, their simplicity and focus on family, [but] then encouraged young women to march in public parades dressed in military-style uniforms. As Fascism exalted the new male (the new Fascist soldier), it glorified the prewar version of the female: big hipped, big breasted, and perfectly shaped for easy birthing.[27]

When referring to leisure, propaganda publications visually presented women in Italian Fascism as modern, liberated, healthy, pretty, graceful, and happy, without reference to marriage or motherhood. The compilation *I Dopolavoro Aziendali* contains several corresponding photomontages of female factory workers and civil servants. On the one hand, working women were courted by the OND and often enrolled in separate physical education groups. On the other hand, female employment was regarded as undesirable. This view even influenced companies' *dopolavoro* circles, which offered maternity prizes and instructional courses on domestic duties.[28] A particularly paradoxical example is given by the glassworks company *S.A. Cristalleria Murano, Milano*, which produced glass for industrial purposes. Photographs show female *dopolavoro* members practicing archery and javelin throwing. In the text that described the circles' activities, the only reference to women workers' leisure activities conveys a completely different image:

> Complementing its activity in all spheres, the Company Dopolavoro of the Murano Glassworks has organized courses of domestic economy for the women workers of the Company. A Fascist School, this is of the highest significance, where Italian women are instructed in a wider and more precise understanding of their duties and are educated in the true cult of the family and motherhood, through those rulings which are necessary for household management and childcare. Family and motherhood are understood by the maturity brought by Fascism, which alone can improve and perpetuate the race.[29]

Can a similar discrepancy be detected with regard to the Fascist views on masculinity? The reactionary impetus which marked Fascist discourses on femininity also characterized its concepts of virility, and the propagandistic image of the Italian man was unidimensional and stereotypical. The lack of differentiation reflected Fascist propaganda's ignorance of the actual living conditions and social stratification. In contrast to this, the OND's actual range was more complex. From the late nineteenth century onward, in Italy as in other Western societies, fears of degeneration due to a masculinity crisis, of effeminacy and of a threat to patriarchal authority had been a central theme, often combined with ruralist, anti-modernist, anti-intellectualist, and eugenicist discourses. At the turn of the century, Italy had undergone significant political, economic, social, and cultural changes. Accelerating industrialization and the resulting urbanization had not only altered work structures but also family life. The traditional extended family had given way to the nuclear one. Birth rates had dropped significantly, and women had entered employment. In the northern cities, modern mass culture had gained popularity among the young. Educational reforms had led to an unprecedented increase in educational opportunities resulting in a rapid drop in illiteracy rates.

Socialist movements had gained influence, especially in urban centers but also among the rural working classes. Despite these structural changes, Italy remained characterized by strong regional differences with regard to working conditions, living conditions, and wages, with abounding poverty, a high level of emigration, and political ruptures.

Perceptions of alienation, of a loss of traditional values and of unfulfilled expectations fuelled feelings of nostalgia and anti-modernist thinking. At the same time, Italy's imperialist ambitions stoked notions of racial superiority and nourished patriotism. Militarism was regarded as a cure for the perceived masculinity crisis. World War I strengthened nationalism among Italians but regionalism continued to define identities. After the war, with its high number of casualties, the denial of some of Italy's territorial claims in the peace settlement was exploited by nationalists, who decried a mutilated victory, a *vittoria mutilata*.[30] The deepening social, political, and economic crisis led to "an attitude of social resentment and explosiveness without precedent in the modern history of Italy, for northern city workers, poor southern peasants, and farm laborers in diverse regions felt exploited and betrayed, leading to a massive new wave of strikes in the north, and land seizures in the south."[31] Political movements fuelled popular radicalization. From the foundation of the first *Fascio di Combattimento* (combat group) in March 1919 onward, a cult of violence was central to Fascist concepts of virility, with an emphasis on militancy and with the Fascist action squads being perceived as the vanguard. "The war acted above all as a grand founding myth of the new Fascist men: the war as training ground of virility, as the extreme experience in which a whole and firm masculinity was formed or reconstituted."[32] Many sporting activities for Fascist men showed clear reference to military training.

The vision of the "Fascist new man," "a heroic, athletic and dynamic member of Fascism's mystical 'community of believers,' ready to sacrifice all for the nation,"[33] reached into the field of leisure. The "Moto Guzzi" motorcycle company, for instance, wrote of its members, the *dopolavoristi*:

> The excursion section produces many amateurs of alpinism and mountain climbing, who invariably have distinguished themselves in various competitions. One of them displayed prodigies of ability and valour on Amba Uork, where he died a glorious death. ... Not only do its members distinguish themselves by their valour and expertness but they are also remarkable for their laudable discipline and gentlemanly sense of loyalty and camaraderie.[34]

The emphasis on militarism seems to have been prominent above all in the public representations, where male participants performed as a modern, dynamic, and disciplined mass. Whereas the range of leisure activities for men in the *dopolavoro* circles was broad and geared towards different age groups and social backgrounds, the image the OND ascribed to its *dopolavoristi* was that of a young military reserve ready for action. The stereotype image of male *dopolavoristi* excluded elderly and physically unfit men.

The Italian Fascists' Grip on Children's Leisure

The influence exerted by the Italian Fascists was also extended to include children's leisure. In 1926, the even more overtly political and paramilitary youth organization Opera Nazionale Balilla, ONB (National Balilla Organization) was founded as an umbrella organization for the existing circles for boys of different age groups and for the newly established equivalents for girls. The name "Balilla" derived from the legend of a Genoese boy who was said to have thrown stones at the city's Austrian occupiers in 1746. The ONB was at first placed under party control, but in 1929 it came under the supervision of the Ministry of National Education. By the mid-1930s, the structure was highly differentiated. For boys and male adolescents, the youth groups established were the Figli della Lupa (wolf-cub groups for boys under eight years of age), the Balilla (for those aged eight to fourteen), the Avanguardisti (avant-gardists, the fifteen to eighteen year-olds) and the Fasci Giovanili di Combattimento (the youth's combat groups). The latter remained under PNF control. For girls and young women, the corresponding groups were the Figlie della Lupa (wolf-cub groups for girls), the Piccole Italiane (little Italians) and the Giovani Italiane (young Italians). Additionally, university students were organized in the Gruppi Universitari Fascisti (Fascist University Groups).

The children's groups were led by adults, often schoolteachers, which closely linked schools to the youth groups on the local level.[35] Educational ideas imparted in the circles were developed in close connection with the school curricula. As with the adult organizations, membership varied and was higher in northern Italy, but it did not meet the expectations of the Fascist party leaders. Even after it had become compulsory in 1939, only 50 percent of Italian children were enlisted.[36]

Other existing youth movements and Church organizations for children were soon forced to dissolve or to confine their activities to religious education. The sporting activities the circles offered ranged from team sports, fencing, athletics, boxing, and shooting for boys, and gymnastics, athletics, and group games for girls.[37] In the Fascist boys' organizations, military training and demands for obedience were omnipresent. Members of the youth groups wore uniforms, which differed in style and thus showed allegiance to their specific age group. At the same time, this made exclusion of non-members highly visible. These uniforms were rather expensive, which put considerable financial pressures on parents.[38] The transition from one age group to the next was celebrated in the manner of military promotion. As with the adults' leisure organizations, the concurrence of inclusion and exclusion, of egalitarianism and rivalry, was an inherent feature of Fascist youth organizations. A meritocratic system was intended to encourage children's participation. Being eager was presented as the key to enjoying the Duce's favor. Correspondingly, the statutes of the Fasci Giovanili di Combattimento emphasized that membership in the Fascist party was not a right acquired by completion of career but a noble title awarded by the Duce to those who, by faith and deeds, had proved worthy.[39] Instructional material conceived for the circles contained almost exclusively patriotic topics and praise for Fascist achievements. With the renaming of the umbrella organization as Gioventù Italiana del Littorio, GIL (Italian Youth of the Lictor) in 1937, more emphasis was laid on imperialist themes and militancy.

Courses for girls were more practical, and orientated toward their future roles as mothers and housewives. Correspondingly, they were taught the principles of childcare, hygiene and first aid, knitting, sewing, and flower arranging. Alternatively, they engaged themselves in local philanthropic work.[40]

Mussolini was presented as a role model for Italian youth and as the caring "Father of the Nation." The image of the Duce as a father figure was essential to Italian Fascist propaganda. Astonishingly, in British fascism there was no equivalence to this theme. The image of Mosley as a leader did not contain reference to fatherhood.

Despite the paradoxical combination of egalitarianism on the one hand, and the emphasis on obedience and subordination under the strict hierarchy and the strongly patriarchal concept of children's leisure on the other, the Italian Fascist youth groups enjoyed vast popularity among children. They offered fun and, for many of their members, an unprecedented degree of independence and responsibility. Membership granted access to sports grounds, which were otherwise scarce. It also provided access to the local Balilla houses, where films were shown and radio broadcasts transmitted. The stress on common identity and service to a higher goal boosted children's self-consciousness and pride.

The Fascist youth organizations placed immense importance on creating a community spirit, which was achieved most successfully at the Fascist summer camps. These were very popular, as for many children they offered their only opportunity for a vacation, or enabled them to escape parental control and spend time with their peers from different Italian regions as well as from the Italian communities abroad. The Fascists considered expatriate Italians to be a vital part of society and thus aimed to extend their influence in their communities. Here, they strongly propagated Fascist visions and tried to establish close relations with expatriate Italians and their children, many of whom had been born in the host countries. The regime presented itself as a guardian of *Italianità* by enabling children of emigrated families to get to know, and build a bond with, their parents' mother country.

British Union of Fascists: Politicizing Sports

To contemporary British culture, mass spectacles of physical exercise and large youth organizations of a paramilitary appearance were not unfamiliar. In their attempts to incorporate young men and women in a subliminal way by offering pastimes, the British fascist movements thus faced strong competition from non-political clubs and organizations that were patriotic but neither fascist nor extremist. In Britain, plans for a national program for improving leisure and recreational behavior, especially that of the working classes, had been widely discussed. For the upper and middle classes, the tone for adequate sporting activities had been set mostly by the public schools' physical education curricula. From the mid nineteenth century onward, female leisure had become a common feature of medical journals and women's magazines. Since the beginning of the twentieth century, a broad physical culture movement had emerged, and the number of sporting and physical culture clubs, institutes concerned with improving fitness, and magazines propagating a healthier lifestyle had increased.[41] During the interwar period, educational, municipal, and work-based sports provision became established across Britain.[42] In the late 1920s, mass sporting events such as the Festivals of Youth, which were held annually at the Crystal Palace, became institutionalized. These events were supported by the League of Nations and brought together youth organizations, physical culture clubs from all over Britain, and also representatives of many other countries.

Youth organizations enjoyed vast popularity at the time. The quickest growing organizations were the Boy Scouts and the Girl Guides, which had been founded in 1908. In 1930 the combined membership topped one million.[43] They were hierarchically organized, provided uniforms and insignia, and offered athletic as well as outdoor activities. They also organized trips to the countryside and camps, and placed strong emphasis on patriotism, discipline, and a sense of duty.

After its foundation in the autumn of 1932, the British Union of Fascists touted British fascism as a movement for youth, vigor and strength, true patriotism, and discipline. In the following years, the BUF tried to attract young men and women from all levels of society. Leisure activities played an important role in this effort. The party organized dances, concerts, dinners, film showings, established sports clubs, martial arts classes, soccer and rugby teams, staged fencing and boxing events, and held holiday camps at the British seaside. The activities that the party organized were heavily advertised in its newspapers. Members were reminded to wear their uniforms at these events, and the BUF sold a wide range of insignia and merchandise in order to foster and visibly display a common identity. As in Italian Fascism, leisure was presented not as an end in itself but as part of the striving for national grandeur and the implementation of a fascist society.

The movement incorporated influences from Italian Fascism, German National Socialism, English nationalism, and imperialism. It was anticommunist and increasingly anti-Semitic, advocating dictatorship and the corporate state. Moreover, it had a strong paramilitary organization. While expressing admiration for the Italian Fascists, the BUF sought to emphasize its British character, its conformity with British traditions and its patriotism for the empire, thus rejecting the accusation that it was a foreign movement. The considerable funds the BUF received from the Italian Fascist regime were transferred in different currencies via Italian embassies and consulates in other countries in order to conceal the financial support from British authorities.[44] The large number of propaganda articles in the movement's weekly and monthly papers in favor of Fascist Italy covered ideological, economic, social, and cultural topics. The propaganda peaked with the BUF's "Mind Britain's Business" campaign after Italy's attack on Ethiopia.[45]

The British authorities closely observed the BUF's contacts with foreign fascist organizations and the visits that the party's members paid to Italy and Germany. The BUF established branches in Italian cities such as Genoa, Rome, Florence, Turin, and Milan.[46] They remained marginal, and conflicts with the headquarters were frequent. From 1933 to 1936, the BUF's chief of staff, Ian Hope Dundas, frequently traveled to Italy in order to establish a closer relationship with the PNF. On one occasion, he presented plans for the organization of soccer matches between Italian and British fascists. Reports instigated by the Italian Foreign Office, and information gathered by British intelligence, demonstrate that attitudes toward Dundas were very ambivalent in Italy. On several occasions, Mussolini even refused to see him. In 1936, Dundas was sent to Rome for six months to act as a liaison officer between the BUF and the PNF. His expenses were met by the Italian Foreign Office. According to a British intelligence report, which nicknamed Dundas "the self-styled ambassador to Rome of the BUF," he was regarded as a nuisance by his Italian contacts.[47]

Relations to the Italian Fascists were largely restricted to the higher ranks of the BUF. Apart from these meetings, mutual visits were paid, in which praise and expressions of solidarity were exchanged. The relationship that existed on a local level between the BUF and the PNF's branches abroad, the Fasci all'Estero, was comparatively distant and characterized by competition rather than cooperation. Despite their close vicinity, common activities were scarce. In contrast to this, Claudia Baldoli has pointed out that according to reports the director of the London *Fascio*, Carlo Camagna, sent to Rome, frequent contacts between the BUF and the *Fascio* occurred. However, these meetings were not publicized in either the *Fascio*'s newspaper or in the BUF's weekly *Blackshirt*.[48] Where the BUF did mention plans for establishing close relationships between Italian and British fascists, such as for its tours to Italy, it remains unclear to what extent these schemes were put into practice, as the BUF did not report on the outcomes.

Referring to the established parties as "the old gangs," the BUF claimed to be the only legitimate representative of British youth. In his book *The Greater Britain*, Mosley had described the so-called "modern movement" as a disciplined army, "grasping and permeating every aspect of national life."[49] Common and interwoven features in the BUF's publications were the perception of severe economic crisis threatening the future of the British Empire and the dichotomy of "old gangs" and "the movement of youth." "No ordinary party of the past, resting on organisations of old women, tea fights and committees, can survive in such a struggle. Our hope is centred in vital and determined youth, dedicated to the resurrection of a nation's greatness and shrinking from no effort and from no sacrifice to secure that mighty end."[50] The image of a disciplined movement created by the BUF was closely connected to notions of athleticism, fitness, militancy, virility, and corresponding leisure activities, which were presented as being rooted in English history: "In our ordered athleticism of life we seek, in fact, a morality of the Spartan pattern. But when the Fascist state is won this must be more than tempered with the Elizabethan atmosphere of Merrie England. The days before the victory of Puritan repression coincided with the highest achievements of British virility and constructive adventure."[51] The BUF rhetoric declared athleticism, the training of body and mind as well as healthy enjoyment, to be a remedy against degeneration. The party portrayed itself to be the only representative of a corresponding lifestyle.[52]

Already in 1931, shortly after Mosley had founded the New Party, he strongly argued for integrating Italian Fascist principles into the party, especially into the party's youth movement. This seemed a thoroughly calculated and strategic decision to his New Party associates.[53] The New Party's paramilitary youth organization NUPA became the direct predecessor of the BUF's Blackshirts. Shortly after the foundation of the BUF, Mosley courted influential members of the British Fascists (BF), which had been founded in 1923. The BUF's Blackshirts now disrupted BF meetings, and a majority of the BF members joined Mosley's movement.

The British Union of Fascists' understanding of youth differed from the concept in Italian Fascism. From the onset, young men and women in their late adolescence and early adulthood were considered to be the youth element in the British movement, while Italian Fascists aimed at incorporating and indoctrinating children from an early age. In British fascism there was no parallel to the Italian propaganda theme of the leader being the father of the nation. Mosley saw himself as a particularly young, virile, and athletic leader, and was presented as such. Many of the female members of the BUF expressed an almost fanatical adoration for Mosley, who was presented by the movement's propaganda as the handsome, hard-working widower.

BUF's Adoption of a Paradox

As in Italian Fascism, concepts of the role of women, of femininity, and of female leisure in British fascism were contradictory. In the BUF, the Women's Section was separated from the Men's Section. With the exception of one day per week, women were not allowed in the movement's headquarters. In the BUF's vision of the corporate state, women's participation was confined to the Domestic Corporation. The movement's publications only vaguely promised women in a fascist state freedom to decide whether they wanted to work or stay at home.

The presence of several former suffragettes in the BUF evoked the perception of the movement as being less misogynist and reactionary, and as allowing female members a significantly higher level of influence on the party's aims and agitation. Furthermore, Julie Gottlieb has argued that the sexually discriminatory rhetoric and structural gender segregation in the BUF did not prevent the female members from participating fully in the construction of the movement.[54] However, this perception is somewhat misleading. The party, indeed, relied heavily on female voluntary work, and women were actively engaged as speakers, canvassers, and fund-raisers for the BUF. But this was due to the fact that the party leaders assumed women would be regarded as more trustworthy and that the militaristic appearance of male members would be a hindrance to canvassing. In addition, in comparison with women's participation in the partly female-led BF, the BUF's hierarchy excluded women from leading positions, thus limiting their sphere of influence. Therefore, Gottlieb's conclusion that there was power sharing on many levels seems to be too euphemistic, and to overestimate female members' authority in the movement.[55]

The BUF claimed to represent British youth, and thus to be aiming at the incorporation of young women. Therefore, the Women's Section organized its own instructional leisure activities such as classes for speakers, foreign languages courses (especially Italian and German), and discussions on the nature of fascism and the perceived benefits of a fascist society. There were marching bands and holiday camps at the seaside exclusively for female members. However, in the context of the varied leisure culture of interwar Britain, the boom in commercialized leisure, and the popularity of organizations such as the Girl Guides, the BUF's activities seem very marginal and far from appealing to the masses of young, unmarried, salaried women.

The Women's Section was first led by Mosley's mother, Maud. Following severe disruptions within the section, as well as between mother and son, it was later handed over to politically experienced middle-aged women.[56] Former female members recalled how Maud Mosley acted as a chaperone for the younger members.[57] The former suffragettes who had joined the BUF were aged in their fifties, and stemmed from the upper and middle classes. Thus, there was a generational as well as a class gap. The Women's Section clearly contrasted to the movement's self-proclaimed role as a youth movement.

But why was the BUF perceived as allowing a higher level of emancipation? The party's use of public relations tools played an important role: for example, the BUF coined an image of its female adherents as an avant-garde of warriors by making their participation in martial arts public. This effectively evoked the image of a feminist combat unit. While flappers and young women who enjoyed commercialized leisure were heavily attacked in the movement's publications, the movement portrayed the ideal young woman as being energetic, fierce, and fearless. Female members of the BUF were offered training in ju-jitsu and fencing. These activities were heavily advertised in the BUF's newspapers and in the 1933–34 *Daily Mail* campaign in favor of the party. Ju-jitsu courses had previously also been part of the BF's leisure activities. Whereas in Italian Fascism young women were presented as athletic, fit, and healthy, but still graceful and feminine, the BUF's focus on martial arts and marching evoked the image of a small elite of female soldiers as a role model for young fascist women. This image, and the decision to present groups of the uniformed paramilitary female stewards at the movement's rallies, functioned as a publicly staged violation of a taboo. Fiona Skillen has argued that sports involving physical contact or even violence, such as soccer and rugby, continued to be widely regarded as unsuitable for women throughout the interwar years. While it seemed acceptable for women to watch these sports, participation was largely confined to men.[58] The BUF set itself apart from the existing organizations by training young women in martial arts, and thus blurred the boundaries between men's and women's spheres of action.

The main target group of the BUF was young men in their late teens and twenties. By focusing on this group, the party turned its attention to an age cohort that was strongly affected by unemployment and not well represented in the contemporary youth organizations. While members of the Defence Corps and many Blackshirts were employed by the movement, and even lived in the party's headquarters, most of its male members throughout Britain attended local branch meetings in their spare time. To some extent, the BUF drew inspiration from British club culture and took up features of gentlemen's clubs such as exclusivity, class-consciousness, and the maintenance of traditional manners. This contrasted to the party's claim of being a classless and dynamic movement. Simultaneously, the BUF regarded fencing, boxing, martial arts, paramilitary training, and motoring as appropriate means to cultivate British sportsmanship and virility. Whereas sports like fencing seem to have attracted especially the upper- and middle-class members, the adoption of rougher sports such as boxing can be seen as being in line with general trends in middle- and working-class leisure during the interwar period. As Matthew Taylor has pointed out, boxing became immensely popular at the time, and boxing clubs mushroomed throughout Britain.[59] Not only was it regarded as one of the most virile sports but it was also seen as a means to instill discipline among young men in deprived areas.

Male leisure activities organized by the BUF were centered on paramilitary marches and demonstrations in public. The party increasingly attracted young men who were willing to engage themselves in violent clashes with opponents, and it benefited from their propensity for violence. By cultivating a form of hooliganism, provoking street fights, and staging pseudo-military parades, which were thoroughly prepared and directed, the movement established a ritual that aroused considerable public attention.

A Youth Movement without Children?

It seems paradoxical that a party that regarded and presented itself as a youth movement hardly mentioned children in its propaganda. Ideas of establishing fascist children's clubs to counter the socialist youth organizations had been prominent in the first British fascist movement. Its female members, such as the movement's founder Rotha Lintorn-Orman, argued for the necessity to incorporate children, but attempts to advertise these clubs in rather poor, densely populated areas failed.[60] In the first four years of its existence, the BUF rarely drew attention to its small groups for boys; these were supervised by members of the Women's Section,[61] possibly a concession to the large number of female members who had formerly been engaged in the BF. With the Women's Section's exclusive influence on these groups, they were far from propagating the movement's ideals of virility and militancy to boys.

But while the BUF's attempts to organize boys were rudimentary, their interest in organizations for girls was non-existent. The latter remained a blind spot in the movement.

In November 1936, an article in *The Blackshirt* claimed that BUF youth organizations had been founded four months earlier and were now to be expanded.[62] Rather than explaining the outline of the newly conceived Cadet and Youth organizations, presenting the activities they were to offer and thus publicizing them, the article stated at length what they were *not* like:

> Italian and German models were carefully examined. The English youth is marked by a self-consciousness which prevents him from those open expressions of patriotism so easy to the Latin temperament. He has not the traditions of the open air which is so marked a feature of Germany. Thus the many excellent points of the Balilla and Avanguardista were regretfully passed over, and likewise, the details of the German Youth Organisation were found to be of a type which would not wholly fit in with British needs. Just as we were compelled to reject models from Fascist countries abroad, so also on examination did we reject the possibility of using existing home juvenile organisations, since their ideology, methods and organisation differed radically from the Fascist conceptions which we wished to encourage.[63]

The youth movement's aim was declared to be that of preparing its members for admission to the adult organizations. The underlying principles were stated to be loyalty, service, and discipline, and the planned BUF youth training was presented as aiming at inculcating ideals of clean healthy living through physical culture, sport, and open air work.[64] According to David Stephen Lewis, the youth movement "failed to grow and was allowed to slip quietly into obscurity."[65]

Conclusion

Both fascist movements propagandistically praised the leisure activities they offered as highly desirable, as unique, and as directed toward a higher goal. Synchronicity, discipline, and fitness were presented as natural and inherent in fascist society. Similarities to, and borrowings from, other fascist movements, contemporary non-political organizations, conceptions, and trends were denied in order to pretend originality and to appeal to nationalist sentiments. Organized and ritualized leisure served to pretend homogeneity and to cover up contradictions and disparities. Despite high-flown aims, political strategies were tempered by reality. In Britain, the fascist movement remained marginal. In Italy, the intended successes were limited by regional and social boundaries: the South showed higher resistance due to the strength of its entrenched milieus and social relations, and in the North less than half of the target group was successfully organized. In both cases, the disparate structure of the project "organizing leisure" reduced its impact. The Italian and British fascists kept in contact for several years, and the BUF received considerable funds from the Italian regime. These relations were largely restricted to the higher ranks. They encompassed propagandistically exploited formal visits and clandestine meetings. Despite substantial ideological and strategic similarities and adoptions, the movements were divided by the impact of their respective national cultures and traditions, nationalism, and power-political aims.

ANNA LENA KOCKS, M.A., studied History and English Literature and Cultural Studies at Humboldt-Universität zu Berlin, and is currently working on a doctoral thesis concerning Italian and British Fascism at Freie Universität Berlin. She is a part-time consultant for corporate history in a management consultancy. Publication: *Lässigkeit als Lebensart. La Sprezzatura nel Libro del Cortegiano di Baldassare Castiglione* (Bristol, 2013).

Notes

1. See Carsten Anckar, "On the Applicability of the Most Similar Systems Design and the Most Different Systems Design in Comparative Research," in *International Journal of Social Research Methodology* 11, no. 5 (2008): 389–401. Jürgen Kocka has discussed the advantages and disadvantages of another kind of asymmetrical comparative research where one unit is analyzed in a detailed manner and brief sketches of other units are used as a foil for the peculiarities of the main unit. Kocka has argued that this can be an enriching approach as it leads to insights into the specifics of the major object of investigation. See Jürgen Kocka, "Asymmetrical Historical Comparison: The Case of the German Sonderweg," in *History and Theory* 38, no. 1 (1999): 40–50.

2. For the self-contradictory nature of fascist movements and their ideological inconsistencies, see Arnd Bauerkämper, *Der Faschismus in Europa 1918–1945* (Stuttgart, 2006), 27–28; for fascist ideology of national renaissance, see Roger Griffin, "Staging the Nation's Rebirth: The Politics and Aesthetics of Performance in the Context of Fascist Studies," in Günter Berghaus, ed., *Fascism and Theatre: Comparative Studies on the Aesthetics and Politics of Performance in Europe, 1925–1945* (Oxford, 1996), 11–29.

3. See, e.g., Daniela Liebscher, *Freude und Arbeit: Zur internationalen Freizeit- und Sozialpolitik des faschistischen Italien und des NS-Regimes* (Cologne, 2009).
4. Achille Starace, *L'Opera Nazionale Dopolavoro* (Verona, 1933), 15–18.
5. From 1927 onward, it was subordinated to the PNF.
6. Stanley Olson, ed., *Harold Nicolson: Diaries and Letters 1930–1964* (London, 1980), 35–36.
7. "Fascism Means Teamwork—and Freedom to Live," *Daily Mail*, 1 Feb.1932, p. 10.
8. Hans Woller, *Geschichte Italiens im 20. Jahrhundert* (Munich, 2010), 118.
9. See, e.g., "Società Italiana Pirelli Milano," in *I Dopolavoro Aziendali in Italia* (Rome, 1938), 380. The compilation *I Dopolavoro Aziendali* presented the companies' *dopolavoro* circles simultaneously in five languages. Quotes are derived from the English version.
10. Woller, *Geschichte Italiens*, 118.
11. Ibid.
12. Ibid, 119.
13. Starace, *L'Opera Nazionale Dopolavoro*, 35.
14. *I Dopolavoro Aziendali*.
15. Giovanni Bertinetti, *Il Libro del Dopolavoro* (Turin, 1928), 3, 10–11.
16. *I Dopolavoro Aziendali*, 48.
17. For the Concorso Ginnico Atletico, see e.g., *Annuario dell'Opera Nazionale Dopolavoro 1938* (Rome, 1938), 102–7.
18. Victoria de Grazia, *The Culture of Consent: Mass Organization of Leisure in Fascist Italy* (Cambridge, 1981), 1.
19. Ibid., 57.
20. Victoria de Grazia, *How Fascism Ruled Women* (Berkeley, CA, 1992), 1.
21. Ibid., 20–22; Elisabeth Dickmann, *Die italienische Frauenbewegung im 19. Jahrhundert* (Frankfurt/Main, 2002), 48–50.
22. De Grazia, *How Fascism Ruled Women*, 26.
23. Allison Scardino Belzer, *Women and the Great War: Femininity under Fire in Italy* (New York, 2010), 2.
24. Ibid., 3.
25. Paul Ginsborg, *Die geführte Familie: Das Private in Revolution und Diktatur 1900–1950* (Hamburg, 2014), 256.
26. De Grazia, *How Fascism Ruled Women*, 202.
27. Scardino Belzer, *Women and the Great War*, 178.
28. *I Dopolavoro Aziendali*, 792, 1056.
29. Ibid., 1056.
30. Bauerkämper, *Der Faschismus in Europa*, 51.
31. Stanley G. Payne, *A History of Fascism 1914–1945* (Madison, WI, 1995), 88.
32. Sandro Bellassai, "The Masculine Mystique: Antimodernism and Virility in Fascist Italy," *Journal of Modern Italian Studies* 10, no. 3 (2005): 317.
33. Perry Willson, "The Nation in Uniform? Fascist Italy 1919–43," *Past and Present* 221 (2013): 240.
34. *I Dopolavoro Aziendali*, 1312.
35. Tracy H. Koon, *Believe, Obey, Fight: Political Socialization of Youth in Fascist Italy 1922–1943* (Chapel Hill, NC, 1985), 95.

36. Carmen Betti, *L'Opera Nazionale Balilla e l'educazione fascista* (Florence, 1984), 177.
37. Koon, *Believe, Obey, Fight*, 96–100.
38. Willson, "The Nation in Uniform?," 267.
39. Achille Starace, *Fasci Giovanili di Combattimento* (Verona, 1933), 20.
40. Koon, *Believe, Obey, Fight*, 97.
41. See Ina Zweininger-Baglielowska, "Building a British Superman: Physical Culture in Interwar Britain," *Journal of Contemporary History* 41, no. 4 (2006): 599–610.
42. See Fiona Skillen, *Women, Sport and Modernity in Interwar Britain* (Bern, 2013).
43. Tammy M. Proctor, "(Uni)Forming Youth: Girl Guides and Boy Scouts in Britain, 1908–1939," *History Workshop Journal* 45 (1998): 104.
44. The National Archives, Kew, Security Service, KV 2/881.
45. In the campaign, the BUF sought to justify Italy's attack on Ethiopia and demanded non-intervention on the part of Britain. Cf., e.g., "The Italian–Abyssinian Dispute," in *The Blackshirt*, 30 Aug. 1935, 7.
46. Claudia Baldoli, *Exporting Fascism: Italian Fascists and Britain's Italians in the 1930s* (Oxford, 2003), 46.
47. The National Archives, Kew, KV 2/881.
48 Baldoli, *Exporting Fascism*, 41–46.
49. Oswald Mosley, *The Greater Britain* (London, 1934), 31–32.
50. Ibid, 33.
51. Ibid, 52.
52. Ibid, 53.
53. Olson, *Harold Nicolson*, 35–37.
54. Julie Gottlieb, *Feminine Fascism: Women in Britain's Fascist Movement* (London, 2003), 65.
55. Ibid.
56. See, e.g., Special Collections, Cadbury Research Library, University of Birmingham, OMN/B/1/1/8 and OMN/B/1/1/9.
57. Nicholas Mosley, *Beyond the Pale: Sir Oswald Mosley and Family, 1933–1980* (London, 1983), 25.
58. Skillen, *Women, Sport and Modernity*, 195–96.
59. Matthew Taylor, "Round the London Ring: Boxing, Class and Community in Interwar London," *The London Journal* 34, no. 2 (2009): 141–42.
60. Gottlieb, *Feminine Fascism*, 13, 20, 26.
61. See "Blackshirts in Camp," in *Action: Britain First*, 30 July 1936, p. 1.
62. "The Fascist Youth Movement in England," in *The Blackshirt*, 28 November 1936, p. 7.
63. Ibid.
64. Ibid.
65. David Stephen Lewis, *Illusions of Grandeur: Mosley, Fascism and British Society, 1931–81* (Manchester, 1987), 73.

Bibliography

Annuario dell'Opera Nazionale Dopolavoro 1938. Rome, 1938.
Guida Generale degli Italiani in Gran Bretagna. London, 1939.
I Dopolavoro Aziendali in Italia, Rome, 1938.

Anckar, Carsten. "On the Applicability of the Most Similar Systems Design and the Most Different Systems Design in Comparative Research," *International Journal of Social Research Methodology* 11, no. 5 (2008): 389–401.
Baldoli, Claudia. *Exporting Fascism: Italian Fascists and Britain's Italians in the 1930s*. Oxford, 2003.
Bauerkämper, Arnd. *Der Faschismus in Europa 1918–1945*. Stuttgart, 2006.
Bellassai, Sandro. "The Masculine Mystique: Antimodernism and Virility in Fascist Italy," *Journal of Modern Italian Studies* 10, no. 3 (2005): 314–35.
Bertinetti, Giovanni. *Il Libro del Dopolavoro*. Turin, 1928.
Betti, Carmen, *L'Opera Nazionale Balilla e l'educazione fascista*. Florence, 1984.
de Grazia, Victoria. *The Culture of Consent: Mass Organization of Leisure in Fascist Italy*. Cambridge, 1981.
———. *How Fascism Ruled Women*. Berkeley, CA, 1992.
Dickmann, Elisabeth. *Die italienische Frauenbewegung im 19. Jahrhundert*. Frankfurt/Main, 2002.
Ginsborg, Paul. *Die geführte Familie: Das Private in Revolution und Diktatur 1900–1950*. Hamburg, 2014.
Gottlieb, Julie. *Feminine Fascism: Women in Britain's Fascist Movement*. London, 2003.
Griffin, Roger. "Staging the Nation's Rebirth: The Politics and Aesthetics of Performance in the Context of Fascist Studies." In Günter Berghaus, ed., *Fascism and Theatre: Comparative Studies on the Aesthetics and Politics of Performance in Europe, 1925–1945*. Oxford, 1996, 11–29.
Kocka, Jürgen. "Asymmetrical Historical Comparison: The Case of the German Sonderweg," *History and Theory* 38, no. 1 (1999): 40–50.
Koon, Tracy H. *Believe, Obey, Fight: Political Socialization of Youth in Fascist Italy 1922–1943*. Chapel Hill, NC, 1985.
Lewis, David Stephen. *Illusions of Grandeur: Mosley, Fascism and British Society, 1931–81*. Manchester, 1987.
Liebscher, Daniela. *Freude und Arbeit: Zur internationalen Freizeit- und Sozialpolitik des faschistischen Italien und des NS-Regimes*. Cologne, 2009.
Mosley, Nicholas. *Beyond the Pale: Sir Oswald Mosley and Family, 1933–1980*. London, 1983.
Mosley, Oswald. *The Greater Britain*. London, 1934.
Olson, Stanley, ed. *Harold Nicolson: Diaries and Letters 1930–1964*. London, 1980.
Payne, Stanley G. *A History of Fascism 1914–1945*. Madison, WI, 1995.
Proctor, Tammy M. "(Uni)Forming Youth: Girl Guides and Boy Scouts in Britain, 1908–1939," *History Workshop Journal* 45 (1998): 103–34.
Scardino Belzer, Allison. *Women and the Great War: Femininity under Fire in Italy*. New York, 2010.
Skillen, Fiona. *Women, Sport and Modernity in Interwar Britain*. Bern, 2013.

Sponza, Lucio. *Divided Loyalties: Italians in Britain during the Second World War.* Bern, 2000.

Starace, Achille. *Fasci Giovanili di Combattimento.* Verona, 1933.

———. *L'Opera Nazionale Dopolavoro.* Verona, 1933.

Taylor, Matthew. "Round the London Ring: Boxing, Class and Community in Interwar London," *The London Journal* 34, no. 2 (2009): 139–62.

Willson, Perry. "The Nation in Uniform? Fascist Italy, 1919–43," *Past and Present* 221 (2013): 239–72.

Woller, Hans. *Geschichte Italiens im 20. Jahrhundert.* Munich, 2010.

Zweininger-Baglielowska, Ina. "Building a British Superman: Physical Culture in Interwar Britain," *Journal of Contemporary History* 41, no. 4 (2006): 595–610.

4

"THE BROTHERHOOD OF YOUTH"
A Case Study of the Ustaša and Hlinka Youth Connections and Exchanges

Goran Miljan

One of the key characteristics emphasized in fascist movements and regimes was youthfulness and the role of the youth.[1] Fascists saw the youth, with its youthful vigor and élan, as the "new" generation free from all the vestiges of past ideas, and were thus stressing it "at the expense of the older generation."[2] As Patrizia Dogliani stated with regards to the youth in Nazi Germany and Fascist Italy, "each of the regimes sought through their youth organizations to insert the children of the populace into collective life and so 'nationalize' them."[3] Dressing their youth in uniforms, gathering them under the new national symbols, and indoctrinating them with an idea of a new national revolution, a revolution of the youth, fascists sought a radical reshaping of their respective societies through their youth organizations. The idea was to impose strict discipline and unconditional obedience, by which younger generations would accept their assigned roles and become obedient citizens and future leaders.

Fascists presented their youth as a symbol of change, a symbol of the new generation that breaks with the old order and opens the path toward "new" national revolution and revival.[4] Therefore, the youth was seen as a *tabula rasa*, as a generation capable of understanding, protecting, and carrying the older generations' struggles, ideas, and values. In order to achieve this, the youth was to be molded according to the radical nationalistic vision seen as opposite to the decadence and destruction of their contemporary world.[5] In such a worldview the youth became a necessary prerequisite for the accomplishment of fascist revolution, and therefore was assigned with the task of carrying out and protecting this radical idea of national regeneration. To achieve this, fascists established their obligatory nationwide youth organizations, whose purpose was to serve as incubators for the creation of this "new man," devoted to his/her national community, leader, and homeland.

The idea and role assigned to the youth was no different in the Ustaša worldview. In fact, Ivan Oršanić, administrative commander of the Ustaša Youth (Ustaška mladež, UM), described the Ustaša idea revolving around the youth as the new generation with these words:

> From this revolutionary core, from this struggle, there is to develop a whole generation that never existed before in Croatia—the Ustaša generation ... The wave of the Ustaša youth generation has to sweep away all that and all those whom we consider evil and unworthy ... the remnants of a generation unable to carry within itself the wholeness of a nation, its aims, struggles, higher values, and virtues.[6]

The Ustaša officials considered it necessary to raise and educate new generations of Croats, the new Ustašas, due to their belief that there was an imminent threat of national decadence and therefore a need for national salvation. In order to prevent such a scenario they established an obligatory party-controlled youth organization assigned to "grind the souls of young Croats and create out of them the Ustašas who shall fill in the ranks of his [the *Poglavnik*'s] faithful Ustašas and replace them once these fall."[7]

Considering the similarities present with regards to the youth in the Slovak Republic (Slovenská republika, SR) and the Independent State of Croatia (Nezavisna Država Hrvatska, NDH), this chapter examines the ideological and organizational similarities and relations established between the Hlinka Youth (Hlinkova mládež, HM) and UM organizations. Both organizations were influenced by, and had relations with, different fascist youth organizations, especially with the Fascist Lictor Youth (Gioventù Italiana del Littorio, GIL) and the Nazi Hitler Youth (Hitlerjugend, HJ). However, the argument presented here is that the relations between these two youth organizations were considered to be more suitable and meaningful by both sides. Professor Luka Halat, a district leader of the Ustaša Youth section, described their relations with these words: "This is not just friendship, but something more and deeper; it is the feeling of fateful connection of common benefit and common aspirations ... These relations of ours are becoming stronger by each day, and they will be built and polished by our Ustaša and their Hlinka Youth."[8]

The "New" Youth for the "New" Future—The European Youth Alliance

Connections and transfers amongst fascist youth organizations were manifold, but often limited to a smaller number of youth organizations coming together. However, during the summer of 1942, fascist youth leaders in Europe decided to change this by establishing a Europe-wide youth alliance. The first of the two major events of that summer occurred from 18 June until 3 July when officials and members of fascist youth organizations from across Europe gathered at Weimar and Florence for what was described as "a cultural manifestation of European youth."[9] This Europe-wide congregation provided an opportunity for the youth members to come together and participate in various cultural events.[10] These events served to establish closer relations amongst the officials and members of the youth organizations, as well as providing the opportunity for exchange and transfer of the youth publications, such as the UM magazines *Ustaška mladež* (Ustaša Youth) and *Novo pokoljenje* (New Generation).[11]

According to one Ustaša article, the initiative for establishing broader cooperation amongst the fascist youth was put forward during this first major Europe-wide youth event.[12] In fact, the Ustaša journal *Hrvatski narod* (Croatian People) interviewed HJ leader Arthur Axmann, in which he spoke of the idea of establishing the European youth alliance, which might be formed "already during the next meeting which will be held in Vienna."[13] The meeting in Vienna was organized by Axmann, together with Baldur von Schirach, then serving as the Gauleiter of Vienna, and the secretary of the National Fascist Party (Partito Nazionale Fascista, PNF), Aldo Vidussoni.[14] It took place from 14 to 18 September 1942, when the youth leaders and members from fourteen European countries assembled.

What is interesting with regards to this meeting is that it took place only two weeks after the United States president, Franklin Delano Roosevelt, gave his speech dedicated to the youth and its role at the International Student Assembly, where members from fifty-six countries gathered in Washington, D.C.[15] In his speech Roosevelt attacked the Axis on the grounds of the youth manipulation and the fact that "the Nazis, the Fascists and the militarists of Japan have nothing to offer to youth—except death."[16] Roosevelt emphasized that today's struggle is the struggle for the youth, and that "the Quislings have organized youth movements too—but these are only movements of youth by the tens of thousands to [be sent to] the slaughter of the Eastern Front, where the Nazis need cannon fodder."[17] These words, broadcast by radio, had an impact on fascist youth leaders. In fact, the

Ustaša newspapers reflected on Roosevelt's speech by stating: "Today, Roosevelt intends to dispute the right of Hitler and Mussolini to lead the European youth, and that means into war."[18] According to them, Roosevelt was destined to lose this fight, since his weapon was that of an old "democratic phrase of individual freedom, while the weapon of New Europe in this fight for the youth is the freedom of nations in all their life space and social justice."[19] The UM leader Oršanić stated that Roosevelt's words are nothing more but "false phrases and hypocrisy," and that it is in fact the youth in America who are "without any ideals and completely disregarded as such."[20] While the initiative for this meeting and the creation of a Europe-wide fascist youth alliance did come from the youth leaders, it can be assumed that Roosevelt's speech had an impact on speeding this process further. This is evident from the fact that Baldur von Schirach also reflected on Roosevelt's speech by criticizing the "irresponsible cowboy-like and scout education of the youth in America," and contrasting it with Europe where the youth is being educated so as to become "a responsible factor in life of its nations and states, and the whole continent."[21]

The meeting held in Vienna in September 1942 established the fascist European Youth Alliance, which comprised fourteen national youth organizations. Arthur Axmann became its president, and Vidussoni its head secretary. This alliance was divided into several working communities, each in charge of conducting and monitoring different aspects of the youth organization, education, and activities. Each community was headed by one or more youth leaders or officials from different national youth organizations. For example, the working community on Youth and Family was to be headed by the leader of the Spanish youth, Elola; the Community of Women was to be headed by Spanish female youth leader Billar Prima de Rivera together with Italian female youth leader Testa and Reich female youth leader Juta Rüdiger. The Community for Sport was to be headed by Reich sports leader Tschammer und Osten; Stabsführer Mückel was to be head of the Community for Constructions and Travellings; Italian representative Celani was to be in charge of Press, Movies, and Radio; and Italian commander Bonnaci was to lead Upbringing. Belgium youth official Lehembre was to take over the Community for Youths' Health, and Bulgarian representative Klečkov the Community for Youths' Rights; Danish representative Jensen was to lead Leisure, Finland's representative Loohivouri was to preside over the Community for Ethical Upbringing, UM leader Oršanić was named head of the Community for Official Youth Upbringing, Dutch Waffen-SS and youth leader Van Geelkerke was put in charge of of Culture and Art,

Norwegian minister Stang of Countryside Service, Romanian general Iliescu was to be in charge of School Education, HM leader Macek was to head the Community for People and its Customs, and Hungarian General-Lieutenant Beldy the Pre-military Youth Education.[22]

As can be seen, the idea here was the same as in most, if not all, national fascist youth organizations, and that was to embrace and control almost every aspect of the youth activities. The difference now being that this was to be attempted at a broader, supranational European level. Oršanić saw the European Youth Alliance as a natural development of the UM organization, since he saw the UM as "a generation of European revolution ... that steps into this alliance with other European youth with joy, because it will find itself in the company of those who are fighting for the same goals and who think alike."[23]

The event itself received broad coverage in the Ustaša and Slovak press. Special emphasis was placed on its Europe-wide significance and on the notion of their respective youth organizations' affiliation with this "New Europe" in the making. As stated by Alojz Macek, "the Slovak Hlinka Youth stands today in joy with the youth of the whole of Europe ... cooperates and fights, and will fight with all loyalty, against the rotten Jewish-Bolshevik-capitalist world gentry for the new national and social Europe."[24] For Oršanić, participation in the alliance was a natural thing for the UM and the Ustaša revolution.[25] It can be argued that for the HM and the UM officials active participation in this alliance served both as a justification of their domestic youth policies and also as a confirmation for their states' existence and their future role in this "new" fascist Europe. However, unlike the Ustaša and Slovak press, the Nazi press was less interested and impressed by the event itself.[26] Koch argues that this has to do with the fact that, on 16 September 1942, Goebbels polemicized with German journalists "against the talk of a 'new Europe.'" The situation, of course, changed profoundly after the Stalingrad disaster in January 1943, when the discourse of "New Europe," a Europe of alliance and comradeship, started gaining more space within Nazi propaganda.[27] Another reason why Nazi propaganda was less eager to talk about the alliance is perhaps the fact that the Spanish delegation, headed by Pilar Primo de Rivera and José Antonio Elola, "managed to circumvent some of the original intentions of the organizers," such as the idea of having a strong condemnation of Jews in the final declaration, which in the end did not occur.[28]

Despite all the efforts and coverage given to this meeting in the Ustaša and Slovak press, this broadly envisioned fascist youth alliance came to almost nothing during only its second meeting in Madrid. Organized in December 1942, under the title "Youth and Family," only half of the national youth organizations present in Vienna attended the Madrid meeting.[29] Nevertheless, despite their failure to create a Europe-wide network of fascist youth organizations, cross-national connections and transfers amongst individual fascist youth organizations continued, one such example being that between the HM and the UM organizations.

Hlinka and Ustaša Youth Organizations

During the nineteenth and twentieth centuries, Croats and Slovaks shared a similar history. Both were part of the Habsburg Monarchy and, after the 1867 *Ausgleich* (compromise) and the creation of the dual Austro-Hungarian Monarchy, both became parts of the Kingdom of Hungary. One major difference at that point was the agreement reached between Hungary and Croatia in 1868, an agreement denied to Slovaks, by which Croatia was allowed to have its *Sabor* (Diet), giving certain freedom in questions of religion and official language as well as educational and judicial affairs.[30] According to Jan Rychlík, the fact that both Croats and Slovaks were part of the same kingdom allowed for the creation of a joint platform against Budapest. This cooperation also continued after 1918 when both nations, though entering voluntarily into the new states of Czechoslovakia and the Kingdom of Serbs, Croats, and Slovenes, felt as though they were simply being assimilated by the Czechs, that is the Serbs.[31] Such a view on the post-1918 period created the feeling of a need to further continue their national struggles for autonomy or independence. The idea of national independence was especially present amongst the more nationalistic parties such as Croatian Party of Rights (Hrvatska stranka prava, HSP) and Hlinka's Slovak People's Party (Hlinkova slovenská l'udová strana, HSLS).[32] It was from these two political parties that both Croatian and Slovak fascist movements emerged.

Both the SR and the NDH owed their existence to Nazi Germany, whose expansionist drive in Central and Southeastern Europe made their establishment possible. However, when the Kingdom of Yugoslavia[33] was occupied, Pavelić and his Ustašas were not the first choice for Hitler, but eventually remained the only one. At first the Nazis offered the leadership of Croatia to Vladko Maček, the leader of Croatian Peasant Party (Hrvatska Seljačka Stranka, HSS). However, when Maček refused to accept this position, the Nazis offered it to Pavelić and his Ustašas, who accepted it. The fact that he was not the Nazis' first choice meant very little to Pavelić, since from the outset his main aim was an independent Croatian state at any cost—an idea which, according to the Ustašas, had now been achieved with the help of their "allies."[34] By the time the NDH was established, in April 1941, the SR had been in existence for more than two years, as had its youth organization, HM.

The HM organization was established in autumn 1938 and was structured on similar principles as the HJ and GIL. Macek, a former member of the Slovak Catholic Scouts, became its assembly leader and Vojtech Tuka became the head of the organization.[35] While both the HJ and GIL influenced the HM organization on both ideological and practical levels, its organizational structure and symbols were more directly influenced by the GIL. The most visible symbolic influence of Fascism is seen in the symbol of the HM, represented by an eagle standing on *fasces* with a double cross in the middle.[36] Organizational influence is seen from the fact that HM was also divided into male and female branches according to their age, with both age sections having male and female names, same as in the GIL. The HM male branch was divided into *vĺčatá* [Wolves] age 6 to 11, *orlov* [Eagles] age 11 to 16, and *junákov* [Heroes] age 16 to 20. The female branch was equally divided into *víly* [Nymphs] age 6 to 10, *tatranky* [Tatras] age 10 to 15, and *devy* [Girls] age 15 to 20.[37]

The UM was also structured on similar principles to the youth in Fascist Italy and SR. It was established by the *Poglavnik*'s Decree on 12 July 1941, which stated that male and female youth was to be organized into the "*Ustaška mladež* as an integral part of the Ustaša movement."[38] The decree divided the organization into male and female branches, each with its own administrative commander deputies. It divided the UM into four categories: *Ustaška uzdanica* [Ustaša Mainstay] age 7 to 11, *Ustaški junak* [Ustaša Hero] age 11 to 15, *Ustaška Starčevićeva mladež* [Ustaša Starčević Youth] age 15 to 18, and *Sveučilišna mladež* [University youth].[39] In November 1941, a new Law Decree on the UM was proclaimed, and contained only one small change concerning the age of those who were to be integrated into the *Starčevićeva mladež* section, increasing the age of membership to 21.[40] As can be seen, there were not many structural or organizational differences between the HM and UM, or the GIL for that matter. One small difference was that of the age at which the youth entered their respective organizations, and the age at which they could leave the organization. Another difference was that the Ustašas did not divide their male and female branches by names, but instead had both male and female sections within one age section under the same name.

Despite the influence of the GIL on both youth organizations, the HM, to my knowledge, never institutionalized its relations with the

GIL. While it was argued that the HM saw the GIL as its model, their relations were confined to organizational transfer and practical youth interactions.[41] On the other hand the UM officials established closer contacts with the GIL and institutionalized their relations in a sense of an official "Agreement." This agreement, signed on 17 September 1941, stated that due to the "complete sameness of spiritual views of Fascist and Ustaša revolutions and the purpose of these movements within the framework of new order," it was necessary to establish closer contacts and cooperation between the two youth organizations and thus give this relation a more "practical, constant, and real content."[42] The agreement elaborated on their mutual connections and transfers, especially with regards to the GIL providing facilities and resources for the UM members. According to the agreement, the GIL made a commitment to provide access for the UM members to its youth academies, as well as to provide practical assistance from its officials with regards to the youth organization, education, and practices.[43] The knowledge gained from such cooperation was then transferred and applied within the UM, especially with regards to the youth education and everyday activities.

Immediately upon the establishment of the UM in July 1941, relations and connections with the HM came to the forefront. In fact, the Ustašas started paying significant attention to the SR immediately upon the establishment of their regime. For example, in May 1941 the football club Gradjanski played a game in Slovakia.[44] In June 1941 a group of Croatian journalists visited Slovakia and reported on various aspects of the Slovakian state and society.[45] In June 1941, the Slovak newspaper *Gardista* also published an article on the *Poglavnik* and his life.[46] Ustaša newspapers wrote extensively on Slovakia and its development. However, this was not one-sided admiration, and the idea was to establish closer contacts and transfer certain organizational, political, and social aspects. The same can be found in the SR, as seen from the visit of Milo Urban, editor-in-chief of *Gardista*, journalist Viliam Kovar, and other reporters in May 1941, when they visited and reported on the NDH, where, according to one article, they were welcomed as "our great Slovak friends."[47]

Descriptions of their mutual relations and cooperation often contained and emphasized the theme of friendship and the similar hardships of the two nations. Both nations were seen as having been thrown into "the servitude of foreign governance and occupation" by the Versailles dictate.[48] According to one article, such close connection was based on a similar or even common past, as well as the fact that the two nations were "connected by their hard fight against two falsely friendly nations, the Czechs and the Serbs."[49] In order to further strengthen their relations, the Croatian-Slovak Society was established on 13 March 1942 in Bratislava, followed by its establishment in Zagreb, "with the purpose of broadening mutual relations."[50] One of the main tasks of this society was to organize various cultural and political events as well as to publish a bilingual journal, *Tatre i Velebit*, in which literary works, poems, short stories, and articles regarding political issues were published.[51]

The youth relations went hand in hand with political and cultural ones. In fact, it could be argued that the HM organization was taken as a more suitable partner for the UM. As early as July–August 1941, official delegations of the UM went on a visit to Slovakia with the purpose of observing and becoming acquainted with their work, because "observation of their work gave us new incentives."[52] The youth officials visited youth camps and schools where future HM leaders and officials were educated.[53] Relations were further strengthened by the visit of the HM delegation, headed by Alojz Macek, to the NDH in October 1941.[54] They arrived in Zagreb on 16 October and traveled further across the NDH, visiting numerous cities throughout the state.[55] One interesting point regarding this visit is Macek's interview in which he was amazed and surprised about the UM's good organization, especially its capacity to organize youth en masse in such a short time.[56] His observation is interesting considering the fact that the UM did face various organizational and practical problems. However, Macek's interview shows that, to some extent, the Ustašas were successful in establishing and organizing their youth organization, at least in its initial phase. This can also be seen from an archival document, which shows that by the end of the 1941 most of the UM officials had been appointed to their respective youth sections, and that various courses and activities, both on a domestic and an international level, had been organized.[57] The fact of this initial success was also acknowledged by the former UM official Ante Brkljačić in his August 1942 report, in which he criticized the lack of coordination, leadership, and clear policy with regards to the UM.[58]

Following Macek's visit, the HM journal *Nová mládež* (New Youth) published an article by Otto J. Matzenauer, leader of an international section of the HM. In his article Matzenauer stated that Ustaša visits to Slovakia served the purpose of seeing how "we organize and see youth in Slovakia."[59] He also emphasized the similarities between the two organizations by describing the organizational structure of the UM, as well as its command structure. One interesting section of his text is that devoted to the comparison of the command structure in the UM with that of the HM. In comparing them, Matzenauer concludes that the UM *stožernik* (district leader) has its equivalent in the *stotinár* within the

HM, while the *logornik* (commune leader) is identical to their *dozorník*, and the *tabornik* (county leader) to their *táborník*. He also emphasized the similarity of their youths' uniforms in saying that the "color and cut of their uniforms are similar to ours."[60] All these organizational and symbolic similarities led Matzenauer to a conclusion that, from what he mentioned here, "we see how many analogous elements there are between the Ustaša Youth and our Hlinka Youth."[61] In December 1941, the UM delegation led by Ivan Oršanić made a return visit to Slovakia, where they were greeted by the highest Slovak representatives, such as Prime Minister Vojtech Tuka,[62] and were also awarded with the HM medals.[63] According to one of the Ustaša newspapers, the purpose of this visit was to "become acquainted with the hierarchy and organization of the Hlinka Youth and Hlinka Guard."[64]

In April 1942, the Administrative Command of the UM sent its official Boris Kregar to Slovakia to "become acquainted with the structure of the Hlinka Youth, especially in the field of pre-military education."[65] A month later, in May 1942, UM official Zvonimir Malvić was appointed envoy of the UM at the HM headquarters, in charge of further developing relations between the two youth organizations.[66] However, while the UM did send their envoy to the HM, which shows an intention of establishing firmer, institutionalized relations, the HM failed to do so. From a letter written to Malvić by Oršanić it is clear that, by November 1942, the HM had not sent one of its member to serve as their envoy at the UM headquarters in Zagreb.[67] In his response, Malvić wrote that he spoke on the phone with Macek and that the reason why this was not done was due to the fact that it "costs quite an amount of money, which the Hlinka Youth does not have, but also because there are simply not enough people currently available, who could take over such [a] function."[68] In fact, as to my knowledge, the HM never appointed their envoy. Whether the reasons for this were those stated by Macek to Malvić, or of some other nature, remains unclear.

As has been shown, mutual visits of official delegations or journalists served the purpose of establishing firmer relations between the SR and the NDH. Nowhere was this intention more clearly visible than in the mutual visits of their youth officials. By examining structures of each other's youth organizations, both sides transferred and adapted certain organizational or symbolic practices. This was made possible by the presumption that ideas and practices of their youth organizations were of equal nature, "directed towards the development of a new man, a man of a new spirit and new comprehensions."[69] Another reason why such contacts were established and emphasized was the fact that the HM and the UM could each measure and present their success much better and more easily by making comparisons to each other, rather than trying to compare themselves with the GIL or the HJ, with their massive memberships, resources, and infrastructures.

Connections and Exchanges

On 7 and 8 December 1941, a Slovak chess delegation came to Zagreb for the first international chess tournament to be played between the two nations. The call for the tournament stated that this was the first time that Croatian chess players had played at an international level, and that both countries had shared a common lack of "freedom, statehood, and independence through the centuries ... [a] common struggle in the past, common enemies, and [now the] same ideals in the present."[70] While the tournament was designed for professionals, one part of it was dedicated to a competition between the representatives of the HM and UM members. In the Ustaša discourse, chess was seen as a noble game that had the capacity to develop young minds and souls.[71] In fact chess was seen as an important, integral part of youth education, able to provide a range of possibilities for youth development and "all things necessary for building the real human."[72] The UM officials considered chess to be an educational tool capable of developing "attention, reasonable judgment, determination, will, stamina, and readiness in decision making."[73] That chess was seen as an important component in youth education, but also in establishing firmer connections between the two youth organizations is seen from the fact that, in July 1942, HM representatives sent an invitation to the UM members for a rematch, which took place on 21–24 August in Trenčianske Teplice in Slovakia. In order to participate in this tournament, all players had to prove that they were members of either the HM or the UM organization, presumably to prevent professionals from competing.[74] There was also an attempt at organizing a trilateral chess tournament between Slovak, Croatian, and Bulgarian representatives, to be held in Zagreb on 25–27 April 1943, but in the end, members of Branik, the Bulgarian youth organization, were not present at this tournament.[75] It can be assumed that both organizations, desiring a total grasp over youth education and recognizing the emerging need for a re-education of their youth due to their neglect in the past, considered chess to be a noble and useful game, capable of developing various aspects of the youth character.[76]

The highpoint of the youth connections and exchanges came during the summer of 1942. Once the official connections and exchanges had been established, the summer of 1942 saw the realization of youth connections on a membership level.[77] The first of such contacts occurred in July 1942, when the HM organized a summer camp in the city of Párnica where twenty-eight members of the UM participated.[78] Only a month later, in August 1942, UM invited thirty members of the HM to attend a joint Croatian–Slovak summer camp, which took place from 5 August at the city of Ozalj.[79] The purpose and goal of such joint camps were described in one Ustaša article as being to educate young males "so that they become qualified to take over the [leadership] duty which will be assigned to them."[80] The camp was an improvised one, with members sleeping in tents, and with signs inscribed with the salutes *Na straž!* and *Za Dom Spremni!* standing above the camp entrance. Their daily schedule was prepared in advance; there was a lecture organized entitled "Croatian–Slovak Hour," and a special course on military pre-education in which the youth members learned how to handle a weapon.[81]

A month later, Ustašas organized a two-month course in the small city of Borovo in eastern Slavonia, where a local UM training school was established. They invited twenty-seven members of the HM to participate.[82] The Borovo School was established to educate future officials and leaders of the UM, and was built and organized according to "similar role-model schools in Germany and Italy."[83] Having members of foreign youth organizations attending this school was used by the Ustašas to emphasize its role and purpose, "since not only Croats shall be educated within, but future Ustaša officials, and also officials of friendly countries. First in line came the Slovaks."[84] The course itself lasted for two months, and the leader of the HM was to be in charge of giving lectures on Slovak history and geography, as well as on the structure and organization of the HM organization.[85] The HM delegation was headed by their leaders Stefan Kassay and Jozef Kuzma.[86] That the HM took this participation seriously is best seen from the fact that it organized a short preparatory camp, from 25 to 29 September at Moravského Sv. Jána, for those selected to attend the course in Borovo.[87] During the Borovo course, members of both organizations were dressed in UM uniforms, with their lectures mostly devoted to learning and understanding each other's organizations, and with additional courses in gymnastics and sports.[88] During the first ten days the youth had only practical courses in military pre-education, gymnastics, and singing, in order to provide time for the HM members to become acquainted with the Croatian language "so they could later understand and listen to our theoretical lectures."[89] This was done through language courses in both Slovak and Croatian, which all members had to attend.[90]

During their stay, the youth members were given a strict schedule with their day commencing at 5 a.m. and lasting till 9 p.m., with a four-hour break from noon till 4 p.m.[91] Special emphasis was placed on pre-military education, which had an important role within the UM organization and the Ustaša worldview in general,[92] but also due to the fact that the HM organization placed less emphasis on it.[93] At the end of the course all attendees had to pass examinations, after which HM members were given various books, brochures, and journals published by the UM.[94] The HM members returned to Slovakia on 29 November. When reporting on their stay in Borovo, their newspaper *Slovak* stated that they had been warmly welcomed and comfortably accommodated, and that "wherever we passed through we were greeted with our salute: *Na straž!*"[95] How important this visit was for the Ustašas can best be seen from the fact that they established a special commemorative sign for those actively participating in the course. The sign consisted of a triple letter "U" with a Slovak double cross in the middle, and an insignia "Borovo 1942" written at the bottom.[96] The right to be awarded with and to carry this sign was given to seventy-two people, of whom sixty-one were youth members, and the remaining eleven were teachers and officials who had actively participated in the course.[97]

Besides mutual, face-to-face gatherings at various meetings, courses, and sports competitions, another crucial aspect in this relation was the exchange of various materials and publications. During their stay at the Borovo School, HM members were given various materials published by the UM organization. Presumably, Slovak members also brought materials of their own to this course. Sources also tell us that twenty-five issues of the female Ustaša journal *Ustaškinja* were sent to Slovakia, and were to be sent in the future "on the principal of reciprocity."[98] Mutual distribution and exchange of various materials published by or for the youth members can also be seen from a memo written by Zvonimir Malvić, which he sent to HM headquarters, in which it was stated that "it is an honor to deliver you various brochures of propaganda editions … monthly journals and editions, as well as the collection of the Ustaša Youth orders with a request to take into knowledge that journals will be sent on a regular basis in the future."[99] Slovak newspapers and journals, such as *Gardista*, *Kocúr*, and *Nový Svet* were also sent to the NDH.[100] Also, prior to the departure of UM official Kregar to Slovakia, the Slovak side was asked to send a "rulebook and handbook on the structure of the Hlinka Youth, and especially handbooks on physical and pre-military education."[101] One interesting case in all these exchanges is that of an Ustaša book *O taborovanju i logorovanju* [On Camping] published by the UM Propaganda Office.[102] This book was intended for the youth officials in charge of organizing and conducting the youth camps. It contained detailed descriptions of how and where to set up a camp, how to set up tents, and how to organize a daily schedule, as well as advising on youth discipline, and on the obligations and duties of members while camping. What is interesting is that no copies of this book exist in either the University and National Library or in the State Archives in Zagreb. Instead, the book can be found in the University Library in Prague. The only conclusion one can draw from this is that at a certain point the book was sent by the UM to the HM, and remained at the University Library in Prague after 1945.

The mutual exchange of various materials, workbooks, and other publications served the purpose of bringing these two nations and their youth organizations even closer. Such exchange and transfer had the role of promoting their own culture and history, and above all their regime and youth organization. However, it also needs to be noted that such exchange, besides serving simple propaganda purposes, also had a role of transferring various structural and organizational youth ideas, and then implementing them in practice. One reason why such exchange was possible and welcomed, even amongst the youth members, was that both the HM and UM members could understand each other much more easily than they could, for example, their Italian or German peers. The Slovak and Croatian languages are very similar, and were perhaps even more similar during the interwar and World War II period, prior to the processes of "language cleansing" done after 1945 and 1989, especially in Croatia.[103] The importance of language was often emphasized in reports describing their mutual connections. For example, one Ustaša member mentioned that during their stay in Weimar and Florence it was easy for them to come to terms with their Slovak comrades.[104] This ability to understand and to speak to each other easily was also emphasized by Matzenauer in his article, where he stated that during their visit "Croats spoke Croatian and we spoke the Slovak language, and there was no misunderstanding between us."[105] Due to such similarity of languages, as well as the constant emphasis on the two nations' similarities, both historically and in the present day, active literary exchanges took place between the two youth organizations. Besides serving the purpose of each becoming acquainted with the other's organization and its activities, it also served the purpose of cultural diplomacy in promoting each country's cultural and political values and ideas.

Despite intense relations, both on the political and practical level during 1941 and 1942, by 1943 these relations had started deteriorating and their intensity almost caused them to come to a halt. One major reason for this was the deteriorating situation on the Eastern Front, especially after the battle for Stalingrad, as well as the growing presence and resistance of partisans both in the SR and the NDH. However, while in Slovakia the major uprising occurred in 1944, in the NDH it can be traced back to the second half of 1941, and especially after late 1942. One reason for such differences in the timing and intensity of resistance can be found in the policy and practice of a widespread terror implemented from the outset in the NDH. Only a month into the existence of their regime, the Ustašas introduced laws that enabled a widespread terror against the "enemies," be they political, ethnic, or racial. In fact, the Ustašas introduced racial laws, aimed against the Jews specifically, on 30 April 1941, some five months prior to the Slovak *Codex Judaicus*, which was proclaimed on 9 September 1941.[106] Such widespread Ustaša terror, aimed against the Serbs, Jews, and Roma people, caused resistance to their regime, especially amongst the Serbs and Jews living on the territory of the NDH. Thus partisan resistance, be it communist or not, presented a major factor during the entire existence of the NDH. With its growing power, especially with Tito's communists gaining broader support, the security and economic situation worsened significantly during the 1943. It comes as no surprise then that it was during this period that mutual relations between the members of the HM and the UM organizations came to a halt. However, diplomatic and political relations remained active until 1945,[107] and Ustaša newspapers and journals continued to publish articles on the HM and the SR, written by youth officials or official delegations that visited Slovakia.[108]

Conclusion

As has been shown, close relations between the HM and the UM were enacted immediately upon the establishment of the Ustaša regime. The two examples of the youth connections described here show the idea of the youth and its role within the newly established regimes, which sought the radical regeneration of their nations. What they also show is that besides such individual relations, both youth organizations strived toward recognition of themselves on an international level through participation in exchanges with other fascist youth organizations. There is no doubt that the HJ and the GIL, with their histories, massive memberships, and developed infrastructures, served as role models. However, despite this, both the SR and the NDH adjusted their youth organizations according to their own ideas of nation and national needs. Thus, it was exactly through relations established between the HM and the UM that both the SR and the NDH claimed their position in this "New Europe" they saw emerging. As Oršanić stated, "the youth actively participates in attaining victory today, but will participate even more in the building of the first peace, new order, and that is its real mission."[109] While their youth organizations served first and foremost to mold a "new" Slovak and a "new" Croat, their mutual connections, as well as those with other fascist youth organizations, served as confirmation of their regimes existence and their youth policies.

How similar fascist youth organizations and their policies were during the interwar and World War II period, and what the relations and exchanges were between them, still requires further scholarly research based on innovative methodology, such as transnational and comparative approaches. Without a doubt, such research will have to include these so-called "peripheral" cases. Not only are these cases under-researched, with an abundance of unknown archival material, but they have a tremendous potential to contribute to our understanding of fascism as Europe-wide, or even global, phenomena. As Constantin Iordachi recently argued, "although fascist movements and regimes took specific or even original forms in different countries, they were shaped by common trans-national conditions, were animated by a common ideology, and shared a sum of common features in terms of their organization, style of politics, social composition, and political evolution."[110]

Fascist youth organizations were products of exactly all the various features that Iordachi mentions, and they therefore require our attention and further research. While mutual connections and transfers between fascist movements and regimes were manifold, they still lack broader research and explanation within fascist studies. Even when such research exists, it mostly focuses on transfers and relations that occurred between the "core" fascist movements and regimes, neglecting the "peripheral" cases, such as those in Central and Southeastern Europe. As shown in this chapter, transnational research on fascist movements and regimes will have to take into account transfers and relations established between this "core" and "periphery," and even more importantly, it will also have to take into account the transnational relations established between the "peripheral" fascist movements and regimes.

GORAN MILJAN is a Postdoctoral Research Fellow in Holocaust and Genocide Studies at the Hugo Valentin Centre, Uppsala University. He earned his PhD at the Department of History, Central European University, Budapest. His research is focused on comparative and transnational fascism, with special emphasis on fascism and fascist youth organizations during the interwar and World War II period in Central and Southeastern Europe. Selected publications: Zrinka

Borovečki and Goran Miljan, "Sport in den totalitären Regimen: Idee, Identität und Zwang—Fallstudie Kroatien," in *Mogersdorf—Geschichte der Körperkultur und des Sports im pannonischen Raum im 19. und 20. Jahrhundert*, ed. Ivica Šute and Željko Holjevac (Zagreb, 2017); "Fascism, Sport, and Youth: Idea and Role of Physical Education and Sport in Educating and Organizing the Ustasha Youth, 1941–1945," *Radovi* 46, no. 1 (2014) [in Croatian]; "'Charismatic' *Poglavnik*? *Poglavnik* and the Formation of Charismatic Community: Applicability and Usefulness of Weber's Concept of Charisma," *Historijski zbornik* 66, no. 1 (2013) [in Croatian].

Notes

1. Unfortunately, there is still a lack of any serious comparative or transnational research on fascist youth organizations in interwar and World War II Europe.
2. George L. Mosse, *Nazi Culture: Intellectual, Cultural and Social Life in the Third Reich* (Madison, WI, 1966), 263.
3. Patrizia Dogliani, "Propaganda and Youth," in *The Oxford Handbook of Fascism*, ed. R.J.B. Bosworth (Oxford and New York, 2010), 195.
4. Bruno Wanrooij, "The Rise and Fall of Italian Fascism as a Generational Revolt," *Journal of Contemporary History* 3 (1987): 401–2.
5. Michael A. Ledeen, "Italian Fascism and Youth," *Journal of Contemporary History* 3 (1969): 137.
6. Ivan Oršanić, "Ustaška mladež," *Ustaša—vijesnik hrvatskog ustaškog oslobodilačkog pokreta*, 3 August 1941, 5.
7. Ivo Korsky, "Ustaška mladež u novoj Hrvatskoj," in *Ustaški godišnjak* (1942): 207.
8. Luka Halat, "Vidjeli smo Slovačku," *Ustaška mladež*, 15 September 1942, 16.
9. "Velika kulturna manifestacija europske mladeži u Weimaru i Florenciji," *Suradnja*, 28 September 1942, 12–15.
10. Ibid.
11. Zdenka Bogner, "Ustaška mladež u Weimaru," *Novo pokoljenje*, 10 August 1942,5–6.
12. M.K., "Zajednica europske mladeži," *Ustaška mladež*, 19 July 1942, 2.
13. "Zajednička fronta mladeži Nove Europe," *Hrvatski narod*, 4 July 1942.
14. H.W. Koch, *The Hitler Youth: Origins and Development, 1922–1945* (New York, 2000), 235; and Wayne H. Bowen, *Spaniards and Nazi Germany: Collaboration in the New Order* (Columbia and London, 2000), 145.
15. William Allan Neilson, "Proceedings of the International Student Assembly," *Educational Research Bulletin* 5 (May 1946), 138.
16. Franklin D. Roosevelt, Address to the International Student Assembly, 3 Sept. 1942. http://www.presidency.ucsb.edu/ws/index.php?pid=16300&st=&st1 (accessed 23 February 2015).

17. Ibid.
18. "Stvaranje saveza europske mladeži," *Nova Hrvatska*, 15 September 1942.
19. Ibid.
20. "HRVATSKA USTAŠKA MLADEŽ U SAVEZU EUROPSKE MLADEŽI," *Hrvatski narod*, 10 September 1942.
21. "Ustaška mladež u Savezu eruopske mladeži," *Hrvatski narod*, 24 September 1942.
22. "Savez Europske mladeži," *Nova Hrvatska*, 16 September 1942.
23. "Hrvatska mladež u europskom savezu," *Nova Hrvatska*, 17 September 1942.
24. Alojz Macek, "Európský sväz mládeže," *Gardista*, 13 September 1942.
25. "HRVATSKA USTAŠKA MLADEŽ U SAVEZU EUROPSKE MLADEŽI," *Hrvatski narod*, 10 September 1942.
26. Koch, *The Hitler Youth*, 235.
27. Ibid., 235–36.
28. Bowen, *Spaniards and Nazi Germany*, 145–46.
29. Ibid., 146.
30. Robert Bideleux and Ian Jeffries, *A History of Eastern Europe: Crisis and Change* (New York, 2007), 251–53.
31. Jan Rychlík, "Odnosi Slovačke i Nezavisne Države Hrvatske, 1941–1945," *Časopis za suvremenu povijest* 3 (2004): 939–40.
32. Hrvatska stranka prava was founded in 1861 by a Croatian politician named Ante Starčević with a political platform of Croatian independence based on Croatian historical rights and its voluntary admission into the Habsburg Empire in 1527. Slovenská l'udova straná was founded in 1913 by Father Andrej Hlinka, and was renamed Hlinkova slovenská l'udova straná in 1925.
33. The name of the state was changed in January 1929 when King Alexander proclaimed a dictatorship. For more on this, see John R. Lampe, *Yugoslavia as History: Twice There Was a Country* (Cambridge, 2000); and Dejan Djokić, *Elusive Compromise: A History of Interwar Yugoslavia* (New York, 2007).
34. *Hrvatski narod*, 10 April 1941.
35. Michal Milla, *Hlinkova mladež 1938–1945* (Bratislava, 2008), 36.
36. See, for example, the front covers of the Hlinka Youth journal *Nová mládež*, where the eagle appears as such (e.g., *Nová mládež*, September 1942).
37. Milla, *Hlinkova mladež 1938–1945*, 69.
38. "Osnovana je 'Ustaška mladež'," *Ustaša—vijesnik hrvatskog Ustaškog oslobodilačkog pokreta*, 19 July 1941, 11.
39. Ibid.
40. *Narodne Novine*, 5 November 1941.
41. Milla, *Hlinkova mladež 1938–1945*, 118–19.
42. "SURADNJA HRVATSKE I TALIJANSKE MLADEŽI," *Hrvatski narod*, 19 September 1941.
43. There were several cases of the UY members attending the GIL academies, as well as cases where the GIL officials provided practical organizational assistance to the UM officials. See, for example, "Ljetna kolonija Ustaške mladeži u Zagrebu," *Nova Hrvatska*, 22 July 1942; "Ustaška mladež na

Academia della GIL," *Hrvatski narod*, 3 December 1941; and "Vijesti Ustaške mladeži," *Novo pokoljenje*, 10 October 1942, 15.
44. "Draga braćo Hrvati," *Gardista*, 31 May 1941; and *Novi List*, 27 May 1941.
45. "Chorvatski novinari na Slovenska," *Gardista*, 8 June 1941; and Hrvatski državni arhiv-HDA, Nezavisna Država Hrvatska—NDH, Slovačko poslanstvo u Zagrebu—SPZ, microfilm D-2852/2-3, "Poziv novinara u Slovačku," 27 June 1941.
46. "Hrdinsky život poglavnika dr. Antona Pavelića," *Gardista*, 13 June 1941.
47. "Zajednički put slovačkog i hrvatskog naroda," *Novi List*, 11 May 1941.
48. "Hrvatska i Slovačka," *Hrvatski krugoval*, 1 November 1941, 14.
49. M.K., "Nova Slovačka i Hrvatska," *Ustaška mladež*, 2 November 1941, 1–2.
50. Rychlík, "Odnosi," 950–52.
51. See, for example, *Tatre i velebit* (Zagreb: Hrvatski državni tiskarski zavod, 14 March 1942).
52. M.B. "Medju Slovacima," *Ustaška mladež*, 2 November 1941, 15.
53. Maca Mimić, "Osada Hlinkine mladeži u Chtelnici," *Ustaška mladež*, 21 September 1941, 14–15; and "Zastupcovia ustaše na ceste po Orave," *Gardista*, 28 August 1941.
54. "Hlinkova mládež na cestah po Chorvatsku," *Nová mládež* (November 1941): 8.
55. "Srdečné privitanie HM v Záhrebe," *Gardista*, 17 October 1941; and "Delegácia HM na ceste do vlasti," *Gardista*, 24 October 1941.
56. "HM sa vrátila z Chorvátska," *Gardista*, 26 October 1941; and "Obetavost Chorvátov za svoj štát nepozná hranic," *Gardista*, 29 October 1941.
57. HDA, ZIG NDH—1549, Group VI/Box no. 196–97.
58. HDA, Sabor NDH—211, Predsjednički spisi—Z-807/2/1, "Izvještaji o Ustaškoj Mladeži," 21 August 1942. Further on HDA, SNDH—211, PS, IUM—Z-807/2/1.
59. J. Matzenauer, "Ustašská mládež," *Nová Mládež* (October 1941): 4.
60. Ibid.
61. Ibid.
62. "Izaslanstvo Ustaške mladeži u Slovačkoj," and "Reprezentanti chorvátskej mládeže na Slovensko," *Gardista*, 10 December 1941.
63. "BRATSKO ZBLIŽAVANJE SLOVAČKE I HRVATSKE MLADEŽI," *Nova Hrvatska*, 14 December 1941.
64. "Reprezentanti chorvátskej mládeže na Slovensko," *Gardista*, 10 December 1941; and "Izaslanstvo Ustaške mladeži u Slovačkoj," *Nova Hrvatska*, 28 December 1941.
65. "Chorvátskemu vyslanectvu",7251/1942, Ma, HDA, Nezavisna Država Hrvatska—NDH, Poslansntvo Nezavisne Države Hrvatske Bratislava—229, 25 April 1942. Further on HDA, NDH, PNDHB—229.
66. "Poslanstvu NDH," 1/42, HDA, NDH, PNDHB—229/2, 1 May 1942.
67. "Gospodinu doktoru Zvonimiru Malviću," 251/42, HDA, NDH, PNDHB—229/2, 4 November 1942.
68. "UPRAVNOM ZAPOVJEDNIČTVU USTAŠKE MLADEŽI," 53/42, HDA, NDH, PNDHB—229/2, 18 November 1942.
69. "Izaslanstvo Ustaške mladeži u Slovačkoj," *Nova Hrvatska*, 28 December 1941.

70. "VELIKI ŠAHOVSKI SUSRET," *Nova Hrvatska*, 7 December 1941.
71. "Ustrojstvo šahovske igre u postrojbama Ustaške mladeži Nezavisne Države Hrvatske," *Dužnostnik—službeni list Ustaške mladeži* 7 (September 1942): 358.
72. "Šahistima Ustaške mladeži," *Ustaška mladež*, 1 July 1943,15.
73. "Ustrojstvo šahovske igre u postrojbama Ustaške mladeži Nezavisne Države Hrvatske," *Dužnostnik—službeni list Ustaške mladeži* 7 (September 1942): 358.
74. "Poziv H.V.H.M. na šahovski turnir," HDA, NDH, PNDHB—229/2, 21 July 1942.
75. "Medjunarodni šahovski troboj Slovačka-Bugarska-Hrvatska u Zagrebu," 552/1943, HDA, NDH, PNDHB, 229/2, 16 March 1943.
76. For a more elaborated view on the role and idea of sport in the Ustaša Youth organization, see Goran Miljan, "Fašizam, sport i mladež—ideja i uloga tjelesnoga odgoja i sporta u odgoju i organizaciji Ustaške mladeži, 1941–1945," *Radovi—Zavod za hrvatsku povijest* 46 (2014): 361–82.
77. For more on the Ustaša idea of youth, its practices and connections, see Goran Miljan, "'To be Eternally Young Means to be an Ustasha': Youth Organizations as Incubators of a New Youth and New Future," in *The Utopia of Terror: Life, Death and Everyday Culture in the Ustasha State, 1941–1945*, ed. Rory Yeomans (Rochester, NY, 2015).
78. "Ustašská mládež na tábore HM," *Gardista*, 5 July 1942; and "Odsunutie terminu započatia Slovensko-nemecko-chorvatskeho Tabora," HDA, NDH, PNDHB, 229/2, June 1942; and "Ustaška mladež stigla u Slovačku," *Nova Hrvatska*, 8 July 1942.
79. "Poziv na taborovanje u Kuparima," 21/1942, HDA, NDH, PNDHB, 229/2, 10 July 1942. This document states that this summer camp was to take place in Kupari near Dubrovnik. However, due to unknown circumstances, the camp was moved to Ozalj, where the first Ustaša Youth summer camp was taking place.
80. "Taborovanje Ustaške mladeži na Ozlju," *Nova Hrvatska*, 11 August 1942.
81. Ibid.
82. "Oršanićevo pismo Malviću vezano uz dolazak predstavnika Hlinkine mladeži," HDA, NDH, PNDHB, 229/2, 20 August 1942.
83. "Svečano otvorenje prve škole dužnostnika Ustaške mladeži u državi," *Novo Borovo*, 26 September 1941.
84. "Godišnjica prve škole ustaških dužnosnika u Nezavisnoj Državi Hrvatskoj," *Novo Borovo*, 2 October 1942.
85. "Oršanićevo pismo Malviću vezano uz dolazak predstavnika Hlinkine mladeži," HDA, NDH, PNDHB, 229/2, 20 August 1942.
86. "Hlinkina maldež! Na straž!," *Novo Borovo*, 2 October 1942.
87. "HM pred cestou do Chorvátska na výcvikové tábory," *Gardista*, 6 September 1942.
88. "Posiet iz Borova" and "Odlazak Hlinkine mladeži iz Borova," *Hrvatski list*, 11 December 1942.
89. "Godišnjica obstanka prve škole za dužnostnike Ustaške mladeži u Borovu," *Hrvatski narod*, 23 October 1942.

90. "GODIŠNJICA USPJEŠNOG RADA ŠKOLE ZA USTAŠKE DUŽNOSTNIKE U BOROVU," *Nova Hrvatska,* 28 October 1942.
91. "Godišnjica prve škole ustaških dužnosnika u Nezavisnoj Državi Hrvatskoj," *Novo Borovo,* 2 October 1942.
92. Ivo Babić, "Potreba i značenje vojne prednaobrazbe," *Plava Revija* 3 (March 1943): 65–75.
93. "Završetak tečaja Hlinkine i ustaške mladeži u Borovu," *Novo Borovo,* 5 December 1942; and "Odlazak Hlinkine mladeži iz Borova," *Hrvatski list,* 11 December 1942.
94. "Završetak tečaja Hlinkine i ustaške mladeži u Borovu," *Novo Borovo,* 5 December 1942.
95. "Dva mesiace v bratskom Chorvátsku," *Slovak,* 12 December 1942.
96. "Naredba o spomen-znaku tečajaca Hlinkine i Ustaške mladeži," *Dužnostnik — službeni list Ustaške mladeži* 5 (May 1943): 3–4.
97. "U smislu Naredbe o spomen-znaku tečajaca," HDA, Zbirka izvornog gradiva NDH—1549, Group VI/199, 21 June 1943.
98. "Časopis Ustaškinja—dostavlja se," HDA, NDH, PNDHB—229/3, 12 July 1943.
99. "Dostava časopisa," HDA, NDH, PNDHB—229/2, 6 May 1942.
100. "Redakcia dennáka 'Gardista'," 1 July 1941; and "Administrácia časopisu 'Kocúr,'" 1 July 1941; and "Redakcia časopisu 'Nový Svet,'" 1 July 1941, HDA, NDH, SPZ, D-2852/2–3.
101. "Chorvátskemu vyslanectvu," 7251/1942, Ma, HDA, NDH, PNDHB—229, 25 April 1942.
102. *O taborovanju i logorovanju* (Zagreb: Promičba Ustaške mladeži, 1942).
103. For more on the politics of language in Croatia, see an excellent study by Snježana Kordić, *Jezik i nacionalizam* (Zagreb, 2010).
104. "S ustaškim Junacima i Junakinjama u Firenzi," *Ustaška mladež,* 19 July 1942,16.
105. Matzenauer, "Ustašská mládež," 4.
106. Stanislav J. Kirschbaum, *A History of Slovakia: The Struggle for Survival* (Houndmills and London, 1995), 197; and Ivo Goldstein, *Hrvatska 1918–2008* (Zagreb, 2008), 256.
107. Rhychlík, "Odnosi," 954–56
108. See, for example, "KAKO SMO DOŽIVJELI SLOVAČKU," *Hrvatski narod,* 8 July 1943; and Janko Skrbin, "PUTEVI SLOVAČKE IZGRADNJE," *Hrvatski narod,* 4 December 1943.
109. M.K., "Predavanje izaslanika ustaške mladeži na Bečkom kongresu europske mladeži," *Ustaška mladež,* 15 October 1942,19.
110. Constantin Iordachi, "Comparative Fascist Studies: An Introduction," in *Comparative Fascist Studies: New Perspectives,* ed. idem (New York, 2010), 4.

Bibliography

Archives
Hrvatski državni arhiv—HDA, Nezavisna Država Hrvatska—NDH
- *Slovačko poslanstvo u Zagrebu—D 2850—2862*
- *Poslanstvo Nezavisne Države Hrvatske Bratislava—229*
- *Zbirka izvornog gradiva NDH—1549*
- *Sabor NDH—211, Predsjednički spisi.*

Newspapers and Journals
Dužnostnik—službeni list Ustaške mladeži
Gardista
Hrvatski krugoval
Hrvatski list
Hrvatski narod
Narodne Novine
Nova Hrvatska
Nová mládež
Novi List
Novo Borovo
Novo pokoljenje
Plava Revija
Suradnja
Slovák
Tatre i velebit
Ustaška mladež
Ustaša—vijesnik hrvatskog ustaškog oslobodilačkog pokreta
Ustaški godišnjak, 1942

Internet Sources
Franklin D. Roosevelt, Address to the International Student Assembly, 3 Sept. 1942. http://www.presidency.ucsb.edu/ws/index.php?pid=16300&st=&st1 (accessed 23 February 2015).

Books and Articles
Bideleux, Robert, and Ian Jeffries. *A History of Eastern Europe: Crisis and Change.* New York, 2007.
Bowen, Wayne H. *Spaniards and Nazi Germany: Collaboration in the New Order.* Columbia and London, 2000.
Djokić, Dejan. *Elusive Compromise: A History of Interwar Yugoslavia.* New York, 2007.
Dogliani, Patrizia. "Propaganda and Youth." In *The Oxford Handbook of Fascism,* ed. R.J.B. Bosworth, 185–202. Oxford and New York, 2010.
Goldstein, Ivo. *Hrvatska 1918–2008.* Zagreb, 2008.

Iordachi, Constantin. "Comparative Fascist Studies: An Introduction." In *Comparative Fascist Studies: New Perspectives*, ed. Constantin Iordachi, 1–50. New York, 2010.

Jelić-Butić, Fikreta. *Ustaše i Nezavisna Država Hrvatska: 1941–1945*. Zagreb: SN Liber i Školska knjiga, 1977.

Kirschbaum, Stanislav J. *A History of Slovakia: The Struggle for Survival*. Houndmills and London, 1995.

Koch, H.W. *The Hitler Youth: Origins and Development, 1922–1945*. New York, 2000.

Kordić, Snježana. *Jezik i nacionalizam*. Zagreb, 2010.

Lampe, John R. *Yugoslavia as History: Twice There Was a Country*. Cambridge, 2000.

Ledeen, Michael A. "Italian Fascism and Youth." *Journal of Contemporary History* 3 (1969): 137–54.

Miljan, Goran. "Fašizam, sport i mladež—ideja i uloga tjelesnoga odgoja i sporta u odgoju i organizaciji Ustaške mladeži, 1941–1945." *Radovi—Zavod za hrvatsku povijest* 46 (2014): 361–82.

———. "'To be Eternally Young Means to be an Ustasha': Youth Organizations as Incubators of a New Youth and New Future." In *The Utopia of Terror: Life, Death and Everyday Culture in the Ustasha State, 1941–1945*, ed. Rory Yeomans. Rochester, NY, 2015.

Milla, Michal. *Hlinkova mládež 1938–1945*. Bratislava, 2008.

Mosse, George L. *Nazi Culture: Intellectual, Cultural and Social Life in the Third Reich*. Madison, WI, 1966.

Neilson, William Allan. "Proceedings of the International Student Assembly." *Educational Research Bulletin* 5 (1946): 138.

O taborovanju i logorovanju. Zagreb, 1942.

Rychlík, Jan. "Odnosi Slovačke i Nezavisne Države Hrvatske, 1941–1945." *Časopis za suvremenu povijest* 3 (2004): 939–57.

Wanrooij, Bruno. "The Rise and Fall of Italian Fascism as a Generational Revolt." *Journal of Contemporary History* 3 (1987): 401–18.

The Estado Novo and Portuguese–German Relations in the Age of Fascism

Cláudia Ninhos

History and Historiographical Debates

On 28 May 1926, a military coup brought the First Portuguese Republic (1910–26) to an end, setting in motion a process that within a short time would lead to the rise of António de Oliveira Salazar and to the institutionalization of a dictatorship that would last until 1974. Salazar became president of the Council of Ministers in July 1932. This was the moment when he began to reinforce his power and build a new regime. It was then institutionalized by the 1933 Constitution, which Salazar himself, with the help of some of his collaborators, had drafted. This document made Portugal a "unitary and corporative republic"[1] whose sovereignty was limited only by "morality and law,"[2] maintained a regime of separation from the Catholic Church, and committed the Estado Novo, the New State, with the creation and development of a corporative economy.

When we analyze Salazar's political speeches, we can see that his predominant line of argumentation was one that always defended the national paradigm. That is to say, the dictator conceived his Estado Novo to be an original, national phenomenon applied to the Portuguese national context. As such, it could not be included in the group of fascist and totalitarian regimes.[3]

However, we should not undervalue the demagogic nature of Salazar's statements and the analysis should go beyond the dictator's discourse. In fact, if we compare the ideological matrix and the political–institutional characteristics of the Estado Novo with those of other regimes, such as National Socialism and Italian Fascism, we can find a plethora of fascist elements. This is the case, for example, of the omnipresent, violent, anticommunist and antiparliamentarian discourse that was in fact characteristic of the political programs of all fascisms. Like National Socialism in Germany and Fascism in Italy, the Portuguese regime was presented as a "Third Way," an alternative to the previous ruling order and to communism. The structuring of the Estado Novo in the form of a dictatorship was made through the alliance between different right wings, and this fact has been used as an argument to reject its fascist nature. In opposition to what he considered to be the crumbling republican parliamentary system, and being against Marxist–Leninist solutions, Salazar appeared as the bearer of a New Order, a New State—the Estado Novo.

This New Order consisted of a wide-ranging project that was not only political in nature but also cultural and economic. At the economic level, it meant breaking with the "old" liberal capitalism. It involved the creation of a corporative state that was to take an active, dirigiste role. At the political level, it meant breaking away from the previous "disorder" caused by the parliamentarianism of the First Republic, subordinating the individual to the state, placing the nation above individual interests and regenerating the "homeland" (*patria*) which was considered to be "sick." There was a unique party, the National Union (Uniaof Nacional, UN), although this party had not conquered the power "on the streets." The political police was restructured, with the State Defence and Surveillance Police (Polícia de Vigilância e de Defesa do Estado, PVDE) appearing in 1933. Special military tribunals were also established, and legislation was passed that moved toward the corporatization of the economy. The dictator used repressive means and propaganda mechanisms, and adopted a charismatic leadership style, in order to ensure his power. Actually, his moral authority was presented as being based on his knowledge, emanating from his status as full professor in Coimbra, which led the Spanish philosopher Miguel de Unamuno to designate the Portuguese regime as "cathedratic *fascism.*" The populist leadership of the dictator was also based on the image of simplicity and austerity, and Salazar was presented as "the savior of the nation."

The new ruler sought to establish totalitarian control over Portuguese society, creating institutions through which to ideologically shape individuals and to repress all those who might deviate from the imposed order. The regime's "totalitarian inclination" was reflected in the need to shape and re-educate the Portuguese people, with a view to creating a "New Man."[4] To this end, institutions such as the National Propaganda Secretariat (Secretariado de Propaganda Nacional, SPN) and the Portuguese Youth Organization (Mocidade Portuguesa, MP) were set up, the latter against the backdrop of the Spanish Civil War. It was because of this same context that Salazar made the army subordinate to the regime, reforming it and, in 1936, appointing himself as minister of war. Along the way he had to remove his opponents. For example, he exiled Rolão Preto, the leader of the National Syndicalist Movement (Movimento Nacional-Sindicalista, MNS),[5] but accepted any of Rolão Preto's former followers who wished to be integrated into the regime and who agreed to accommodate to the Salazarist solution. The pressure exercised by this faction led to the creation of institutions such as the Portuguese Legion (Legião Portuguesa, LP) and the National Foundation for Joy at Work (Fundação Nacional para a Alegria no Trabalho, FNAT), which were both greatly influenced by similar Italian and German organizations.

Contemporaries were aware of the affinities existing between the German dictatorship and the Portuguese regime, and sought to highlight them publicly. They looked with admiration at Germany and forced themselves to view the "National Revolution"[6] that had occurred in Portugal alongside what had occurred in Germany. Although the attraction for National Socialism was not consensual, one part of the Portuguese elite enthusiastically welcomed Hitler's rise to power, expressing "a political passion favorable to Germany."[7] These individuals therefore made a huge effort to demonstrate the ideas and ideologies shared by the two countries, and some of them immediately established contacts with Nazi Germany. According to Oswald von Hoyningen-Huene, the German minister plenipotentiary in Portugal (1934–44), his country had many friends and admirers at the very heart of the government, and the National Syndicalists were particularly enthusiastic.[8] The Germans, like the Portuguese, also made a great effort to demonstrate the existence of a "kinship of spirit and feelings"[9] or even a *Schicksalsgemeinschaft*, a "community of destiny."[10]

In point of fact, the Estado Novo had more in common with Germany and Italy than with countries with liberal governments such as Great Britain. German diplomacy took advantage of the state's political-ideological bases, and during the war it even used the fact that Salazar's opponents were hoping for an Allied victory to convince government circles that it was Germany that was Portugal's true ally.[11] German victories in the war were always widely publicized and even praised in the Portuguese press. This enthusiasm increased even more with the opening of the Eastern Front and the start of the "crusade" against communism.[12]

There were of course important differences. One of these is the fact that, unlike Italian Fascism and German National Socialism, there was no mass movement, which led Manuel de Lucena to claim that Salazarism was a "fascism without a fascist movement."[13] This very fact was noted and highlighted at the time by contemporaries. According to Hans Freytag, the German minister plenipotentiary in Lisbon, not even National Syndicalism, which ideologically showed a greater proximity to the Nazi regime, could be considered as a mass movement, since the overwhelming majority of the Portuguese population were illiterate.[14] For Hoyningen-Huene, Freytag's successor in Lisbon, the Portuguese dictatorship did not choose to become a major fascist movement with a revolutionary dynamic, but limited itself to sympathizing with National Socialist and fascist ideology.[15] Although Salazar knew the benefits of introducing fascism under his own leadership, there were three factors that prevented him from taking this course: first, the opposition of the army, which did not want to relinquish its influence to a large popular movement; second, Salazar's personal aversion to a populist leadership that would mean personal contact with the masses; and finally, the fear that the "Portuguese temperament" would not adjust to the internal and perpetual tension that fascism demanded from each individual. Huene had shrewdly identified two key differences between Salazarism and National Socialism: the Portuguese New State was not based on a popular revolutionary movement; and the aversion of Salazar towards the masses.

Another crucial difference was anti-Semitism, which was a central tenet of Nazi ideology. In Portugal, however, it was not part of the regime's ideology and was just a "marginal" phenomenon.[16] In fact, German diplomats themselves said there was a lack of understanding about the racial issue in Germany, which, in their opinion, was due to the large amount of miscegenation that existed in Portugal.[17]

The comparative studies about the political nature of the Portuguese regime, written by historians and political scientists, tend to emphasize the differences and uniqueness, and exclude the Estado Novo from the "fascist" category.[18] However, this is not a consensual interpretation, and for other historians Salazarism fits unquestionably into the typology of fascism.[19]

It is not our intention to take this discussion further in this chapter. However, we consider that fascism should not be understood as a monolithic and immutable block but rather as an ideology that spread a little throughout the whole of Europe in the interwar period. In some countries it managed to come to power and put its political-ideological project into practice; in others it did not. Despite sharing a common nature, however, the ideology was adapted to suit national conditions.

This chapter thus seeks to contribute to a better understanding of the transnational communications, exchanges, and transfers between National Socialism and the Estado Novo, because, besides those few comparative studies, the transnational dimension of the Estado Novo and the countless cross-border communications have not received the attention they deserve. Our main aim though is to analyze the relationship between the Portuguese regime and National Socialist Germany, focusing on a single aspect of the many transnational exchanges and transfers during the period.

We assert that Portugal and Germany were very close and that there was intensive cooperation between the two regimes. For example, Portuguese organizations like the MP or FNAT were set up to mirror their German counterparts. Why are these organizations so important? It is because they were created at the time when the greatest fascistization of the Portuguese regime was taking place and at the very moment when neighboring Spain was experimenting with a Manichaeistic struggle between the republicans and the nationalists led by General Francisco Franco. Moreover, it was the regime itself that asked the German Legation for information about the Nazi organizations.[20]

This was naturally well received by the German authorities. Hoyningen-Huene, at the time the German minister plenipotentiary in Portugal, told the German Ministry of Foreign Affairs (Auswärtiges Amt, AA) that it was of great "interest that Portugal should also proceed with this organization [the LP] according to our model, because it is to be hoped that new advances in promoting understanding for our National Socialist Germany might result from it."[21] This proves that there was a desire on the part of at least some members of the regime to make National Socialist Germany the model to be followed. It also shows that it was important for the Germans that Portugal use German organizations as their model so that National Socialism might be better understood. The interest was, therefore, reciprocal. Thus it can be seen that Germany, like Italy, became a center that sought to spread its hegemony throughout Europe, influencing other countries both politically and ideologically.

The thesis we will present in the following pages claims that Portuguese young people were one of the main focuses of attention for German diplomacy. We will seek to analyze the relationship between the Third Reich and the Estado Novo, focusing on academic exchanges and especially the interaction between the two regimes' youth organizations. This choice is not in any way random. After consulting documentation in German archives, we concluded that German diplomacy managed to set up a large network of contacts, whose main actors were young people and academics who connected Germany to Portugal in a strategy that aimed, ultimately, at bringing the two regimes closer together.

The Importance of Cultural Exchange in the Normalization of Portuguese–German Relations

With Portugal's entry into World War I on the side of Britain, relations between Portugal and Germany were broken off for some years. It was only in the 1920s that exchanges between the two countries returned to normal. But even so they continued to be very much affected by postwar problems and by the resolution of such questions as war reparations and the return of goods belonging to Germans that the Portuguese government had seized in 1916, as described in reports sent back by German diplomatic representatives in Lisbon.[22]

In the face of such obstacles, it was cultural and scientific diplomacy that, in our opinion, helped lead to the normalization of diplomatic relations. Indeed, German diplomats realized early on the potential of German culture as an exportable "product" to Portugal. The "Notes for the Reception of the Portuguese Envoy by Hitler," dating from 1933, lamented that the negotiations referred to above had gone on for so long, but stressed that cultural relations between the two countries had intensified in the last few years.[23] A few years before, in March 1929, Albert von Baligand, the German minister plenipotentiary in Lisbon, called the attention of the AA to the fact that four university professors had been part of the last government. "As we know, scientific circles have considerable influence in politics there," wrote Baligand. Most of the better-known university teachers had already occupied ministerial places on one or more occasions. The diplomat therefore considered it very important that the political activity of the legation should continue to foment constant contact with these circles, and also offer them the chance to work alongside Germans.[24]

The Portuguese elite were in effect the main target of German diplomacy in Portugal. This fact seemed to be obvious to their contemporaries. In the final years of the Weimar Republic, the Germans were already maintaining a cultural policy in Portugal in response to the strategy of the other powers, as reports sent back to Berlin by the legation mention. At that time Britain did not overly concern the Germans, who were more interested in expanding their contacts with those Portuguese who had studied in German universities and who wanted to maintain close ties to "German" science. They therefore considered it a good idea to create the means necessary to grant scholarships to Portuguese students and to pay for Portuguese professors to travel to Germany.[25] Such an opportunity arose in 1929 when the National Education Board (Junta de Educação Nacional, JEN) was founded, as this institution was responsible for awarding study scholarships to students in Portugal and abroad. It is therefore understandable that at the beginning of May 1930, in a report on Portuguese cultural propaganda abroad, Baligand drew the attention of the AA to an interview given by Simões Raposo[26] to a Portuguese newspaper, even saying that JEN was "the central organ for Portuguese cultural propaganda."[27] Thus the Germans started to direct their attention at this organization, and this was reflected in the number of scholarship holders sent to Germany.

This immediate and close relationship with JEN can be explained by the fact that Germany was traditionally one of the main destinations for Portuguese scholarship holders and interns. What is more, the German pedagogic and university model had been used as a blueprint for Portugal,[28] and German institutions certainly served as a model when JEN was set up. Furthermore, at the head of the board were figures who maintained an umbilical cord relationship with Germany, as was the case of Gustavo Cordeiro Ramos, the minister for education and a university professor. Germany, together with France, then became the main destination for Portuguese scholarship holders and, even after Hitler's rise to power, the relationship between the board and Germany was strengthened and institutionalized, as an academic exchange service with the German Academic Exchange Service (Deutscher Akademischer Austauschdienst, DAAD) was inaugurated in the academic year 1934/35.[29] JEN, and later the Institute for High Culture (Instituto para a Alta Cultura, IAC) which replaced it in 1936, became the partner par excellence of the Nazi cultural and academic institutions in Portugal, with whom they exchanged books, academics, and scholars.[30]

From 1933 on, relations between Portugal and Germany intensified, especially with the arrival in Lisbon of a new diplomat, Baron Oswald von Hoyningen-Huene, who, as mentioned earlier, remained as German minister plenipotentiary until 1944. This aristocrat, who had started working for the AA during the Weimar Republic, was not a radical Nazi and only joined the National Socialist German Workers' Party (Nationalsozialistische Deutsche Arbeiterpartei, NSDAP) in 1937, probably under pressure. In Portugal he sought to restrain the local Nazi Party Group (NSDAP-Landesgruppe Portugal), setting himself up as the only official representative of the regime. Huene had the prudence of curbing the impulses and desires of the Nazi organizations in Portugal, restricting their activities to the Germans living in that country. The Nazi indoctrination was mostly made in private "spaces," such as the German schools, the German Club, and even onboard the ships of the Kraft durch Freude ("Strength through Joy," Nazi leisure organization). Although some Portuguese also participated, the most visible ideological indoctrination took place behind closed doors and not in public spaces. The limitation of the activities of the party to the German citizens living in Portugal was the main reason of tension with the *Landesgruppenleiter* (National group leader of the Nazi Party in Portugal), who acted under the directives of the AO, often against von Hoyningen-Huene's will. Huene feared that a parallel diplomacy could damage the political strategy of the legation, or even threaten the trust he had with the Portuguese dictator.[31] He was aware that the party's activity should be more reserved, so as not to cause protests from the Portuguese government.[32] His attitude was very important to win the confidence of the Portuguese dictator, and differed from that of the British embassy and the British citizens living in Portugal, which led Salazar to praise the Germans.[33]

Nevertheless, Hoyningen-Huene faithfully served the Nazi regime's interests, which explains why he remained so long at the head of the German Legation in Lisbon. He even became a friend of Salazar, which strengthened his position, thus enabling him to fulfill his political objectives. Huene's strategy involved Germany moving closer to Portugal in the economic and military spheres, taking advantage of the strained relations between Portugal and Britain that had been caused by the outbreak of civil war in neighboring Spain. This had led to major changes being introduced in Salazar's domestic and foreign policy,[34] as he supported the faction led by Franco. The Germans sought to tighten the economic ties between the two countries, even managing during World War II to become one of Portugal's main commercial partners. This came in the wake of relations between the two countries becoming closer on a military level, since Germany had taken a great interest in the Portuguese rearmament program early on. The Nazis also took advantage of the terrain left vacant by Britain, which had been very reticent to supply the Portuguese national army in view of the support given by the regime to General Franco. From then on, Germany began to facilitate financing for the army, and welcomed Portuguese missions that went to the Reich to choose military material and equipment, and which received technical training there.[35] The PVDE had also established an important collaboration with the Gestapo and the Abwehr, especially under the impulse of the Captain Paulo Cumano, a well-known Germanophile who had studied mining engineering in Germany. Erich Emil Schroeder was the Security Service (Sicherheitsdienst, SD) agent in charge of police liaison with the PVDE.[36]

Right from the first moment, the strategy conceived by Huene was designed to be carried out over the long term, and he even admitted in confidence that Portuguese–German relations should be constructed through a "century's worth of work." Furthermore, the Germans were committed to the idea of continuity—whereas the British Embassy had had four ambassadors in ten years, only one minister plenipotentiary had passed through the German Legation. Huene's strategy was based on "long and patient work," which he carried out for over a decade.[37] Part of this effort involved forging closer links with the younger generation, promoting numerous activities run by the German cultural institutions in the country such as the German–Portuguese Society (Deutsch–Portugiesische Gesellschaft, DPG), and developing contacts with the Ministry for Public Education and the MP. Huene's strategy, like that of his predecessors, was profoundly elitist. In other words, it was centered on the political, scientific, and cultural elite of the Estado Novo and not on the uneducated masses, who carried no weight in the political decision-making process of a regime where censorship was in force and freedom did not exist.[38]

Huene also continued to instrumentalize German culture and Germany's supposed "scientific superiority" so as to impose the cultural, scientific, and, consequently, ideological hegemony of the country he represented in Portugal. To this end, he set out early on to win over the Portuguese elite who, by tradition, were culturally "Francophile" and "Francophone." Culture and science in fact played a central role in his activity, to such an extent that he fought hard for a Cultural Agreement to be signed between the two countries—an accord that Portugal never wanted to sign. In fact, in the terms in which it was drawn up, the agreement transformed the cooperation that took place on various levels—both official and unofficial—and between various organizations into an official state relationship that placed Portugal within the sphere of the ideological and political influence of the Reich. Despite this setback, during the first few years that Huene was in Lisbon the German diplomatic apparatus increased in size, while the academic and scientific exchanges became even more numerous. Visits by ships of the KdF also increased in number, as did the exchange of delegates between the MP, founded in 1936, and the Hitlerjugend (HJ).

Exchange between Youth Organizations

In the summer of 1937, Gertrud Richert, head of the Portugal and Spain Section at the Ibero-American Institute, gave an interview to the newspaper *A Voz* on the subject of German–Portuguese cultural relations. When asked what would be useful to strengthen exchange between the two countries, Richert replied:

It would seem to me very important to bring the youth of our two countries closer together, something many people have already taken an interest in doing. The reciprocal visits between the Portuguese Youth Organization and the Hitler Youth Organization could become a stimulus for the exchange of high school students, which could be arranged at the same time. I also hope that exchanges between the women's movements in Germany and in Portugal might take place, and with good results.[39]

This exchange between the MP and the HJ is in fact one of the clearest examples of "cross-border cooperation" between fascist-type regimes. The Hitler Youth, which inspired and supported youth organizations throughout Europe, was not indifferent to its Portuguese counterpart. It quickly became an inspirational model for the Portuguese Estado Novo, and is an example of what attracted it to Nazism. This influence was also seen in the School Action Vanguard (Acção Escolar Vanguarda, AEV), set up in 1934. There was a constant exchange of delegations, and both the German minister plenipotentiary and the representative of the Nazi party in Lisbon, Wilhelm Berner, were represented at the São Carlos Theater when the movement was officially presented,[40] where they listened to Salazar's speech in which he referred to communism as "the great heresy of our age."[41] Shortly afterwards, the Vanguardists organized a demonstration in support of Salazar, and the "Green Shirts" of the AEV appeared for the first time, differentiating themselves in this way from the "Blue Shirts" of the National Syndicalists. The new organization, born out of the dissolution of the National Syndicalist Movement that Salazar had closed down in July 1934, ended up incorporating symbols (uniforms) and rituals (political meetings, the salute) shared by the different fascisms. This was meant to show that throughout Europe the time had come to fight communism, a fight that was in fact one of the driving forces behind all these fascisms.

From its creation until its extinction in 1936, Wilhelm Berner, at the time secretary of the German–Portuguese Society, was the true doctrinal mentor of the AEV and a propagandist of Nazi Germany who used the newspaper *Avante!* to carry his message.[42] As well as Berner's texts, anonymous articles about German youth appeared in this paper,[43] and every issue included some small piece of information about Germany.

The Nazi indoctrination made through these texts was afterwards reinforced by means of other activities such as the showing of films and documentaries in the legation or in the DPG to which the Vanguardists were also invited. These films helped to consolidate the knowledge about young Germans that had been acquired from newspapers, books, and magazines, thus increasing even more the admiration nurtured for Nazism.[44] In the pages of *Avante!*, German language and culture courses organized by the German–Portuguese Society were advertised,[45] as were other events organized by German institutions in Portugal, which the Portuguese elite made a point of attending. These institutions sought to influence Portugal's younger generation, in particular high school students.

Visits by Portuguese leaders to the Reich were also very common. In 1935, for example, António Almodôvar traveled to Germany to study how the German government managed the task of integrating young people, which he considered to be a decisive element of the "work for the political–social renovation of the Third Reich."[46] The invitation to go to Germany came from the Ministry of Propaganda, who suggested that the German minister plenipotentiary in Lisbon should invite a leader of the AEV to attend the annual rally of the Nazi Party in Nuremberg so that he could "form a true impression of the new Germany." The suggestion was welcomed by the legation, which considered that Germany should not "leave this terrain solely to Italian propaganda,"[47] and by the AEV itself.

Such important exchanges, however, did not stop strong criticism of National Socialism being voiced within the AEV. While some highlighted the singularity of the Portuguese Estado Novo, allegedly constructed in accordance with the national "character," others rejected external influences and exogenous models that could lead Portugal into the "Germanic sphere of influence in the world."[48] Other aspects of Nazism that were strongly criticized were imperialism and the position taken toward the Church and Catholics in Germany. Nazi paganism and the way the German regime antagonized the Church did not please Portuguese Catholic circles. News of priests being imprisoned and Catholic organizations being dissolved reached Portuguese ears despite censorship being in place. One article published in *Avante!* even went so far as to praise the way that the Church in Germany was resisting and opposing the sterilization law.[49] How can such condemnation by a newspaper and an organization that were both clearly pro-Nazi be explained? These criticisms were possible as there was not, in fact, any consensual opinion about Germany and the benefits that importing the Nazi model would bring Portugal. Indeed, certain sectors of the regime's elite had always harbored strong reservations about Nazism. Many continued to prefer the influence of Italian Fascism because they considered it more suited to the supposedly Latin and Christian Portuguese "character."[50] Even Salazar himself perceived Mussolini "more cautious, more Latin,"[51] while the Portuguese Catholic Church was vehemently opposed to the youth exchanges with Nazi Germany.

However, even despite these critical voices, the AEV continued to favor the relationship with Germany, as can be seen in *Avante!* In fact, the person responsible for the DPG, Johannes Roth, assured the legation at the end of 1935 that interest in the New Germany had grown of late in Portugal and that, almost daily, there were requests for information from intellectual circles about the HJ, *Winterhilfe* (Winter Relief), the National Socialist People's Welfare Organization (Nationalsozialistische Volkswohlfahrt, NSV) and KdF.[52]

The Decline of the Vanguard Movement and the Creation of the MP

Over time, the Portuguese Vanguard movement, the AEV, began to lose its dynamism. When the Estado Novo no longer had need of it, it ceased to be able to count on the regime's support, and ended up fading away. By appointing António Almodôvar to head this organization, the Ministry for Public Education broadened, as it had wanted, its sphere of action, and brought under its own control an organization that had been born with its umbilical cord tied to the SPN. Its life span proved to be very short and the AEV was, according to Homem Cristo, never anything more than a modest "version" of the "youth organizations that were more or less sportive, more or less political, more or less military" that had been created in Italy and in Germany.[53] A better organizational model would only appear in 1936 within the Ministry of Education, but calls in this direction could already be found in the last few issues of *Avante!*:

> It is urgent to work so that the day might shortly come when our youth—within our Latin temperament and given our educational processes—can start being prepared to indisputably ensure the continuation of the magnificent work of salvation that we owe to a few good Portuguese citizens.[54]

This pressure came not only from the Vanguard movement itself but also from the Ministry of Internal Affairs and from some of the National Union's leaders.[55] Curiously enough, it was following António Almodôvar's trip to Germany when it was decided to create a new organization, given the decline of the AEV, but under the aegis of the Ministry for Public Education. Based on what he had seen and heard when in the Reich, Almodôvar highlighted how the Germans operated in terms of physical preparation and "political–social training." The former ensured a type of pre-military technical preparation acquired through practicing sport, marching, gliding, and handling weapons. The latter, on the other hand, ensured a form of "nationalist training" through lectures and readings that were, obviously, guided. Finally, this was also seen as one of the ways to guarantee the "strengthening of the race" through excursions, camping, and sport; in short, through life in the open air.[56]

In the context of the educational reform headed by the minister, António Carneiro Pacheco, the MP was set up. This covered all young people between the ages of 14 and 17, even if they did not attend school.[57] Both in the decree that instituted the organization and in the regulatory ordinance published some months later, it was made very clear that the new organization was not merely aimed at promoting the physical and pre-military education of young Portuguese people, but at providing both a moral and a civic education. Naturally this was a nationalist education because it proposed to stimulate "devotion to the fatherland in terms of order, a fondness for discipline, and the cult of military duty."[58] The Regulatory Ordinance of the MP further pledged to foment a Christian education and would therefore not admit, for example, members with no religion.[59]

Its first commissar had a very different project though. In a highly radicalized period, owing to the outbreak of the Civil War in Spain, Francisco Nobre Guedes wanted to make the MP the instrument by which all young people could be shaped in a totalitarian way. He encouraged an intensive exchange program with the HJ, which served as his model. The first public appearance of the MP was in Germany when a group of twenty-nine members (students from the Colégio Militar and sons of leaders of the MP) took part in an international youth camp at the time of the Olympic Games in August 1936. After this, the young Portuguese students traveled around Germany for one week.[60] In Dresden they were received by the *Gauleiter* who "praised" Portugal, claiming it was "walking at Germany's side in the fight against false ideas," and in Munich "the Germans exceeded all expectations in terms of kindness." When he thanked the "friendly" way in which the MP had been received in the Reich, the minister of education, Carneiro Pacheco, assured the German minister plenipotentiary that the boys of the Mocidade would retain "an unforgettable memory of their stay in Germany."[61] He went on to say:

> I hope that this visit will be the beginning of a continuous exchange, and that bringing the youth of our two countries into contact with each other might enable them to have a fuller understanding of each other and might be the guarantee that Portugal and Germany will always know how to show mutual respect and understanding for each other. The similarity of our social objectives and our shared efforts to defend Christian civilization are the guarantee that this work of bringing them closer together is solid and will enjoy a wider projection.

Huene made a point of sending a copy of Carneiro Pacheco's letter to Friedhelm Burbach, *Auslandskommissar* of the NSDAP for Spain and Portugal, saying that it proved the reception of the Portuguese boys in Germany had been appreciated and that, through the visit, "a new stone in the building of German–Portuguese friendship, for which we are all working together, had been laid."[62]

The visit lent added force to exchanges between the two countries because news appeared in the press during the month of September about a possible trip to Lisbon of leaders of the HJ at the invitation of Carneiro Pacheco. This, according to the same newspapers, was proof that the collaboration between the young people of the two countries had been a success.[63] The Germans, ever attentive to developments in Portugal, immediately took an interest in the MP and appointed a delegate to be in charge of relations with the new organization. The Nazis in fact showed an interest in all the youth movements that were appearing in various countries. This led the leader of the HJ to try to set up an office that could impose the German model's leadership on the foreign youth organizations. He thus became responsible for collecting information during his frequent trips abroad. The HJ also asked the AA about youth movements and organizations in other countries and, in due course, about the most important legislation in this domain, as well as quarterly reports about youth work, magazines, and newspapers.[64]

In Portugal, the German authorities made a point of emphasizing the affinities between the youth organizations of the two countries, and the numerous visits arranged were seen as proof of their very close relationship. These contacts became even closer in the following years. They were of as much interest to the Germans as to the Portuguese, with IAC being the intermediary for the exchanges. These were very important occasions, enabling ideas to be exchanged and strengthening the bonds that linked the two organizations.

The Portuguese–German exchanges in this area continued, despite some criticism and reluctance, reaching their highest point in 1937–38. A report from the British Embassy said that "the year 1938 witnessed the continuation of the struggle for Portugal."[65] Throughout this year the British continued to feel threatened by Germany's behavior, believing that the German Legation in Lisbon and various other organizations were working intensively to prepare the way to later dominate the country. For the British, it was obvious that the German policy was to "gain control of the Mocidade Portuguesa."[66] They were aware that the organization was similar to the German one in its methods and practices, despite Nobre Guedes having tried to reassure the British and guaranteeing to Lord Lloyd that there was no cause for alarm in relation to any possible Germanization of the organization. This also caused deep discontent among Catholics, and in particular amongst those who gravitated around the patriarch cardinal, Manuel Gonçalves Cerejeira, who looked with growing apprehension at how the movement was developing.[67] In the collective pastoral letter of 18 April 1938, God was called upon to prevent the totalitarian state's paganism from seducing the youth of Portugal. The patriarch cardinal expressed his surprise to the minister of Education at the invitation proffered to the *Reichsjugendführer*, Baldur von Schirach, to take part in the MP's camp on 28 May 1938. In his opinion, intensifying relations "would not only be offensive and dangerous for Portuguese Catholic consciences but also not at all worthy of our national pride, as we know the inferior idea the Germans have of us, children (according to them) of an inferior and negroid race."[68]

The mobilization of Portuguese youth, following the German model, continued to be a systematic target for attacks by the Catholics, which the national commissar responded to by guaranteeing that it was a "mistake" to fear "contagion and absorption," considering that "meetings of good camaraderie with foreigners … do not alter our boys' way of being and way of feeling, but rather give them reasons to always take pride in their nationality, an awareness of their patriotism."[69] The growing reluctance led Hoyningen-Huene himself, ever cautious, to advise that exchanges be increased. The diplomat must have felt that, of late, political Catholicism had exerted a strong influence on the education of young Portuguese people, which had forced the MP to slow down its joint projects with the German youth movement, particularly when this work was highly visible. Given the circumstances, Huene advised that four exchange trips with Portugal should be organized, including during the summer months. He also recommended that a group of HJ should visit Porto. In his opinion, if there were a reduction in the number of visits, German–Portuguese relations in the area of youth education, still in its initial (but auspicious) stages—so wrote Huene—could suffer a setback due to the influence of Catholic political circles.[70]

In May 1938, more members of the HJ arrived in Lisbon.[71] In July of the same year, fourteen Germans, all members of the HJ, came to Portugal in the company of Walter Prinzhorn at the invitation of the director of the Infante de Sagres College. Then in the summer of 1938 the commissar, Nobre Guedes, went to Germany to take part in the International Congress on Technical Education as the representative of Portugal.[72] News of his trip was reported in both the Portuguese[73] and the German[74] press. At the invitation of the MP's commissariat, three leaders of the HJ—Georg Berger, Josef Forster, and Werner Lamann—visited Portugal in December 1938.[75] For a whole week they visited various centers of the MP as well as the German School.[76] *The Times* newspaper of 6 December 1938 also reported the presence of the three leaders.[77]

Despite the outbreak of war in September 1939, the exchange program continued. Contrary to what Simon Kuin claims,[78] the two organizations remained close, although relations were less intensive and less visible, as Orlando Grossegesse has already noticed.[79] There were naturally moments when war developments forced initiatives to be cancelled. This happened, for example, following the sinking of the Portuguese ship *Corte Real* by a German submarine in 1941, which led to the cancellation of a visit by members of the HJ. Despite the Portuguese government's desire to receive the young Germans, it was thought that people would not understand such an expression of friendship toward the Germans; and so the visit, considered inopportune, was cancelled.[80]

The exchanges continued despite the war and the replacement of the Germanophile Nobre Guedes[81] by Marcelo Caetano. In 1941 the Portuguese Consulate in Berlin asked the Portuguese Ministry of Foreign Affairs (Ministério dos Negócios Estrangeiros, MNE)[82] if it could give visas to two older HJ members, Lutz Hassenpflug and Werner Lamann, who were going to Lisbon to visit the MP and to prepare the arrival of a group of gymnasts from the HJ that was planned for October.[83] In the same year, on 3 September, the Portuguese Legation in Berlin mentioned the presence in Germany of an official mission from the MP who were taking part in the Breslau Sports Festival.[84] In July 1942 the legation communicated to the MNE that a visit to Berlin was expected from Captain Quintino da Costa and a group of boys from the MP.[85] In the same year the MP was officially represented at the meeting at which the European Youth Association was created.[86] These exchanges did not pass unnoticed by the British. In 1942 an official memo from the Portuguese ambassador in London, Armindo Monteiro, to Salazar reported a conversation he had had with the head of the British Council, who expressed his displeasure at the position taken by the MP. He did not understand how an official organization of a country that was "an ally of England" could at that moment continue to "accept invitations to visit Berlin." This was not in fact the first complaint made by Britain regarding the behavior of the MP, who refused to accept any British assistance, even technical. Monteiro believed that the organization was about to be "put on the Black List" by the British, and he lamented that "the people who lead the 'Mocidade' are not aware of the external repercussions of their acts."[87]

Collaboration between the youth organizations of the two countries began, as has been seen, very early on. It responded to the interests of both, although it was not consensual in Portugal where it encountered opposition from Catholic circles who feared the assimilation of the German model, which they characterized as totalitarian, pagan, and militarist. These contacts were maintained, although in a somewhat reduced form, during World War II. As the war spread throughout Europe, it became increasingly difficult to travel. In addition, Oliveira Salazar always remained intransigent in his defense of neutrality, which helps us understand the reason why news about these exchanges ceased to appear on the front pages of the newspapers. It also explains why he did not give in to pressure from the German Legation which, following instructions from the AA, made a great effort to persuade Portugal to send a volunteer force of Legionnaires to fight Bolshevism in the East.[88] It is obvious that for Salazar, who wanted to keep the Iberian Peninsula out of the conflict, sending a sort of Portuguese "Blue Division" would be a clear breach of neutrality and would lead to a strong response from Britain.[89] During the war, his main concern was to keep the country out of the conflict, demonstrating a tremendous ability to adapt to circumstances. Thus, he moved closer to Nazi Germany when victory seemed certain, sending diplomats there—Nobre Guedes and Tovar de Lemos—who would help this rapprochement. But he gave in to pressure from the Allies when their victory became very obvious, ceding the military base of Lages in the Azores and putting an embargo on the sale of wolfram. Salazar, who would have preferred a peace "with neither winners nor losers," as he put it, had to prepare himself for the new postwar order that was marked by the defeat of Nazi Fascism.

Final Remarks

António de Oliveira Salazar was not an enthusiastic supporter of the National Socialist regime. The dictator rejected paganism and the imperialist thrust of the German regime. He feared for the survival of small nations like Portugal should the Germanization of Europe come about. In official speeches Salazar systematically sought to differentiate his Estado Novo from totalitarianism and Nazism, arguing that the Portuguese regime was original and that it was a *sui generis* solution applied to the Portuguese case.

However, among the political–cultural elite of the Estado Novo, and even within its institutions, could be found great enthusiasm for the Third Reich. Within the regime's organizations, such as the MP, the LP, and FNAT, relations with their German counterparts were very close.

This rapprochement was not only encouraged by German functionaries and diplomats but it was also sought by Portuguese leaders who looked at the HJ and the KdF as models to be imitated in order to help create the Portuguese "New Man." Despite some reservations regarding Nazi racist doctrines and German expansionism, many viewed Hitler's rise to power with enthusiasm. The Third Reich became a "dominant model," and both organizations and German diplomacy tried to project the image of an omnipotent and omnipresent Germany.[90]

In the case of Portugal, this rapprochement benefited from the Spanish Civil War when the biggest period of "fascistization" of the regime occurred with the creation of paramilitary and other organizations to shape the population. During these years the exchanges of delegations multiplied. By means of these contacts, as well as through articles they wrote in Portuguese newspapers and magazines and intensive propaganda, the Nazi leaders managed to make their influence permeate the Portuguese regime.

The profile of the individuals involved is very similar. There were men of the regime, leaders of the most fascistized organizations, ministers, journalists, and university professors; but there were also young people, members of the MP and the LP, high school students and even university students. Drawn from the well-educated upper class, they were part of an intellectual tradition that regarded Germany as the cradle of erudite music and literature, philosophy, and the most advanced technical knowledge. They spoke German and in most cases attended German universities, with many of them receiving scholarships under the agreement established between DAAD and IAC. All of them showed their sympathies for Germany through magazines and newspapers, in which they let it be known that they vehemently believed in an authoritarian, antiliberal and anti-Marxist solution.

For peripheral countries like Portugal and Spain, Germany appeared in the eyes of their intellectuals and scientists to be in the vanguard of culture and technology. Through personal contacts, visits to the Reich, and cultural events organized by the Nazi institutions in Portugal, Germany tried to draw Portugal into its sphere of influence. Indeed, the Reich became a veritable "magnetic field" for the Portuguese Estado Novo. It sold armaments, it received military missions; it sent teachers, it received students in its universities where it trained and shaped them. Without a doubt, this was a relationship that was intended to be global and to cover all areas—from the military to the artistic, the scientific to the economic. The strong commitment to a strategy based on cultural relationships did not, however, prevent the traditional strategic paths of politics and economics from being maintained and strengthened.

Nevertheless, culture was the domain in which the Germans could act with greater freedom until the end of the conflict. They did not face any strong competition from the British in the first phase. On the contrary, the latter were forced to follow the German strategy on the cultural level, organizing lectures and, among other initiatives, encouraging the teaching of English. Besides, a propaganda strategy focused on culture could slip past unnoticed, despite its aggressiveness and the fact that it contained a political message that was easily dissimulated. German propaganda acted on those people with influence, on the regime's elite, and on the young, who, in the future, would ensure the continuation of German influence. Moreover, it rapidly shifted from being a strong cultural factor to being a political and ideological influence. Culture served as a political instrument, but it also facilitated economic penetration. It is in this context and within this logic that the Portuguese–German relationship should be understood—and especially the exchanges established with the Mocidade Portuguesa and the JEN/IAC. However, this relationship between the Portuguese Estado Novo and National Socialism was but one of the many faces of the intensive transnational communication and interaction among the fascisms of Europe.

CLÁUDIA NINHOS is researcher at the Faculty of Social and Human Sciences of the New University of Lisbon. Her research focuses on the Holocaust, National Socialism, fascism, and German–Portuguese relations. Her publications include *Salazar, Portugal and the Holocaust*, with Irene Pimentel (2013, in Portuguese); and two co-edited volumes, with Fernando Clara: *The Anxiety of Influence: Politics, Culture and Science in Germany's Relations with Southern Europe, 1933–45* (2014, in Portuguese); and *Nazi Germany and Southern Europe, 1933–45: Science, Culture and Politics* (2016).

Notes

1. Constitution of 11 April 1933, article 5.
2. Ibid., article 4.
3. The National Archives (TNA), GFM 33/4334, L053438-L053452, "Übersicht über die Ereignisse des Jahres 1933."
4. Fernando Rosas, "O salazarismo e o homem novo: ensaio sobre o Estado Novo e a questão do totalitarismo," *Análise social* 35(157) (2001): 1031–54.
5. António Costa Pinto, *Os Camisas Azuis: ideologia, elites e movimentos fascistas em Portugal, 1914–1945* (Lisbon: Editorial Estampa, 1994).

6. Name by which the military coup of 28 May 1926 was known at the time.
7. Dez Anos de Política Externa (1936–1947). *A Nação Portuguesa e a Segunda Guerra Mundial*, vol. 9 (Lisbon, 1974), 198.
8. The National Archives GFM 33/4334,L053458-L05474, "Jahresbericht," 15/27/1935.
9. *Deutsche Allgemeine Zeitung, apud Jornal da MP*, Ano I, n. 24, 15/11/1938, 2.
10. "Empfang des Ibero-Amerikanischen Instituts," *Abend und Nacht-Ausgabe. Deutsches Nachrichtenbüro* (4 April 1939): 1.
11. TNA, FO 371/26858, C 1094, 25.1.1941.
12. Alfredo Pimenta, "A hora das decisões," *A Jovem Europa [Junges Europa]. Folhetos da Juventude Académica da Europa*, vol. 1/2 (1942): 6–7.
13. Lucena was one of the first academics to investigate the relationship between the Portuguese regime and fascism. In 1971 he presented a thesis in France on the Portuguese corporative system. It was only published in Portugal in 1976.
14. TNA, GFM 33/4334, L053740–L053746, "Die innerepolitische Lage in Portugal ...," 23/11/1933.
15. PAAA, R102412, "Jahresbericht," 20.1.1937.
16. Irene Pimentel, "Marginal e importado: o anti-semitismo português na primeira metade do século XX," *História* 15 (June 1999): 42–53.
17. TNA, GFM 33/4334, L053438–L053452, "Übersicht über die Ereignisse des Jahres 1933."
18. Stanley G. Payne, *Fascism, Comparison and Definition* (Madison, WI, 1980); Ernst Nolte, *Die faschistischen Bewegungen: Die Krise des liberalen Systems und die Entwicklung der Faschismen* (Munich, 1966); Pierre Milza, *Les Fascismes* (Paris, 1991); Yves Léonard, *Salazarisme et Fascisme* (Paris, 1996). Portuguese authors: António Costa Pinto, *O Salazarismo e o fascismo europeu: problemas de interpretação nas ciências sociais* (Lisbon, 1992); idem, *Os Camisas Azuis*; Manuel Braga da Cruz, *As Origens da democracia cristã e o Salazarismo* (Lisbon, 1980); idem, *O partido e o Estado no salazarismo* (Lisbon, 1988); Filipe Ribeiro de Meneses, *Salazar. Uma biografia política*, 4th ed. (Alfragide, 2010), 187.
19. Manuel de Lucena, *A Evolução do Sistema Corporativo Português* (Lisbon, 1976); Fernando Rosas, "Cinco pontos em torno do estudo comparado do fascismo," *Vértice* 13 (1989): 21–29; idem, "O salazarismo e o homem novo"; Luís Reis Torgal, "Estado Novo e Fascismo," in *Estados Novos: Estado Novo* (Coimbra, 2009), 289–367; idem, "Estado Novo: um totalitarismo à portuguesa?" in *Estados Novos: Estado Novo* (Coimbra, 2009), 249–88; João Paulo Avelãs Nunes, "Tipologias de regimes políticos: Para uma leitura neo-moderna do Estado Novo e do Nuevo Estado," *Revista Portuguesa de História* 24 (2000): 305–48; Manuel Loff, *O nosso século é fascista: o mundo visto por Salazar e Franco (1936–1945)* (Porto, 2008).
20. João Pinto da Costa Leite (Lumbrales), who had been appointed by the government to run the Portuguese Legion, asked the German Legation for information about the SA (Sturmabteilung) and the SS (Schutzstaffel) so that the Portuguese Legion might follow the same model. António Louçã, *Portugal visto pelos Nazis: documentos 1933–1945* (Lisbon, 2005), 51.

21. António Louçã, *Conspiradores e traficantes Portugal no tráfico de armas e de divisas nos anos do nazismo (1933–1945)* (Cruz Quebrada–Dafundo, 2005), 51.
22. TNA, GFM 33/4334, L053394–L053432.
23. TNA, GFM 33/3171, E 592399–592400, "Aufzeichnung für den Empfang des Portugiesischen Gesandten durch den Herrn Reichskanzler," 18.10.1933.
24. Politisches Archiv des Auswärtigen Amt (PAAA), R 71629, "Förderung deutscher Geschichtsstudium in Portugal," 7.3.1929.
25. PAAA, R 71629, "Kulturpolitik fremder Mächte in Portugal," 1.5.1930.
26. Simões Raposo was, at that time, the first secretary of the National Education Board.
27. PAAA, R 61253, "Portugiesischer Kulturpropaganda im Ausland," 1.5.1930.
28. Cláudia Ninhos, "À procura de uma 'Aliança Espiritual' com a Alemanha. Do Ultimato Britânico à ascensão do Nacional-Socialismo," *A Angústia da Influência: Política, Cultura e Ciência nas relações da Alemanha com a Europa do Sul, 1933–1945*, ed. Fernando Clara and Cláudia Ninhos (Frankfurt/Main, 2014), 67–96.
29. Arquivo Histórico do Instituto Camões (AHIC), 1537/1 Deutscher Akademischer austausdienst [*sic*]—Berlin, Document 61.
30. Cláudia Ninhos, "Portugal at the 'Third Front'," *Nazi Germany and Southern Europe, 1933-45. Science, Culture and Politics*, ed. Fernando Clara and Cláudia Ninhos (New York, 2016), 120–40.
31. TNA, GFM 33/143, 121189–121191, "Auszug aus meiner Dienstreise nach Lissabon, Madrid und Paris," sd.
32. TNA, GFM 33/143, 121166, "Telegramm," 8/9/1941.
33. DGARQ, AOS/CD-8-P.2, Carta de salazar a Armindo Monteiro, 14–16.2.1941.
34. TNA, FO 371/22601, "Annual Report on Portugal for 1937," 11.3.1938.
35. Telmo Faria, *Debaixo de fogo! Salazar e as Forças Armadas (1935–41)* (Lisbon, 2000).
36. Irene Pimentel and Cláudia Ninhos, *Salazar, Portugal e o Holocausto* (Lisbon, 2013), 129–34.
37. TNA, FO 371/39596, Sir R. Campbell to Mr Eden, 23.11.1944.
38. Cláudia Ninhos, "'Com luvas de veludo': A estratégia cultural alemã em Portugal (1933–1945)," *Relações Internacionais (R:I)* 35 (September 2012): 103–18.
39. A news cutting from the newspaper *A Voz* entitled "Intercâmbio Intelectual: As relações culturais germano-portuguesas" [Intellectual Exchange: German–Portuguese Cultural Relations] (AHIC, 1207/18—Instituto Ibero-Americano de Berlim, document 23, 15.08.1937).
40. "Apoteose vanguardista em S.Carlos," *Avante!* 2 (1934).
41. António de Oliveira Salazar, *Discursos*, 5th ed., vol. I (Coimbra, 1961), 312.
42. Wilhelm Berner, "História e Organização da Juventude Hitleriana," *Avante!* 6 (2 March 1934); idem, "O antigo quartel-general do Comunismo na Alemanha," *Avante!* (24 March 1934); idem, "A ditadura alemã," *Avante!* 16 (27 May 1934); idem, "Educação política da juventude alemã," *Avante!* 5 (23 February 1934).

43. "Contribuições para organização da juventude portuguesa", *Avante!* 3 (1934).
44. *Avante!* 19 (24 February 1935): 2.
45. *Avante!* 14 (20 January 1935).
46. António Almodôvar, "A Educação da Juventude, Escola Portuguesa," *Boletim do Ensino Primário Oficial* 55 (31 October 1935).
47. PAAA, R 71631, "Ernesto da Silva, Führer der 'Acção Escolar Vanguarda,'" 17.8.1934.
48. Anon., *Contra todas as Internacionais* (Lisbon, 1934), 38.
49. "Germânia," *Avante!* 8 (1934); António Costa Pinto and Nuno Afonso Ribeiro, *A Acção Escolar Vanguarda (1933–1936): a juventude nacionalista nos primórdios do estado novo* (Lisbon, 1980), 102–3.
50. Anon., *Contra todas as Internacionais*; Costa Pinto and Ribeiro, *A Acção Escolar Vanguarda*, 100–101.
51. António Ferro, *Entrevistas a Salazar* (Lisbon, 2007), 140.
52. PAAA, Lissabon 45, "Roth an die Deutsche Gesandtschaft," 6.11.1935.
53. Fernando Homem Cristo, "Palavras aos Vanguardistas", *Avante!* 24 (1935): 3; Costa Pinto and Ribeiro, *A Acção Escolar Vanguarda*, 109–10.
54. *Avante!* 3 (16 December 1935).
55. Simon Kuin, "A Mocidade Portuguesa nos anos 30: anteprojectos e instauração de uma organização paramilitar da juventude," *Análise social* 28 (122) (1993): 564.
56. Almodôvar, "A Educação da Juventude."
57. Decree-Law n. 26 611 of 19 May 1936
58. Ibid., Art. 40.
59. Decree-Law n. 27 301 of 4 December 1936: Regulatory Ordinance Governing the Organização Nacional Mocidade Portuguesa [National Organization of Portuguese Youth].
60. *Diário da Manhã*, 30 August 1936.
61. PAAA, Lissabon 46, letter from Carneiro Pacheco to the German minister, 14.9.1936.
62. PAAA, Lissabon 46, von Huene an den Auslandskommissar der NSDAP für Spanien und Portugal, Friedhelm Burbach, 19.9.1936.
63. PAAA, Lissabon 46, von Huene an den Gebietsführer Herrn Schulze, 25.9.1936.
64. PAAA, Lissabon 46, Kaufmann an Aschmann, Auswärtiges Amt, 1.10.1937.
65. TNA, FO 371/24071, "Annual Report on Portugal for 1938," 28.2.1939.
66. Ibid.
67. Ibid.
68. Kuin, "A Mocidade Portuguesa nos anos 30," 585.
69. Direcção-Geral de Arquivos (DGARQ), Arquivo Oliveira Salazar (AOS), CD-2, no. 207-236, letter from Nobre Guedes to Oliveira Salazar, 3.12.1938.
70. PAAA, Lissabon 45, "Portugalfahrten der Hitlerjugend," 4.5.1938.
71. "Estiveram em Lisboa alguns rapazes da 'Hitler Yuguend'", *Jornal da M.P.*, 15 May 1938.
72. "Está na Alemanha o Comissário Nacional da 'M.P.'", *Jornal da M.P.*, 1 August 1938.
73. See, for example: *Diário da Manhã*, 16 July 1938, in PAAA, Lissabon 46.

74. *Hamburger Fremdenblatt*, 23 July 1938, in PAAA, Lissabon 46.
75. "A Visita a Portugal de 3 dirigentes da Juventude Hitleriana," *Jornal da M.P.*, 15 December 1938.
76. PAAA, Lissabon 45, "Bericht über den Portugalaufenthalt von Reichskassenverwalter Gebietsfuehrer Georg Berner ...," 14.12.1938.
77. *The Times*, 6.12.1938, in PAAA, Lissabon 45.
78. Kuin, "A Mocidade Portuguesa nos anos 30", 573.
79. Orlando Grossegesse, "A lição alemã na Mocidade Portuguesa," in *Portugal-Alemanha-África: Do colonialismo imperial ao colonialismo político*, ed. A.H. Oliveira Marques, Alfred Opitz, and Fernando Clara (Lisbon, 1996), 185–97.
80. DGARQ, AOS/NE-7, pt 28, Notes on the conversation with the German Minister about the visit to Portugal of a group of HJ members, 15.10.1941.
81. Salazar sent him to Berlin to head the Portuguese legation in Germany, given his sympathy for and ideological proximity to National Socialism.
82. Arquivo Histórico-Diplomático do Ministério dos Negócios Estrangeiros (AHDMNE), Telegrams received 1941, Berlin, From the Portuguese Consulate in Berlin.
83. The visit was cancelled after the sinking of the *Corte Real*.
84. AHDMNE, Telegrams received 1941, Berlin, 3.9.1941.
85. AHDMNE, Telegrams received 1941, Berlin, From the Portuguese Legation in Berlin, 17.7.1942.
86. Gründungstagung des Europäischen Jugendverbandes [Founding Meeting of the European Youth League]. (Cf. Kühberger, Europa, 2009, p.16 note 27).
87. DGARQ, AOS/CD-8-P.2, n. 384–400, Official memo from Armindo Monteiro, 26.10.1942.
88. TNA, GFM 33/143, 121120, "Telegramm," 27.7.1941.
89. For Berlin, even if only small, it would give "a visible sign of Europe's solidarity in the fight against Bolshevism" (DGARQ, AOS/ND-1, pt.1, 6.7.1941). The question was discussed with Salazar, and the MNE, who retreated behind the excuse that sending a volunteer force of Portuguese nationals to fight Bolshevism in the Soviet Union would serve no useful purpose since it would only be a small force and would have no effect on the final outcome of the struggle. Even so, Salazar agreed to think about a possible public manifestation of how the fight against Bolshevism was positively viewed in Portugal. In July, the Central Board of the LP (Junta Central da Legião Portuguesa) issued a Service Order in which it declared its solidarity with the fight against the Soviet Union: "The great size of the armed forces that today are facing Russian communism have no need of our collaboration on the battle front, but we should consider ourselves mobilized and ready to join the struggle as soon as it might be deemed necessary in this western extremity of Europe." "Ordem de Serviço à Legião Portuguesa," in *Boletim da Legião Portuguesa* 47 (July 1941): 3–4.
90. Arnd Bauerkämper, "Ambiguities of Transnationalism: Fascism in Europe between Pan-Europeanism and Ultra-Nationalism 1919–39," *Bulletin of the German Historical Institute London* 29 (2) (2007): 58–60.

Bibliography

Archives
Germany: Politisches Archiv des Auswärtigen Amtes (PAAA).
Portugal: Arquivo Histórico do Instituto Camões (AHIC).
Portugal: Arquivo Histórico-Diplomático do Ministério dos Negócios Estrangeiros (AHDMNE).
Portugal: Direcção-Geral de Arquivos (DGARQ).
United Kingdom: The National Archives (TNA).

Published Sources
AAVV. *O Fascismo em Portugal: actas do Colóquio realizado na Faculdade de Letras de Lisboa em Março de 1980.* Lisbon, 1982.
———. *O Estado Novo: das origens ao fim da autarcia 1926–1959.* Lisbon, 1987.
Almodôvar, António. "A Educação da Juventude: Escola Portuguesa." *Boletim do Ensino Primário Oficial* 55 (1935): 34–35.
Anon. "Apoteose vanguardista em S. Carlos." *Avante!* 2 (1934).
———. "Contribuições para organização da juventude portuguesa." *Avante!* 3 (1934).
———. "Germânia." *Avante!* 8 (1934): 3.
———. "Portugal Novo." *Avante!* 12 (1934): 2.
———. *Contra todas as Internacionais.* Lisbon, 1934.
———. "A Visita a Portugal de 3 dirigentes da Juventude Hitleriana." *Jornal da M.P.* 26 (1938): 3.
———. "Está na Alemanha o Comissário Nacional da 'M.P'." *Jornal da M.P.* 17 (1938): 3.
———. "Estiveram em Lisboa alguns rapazes da 'Hitler Yuguend'." *Jornal da M.P.* 12 (1938): 2.
———. "Ordem de Serviço à Legião Portuguesa." *Boletim da Legião Portuguesa* 47 (July 1941): 3–4.
Bauerkämper, Arnd. "Ambiguities of Transnationalism: Fascism in Europe between Pan-Europeanism and Ultranationalism, 1919–39." *Bulletin of the German Historical Institute London* 29, 2 (2007): 43–67.
Berner, Wilhelm. "Educação política da juventude alemã." *Avante!* 5 (1934): 4.
———. "História e Organização da Juventude Hitleriana." *Avante!* 6 (1934).
———. "O antigo quartel-general do Comunismo na Alemanha." *Avante!* (1934): 9.
———. "A ditadura alemã." *Avante!* 16 (1934): 3.
Cristo, Fernando Homem. "Palavras aos Vanguardistas." *Avante!* 24 (1935): 3.
Cruz, Manuel Braga da. *As Origens da democracia cristã e o Salazarismo.* Lisbon, 1980.
———. *O partido e o Estado no salazarismo.* Lisbon, 1988.
Dez Anos de Política Externa (1936–1947). *A Nação Portuguesa e a Segunda Guerra Mundial,* vol. 9. Lisbon, 1974.
Faria, Telmo. *Debaixo de fogo! Salazar e as Forças Armadas (1935–41).* Lisbon, 2000.
Ferro, António. *Entrevistas a Salazar.* Lisbon, 2007.

Grossegesse, Orlando. "A lição alemã na Mocidade Portuguesa." In *Portugal–Alemanha–África: Do colonialismo imperial ao colonialismo político*, ed. A.H. Oliveira Marques, Alfred Opitz, and Fernando Clara, 185–97. Lisbon, 1996.

Kühberger, C. "Europa als 'Strahlenbündel nationaler Kräfte'. Zur Konzeption und Legitimation einer europäischen Zusammenarbeit auf der Gründungsfeierlichkeit des "Europäischen Jugendverbandes" 1942." *Journal of European Integration History* 15, 2 (2009): 11–28.

Kuin, Simon. "A Mocidade Portuguesa nos anos 30: anteprojectos e instauração de uma organização paramilitar da juventude." *Análise Social* 28, 122 (1993): 555–88.

Léonard, Yves. *Salazarisme et Fascisme*. Paris, 1996.

Loff, Manuel. *O nosso século é fascista: o mundo visto por Salazar e Franco (1936–1945)*. Porto, 2008.

Louçã, António. *Conspiradores e traficantes Portugal no tráfico de armas e de divisas nos anos do nazismo (1933–1945)*. Cruz Quebrada–Dafundo, 2005.

———. *Portugal visto pelos Nazis: documentos 1933–1945*. Lisbon, 2005.

Lucena, Manuel de. *A Evolução do Sistema Corporativo Português*. Lisbon, 1976.

Meneses, Filipe Ribeiro de. *Salazar: Uma biografia política*, 4th ed. Alfragide, 2010.

Milza, Pierre. *Les Fascismes*. Paris, 1991.

Ninhos, Cláudia. "'Com luvas de veludo': A estratégia cultural alemã em Portugal (1933–1945)." *Relações Internacionais (R:I)* 35 (September 2012): 103–18.

———. "À procura de uma 'Aliança Espiritual' com a Alemanha. Do Ultimato Britânico à ascensão do Nacional-Socialismo." In *A Angústia da Influência: Política, Cultura e Ciência nas relações da Alemanha com a Europa do Sul, 1933–1945*, ed. Fernando Clara and Cláudia Ninhos, 67–96. Frankfurt/Main, 2015.

———. "Portugal at the 'Third Front.'" In *Nazi Germany and Southern Europe, 1933–45: Science, Culture and Politics*, ed. Fernando Clara and Cláudia Ninhos, 120–40. New York, 2016.

Nolte, Ernst. *Die faschistischen Bewegungen: Die Krise des liberalen Systems und die Entwicklung der Faschismen*. Munich, 1966.

Nunes, João Paulo Avelãs. "Tipologias de regimes políticos: Para uma leitura neo-moderna do Estado Novo e do Nuevo Estado." *Revista Portuguesa de História* 34 (2000): 305–48.

Payne, Stanley G. *Fascism, Comparison and Definition*. Madison, 1980.

Pimenta, Alfredo. "A hora das decisões." *A Jovem Europa [Junges Europa]. Folhetos da Juventude Académica da Europa* 1/2 (1942): 6–7.

Pimentel, Irene. "Marginal e importado: o anti-semitismo português na primeira metade do século XX." *História* 15 (June 1999): 42–53.

Pimentel, Irene, and Cláudia Ninhos. *Salazar, Portugal e o Holocausto*. Lisbon, 2013.

Pinto, António Costa. *O Salazarismo e o fascismo europeu: problemas de interpretação nas ciências sociais*. Lisbon, 1992.

———. *Os Camisas Azuis: ideologia, elites e movimentos fascistas em Portugal, 1914–1945*. Lisbon, 1994.

Pinto, António Costa, and Nuno Afonso Ribeiro. *A Acção Escolar Vanguarda (1933–1936): a juventude nacionalista nos primórdios do estado novo.* Lisbon, 1980.

Rosas, Fernando. "Cinco pontos em torno do estudo comparado do fascismo." *Vértice* 13 (1989): 21–29.

———. "O salazarismo e o homem novo: ensaio sobre o Estado Novo e a questão do totalitarismo." *Análise social* 35, 157 (2001): 1031–54.

———. *Salazar e o poder: a arte de saber durar.* Lisbon, 2012.

Salazar, António de Oliveira. *Discursos,* 5th ed., vol. I. Coimbra, 1961.

Torgal, Luís Reis. "Estado Novo: um totalitarismo à portuguesa?" In *Estados Novos: Estado Novo,* 249–88. Coimbra, 2009.

———. "Estado Novo e Fascismo." In *Estados Novos: Estado* Novo, 289–367. Coimbra, 2009.

✺ 6

INTER-FASCIST CONFLICTS IN EAST CENTRAL EUROPE
The Nazis, the "Austrofascists," the Iron Guard, and the Organization of Ukrainian Nationalists

Grzegorz Rossoliński-Liebe

Introduction

The history of European fascism is characterized by both cooperation and conflicts between movements, regimes, and individuals. Hyper-nationalism and racism, two intrinsic elements of fascism, simultaneously united and divided the leaders, members, and adherents of movements and regimes. The Italian Fascists, the German Nazis, and a number of other similar movements and regimes wanted to unite and create Europe on their terms. They usually called it "New Europe," but they did not agree on which countries ought to be included as self-governing nation-states, and which ones should be subordinated to the major regimes. A huge problem for the creation of a fascist Europe and also of a fascist European community was the obsession with violence, including the belief that conflicts should be resolved by war. Nevertheless, it was neither violence nor the ultranationalist and racist nature of fascism that caused the most brutal conflicts between fascists. As this chapter will demonstrate, inter-fascist clashes frequently resulted from pragmatic subjects, the desire to keep "order" in particular parts of Europe, and sometimes also from cultural and political misunderstandings.

All four movements analyzed in this chapter—the German National Socialists, the "Austrofascists," the Romanian Iron Guard, and the Organization of Ukrainian Nationalists—had their own specifics that made them idiosyncratic. Notwithstanding this, they still show a large number of similarities. This demonstrates that despite cultural, political, and social differences they belonged to the same family of movements.

They were united by similar ideologies and orientations, and they wanted to eliminate the same kind of enemies in their states. The four movements shared a sense of belonging to each other, and emphasized this on various occasions. Yet they were not equal, and they pursued different geopolitical goals. In 1933 the National Socialists took power in Germany and became a regime controlling one of the most powerful European states. The "Austrofascists" took power as well, in a much smaller country but with a German language and a Germanic culture. The Iron Guard, a Southeast European movement united first of all by religion and religious mysticism, fascinated many young Romanians, but it ruled a state only in late 1940 and early 1941, sharing power with the military dictator Ion Antonescu, who remained skeptical about the revolutionary spirit of fascism. The Organization of Ukrainian Nationalists (Orhanizatsia Ukraïns'kykh Natsionalistiv, OUN) aimed to establish a fascist regime, but it did not have a state in which it could implement its program. Thus, it combined the fight for an independent state with integration into the community of fascist regimes, similar to the Slovak Hlinka Party and the Croatian Ustaša.

Following Roger Griffin's definition of generic fascism, and defining this phenomenon also according to futures typical of the ideal type of fascism, it makes sense to regard all four movements or regimes analyzed here as fascist or semi-fascist. Griffin has defined fascism as "a genus of political ideology whose mythic core in its various permutations is a palingenetic form of populist ultranationalism."[1] Thereby he emphasized that fascist movements or regimes wanted to prevent the "degeneration" of a nation through palingenesis—a radical cultural, political, and ultranationalist "regeneration." Some most important futures of an ideal type of fascism are the *Führerprinzip*, ultranationalism, populism, racism, anti-Semitism, antidemocratism, antiliberalism, anti-Marxism, anticonservatism, totalitarianism, and militarism or obsession with violence, which fascist movements regard as an extension of politics.[2] In general, movements or regimes absorbed these futures in different proportions, and they combined them with their national traditions or non-fascist other political orientation, such as conservatism or nationalism. Thus we should differentiate between fascist and semi-fascist movements, and try to explain the various forms of cultural amalgamations and political hybridizations.

The purpose of this chapter is to explain why some movements, despite their ideological similarities, did not collaborate with each other, but remained in unfriendly relations, detained the members of other organizations, or even combated one another. The inter-fascist conflicts investigated in this study had different causes, and they illustrate three different types of encounter. By analyzing them, we will elaborate the aims and main features of the movements, and then work out what prevented the collaboration between them. Finally, the three examples will be compared in order to find out if there were some similar reasons for the conflicts or if they were accidental and resulted from random misunderstandings.

The Nazis and the "Austrofascists"

As a small, German-speaking country created from a central part of the Habsburg Empire in 1918, Austria was home to two fascist or semi-fascist movements. The first was the National Socialists, and the second the Home Guard (Heimwehr) and the Fatherland Front (Vaterländische Front). The latter became known as the "Austrofascists" after World War II. The Home Guard emerged from groups composed of vigilantes, peasants, and petit-bourgeois who sought to protect their property and defend "order" during the period of chaos after World War I. It was a paramilitary, far-right movement with sympathies for the Christian Socialist Party (Christlichsoziale Partei, CS). With the exception of the branches in Styria (Steiermark), the Home Guard supported the idea of Austrian independence, opposing the pan-German idea of the unification of Austria and Germany. The Home Guard regarded as its main enemies the socialists and the communists. Its most important aims were the protection of the *Volk* (people) against elements that could weaken its ethnic and national unity, and the strengthening of authoritarianism and corporatism in Austrian society. During the 1920s and early 1930s, the Home Guard adopted many fascist elements from Italian Fascism, and elaborated Austrian fascism which was later absorbed by the Fatherland Front.[3]

The Austrian Nazi Party was a pan-German movement, but it was not the carbon copy of the National Socialist German Workers' Party (Nationalsozialistische Deutsche Arbeiterpartei, NSDAP). It had been founded as early as 1903 as the German Workers' Party (Deutsche Arbeiter Partei, DAP), years before the NSDAP was established in Germany in 1920. For several years it was called the Austrian German Nationalist Workers' Party (Deutsche Nationalsozialistische Arbeiterpartei, DNSAP). In its beginnings it was not fascist but *völkisch*, anti-Semitic and pan-German. In the early 1920s, the Austrian Nazi party was relatively stronger than its counterpart, the German NSDAP. Like many other European fascist movements, the Austrian Nazis were divided into two generations. In 1926, the party split into a young faction that accepted Hitler's supremacy and called itself the NSDAP-Hitlerbewegung. The other faction remained loyal to their leader Karl Schulz, preserved the name of DNSAP, and took socialism more seriously than nationalism. The two groups bitterly fought each other and remained equally weak until the late 1920s. By the early 1930s, the NSDAP-Hitlerbewegung had prevailed, largely due to the triumph of Nazism in Germany.[4]

The Austrian Nazi movement was composed of Austrian members (for example, Alfred Proksch and Hermann Neubacher) as well as Germans such as Theodor Habicht. The latter strengthened the Austrian Nazi party, which suffered from internal conflicts. The Austrian Nazis tried to recruit new members from the pan-German elements. Many of them were in the Home Guard, especially in the province of Styria where the organization even considered collaborating with the Austrian Nazis. The latter relied on a clearer ideology than the Home Guard, and they were politically more radical, anti-Semitic, and racist. The main point of disagreement between the Austrian Nazis and the Home Guard was the question of whether Austria should become a part of Germany or exist as an independent state. With the exception of the pan-German elements in Styria, the Home Guard voted for an independent Austrian state. Although the pan-German movement was quite strong in Austria, the first regime was established by the conservative Christian Socialist Party, which stood close to the Home Guard and opposed the Austrian Nazis.[5]

Unlike in Germany and Italy, the Austrian fascist regime continued to be based on conservative and right-wing elements. In May 1932, Engelbert Dollfuss (1892–1934), a member of the Christian Socialist Party, was appointed chancellor. A year later, he established the Fatherland Front which allied with the Home Guard, and prohibited or eliminated all other parties. Dollfuss, the youngest and shortest European leader, turned Austria into a clerical-fascist or semi-fascist state, which modeled itself on Italian Fascism but was more conservative than the Italian model. Austria's government sought the protection of Mussolini in order to preserve the country's independence. Fascistization of the regime was intended to improve these relations and to shield the country against Germany's plans for incorporation. The Fatherland Front invented Austrian fascist symbols and rituals, and militarized the society. The main sign of the Fatherland Front became the *Kruckenkreuz*, a kind of double-sided swastika. Dollfuss was appointed the leader (*Führer*) of the Fatherland Front and the dictator of the *Ständestaat* (corporate state), which was to "overcome the class struggle." Accordingly, it was glorified as "the personification of the whole *Volk*."[6]

The members of the Fatherland Front owed the Führer unconditional obedience, and Dollfuss and his follower Kurt Schuschnigg referred to their form of government as *Führerstaat* (leader state).[7] The ideology of the Austrian regime was a form of "Germanism," including elements of Italian Fascism. It defined as its enemies the Bolsheviks, socialists, communists, democrats, liberals, capitalism, individualism, and the democratic-parliamentary party system. The Fatherland Front was less anti-Semitic than the German and Austrian Nazis, but it did not hide its intention to "clean" the nation of political and national enemies. It combined corporatism, violent paramilitarism, and religious conservatism, as well as racist and anti-Semitic nationalism.[8] Catholicism played an especially important role in the ideology of the "Austrofascists" because it emphasized their distinctiveness from the German Nazism, which was perceived in Austria as pagan or protestant, although there were many Catholics among the German Nazis, and Hitler even maintained his membership of the Catholic Church until his death. For this reason Dollfuss and Schuschnigg frequently called its authoritarian state, the *Christlicher Ständestaat* (Christian corporatist state).[9]

The politics of Dollfuss's regime and of the Nazis were irreconcilable. In May 1933 Hitler decided to topple the Austrian dictatorship with the help of propaganda and terror. In July 1933, a series of eighty-four speeches by Nazis began to be transmitted from Munich, Leipzig, Breslau, and Stuttgart. They ridiculed the Austrian government and incited Austrian National Socialists to conduct terror acts. In addition, German planes dropped leaflets over Austria. They urged the population to withdraw their bank deposits, and called for a tax boycott.[10] Moreover, Dollfuss was mocked for being short. The Nazis printed postcards that depicted the Austrian dictator as a uniformed boy with flowers standing next to Hitler who, together with some uniformed Nazis behind his back, could not help laughing while looking at the cute "little Kanzler."[11] During the first waves of terror in the summer of 1933, there were several explosions in Austria each day. As a result, Habicht and 1,142 other Nazis were deported to Germany as early as 13 June 1933. On 19 June 1933 in Vienna, two Nazis armed with hand grenades killed one man and seriously wounded thirteen others. On the same day, Dollfuss outlawed the Austrian Nazi party, all its subordinate organizations, and the Styrian Home Guard. The deported Austrian National Socialists established their new headquarters in Munich. They also prepared further terror campaigns in collaboration with Hitler and his German Nazi followers. By April 1934, about fifty thousand Austrian Nazis had been convicted of various offenses, and in June 1934 the death penalty was reintroduced for the possession of explosives.[12]

The coup d'état against Dollfuss took place on 25 June 1934. It was initiated and approved by Hitler, but the German Nazis distanced themselves from it. The main organizers of the overthrow were Theodor Habicht, Rudolf Weydenhammer, a German industrialist and NSDAP member, Eduard Frauenfeld, the head of the Vienna NSDAP, and Fridolin Glass, the military leader of the coup. The principal aim of the overthrow was to establish the right-wing Christian Social Party member Anton Rintelen as the new leader of the country, as he would accept the German supremacy over Austria. Hitler, who during the putsch stayed in Bayreuth, ordered a special plane to be prepared, which would take him to Vienna where he would embrace the new regime. On the radio, some Nazi rebels announced the abdication of Dollfuss's regime as an incentive for an uprising. Yet Dollfuss was shot, apparently accidentally, by Otto Planetta, and he died a few hours later. The Vienna rebels were disarmed on the evening of 25 June 1934. In some other parts of Austria, the Nazis revolted for the next two days. These events extremely annoyed Mussolini, who ordered Italian troops to parade on the Austrian–Italian border and considered an intervention if Hitler should try to seize power in Austria. The coup d'état turned out to be a disaster for Hitler. Although one of main reasons for overthrowing the regime of Dollfuss was to improve Germany's international situation and break up its isolation, the rebellion brought opposite results. After the coup, Hitler forced the Austrian Nazis to claim that they conducted it on their own and without any orders from him. All documentary evidence was destroyed. Nevertheless, at least a number of people— including Mussolini, who had discussed the political situation in Austria with the Führer on 14 June 1934—were quite sure about the proceedings and the actual instigators of the rebellion.[13]

During the coup d'état, over two hundred people were killed, and thirteen Nazis were executed shortly afterwards. Many Nazis escaped from Austria to Germany, but hundreds were arrested and detained in camps. The largest and most famous of those sites was Wöllersdorf near the Wiener Neustadt. By October 1934, 5,302 people had been imprisoned in this camp, of whom 4,747 were Nazis.[14] The British journalist G.E.R. Gedye, who visited the camp in April 1934, described life there as "easy if boring."

> There were no cells, no plank beds. All the inmates, mostly young men, had photos of their best girls upon the walls. There were no restrictions on smoking and no hard labor to be done, as in the German camps … Except for a few simple chores the time was their own and seemed to be devoted chiefly to football, sunbathing, or reading under the trees.[15]

Frauenfeld, who was imprisoned at Wöllersdorf from December 1933 to May 1936, described the conditions in the camp in a less favorable light and complained about the homosexual commandant of the camp, Emanuel Stillfried.[16]

Kurt Schuschnigg, the federal minister of justice and education up to 1934, became Austria's new leader. He continued the policies of fascistization that Dollfuss had pursued in Austria. In 1936 the organization Neues Leben (New Life), an equivalent to the Italian Dopolavoro (After Work) and the German Kraft durch Freude (Strength through Joy), was established. The same year the Frontmiliz (Voluntary Militia) was set up, whereas the Home Guard other old militia formations had to dissolve. In 1937, the Sturmkorps (Storm Troops), an elite military formation modeled on the Nazi SS, was created. Its slogan Unser Wille werde Gesetz (Our Will Shall Be Law) resembled the SS motto Unsere Ehre heisst Treue (Honor for Us Means Loyalty). Bruce Pauley, a specialist of Austrian Nazism, has called this politics "positive fascism."[17] The Fatherland Front gained more and more supporters. By 1936 it counted about 2 million members, and by March 1938 3.3 million, almost half of the country's population, had joined.[18] Some contemporary observers pointed out that fascism in Austria resembled German Nazism. On 2 February 1937, for example, Hermann Göring wrote to Guido Schmidt, the Austrian secretary of foreign affairs:

> I have heard many Austrians who tell me that they cannot understand it when the [Austrian] government on the one hand rejects everything which is National Socialist and says National Socialism is not for Austria, and on the other hand copies German National Socialism in its own state structure, that is to say the same forms, the same organizations, the same expressions, the same laws, the same methods, only with reversed insignia. They say that in Austria one only has to substitute the Kruckenkreuz for the Hakenkreuz and the word patriotic [vaterländisch] for National Socialist in order to have in Austria the living mirror image of Germany.[19]

After the July coup, the Austrian Nazi movement was very weak but it gradually recovered. In October 1935, Italy started the war against Ethiopia. As it needed Germany's support, Austria lost its main defender. Schuschnigg started negotiations with Hitler. They resulted in the Austro-German Agreement of 11 July 1936. The published part of this treaty said that Germany recognized the "full sovereignty" of Austria. In exchange, the Austrian Nazis were granted amnesty, equality of rights, and representation in the government.[20] In the following months, Schuschnigg gradually became more and more dependent on Germany. On 11 March 1938, the German and Austrian Nazis pressurized him to resign. He gave in and announced his resignation on the radio on the same day.[21] The Austrian Nazis had already occupied some offices in the capitals of provincial states such as Graz, Linz, and Innsbruck, and were present on the streets of many other communities. It was obvious that there would be a new takeover of power, but it was not clear if Austria would rescue some independence under the rule of Austrian Nazis. Moreover, it had not yet been decided if it would be incorporated into the German Reich and directly ruled by the German Nazis. Although the Austrian Nazis preferred the first scenario, the latter came true. On 12 March, the German Nazis invaded Austria and officially annexed the country on the next day (*Anschluss*). While marching into Austria, the German troops were greeted enthusiastically in Vienna and many other locations.[22]

Another wave of arrests started on the same day, when a number of Austrian politicians of the Fatherland Front were detained and then deported to Nazi concentration camps together with Jews, communists, socialists, and other enemies of the new regime. In 1938, eight thousand Austrians were sent to Dachau; some of them were politicians of the Fatherland Front. Altogether, up to seventy-six thousand Austrians were arrested in the first weeks after the *Anschluss*, although many of them were released after a few weeks. Others remained in concentration camps much longer, some until the end of the war, and several died in the camps.[23]

Schuschnigg was arrested on 12 March 1938. He was detained as a special political prisoner, *Sonderhäftling* or *Ehrenhäftling*, of the SS. First he was kept in the house of the gardener of the Belvedere palace in Vienna, and from May 1938 onwards in the Vienna Gestapo headquarters, the Metropol Hotel. He was imprisoned on the fifth floor in the company of the banker Louis Nathaniel von Rothschild, and was was allowed to marry Vera Czernin von und zu Chaudenitz. The church marriage, however, happened by proxy; Schuschnigg was represented by his brother. On 29 October 1939, both moved to Munich, where their daughter was born on 23 March 1941. On 8 December of that year, they were brought to the concentration camp of Sachsenhausen, in which they stayed until February 1945. They lived there in a one-family house together with a maidservant. The house was in a special area of the camp among other one-family houses for special political prisoners. His wife was allowed to go shopping in Berlin, and his son attended a high school. Nevertheless, Schuschnigg was not allowed to meet the other prisoners, although he knew who lived in other houses on the site. His brother Artur stayed in the same camp but as an ordinary political prisoner, and he had to perform forced labor. On 7 February 1945, when the Red Army approached Berlin, Schuschnigg and his family were taken to the concentration camp Flossenbürg, where they stayed together with other special political prisoners. On 8 April 1945, they were brought to Dachau, where they met some other prominent prisoners including Miklós Horthy, the son of the Hungarian dictator. At the end of April 1945, they were moved to Niederdorf near Innsbruck, where the Americans were to liberate them.[24]

The Providnyk and the Führer

Ukrainians had lived in two empires throughout the nineteenth century: about 80 percent of them in the Russian Empire and about 20 percent in the Habsburg Monarchy.[25] In November 1917 they proclaimed a separate state in Kiev, and a year later another one in Lviv, but they did not succeed to keep either of them. Their neighbors—Poles and Russians—were stronger, and the Ukrainian alliance with Germany made the winners of World War I skeptical about the establishment of a Ukrainian state. Thus, during the interwar period, about 20 percent of Ukrainians lived in Poland and 80 percent in the Ukrainian Soviet Socialist Republic (USSR).[26] The idea of restoring a separate state, however, became the central aim of the Ukrainian national movement, which radicalized and fascistized in this period. It was rooted in Poland, but its leaders and founders lived in exile. The Soviet Ukraine was not affected by this movement.[27]

In 1920 in Prague, a group of Ukrainian veterans of World War I established the Ukrainian Military Organization (*Ukraïns'ka Viis'kova Orhanizatsiia*, UVO), and the Organization of Ukrainian Nationalists (*Orhanizatsia Ukraïns'kykh Natsionalistiv*, OUN) was founded in Vienna in 1929. The UVO was at first a small group of war veterans who worked with the German military intelligence (*Abwehr*) and the Lithuanian government. During the 1920s, however, it absorbed more and more other political groups and attracted young Ukrainians who wanted to fight for the independence of their country. The OUN became a mass movement of several thousand members. It resembled the Slovak Hlinka Party and the Croatian Ustaša. In terms of ideology, it combined radical nationalism with anti-Semitism, racism, cult of war and mass violence, as well as contempt for democracy and communism. It saw itself as a fascist movement, but it called itself the Organization of Ukrainian Nationalists and not the Organization of Ukrainian Fascists. The members of the movement called themselves the Ukrainian nationalists, too, but they claimed to be related to movements such as the Italian Fascists, the German Nazis, the Ustaša, and the Iron Guard. Mussolini trained Ukrainian nationalists together with Ustaša revolutionaries in Sicily, and the OUN had offices in Berlin and Vienna.[28]

The OUN was divided into two generations; the older one was born around 1890, and the younger one around 1910. The latter generation controlled the homeland executive in Poland, whereas the older members and founders of the movement lived in countries such as Germany, Italy, Czechoslovakia, and Switzerland. The first leader of the OUN, Ievhen Konovalets, resided in Germany and Switzerland, among others. He was assassinated on 23 May 1938 in Rotterdam. His successor, Andrii Mel'nyk, also belonged to the older generation. Unlike Konovalets, he was disliked by the younger generation, most of whose favorite leader was Stepan Bandera. During the interwar period the OUN killed several Jews, Poles, Ukrainians, and Russians. The most famous victim of the organization was Polish Interior Minister Bronisław Pieracki. A central strategic plan of the Ukrainian nationalists was a "national revolution" or an uprising that would enable the OUN to take power and establish a state. In order to put this plan into practice, the OUN needed a convenient occasion such as an international conflict between Poland and Russian or a European war.[29]

The OUN considered conducting a revolution after Germany's attack on Poland on 1 September 1939. However, the organization's leaders abandoned this plan because of the German–Soviet agreement that led to the incorporation of Western Ukraine into the USSR. Instead several hundred OUN members left the territories occupied by the Soviet authorities and went to the General Government (*Generalgouvernement*) in Poland where they collaborated with the Germans and prepared themselves for the invasion of the Soviet Union. In 1940, the OUN split into the OUN-B (leader Stepan Bandera, younger generation) and the OUN-M (Andrii Mel'nyk, older generation). In order to distinguish itself from the *Vozhd'*, Andrii Mel'nyk, the title of *Providnyk* was bestowed upon Bandera. Both factions prepared the "national revolution" which was planned to begin simultaneously with the German attack on the USSR ("Operation Barbarossa"). The nationalist underground in western Ukraine was largely controlled by the OUN-B, and it was this faction that established a state after the German attack on the Soviet Union on 22 June 1941. It also committed many crimes against Jews and other civilians.[30]

An independent state was announced by the leading OUN-B member, Iaroslav Stets'ko, in Lviv on 30 June 1941. Bandera's representative thereby followed the examples of Slovakia, where the Hlinka Party had established a collaborationist state on 14 March 1939, and of Croatia, where Pavelić's representative Slavko Kvaternik had proclaimed statehood on 10 April 1940. Bandera could not come to Lviv, because the Reich Security Main Office (Reichssicherheitshauptamt, RSHA) forbade him to go to the "newly occupied territories." Nevertheless, his spirit was very much with the revolutionary nationalists in Lviv. Shortly after the proclamation, Stets'ko wrote letters to the Führer Adolf Hitler, the Duce Benito Mussolini, the Caudillo Francisco Franco, and the Poglavnik Ante Pavelić. He greeted them in the name of the Providnyk and asked them to acknowledge the new Ukrainian state. Yet Nazi Germany had different plans for the Ukraine and other territories released from Soviet occupation. Contrary to Slovakia and Croatia, the Nazis did not intend to allow any collaborationist states to be established in the former USSR. Bandera was arrested as early as 5 June and Stets'ko four days later. Both were taken to Berlin. They shared the fate of Kazys Škirpa, the leader of the Lithuanian Activist Front (Lietuvos aktyvistų frontas, LAF), who proclaimed statehood in Kaunas on 23 June 1941. The LAF organized pogroms together with the Germans, as the OUN-B did in western Ukraine.[31]

Bandera tried to negotiate with the Reich minister for the Occupied Eastern Territories, Alfred Rosenberg. The latter, however, was not interested in any cooperation with the radical OUN-B, and ignored Bandera's offer.[32] Hitler included eastern Galicia as "Distrikt Galizien" into the General Government, and central and eastern Ukraine became the "Reichskommissariat Ukraine." It was governed by Germans and submissive Ukrainian collaborators such as Volodymyr Kubiiovych, the head of the Ukrainian Central Committee (Ukraïns'kyi Tsentral'nyi Komitet, UTsK). In the following months, the Germans arrested a further several hundred OUN members. Some leading OUN activists such as Bandera and Stets'ko were kept by the Gestapo as special political prisoners (*Ehrenhäftlinge* or *Sonderhäftlinge*) in Berlin, and in the concentration camp of Sachsenhausen near the German capital where they resided in a building in a special area of the camp with solitary cells. At that time, Bandera's wife and daughter lived in Berlin-Charlottenburg, and they were allowed to visit Stepan on a regular basis. Bandera's contact with the movement in Ukraine was limited, and he does not seem to have made a major impact on politics in Ukraine, although the OUN members still regarded him as their spiritual leader. The majority of the other OUN activists who had been confined by the Germans remained as ordinary political prisoners in different German concentration camps, including Auschwitz. About thirty prisoners, or 20 percent of all OUN members who were confined in Auschwitz, did not survive this camp. Bandera's two brothers Vasyl' and Oleksandr were not among the survivors. Bandera, Stets'ko, and several other leading members were released in September 1944, when Germany resumed collaboration with them. Others remained in concentration camps until the end of the war. According to Dmytro Shandruk, the head of the collaborationist Ukrainian National Committee (Ukraïns'kyi Natsional'nyi Komitet, UNK) established by Rosenberg, Bandera promised the Nazis his "full support to the end, whatever it may be," in January 1945. In early February, however, he left Berlin and went to Vienna.[33]

When Bandera and other OUN members were confined in Berlin and Sachsenhausen, the OUN-B in Ukraine remained underground and did not officially collaborate with the Germans. Nevertheless, the organization sent many of its members to the Ukrainian police, which helped the Germans to annihilate the Jews. Although the Nazis generally attempted to purge the police of OUN members, many remained in the police and more and more joined it. The Ukrainian policemen were involved in the annihilation of almost 1.6 million Jews, eight hundred thousand of whom were killed in eastern Galicia and Volhynia, the area of OUN activity.[34] In early 1943, the OUN formed the Ukrainian Insurgent Army (Ukraïns'ka Povstans'ka Armiia, UPA), which in spring 1943 began to "cleanse" Volhynia of the Polish population. At that time, about five thousand Ukrainian policemen deserted and joined the UPA. They used the knowledge that they had obtained in the police to slaughter the Poles. Altogether between seventy thousand and one hundred thousand Polish civilians were killed by members of the OUN and partisans of the UPA, who called themselves "Banderites" (after Stepan Bandera), and were identified as such by their victims.[35]

Iron Guard, Antonescu, and Hitler

Unlike Germany, Hungary, Croatia, Ukraine, and some other countries in which fascist movements came up after 1918, Romania had emerged victorious from World War I. Its territory had doubled. Nevertheless Romania became the home to the third largest European fascist movement.[36] In the beginning, it was shaped to a large extent by students. Its first charismatic leader, Corneliu Codreanu, had studied in Jena, Berlin, and at the University of Jassy, where the anti-Semitic professor, Alexandru Cuza, had served as his mentor and infused young Romanian radicals with his radical ideology. Codreanu admired Adolf Hitler and especially Mussolini, whose "March on Rome" in October 1922 popularized Fascism among many ultranationalist, antidemocratic, and revolutionary movements in Europe. Codreanu and other young radical nationalist Romanians were first united in the National-Christian Defense League (Liga Apărării Național Creștine, LANC), an anti-Semitic party that had been established by Cuza in 1923. In 1927, Codreanu and some other young Romanians created their own fascist organization, the Iron Guard, known also as the Legion of the Archangel Michael and its members as legionaries. Its first and unquestioned leader became the charismatic Codreanu.[37]

The Iron Guard was a typical East Central European fascist movement rooted in populism, religion, and peasant nationalism. Codreanu and many other legionaries frequently wore embroidered shirts which emphasized their connection to the people, soil, and the peasant culture, and served as their unofficial uniform. The core of the movement's ideology was religious mysticism, which the Iron Guard combined with anti-individualism, anti-Semitism, racism, hostility toward democracy and toward communism. The religious mysticism let the Iron Guard appear like a kind of heretical Christian sect of peasants who expected "The spiritual resurrection! The resurrection of nations in the name Jesus Christ!"[38] The main enemies of the movement were the Jews. In order to become a member, a candidate had to swear to obey six fundamental laws (discipline, work, silence, education, mutual aid, and honor), write oaths in his own blood, and pledge to kill when so ordered. By the late 1930s, the Iron Guard commanded over two hundred thousand members.[39] Nevertheless, the organization lacked the capacity to successfully conduct a coup d'état.[40]

From 1918 to 1938, Romania was a constitutional monarchy with a parliamentary system. From 1930 to 1940 its ruler was King Carol II. In 1931, the Iron Guard participated in a nationwide general election, and Codreanu was elected to the parliament. Because of the regular clashes between the legionaries and state officials, however, the movement was banned over and over again. After suppressing the Iron Guard on 10 December 1933, Prime Minister Ion Duca was assassinated in retaliation.[41]

An important propaganda event in the history of the movement was the funeral of the legionaries Ion Moța and Vasile Marin, who had fallen on 13 January 1937 in the Spanish Civil War. This incident increased the popularity of the Iron Guard in Romania. In the parliamentary elections in December 1937, the Iron Guard gained 15.5 percent of the vote. In February 1938, however, Carol II, a person deeply disliked by the legionaries, dissolved the parliament and introduced a royal dictatorship. Codreanu was arrested in April 1938 and executed, together with thirteen other legionaries, on the night of 29/30 November

1938. The new leader of the movement became Horia Sima. He was another charismatic personality, albeit less popular.[42]

The parliamentary elections in December 1937 were the last in interwar Romania. After dismissing the government and instituting a royal dictatorship, the king intended to fascistize his dictatorial state by borrowing many elements from contemporary fascist movements and regimes. A cult was established around the charismatic leadership of the king, and the Front of National Rebirth (Frontul Renașterii Naționale, FRN), a mass political organization, was formed on 15 December 1938. Because all parties and associations had been forbidden, the FRN was the single political organization in Carol II's dictatorial Romania. The FRN elaborated its own ideology, which was based on the cult of the monarch, the national idea, Christian and conservative family values, and corporatism. Further organizations established during the process of fascistizing the royal monarchy were: the National Guard (Garda Națională) of the FRN; Work and Leisure (Muncă și Voe Bună), an equivalent of the Nazi *Kraft durch Freuede*; and the youth organization The Sentinel of the Motherland (Straja Țării), which followed the motto "Faith and Labor for the Fatherland and the King." The Sentinel of the Motherland gave military training to all citizens between the ages of seven and twenty-one, and held a monopoly over the education of the young. On 22 June 1940 the FRN was renamed Party of the Nation (Partidul Națiunii, PN). On 8 August 1940, in the course of fascistization, the Jews in Romania were stripped of their rights. Despite these efforts to fascistize Romanian society and to cooperate with the Iron Guard, Carol II's policies were unsuccessful and his popularity was restrained.[43]

The legionaries were at odds with Carol II but they had good relations with some circles of the German Nazis, who regarded the Iron Guard as an organization spiritually related to them. Thus, the Nazis supported the legionaries' struggle against the old system and the Jews in Romania. Both the Nazis and the legionaries disliked Carol II, who was a royalist and not a fascist dictator, despite his attempts to fascistize his monarchy. On 21 September 1939, the legionaries assassinated another Romanian prime minister, Armand Călinescu. Carol II and his regime answered by executing 253 imprisoned legionaries. Sima, who was involved in the assassination of Călinescu, escaped to the German capital Berlin, which was the main foreign basis of the movement.[44]

The Soviet–Nazi Ribbentrop–Molotov Pact of non-aggression from 23 August 1939 weakened Romanian sovereignty. In order to avoid confrontation with the Soviet Union, and under pressure from Germany, Carol II gave up several Romanian territories: Bessarabia and Northern Bukovina went in the summer of 1940 to the Soviet Union, Southern

Dobrogea was ceded to Bulgaria, and Hungary incorporated Northern Transylvania. This loss of territories led to mass demonstrations and caused a deep crisis of legitimation for Carol II's regime. Two days before his abdication, on 6 September 1940, the king had ordered former Defense Minister Marshal Ion Antonescu to establish a new government. The latter allied with the Iron Guard, and they formed the so-called National Revolutionary State, governed by two leaders: Antonescu and Sima. Although the marshal and the Iron Guard presented themselves in public as a harmonious team, conflicts between them emerged. Antonescu and Sima belonged to different generations, and they had dissimilar political interests and expectations.[45]

The Nazis tried to mediate between the two groups of the National Revolutionary State, but legionaries' terror against Jews and other groups such as communists and socialists fuelled conflicts and made mediations difficult. At the end of November 1940, Antonescu initially considered his abdication but then decided to pressurize Sima to resign. The formal transfer and burial of Codreanu's remains, on 30 November 1940, which was turned into a huge public event with the attendance of German and other fascist representatives, postponed the resolution of the conflict. Antonescu was angry with Sima, because he did not control the radical groups of the legionaries who terrorized the Jews, marauded, and destabilized the country. Hitler needed to find a solution to this dissatisfying state of affairs in order not to lose an important ally in his upcoming war against the Soviet Union. He invited both Antonescu and Sima to a meeting in Obersalzberg on 14 January 1941. However, the marshal was the only guest who showed up. He informed the Führer that he had an obligation to rescue the country with, without, or against the Iron Guard. Hitler responded that organizations with a certain ideological profile do not suit all countries, and explained to Antonescu that the stability of the country was more important than ideology. Six days later, during a meeting with Mussolini, Hitler informed his Italian counterpart that one of the two Romanian leaders had to resign. The Duce assumed that it would not be Antonescu.[46]

After the meeting between Hitler and Mussolini, the military conflict between the legionaries and Antonescu's troops escalated. The marshal denounced Sima and the other leaders of the Iron Guard as rebels. Germany backed him up, but offered asylum to the legionaries. On the other hand, Reinhard Heydrich, the head of the RSHA, wanted to support Sima. Goebbels, too, sympathized with the legionaries, but the final decision was taken by Hitler.[47] According to Goebbels, the Führer supported Antonescu because he needed his military assistance. Hitler was not convinced by Sima, and found him politically unsophisticated (*unterklassig*). The Iron Guard was for him too mystic, and insufficiently pragmatic.[48]

In late January 1941, Antonescu formed a new government, banned the Iron Guard, and began forming his own cult of personality. Some less radical elements were integrated into the new regime, but over ten thousand legionaries were arrested and about 250 killed. About three hundred Romanian fascists, including Sima, fled to Germany; some twenty thousand went into hiding in Romania.[49] From May 1941 to December 1942, the fascist refuges were confined in Berkenbrück and Rostock. The RSHA was responsible for their well-being. Every legionary had to swear not to pursue any political goals, nor to intervene in the relations between Germany and Romania.[50] The fourteen leading members of the Iron Guard were settled in a villa in Berkenbrück, seventy kilometers from Berlin. About fifty further legionaries were detained in "Paul Nortmann," a recreational home of the SS in the same village. The other members of the Iron Guard stayed in Rostock where they worked in an aircraft factory. Professor Ernst Heinkel, who supervised them, praised their discipline.[51]

Although the legionaries were forbidden to intervene in the political affairs of Romania, they did so with the help of informal channels. Antonescu knew this, and arrested some further members of the Iron Guard in Romania.[52] The marshal asked Hitler to extradite Sima, but the Germans expected Antonescu to kill the leader of the Iron Guard. This would have turned him into a martyr and complicated the already difficult state of affairs in Romania. Moreover, the Germans wanted to keep Sima in case the marshal and his regime started to cause problems, in which case they would need new Romanian allies.[53]

On 16 December 1942, during the battle of Stalingrad, Sima escaped to Italy and attempted to meet Mussolini. His escape alarmed Antonescu and Hitler, who asked the Duce to deliver Sima to Berlin as soon as possible. The leader of the Romanian fascists was arrested in Rome on 27 December 1942 and transported to Berlin by plane on the next day.[54] According to Goebbels, Hitler was so infuriated by Sima's escape that he initially wanted to assassinate him, but in the end changed his mind.[55] Nevertheless, relations between the Iron Guard and the Nazis remained troubled. In mid-January 1943, Sima and his adjutant, Traian Borubaru, were interned in the concentration camp of Buchenwald, where they stayed as special political prisoners (*Ehrenhäftlinge* or *Sonderhäftlinge*) in a villa in a special area of the camp.[56] At the same time, 130 legionaries from Rostock were moved to Buchenwald as well. They lived in a barrack, but wore their own civilian clothes. On 24 April

1943 they were moved to a new camp constructed specially for them in Fichtenhain, where they lived in three barracks behind an electric barbwire. The wives of the legionaries moved into a fourth barrack, which was finished in May 1943.[57]

After the relocations, the Romanian legionaries stayed in Rostock, Dachau, Fichtenhain, Sachsenhausen, and Ravensbrück. Similar to the members of the OUN, they were confined as political or special political prisoners, and enjoyed much better treatment than ordinary prisoners of German concentration camps.[58] In late March 1943, Sima and Borubaru were confined in a special area of the camp in Sachsenhausen. Bandera and some other OUN members were arrested and placed in solitary cells in the same building. Sima and his adjutant, on the other hand, stayed in a part of the building composed of a living and sleeping cell as well as a washroom with a shower. One of the purposes of placing Sima there was to isolate him from the other legionaries and from prisoners who had connections to Romania.[59]

Yet in 1943, relations between the Nazis and Antonescu began to deteriorate. The Germans suspected the marshal of seeking a ceasefire with the Allies in order to secure his interests in case Germany lost the war. Antonescu and his government, on the other hand, suspected the Nazis of supporting legionaries' plans for a plot against him.[60] A few months later, the relations between the Nazis and Antonescu seriously deteriorated. In April 1944, the Red Army reached North Bukovina, and on 23 August 1944 the Antonescu regime was overthrown.[61] Just two days later, Hitler met Sima in his military headquarters, the "Wolfsschanze." The Führer was kind and warm toward the leader of the legionaries, who promised Hitler he would form a government that would mobilize Romanians to fight against the Red Army—the common enemy of all European fascists. On 26 August 1944, Sima proclaimed his new Romanian state on air from Vienna, and he kept mobilizing the Romanians in the following days in numerous radio broadcasts.[62]

Sima was not the only fascist who continued this hopeless fight against the Soviet Army and the Allies. On 16 October 1944, the SS forced Miklós Horthy to abdicate in Hungary. Ferenc Szálasi, the leader of the Arrow Cross Party, became the new leader of the country. He welcomed Sima in a letter as a comrade in their faith for the "New Europe."[63] Sima's possibilities were, however, limited. He planned to send a man to Bucharest in order to overthrow the government and to found a Romanian national army with the help of the Waffen-SS. But these efforts remained mere plans. Nevertheless, formally the Iron Guard leader and his government remained faithful to the fascist goal of a "New Europe," and supported Nazi Germany until the end of April 1945.[64]

Conclusion

The three cases analyzed in this chapter show that conflicts are important elements of the history of European fascism. They need to be investigated as extensively as friendly encounters and all kinds of cultural, political, and military cooperation in order to understand the nature of transnational fascism. The history of inter-fascist conflicts can obviously not be reduced to the three examples presented here. It would require a group of experts from several parts of Europe to illuminate and write this kind of history. One point of departure could be the German concentration camps in which our three protagonists —Schuschnigg, Sima, and Bandera—were confined. Nevertheless, the history of European fascism appears to be so complex that several other approaches and methods would be necessary to unveil other forms of inter-fascist conflicts and misunderstandings.

Ideology was a crucial component of fascist movements and regimes. It provided them with orientation and facilitated transnational cooperation, despite the ultranationalist cores rooted in fascist ideologies. Nevertheless, it would be wrong to assume that the programs of the three analyzed movements were identical. Anti-Semitism was more essential in German Nazism than it was in the worldview of the Fatherland Front. Religion was absolutely essential for the Iron Guard, but not for the German Nazis. The struggle for an independent state was not the aim of the Austrian, German, or Romanian fascists, because they already had one. However, it was not, in the first instance, the ideological differences that caused conflicts between fascist movements. In fact, it was first of all pragmatic issues that led to or even caused the clashes, and that convinced Hitler to cooperate with military leaders and conservative elites like in Hungary and Romania, and not with fascist or semi-fascist movements. In the case of Austria, it was Hitler's determination to break up Germany's international isolation and to control a country which, as the Nazis believed, historically belonged to Germany. Ukrainian nationalists were not allowed to collaborate politically with the Nazis, because the Germans did not want to establish any states in the territories of the former USSR. Although the Iron Guard was a subject of admiration for many leading Nazi politicians, Antonescu could govern Romania more efficiently and provide stronger support for the war against the Soviet Union than the legionaries.

Thus, there is no universal answer to the question of what caused the conflicts among fascist movements and regimes, or of what facilitated their cooperation. The Nazis sympathized with fascists but they were concerned more about pragmatic matters than about ideological or spiritual similarities. The worldview of authoritarian conservative leaders was also not entirely alien to the Nazis, and they could find enough similarities such as racism and nationalism to cooperate with them. Thus, when it was convenient for the Nazis, they collaborated with authoritarian conservative forces and imprisoned the fascists. Yet they repeatedly altered their position in different contexts, and initiated collaboration with fascists when they felt that they might lose the war or that conservative authoritarians might not want to support them anymore.

Contrary to their expectations, the Germans did not benefit from detaining and combating the fascists. Even if in the short run they took advantage of the collaboration with conservatives, in the long run they needed the fascist movements, who proved to be faithful and loyal, even after years of imprisonment. The conflicts also did not exclude any kind of collaboration. While the elite of the OUN were confined in concentration camps, Ukrainian policemen, including many OUN members, helped the Nazis annihilate the Jews. Some legionaries were integrated into Antonescu's regime and fought on the eastern front, even if many were persecuted. Numerous former members of the Fatherland Front and the Home Guard helped the Nazis on the eastern front as well, while some of them spent the war in concentration camps.

Apparently, all fascists who were imprisoned by the Nazis benefited from their "accidental" imprisonment. After the war, they could argue that they had opposed the Nazis and their genocidal policies toward the Jews. Bandera, for instance, presented himself as an opponent of Nazi Germany and as a freedom fighter during the Cold War. Stets'ko founded and led the Anti-Bolshevik Bloc of Nations, which united veterans of several East European fascist movements, including the Ustaša, the Iron Guard, and the Hlinka Party. Some more Ukrainian nationalists, who were confined in Nazi concentration camps, worked as professors at Western universities. Horia Sima was not apprehended and executed like Antonescu, but died in Madrid in 1993. During his second life, he was one of the main anticommunist Romanian exile leaders. Schuschnigg moved to the United States in 1948, becoming an American citizen and a professor of political science at Saint Louis University. In 1968 he returned to Austria and published an almost 500-page book *Im Kampf gegen Hitler* (The Struggle against Hitler), in which he did not have much to say about the fascist nature of the Fatherland Front and the regime that he had headed, but a lot about his antifascist resistance against Nazi Germany.[65]

GRZEGORZ ROSSOLIŃSKI-LIEBE, researcher and lecturer at the Freie Universität Berlin, studied History and Cultural Studies at the Viadrina European University. Selected publications: *Stepan Bandera: The Life and Afterlife of a Ukrainian Nationalist: Fascism, Genocide, and Cult* (Stuttgart, 2014); "The Fascist Kernel of Ukrainian Genocidal Nationalism," *The Carl Beck Papers in Russian and East European Studies* 2402 (May 2015); *Alma mater antisemitica: Akademisches Milieu, Juden und Antisemitismus an den Universitäten Europas zwischen 1918 und 1939* (Vienna, 2016).

Notes

1. Roger Griffin, *The Nature of Fascism* (London, 1991), 26.
2. Roger Eatwell, "The Nature of 'Generic Fascism': The 'Fascist Minimum' and the 'Fascist Matrix,'" in *Comparative Fascist Studies: New Perspectives*, ed. Constantin Iordachi (London, 2009), 136–39.
3. Gerhard Botz, "The Coming of the Dollfuss-Schuschnigg Regime and the Stages of its Development," in *Rethinking Fascism and Dictatorship in Europe*, ed. António Costa Pinto and Aristotle Kallis (London, 2014), 126–29.
4. Bruce Pauley, "From Splinter Party to Mass Movement: The Austrian Nazi Breakthrough," *German Studies Review* 2, no. 1 (1979): 7–9, 14–15; Bruce Pauley, *Hitler and the Forgotten Nazis. A History of Austrian National Socialism* (Chapel Hill, 1981), 246–47.
5. Pauley, "From Splinter Party to Mass Movement," 24–27.
6. Michael Mann, *Fascists* (Cambridge, 2004), 210.
7. Botz, "The Coming of the Dollfuss-Schuschnigg Regime," 121.
8. Mann, *Fascists*, 208–11; Pauley, *Hitler and the Forgotten Nazis*, 162.
9. Botz, "The Coming of the Dollfuss-Schuschnigg Regime," 121.
10. Pauley, *Hitler and the Forgotten Nazis*, 114–15.
11. Kurt Bauer, *Hitlers Zweiter Putsch: Dollfuß, die Nazis und der 25. Juli 1934* (Vienna, 2014), 160.
12. Bauer, *Hitlers Zweiter Putsch*, 13; Pauley, *Hitler and the Forgotten Nazis*, 106–9.
13. Bauer, *Hitlers Zweiter Putsch*, 41–91, 127–57, 193.
14. Pauley, *Hitler and the Forgotten Nazis*, 111.
15. Quoted in ibid., 111.
16. Ibid., 111–12.
17. Ibid., 162.
18. Botz, "Coming of the Dollfuss-Schuschnigg Regime," 138.
19. Quoted in Pauley, *Hitler and the Forgotten Nazis*, 163.
20. Ibid., 164–65.
21. Ibid., 208–11.
22. Ibid., 206. See also Peter Stachel, *Mythos Heldenpatz* (Vienna, 2002), 15–22.
23. Wolfgang Neugebauer and Peter Schwarz, *Stacheldraht, mit Tod geladen … Der erste Österreichertransport in das KZ Dachau 1938* (Vienna, 2008), 5, 8, 24.

24. Ibid., 10; Volker Koop, *In Hitlers Hand: Sonder- und Ehrenhäftlinge der SS* (Cologne, 2010), 95–109. In general on Schuschnigg, see Anton Hopfgarten, *Kurt Schuschnigg: Ein Mann gegen Hitler* (Graz, 1989).

25. For the history of Ukraine, see Andreas Kappeler, *Kleine Geschichte der Ukraine* (Munich, 2009); Serhy Yekelchyk, *Ukraine: Birth of a Modern Nation* (Oxford, 2007).

26. Iaroslav Hrytsak, *Narys istorïi Ukraïny: Formuvannia modernoï ukraïn's'koï natsïi XIX–XX stolittia* (Kiev, 2000), 111–59; Frank Golczewski, *Deutsche und Ukrainer 1914–1939* (Paderborn, 2010), 414–21.

27. For the history of the Organization of Ukrainian Nationalists (*Orhanizatsia Ukraïns'kykh Natsionalistiv*, OUN), see Franziska Bruder, *"Den ukrainischen Staat erkämpfen oder sterben!" Die Organisation Ukrainischer Nationalisten (OUN) 1929–1948* (Berlin, 2007); Grzegorz Rossoliński-Liebe, *Stepan Bandera: The Life and Afterlife of a Ukrainian Nationalist: Fascism, Genocide, and Cult* (Stuttgart, 2014).

28. Golczewski, *Deutsche und Ukrainer*, 547–69; Bruder, *"Den ukrainischen Staat erkämpfen,"* 32–51; Rossoliński-Liebe, *Stepan Bandera*, 67–89.

29. Golczewski, *Deutsche und Ukrainer*, 561; Rossoliński-Liebe, *Stepan Bandera*, 69–70. For the concept of revolution, see Grzegorz Rossoliński-Liebe, "The Fascist Kernel of Ukrainian Genocidal Nationalism," *The Carl Beck Papers in Russian and East European Studies* 2402 (2015): 35–37.

30. Grzegorz Rossoliński-Liebe, "Der Verlauf und die Täter des Lemberger Pogroms vom Sommer 1941: Zum aktuellen Stand der Forschung," *Jahrbuch für Antisemitismusforschung* 22 (2013): 207–43; John-Paul Himka, "The Lviv Pogrom of 1941: The Germans, Ukrainian Nationalists, and the Carnival Crowd," *Canadian Slavonic Papers* LIII, nos. 2–4 (2011): 209–43; Grzegorz Rossoliński-Liebe, "The 'Ukrainian National Revolution' of Summer 1941: Discourse and Practice of a Fascist Movement," *Kritika: Explorations in Russian and Eurasian History* 12, no. 1 (2011): 86–95.

31. Rossoliński-Liebe, *Stepan Bandera*, 194, 199, 247; idem, "The Ukrainian National Revolution," 89.

32. "Stepan Bandera an Reichsminister Alfred Rosenberg. Berlin, den 14. August 1941," in *Akten zur deutschen Auswärtigen Politik 1918–1945*, series D, vol. XIII, ed. Walter Bußmann (Göttingen, 1970), 261–62; Bandera's memorandum to Alfred Rosenberg, Berlin, 9 December 1941, in *OUN v 1941 rotsi: Dokumenty chastyna 1*, ed. Stanislav Kul'chyts'kyi (Kiev, 2006), 564.

33. Rossoliński-Liebe, *Stepan Bandera*, 249, 251, 285–88; Adam Cyra, "Banderowcy w KL Auschwitz," *Studia nad faszyzmem i zbrodniami hitlerowskimi* 30 (2008): 388–402.

34. Bohdan Kazanivs'kyi, *Shliakhom Legendy: Spomyny* (London, 1975), 263–66; Gabriel N. Finder and Alexander V. Prusin, "Collaboration in Eastern Galicia: The Ukrainian Police and the Holocaust," *East European Jewish Affairs* 34, no. 2 (2004): 103–12; Alexander Kruglov, "Jewish Losses in Ukraine, 1941–1944," in *The Shoah in Ukraine: History, Testimony, Memorialization*, ed. Ray Brandon and Wendy Lower (Bloomington, 2008), 273.

35. Grzegorz Motyka, *Ukraińska partyzantka 1942–1960: Działalność Organizacji Ukraińskich Nacjonalistów i Ukraińskiej Powstańczej Armii* (Warsaw, 2006), 410–12.
36. Stanley G. Payne, *A History of Fascism, 1914–1945* (Wisconsin, 1995), 277.
37. Mann, *Fascists*, 265.
38. Quoted in Payne, *History of Fascism*, 288.
39. Ibid., 277–85.
40. Constantin Iordachi, "A Continuum of Dictatorships: Hybrid Totalitarian Experiments in Romania, 1937–1944" in *Rethinking Fascism and Dictatorship in Europe*, ed. António Costa Pinto and Aristotle Kallis (London, 2014), 246.
41. Armin Heinen, *Die Legion "Erzengel Michael" in Rumänien. Soziale Bewegung und politische Organisation: Ein Beitrag zum Problem des internationalen Faschismus* (Munich, 1986), 99–151, 252–57.
42. Ibid., 309–10, 364–80.
43. Iordachi, "Continuum of Dictatorships," 248–53.
44. Heinen, *Die Legion "Erzengel Michael,"* 364–79; Gerhard Köpernick, *Faschisten im KZ. Rumäniens Eiserne Garde und das Dritte Reich* (Berlin, 2014), 47–48.
45. Ibid., 45–70; Iordachi, "Continuum of Dictatorships," 253.
46. Köpernick, *Faschisten im KZ*, 70–79.
47. Ibid., 94–100.
48. Ibid., 102.
49. Ibid., 129, 140, 142.
50. Ibid., 110–11.
51. Ibid., 113–15, 120, 142–43.
52. Ibid., 148, 153.
53. Ibid., 159.
54. Ibid., 180–83.
55. Ibid., 184, 191–93.
56. Ibid., 194.
57. Ibid., 194–95.
58. Ibid., 201.
59. Ibid., 205.
60. Ibid., 211.
61. Ibid., 216–17.
62. Ibid., 223–24.
63. Ibid., 234–35. Szálasi was a personal enemy of Horthy, like Sima of Antonescu. See, on this, Johannes Dafinger's chapter in this volume.
64. Ibid., 236–48.
65. Kurt Schuschnigg, *Im Kampf gegen Hitler: Die Überwindung der Anschlussidee* (Vienna, 1969).

Bibliography

Bauer, Kurt. *Hitlers Zweiter Putsch: Dollfuß, die Nazis und der 25. Juli 1934*. Vienna, 2014.

Botz, Gerhard. "The Coming of the Dollfuss-Schuschnigg Regime and the Stages of its Development." In *Rethinking Fascism and Dictatorship in Europe*, ed. António Costa Pinto and Aristotle Kallis. London: Palgrave, 2014.

Bruder, Franziska. *"Den ukrainischen Staat erkämpfen oder sterben!" Die Organisation Ukrainischer Nationalisten (OUN) 1929–1948*. Berlin, 2007.

Bußmann, Walter, ed. *Akten zur deutschen Auswärtigen Politik 1918–1945*, series D, vol. XIII. Göttingen, 1970.

Cyra, Adam. "Banderowcy w KL Auschwitz." *Studia nad faszyzmem i zbrodniami hitlerowskimi* 30 (2008): 383–432.

Eatwell, Roger. "The Nature of 'Generic Fascism': The 'Fascist Minimum' and the 'Fascist Matrix.'" In *Comparative Fascist Studies: New Perspectives*, ed. Constantin Iordachi, 134–161. London, 2009.

Finder, Gabriel N., and Alexander V. Prusin. "Collaboration in Eastern Galicia: The Ukrainian Police and the Holocaust." *East European Jewish Affairs* 34, no. 2 (2004): 95–118.

Golczewski, Frank. *Deutsche und Ukrainer 1914–1939*. Paderborn, 2010.

Griffin, Roger. *The Nature of Fascism*. London, 1991.

Heinen, Armin. *Die Legion "Erzengel Michael" in Rumänien. Soziale Bewegung und politische Organisation: Ein Beitrag zum Problem des internationalen Faschismus*. Munich, 1986.

Himka, John-Paul. "The Lviv Pogrom of 1941: The Germans, Ukrainian Nationalists, and the Carnival Crowd." *Canadian Slavonic Papers* LIII, nos. 2–4 (2011): 209–43.

Hopfgarten, Anton. *Kurt Schuschnigg: Ein Mann gegen Hitler*. Graz, 1989.

Hrytsak, Iaroslav. *Narys istoriï Ukraïny: Formuvannia modernoï ukraïn's'koï natsiï XIX–XX stolittia*. Kiev, 2000.

Iordachi, Constantin. "A Continuum of Dictatorships: Hybrid Totalitarian Experiments in Romania, 1937–1944." In *Rethinking Fascism and Dictatorship in Europe*, ed. António Costa Pinto and Aristotle Kallis. London, 2014.

Kappeler, Andreas. *Kleine Geschichte der Ukraine*. Munich, 2009.

Kazanivs'kyi, Bohdan. *Shliakhom Legendy: Spomyny*. London, 1975.

Koop, Volker. *In Hitlers Hand: Sonder- und Ehrenhäftlinge der SS*. Cologne, 2010.

Köpernick, Gerhard. *Faschisten im KZ: Rumäniens Eiserne Garde und das Dritte Reich*. Berlin, 2014.

Kruglov, Alexander. "Jewish Losses in Ukraine, 1941–1944." In *The Shoah in Ukraine: History, Testimony, Memorialization*, ed. Ray Brandon and Wendy Lower. Bloomington, 2008.

Kul'chyts'kyi, Stanislav, ed. *OUN v 1941 rotsi: Dokumenty chastyna 1*. Kiev, 2006.

Mann, Michael. *Fascists*. Cambridge, 2004.

Motyka, Grzegorz. *Ukraińska partyzantka 1942–1960: Działalność Organizacji Ukraińskich Nacjonalistów i Ukraińskiej Powstańczej Armii*. Warsaw, 2006.

Neugebauer, Wolfgang, and Peter Schwarz. *Stacheldraht, mit Tod geladen … Der erste Österreichertransport in das KZ Dachau 1938*. Vienna, 2008.

Pauley, Bruce. "From Splinter Party to Mass Movement: The Austrian Nazi Breakthrough." *German Studies Review* 2, no. 1 (1979): 7–29.

———. *Hitler and the Forgotten Nazis: A History of Austrian National Socialism.* Chapel Hill, 1981.

Payne, Stanley G. *A History of Fascism, 1914–1945.* Wisconsin, 1995.

Rossoliński-Liebe, Grzegorz. "The 'Ukrainian National Revolution' of Summer 1941: Discourse and Practice of a Fascist Movement." *Kritika: Explorations in Russian and Eurasian History* 12, no. 1 (2011): 83–114.

———. "Der Verlauf und die Täter des Lemberger Pogroms vom Sommer 1941: Zum aktuellen Stand der Forschung," *Jahrbuch für Antisemitismusforschung* 22 (2013): 207–43.

———. *Stepan Bandera: The Life and Afterlife of a Ukrainian Nationalist: Fascism, Genocide, and Cult.* Stuttgart, 2014.

———. "The Fascist Kernel of Ukrainian Genocidal Nationalism," *The Carl Beck Papers in Russian and East European Studies* 2402 (May 2015).

Schuschnigg, Kurt. *Im Kampf gegen Hitler: Die Überwindung der Anschlussidee.* Vienna, 1969.

Stachel, Peter. *Mythos Heldenpatz.* Vienna, 2002.

Yekelchyk, Serhy. *Ukraine: Birth of a Modern Nation.* Oxford, 2007.

⌁ 7

FASCIST POETRY FOR EUROPE
Transnational Fascism and the Case of Robert Brasillach

Marleen Rensen

Robert Brasillach (1909–1945) was a literary critic and writer who became a prominent spokesman of French fascism in the 1930s. He never aligned himself to a political party, but he endorsed fascism wholeheartedly as the editor in chief of the fascist, anti-Semitic weekly *Je Suis Partout*. Historians count him among the hard core fascists who actively pursued a policy of collaboration with Nazi Germany in World War II. On 6 February 1945, shortly after the liberation of France, Brasillach was executed for treason. This followed a hotly discussed trial that marks a still contested episode in the history of France and French fascism.[1]

His case, however, goes beyond the national paradigm. Brasillach was an advocate of a fascist Europe, and he contributed considerably to the conception of fascism as a pan-European ideology and movement. As a journalist, he had many opportunities to go abroad and report from political gatherings in various parts of Europe. He consistently discussed the case of France through an international prism, while expressing the desire to forge a genuine French fascism.

Like other French fascists in the 1930s and 1940s, Brasillach despaired over his country, regretting that a singular large fascist movement had failed to materialize. The various parties and movements that were considered fascist or belonging to the far-right, such as the Faisceau, the Jeunesses Patriotes, the Francistes, the Croix de Feu, and the Parti Populaire Français, never managed to establish a unified front. As a consequence, French fascists were particularly challenged to accommodate successful foreign fascisms, while maintaining a strong national identity.

The relationship to foreign fascist models is a crucial issue in the historiographical debate about French fascism. The fact that no fascist movement ever succeeded in taking over power is regarded by some as proof for the thesis that France was "immune" from the fascist force.[2] If there ever was any fascism in France, it has to be considered a foreign import, they say. Other historians, however, conceive fascism as a genuine French product. Zeev Sternhell, who most powerfully expressed this view, pointed out that fascist ideology was rooted in the thinking of Sorel, Péguy, Lagardelle, and other French intellectuals: "French fascism was in every respect an indigenous school of thought."[3]

It is not the purpose of this chapter to take sides in this debate. Rather, it aims to inspect the case of Brasillach more closely in order to provide further insight into the tension between the nationalist and transnationalist elements in his understanding of fascism. It will focus on his perceptions of foreign models and look particularly at his attempts to adopt and transform them into a specific French fascism. Moreover, it explores Brasillach's cross-border connections and interactions that can help better understand the practice of transnational fascism.

Facets of European Fascism

In his memoirs, "Notre avant-guerre", published in 1941, Brasillach devoted an entire chapter to the birth of fascist man in Europe. This "new man" was born in Mussolini's Italy, yet he can claim to the international label of homo fascista, Brasillach notes. Inserting parts of the reports he made as a journalist, he presents a patchwork of colorful pictures of fascists across Europe.

After the emergence of Italian Fascism, Brasillach writes, nationalist movements emerged everywhere in Europe, one after the other: Salazar's Portugal followed up on Mussolini, and then came Germany, which accomplished her "revolution" in the early 1930s. Providing additional evidence for the manifestation of fascism on a European-wide scale, Brasillach draws on a whole list of nationalist movements spread across the continent: the Spanish Falange, the British Union of Fascism, the Rex Movement in Belgium, Codreanu's Iron Guard in Romania, the Dutch National Socialist Movement of Mussert, and many others. Brasillach was well aware of the fact that each movement had its own particularisms: Salazar, for example, favored a corporatist state based on catholic values, whereas Hitler practiced a near pagan religion.

The cross-fertilizations between the various movements contributed, in his view, to the emergence of a new transnational force: "All these nationalist movements—whether they had won or were still striving to seize power—carried over some of their characteristics to other movements, no matter how much they differed in nature. In this way, they reinforced the sense of a universal revolution, comparable to the one in 1848."[4] Everywhere in Europe, the nations "reawakened" due to the fascist movements. They lit the "nationalist flame" and formed altogether a grand European revolution; as Brasillach writes: "Europe was burning, Europe sang and became an ever-increasing unity."[5]

Like many fascists of his day, Brasillach was convinced of the decline of France and Europe at large. Along with the diagnosis of crisis, he expected that fascism would lead to a spiritual and cultural renewal. In his consideration of fascism is much that supports Roger Griffin's thesis that fascist ideology is characterized by an ultranationalist form of the political myth of "palingenesis," meaning "rebirth." At the core of this ideology, Griffin argues, is the belief that the nation can be newly born and arise "Phoenix-like" from the political and cultural decadence.[6]

The desire to revitalize the nation was particularly pertinent to France. Apart from general discontent with modern bourgeois society, other symptoms of decay were perceived as particular French problems. The country suffered from a conspicuous decline in birthrate and, ever since the defeat in the Franco-Prussian war of 1870, it feared a loss of military power and male force. French intellectuals across the political spectrum, but fascists in particular, were preoccupied by the specter of decline.[7] Many blamed the Third Republic for everything that was perceived to be corrupt, weak, and decadent. The Popular Front government of the Jewish socialist Léon Blum was vilified most ferociously. Adopting the rhetoric of decadence and regeneration, Brasillach argued time after time that France needed to be revitalized by overthrowing the parliamentary democracy and installing a fascist order.

Fascist ideology, as Brasillach conceived it, was a revolt against decadent democracy, capitalism, liberalism, and Marxism. He presented it as a fusion of nationalist and socialist strands of thought, and often used the terms "fascism" and "national socialism" interchangeably.[8] However, rather than a political or economic doctrine, for Brasillach fascism meant foremost a "poetry" and a "spirit" of joy, youth, fraternity, and faith in the nation.[9] It is typical of his poetic approach that the chapter of his memoirs that he devoted to fascism is called "Notre mal-du-siècle, le fascisme."

One may wonder whose fascism Brasillach describes: the inner circle of his friends, his generation in France, or the cohort of his age group in the whole of Europe? Whereas his home country dominates the story in the first chapters of the book, the scope gradually extends to Europe and events in the mid and late 1930s. In a way, this structure adequately reflects his political progression from right-wing nationalism to European fascism.

From Nationalism to European Fascism

Unlike the French fascist writer Pierre Drieu la Rochelle, who already called for a federate Europe in the 1920s, Brasillach's outlook was predominantly French in the early phase of his formative years. Educated at the Lycée Louis-le-Grand and the École Normale Supériere, he was primarily interested in classical and French authors like Virgil, Corneille, Rimbaud, and Giraudoux. Crucial for his way to fascism was the influence of Charles Maurras, the leader of the ultranationalist and royalist movement Action Française, whom he met in the Quartier Latin.

In his 1941 memoirs, Brasillach anticipated his development toward fascism with the remark that Maurras's party aired "a kind of pre-fascism," representing best "the aspirations of nationalist youth." By contrast, Valois' "Le Faisceau," he noted, was only "a pale imitation" of the Italian Fascism he admired in his days at the Louis-le-Grand.[10] Brasillach began his career by writing literary critics for Maurras's daily paper *Action Française*, which is indicative of the fact that he was more occupied with literature than with politics in the late 1920s.

The Parisian riots of 6 February 1934 were of vital importance for Brasillach's political "awakening." This violent street protest was provoked by right-wing press revelations that the government was involved in a corruption scandal, known as the Stavisky affair. Although it was not an actual fascist coup d'état, left-wing parties regarded the uproar as the expression of "an international fascist plot" calling to mind the takeovers of Mussolini and Hitler.[11] Brasillach, and many other rightists, glorified it as the birth of a fascist movement in France, and transformed the event into a nationalist myth. With the purpose of perpetuating the remembrance of that particular day in 1934, he kept evoking it over the years and amply discussed "its invincible hope in a National Revolution."[12]

Although Brasillach did not openly convert to fascism after the uproar of 1934, like Drieu for instance did, it is certain that his interest in politics increased from the mid-1930s onward. Mussolini's invasion of Ethiopia in 1935 triggered his political involvement beyond the confines of the French nation-state.[13] Protesting against the subsequent sanctions against Italy, he posed—with Henri Massis—as defender of the West. One year later, in 1936, Brasillach began to actively advocate fascism when the ideologically charged atmosphere reached a peak. In May, the Popular Front won the national elections in France, provoking hostile reactions from right-wing parties and organizations. The Spanish Civil War, which broke out some months later, further widened Brasillach's perspective.

By that time, he regularly contributed to *Je Suis Partout*. The weekly had been founded in 1930 and was led by a group of young adherents of Maurras, among them Pierre-Antoine Coustau, Pierre Gaxotte, Lucien Rebatet, and Maurice Bardèche, Brasillach's friend and brother-in-law. While they remained loyal to Maurras in many ways, they tended to be more revolutionary and internationally minded.[14] *Je Suis Partout* was primarily addressed to the French readership, but the paper specialized in the coverage of foreign politics and had a number of correspondents across Europe and beyond.

The title *Je Suis Partout,* meaning both "I am everywhere" and "I follow everywhere," testifies to this international scope, spanning over different national contexts. It may be inadequate to call the newspaper *l'organe officiel du fascisme international,* as contemporaries did, but it is indisputable that it provided support for fascist movements in Europe. Moreover, the weekly was an important channel for the cross-border dissemination of fascist ideology. It published, for instance, an interview with Mussolini, and translated extracts from Codreanu's book *Pentru Legionari* (For my Legionaries).[15]

Especially after the elections in May 1936, the team of *Je Suis Partout* started to look beyond France's borders for inspiration and guidance. In accordance with the "fever of travel" among the French Right in this period, the staff members of *Je Suis Partout* traveled widely, thus receiving a "European education."[16] As Brasillach claimed in his memoirs, he was initially attracted to the fascist spirit by Léon Degrelle, the leader of the Belgian Rex Party. As a number of French-speaking Belgian journalists, like Pierre Daye, were associated to *Je Suis Partout*, the weekly had close ties with Belgium.

Léon Degrelle and the Belgian Rexist Party

Degrelle, who was of French origin and strongly influenced by the Catholic Right of Maurras and Péguy, had founded the militant Rex Party in 1935 and gained widely in the next year's national election. Shortly afterwards, in June 1936, Brasillach joined a delegation of journalists on a journey to Belgium in order to meet the leader in person. In his report of this visit, Brasillach took note of the Rex Party's national program. It aimed to carry out a moral revolution, in the fashion of Mussolini and Salazar. Most of all, however, he displays his attraction to the personality of the leader of the party, who was full of energy and had a lust for life.

Degrelle, who had just turned thirty, seemed the reverse of French politicians, whom Brasillach judged to be old, sterile, and decadent.

The juxtaposition of "old" versus "young" was of course symptomatic of the widespread discourse of national renewal. Not all members who surrounded the leader were young, Brasillach noted, but the Rexist movement as a whole radiated a joyful spirit of youth and dynamic energy. "When will we have such a movement of youngsters in France?," he asked enviously in *Je Suis Partout*.[17] Over the years, Brasillach would constantly repeat this sentence, full of regret.

Youth, as incarnated by Degrelle, became the very essence of Brasillach's fascism. Wherever he traveled in fascist countries, he witnessed a similar exaltation among young fascists, who espoused revolt, comradeship, and, more than anything, a lust for life. The following line from "Introduction à l'esprit fasciste" (1938) sums it up best: "The young fascist, supported by his race and his nation, proud of his vigorous body, of his lucid mind, scornful of the abundant goods of this world, the young fascist in his camp, with his comrades in peace who can become his comrades in war, the young fascist who sings, who marches, who works, who dreams, he is above all a joyous creature."[18] Since Brasillach reproduced this fragment over and over again in his writings, it can be considered his essential conception of the new fascist man.

For Brasillach, Degrelle not only exemplified this "new man." He also came to represent a whole new style of politics. The Belgian leader had no interest in political theory. Politics was all about emotions, feelings, and instinct, Brasillach remarks. As he rightly observed, the leader was a charismatic orator who incited popular enthusiasm with his "physical radiance, a certain animal attraction."[19] In *Léon Degrelle et L'avenir de Rex*, the book he published in November 1936, Brasillach elaborates on his "Rex Appeal" in more depth.[20]

Another feature of Degrelle's political style is the use of mythic imagery. Brasillach gives a romanticized account of his conversation with the leader on a nocturnal journey by car, driving from Namur to Brussels. "Magical" and "unforgettable" are the words Brasillach used to describe the mesmerizing enchantment of Degrelle, telling stories, evoking his native region and the close community he grew up in. This young man, he says, was a "poet of action" who seduced the masses with compelling mythic images of the nation. His politics rested on a "profound poetry," a style he recognized in other fascist leaders:

> When he speaks to the Italians about their native land and their lands across the seas, Mussolini is a great poet, a descendant of the Latin poets of old, evoking eternal Rome, and galleys on the *Mare nostrum*; and he is a poet, too, this Hitler who invents Walpurgis nights and May festivals, who mingles in his songs the Romanticism of the Cyclops and the

Romanticism of the 'blue flower', … and he is a poet, too, the Romanian
Codreanu with his Legion of the Archangel Michael.[21]

Brasillach admitted that Degrelle "helped him understand" the language
of the "leaders of Europe" who succeeded in winning over the masses.[22]

It is noteworthy that Degrelle was a journalist too. Writing for the
Brussels daily *Le XXe siècle* (The Twentieth Century), he reported from
foreign countries and he established contacts with Mussolini, Hitler,
Codreanu, and Primo de Rivera. After 1936, Rex was also financially
sponsored by both Mussolini and Hitler, who attempted to find
support for fascism throughout Europe.[23] After a visit to Italy, Degrelle
praised Mussolini's fascism as a political model for right-wing parties
in Belgium. In the late 1930s, however, he began to favor Nazi Germany
as an example for his country.[24]

In a similar vein, Brasillach brought Degrelle's ideas to the attention
of the French public, hoping that they could draw lessons from the
Belgian case. In October 1936, an entire issue of *Je Suis Partout* was
devoted to Rex, containing an open letter of Degrelle himself, addressing
the French people: "Qu'est-ce que Rex?" (What is Rex?). He points to
the cultural closeness with France, resting upon a shared language,
history, and political tradition. "Do not link us up to Berlin," Degrelle
says; "we want to get along with all our neighbors and organize with
all regenerated peoples the resistance to communism." Aside from his
concern for Belgium and "European civilization," he aimed to give
back to France her "purity, youth, and joie de vivre."[25]

Although the massive appeal of Rex was short lived, Brasillach's
admiration for Degrelle remained undiminished, even until the end
of World War II, when the Belgian politician collaborated and fought
on the Eastern Front as a volunteer for the Waffen SS. Writing in 1942,
Brasillach adapted Degrelle's poem "Mon pays me fait mal" (1927) to
the national context of France in wartime.[26] Elaborating on the theme of
Degrelle's poem, Brasillach expressed bitter repulsion of the weak and
corrupt democratic regime in his own country, and urged for renewal.

Latin-Mediterranean Fascism

By the time Brasillach published his book on Rexism, his attention
was more and more drawn to the Spanish Civil War. As historians
have illustrated, the conflict in Spain was of crucial significance for
international fascism, because it lent the efforts to forge transnational
alliances a new impetus.[27] Like many other intellectuals, Brasillach
became increasingly engaged in cross-border mobility because of the

Spanish conflict. With the "gang" of *Je Suis Partout*, he made several tours through Spain in 1936 and 1938 and was, among others, received by Franco's director of propaganda.[28] Speaking of this period, Brasillach observed: "It was the time when, in the face of other nationalisms, French nationalism became more clearly conscious of itself ... but it was also the time when it [French nationalism] listened better than ever to [what was transpiring] beyond its borders."[29]

Brasillach's manifold publications on the war give evidence of an explicit European framing of the political developments. The book *Histoire de la guerre d'Espagne* (1939) that he wrote with Bardèche depicts the war as a European battleground where fascists from diverse countries were fighting side by side against bolshevism: "In the grey smoke of shellfire, under a sky crisscrossed by Russian and Italian fighter planes, the ideological contradictions were being resolved in this ancient land of conquerors and acts of faith. Spain was conferring its blessing and its nobility upon the war of ideas."[30] Here, anti-bolshevism is foregrounded as a prominent feature of the European fascism that was taking shape on Spanish ground. The authors frame the conflict as a Holy "crusade" between "Marxist decadence and fascist spirituality."[31] This vision came to dominate Brasillach's view on international fascism, and he would continue to convey it during World War II.

The use of religious rhetoric is a perfectly conscious procedure that is related to the Christian character of the various fascist movements in Spain that Brasillach endorsed. He most strongly admired the Falangist Movement, who represented for him a new "Catholic fascism."[32] Similar to his adoration of Degrelle, Brasillach idolized the young Falangist leader José Antonio Primo de Rivera as a "prince of youth" and "sacrifice."[33]

While reminding of Sorel's philosophy of mythmaking, he created political myths of the pan-European fascist struggle to rival the communist mythologies. Critics who dismiss the image of Brasillach as a mere "romantic" writer have noted that this was a "calculated" approach to "move and mobilize the masses."[34] *Les Cadets de l'Alcazar* (1936), written with Henri Massis, illustrates his approach perfectly. The fascists in Toledo who defended the Alcazar against Republican forces are fashioned into heroic martyrs, prepared to die for the national cause. The authors see the defense of the old fortress as part of the "eternal war of Spain, that of the Reconquista and that of Rodrigue and that of the Cid." The setting of Alcazar serves as a powerful symbol of Roman and Catholic traditions, connected to the Spanish history of kings "from the Visigoths to Charles V, ... from El Cid, who was its first governor, to the Cadets..."[35]

Critics have demonstrated that these references are not only meant to evoke Spanish history, but also to recall the literary tradition of writing about the Cid, the warrior knight of medieval Spain, who was glorified as a national hero for his role in the wars of reconquest. Brasillach probably alludes here to the Spanish epic *Poema de Mio Cid* and the French classic play *Le Cid* of Pierre Corneille, which both express a chivalric ideal of brave and honorable combat. In this manner, he displays a Franco-Spanish connection, and turns Spain into an example for France.[36]

The myth of "eternal Spain" further exceeds the confines of the nation, because the Spanish soil is cast as a timeless battleground where Christians have always resisted foreign domination, especially during the Reconquista. In the revised version of *Les cadets de l'Alcazar*, which appeared in 1939, Brasillach and Massis suggest that the fascists in Alcazar defended the Catholic Occident and the whole of Western civilization, France included. Their fight was comparable to the Christian combat against the Muslims, the enemy of the East, centuries before. Framing the Spanish conflict this way was a central trope in the writings of the far right in France.[37]

At the root of the linkage with Spain was the doctrine of Latin culture, which was widespread at the time in France and Italy.[38] Maurras, who contributed significantly to the cult of Latinity, glorified Latin-Mediterranean cultures and held up France as the guardian of the classical tradition. Restoring the ties to the heritage of classical civilizations seemed to pave the way to overcoming modern decadence, in both culture and politics. From this perspective, he saw natural allies in the "Latin dictators" of Italy, Spain, and Portugal. Brasillach often evidenced his affections for the Latin-Mediterranean culture and literature. In his first book on Virgil, for instance, written in 1931, he portrayed the Latin writer as "an emblem of Mediterranean genius."[39] On a more personal level, he related his kinship with Spain and the Mediterranean to the fact that his ancestors were Spanish and that he had spent his early childhood in Perpignan, close to the southern border of France.[40]

By referring to the Christian and classical traditions, Brasillach integrated Spanish fascism into the wider frame of Latin-Mediterraneanism. In earlier pieces he praised the Latin "poet" in the Duce,[41] and he noted the traditions of "Latin Wallonia" in Degrelle's politics.[42] The notion of a distinct Latin or Mediterranean type of fascism was a way to stress the difference from National Socialism in the Third Reich. Whereas Brasillach could see France being aligned to Italy, Spain, and Portugal in a Latin fascist bloc, Germany, in his view, was distinct, if not essentially different. He thus defined the French brand of fascism foremost against the German version, which was no doubt the most complicated variant of fascism he encountered.[43]

Nazi Germany, France's "Other"

In September 1937, Brasillach attended the Nuremberg party rally with some team members of *Je Suis Partout*. They took part in several party festivities and had the privilege of meeting Hitler and other Nazi functionaries in person. The trip, with the formal purpose of covering the party rallies in the press, was partly arranged by Rive Gauche, an association of the young Right created by Annie Jamet. When she organized a series of lectures on fascism, she not only invited French journalists of *Je Suis Partout* and other newspapers, but also engaged Filippo Marinetti and Otto Abetz.

Even if these foreign lectures did not seem to have a transformative impact on Brasillach's political outlook,[44] Rive Gauche provided him with contacts beyond France's borders—with Abetz, for example, whom he met several times in the late 1930s. Annie Jamet died in 1938, but her association continued to exist. In occupied France, Rive Gauche returned in the form of a Parisian bookstore, facilitating the exchange of French and German books. As a member of the board, Brasillach was still involved in the project, as was Bardèche.[45]

When Brasillach was traveling to Nuremberg in 1937, he did not know much about German literature, and he certainly did not have a good command of the German language. Yet, he was not entirely unfamiliar with Germany or Nazism. As a film critic he had studied Leni Riefenstahl's *Triumph des Willens*, which he qualified in 1935 as "monotonous and occasionally magnificent."[46] Moreover, he knew the favorable impressions of Hitler's Third Reich conveyed by Massis and some fellow journalists of *Je Suis Partout*. They may have made Brasillach receptive to the "new" Germany.

At any rate, he recommended the Third Reich as a "model" for his country in the lecture series he held for Rive Gauche in November 1936, centering on the question "Will Europe be fascist?" National Socialism was actually rooted in France, he reasoned, because it had been conceptualized by Maurras.[47] Similar to fascist compatriots, Brasillach claimed France's credit by locating the French sources in the fascist ideology.[48] Espousing the "universal truths" of fascism, he reminded his fellow Frenchmen that Mussolini himself had acknowledged what he owed to Sorel and Proudhon.[49]

Although Brasillach aligned German National Socialism to Maurrasian thought, he was cautious of Germany precisely because he was a disciple of Maurras. Several book reports demonstrate that his distrust was largely based on stereotypical images of Germany as a "romantic" and "musical" nation. He warned of "ancient German paganism" and, referring to German thought as a "force without reason," Brasillach declared: "These dangerous types of music are for other peoples, and we will never understand them."[50] In line with the conceptual framework of Maurras, he described German culture in terms of irrationalism, disorder, and anarchy, as opposed to the supposedly French classical culture of order and harmony.

As we can conclude from Brasillach's report "Cent heures chez Hitler," published in 1937 in *Revue Universelle*, his visit to Germany left him with mixed feelings. His praise of the Hitler Youth is plain and unreserved. The outdoor camps, full of singing, playing, and sporting children, brought back pleasant memories of the "fascist joy" he had witnessed on his earlier trips to Belgium and Italy. The young Germans he met were, he observed, all physically strong and passionately devoted to their country.

However, his account of the party rallies is full of ambiguities. It is a well-known fact that Brasillach once called the Nuremberg rallies "the highest artistic creation of our times."[51] He wrote this controversial praise in 1943, but the general idea is already manifest in his report of 1937. The record of his impressions gives a detailed account of the enchanting theatrical orchestration of nocturnal ceremonies with choruses, liturgical rites, torches, and special light effects. For Brasillach, this political mass celebration was an uplifting aesthetic experience that constituted a real experience of national community.

Nevertheless, he found the new Nazi "religion" overwhelming and deeply alienating. Stressing the radical otherness of Germany, Brasillach emphasizes that it was "a *strange* country" to the French. He even describes Germany as "farther than the most distant parts of the Orient."[52] As the songs and ceremonies were seductive, he warns the French to be alert to the delusional "charm" of this aesthetic form. However, such critical or alarming notes are altered or simply left out in the revised version of the report that he presented in *Notre avant-guerre*.

The account of Hitler's Germany is comparative in nature, similar to his writings about Belgium and Spain. Yet in accordance with a long-standing French tradition, Germany serves more than any other country as an "inverted mirror" to France.[53] The features of Nazism that he viewed with suspicion were precisely the characteristics that he exalted in French culture, and the qualities that he praised in

Germany were exactly the virtues that he perceived to be missing in France. These projections testify to the complex relationship between Brasillach's French nationalism and his adulation of German Nazism. This was not simply a matter of appropriating a foreign model: "We saw in Germany many things that diverged from what we, the French people, needed: things we certainly did not need to love. ... However, since our visit, nobody could stop us from converting these new ideas in our own country, in our own way."[54] The valuable elements could be imported to France, Brasillach suggested, and the components that he perceived to be foreign would be rejected in the French version. The irrational and mystical side of Nazism would not be appropriate for France, he thought, but the sense of belief, sacrifice, and honor would undoubtedly appeal. Moreover, the young people in France, who were, in his view, miserable and gloomy, needed the refreshing energy and joy he observed in the youth camps of the Third Reich.

According to Brasillach, France needed to establish an alternative fascism with a specific French form and content: "To succeed the French must find their poetry, their myths, their French images, as well as confidence in themselves and in a national ideal."[55] In 1941, when he reported from his trip to the Writer's Conference on European Literature in Weimar, he repeated that the French could adapt the fascist aesthetics of Nazi Germany, which exposed "continuity with the vitality from the past": "we can make it ours, not by a useless copy or imitation but by a more developed knowledge of who we are."[56]

As David Carroll argues, Brasillach found in Nazi Germany "the model for an aesthetic *operation*, an aesthetic-political strategy for the self-fashioning of a people, that France could emulate."[57] Comparable to other French "literary fascists" Carroll examined—Drieu la Rochelle, Lucien Rebatet, Thierry Maulnier, and Louis-Ferdinand Céline— literature and art are intrinsic to Brasillach's fascist thought. The ultimate experience of fascism, as he saw it, was a fusion of art and politics, past and present, individual and crowd, which constituted a sense of national community. According to Roger Griffin, the theatrical "staging of the nation's rebirth" played a crucial role in both Fascist Italy and Nazi Germany.[58] But even if the aesthetic creation can be considered a transnational aspect of fascism, national interests come into play in terms of form and content.

Brasillach's fictional treatment of fascism in *Les sept couleurs* (1939) can be regarded as an attempt to conceptualize an authentic French variant of fascism. The form of the novel, which tells the story of a fascist apprenticeship, fuses tradition and modernity. The narrative is composed of seven different literary styles and, as a whole, embedded in the intertextual framework of *Polyeucte*, Corneille's tragedy on Christian martyrdom. Brasillach, who had identified Corneille as a "pre-fascist" in a politically charged book,[59] thus actively renews the classical tradition of French literature. As such, the novel perfectly illustrates the transfigurative role of the literary-aesthetic fascism as Brasillach conceived it.[60] As Mary Ann Frese Witt has demonstrated, the form of modern tragedy, which was equally explored by other French literary fascists, exhibits a connection to the "sister Latin nation," Italy, where D'Annunzio, Pirandello, and others revived the classical legacy within the national theatrical tradition.[61]

Building on the conventional French–German antagonism, *Les sept couleurs* implicitly opposed the literary or verbal, more rational French culture to the musical, emotional and non-verbal aspects of its German counterpart.[62] The part on Hitler's Germany, which is largely based on *Cent heures chez Hitler*, highlights the musical enchantment of the singing choruses at the congress that he perceives to be essential for Hitler's movement. The closure of the novel, ending in the Spanish Civil War, imagines a fascist Europe to come, and is based on the Spanish or Latin form rather than the German.[63]

Even if Brasillach was increasingly attracted to German National Socialism from 1937 onward, his series of articles on "the fascist spirit" in *Je Suis Partout* attests to a remaining resistance toward Hitlerism.[64] Obviously, his attitude toward Germany became further complicated after the outbreak of World War II.

War and Occupation: A Franco-German Couple?

The fall of France led Brasillach, and many others, to believe that the country was neither strong enough to regenerate itself nor in a position to withstand the Soviet Union on her own. Contrary to Maurras, who remained deeply anti-German and refused to collaborate, Brasillach claimed to defend the national interest by cooperating with the German occupier. His primary concern was to reintegrate France into Europe by installing a genuinely French "national socialist party."[65]

Brasillach envisaged a new European order in which Germany would take the lead and help France overcome its weakness and deficit in manliness. He therefore approved the occupation of France, even when Hitler expanded it to a total takeover in 1942. Like Drieu and other French intellectuals, Brasillach believed that France could ultimately become a privileged partner of Germany in Hitler's New European Order. The German collaborators fed this "Grand Illusion" by making serious efforts to convince French intellectuals that they esteemed French culture, and tried to make it flourish under the occupation.[66]

Only for a short period, Brasillach had faith in the "National Revolution" that Pétain tried to carry out in the unoccupied zone. Because he was captured by the Germans shortly after he had been mobilized by the French army, Brasillach could only follow the events from a distance. Writing from a prisoner-of-war camp in Soest, he initially praised Pétain. Although Brasillach continued to write favorably on the new head of state after his liberation in 1941, at the request of Vichy, he became impatient and gradually more critical.[67] Other policies were needed, he believed, to make France enter the "universal revolution" that he yearned for.

Brasillach voiced this message in various writings, most notably in his contributions to *Je Suis Partout*. Back in Paris in 1941, he resumed the task of editor in chief, the position he had held since 1937. Under the German occupation regime, *Je Suis Partout* soon became the leading journal in the French collaborationist press. The circulation, which was 40,000 in 1936, rose to 150,000 in 1941, 250,000 in 1942, and came close to 300,000 in 1944.[68] Whether *Je Suis Partout* was sponsored by Nazi Germany or not,[69] Brasillach adopted an overt pro-German stance, and he continued his campaign for the establishment of a French fascism.

In the article "Pour un fascisme français" of November 1942, he reminded his readers of the fascist revolution in Italy twenty years earlier. Citing Mussolini's statement that fascism was a "universal revolution," he urged the French not to forget the ideal of "a pure nation, a pure history, a pure race."[70] Elsewhere, he encouraged the adoption of policies and practices from Mussolini's Italy and Hitler's Germany, such as the creation of a single party, the installment of "grand ministries," and, most importantly, the creation of youth centers for the restoration of a healthy virile youth.[71]

One should not be ashamed of taking inspiration abroad, as he repeatedly insisted. As late as April 1943, Brasillach reassured that "[a] French nationalist, anxious for his own dignity and the future of his country, has no more reason to be embarrassed at looking toward, at admiring, and at adopting the political truths discovered by its former conquerors than a German nationalist had to be embarrassed at adopting the metric system during the French Revolution."[72]

The German occupation of France obviously led to increasing interactions with the "foreign other" in everyday life. Building on networks and structures from the interwar period, cultural institutions were created with the intention of promoting a positive image of Germany in occupied France: the German Embassy, the German

Institute, and the Propaganda-Abteilung. Nazi officials like Otto Abetz, Karl Epting, and Gerhard Heller cultivated friendship and built up affective relationships with French intellectuals in occupied Paris.

As he recorded in his *Journal d'un homme occupé*, Brasillach frequented the German institutes and socialized with several Nazi intellectuals. He had the closest ties to Karl-Heinz Bremer, the associate director of the German Institute in Paris, who was known to be a Francophile. Brasillach was attracted to the charm of this "tall blond young man" and idolized the "young Siegfried" as an emblematic young fascist.[73] When Bremer was sent to the Eastern front and killed in 1942, Brasillach expressed his deep-felt sadness: "Dear Karl-Heinz, we had made plans together; once peace came we wanted to go walking, go camping, find twin landscapes, fraternal cities of our towns."[74] Their friendship served him as a perfect symbol of the Franco-German rapprochement and collaboration. As Brasillach insisted, his friend "had not for a single second renounced being German," and "demanded that we be French." The friendship had a profound impact on Brasillach who proclaimed in 1943 that he had been "a collaborationist of reason" but had become "a collaborationist of heart" too.[75]

Like much of Brasillach's writing on fascists, the portrait of Bremer does not conceal his erotic attraction. Critics have supposed or speculated about a love affair between the two men. Whatever Brasillach's sexual preferences, contemporaries and critics have regarded him as an exemplary intellectual who represented the fusion of male eroticism and fascism. This became particularly pertinent in the discussion about his role as a collaborator in wartime France. As Alan Riding contends, the theory that homosexuals were more inclined to collaborate "often blended with the view that, like a woman, France had surrendered to Germany's masculine force."[76]

This was a crucial topic in Brasillach's trial in January 1945. Alice Kaplan has observed that "the metaphoric charge of the prosecution [was] that Brasillach's attraction to Germany was homosexual in nature."[77] The following very forceful quote was brought up in the trial: "I was not a Germanophile before the war … I have contracted a liaison with the German genius [*génie*], I will never forget it … Like it or not, we have lived together: French[men] of some reflection during these few years will have more or less slept with Germany, and the memory of it will remain sweet to them."[78]

The partnership of France and Germany became central to Brasillach's conception of a new European fascist order. Unlike Drieu and other fascist Europeanists, he never spoke out for the forging of a federate Europe. According to some critics, Brasillach was "the most nationalist" of French fascist collaborators.[79] As he plainly stated, the unity of France was his primary concern. The alliance with Europe and the West came second.[80] Similar to other French fascists, Brasillach barely reflected on the proclaimed European order, and seemed to care little about the question of how it would be constructed.[81] Nevertheless, he adopted a European mindset on numerous occasions.

Shortly before the Weimar Conference on European Literature in 1941, when he claimed that Hitler fought for "all of Europe," he brought up "the shared civilization of Racine, Shakespeare, Dante, and Goethe."[82] And in the report of this conference, where he visited the tombs of Goethe and Schiller, he stressed once more that the vital connection to ancient national traditions was "a lesson" for all countries."[83] Brasillach, however, did not see—or neglected the fact—that the Nazis' cultural policies were chiefly intended to rival the hegemony of the French classical model in the cultural realm.[84]

Europe, as Brasillach conceived of it, was foremost defined against Bolshevism and Jewishness. After the invasion of the Soviet Union in June 1941, he plainly encouraged a Franco-German military alliance in the "European struggle against bolshevism." According to this logic, which was fully in tune with the Nazi propaganda,[85] he also endorsed the anticommunist "Légion des volontaires Français contre le Bolchévisme," at least until 1943.[86]

Aside from communists and French resistance fighters, both of whom Brasillach liked to see arrested,[87] Jews were considered the primary enemy, responsible for weakening France and dragging it into war. Since the late 1930s, *Je Suis Partout* had made itself known as a venomous anti-Semitic weekly by praising or pardoning anti-Jewish policies in Germany. As a consequence, opponents branded the newspaper as a mouthpiece of Hitler. Brasillach, however, advanced his usual argument that anti-Semitism was "not a German invention but a French tradition," going back to King Louis XI.[88] In a similar fashion, he stated in 1941 that the Nazis had built on the racial theories of Count Gobineau (1816–1882).[89]

In *Je Suis Partout*, Brasillach campaigned for a moderate "anti-Semitism of reason." It was supposed to be a specifically French version, distinct from the German brand that he judged as racial, instinctual, and excessively violent. "We do not want to kill anyone, we do not want to organize pogroms," he proclaimed in the first special issue on "the Jewish Question" in 1938.[90] "Instinctual" hatred of Jews should be converted into legislation at state level, symbolizing French reason. This so-called "moderate" position by no means prevented Brasillach from offering solutions that reminded of Nazi racial policies, as for instance a special status for Jews in France that would deprive them of their citizenship.[91]

Pursuing this line of thought in World War II, Brasillach conveyed a more "intensified" anti-Semitism.[92] The Vichy regime attributed to Jews the special status he had called for, and yet, in his opinion, it did not go far enough. On a regular basis, *Je Suis Partout* revealed the pseudonyms and addresses of Jews in hiding, and expressed anti-Jewish sentiments in a particularly vicious rhetoric. After the roundup of Vel d'Hiv in 1942, Brasillach issued the most cruel and much-quoted call to "separate the Jews en bloc and do not keep the little ones."[93]

The year 1943 marked for Brasillach a moment of disillusionment. Since the outbreak of the war he had been convinced that Germany would triumph, but by now he began to have serious doubts.[94] This eventually caused his break with *Je Suis Partout*, which was taken over by the hardliners who persisted in their advocacy of collaboration. Brasillach's subsequent public statements in *La Révolution Nationale* and other journals gave no evidence of defeatism, but the thoughts he recorded privately betray sentiments of pessimism.[95] He remained committed, though, to the dream of a young, fascist Europe until the very bitter end of his trial in 1945, where he justified his pursuit of the policy of collaboration by claiming to have served the interests of his country.

Conclusion

As a journalist and writer, Brasillach contributed considerably to the understanding of fascism as a transnational phenomenon. Through the exploration of foreign fascisms that he encountered on his travels to Belgium, Italy, Spain, and Germany, he came to conceive of fascism as a pan-European force and ideology. Committed to the task of bringing the French nation into line with the turn to fascism elsewhere in Europe, Brasillach tried to disseminate the universal fascist spirit across national borders by adopting certain fascist ideas and themes and ignoring others. He thus made myths of the pan-European fascist fight against communist and Jewish decadence, intended to bring forth spiritual and cultural renewal.

Most importantly, the aesthetic practices of foreign fascisms inspired him to search for a peculiarly French fascist "poetry," while avoiding servile imitation or import. If Brasillach conceived of aesthetic fascism in transnational terms, its essential foundation was the expression of the universal "fascist spirit" through the creative renewal of the national cultural tradition. Initially, he aligned the French brand primarily to the

Latin-Mediterranean type of literary fascism, as opposed to the more musical variant of German National Socialism. Yet, due to collaboration benefits in World War II, Brasillach endorsed a Franco-German alliance in the wider frame of a universal fascist poetry for Europe. Although he never ignored the particularisms of French and German fascism, he increasingly softened the "danger" of German music, and obscured the tensions between the nationalist and transnationalist elements of his fascist thought.

MARLEEN RENSEN, Assistant Professor of Modern European Literature at the University of Amsterdam, studied Arts and Culture at the University of Maastricht. She received her PhD in literature from the University of Amsterdam. Her research focuses on politically engaged artists in the interwar years. Selected publications: *European Encounters: Intellectual Exchange and the Rethinking of Europe 1914–1945* (Amsterdam and New York, 2014) edited with Carlos Reijnen; and *Lijden aan de tijd. Franse intellectuelen in het interbellum* (Soesterberg, 2009).

Notes

1. Alice Kaplan presents an in-depth study of Brasillach's trial in *The Collaborator: The Trial and Execution of Robert Brasillach* (Chicago, 2000).
2. Brian Jenkins, *France in the Era of Fascism: Essays on the Authoritarian Right* (New York and Oxford, 2007), 1–22.
3. Zeev Sternhell, *Neither Left nor Right: Fascist Ideology in France* (Princeton, NJ, [1986] 1996), 27.
4. Robert Brasillach, *Notre Avant-Guerre*, in *Oeuvres Complètes*, vol. VI (Paris, 1964), 231.
5. "L'univers flambait, l'univers chantait et se rassemblait, l'univers travaillait." Brasillach, *Notre Avant-Guerre*, 230–31. Peter Tame has translated "l'univers" as "Europe." This seems adequate, as Brasillach remarks that the revolution of 1848 "brûla toute l'Europe."
6. Roger Griffin, "Europe for the Europeans: Fascist Myths of the New European Order, 1922–1992," in *A Fascist Century: Essays by Roger Griffin*, ed. Matthew Feldman (New York, 2008), 135.
7. I have written elsewhere on the idea of decadence in the works of French left-wing writers: Marleen Rensen, *Lijden aan de tijd: Franse intellectuelen in het interbellum* (Soesterberg, 2009).
8. William Tucker, *The Fascist Ego: A Political Biography of Robert Brasillach* (Berkeley and London, 1975), 229.
9. Brasillach declares that fascism was not a political or economic doctrine, *Notre Avant-Guerre*, 279.
10. Ibid., 39–41.

11. See, for example, Richard Griffiths, *Fascism* (London and New York, 2005), 79–80.
12. Brasillach, *Notre Avant-Guerre*, 154.
13. Gisèle Sapiro, *The French Writers' War 1940–1953*. English trans. (Durham, NC and London, 2014), 112.
14. Pierre-Marie Dioudonnat, *Je Suis Partout 1930–1944: les maurassiens devant la tentation fasciste* (Paris, 1973), 133–34; Paul Mazgaj, *Imagining Fascism: The Cultural Politics of the French Young Right, 1930–1945* (Newark, 2007), 182–83.
15. Leon Volovici, *Nationalist Ideology and Antisemitism: The Case of Romanian Intellectuals in the 1930s* (Oxford, 1991), 67.
16. The term is used in Dioudonnat, *Je Suis Partout 1930–1944*, 143.
17. Robert Brasillach, "Visite à Léon Degrelle," *Je Suis Partout*, 20 June 1936.
18. Robert Brasillach, "Introduction à l'esprit fasciste part III," *Je Suis Partout*, 8 July 1938. This passage is reproduced in *Notre Avant-Guerre*, 279. See also: David Carroll, *French Literary Fascism: Nationalism, Anti-Semitism and the Ideology of Culture* (Princeton, NJ, 1995), 119–20; Tucker, *The Fascist Ego*, 112–14.
19. Cited in Mazgaj, *Imagining Fascism*, 190.
20. Brasillach narrates that the handsome leader was so famous for his charm to women that the male members of the movement spoke with some irony of his "Rex Appeal"; Robert Brasillach, *Léon Degrelle et l'avenir de Rex*, in *Oeuvres Complètes*, vol. V, 9.
21. Brasillach, *Léon Degrelle et l'avenir de Rex*. 58. These lines are reproduced in his memoirs, *Notre Avant-Guerre*, 238–39. See also Griffiths, *Fascism*, 116.
22. Brasillach, *Notre Avant-Guerre*, 234.
23. Arnd Bauerkämper, "Transnational Fascism: Cross-Border Relations between Regimes and Movements in Europe 1922–1939," *East Central Europe* 37 (2010): 218, 224.
24. Griffiths, *Fascism*, 120.
25. Léon Degrelle, "Qu'est-ce que Rex? Lettre aux Français", *Je Suis Partout*, 24 October 1936. For a discussion on the special issue on Rex, see Dioudonnat, *Je Suis Partout 1930–1944*, 145–46.
26. Robert Brasillach, "Mon pays me fait mal…," *Je Suis Partout*, 20 November 1942, in *Oeuvres Complètes*, vol. 12, 505–8.
27. Bauerkämper, "Transnational Fascism," 230.
28. Tucker, *The Fascist Ego*, 206.
29. Brasillach, *Notre Avant-Guerre*, 229. Cited in Mazgaj, *Imagining Fascism*, 189.
30. Robert Brasillach and Maurice Bardèche, *Histoire de la guerre d'Espagne*, *Oeuvres completes*, vol. V, 79. See also Martin Hurcombe, *France and the Spanish Civil War: Cultural Representations of The War Next Door, 1936–1945* (Farnham and Burlington, VT, 2011), 46.
31. Robert Soucy, *French Fascism: The Second Wave, 1933–1939* (New Haven, CT and London, 1995), 295.
32. Griffiths, *Fascism*, 118.
33. Brasillach continued to idolize Antonio Primo de Rivera in his writings. This particular quote comes from his acticle "L'absent," *Je Suis Partout*, 4 December 1942.

34. Mazgaj, *Imagining Fascism*, 186.

35. Robert Brasillach and Henri Massis, *Les Cadets de l'Alcazar* (Paris, 1936), respectively 73, 11–12. Cited in Paul Schue, "Remember the Alcazar! The Creation of Nationalist Myths in the Spanish Civil War: The Writings of Robert Brasillach," in *National Identities* 10, no. 2 (June 2008), respectively 136, 135.

36. Schue, "Remember the Alcazar!", 135–49.

37. Sapiro, *The French Writers' War*, 115; Hurcombe, *France and the Spanish Civil War*, 46.

38. Catherine Fraixe, Lucia Piccioni, and Christophe Poupault, eds., *Vers une Europe latine: Acteurs et enjeux des échanges culturels entre la France et l'Italie* (Brussels, Bern, and Vienna, 2014).

39. Robert Brasillach, *Présence de Virgile* (Paris, 1931). Cited in Kaplan, *The Collaborator*, 9.

40. Robert Brasillach, *Notre Avant-Guerre*, 160. See also, Tucker, *The Fascist Ego*, 105–6.

41. Robert Brasillach, *Léon Degrelle et Rex*, 58.

42. Ibid., 20. Citing Degrelle, Brasillach refers to "sa Wallonie latine".

43. As William Tucker notes, Brasillach's writings of the early 1930s attest to his struggle to reconcile the classic and romantic traditions; Tucker, *The Fascist Ego*, 73. See also, Mary Ann Frese Witt, *The Search for Modern Tragedy: Aesthetic Fascism in France* (Ithaca, NY and London, 2001), 149.

44. In his record of the the the lecture series, Brasillach only mentions "a Swiss" with a terrible accent and "a German" who lectured on the Nazi youth but could not speak French; *Notre Avant-Guerre*, 234; *Oeuvres Complètes*, 220–21. It is possible that this description refers to lectures of an earlier period. See Tucker, *The Fascist Ego*, 155–57.

45. Albrecht Betz and Stefan Martens, *Les intellectuels et l'occupation 1940–1944: Collaborer, partir, résister* (Paris, 2004), 77–78.

46. Maurice Bardèche and Robert Brasillach, *Histoire du cinéma* (Paris, 1935), in *Oeuvres Complètes*, vol. X, 397.

47. Kaplan, *The Collaborator*, 13

48. Mazgaj, *Imagining Fascism*, 233.

49. For the universal truths of fascism, see Robert Brasillach, "Devant l'equivoque," in *Je Suis Partout*, 3 July 1942, 457–60. For the French "roots" of fascism, see "La République est crévée, qu'on le veuille ou non," in *Je Suis Partout*, 16 June 1941, in *Oeuvres Complètes*, vol. 12, 345–48; "Pour un fascisme français," *Je Suis Partout*, 6 November 1942, in *Oeuvres Complètes*, vol. 12, 499–502.

50. Robert Brasillach, "Henri Massis, Débats," in *L'Action Française*, 13 December 1934, in *Oeuvres Complètes*, vol. XI, 487. Cited in Carroll, *French Literary Fascism*, 115. His wariness is particularly notable in his review of Alphonse de Châteaubriant's *La Gerbe des Forces* (1937), in which he criticizes the author for not having been able to resist the German "charm." See Robert Brasillach, "A. de Chateaubriant 'la Gerbe des forces,'" and H. de Montherlant, "le Démon du bien," in *L'Action Française*, 8 July 1937, in *Oeuvres Complètes*, vol. 12, 63–66.

51. Robert Brasillach, "Les Leçons d'un anniversaire," in *Je Suis Partout*, 29 January 1943, in *Oeuvres Complètes*, vol. 12, 525.
52. Robert Brasillach, "Cent heures chez Hitler," in *La Revue Universelle*, 1 October 1937. Cited in Karen Fiss, *Grand Illusion: The Third Reich, the Paris Exposition and the Cultural Seduction of France* (Chicago, 2009), 177.
53. Michael Nolan, *The Inverted Mirror: Mythologizing the Enemy in France and Germany, 1898–1914* (Oxford, 2005).
54. Brasillach, *Notre Avant-Guerre*, 267.
55. Cited in Kaplan, *The Collaborator*, 13.
56. Robert Brasillach, "De la cité de Goethe au nouvel 'axe' de Berlin," *Je Suis Partout*, 8 November 1941. This article is reproduced in *Journal d'un homme occupé*, in *Oeuvres Complètes*, vol. VI, 481. Cited in Carroll, *French Literary Fascism*, 116.
57. Carroll, *French Literary Fascism*, 117.
58. Roger Griffin, "Staging the Nation's Rebirth: The Politics and Aesthetics of Performance in the Context of Fascist Studies," in *Fascism and Theatre: Comparative Studies on the Aesthetics and Politics of Performance in Europe, 1925–1945*, ed. Günter Berghaus (Oxford, 1996), 11–30.
59. Robert Brasillach, *Pierre Corneille: L'homme et son oeuvre* (Paris, 1938).
60. Carroll, *French Literary Fascism*, 106–7, 124; Luc Rasson, *Littérature et fascisme: les romans de Robert Brasillach* (Paris: 1991), 111–37.
61. Witt, *The Search for Modern Tragedy*, especially 160 and 233. On the part of literary fascism, Luc Rasson has illustrated that Brasillach refers to "the alliance of poetry and action" in Italian Fascism, as embodied by the connection between D'Annunzio and Mussolini; in Rasson, *Littérature et fascisme*, 115.
62. Witt, *The Search for Modern Tragedy*, 150–52.
63. Hurcombe, *France and the Spanish Civil War*, 88, 211. See also Peter Tame, *The Ideological Hero in the Novels of Robert Brasillach, Roger Vailland, and André Malraux* (New York, 1998), 88–115.
64. Robert Brasillach, "Introduction à l'esprit fasciste," *Je Suis Partout*, 1938, part I on 24 June, part II on 1 July, and part III on 8 July. See also Carroll, *French Literary Fascism*, 116.
65. Tucker, *The Fascist Ego*, 221.
66. The term refers to Karen Fiss's book, *Grand Illusion*.
67. Mazgaj, *Imagining Fascism*, 231–32.
68. Soucy, *French Fascism*, 43.
69. Tucker, *The Fascist Ego*, 202.
70. Robert Brasillach, "Pour un fascisme français," *Je Suis Partout*, 6 November 1942.
71. For the ministries, see Tucker, *The Fascist Ego*, 241. For the creation of French youth centers, see Brasillach's account of his visit to a Vichy youth camp: "Une journée dans un Centre de jeunesse," *Je Suis Partout*, 10 January 1942, in *Oeuvres Complètes*, vol. 12, 403. For the obsession with masculinity, see Joan Tumblety, "Revenge of the Fascist Knights: Masculine Identities in *Je Suis Partout*, 1940–1944," in *Modern & Contemporary France* 7(1) (1999): 11–20.

72. Robert Brasillach, "Les leçons d'un anniversaire," *Je Suis Partout*, 29 January 1943, in *Oeuvres Complètes*, vol. 12, 527. Cited in Mazgaj, *Imagining Fascism*, 251.

73. Robert Brasillach, "Sur la mort d'un ami allemande," *Je Suis Partout*, 18 September 1942, in *Oeuvres Complètes*, vol. 12, 479. Cited in Mazgaj *Imagining Fascism*, 240.

74. Ibid., 479.

75. Robert Brasillach, "Naissance d'un sentiment," *Révolution Nationale*, 4 September 1943. Cited in Griffiths, *Fascism*, 240.

76. Alan Riding, *And The Show Went On: Cultural Life in Nazi-Occupied Paris* (New York, 2010), 247. At the time, imagining France and Germany as a couple was a common way of understanding the special relationship between the countries. The long-standing French–German antagonism had fed the belief that France and Germany could make a happy couple, as opposites attract.

77. Kaplan, *The Collaborator*, xii.

78. Robert Brasillach, "Lettre à quelques jeunes gens," *Révolution nationale*, 19 February 1944.

79. David Charles Lewis, *European Unity and the Discourse of Collaboration: France and Francophone Belgium: 1938–1945*, PhD dissertation, University of Toronto (1996), 162, 200.

80. See, for example, Robert Brasillach, "Pour un fascisme français," *Je Suis Partout*, 6 November 1942, in *Oeuvres Complètes*, vol. 12, 499–502.

81. Bernard Bruneteau, *L'Europe nouvelle de Hitler: Une illusion des intellectuels de la France de Vichy* (Monaco, 2003).

82. Robert Brasillach, "Les crimes sont signés," *Je Suis Partout*, 13 September 1941, in *Oeuvres Complètes*, vol. 12, 376–77. In a different article, "Les leçons d'un anniversaire" of 29 January 1943, Brasillach points out that Shakespeare was "perfectly English," like Goethe was "perfectly German" and Corneille who was "perfectly French," in *Oeuvres Complètes*, vol. 12, 526.

83. Brasillach, "De la cité de Goethe." This article is reproduced in *Journal d'un homme occupé*, *Oeuvres Complètes*, vol. VI, 481.

84. Benjamin George Martin, "European Literature in the Nazi New Order: The Cultural Politics of the European Writers Union, 1941–43," *Journal of Contemporary History* 48(3) (2013): 486–508.

85. Lewis, *European Unity*, 125.

86. Tucker, *The Fascist Ego*, 254.

87. See, for example, Robert Brasillach, "Pas de pitié pour les assassins de la patrie," *Je Suis Partout*, 25 October 1941, in *Oeuvres Complètes*, vol. 12, 385–87.

88. Robert Brasillach, "Les Français devant les Juifs," *Je Suis Partout*, 17 February 1939 (special issue on "Les Juifs et la France"). See also Sandrine Sanos, *The Aesthetics of Hate: Far-Right Intellectuals, Antisemitism, and Gender in 1930s France* (Stanford, CA, 2013), 235.

89. Robert Brasillach, "La République est crevée, qu'on le veuille ou non," *Je Suis Partout*, 16 June 1941, in *Oeuvres Complètes*, vol. 12, 346.

90. Robert Brasillach, "La Question Juive," *Je Suis Partout*, 15 April 1938, special issue on "Les Juifs."
91. Brasillach only wanted to make an exception for a few individuals who had special importance for France, like the philosopher Henri Bergson. See also Tucker, *The Fascist Ego*, 167.
92. Kaplan, *The Collaborator*, 36.
93. Robert Brasillach, "Les sept Internationales contre la patrie," *Je Suis Partout*, 25 September 1942, in *Oeuvres Complètes*, vol. 12, 481.
94. Tucker, *The Fascist Ego*, 254.
95. Mazgaj, *Imagining Fascism*, 252–53.

Bibliography

Bauerkämper, Arnd. "Transnational Fascism: Cross-Border Relations between Regimes and Movements in Europe 1922–1939." *East Central Europe* 37 (2010): 214–46.
Betz, Albrecht, and Stefan Martens. *Les intellectuels et l'occupation 1940–1944. Collaborer, partir, résister*. Paris, 2004.
Brasillach, Robert, and Henri Massis. *Les Cadets de l'Alcazar*. Paris, 1936.
Brasillach, Robert. *Oeuvres Complètes de Robert Brasillach*. Edited and annotated by Maurice Bardèche. 12 vols. Paris, 1963–1966.
———. "Visite à Léon Degrelle." *Je Suis Partout*, 20 June 1936.
———. "Cent heures chez Hitler." *La Revue Universelle* 71, 1 October 1937.
———. "Introduction à l'esprit fasciste I, II, III." *Je Suis Partout*, 24 June, 1 July, and 8 July 1938.
———. "Les Français devant les Juifs." *Je Suis Partout*, 17 February 1938.
———. "La Question Juive." *Je Suis Partout*, 15 April 1939.
Bruneteau, Bernard. *L'Europe nouvelle de Hitler. Une illusion des intellectuels de la France de Vichy*. Monaco, 2003.
Carroll, David. *French Literary Fascism: Nationalism, Anti-Semitism and the Ideology of Culture*. Princeton, NJ, 1995.
Degrelle, Léon. "Qu'est-ce que Rex. Lettre aux Français?", *Je Suis Partout*, 24 October 1936.
Dioudonnat, Pierre-Marie. *Je Suis Partout 1930–1944*. Paris, 1973.
Fiss, Karen. *Grand Illusion: The Third Reich, the Paris Exposition and the Cultural Seduction of France*. Chicago, 2009.
Fraixe, Catherine, Lucia Piccioni, and Christophe Poupault, eds. *Vers une Europe latine. Acteurs et enjeux des échanges culturels entre la France et l'Italie*. Brussels, Bern, and Vienna, 2014.
Griffin, Roger. "Europe for the Europeans: Fascist Myths of the new European Order, 1922–1992." In *A Fascist Century. Essays by Roger Griffin*, ed. Matthew Feldman, 132–80. Houndmills and New York, 2008.
———. "Staging the Nation's Rebirth: The Politics and Aesthetics of Performance in the Context of Fascist Studies." In *Fascism and Theatre: Comparative Studies on the Aesthetics and Politics of Performance in Europe, 1925–1945*, ed. Günter Berghaus, 11–30. Oxford, 1996.

Griffiths, Richard. *Fascism*. London and New York, 2005.

Hurcombe, Martin. *France and the Spanish Civil War: Cultural Representations of The War Next Door, 1936–1945*. Farnham and Burlington, VT, 2011.

Jenkins, Brian. *France in the Era of Fascism: Essays on the Authoritarian Right*. New York and Oxford, 2007.

Kaplan, Alice. *The Collaborator: The Trial and Execution of Robert Brasillach*. English trans. Chicago, 2000.

Lewis, David Charles. *European Unity and the Discourse of Collaboration: France and Francophone Belgium, 1938–1945*. PhD dissertation. University of Toronto, 1996.

Martin, Benjamin George. "European Literature in the Nazi New Order: The Cultural Politics of the European Writers Union, 1941–43." *Journal of Contemporary History* 48(3) (2013): 486–508.

Mazgaj, Paul. *Imagining Fascism: The Cultural Politics of the French Young Right, 1930–1945*. Newark, 2007.

Nolan, Michael. *The Inverted Mirror: Mythologizing the Enemy in France and Germany, 1898–1914*. Oxford, 2005.

Rasson, Luc. *Littérature et fascisme: les romans de Robert Brasillach*. Paris, 1991.

Rensen, Marleen. *Lijden aan de tijd: Franse intellectuelen in het interbellum*. Soesterberg, 2009.

Riding, Alan. *And The Show Went On: Cultural Life in Nazi-Occupied Paris*. New York, 2010.

Sapiro, Gisèle. *The French Writers' War 1940–1953*. English trans. Durham, NC and London, 2014.

Sanos, Sandrine. *The Aesthetics of Hate: Far-Right Intellectuals, Antisemitism, and Gender in 1930s France*. Stanford, CA, 2013.

Schue, Paul. "Remember the Alcazar! The Creation of Nationalist Myths in the Spanish Civil War: The Writings of Robert Brasillach." *National Identities* 10, no. 2 (June 2008): 131–47.

Soucy, Robert. *French Fascism: The Second Wave, 1933–1939*. New Haven, CT and London, 1995.

Sternhell, Zeev. *Neither Left nor Right: Fascist Ideology in France*. English trans. Princeton, NJ, 1996.

Tame, Peter. *The Ideological Hero in the Novels of Robert Brasillach, Roger Vailland, and André Malraux*. New York and Paris, 1998.

Tucker, William. *The Fascist Ego: A Political Biography of Robert Brasillach*. Berkeley and London, 1975.

Tumblety, Joan. "Revenge of the Fascist Knights: Masculine Identities in *Je Suis Partout*, 1940–1944." *Modern & Contemporary France* 7(1) (1999): 11–20.

Volovici, Leon. *Nationalist Ideology and Antisemitism: The Case of Romanian Intellectuals in the 1930s*. Oxford, 1991.

Witt, Mary Ann Frese. *The Search for Modern Tragedy: Aesthetic Fascism in France*. Ithaca, NY and London, 2001.

ᴏ 8

Nᴀᴛɪᴠᴇ Fᴀsᴄɪsᴛs, Tʀᴀɴsɴᴀᴛɪᴏɴᴀʟ Aɴᴛɪ-Sᴇᴍɪᴛᴇs
The International Activity of Legionary Leader Ion I. Moța

Raul Cârstocea

Introduction

Studies of fascism have interpreted it as either limited to the specific case of the Fascist regime in Italy or to the two established regimes in Italy and Germany, arguing that "international fascism is unthinkable, a contradiction in terms,"[1] or, alternatively, as a "global" or "universal" phenomenon.[2] Positioning themselves between these two opposing poles, recent studies have increasingly emphasized the transnational or international character of fascism.[3] As the introduction to this volume points out, such an attempt transcends (while being inclusive of) both comparative analyses and studies that focus on the attempts of both the Italian and the German regimes to "export" their respective models, as well as the tensions ensuing due to the competition among them. Furthermore, such an approach also encompasses the diverse and complex examples of interactions and entanglements between fascist movements and regimes, revealing an international dimension to the phenomenon that could also prove relevant for the analysis of contemporary connections between far right groups, organizations, and parties.

The conceptualization of fascism as a transnational political movement is also part and parcel of the established "new consensus" in fascist studies, geared towards "taking fascist self-descriptions and self-representations more seriously than previously."[4] Along these lines, taking into account not only the pragmatic self-interest on behalf of the two established regimes to promote the influence of Italian Fascism and German National Socialism in Europe, but also the ideological affinities between fascist organizations that led some of these to look for guidance or even sponsorship from Italy or Germany (or both), as well as for contacts with other non-state movements, is also helpful for emphasizing the shared features, or indeed the common core that the various attempts at defining fascism as an international phenomenon have been striving to identify.[5] Viewed from this perspective, the self-identified similarities between what legionary commander Ion I. Moța, on whose international activity this chapter focuses, identified as "movements of national regeneration"[6] seem to confirm the importance of the palingenetic element in fascist ideology, which is central to Roger Griffin's definition of the phenomenon, as well as the revolutionary character of fascism, central to the "new consensus."[7]

Outside of the thoroughly researched cases of Fascist Italy and Nazi Germany, cases of what had all too often been identified as "minor" or "peripheral" fascist movements—while being neither, as with the case of the legionary movement in interwar Romania—might shed light on fascism's transnational character, and on the tension between the international links that such movements sought and the specificities related to their ultranationalist character, which eventually prevented the development of enduring connections and cooperation between them. Exploring the diversity and entanglements of the relationships between the Legion of the Archangel Michael, Romania's interwar fascist movement (also known as the Iron Guard after 1930), and similar organizations in Europe, as well as with the regimes in Italy and Germany, would far exceed the scope of this single chapter, which will focus instead on one of the prominent leaders of the legionary movement and his personal involvement in some of the transnational connections that the organization established. The case is that of Ion I. Moța, the faithful lieutenant of Corneliu Zelea Codreanu (founder and undisputed leader of the movement), whose career was marked by international experiences, until his death fighting in the Spanish Civil War in January 1937. Characterized by unsympathetic contemporary observers of the movement as "certainly the most intelligent among the leaders of the Iron Guard,"[8] and by the legionary author of a short biography as "the first and most perfect of the Captain's legionaries,"[9] Moța was one of the most influential ideologists of the movement, second only to Codreanu himself.[10] He was also the Romanian delegate at the fascist congress in Montreux in December 1934, as well as the correspondent on behalf of the Legion with the Welt-Dienst (World Service), the international anti-Semitic news agency.

Focusing on Ion I. Moța's international activity, I argue that members of the legionary movement were interested in transnational cooperation along the lines of combating what they perceived as common enemies

(Jews and communists, where the latter were consistently subsumed to the former), while being simultaneously keen on affirming their native character and their distinction from any purported Italian or German influence. As mentioned above, the latter feature is one that eventually accounted for the frequent breakdown of collaboration between fascist movements and regimes, and prevented the development of any stable structures for formal cooperation. The chapter will make this argument by focusing primarily on the views and statements of Moța, both published in the press articles he authored and as expressed in his correspondence and the statements he made at the Montreux conference. As such, it is important to note that this short chapter by no means attempts to provide a comprehensive analysis of the transnational connections involving the legionary movement, not dealing for example with the extent to which the movement, and especially its leader, Codreanu, represented potential models for other fascist organizations abroad.[11] Instead, this paper purposely limits itself to an exploration of the legionaries' own conceptualizations of their perceived need for transnational cooperation, as well as the limits they themselves saw to this project, viewed through the lens of Ion I. Moța's international activity.

Early Beginnings: Moța and Codreanu before the Establishment of the "Legion"

The "Legion of the Archangel Michael" was established on 24 June 1927 by a group of five students, who would later call themselves "The Knights of the Annunciation." The trope of the Annunciation, frequently employed by the movement in its rhetoric, departed however from its Christian connotation related to the birth of Jesus, and became associated with the heralding of the Legion's own notion of Romania's revolutionary rebirth, a distinctly fascist metaphor that was central to the ideology of the movement.[12] As one of the initial founders of the movement and Codreanu's loyal second-in-command until his death in 1937, Moța was one of the self-proclaimed "Knights," and the religious language that thoroughly permeated the movement's rhetoric was to a significant extent indebted to the contribution of one who was famed within the Legion for his piety.[13]

Born on 5 July 1902 in Orăștie, a town in Transylvania that was at the time part of the Austro-Hungarian Empire, Moța grew up in a very religious and nationalist family.[14] His father, Ioan Moța, was an Orthodox priest, as were both his grandfathers.[15] In the year he was born, his father began editing the newspaper *Libertatea* (Freedom), a nationalist weekly that militated for the rights of the Romanians in Transylvania.[16] A mainstream nationalist newspaper that would, however, take a radical turn in the 1930s and openly support the legionary movement,[17] *Libertatea* was among the most popular Romanian-language newspapers in Transylvania before the war, making Father Ioan Moța into a well-known personality of the national movement.[18] During World War I, Ion I. Moța moved first to Bucharest and then Iași, following his father who had traveled to the Old Kingdom of Romania in 1914 to promote the country's entering the war on the side of the Triple Entente and against the Central Powers, an activity that led to his condemnation to death by the Austro-Hungarian Empire.[19] Aged fourteen at the time of Romania's entry into the war, Moța was too young for military service and consequently volunteered in agricultural work to supply the soldiers at the front.[20] After the war, he obtained his baccalaureate from the prestigious Gheorghe Lazăr high school in Bucharest, leaving in 1920 for the Sorbonne, to study law.[21] The fact he was denied a state scholarship, despite his good results in the examinations, represented a profound disillusionment for him, and a personal factor that contributed to his lifelong anti-Semitism, as he believed that Jewish students benefited from preferential treatment from the Romanian state.[22]

Following his return from Paris, Moța enrolled as a law student at the University of Cluj in 1921, and was at the forefront of the anti-Semitic student protests that erupted in December 1922 on all university campuses in the country.[23] It was at this time that he met Corneliu Zelea Codreanu, himself a founding leader of the anti-Semitic "Association of Christian Students" at the University of Iași, and already notorious for his violent attacks on Jewish students.[24] Codreanu had just returned from Germany, where he had been attending courses at the University of Berlin since autumn, but where he had left primarily "to study the organization of the anti-Semitic action undertaken by the German student body."[25] The two became close friends and, later, when Moța married Codreanu's sister Iridenta in August 1927, brothers-in-law.[26] Their personal relation was accompanied by close political cooperation. Following the establishment on 4 March 1923 of the League of National-Christian Defense (Liga Apărării Național-Creștine, LANC), the first anti-Semitic political organization in post–World War I Romania, led by the notorious anti-Semite Alexandru C. Cuza, Codreanu became the leader of its youth section at the national level.[27] In the course of the same year, Moța, who had himself been recently elected president of the Petru Maior student center in Cluj, founded Romanian Action (Acțiunea

Românească, AR), an organization whose very name suggests the strong influence of Action Française on the future legionary leader.[28] Together with a number of other small organizations established as imitations of radical right or fascist movements abroad (like the Romanian National Fascia), Acţiunea Românească later joined LANC, mostly due to the popularity of Codreanu.[29]

This popularity was the direct result of an escalation of Codreanu's violence, whose emphasis on "direct action" and "military discipline" had led to divergences with his mentor, Cuza, ever since LANC's establishment.[30] Moţa was from the onset an adept of Codreanu's conception of the path that the nationalist movement should follow. After translating into Romanian the infamous "Protocols of the Elders of Zion," published at his father's printing house *Libertatea* in the summer of 1923,[31] he became part of a student plot envisaged by Codreanu to assassinate six representatives of "Jewish power" (prominent rabbis, bankers, and journalists) and six Romanian government ministers they held responsible for the voting of the 1923 Constitution,[32] which had finally granted citizenship and equal civil and political rights to Jews, making Romania the last country in Europe to emancipate its Jewish population. Although the plan was unrealistic (the six students had only one revolver), the subsequent trial brought the students to fame. An intense propaganda campaign of LANC turned public opinion in their favor and eventually ensured their acquittal. While in prison, Moţa shot and severely wounded Aurel Vernichescu, the student who had revealed the plot to the police, yet he was also acquitted for his attempted murder.[33]

The beginnings of the legionary movement can be traced back to this first prison experience of its future founders. According to Codreanu's memoirs, it was in the prison of Văcăreşti that he came up with the plans for a new youth organization, functioning within LANC structures, but as a movement with different goals, "of education and combat."[34] Meant to be called "The Archangel Michael," this organization was to have three sections: students, rural youth, and high school pupils.[35] Of the three, only the last (known as "Brotherhoods of the Cross") materialized before 1927, and Moţa was appointed its leader.[36] The activity of the "Brotherhoods" was, however, intermittent prior to 1927, as its leaders were again imprisoned following Codreanu's assassination of police prefect Constantin Manciu on 25 October 1924, and then left for Grenoble to pursue their doctoral studies following Codreanu's acquittal in May 1925.[37]

Anti-Semitism as the impetus for transnational cooperation of Ion I. Moța and the "Legion of the Archangel Michael"

In the summer of 1925, Moța accompanied two of the senior figures of LANC, professors A.C. Cuza and Corneliu Șumuleanu, to the International Anti-Semitic Congress held in Budapest.[38] There, he acted as the representative of Romanian youth, and even took on the task of editing "the statutes of the world anti-Semitic youth section."[39] It was at this point that Moța became directly involved in efforts at international cooperation between different nationalist, anti-Semitic movements, or, as his biographer puts it, "the first time when [he] put forth, at a global congress, the idea of the brotherhood of all Christian nations against the Jewish threat."[40] He would later recall the very good reception that Romanian delegates enjoyed at the congress, which is quite remarkable coming from a Transylvanian who was the son of a nationalist condemned to death during the war by the Austro-Hungarian Empire and who always remained suspicious of Hungary and its revisionist claims.[41] As such, this aspect demonstrates his commitment to establishing transnational links with similar organizations abroad, driven primarily by his anti-Semitism. According to Armin Heinen, this is also where he met Georg de Poterre, the notorious Banat-born anti-Semite who would later be Moța's interlocutor in his correspondence with the *Welt-Dienst*.[42]

Moța's participation at this congress was prompted by his notion of the need for transnational cooperation against an alleged "Jewish threat" or "conspiracy," to which his deep-seated anticommunism was subsumed. This was the expression of a worldview that is consistently expressed in his writings, from the early articles written in his student days up to the last letters from the Spanish front, which were subsequently published, at the explicit request of the author, in his father's newspaper, *Libertatea*.[43] In line with his profound religiosity, Moța viewed this as a "Jewish criminal plan of world domination,"[44] aimed at the destruction of Christianity and the Christian Church, and as an international problem that had manifested itself from the period before the French Revolution and had culminated with the triumph of atheistic communism in Russia.[45] Consequently, his envisaged "solution" to the problem also took on an international dimension, consisting in the aforementioned cooperation of "Christian nations" in combating this threat. This orientation would increasingly become apparent after the establishment of the Legion, when emphases on the movement's specificity and distinctness from other fascist movements were doubled by appeals to international collaboration, primarily aimed at establishing a common anti-Semitic platform.

In turn, this feature was not a novelty of the legionary movement (despite the fact that its anti-Semitism was far more radical than the prewar varieties), but was instead coherent with the tradition of nineteenth-century Romanian anti-Semitism. Ever since the crystallization of modern anti-Semitism in Romania during the late 1870s, anti-Semitic writers and politicians had borrowed heavily from notions developed elsewhere—in Austria-Hungary, France, and Germany.[46] Moreover, prewar Romanian anti-Semites, while deploring the international pressure to emancipate the country's Jews, had themselves sought to establish links with organizations or politicians that held similar views abroad. The country had hosted an international anti-Semitic congress in 1886, and the Alliance Anti-semitique Universelle, meant to be a response to the Alliance Israelite Universelle (which had militated for the emancipation of the Jews in Romania at the Congress of Berlin), was established by A.C. Cuza in Bucharest in 1895.[47]

Indeed, at least in the beginning, following its establishment as a result of a split within LANC, the Legion announced its continuity with Cuza's anti-Semitism.[48] The difference lay with the pronounced fascist character of the movement, visible from its inception and in sharp contrast with LANC, which was meant to function within the limits of parliamentary politics, as an anti-Semitic political party.[49] Also from the outset, and different from Codreanu's earlier prison plans, the movement was organized into four sections: (1) of youth (with the subsection "Brotherhoods of the Cross"); (2) of protection (by mature nationalists supporting the legionary youth); (3) of help (as clarified in a later article, by Romanian women); and (4) international.[50] The purposes of the international section, as outlined in the statutes published in *Pământul Strămoşesc* (Ancestral Land), the first legionary publication, were the following:

> (a) to bring together all the Romanians outside the borders of the country; (b) to preach the truth about the invasion of the Romanians' ancestral land by the Jews, through a magazine that will be printed in Paris, entitled *L'Archange Michel*; (c) to collect all the calumnies uttered by Jews about the Romanians [abroad] and to publish them in the country; (d) to establish connections with all similar organizations in the world, with the purpose of the resolution of the Jewish problem.[51]

As it can be clearly inferred from the presentation above, anti-Semitism was central to the purpose of the international section of the Legion. This entailed both monitoring and reporting on the articles issued in the foreign press dealing with the Jewish minority in Romania and with the growing anti-Semitism in the country, and the "export" of Romanian anti-Semitism abroad through a French-language publication (which in the end was never issued), as well as the attempt to forge transnational links with other anti-Semitic organizations. Moreover, the permanent "foreign affairs" section in *Pământul Strămoşesc*, appearing from the fifth issue of the newspaper onward, was suggestively entitled "Anti-Semitic World News."[52] And while the activity of the "international section" of a movement that, in the beginning at least, could barely raise the funds needed for its domestic functioning was limited to sporadic contacts between legionary sympathizers who found themselves in other countries and local fascists, radical nationalists, and anti-Semites, it was in the last of its four "purposes" that the organization (and Moţa in particular) eventually invested the most. As mentioned above, this was in line with his dualist understanding of the modern world, and Europe in particular, as the site of a Manichaean conflict between the "Jewish spirit" and Christianity. As Philip Morgan notes, it was indeed the movement's "claim to be an integral part of a more general life-and-death struggle between 'civilizations,' or between different versions of European civilization" that rendered the Legion "one of the most 'international' and 'internationalist' of European fascist movements."[53]

Moţa clearly expressed this view in an article included in the issue of *Pământul Strămoşesc* subsequent to the one which had announced the international section of the Legion. In a "response" he gave to Lord Rothermere's editorial "Hungary's Place in the Sun," published in the *Daily Mail* on 21 June 1927, which argued for the revision of the Treaty of Trianon in favor of Hungary, Moţa integrated Rothermere's advocacy with his lifelong obsession, the international Jewish conspiracy, and dubbed Rothermere—the sympathizer of both Italian Fascism and German National Socialism—a "Jew."[54] In his interpretation of Hungarian revisionism, this was "without a doubt" nothing but "the counter-strike decreed by the supreme Zionist leadership … to try *to spoil the brotherhood of Christian peoples that was foreshadowing on the horizon.*"[55] By this "brotherhood," Moţa meant the "powerful anti-Semitic movements and even attempts at international agreements for the resolution of the Jewish problem" that had recently emerged all over Central and Eastern Europe (naming Romania, Poland, and Hungary as examples, and making a reference to the anti-Semitic congress he had attended in Budapest in 1925) and that were "extremely dangerous for the Jews."[56] His argument concluded with a statement that, while always prepared to defend themselves against Hungarian aggression, Romanian nationalists, "as good Christians," did not wish for such a conflict; instead, Moţa summed up, their desire was for "a brotherhood with all nations against the Jews, and we will work towards accomplishing it."[57]

This chapter captures some of the most important features of the Legion's "internationalist" impetus, as well as touching upon some of the specificities of the movement that prevented it from identifying with any of the established fascist regimes, in Italy and later in Germany. The context for the legionaries' view of the need for cooperation among radical nationalist organizations was that of the aforementioned all-encompassing conflict between the Christian world and what they perceived as a coordinated international action of the Jews. This displacement of all existing or potential conflicts and antagonisms, either internal or external to Romania, unto the presumed agency of a "leadership" of a united "world Jewry" was the defining element that conferred legionary anti-Semitism its specific, murderous radicalism and that also prompted the movement, more than anything else, to seek like-minded allies abroad.[58] On the other hand, it is important to note that this worldview is consistently framed as a struggle involving Christianity as a religion and the Christian nations, rather than having race or geopolitics at its core.[59]

Following an initial period of stagnation between 1927 and 1930, when the Legion was no match for the more established and better-funded LANC, the movement witnessed a significant increase in popularity in the early 1930s, in the context of the social, economic, and political crises affecting Romania.[60] By this time, the initial interest of the movement in Italian Fascism was doubled by increasing attention to developments in Germany. In December 1928, Pământul Strămoşesc reported on the "great anti-Semitic movements in Germany and Poland," as well as in Vienna and Prague, and bestowed praise on the "German leader of the powerful anti-Semitic army."[61] In 1929, Codreanu wrote to a Romanian living in Munich in an attempt to contact Hermann Esser, editor of Völkischer Beobachter, and was apparently contemplating a visit to Germany to meet members of the National Socialist German Workers' Party (Nationalsozialistische Deutsche Arbeiterpartei, NSDAP). There was, however, no interest on the German part in the insignificant legionary movement, and Codreanu's visit did not take place; as Armin Heinen notes, referring to the severe shortage of funds that the movement faced at this time, "the Legion had indeed more stringent problems than a strengthening of its links with parties abroad."[62]

Between Fascist Italy and Nazi Germany: The Legionary Movement in the 1930s

By the time of Hitler's coming to power in 1933, the situation had changed significantly. In the extremely volatile political situation in Romania, where elections were held every year between 1931 and 1933, the Legion had scored its first electoral successes, first sending Codreanu and his father to parliament in two by-elections and then obtaining five seats in the general elections of July 1932.[63] Police reports at this time began to take the movement much more seriously than previously, and directly identified it as a fascist organization, comparing its rhetoric and propaganda style to those employed by Mussolini and Hitler.[64] The adherence of a group of young intellectuals to the movement had given it a "voice" in the pages of three major Bucharest-based newspapers (the dailies *Cuvântul* and *Calendarul*, and the bi-weekly *Axa*), conferring the movement the intellectual prestige it had hitherto lacked. These intellectuals were quick to identify the Legion as "doubtlessly the Romanian 'representative' of Fascism and National Socialism."[65]

As the Legion declared its support for German National Socialism and celebrated its victory, the accusations that the movement had close connections with Hitler and was even subsidized by Germany multiplied. However, as Armin Heinen convincingly showed, this was not the case, and the legionary movement was in fact the least preferred Romanian partner for the NSDAP at this time.[66] The concerns of the Nazis lay first and foremost with the German minority in Romania, who they believed would be better served by Cuza's party, viewed as "entirely philo-German," than by the Legion, which they saw as inclining more toward Fascist Italy than Germany, and as more intransigent toward all national minorities in Romania.[67] A report of the leadership of German youth, cited by Heinen, identified the legionary movement as the Romanian party that comes closest to fascism, while concluding that "the very probable success of Codreanu is not at all desirable in view of Germany's interest."[68]

Moța's articles at this time seem to indicate that the Nazi assessment of the Legion's position was not off the mark, at least with respect to the movement's ultranationalism and its attitude toward minorities. In response to the "infamous" and "ridiculous" accusations that the movement was subsidized by Hitler in an attempt to undermine Romania, Moța wrote that in the face of such a *"Hitlerist* threat to our borders, nothing would be able to face it with more determination, with more élan and crushing force, than a legionary Romania, fortified in its ethnic constitution."[69] Accusing in turn the Liberal Party of having sacrificed Romania's interests to foreign ones (French, or "pan-European"), he clarified that the Legion's "applauding of Chancellor Hitler for the destruction of Marxism and the libertarian philosophy of the French Revolution" would never entail any compromise "of Romanian realities for the sake of some *Hitlerist* international."[70] In a later article, addressing the propagation of National Socialism among ethnic Germans in Romania, Moţa was very clear on his position toward national minorities in the country, whose loyalty, he argued, had to rest primarily with their host Romanian state. As such, their allegiance to a foreign leader in their kin state was inconceivable, and would transform them into traitors and enemies of the Romanian nation.[71] Moţa praised once again "the Führer so appreciated and esteemed by us all, up to the limit of Romanian interests," and foresaw "an accentuation of the political rapprochement of Romania and Germany in the future—and the future global resolution of the Jewish problem, as well as the fascist reconstruction of States will engender a close collaboration and brotherhood of all fascist States." However, he concluded that "without having the right to forbid Saxons a spiritual participation, limited and conditioned, to the German rebirth, yet we cannot accept a full-fledged *Hitlerism* of Saxons and Germans in Romania."[72] These "limits and conditions" were explicitly those of Romania's interests and of the unconditional allegiance required of all its citizens to them, regardless of nationality. Thus, while drawing attention to the element of "rebirth" in National Socialism and the anticipation of a common fascist front that would address "the Jewish problem" globally, the limit of the legionary impetus toward cooperation with other fascist movements and regimes remained with the native character of the movement and its ultranationalism.

The second consideration of the aforementioned German report, that the Legion was closer to Italian Fascism, is harder to assess. In the context of the tensions between Germany and Italy in 1933–35 and of the Austrian crisis, the openings of the newly established Action Committees for the Universality of Rome (Comitati d'Azione per l'Universalità di Roma, CAUR) toward the legionary movement and the visit of Eugenio Coselschi to one of the Legion's voluntary work camps were probably the reasons prompting this assessment.[73] By this time, Mussolini had abandoned his earlier views that fascism was not "merchandise for export," and was much more interested in transferring the model, as long as this would occur under Italian leadership.[74] However, these contacts with the legionary movement did not develop beyond the level of sporadic mutual visits, and, from the Italian side, the centrality of anti-Semitism in legionary ideology was a disturbing element.[75] As legionaries were keenly following the situation in Austria, the movement's person in charge of foreign affairs, Mihail Polihroniade, extensively discussed its importance for Italo-German relations, noting after the establishment of the Austrian dictatorship that, while it represented a new blow for democracy and a further success for Italian Fascism, about which the legionaries were understandably enthusiastic, the regime in Austria was not a proper fascist one. This was due to the fact that it lacked popular support, being instead an "*anti-national* dictatorship, unnatural …, a police state" and, "what is worse," "a vassal of Rome."[76] These considerations show once again the interest, on the one hand, of the legionary movement in the "internationalization" of fascism, and, on the other, their contempt for any import, imitation, or adoption of the model as a result of outside pressures. Striving to accomplish their own national revolution that would transform the Romanian state into one of legionary making, legionaries were keen on establishing links with similar organizations abroad, while wary of falling under the influence of any of the two established regimes.

At the time when relations between Fascist Italy and Nazi Germany had reached an all-time low after the assassination of the Austrian chancellor Engelbert Dollfuß, Moța's participation in the Montreux Congress of December 1934, the first such gathering of European fascists, under Italian auspices, appears interesting, especially since the Legion had refused an earlier invitation to a congress organized by the *Welt-Dienst*, the anti-Semitic news agency sponsored by the Nazis, on 26 August.[77] It must be noted that the *Welt-Dienst* was not an official Nazi publication and that its founder's relationship with the regime was occasionally problematic and deteriorated toward the end of the 1930s. Eventually, the Foreign Affairs Bureau of the NSDAP took over the publication in 1939, removing its founder, Ulrich Fleischhauer, from his editorial position, and reissuing it in 1940 in a new format. The problematic relationship of the *Welt-Dienst* with the Nazi regime was due partly to the ambivalence of several prominent leaders of the NSDAP toward the publication and toward Fleischhauer himself, and partly to the conscious attempts by the latter to distance it from the "official" party line and conceal its support, in an attempt to make it appear more independent of the German state and thus more appealing to an international audience, particularly in the crisis years following the Nazi takeover. Nevertheless, evidence indicates that between 1933 and 1937, so at the time of Moța's correspondence with the *Welt-Dienst*, the news agency was financed by Goebbels' Ministry of Propaganda, albeit not openly.[78]

In his correspondence with Georg de Poterre, his interlocutor on behalf of the *Welt-Dienst*, Moța invoked the movement's "terrible poverty" as the reason for not attending the German congress, yet this was no longer the case in mid-1934, so his was primarily an excuse, all the more apparent since the *Welt-Dienst* had offered to cover all the costs for a legionary delegation.[79] The Legion would later also decline repeated invitations to other international anti-Semitic congresses (where, in addition to covering the costs, de Poterre even suggested they could "name their conditions" and set the date themselves) and to the seventh Nürnberg Nazi Party rally, in September 1935.[80] Thus, the Montreux congress was one of the extremely rare instances when a prominent legionary leader participated at an international fascist event as an official representative of the movement, rather than in a personal capacity. As such, Moța's stance at the congress, and his own reflections on his participation, expressed in the correspondence with de Poterre, appear particularly relevant for understanding his, and implicitly the legionary view of transnational cooperation between fascist movements and regimes.

Native Fascists, Transnational Anti-Semites

The congress organized by CAUR in Montreux, Switzerland, on 16–17 December 1934 brought together representatives from Austria, Belgium, Denmark, France, Ireland, Italy, Lithuania, the Netherlands, Norway, Portugal, Romania, Spain, and Switzerland.[81] Significantly for the state of Italo-German relations at this time and for the purposes of the congress, no representatives of the NSDAP were invited. This was in line with the mandate of the congress (and of CAUR generally, as its very name suggested) to export Italian Fascism as a revolutionary solution to the crises affecting Europe, adaptable to different national contexts yet firmly anchored in the idea of the corporatist state and the "universality of Rome."[82] In the context of the rivalry between Fascist Italy and Nazi Germany, at a time when Mussolini derided Hitler's racism, anti-Semitism had no place on the Italian agenda, all the more so as he personally had many Jewish collaborators and "the Fascist movement itself was disproportionately Jewish—that is, Jews made up a greater proportion of the party at all stages of its history than of the Italian population as a whole."[83]

This context was lost on Moța, who was surprised at the absence of German representatives and who, true to his own (and the Legion's) agenda, considered "the discussion of the Jewish problem … the essential work of this congress," having raised the issue himself.[84] In consequence, his statement had "split the congress and catapulted [him] in the position of faction chief."[85] One of the Belgian delegates, Paul Hoornaert, the Irish Eoin O'Duffy, the Portuguese Eça de Queiroz, the Greek George Mercouris, the Austrian Rinaldini, and the Italian delegation opposed his motion of adopting an "unequivocal" stance on the "Jewish issue," whereas the other Belgian representative, Somville, the Dutch Arnold Meijer, the Swiss Fonjallaz, and the Danish Clausen supported it.[86] Eventually, the statement adopted by the congress was more moderate and qualified than Moţa would have preferred; nevertheless, insofar as it represented a joint statement and resolution, and thus, in his view, a step toward "the establishment of a global anti-Jewish front," which was the common goal he shared with the *Welt-Dienst*, he interpreted it as a success.[87] Reproduced upon his return by the legionary secretariat and sent to all commanders of county chapters, it opened with the statement that "the Jewish question could not be resolved by a universal campaign of hatred against the Jews," continuing, however, with a denunciation of "some groups of Jews' ... nefarious influence on the moral and material interests" of their host countries, destructive "of the idea of Patria and of Christian civilization" and concluding with a "pledge to combat them."[88] In addition, Moţa had "demanded that at future reunions the Germans are no longer avoided, but invited."[89]

Moţa's stance at the Montreux congress confirms the primacy of anti-Semitism as the main impetus for transnational cooperation of the legionary movement. However, his correspondence with de Poterre also reveals his position on the crucial issue of racism, pointing toward the key element that differentiated legionary anti-Semitism from the Nazi one. As such, he tells his interlocutor that he avoided linking anti-Semitism to racism, leaving space for different, "spiritualist" interpretations of the Jewish issue "in the Franco-Italian manner" (one can recall Moţa's admiration for Action Française), adding that "a German–Italian understanding would be easier to accomplish by avoiding the presentation of the Jewish problem as explicable only through racial doctrine, and thus by asking to indissolubly link the anti-Jewish action to the racial one."[90] He continues his letter by explaining his own position on racism, one that deserves to be cited in full: "Myself, I admit, I am a racist, but with reservations: for example, I do not accept that religion is based on the specificity of the race; a specificity that it can have in its exterior forms, its ritual; but not in its content, which is not of human but divine essence, which we acquire through revelation and not through the genius of the race."[91] A lot has been made of Moţa's admission of racism, most recently in an article by Mircea Platon, which argues that his participation in the congress was meant to send "an international signal of the Legion's commitment to racism."[92] Most of Platon's conclusions—such as Moța's belief in the necessity of establishing an international anti-Semitic front, or his conviction that the solution to the "Jewish problem" could be formulated only in the context of fascist politics, wherein lay the Legion's main distinction from LANC[93]—are in agreement with the argument put forth in this chapter. However, his straightforward identification of an alleged commitment of the legionary movement to racism is very problematic and unwarranted by Moța's statement cited above, by his activity at the congress, and generally by his views as reflected in his publications, from his student days up until 1937.

To begin with, it is difficult to understand why Moța would choose to air his racism at a congress organized by CAUR, in the context of Italo-German rivalry, while refusing to attend explicitly anti-Semitic international reunions organized by the explicitly racist *Welt-Dienst*—all the more so since Cuza took part in the latter and would subsequently accuse Moța of participating in a "Masonic" event (the Montreux congress).[94] Then, if this was indeed his purpose, why would he avoid the topic of racism rather than address it directly? As such, and in line with a further statement in the same letter, once again on the topic of "our common [anti-Semitic] action" and which opens with the words "while not being a racist [*Mais tout en n'étant pas raciste*],"[95] it is more likely that Moța's "reservations," and primarily the religious one he mentions, were more important for him to convey to his interlocutor than his "reserved" "racism." Indeed, as previously assessed by Armin Heinen, the entire correspondence with the *Welt-Dienst* gives the impression that Moța—who "answered intermittently, with long pauses"—was "more likely infuriated by the requests of the other [de Poterre]"[96] rather than of his subscribing to the "New European Order" of Nazi making that Platon suggests.[97]

Instead, it is more likely that in the statement above Moța took the opportunity to reaffirm his belief in the primacy of religion, which is a constant in his writings and which was the main element that, in the self-identifications and self-descriptions provided by legionary leaders, which we resolved to take seriously, distinguished the movement from Italian Fascism and German National Socialism. In a statement made at his trial in 1938, Codreanu described Fascism's preoccupation with the state as the "coat," the exterior form; National Socialism's racism as the "blood" and the "body"; while "legionarism" was "located … in the soul of the individual and the nation, without neglecting either the idea of state or that of race; however, our essential point, the root, is placed here, in the soul"; in the view of the leader of the legionary movement, this accounted for "the superiority of the legionary idea over Fascism and National Socialism."[98] As such, Platon's argument that "Moța and other Iron Guardist leaders ... did not recognize any incompatibility between their own manifest Christianity and the German brand of anti-Semitism"[99] does not appear to be supported by the available evidence. Instead, it seems more reasonable to conclude, as Armin Heinen does, that "the National Socialist racial theory was irrelevant for the legionaries. Their nationalism was not directed against the Christian heritage, but merged with the desire for a religious revival."[100]

"In Defense of the Holy Cross"—Ion I. Moța on the Spanish Front

The final chapter of Moța's life provides yet another example of his commitment to a transnational cooperation whose aim he perceived along the lines of his lifelong obsession: the "defense of Christianity" from an alleged "Judeo-Bolshevik threat."[101] Part of a small legionary delegation under the command of General Gheorghe Cantacuzino, Moța left for Spain on 25 November 1936. The mission of the legionary team was to be a purely symbolic gesture of support for the Spanish nationalists, presenting Colonel José Moscardó Ituarte, the defender of Alcazar, with the gift of a sword.[102] In light of the fact that at this time the movement was preparing to come to power and that all eight legionaries were among its most prominent leaders, Codreanu gave specific orders to the team that they were not to exceed the term of one month and should return by 1 January 1937, and that they should not engage in active combat and put their lives at risk.[103]

In an extremely rare act of defiance against a direct order from Codreanu, Moța resolved to stay on and enlist himself and the other legionaries (with the exception of General Cantacuzino, who was seventy-seven years old) in the Foreign Legion, a voluntary unit consisting mostly of Spanish nationalists but also including foreign volunteers who, in his own interpretation, had "come to fight in Spain for the defense of the Cross and the destruction of communism in the entire world."[104] In his letters from the Spanish front, published after his death in his father's newspaper *Libertatea*, Moța mentions meeting the Irish nationalists under the command of General Eoin O'Duffy, whom he knew from the Montreux congress, as well as the very good reception the legionaries had enjoyed from the Portuguese nationalists.[105] Among the Spanish organizations fighting on the nationalist side, he was most impressed with the Falange, whose headquarters he visited and which he identified as the one that "resembles the most our Legion in Romania."[106]

Moreover, and most importantly for the purposes of this chapter, in all his letters from Spain Moța also elaborates extensively on his reasons for choosing to fight in the Spanish Civil War, in an attempt to explain the paradox of a nationalist fighter committing to a cause that was in all appearances foreign to the interests of Romania. In one of his most synthetic such explanations, covering all aspects of his vision of transnational cooperation between fascist movements and regimes, he states:

> No power, no love, is above the Nation and cannot be fulfilled outside of the Nation—except for the power of Christ and the love for Him. When a devilish army rises to banish Christ from the world, when they attack the luminous face of the Savior with machine guns and bayonets, then all the people, of all nations, must come to the defense of the Cross! All the more so as those who attempt now to destroy Christianity in Spain will attack tomorrow the Christian and Romanian [sic!] order of all nations, thus also of our Romania. But if the love of Christ, the power of Christ, which is above all Nations, could bring us Romanians to fight for the Cross in the foreign land of Spain, together with the Spanish, the Germans and the Italians—this does not mean that the power of Christianity and the love of Christ remove us from our nation, alienate us from it. By defending Christianity, even on foreign soil, we defend a power that is the source of our nation's power, and by listening to the call of our love for the Cross, we obey, here in Spain, our love for our Romanian nation.[107]

The statement above, continued in a subsequent letter (the very last to be published) with a further explanation, that "here, we fight and we fall for the defense of *our* ancestral law, for the happiness of the Romanian nation, for its resurrection through the fight of the Legion and the new creation that the Captain brings,"[108] sums up synthetically Moța's views of nationalism, of its relationship with religion, and of the palingenetic element that was central to legionary ideology, as well as of the common cause that transcended national interests and subsumed them. Unmistakably, the latter could only be justified for Moța by Christianity (and not race, nor a new European geopolitical order), the only cause he viewed as superior to the national one, which, in turn, was entirely dependent on its Christian "source." It was according to his typically dualist understanding of the contemporary world as the site of a life and death struggle between Christianity and its mortal enemies—identified in the context of the Spanish Civil War alternatively as "the invasion of Satanic communism" and "the Jewish dream"[109]—that he saw a need for cooperation between the members of all (Christian) nations who shared similar views. And just as the legionary palingenesis was consistently expressed in the Christian language of "resurrection," this key aspect in legionary ideology was the specific factor that on the one hand allowed the movement to proclaim its native version of fascism as distinct from, and superior to the Italian and German models, and on the other hand led to the radical exclusion of the Jews (on religious rather than racial grounds) from the legionary dream of a "community of faith."

To conclude, by tracing the international activity of Ion I. Moța, legionary leader and lieutenant of Corneliu Zelea Codreanu, this chapter has shed light on his views of transnational connections between fascist movements and regimes. Due to his prominent position within the organization and his influence on its ideology, the latter can be considered as representative of the legionary perception of the need for international collaboration in combating what the movement perceived as common enemies. Identified by Moța and the Legion generally as "Jews" and "communism," where the latter was subsumed in the former in the virulently anti-Semitic legionary ideology, it was the international and internationalist character of these "enemies" that, in the legionaries' vision, called for transnational cooperation between the "movements of national regeneration" in Europe.[110] As such, as its title suggests, this chapter has argued that the main impetus for international collaboration of the legionary movement was provided by its anti-Semitism, whereas the limits to such cooperation lay with the native fascist character of the movement and its specificity, conferred by the importance placed on religion within its ideology. In the search of like-minded allies abroad, particular attention was consistently devoted to the palingenetic element in the ideology of such movements, as well as to their revolutionary character, aspects which, according to the "new consensus" in studies of fascism, allow distinguishing fascist movements and regimes from other radical right or conservative authoritarian organizations. Thus, the movement's distinctly fascist vision of both Romanian interests and international relations simultaneously led it to seek transnational links for combating the perceived enemies of a nationalist and Christian Europe, and to set itself apart, due to an ultranationalism doubled by religious fervor, from the other contemporary fascist movements and regimes.

Epilogue

On 13 January 1937, after less than two weeks of combat, Moţa and another legionary commander, Vasile Marin, were killed during a Republican attack near Majadahonda.[111] However, the transnational entanglements of Moţa's life were to continue even after his death, and would eventually prove fateful for the Legion. A grandiose funeral of its two "martyrs" organized by the movement in Bucharest on 13 February 1937 was attended by representatives of the German, Italian, Portuguese, and Spanish diplomatic missions to Romania, despite the fact that the event was not sanctioned by the Romanian state.[112] Even before the funeral itself, the train that crossed all of Europe to bring back the coffins of the two legionary leaders had been honored by members of the SA and the SS (including Hitler's personal guard), by Italian *squadristi*, and by members of the Falange.[113] The international support for an extremist, antiestablishment movement prompted a diplomatic crisis, and the unprecedented scale of the funeral, as well as the discipline displayed by the thousands of uniformed legionaries who had come from across Romania to attend it, spread fear in the government and deeply worried King Carol II.[114] As a result, the king acted decisively against the Legion after the establishment of his personal dictatorship in February 1938. The persecution of the movement, culminating with the assassination of Codreanu in November 1938 and of almost the entire first-rank legionary leadership in September 1939, put an end to the constant rise in popularity the Legion had experienced in the 1930s, and ensured that when it did eventually come to power, in September 1940, it was no longer the uncompromising native fascist movement that Moţa had represented, but one that was much more opportunistic and prone to foreign influences.

RAUL CÂRSTOCEA is Senior Research Associate at the European Centre for Minority Issues (ECMI), Flensburg, Germany. He studied History and Politics at University College London, Central European University, University of Bologna, and the American University in Bulgaria. He specializes in the history of anti-Semitism in Romania, and the Romanian interwar fascist movement, the "Legion of the Archangel Michael." Selected publications: "Breaking the Teeth of Time: Mythical Time and the 'Terror of History' in the Rhetoric of the Legionary Movement in Interwar Romania," *Journal of Modern European History* 13, 1 (2015): 79–97; "Anti-Semitism in Romania: Historical Legacies, Contemporary Challenges," *ECMI Working Paper* 81 (2014): 1–39.

Notes

1. Walter Laqueur, *Fascism: Past, Present, Future* (New York, 1996), 218. See Arnd Bauerkämper, "Transnational Fascism: Cross-Border Relations between Regimes and Movements in Europe, 1922–1939," *East Central Europe* no. 37 (2010): 216–17; and Roger Eatwell, "Towards a New Model of Generic Fascism," *Journal of Theoretical Politics* no. 4 (1992): 163–65 for further examples of authors supporting this view.

2. See Eatwell, "Towards a New Model," 170–72. For a criticism of Ernst Nolte's argument of fascism as a "metapolitical" phenomenon, which Eatwell does not discuss, see Roger Griffin, ed., *International Fascism: Theories, Causes and the New Consensus* (London, 1998), 47–49.

3. Bauerkämper, "Transnational Fascism"; Constantin Iordachi, "Fascism in Interwar East Central and Southeastern Europe: Toward a New Transnational Research Agenda," *East Central Europe* no. 37 (2010): 161–213.

4. Sven Reichardt, "Violence and Consensus in Fascism," *Fascism. Journal of Comparative Fascist Studies* 1, no. 1 (2012): 59.

5. See e.g. Roger Griffin, *The Nature of Fascism* (New York, 1991); Stanley Payne, *A History of Fascism, 1914–1945* (Madison, WI, 1995).

6. Ion I. Moța, *Corespondența cu "Serviciul Mondial" (1934–1936)* (Rome, 1954), 31.

7. For theoretical interpretations of fascism that emphasize its revolutionary character, see e.g. Griffin, *The Nature of Fascism*; Zeev Sternhell, Mario Sznajder, and Maia Asheri, *The Birth of Fascist Ideology: From Cultural Rebellion to Political Revolution* (Princeton, NJ, 1994); Payne, *History of Fascism*; George Mosse, *The Fascist Revolution: Toward a General Theory of Fascism* (New York, 1999).

8. Constantin Argetoianu, *Însemnări zilnice*, vol. 1 (Bucharest, 1998), 275.

9. Andrei Ionescu, "Viața și moartea vitejească a lui Ion I. Moța," in *Almanahul Cuvântul* (Bucharest, 1941), 130.

10. Arguably, Horia Sima, the leader of the movement after Codreanu's death in 1938, could be considered more important than Moța in terms of his later impact on legionary ideology. However, during the period under consideration in this chapter (until Moța's death in 1937), Sima was only a minor, regional leader who remained virtually unknown to the central leadership of the organization.

11. Samuel Goodfellow, "Fascism as a Transnational Movement: The Case of Alsace," *Contemporary European History* 22, no. 1 (2013): 96–99.

12. Ion Țurcan, "Tabere și șantiere," *Însemnări sociologice* 2, no. 9 (1936), 22.

13. Interview with Ștefan Iacobescu, carried out by Virginia Călin, 9 March 1994, *Arhiva de istorie orală a Societății Române de Radiodifuziune* (henceforth AIOSRR), Tape C67.

14. Ionescu, "Viața și moartea," 130.

15. Ibid.

16. Nicolae Roșu, *Orientări în veac* (Bucharest, 1937), 255–56.

17. "Libertatea—foaie verde," *Libertatea*, 12 April 1936.

18. Nicolae Teban, "Înmormântarea lui Moța și Marin," in *Ion Moța și Vasile Marin — 25 ani dela moarte* (Madrid, 1963), 218; Armin Heinen, *Legiunea "Arhanghelul Mihail": O contribuție la problema fascismului internațional* (Bucharest, 2006), 126.
19. Ionescu, "Viața și moartea," 131–32.
20. Ibid., 132.
21. Ibid.
22. Heinen, *Legiunea*, 126; Ion I. Moța, "Răspuns (La invitația d-lui Prof. G. Bogdan-Duică)," Pământul Strămoșesc, 1 January 1928.
23. Ionescu, "Viața și moartea," 132.
24. Corneliu Zelea Codreanu, *Pentru legionari* (Sibiu, 1936), 60–64; "Teroarea haimanalelor din Iași," *Aurora*, 21 May 1922.
25. *Consiliul Național pentru Studierea Arhivelor Securității* (henceforth CNSAS), *Fond Penal* (henceforth Fund P), File 13207, vol. 2, 319.
26. "Nunta lui Moța," *Pământul Strămoșesc*, 1 September 1927. The couple had two children (a daughter, Gabriela, and a son, Mihai), suggestively bearing the names of the two archangels, Michael and Gabriel.
27. Codreanu, *Pentru legionari*, 123.
28. Ionescu, "Viața și moartea," 134; Constantin Iordachi, *Charisma, Politics and Violence: The Legion of the "Archangel Michael" in Inter-war Romania* (Trondheim, 2004), 35–36.
29. *Arhivele Naționale Istorice Centrale* (henceforth ANIC), *Fond Direcția Generală a Poliției* (henceforth Fund DGP), File 121/1924–1926, 182–83.
30. Codreanu, *Pentru legionari*, 124.
31. *Protocoalele Înțelepților Sionului* (Orăștie, 1923).
32. CNSAS, Fund P, File 13207, vol. 2, 179–80; *Arhivele Naționale ale Republicii Moldova* (henceforth ANRM), *Fond Direcția Generală a Poliției* (henceforth Fund DGP), File 103/1933, 225–26.
33. CNSAS, Fund P, File 13207, vol. 3, 169; Francisco Veiga, *Istoria Gărzii de Fier 1919–1941: Mistica ultranaționalismului* (Bucharest, 1993), 76–77.
34. Codreanu, *Pentru legionari*, 179.
35. Gheorghe Istrate, *Frăția de cruce* (Madrid, 1952), 9.
36. Ibid., 7, 14.
37. Ibid., 14–21.
38. Ionescu, "Viața și moartea," 141.
39. Ibid.
40. Ibid.
41. Ion I. Moța, *Cranii de lemn* (Bucharest, 1940), 81.
42. Heinen, *Legiunea*, 304.
43. See e.g. Ion I. Moța, "Cauza noastră e justă în ordinea morală și servește progresul social," *Dacia Nouă*, 23 December 1922; idem, "Necesitatea naționalismului radical," *Dacia Nouă*, 20 January 1923; idem, "Ce ne dați în locul 'cântecelor care pier'?," *Cuvântul Studențesc*, 4 March 1924; idem, "Înțelesul plecării noastre în Spania," *Libertatea*, 6 December 1936; idem, "Prezent!," *Libertatea*, 1 July 1937.
44. Moța, "Necesitatea naționalismului radical."
45. Moța, "Ce ne dați"; Ion I. Moța, "Aufruf zur Treue!—Apel la fidelitate," *Pământul Strămoșesc*, 15 November 1928.

46. Raul Cârstocea, "Uneasy Twins? The Entangled Histories of Jewish Emancipation and Anti-Semitism in Romania and Hungary, 1866–1913," *Slovo* 21, no. 2 (2009): 74-75.
47. Iulia Onac, "The Brusturoasa Uprising," in *Sites of European Antisemitism in the Age of Mass Politics, 1880–1918*, ed. Robert Nemes and Daniel Unowsky (Waltham, MA, 2014), 88.
48. Corneliu Zelea Codreanu, Ion I. Moța, Ilie Gârneață, Corneliu Georgescu, and Radu Mironovici, "Legiunea Arhanghelul Mihail," *Pământul Strămoșesc*, 15 August 1927.
49. For a clear distinction between the legion and LANC, identifying the former's specificity in its "revolutionary legionary spirit" and directly associating it with the "movements" of Mussolini and Hitler, see Ion I. Moța, "Legiunea și LANC," *Axa*, 1 October 1933.
50. Codreanu et al., "Legiunea Arhanghelul Mihail"; Corneliu Zelea Codreanu, Ion I. Moța, Ilie Gârneață, Corneliu Georgescu, and Radu Mironovici, "Organizarea Legiunii Arhanghelul Mihail," *Pământul Strămoșesc*, 1 October 1927.
51. Codreanu et al., "Legiunea Arhanghelul Mihail."
52. "Vești antisemite din lume," *Pământul Strămoșesc*, 1 October 1927 and subsequent issues.
53. Philip Morgan, "Studying Fascism from the Particular to the General," *East Central Europe* 37, nos. 2–3 (2010): 336.
54. Ion I. Moța, "O vorbă ardelenească pentru 'lordul' Rothermere—'Ungaria mare' și planurile Jidănești," *Pământul Strămoșesc*, 1 September 1927. See also Eugen Weber, "Romania," in *The European Right*, ed. Hans Rogger and Eugen Weber (Berkeley, CA, 1966), 521. For Lord Rothermere's fascist sympathies, see Bauerkämper, "Transnational Fascism," 219.
55. Moța, "O vorbă ardelenească" (emphasis in the original). All emphases are in the original unless specified otherwise.
56. Ibid.
57. Ibid.
58. For a comprehensive overview of legionary anti-Semitism, see Raul Cârstocea, "The Role of Anti-Semitism in the Ideology of the 'Legion of the Archangel Michael,' 1927–1938," PhD dissertation (University College London, 2011).
59. For a short comment on the importance of religion for the understanding of legionary anti-Semitism, see Raul Cârstocea, "The Path to the Holocaust: Fascism and Antisemitism in Interwar Romania," *S:I.M.O.N. (Shoah: Intervention, Methods, Documentation)* 1 (2014), 1–11, available at http://simon.vwi.ac.at/index.php/working-papers/carstocea-raul.
60. See e.g. ANIC, *Fond Ministerul de Interne, Diverse* (henceforth Fund MI), File 9/1927, 319–20, 344. See also Horia Sima, *History of the Legionary Movement* (Liss, 1995), 62–68.
61. "Din străinătate," *Pământul Strămoșesc*, 15 December 1928.
62. Heinen, *Legiunea*, 132.
63. ANIC, *Fond Parlament* (henceforth Fund PR), File 2374/1932, vol. 2, 475, 481–84.

64. CNSAS, Fund P, File 11784, vol. 14, 80; vol. 2, 94; ANIC, Fund MI, File 4/1932, 560–61; ANRM, Fund DGP, File 107/1931, 1.
65. Mihail Polihroniade, "Rostul 'Gărzii de Fier,'" *Calendarul*, 18 July 1932.
66. Heinen, *Legiunea*, 224.
67. Ibid., 228–29.
68. Cited in Ibid., 229.
69. Ion I. Moța, "3-22-250 (Răspuns cifrat d-lui Titeanu)," *Axa*, 1 August 1933. The term "Hitlerism" was the most frequent one used in interwar Romania to refer to National Socialism; thus, when citing publications from the epoch, I maintain its original usage.
70. Ibid.
71. Ion I. Moța, "Hitlerismul germanilor din România," *Axa*, 15 October 1933.
72. Ibid.
73. Heinen, *Legiunea*, 223–24, 228.
74. Michael Ledeen, "Italian Fascism and Youth," *Journal of Contemporary History* 4, no. 3 (1969): 138–39.
75. Jerzy W. Borejsza, *Il fascismo e l'Europa orientale: dalla propaganda all'aggressione* (Rome, 1981), 133.
76. Mihail Polihroniade, "Dictatură în Austria," *Axa*, 19 September 1933.
77. Moța, *Corespondența cu "Serviciul Mondial,"* 13.
78. Eckart Schörle, "Internationale der Antisemiten: Ulrich Fleischhauer und der 'Welt-Dienst,'" *Werkstatt Geschichte* 51 (2009): 59–61, 67–69.
79. Moța, *Corespondența cu "Serviciul Mondial,"* 13.
80. Ibid., 26–27, 33.
81. Payne, *History of Fascism*, 229–30; Philip Morgan, *Fascism in Europe, 1919–1945* (London, 2003), 169–70; Roland Clark, "European Fascists and Local Activists: Romania's Legion of the Archangel Michael (1922–1938)," PhD dissertation (University of Pittsburgh, 2012), 259–60.
82. Eugenio Coselschi, in Comités d'Action pour l'Universalité de Rome, *Réunion de Montreux 1617 decembre 1934XIII*, (Rome, 1935), 28–42.
83. Payne, *History of Fascism*, 240.
84. Moța, *Corespondența cu "Serviciul Mondial,"* 15.
85. Mircea Platon, "The Iron Guard and the 'Modern State': Iron Guard Leaders Vasile Marin and Ion I. Moța, and the 'New European Order,'" *Fascism* 1, no. 2 (2012): 82.
86. Ibid.
87. Moța, *Corespondența cu "Serviciul Mondial,"* 15–16.
88. ANIC, Fund DGP, File 232/1935, vol. 2, 45.
89. Moța, *Corespondența cu "Serviciul Mondial,"* 16.
90. Ibid., 15.
91. Ibid.
92. Platon, "The Iron Guard," 82. Philip Morgan also argues that "the Iron Guard … adopted a xenophobic and anti-Semitic racism." Morgan, *Fascism in Europe*, 170.
93. Platon, "The Iron Guard," 85–89.
94. Moța, *Corespondența cu "Serviciul Mondial,"* 17.
95. Ibid., 16.
96. Heinen, *Legiunea*, 304.

97. Platon, "The Iron Guard," 89.
98. CNSAS, Fund P, File 11784, vol. 6, 152–53.
99. Platon, "The Iron Guard," 89.
100. Heinen, *Legiunea*, 121.
101. Moța, "Înțelesul plecării noastre în Spania."
102. Vasile Marin, "Note din drumul spre frontul spaniol," *Porunca Vremii*, 12 December 1936.
103. CNSAS, Fund P, File 11784, vol. 11, 251.
104. Ion I. Mota, "Răvașe dela Legionarii Români de pe Frontul Crucii, din Spania," *Libertatea*, 1 April 1937.
105. Ibid.
106. Mota, "Răvașe IV," *Libertatea*, Easter [19 April] 1937.
107. Ion I. Mota, "Prezent!," *Libertatea*, 1 July 1937. Even the one mistake in the paragraph cited above is indicative of the legion's uncompromising ultranationalism.
108. Mota, "Prezent! II," *Libertatea*, 8 July 1937.
109. Mota, "Înțelesul plecării noastre în Spania."; Ion I. Mota, "Dragostea lor de țară," *Libertatea*, 13 December 1936.
110. Moța, *Corespondența cu "Serviciul Mondial,"* 31.
111. Corneliu Zelea Codreanu, *Circulări și manifeste* (Madrid, 1951), 118.
112. See Valentin Săndulescu, "Sacralised Politics in Action: The February 1937 Burial of the Romanian Legionary Leaders Ion Moța and Vasile Marin," *Totalitarian Movements and Political Religions* 8, no. 2 (2007): 259–69.
113. See *Libertatea*, 11, 18, 25 March 1937.
114. ANIC, Fund MI, File 4/1937; Constantin Argetoianu, Însemnări zilnice, vol. 2 (Bucharest, 1999), 68–77.

Bibliography

Archives

AIOSRR—*Arhiva de istorie orală a Societății Române de Radiodifuziune* (The Oral History Archive of the Romanian Radio Broadcasting Society), Bucharest, Romania.

ANIC—*Arhivele Naționale Istorice Centrale* (The Central National Historical Archives), Bucharest, Romania.

ANRM—*Arhivele Naționale ale Republicii Moldova* (The National Archives of the Republic of Moldova), Chișinău, Moldova.

CNSAS—*Consiliul Național pentru Studierea Arhivelor Securității* (The National Council for the Study of the *Securitate* Archives), Bucharest, Romania.

Published Sources

"Teroarea haimanalelor din Iași." *Aurora*, 21 May 1922.

Protocoalele Înțelepților Sionului. Orăștie, 1923.

"Nunta lui Moța." *Pământul Strămoșesc*, 1 September 1927.

"Vești antisemite din lume." *Pământul Strămoșesc*, 1 October 1927.

"Din străinătate." *Pământul Strămoşesc*, 15 December 1928.
"Libertatea—foaie verde." *Libertatea*, 12 April 1936.

Argetoianu, Constantin. Însemnări zilnice, vol. 1. Bucharest, 1998.
———. Însemnări zilnice, vol. 2. Bucharest, 1999.
Bauerkämper, Arnd. "Transnational Fascism: Cross-Border Relations between Regimes and Movements in Europe, 1922–1939." *East Central Europe* 37, nos. 2–3 (2010): 214–46.
Borejsza, Jerzy W. *Il fascismo e l'Europa orientale: dalla propaganda all'aggressione*. Rome, 1981.
Cârstocea, Raul. "Uneasy Twins? The Entangled Histories of Jewish Emancipation and Anti-Semitism in Romania and Hungary, 1866–1913." *Slovo* 21, no. 2 (2009): 64–85.
———. "The Role of Anti-Semitism in the Ideology of the 'Legion of the Archangel Michael,' 1927–1938." PhD dissertation. University College London, 2011.
———. "The Path to the Holocaust: Fascism and Antisemitism in Interwar Romania." *S:I.M.O.N. (Shoah: Intervention, Methods, Documentation)* 1 (2014): 1–11.
Clark, Roland. "European Fascists and Local Activists: Romania's Legion of the Archangel Michael (1922–1938)." PhD dissertation. University of Pittsburgh, 2012.
Comités d'Action pour l'Universalité de Rome. *Réunion de Montreux 1617 decembre 1934XIII*. Rome, 1935.
Eatwell, Roger. "Towards a New Model of Generic Fascism." *Journal of Theoretical Politics* 4, no. 2 (1992): 161–94.
Goodfellow, Samuel. "Fascism as a Transnational Movement: The Case of Alsace." *Contemporary European History* 22, no. 1 (2013): 87–106.
Griffin, Roger. *The Nature of Fascism*. New York, 1991.
———, ed. *International Fascism: Theories, Causes and the New Consensus*. London, 1998.
Heinen, Armin. *Legiunea "Arhanghelul Mihail": O contribuţie la problema fascismului internaţional*. Bucharest, 2006.
Ionescu, Andrei. "Viaţa şi moartea vitejească a lui Ion I. Moţa." In *Almanahul Cuvântul*. Bucharest, 1941.
Iordachi, Constantin. *Charisma, Politics and Violence: The Legion of the "Archangel Michael" in Inter-war Romania*. Trondheim, 2004.
———. "Fascism in Interwar East Central and Southeastern Europe: Toward a New Transnational Research Agenda." *East Central Europe* 37, nos. 2–3 (2010): 161–213.
Istrate, Gheorghe. *Frăţia de cruce*. Madrid, 1952.
Laqueur, Walter. *Fascism: Past, Present, Future*. New York, 1996.
Ledeen, Michael. "Italian Fascism and Youth." *Journal of Contemporary History* 4, no. 3 (1969): 137–54.
Marin, Vasile. "Note din drumul spre frontul spaniol." *Porunca Vremii*, 12 December 1936.
Morgan, Philip. *Fascism in Europe, 1919–1945*. London, 2003.

————. "Studying Fascism from the Particular to the General." *East Central Europe* 37, nos. 2–3 (2010): 334–37.

Mosse, George. *The Fascist Revolution: Toward a General Theory of Fascism.* New York, 1999.

Moța, Ion I. "Cauza noastră e justă în ordinea morală și servește progresul social." *Dacia Nouă*, 23 December 1922.

————. "Necesitatea naționalismului radical." *Dacia Nouă*, 20 January 1923.

————. "Ce ne dați în locul 'cântecelor care pier'?" *Cuvântul Studențesc*, 4 March 1924.

————. "O vorbă ardelenească pentru 'lordul' Rothermere—'Ungaria mare' și planurile Jidănești." *Pământul Strămoșesc*, 1 September 1927.

————. "Răspuns (La invitația d-lui Prof. G. Bogdan-Duică)." *Pământul Strămoșesc*, 1 January 1928.

————. "Aufruf zur Treue!—Apel la fidelitate." *Pământul Strămoșesc*, 15 November 1928.

————. "3-22-250 (Răspuns cifrat d-lui Titeanu)." *Axa*, 1 August 1933.

————. "Legiunea și LANC." *Axa*, 1 October 1933.

————. "Hitlerismul germanilor din România." *Axa*, 15 October 1933.

————. "Înțelesul plecării noastre în Spania." *Libertatea*, 6 December 1936.

————. "Dragostea lor de țară." *Libertatea*, 13 December 1936.

————. "Răvașe dela Legionarii Români de pe Frontul Crucii, din Spania." *Libertatea*, 1 April 1937.

————. "Răvașe IV." *Libertatea*, 19 April 1937.

————. "Prezent!" *Libertatea*, 1 July 1937.

————. "Prezent! II." *Libertatea*, 8 July 1937.

————. *Cranii de lemn.* Bucharest, 1940.

————. *Corespondența cu "Serviciul Mondial" (1934–1936).* Rome, 1954.

Onac, Iulia. "The Brusturoasa Uprising." In *Sites of European Antisemitism in the Age of Mass Politics, 1880–1918*, ed. Robert Nemes and Daniel Unowsky. Waltham, MA, 2014.

Payne, Stanley. *A History of Fascism, 1914–1945.* Madison, WI, 1995.

Platon, Mircea. "The Iron Guard and the 'Modern State': Iron Guard Leaders Vasile Marin and Ion I. Moța, and the 'New European Order.'" *Fascism* 1, no. 2 (2012): 65–90.

Polihroniade, Mihail. "Rostul 'Gărzii de Fier.'" *Calendarul*, 18 July 1932.

————. "Dictatură în Austria." *Axa*, 19 September 1933.

Reichardt, Sven. "Violence and Consensus in Fascism." *Fascism. Journal of Comparative Fascist Studies* 1, no. 1 (2012): 59–60.

Roșu, Nicolae. *Orientări în veac.* Bucharest, 1937.

Săndulescu, Valentin. "Sacralised Politics in Action: The February 1937 Burial of the Romanian Legionary Leaders Ion Moța and Vasile Marin." *Totalitarian Movements and Political Religions* 8, no. 2 (2007): 259–69.

Schörle, Eckart. "Internationale der Antisemiten: Ulrich Fleischhauer und der 'Welt-Dienst.'" *Werkstatt Geschichte* 51 (2009): 57–72.

Sima, Horia. *History of the Legionary Movement.* Liss, 1995.

Sternhell, Zeev, Mario Sznajder, and Maia Asheri. *The Birth of Fascist Ideology: From Cultural Rebellion to Political Revolution.* Princeton, NJ, 1994.

Teban, Nicolae. "Înmormântarea lui Moţa şi Marin." In *Ion Moţa şi Vasile Marin—25 ani dela moarte*. Madrid, 1963.

Ţurcan, Ion. "Tabere şi şantiere." Însemnări sociologice 2, no. 9 (1936): 10–22.

Veiga, Francisco. *Istoria Gărzii de Fier 1919–1941: Mistica ultranaţionalismului*. Bucharest, 1993.

Weber, Eugen. "Romania." In *The European Right*, ed. Hans Rogger and Eugen Weber. Berkeley, CA, 1966.

Zelea Codreanu, Corneliu. *Pentru legionari*. Sibiu, 1936.

———. *Circulări şi manifeste*. Madrid, 1951.

Zelea Codreanu, Corneliu, Ion I. Moţa, Ilie Gârneaţă, Corneliu Georgescu, and Radu Mironovici, "Legiunea Arhanghelul Mihail." *Pământul Strămoşesc*, 15 August 1927.

———. "Organizarea Legiunii Arhanghelul Mihail." *Pământul Strămoşesc*, 1 October 1927.

9

ITALIAN FASCISM FROM A TRANSNATIONAL PERSPECTIVE
The Debate on the New European Order (1930–1945)

Monica Fioravanzo

Following World War I, in the midst of tension that had been engendered by the conflict itself and a radical upheaval affecting European politics and demographic conditions caused by the various peace treaties, a broad debate developed. It aimed at establishing a new supranational balance capable of solving Europe's political crises as well its issues of identity.[1] For over a decade this discussion was influenced and colored by both conservative and liberal-democratic political stances relating to the reorganization of Europe, which had been destabilized and damaged as a consequence of the war. Prime examples are the Pan-European movement founded by Richard Nikolaus Coudenhove-Kalergi in 1923, and the Memorandum of the French foreign minister, Aristide Briand, drawn up in 1929 to present a project for a Federal Union of Europe. One might also consider the German "Mitteleuropa" movement, which had taken its name from the title of Friedrich Naumann's work *Mitteleuropa!* (1915), as well as the group linked with the Catholic journal *Abendland — Monatshefte für Europäische Kultur, Politik und Wirtschaft* (1925–29), edited by Friedrich Schreyvogl.[2]

Throughout the 1920s, Italian Fascism had remained largely aloof from the ongoing debate, and in March 1928, Mussolini even opined that Fascism was not "merchandise that could be exported." This claim was subsequently refuted in 1930. However, the predominantly domestic bias of the Fascist political outlook was aptly reflected by the comment at that time.[3] Nor did the "Italian Fasci Abroad" (Fasci italiani all'estero) intend to propose a New European Order (NEO). This network, which was officially acknowledged in 1922, primarily focused on foreign groups and movements, and not on governments. Its aim was to "inform" Italian emigrant communities about the basic tenets of Fascist ideology so as to promote consent of Fascist ideals in other countries as well.[4] Mussolini continued to feel the need to consolidate his regime, isolating any possible dissent and imposing the power and prestige of Fascism on competing powers such as the Church and the Crown. Although the Fascist conception of the State, intended as a "will to power and will to govern," essentially contained the idea of a preeminent international role for Fascist Italy, initially these concepts remained latent.[5]

The idea of a NEO and plans for an economic, political, and social "balance" in Europe were introduced by the Fascist movement in the early 1930s, after the regime had become internally consolidated (partially as a consequence of the Lateran Pacts with the Catholic Church in 1929). On the one hand, the 1929 crisis and its social and economic effects led to a sense of profound upheaval in Europe, and the leitmotif was in fact the perception of a European crisis.[6] On the other hand, Italian Fascism feared the growth of National Socialism in Germany. It certainly perceived the Nationalsozialistische Deutsche Arbeiterpartei (National Socialist German Party, NSDAP) as an ideological ally in its opposition to Western democracies. Yet Mussolini also saw the NSDAP as a contender for the leading role over other rightist European movements, which up to then had been held by Italian Fascism. Hence, the particular urgency to propose a "Fascist solution" to cope with the decline of Europe before Germany could have a say in the matter. More specifically, the attention dedicated to European affairs by the Fascists would involve a redefinition of relations among the European nations. Moreover, they envisioned a reshuffling of relations between Europe and the other continents in accordance with the Fascist mission and its ideas concerning European identity. A transnational aspect was thus evident in the Fascist debate on Europe. Its development was concurrent with the rise of the NSDAP. From the beginning, the debate was a "crossroads" and a symbolic point of interaction and tension between the European fascist groups. In this constellation, relations to National Socialism assumed a crucial importance.[7] Starting in the early 1930s[8]—officially in 1932, with the Volta Conference on Europe, which celebrated the first decade of the regime's existence (1922–1932)—the debate on a "New Order" was renewed following the alliance with Nazi Germany and Hitler's visit to Italy in 1938 and, finally, with the outbreak of World War II.[9]

In this chapter, I intend to demonstrate how the Fascist design of the NEO, which fundamentally conflicted with the Nazi perspective, changed over time with respect to the international arena and, above all, to relations with the Third Reich. During the last years of the war, the concept was modified in relation to minor allies. Initially an ambitious project for the reordering of Europe in accordance with Fascist standards, it gradually became a means of competing with the Third Reich. In fact, the Repubblica Sociale Italiana (Italian Social Republic, RSI) attempted to propose a last, alternative vision of this European order in 1943–44. In contrast with previous designs, this final conception of a new Axis Europe was tied to an order utterly dominated by National Socialism.

The Early Thirties

During this initial stage, plans for a NEO were based on a resurgence of the myth of Rome. On the occasion of the tenth anniversary of the regime, the official Fascist journal *Gerarchia*, founded by Mussolini himself, inaugurated the celebrations with a special edition dedicated to the "Universal Mission of Rome." With its spirit and ideals, the Roman world was presented as capable of playing a "mediating role" with respect to "antithetical universal ideas existing between the East and the West." It was seen as the precondition of the universal (and European) role of Fascism, acting as its sole heir.[10] However, the journal assigned the task of understanding the reasons underlying the European crisis to the Conference on Europe, organized by the Alessandro Volta Foundation and to be held in Rome in November 1932. Furthermore, it had to deal with the role to be assumed by Fascist Italy in a Europe restored to its authentic historical and political mission.[11]

The conference was attended by roughly one hundred guests and speakers hand-picked by Mussolini from amongst the most authoritative Italian and foreign academics and politicians of the time. Besides its "scientific" purpose, whereby solutions would be sought for the European crisis, it also had "political" aims. The conference proposed Fascist Italy, the heir to the traditions of ancient Rome, as a guiding force for a new Europe and as a model of order and stability. However, this ideological and propagandistic perspective lacked any real economic or juridical basis. The myth of ancient Rome was then propagated at the operative level by the Comitati d'Azione per l'Universalità di Roma (Action Committees for the Universality of Rome, CAUR), founded in 1933 by Eugenio Coselschi. The aim of these committees was to spread the classical ideals of Roman culture (*Romanità*), embodied in Fascism, to movements and groups throughout Europe. According to this ideology, only Rome could ensure the "political restoration" of a "divided and tormented world."[12]

Based on the interventions of the Fascist speakers, including Francesco Orestano, Francesco Coppola, and Paolo Orano, a moderate model of Imperial Rome emerged, prevalently referring to the ideal of a universal peace (*pax*) rather than Roman power (*potestas*). An "order" was proposed, but a hierarchy of European nations was not explicitly mentioned. The emphasis appeared to be placed on the "natural dominion of Europe" over the other continents.[13] Just as Rome had once dominated the ancient world, so too would Fascist Europe exercise its "legitimate" hegemony over other continents.[14] The academic Francesco Coppola pointed out that on three occasions, "with the Roman Empire, the Catholic Church and the Renaissance, the Italian nation had created and recreated European civilization." He concluded his speech by indicating Italy as the country to which "the duty and glory of saving the civilization of Europe and of the entire world should be entrusted for the fourth time...."[15] Although most of the political leaders and intellectuals invited to the conference harbored no particular prejudices against the idea of a preeminent role for Fascist Italy in Europe, quite a few authoritative representatives of the liberal-democratic position participated in the meeting, for instance British politician Christopher Dawson, and Czechoslovakian jurist *František* Weyr, rector of the University of BRNO.[16]

In the German delegation, conservative or even pro-Nazi positions were entirely dominant, with the exception of sociologist Alfred Weber, professor at the University of Heidelberg until his dismissal following criticism of Hitlerism in 1933. Nonetheless, a clear rejection of the Fascist claim to leadership in Europe came not from within the liberal-democratic faction, but rather from the National Socialists. The most important ideologist of the NSDAP, Alfred Rosenberg, participated in the conference. As his recently discovered diaries have demonstrated, he would also become a leading figure in the Nazi regime and significantly influence Hitler during the war.

Rosenberg spoke about a strict hierarchy of European nations in his lecture entitled "Krisis und Neugeburt Europas" (Crisis and Rebirth of Europe); it was to be an unchangeable hierarchy, in which Germany was at the top. He referred to the "blood myth," thereby rejecting the Roman tradition, which he considered to be outdated. Rosenberg's view was in line with the spirit of a hierarchical Europe; in fact, he was far more outspoken about this than his cautious Italian counterparts. However, Rosenberg refuted the idea of a hegemonic role for Fascism. In his diaries, he often recalls his speech before the Congress, suggesting that Mussolini himself regarded his contribution as the most important one given at the conference.[17] In any case, it should be noted that any opposition from the Fascists remained unspoken at this time. In this initial public context, Mussolini wished to avoid opposition. Thus, in the closing speech of the conference, Francesco Orestano, the leading Italian academic, had to soften any differences, emphasizing a unified purpose.[18]

In its report of the conference, the French magazine *Le Temps* referred to the "multiples apologies du fascisme et certaines critiques à l'égard des méthodes libérales" (many celebratory views promoting Fascism and certain criticisms with respect to the liberal approach), and also to a will to facilitate the "rayonnement des idées mussoliniennes" (influence of Mussolini's ideas).[19]

The Axis (1936–1939)

Hitler's rise to power in January 1933 shifted Europe's political equilibrium. Germany's alliance with Fascist Italy, enshrined in the Pact of Friendship and Alliance of 1936 (which led to the notorious Rome–Berlin Axis), put an end to Germany's political isolation after World War I. The new situation gradually distanced Italy from France and Great Britain, the victors and its former allies, producing a division in Europe between states with a liberal-democratic perspective on one side, and authoritarian, antidemocratic states on the other.

The period from 1936 to 1939 was the phase of greatest convergence between Italy and Germany. At this time, in the view of the Fascists, there was an interweaving of Italy's political aims in terms of its imperialistic ambitions, and the privileged—though as yet not "subordinate"—relationship with the Third Reich. The pact between the two countries was seen as an instrument capable of upsetting the balance established at Versailles, and of potentially facilitating the "natural" hegemony of totalitarian powers in Europe. The importance of the pact pushed the Fascist regime to highlight the necessary, intrinsic harmony between the two countries and the two "revolutions," while also taking into consideration Italian public opinion, which was partially averse to Germany. From the National Socialist point of view, once disagreements over Austria were resolved, tension and competition with Italy would be somewhat limited on account of differing, yet still complementary, foreign policy aims.

The Mediterranean interests of Italy were welcomed by the Third Reich as they were consistent with continental policies relating to German expansionism.[20] In this regard, it is worth recalling the meeting between Italian foreign minister, Galeazzo Ciano, and Adolf Hitler at Berchtesgaden in October 1936 when the pact was signed; on this occasion, and assuming a belligerent stance with the British, the Führer had declared that the "Mediterranean is an Italian sea and any future modification of the balance in the Mediterranean must occur in a manner that will benefit the Italians."[21] Throughout the 1930s the Reich benefited from Italy's support on the level of international legitimacy: Italy, in fact, remained within the Society of Nations until 1937, where it supported German interests even after its departure in 1933.[22]

Two years after the establishment of the Axis, and following Mussolini's short stay in Germany in September 1937, Hitler visited Italy in May 1938. This was his first state visit to Italy following his private meeting with Mussolini in 1934. It was the occasion when the military alliance between the two was sealed. The meeting was highly significant, partly because it occurred shortly following the Austrian *Anschluss* and the proclamation of the Italian Empire.[23] Although the consequences of the two events differed considerably, they were extremely important at the international level, and affected Italy's image and international profile, as well as its relations with its ally. From Mussolini's point of view, in spite of the *Anschluss* and perhaps in order to avoid or to limit negative repercussions in popular opinion, Mussolini was determined to exploit the Führer's visit to consolidate Italy's image of strength, wealth, control, and power. Furthermore, at the level of a "presumed superiority," it was used to reinforce its alliance with Germany.[24] This tie provided a form of compensation for—and to some extent mitigated—Italy's political isolation vis-à-vis France and Great Britain, following Mussolini's invasion of Ethiopia. Deriving strength from his new alliance, the Duce believed he would be in a better position to negotiate with these two countries.[25] On the other hand, although the *Anschluss* undoubtedly represented a serious injury for Italy, it had been Fascist Italy—following Mussolini's ardent statement—that had welcomed "the reappearance of the Empire upon the fateful hills of Rome after fifteen centuries."[26]

There was a strong conviction that, in the understanding between European nations, Fascist Italy was "the sole solid point of reference for European reorganization and pacification," as it "put an end to the social, political, and moral disorder and uncertainty the former allies were and still are subject to." As far as Germany was concerned, Italy pointed out that even the oldest German traditions had recognized "the superior dignity of the imperial symbol of Rome."[27] Thus, Mussolini counted on a relative political and international advantage, and this led him to consider the Axis as a condition that was useful toward achieving the objectives concerning the expansion and reorganization of Europe, which Fascism had already planned and for which the time now seemed ripe. As Paolo Orano stated, "The Rome–Berlin axis …

clarifies and brings into broad daylight conditions and relations existing between national and state entities."[28]

The collective work *L'Asse nel pensiero dei due popoli. Die Achse im Denken der beiden Völker* (The Axis in the Tought of the Two Peoples), edited by Paolo Orano, rector of the Royal University of Perugia, celebrated the Führer's visit to Italy. Presenting texts by Italian and German authors with side-by-side translations, the book reflects a sense of "faith" in the Italian–German alliance as a means of constructing a Fascist Europe. Presenting images conjured up by Giorgio Umani, a poet who today is almost unknown, the book celebrated the "specular" nature of the Axis:

Europa di Ginevra	*Europa von Versailles*
Europa di Versaglia	*Europa von Genf*
nodo che non si scioglie	*Knoten der sich nicht löst*
ma nodo che si taglia.	*sondern Knoten den man zerschneidet.*
Spada d'acciaio fino	*Schwert reinsten Eisens*
Asse Roma-Berlino.	*ist die Achse Rom-Berlin.*
Tu, Duce dei Latini,	*Oh Du Duce der Lateiner*
Tu, Führer dei Germani,	*Oh Du Führer der Deutschen*
Hitler–Mussolini	*Hitler und Mussolini*
Europa di domani.	*Europa von morgen.*
Sigillo del destino	*Siegel des Schicksales*
Asse Roma–Berlino.	*Achse Rom–Berlin.*

—Giorgio Umani[29]

The *Anschluss* was seen as linked to a greater plan, which justified annexation: "The Empire of Ethiopia and the annexation of Austria are two powerful acts which at the time may have appeared as arbitrary and violent but were then immediately seen as admirable on account of their fruitful European results." Only with Mussolini and Hitler, "the two greatest Europeans, was it possible to promulgate the law which will save Western civilization from a debacle."[30]

In the process of a "strong Germany joining forces with a strong Italy," it was Italy that maintained the leading position, by virtue of the Roman tradition and Mussolini's right to rule by primogeniture.[31] In the words of Orano, "The idea that engenders strength in Fascism is 'Primacy' and the Duce has made it a lever whereby it becomes possible to reawaken all latent virtues required to achieve the heights of power and civilization." And Germany, "a nation emulating Rome, was its dialectic term": "Adolf Hitler, the German Führer, thus came to pay a visit to the Leader of Fascist Italy, the first planner of a Europe of strong elements and the founder of an empire."[32]

On the basis of such premises, which would later be revealed in their true light as reckless and foolhardy ambition, Fascism nurtured the conviction that together with Germany it would be able to generate and build a "new Europe."[33] This would be "the logical consequence of a perennial and ideal 'revolution,' which, from Rome to Catholicism and to the Renaissance ... has shaped the spirit of the West."[34] The will to entrench the projects within the Axis that would establish a Fascist hegemony in Europe was so strong that previous differences and conflicts were ignored or played down. Therefore, in order to safeguard an alliance deemed a priority by the Fascist regime, the observations of Werner A. Eicke (published in the celebratory work *The Axis in the Thought of the Two Peoples*, which affirmed the "Aryan" character of a New Europe) were not fully translated into Italian. Furthermore the regime omitted or changed various passages of the text in order not to offend the sensibility of Italian readers, considering racial laws had not yet been enacted, and that the Church and the masses did not hide their reservations about the Germans.[35] Moreover, for the specific purpose of overcoming that diffidence inherent in public opinion in terms of a future Europe based on the Axis, the regime facilitated and intensified exchange and contact of the political, recreational, and cultural nature. Not only leaders and higher-ranking members of society, but also Italian and German youth and mass organizations were involved, with "twin" arrangements established between cities, and the development of common German–Italian projects in view of the World Exhibition that was to be held in Rome in 1942.[36]

The War (1939–1945)

With the outbreak of war, the issue became even more important in the cultural, political, and economic debate. In view of a victory that was held for certain in 1939–40, the Fascist plan for Europe was becoming inevitable, even urgent. *Geopolitica*, a monthly journal, was first published in 1939 with the initiative of the minister of education, Giuseppe Bottai, and the biweekly journal *Primato* was launched in 1940. These journals provided a means by which the economic, territorial, political, and cultural aspects of peace might be contemplated. In these "war journals" the Fascist intellectual elites laid out the theoretical foundations of Italian hegemony in the new Europe.[37] *Geopolitica* and *Primato* documented the planning of a large Euro-Afro-Asian "vital space," seen as "the union of the two imperialisms in the Axis," under whose control the nations were subordinate to a hierarchy established by

Italy and Germany. The liberal principle of an "expected parity among states" was negated, as "only the Fascist and Socialist interpretations of the State are adequate for the new tasks ... and for the vast areas" of Axis Europe. The war clearly made manifest the crisis of the liberal system, and thus justified the claim of the "revolutionary" powers to impose their values in light of the failure of Great Britain and France.[38]

Fascist enthusiasm in this first phase of the conflict is documented by many journals, such as *Giovane Europa* (1942) and *Europa Fascista* (1941), published by Luigi Pinti, and formerly called *Giovanissima*. *Giovane Europa*, first brought out in Italian in 1942, was distributed from 1941 in German under the title *Junges Europa*, with articles by German and Italian writers. It expounded the views of a *"combattentismo universitario europeo"* (European University Fight) among the soldiers on the Eastern Front.[39]

Propaganda efforts were accompanied by training and cultural activities, as shown by the numerous congresses that were organized, such as the Inter-University National Congress of the Gruppi Universitari Fascisti (GUF, Fascist University Circles) held in Padua (8–11 February 1942), involving young university students in particular; the Congress on Economic Problems of the New Order in Pisa (18–23 May 1942); and the Congress on the Idea of Europe organized by the National Institute of Fascist Culture in Rome (23–24 November 1942). Plans were also drawn up for an Imperial Fascist Community that would extend to the Balkans and to Switzerland.[40] Quite paradoxically, while the political and military alliance with Nazi Germany was reinforced as the basic premise for a new Europe overseen by the Axis, differences and rivalries occurring between the Fascist and Nazi plans for a new Europe became increasingly evident.

Italy's propaganda efforts and its expansionary goals were noted by the Nazis and aroused suspicion, not least because, following the Tripartite Pact of 1940, the "New Order" project was publicly silenced in Berlin. On the other hand, German reticence and methods of Germanic dominion in Europe also began to worry the Fascist regime, which was aware of its own weakness compared to its ally. It suffices to think of the catastrophic outcome of the military operations in North Africa and Greece.

However, already in 1940 and, more significantly, following Italy's entry into the conflict and the beginning of Italy's disastrous campaign in Africa, in the work entitled *Revolution im Mittelmeer* by Paul Schmidt, head of the Press Office of the Ministry for Foreign Affairs of the Third Reich, the Germans clearly stated their interest in the Mediterranean. As Schmidt pointed out: "The future colonial configuration will also increase the importance of the Mediterranean for Germany, thus the action taken by Italy for its dominance is a struggle that concerns German interests as well."[41] The point for Italy was to avoid being subjected to "Germanization," and such a need was becoming increasingly evident.[42]

A new phase began in the ongoing conjecture and plans concerning the future "New Order." Until that time, a new Europe had been conceived by the Fascists as a "union of the two imperialist forces of the Axis," which had equal rights. It was also understood that Italy would retain a role of primacy on account of Mussolini's right of "primogeniture" and the Roman tradition. However, the debate became colored by a vein of defensive reaction and reservations concerning Germany. In the journal *Gerarchia*, the official publication of the regime that had been founded by Mussolini himself, Francesco Orestano, the president of the Italian Philosophical Society,[43] published two articles on the NEO: the "Nuovo ordine europeo" (New European Order) (January 1942) and "Vita religiosa nella nuova Europa" (Religious Life in the New Europe) (December 1942). The author of these articles criticized the concept of a super-race and claimed the spiritual superiority of Italy. The New Order was not intended to be built using only weapons or interests but was to be constructed based on ideas. Moreover, Italy could create and guide the New Europe, due to its Christian tradition, which strongly linked it to Europe, in contrast to the secessionist and irreligious Germany.[44]

Joachim von Ribbentrop, the German foreign minister, defined the work as a *Hetzartikel*, an act of incitation. Joseph Goebbels, the minister for propaganda, commented: "Italians are trying … to claim a right to spiritual supremacy in Europe, given that both military and political power slipped from their hands." The German embassy in Rome presented a written complaint demanding an explanation for the incendiary articles.[45] The Fascist regime was in fact claiming its spiritual superiority over Nazism and proposed itself as a moral guide for the New Europe, which it conceived as a vast empire having a hierarchical structure. It was still believed that the conflict would have a successful outcome and that the Axis would win the war, but the regime did not want to let Germany guide Europe on its own through the superiority of its army. The fear was indeed entirely comprehensible in the light of Nazi designs regarding a new Europe, which remained unknown to the Italian ally. The German policies attributed exclusive priority to the interests of the Third Reich.[46]

During 1943 the Fascist perspective concerning Europe changed once again due to the events in the conflict. While the political and military situation was becoming more critical for Nazi Germany (from the landings of the Allies in Algeria and Morocco in November 1942 to the defeat at Stalingrad in January–February 1943) and the outcome of the conflict increasingly uncertain, Italy reconsidered its relations with its minor allies, configuring the "New Order" as a "Europe of Nations." During this phase, the debate was essentially promoted by the diplomatic elite, therefore, in terms that were political rather than theoretical. Proponents included the ambassador in Berlin, Dino Alfieri, and Filippo Anfuso, the plenipotentiary minister in Budapest. The outlook focused on continental Europe and re-emphasized the role of smaller states, from Hungary to Romania.

From February 1943 onward, Giuseppe Bastianini, the undersecretary for foreign affairs, was the main proponent of a Charter of Europe including the borders of the "New Order" of the Axis. This was also to reassure minor allies, who were frightened by the exploitative policies of the Third Reich in the occupied countries, and dismayed by Germany's silence, too.[47] In order to gain the favor of the minor allies, Bastianini raised seven points to define the principle of nationality, full sovereignty, and the independence of the European states in the future "New Order".[48] Amended by Mussolini, the plan was further adjusted by Ribbentrop, who, at the Congress held at Salzburg on 7 April 1943, merely stated in a communiqué that "the victory of the Tripartite Pact would guarantee peace in Europe and the collaboration among nations on the basis of common interests and an equal distribution of the economic resources of the world." It was the first official statement after a long period of silence, and it aroused great interest despite its ambiguity. Nonetheless, it was the most that Ribbentrop would offer, and Bastianini's proposal for a Charter of Europe as opposed to the Atlantic Charter was rejected. Ribbentrop declared that strength was the only method to impose the will of the Axis in Europe, and that any declaration was a sign of weakness.[49]

Certainly, the idea of a Europe of nations was instrumental for Italy, linked to the crisis of the moment; it was proposed in accordance with talks the government was initiating with Romania and Hungary in view of a potential separation from Germany. However, the distance that had been created to the policies of the Third Reich had now become extreme: the only possible Europe for Germany was based on racial supremacy and weaponry.

On 25 July 1943, the fall of Mussolini and the collapse of Fascism changed the international setting, and Germany remained isolated in Europe. It is significant how the Fascism of Salò, which emerged after Mussolini's liberation in a context of near total subordination to the Reich, returned to shine over Europe, though in ways that were very different from before.[50] References were no longer made to any specific areas of exclusive Italian influence. All the proud claims to an Italian primacy in the spiritual leadership of the "New Order" had disappeared. In general, ever less reference was made to the freedom and independence of the minor nations that Bastianini had envisioned— albeit in an instrumental manner—in view of the meeting at Salzburg in April 1943. The "New Europe" advocated by the Repubblica Sociale Italiana (Italian Social Republic, RSI), commonly referred to as the Republic of Salò, was now a supranational Europe, lacking a clear distinction between German and Italian contributions.[51]

It appeared rather that Italy and Germany represented soul against matter (the Allies). Hence the apparent need for a common path, whereby "the process of Italy's rebirth and the strengthening of Germany originate from the same spirit and attain the same result."[52] But here it was Germany that acted as the guiding light for Fascism. Based on the Nazi model, Italy had also to become "a lively construction site, a great workshop, a huge barracks," invincible, and ready to defend not only itself but all of Europe from the "new barbarians," thanks to a united war.[53] Moreover, the imagined Europe would be founded not on freedom, which its peoples were not interested in, but on a poorly defined "principle of justice." The latter was as vague as Mussolini's economic policies, which proposed nothing more than a "third" course of action, antithetical to the perspectives of both bolshevism and capitalism.[54]

The creation of a "New Europe" was now seen as fully coinciding with the elimination of the presence of "Judaism." As a symptom of the degeneration of the culture and identity of Europe, it would be removed like a "dry skin," once Europe had managed to recognize once again its "highest intellectual and moral vocation."[55] Though weak and oppressed by the Third Reich, Mussolini, in a worldwide perspective, reaffirmed his faith in an even broader alliance: "[T]he future world will be dominated by this alliance", consisting of Rome, Tokyo, and Berlin, the custodians of the "grandest ideal of all humanity."[56]

Conclusion

This further shift in the design of a "New Europe" composed of republican Fascism, now "indiscriminately allied with Germany,"[57] and in an entirely prostrate position with respect to a future new National Socialist order, appeared only to generate skepticism on the side of Italy's ally. Republican Fascism, too, was considered unworthy of standing alongside the Third Reich in Axis Europe.[58] A document issued by the taskforce commanded by Rosenberg (Einsatzstab

Reichsleiter Rosenberg, Reichsleiter Rosenberg Taskforce), one of the Reich's most efficient organizations for divesting subjugated peoples and property) was dedicated to the "Italian Perspective regarding the Concept of European Unity." It held that "in its form renewed after September 1943," the Fascism of the Italian Social Republic (RSI) did not manage to instill a European mentality in the Italian people, and even less an imperial mentality. Incapable of representing a movement for the moral and ideological (*weltanschaulich*) renewal of Italy, Fascism could not be expected to offer any solution to the problem of moral and political reconstruction in Europe following the Axis victory.

The deep sense of contempt that Nazi Germany felt towards this last and most "obedient" Fascism was obvious and evident. For the Nazi leadership, a "New Europe" was simply "a European community under German leadership ...", where German influence, in both economic and racial matters, had to be predominant," and in which the *Großdeutsches Reich* would prevail.[59] The "New European Order" would be solely a Nazi Order based on the doctrine of the superiority of the German race and German blood, as Rosenberg had declared in 1932 at the Volta Conference in Rome. Rosenberg later applied this doctrine in 1941, when Hitler declared his "hour had come," and nominated him Reichsminister für die besetzten Ostgebiete (Minister for the Occupied Eastern Territories).[60]

This chapter has traced the origins and developments of the Fascist idea of Europe from the 1930s to the end of World War II, beginning from the myth of Rome to the idea of a spiritual supremacy based on Christianity, and ending with the RSI and its design for Europe. It has highlighted the close link between plans for Fascist hegemony in Europe and the world, and Italy's evolving relationship with the Reich: from collaboration to fear, and from competition to "resignation," all within the context of a rapidly changing wartime Europe.

MONICA FIORAVANZO, associate professor of Contemporary History at the Università degli Studi of Padua, studied History at the universities of Padua and Venice, and received a PhD at the latter. Selected publications: *Élites e generazioni politiche: democristiani, socialisti e comunisti veneti, 1945–62* (Milan, 2003); *Mussolini e Hitler. La Repubblica sociale sotto il Terzo Reich* (Rome, 2006); *La stampa politica femminile della DDR e la costruzione del consenso (1946–1949)* ("Clio", 2013).

Notes

1. Mark Hewitson and Matthew D'Auria, eds., *Europe in Crisis: Intellectuals and the European Idea, 1917–1957* (New York, 2012), 15–34; Yves Hersant and Fabienne Durand-Bogaert, *Europes. De l'antiquité au XXe siècle anthologie critique et commentée* (Paris, 2000), 157–72.
2. Emilia Vigliar, *L'unione europea all'epoca del progetto Briand* (Milan, 1983), 143–50; Vanessa Conze, *Das Europa der Deutschen: Ideen von Europa in Deutschland zwischen Reichstradition und Westorientierung (1920–1970)* (Munich, 2005), 31–37; and Jürgen Elvert, *Mitteleuropa! Deutsche Pläne zur europäischen Neuordnung (1918–1945)* (Stuttgart, 1999), 20–23.
3. Benito Mussolini, "Discorso alla Camera," 3 March 1928, in *Opera omnia*, XXIII, *Dal discorso dell'Ascensione agli accordi del Laterano (27 maggio 1927–11 febbraio 1929)*, ed. Edoardo and Duilio Susmel (Florence, 1957); and idem, *Messaggio per l'anno Nono*, 27 October 1930, in idem, *Opera omnia*, XXIV, *Dagli accordi del Laterano al dodicesimo anniversario della fondazione dei Fasci (12 febbraio 1929–23 marzo 1931)*, ed. Edoardo and Dulio Susmel (Florence, 1958), 278–85.
4. Emilio Gentile, "La politica estera del partito fascista: Ideologia e organizzazione dei Fasci italiani all'estero (1920–1930)," *Storia contemporanea*, no. 6 (1995), 897–956; Arnd Bauerkämper, "Ambiguities of Transnationalism: Fascism in Europe between Pan-Europeanism and Ultra-Nationalism, 1919–39," *German Historical Institute Bulletin* 29, no. 2 (2007), 5–9, 43–47; Claudia Baldoli, *Exporting Fascism: Italian Fascists and Britain's Italians in the 1930s* (Oxford and New York, 2003), 21–30; and Benedetta Garzarelli, *Parleremo al mondo intero: La propaganda del fascismo all'estero* (Alessandria, 2004), 12–27.
5. Benito Mussolini, "Fascismo," in *Enciclopedia italiana* (Milan, 1932), 851.
6. Giorgio Rumi, *Alle origini della politica estera fascista (1918–1923)* (Bari, 1968), 186–87; Nicola Labanca, "L'Italia, potenza imperiale? Nuovi appunti di storiografia," in *Nazione, interdipendenza, integrazione: Le relazioni internazionali dell'Italia (1917–1989)*, ed. Federico Romero and Antonio Varsori (Rome, 2005), 79–82.
7. Meir Michaelis, "I rapporti tra fascismo italiano e nazismo prima dell'avvento di Hitler al potere (1922–1933)," *Rivista storica italiana* 3 (1973): 569–78.
8. Asvero Gravelli's journal *Antieuropa* was first published in 1929. See Marco Cuzzi, *Antieuropa. Il fascismo universale di Mussolini* (Milan, 2006), 30–45.
9. Monica Fioravanzo, "Die Europakonzeptionen von Faschismus und Nationalsozialismus (1939–1943)," *Vierteljahrshefte für Zeitgeschichte* 4 (2010): 509–41.
10. *Gerarchia* 10 (October 1932): 800–805.
11. Carlo Foà, "Cultura e scuola nel primo decennio fascista," *Gerarchia* 10 (October 1932): 909; Simona Giustibelli, "L'Europa nella riflessione del convegno della Fondazione Volta (Roma, 16–20 novembre 1932)," *Dimensioni e problemi della ricerca storica* 1 (2002): 212; and Bernd Sösemann, "'L'idea dell'Europa'. Die faschistische Volta-Konferenz von 1932 und

der nationalsozialistische Kongreß von 1941 im Kontext der Europa-Konzeptionen des 20. Jahrhunderts," *Vigonianae* 1 (2010): 49–95.

12. CAUR, "Manifesto Statuto," 3, in Marco Cuzzi, *L'internazionale delle camicie nere: I CAUR, Comitati d'azione per l'universalità di Roma 1933–1939* (Milan, 2005), 96.

13. Francesco Coppola, "La crisi dell'Europa e la sua cattiva coscienza," in *Convegno "Volta", Roma, 14–20 novembre 1932-XI. Relazioni e comunicazioni,* ed. Reale Accademia d'Italia (Rome, 1932), 4–9.

14. Girolamo Carcopino, "Impero Romano ed Europa," in *Convegno "Volta", Roma, 14–20 novembre 1932-XI. Relazioni e comunicazioni,* ed. Reale Accademia d'Italia (Rome, 1932), 7, 11.

15. Coppola, "La crisi dell'Europa," 20.

16. Christopher Dawson, "Interracial Cooperation as a Factor in European Culture," and Frantisech Weyr, "Zur Idee eines geeinten Europas," in *Convegno "Volta"*, 3–4.

17. Jürgen Matthäus and Frank Bajohr, eds. *Alfred Rosenberg: Die Tagebücher von 1934 bis 1944* (Frankfurt am Main, 2015), 22, 200, 257, 393.

18. Alfred Rosenberg, "Krisis und Neugeburt Europas," in *Convegno "Volta"*, 1–3; Francesco Orestano, "Riassunto generale e conclusioni del 'Convegno Volta': Discorso di chiusura," in *Convegno "Volta"*, 2.

19. "Le congrès de l'Europe," *Le Temps* (19 November 1932), 2; and (23 November), 3.

20. Paul Hiltebrandt, "Grundzüge der italienischen Aussenpolitik," *Erwachendes Europa, Monatsschrift für nationalsozialistische Weltanschauung, Außenpolitik und Auslandskunde* 5 (1934): 131–35, 139–40.

21. *Colloquio del ministro degli Esteri Ciano con il cancelliere del Reich Hitler,* Berchtesgaden, 24 October 1936, in *Documenti diplomatici italiani,* s. VIII: (1935–1939), V (Rome, 1994): 317.

22. Simone Duranti, "La politica estera fascista: Fra storia politica e storia diplomatica," *Studi Storici* 1 (2014): 264.

23. Wolfgang Schieder, *Faschistische Diktaturen: Studien zu Italien und Deutschland* (Göttingen, 2008): 436–39.

24. Arnd Bauerkämper, "Die Inszenierung transnationaler faschistischer Politik: Der Staatsbesuch Hitlers in Italien im Mai 1938," in *Ideengeschichte als politische Aufklärung. Fs. Wolfgang Wippermann zum 65. Geburtstag,* ed. Stefan Vogt et al. (Berlin, 2010), 129–53.

25. Emilio Falco, "'Civiltà fascista' durante la presidenza di De Francisci dell'Istituto nazionale di cultura fascista dal marzo 1937 al marzo 1940," *Clio* 4 (2012): 587–90.

26. Benito Mussolini, "Discorso per la proclamazione dell'Impero," 9 May 1936, in *Opera Omnia*, XXVII, *Dall'inaugurazione della Provincia di Littoria alla proclamazione dell'Impero (19 dicembre 1934–9 maggio 1936),* ed. Edoardo and Duilio Susmel (Florence, 1959), 268–69; Lorenzo Braccesi, *L'antichità aggredita: Memoria del passato e poesia del nazionalismo* (Rome, 2006), 34–35.

27. G. Cavallucci, "Imperialismi antieuropei e idea imperiale fascista," *Critica fascista* 3 (1936): 4.

28. Paolo Orano, "Il fato, il fatto, il fasto. Das Geschehen, das Geschick, die Pracht," in *L'Asse nel pensiero dei due popoli. Die Achse im Denken der beiden Völker*, ed. Paolo Orano (Rome, 1938), 19.

29. Giorgio Umani, "L'Asse die Achse," in *L'Asse nel pensiero*, 169. Giorgio Umani (1892–1965), a lawyer and famous entomologist, also composed poetical works that were published in various collections. Translation: "The Europe of Geneva, the Europe of Versailles, a knot to be severed rather than simply loosened. The Rome–Berlin Axis is a sword of fine steel. You, Leader of the Latin people, and you, Führer of the German folk. Hitler and Mussolini represent the Europe of tomorrow. The Rome–Berlin Axis: the seal of our destiny."

30. Orano, "Il fato," 21; and D.M. Tuninetti, "Il Congedo Der Abschied," 193, in *L'Asse nel pensiero*.

31. Orano, "Il fato," 26.

32. Orano, "Il fato," 18, 22.

33. MacGregor Knox, *Destino comune: Dittatura, politica estera e guerra nell'Italia fascista e nella Germania nazista* (Turin, 2003), 90.

34. G. Engely, "Costruendo la Nuova Europa," *Critica fascista* 1 (1936), 4.

35. Werner A. Eicke, "Die Achse Berlin-Rom," in *L'Asse nel pensiero*, 78–85.

36. Andrea Hoffend, *Zwischen Kultur-Achse und Kulturkampf: Die Beziehungen zwischen 'Drittem Reich' und faschistischen Italien in den Bereichen Medien, Kunst, Wissenschaft und Rassenfrage* (Frankfurt am Main, 1998), 269–355. Luca La Rovere, *Storia dei Guf: Organizzazione, politica e miti della gioventù universitaria fascista 1919–1943* (Turin, 2003), 206–7, 255–61.

37. Renzo De Felice, *Mussolini il duce, II: Lo Stato totalitario 1936–1940* (Turin, 1981), 728–31; and Luisa Mangoni, ed., *"Primato" 1940–1943* (Bari, 1977), 13.

38. Renzo Sertoli Salis, "Considerazioni geopolitiche inattuali," *Geopolitica* 4 (1940), 164–66; idem, *Italia, Europa, Arabia* (Milan, 1940); and Davide Rodogno, *Il nuovo ordine mediterraneo: Le politiche di occupazione dell'Italia fascista in Europa (1940–1943)* (Turin, 2003), 71–79.

39. *Giovane Europa* 1–2 (January 1942), and "Gli elementi dell'Unità europea," *Giovane Europa* 3 (January 1942): 5; "Perché Europa Fascista," *Europa Fascista—Giovanissima—Rassegna di Politica* XI, no. 1 (March 1941): 2–3.

40. Ugoberto Alfassio Grimaldi and Marina Addis Saba, *Cultura a passo romano: Storia e strategie dei Littoriali della cultura e dell'arte* (Milan, 1983), 114–43; La Rovere, *Storia dei Guf*, 350–60; *Convegno per lo studio dei problemi economici dell'ordine nuovo* (Pisa, 1942–43); Gisella Longo, ed., *Il fascismo e l'Idea d'Europa. Il convegno dell'Istituto nazionale di cultura fascista (1942)* (Rome, 2000), 1–45; and Carlo Costamagna, "L'idea dell'Europa e la guerra," *Lo Stato* 3 (1943), 65–78.

41. Paul Schmidt, ed., *Rivoluzione nel Mediterraneo: La lotta per lo spazio vitale dell'Italia* (Milan, 1942), 14.

42. Luca Pietromarchi, *Diario 15 gennaio 1941–20 dicembre 1942*, dated 26 March 1942, in Renzo De Felice, *Mussolini l'alleato: I. L'Italia in guerra 1940–1943, t. I, Dalla guerra "breve" alla guerra lunga* (Turin, 1996), 447–48; and Ruth Nattermann, ed., *I diari e le agende di Luca Pietromarchi (1938–1940): Politica estera del fascismo e vita quotidiana di un diplomatico romano del '900* (Rome, 2009), 11–21.

43. For more about Francesco Orestano (1873–1945), president of the Philosophical Italian Society since 1931, and professor of Moral Philosophy and then of History of Philosophy at the University of Palermo, see Eugenio Garin, *Cronache di filosofia italiana (1900–1943)* (Bari, 1955), 150–64. In 1941 Orestano published the volume *Verso la nuova Europa* (Milan, Fratelli Bocca).
44. Francesco Orestano, "Nuovo ordine europeo," *Gerarchia* 1 (1942): 3–9; and idem, "Vita religiosa nella nuova Europa," *Gerarchia* 12 (1942): 476–84.
45. Politisches Archiv des Auswärtigen Amts [PAAA], Inland I/D, 7.10/ 18. and 19.8 (1941–44), "Italien Kirche" 6, Ribbentrop, Vortragsnotiz, zu D XII—10/43, Berlin, 12 January 1943; Elke Fröhlich, ed., *Die Tagebücher von Joseph Goebbels*, Part II, Diktate 1941–1945, vol. 6, October–December 1942 (Munich, 1996), 466 (18 December 1942).
46. PAAA, Inland g II, *Geheime Reichssachen*, Auswärtiges Amt, Berlin, den 18. September 1942, "Entwurf über die Bildung eines Europa-Ausschusses des Deutschen Reiches"; Lutz Klinkhammer, "L'occidentalizzazione (nazionalsocialista) del concetto di'Europa: alcune riflessioni," in *La rinascita dell'occidente: Sviluppo del sistema politico e diffusione del modello occidentale nel secondo dopoguerra in Italia e Germania*, ed. Stefano Cavazza (Soveria Mannelli, 2006), 17–19.
47. Giuseppe Bastianini, *Volevo fermare Mussolini: Memorie di un diplomatico fascista* (Milan, 2005), 96–98, 304–5.
48. *Documenti Diplomatici Italiani*, s. IX (1939–1943), X (7 February–8 September 1943), (Rome, 1990), no. 198, *Il sottosegretario agli Esteri, Bastianini, al Capo del governo e Ministro degli Esteri, Mussolini*, 6 April 1943, 253–54, and no. 219, *'Appunto', Il sottosegretario agli Esteri, Bastianini, al capo di gabinetto, Babuscio Rizzo*, Rome, 12 April 1943, 286–87.
49. PAAA, Büro Reichsminister, *Handakten Dolmetscher Schmidt*, Akten betreffend: 1943 (Teil II), vom Mai 1943 bis Dezember 1943, 25–40; and Klinkhammer, "L'occidentalizzazione," 21–23.
50. Monica Fioravanzo, "Idee e progetti italiani di Nuovo Ordine Europeo nei rapporti con il Reich nazista (1939–1943)," *Rivista Storica Italiana* 1 (2009): 388–429.
51. A. Pugliese, "Ricostruzione europea," *La repubblica fascista* (19 August 1944): 1; C. Ginelli, "Europa che nasce Europa che muore," *Il fabbro* (15 January 1945): 2.
52. Benito Mussolini, "Brenno a Jalta," 18 February 1945, 451–53; and idem, "Bilancio di un viaggio," 30 July 1944, 387–88, in *Opera omnia*, XXXII (Florence, 1960).
53. F. Brunelli, "Il compromesso alla sbarra," *Dottrina fascista* (23 March 1945): 3; and Nino D'Aroma, "Noi e i tedeschi," *Orizzonte* n.u. (1945): 1; Carlo Borsani, "Scoperta dell'Europa," *La Repubblica fascista* (18 June 1944): 1.
54. Ginelli, "Europa che nasce Europa che muore," 1; and E. Pezzato, "Vittoria Europea e bolscevismo," *La Repubblica fascista* (17 December 1944): 2.
55. Barna Occhini, "Degli ebrei," *Italia e civiltà* (13 May 1944): 2; and A. Mussano, "Repubblica e razza," *La Riscossa* (23 March 1944): 1.
56. Benito Mussolini, "Roma–Berlino–Tokio," 4 October 1943, in *Opera omnia* XXXV (Florence, 1962), 403.

57. Pietro Sella, "Cinquant'anni dopo: repubblica sociale, fascismo, Germania nazionalsocialista," *L'uomo libero* 36 (1993): 6.
58. Robert Grunert, *Der Europagedanke westeuropäischer faschistischer Bewegungen 1940–45* (Paderborn, 2012), 227.
59. Bundesarchiv Berlin-Lichterfelde West [BARCH], NS 30/76, Einsatzstab Reichsleiter Rosenberg, Sonderkommando Süden, den 15.2.1945, E. von Ebenthall, *Einstellung der Italiener zum Gedanken der europäischen Einigung,* 8–9, 12.
60. Matthäus and Bajohr, *Alfred Rosenberg,* 14, 364, 393; Boris Schilmar, *Der Europadiskurs im deutschen Exil 1933–1945* (Munich, 2004), 126.

Bibliography

Alfassio Grimaldi, Ugoberto, and Marina Addis Saba. *Cultura a passo romano: Storia e strategie dei Littoriali della cultura e dell'arte.* Milan, 1983.
Baldoli, Claudia. *Exporting Fascism: Italian Fascists and Britain's Italians in the 1930s.* Oxford and New York, 2003.
Bastianini, Giuseppe. *Volevo fermare Mussolini: Memorie di un diplomatico fascista.* Milan, 2005.
Bauerkämper, Arnd. "Ambiguities of Transnationalism: Fascism in Europe Between Pan-Europeanism and Ultra-Nationalism, 1919–39." *German Historical Institute Bulletin* 29, no. 2 (2007): 43–67.
———. "Die Inszenierung transnationaler faschistischer Politik: Der Staatsbesuch Hitlers in Italien im Mai 1938." In *Ideengeschichte als politische Aufklärung. Fs. Wolfgang Wippermann zum 65. Geburtstag,* ed. Stefan Vogt, 129–53. Berlin, 2010.
Borsani, Carlo. "Scoperta dell'Europa." *La Repubblica fascista* (1 June 1944): 1.
Braccesi, Lorenzo. *L'antichità aggredita: Memoria del passato e poesia del nazionalismo.* Rome, 2006.
Brunelli, F. "Il compromesso alla sbarra." *Dottrina fascista* (23 March 1945): 3.
Cavallucci, Guido. "Imperialismi antieuropei e idea imperiale fascista." *Critica fascista* 3 (1936): 4.
Cavazza, Stefano, ed. *La rinascita dell'occidente: Sviluppo del sistema politico e diffusione del modello occidentale nel secondo dopoguerra in Italia e Germania.* Soveria Mannelli, 2006.
Convegno per lo studio dei problemi economici dell'ordine nuovo. Pisa, 1942–43.
Conze, Vanessa. *Das Europa der Deutschen: Ideen von Europa in Deutschland zwischen Reichstradition und Westorientierung (1920–1970).* Munich, 2005.
Costamagna, Carlo. "L'idea dell'Europa e la guerra." *Lo Stato* 3 (1943): 65–78.
Cuzzi, Marco. *L'internazionale delle camicie nere: I CAUR, Comitati d'azione per l'universalità di Roma 1933–1939.* Milan, 2005.
———. *Antieuropa: Il fascismo universale di Mussolini.* Milan, 2006.
D'Aroma, Nino. "Noi e i tedeschi." *Orizzonte* n.u. (1945): 1.
De Felice, Renzo. *Mussolini il duce, II: Lo Stato totalitario 1936–1940.* Turin, 1981.
———, *Mussolini l'alleato: I, L'Italia in guerra 1940–1943, t. I, Dalla guerra "breve" alla guerra lunga.* Turin, 1996.

Duranti, Simone. "La politica estera fascista: Fra storia politica e storia diplomatica." *Studi Storici* 1 (2014): 264.

Elvert, Jürgen. *Mitteleuropa! Deutsche Pläne zur europäischen Neuordnung (1918– 1945)*. Stuttgart, 1999.

Engely, Giovanni. "Costruendo la Nuova Europa." *Critica fascista* 1 (1936): 4.

Falco, Emilio. "'Civiltà fascista' durante la presidenza di De Francisci dell'Istituto nazionale di cultura fascista dal marzo 1937 al marzo 1940." *Clio* 4 (2012): 587–90.

Fioravanzo, Monica. "Idee e progetti italiani di Nuovo Ordine Europeo nei rapporti con il Reich nazista (1939–1943)." *Rivista Storica Italiana* 1 (2009): 388–429.

———, "Die Europakonzeptionen von Faschismus und Nationalsozialismus (1939–1943)." *Vierteljahrshefte für Zeitgeschichte* 4 (2010): 509–41.

Fröhlich, Elke, ed. *Die Tagebücher von Joseph Goebbels*. Part II, *Diktate 1941–1945*, vol. 6, October–December 1942. Munich, 1996.

Garin, Eugenio. *Cronache di filosofia italiana (1900–1943)*. Bari, 1955.

Garzarelli, Benedetta. *Parleremo al mondo intero: La propaganda del fascismo all'estero*. Alessandria, 2004.

Gentile, Emilio. "La politica estera del partito fascista: Ideologia e organizzazione dei Fasci italiani all'estero (1920–1930)." *Storia contemporanea* 6 (1995): 897–956.

Ginelli, C. "Europa che nasce Europa che muore." *Il fabbro* (15 January 1945): 2.

Giustibelli, Simona. "L'Europa nella riflessione del convegno della Fondazione Volta (Roma, 16–20 novembre 1932)." *Dimensioni e problemi della ricerca storica* 1 (2002): 181–234.

Grunert, Robert. *Der Europagedanke westeuropäischer faschistischer Bewegungen 1940–45*. Paderborn, 2012.

Hersant, Yves, and Fabienne Durand-Bogaert. *Europes: De l'antiquité au XXe siècle anthologie critique et commentée*. Paris, 2000.

Hewitson, Mark, and Matthew D'Auria, eds. *Europe in Crisis: Intellectuals and the European Idea, 1917–1957*. New York, 2012.

Hiltebrandt, Philipp. "Grundzüge der italienischen Aussenpolitik," *Erwachendes Europa, Monatsschrift für nationalsozialistische Weltanschauung, Außenpolitik und Auslandskunde* 5 (1934): 129–40.

Hoffend, Andrea. *Zwischen Kultur-Achse und Kulturkampf: Die Beziehungen zwischen 'Drittem Reich' und faschistischen Italien in den Bereichen Medien, Kunst, Wissenschaft und Rassenfrage*. Frankfurt am Main, 1998.

Knox, MacGregor. *Destino comune: Dittatura, politica estera e guerra nell'Italia fascista e nella Germania nazista*. Turin, 2003.

La Rovere, Luca. *Storia dei Guf: Organizzazione, politica e miti della gioventù universitaria fascista 1919–1943*. Turin, 2003.

Longo, Gisella, ed. *Il fascismo e l'Idea d'Europa: Il convegno dell'Istituto nazionale di cultura fascista (1942)*. Rome, 2000.

Mangoni, Luisa, ed., *"Primato" 1940–1943*. Bari, 1977.

Matthäus, Jürgen, and Frank Bajohr, eds. *Alfred Rosenberg: Die Tagebücher von 1934 bis 1944*. Frankfurt am Main, 2015.

Michaelis, Meir. "I rapporti tra fascismo italiano e nazismo prima dell'avvento di Hitler al potere (1922–1933)." *Rivista storica italiana* 3 (1973): 569–78.

Mussano, A. "Repubblica e razza." *La Riscossa* (23 March 1944): 1.

Mussolini, Benito. "Fascismo." In *Enciclopedia italiana*. Milan, 1932.

———. *Opera omnia*, XXIII, *Dal discorso dell'Ascensione agli accordi del Laterano (27 maggio 1927–11 febbraio 1929)*, ed. Edoardo and Duilio Susmel. Florence, 1957.

———. *Opera omnia*, XXIV, *Dagli accordi del Laterano al dodicesimo anniversario della fondazione dei Fasci (12 febbraio 1929–23 marzo 1931)*, ed. Edoardo and Duilio Susmel. Florence, 1958.

———. "Discorso per la proclamazione dell'Impero," 9 May 1936. In *Opera Omnia*, XXVII, *Dall'inaugurazione della Provincia di Littoria alla proclamazione dell'Impero (19 dicembre 1934–9 maggio 1936)*, ed. Edoardo and Duilio Susmel. Florence, 1959.

———. *Opera omnia*, XXXII, *Dalla liberazione di Mussolini all'epilogo: la Repubblica sociale italiana (13 settembre 1943–28 aprile 1945)*, ed. Edoardo and Duilio Susmel. Florence, 1960.

———. *Opera omnia*, XXXV, *Aggiunte: Scritti e discorsi, Lettere, Telegrammi, Messaggi, Cronologia essenziale dal 13 settembre 1943 al 28 aprile 1945*, ed. E. and D. Susmel. Florence, 1962.

Nattermann, Ruth, ed. *I diari e le agende di Luca Pietromarchi (1938–1940): Politica estera del fascismo e vita quotidiana di un diplomatico romano del '900*. Rome, 2009.

Occhini, Barna. "Degli ebrei." *Italia e civiltà* (13 May 1944): 2.

Orano, Paolo, ed. *L'Asse nel pensiero dei due popoli. Die Achse im Denken der beiden Völker*. Rome, 1938.

Orestano, Francesco. "Nuovo ordine europeo." *Gerarchia* 1 (January 1942): 3–9.

———, "Vita religiosa nella nuova Europa." *Gerarchia* 12 (December 1942): 476–84.

Pezzato, E. "Vittoria Europea e bolscevismo." *La Repubblica fascista* (17 December 1944): 2.

Pugliese, A. "Ricostruzione europea." *La Repubblica fascista* (19 August 1944): 1.

Reale Accademia d'Italia, ed. *Convegno "Volta", Roma, 14–20 novembre 1932-XI. Relazioni e comunicazioni*. Rome, 1932.

Rodogno, Davide. *Il nuovo ordine mediterraneo: Le politiche di occupazione dell'Italia fascista in Europa (1940–1943)*. Turin, 2003.

Romero, Federico, and Antonio Varsori, ed. *Nazione, interdipendenza, integrazione. Le relazioni internazionali dell'Italia (1917–1989)*. Rome, 2005.

Rumi, Giorgio. *Alle origini della politica estera fascista (1918–1923)*. Bari, 1968.

Schieder, Wolfgang. *Faschistische Diktaturen: Studien zu Italien und Deutschland*. Göttingen, 2008.

Schilmar, Boris. *Der Europadiskurs im deutschen Exil 1933–1945*. Munich, 2004.

Schmidt, Paul, ed. *Rivoluzione nel Mediterraneo: La lotta per lo spazio vitale dell'Italia*. Milan, 1942 (1940).

Sella, Piero. "Cinquant'anni dopo: repubblica sociale, fascismo, Germania nazionalsocialista." *L'uomo libero* 36 (1993): 2–10.

Sertoli Salis, Renzo. *Italia, Europa, Arabia*. Milan, 1940.

———. "Considerazioni geopolitiche inattuali." *Geopolitica* 4 (1940): 164–66.

Sösemann, Bernd. "'L'idea dell'Europa': Die faschistische Volta-Konferenz von 1932 und der nationalsozialistische Kongreß von 1941 im Kontext der Europa-Konzeptionen des 20. Jahrhunderts." *Vigonianae* 1 (2010): 49–95.
Vigliar, Emilia. *L'unione europea all'epoca del progetto Briand*. Milan, 1983.

☙ 10

THE NAZI "NEW EUROPE"
Transnational Concepts of a Fascist and Völkisch Order for the Continent

Johannes Dafinger

Introduction

Europa and the bull decorated the front cover of a special edition of *Illustrirte Zeitung Leipzig* in December 1944.[1] The kidnapped princess who had already served in ancient Greece as an allegory for Europe appeared this time on a glossy magazine which was devoted to the cause of a National Socialist "New Europe." A big part of the magazine consisted of advertisements of private German companies avowing themselves to a Nazi-dominated Europe. The aircraft company Focke-Wulf, for example, presented the building of military airplanes as a contribution "to solve the great tasks of the day, the fulfillment of which will bring about a New Order in Europe." Naturally, the "fulfillment" of the "great tasks" would have been a German victory in the "fight for self-determination of continental Europe," as the advertisement was calling World War II. Focke-Wulf would subsequently "continue its peacetime production and build with the gained knowledge and the proven strong productivity better and better airplanes to meet the high demands of coming European air traffic."[2] On the ground, Henschel's locomotives were rolling "in the service of unifying the peoples" (*im Dienst des völkerverbindenden Verkehrs*).[3] A producer of a paste used by house-painters and decorators was sure that Europe was "a unity in a higher sense." Cultural monuments erected together by artists from different European nations seemed to prove this.[4] And the Dresdner Bank confessed: "The fundament of peace is a healthy European economic policy."[5] An engineering company put it with brevity: "Europe is moving closer together."[6]

A contour drawing of Europa and the bull is also reproduced on the cover of a semi-official, bulky compendium entitled *Europa: Handbuch der politischen, wirtschaftlichen und kulturellen Entwicklung des neuen Europa* (Europe: Handbook for the Political, Economic, and Cultural Development of the New Europe). This *Europa-Handbuch*, as it is abbreviated in the front matter, and as I will call it in the following, contains on over three hundred large pages about two dozen programmatic contributions of German and non-German authors to the discourse about a Nazi "New Europe," a "chronicle of the new Europe," lexical entries on the history, economy, and culture of European states, as well as extracts from public speeches by Hitler and other prominent Nazis. It was published by the Berlin-based think tank Deutsches Institut für Außenpolitische Forschung (German Institute for Foreign Policy Research), founded by Foreign Minister Joachim von Ribbentrop and working for him.[7]

The special edition of *Illustrirte Zeitung Leipzig* appeared in print at a time when Nazi Germany had lost nearly all of its European allies and military control over large parts of Europe. The references to a Europe unified under German guidance had therefore something of an invocation. Yet the *Europa-Handbuch* had been prepared under completely different circumstances. Published in the first half of 1943,[8] it must have been drafted before the German defeat at Stalingrad and hence at a time when the involved parties were still counting on a German victory.

The *Europa-Handbuch* is an outstanding document. The compendium should not be taken as a publication reflecting solely visions of Europe developed in the power circle around Ribbentrop and his ministry. As a matter of fact, Ribbentrop's Foreign Office was behind many initiatives to anchor the "New Europe" in Nazi thought and practice. But in addition to chapters that were authored by members of the Foreign Office, it included contributions by the Reich minister of economics, Walther Funk; by the Reich student leader and member of the SS, Gustav Adolf Scheel; by the head of the Amt Musik (Office for Music) in the Amt Rosenberg, Herbert Gerigk; by the president of the People's Court, Roland Freisler; by the sports administrator Carl Diem—and others. Extracts from public speeches by Reich Minister of Propaganda Joseph Goebbels were published in the volume, too, and a very positive review of it appeared in the journal of the Antijüdische Aktion (Anti-Jewish Action), which was closely associated with Goebbels' ministry.[9] No other single publication represented the Nazi discourse about Europe more broadly.

The inclusion of non-German authors in the *Europa-Handbuch* is particularly interesting, too. It reflects the importance of contributions of non-Germans from allied or, in the war, occupied countries to the discourse about Europe in the National Socialist sphere of influence. The layout of the *Handbuch* argues against the assumption that its main objective was propaganda among those who collaborated with Nazi Germany. The regime had other publications that were intended to reach an international audience and to help win non-German Europeans for the Nazi German side. One of the most famous and widely distributed magazines of that type was *Signal*,[10] another one *Junges Europa*.[11] Both were published in several languages. By contrast, the *Europa-Handbuch* was probably directed at a German audience. Its almost encyclopedic approach gives the impression that it was to appeal to professionals who took part in the Nazi discourse about Europe.

This makes the *Europa-Handbuch* an excellent source for historical studies of the discourse about Europe in the National Socialist sphere of influence. What did the concepts of a Nazi "New Europe" actually look like? How did they fit into Nazi ideology? What role would Germany play in the "New Europe"? Which parts were assigned to the other European countries? Was the Nazi "New Europe" a "fascist International"? How did conservative-authoritarian allies of the Nazis relate to the Nazi concepts of Europe? What were the outer borders of Europe in these concepts, and which groups were to be excluded from "New Europe"? My aim in this chapter is to deal with these questions. The investigation is based on an evaluation of the articles in the *Europa-Handbuch*, first of the German authors and then of the non-German ones. Finally, I will address the transnational connections and cooperations that the authors of the *Europa-Handbuch* took part in.

Not all participants in the discourse about the Nazi "New Europe" adopted fascist elements into their worldview. Many European conservatives—most importantly those who formed the administrations of Nazi Germany's allies—were of course influenced by the rise of fascist movements and their takeover in Italy and Germany since 1922, which has led to them being characterized as "fascistized" conservatives or even as "para-fascists," "semi-fascists," "quasi-fascists," "pseudo-fascists," and the like.[12] Without doubt, there is a considerable overlap of their discourse and their exercise of power with fascism. Nevertheless, the term proposed here to describe them is *"völkisch conservative."* The adjective *völkisch*, derived from *Volk*, is not translatable into English. It describes a specific form of being national whereupon the nation (in German here: *das Volk*) is understood as something primordial, rooted either in racial origin or in natural-geographical environment,[13] or in longtime and virtually unchangeable traditions, cultural habits, and language[14] (or in a combination of these elements). The multifaceted *völkisch* movement had already developed long before World War I.[15] National Socialism built on the *völkisch* worldview[16] and combined it with fascist elements. The revolutionary, transcendent (aiming at a New Society and a New Man), and imperialist orientation of fascism had been foreign to the *völkisch* movement before 1920. Thus, National Socialism was both *völkisch* and fascist. *Völkisch* conservatives differed with them and other fascists in their objective to preserve traditional power relations and cultural patterns (including the role of the churches), but they shared with fascists the ideology of primordial ethnonationalism.

"New Europe" in Germany

The "chronicle of the new Europe" and the extracts from treaties and speeches in the *Europa-Handbuch* show that "Europe" was a constant theme in the German public since about 1936 when the Spanish Civil War began. This war involved not alone Franco's nationalist movement, but also European fascists and National Socialists who supported the *Caudillo* in his military conflict with republicans and communists. Later that year, the Anti-Comintern Pact was signed. Initially a treaty only between Germany and Japan, it was ratified by other European countries allied with Germany in the following years. In the *Europa-Handbuch*, the pact was presented as the "backbone of the European united front" fighting against "Bolshevism."[17]

Before addressing other elements of the discourse about such a united Europe, the "iron law" of all National Socialist concepts for a "New Order" in Europe has to be mentioned: that Nazi Germany would be the leading European power.[18] This claim was not open for debate, but the Nazis tried to justify it by referring to allegedly superior "German" qualities (for example, the notion that Germans were more hard-working and talented than any other nations of the continent) and "German" military, economic, and cultural accomplishments. Germans supposedly had a predestination or "mission to lead."[19] In addition, National Socialists argued that it was their ideology that gave them their particular strength for their role as leaders.[20]

Hitler made his clearest remarks about Europe in December 1941 in his speech in front of the Reichstag, which at that time was disempowered as a parliament and gathered only to listen to the Führer. The *Europa-Handbuch* contains extracts from a transcript of that speech. "What is Europe?", Hitler asked the delegates, and gave the answer himself:

> There is no geographic definition of our continent, but only a *völkisch* [*volkliche*] and cultural one. It is not the Urals that form the border

of this continent, but this line that separates the attitude to life [*Lebensbild*] of the West from the one of the East. Europe was a family of peoples [*Völkerfamilie*], which might be as differentiated and divided [*auseinanderweichend*] in its political configuration and objectives as it wants, but which does constitute, considering the overall picture, a partly identical, partly complementary unity with regard to blood and culture [*blutmäßig und kulturell*].[21]

For Hitler, Europe was defined racially and culturally, whereupon culture was a deviate of race. In ancient times, "Europe" had been first "this Greek island into which Nordic tribes had expanded," a little later "the Greek–Roman world," and finally it had incorporated the Germanic tribes as well. Together, Romans and Teutons had defended Europe, or the "Occident" (*Abendland*), in the Battle of the Catalaunian Plains in a "fight of destiny" (*Schicksalskampf*) for the first time. In the following centuries, the defense of Europe had become "mainly … the task of the Teutons [*Germanen*]."[22]

This definition of Europe in 1941 was consistent with what Hitler had already written in *Mein Kampf*. The above-mentioned special issue of *Illustrirte Zeitung Leipzig* quoted as a preamble from his book: "The struggle that rages today involves very great aims: a culture fights for its existence, which combines millenniums and embraces Hellenism and Germanity [*Griechen- und Germanentum*] together."[23] In the preceding sentence in *Mein Kampf*, the unity of different "peoples"[24] connected by this common culture is described as a "racial community" (*Rassegemeinschaft*).[25]

As such, Europe had no stable geographical borders. In one of his "monologues in the Führer's headquarters" some weeks before his speech in the Reichstag, Hitler stated explicitly that he wanted to determine the location of the borders, more precisely the eastern borders of Europe: "The border will be there where the Germanic-German ethnos [*Volkstum*] parts from the Slavic ethnos [*wo sich das germanisch-deutsche Volkstum vom slawischen scheidet*]." This border should be placed "where we want it to be."[26]

Some of the German authors of contributions in the *Europa-Handbuch* joined in this racial definition of Europe, which used biological arguments to determine the outer borders of Europe. An article written under a pseudonym answers the question of how a European sense of cultural and political belonging could develop among the "peoples" of Europe, in spite of "a contrarious history," as follows: "[T]here is only one explanation, namely the one of the kindredship of the European peoples. They have something in common [*etwas Gemeinsames*], *one* root, *one* origin. … Primordial and common to all is and remains the blood which allows to sense common strength in common [*Ursprünglich ist und bleibt allen gemeinsam das Blut, das gemeinsame Höhe gemeinsam empfinden läßt*]."[27] As Hitler in his speeches, the unknown author interprets Europe as a "racial community." The mythical assumption of the transmission of characteristics by "blood" has to function as proof of a stronger connection of "peoples" within Europe than of "peoples" in other regions.

One important element of the definition of Europe as a "racial community" was the exclusion of Jews from this community, with the argument that they belonged to another "race." Theodor Wilhelm, a young professional who published a pedagogical journal (and became a professor in Kiel in the 1950s),[28] writes with frightening openness in the *Europa-Handbuch* that the current war "is ... the final act to a European overall solution [*Gesamtlösung*] of the Jewish problem." With examples from a number of European countries, he shows that "in Europe the front against Jewry today has already, aside from some disfigurements [*Schönheitslücken*], closed ranks."[29]

In its internal affairs, Europe was to be structured along "borders between peoples" (*Volksgrenzen*).[30] While belonging all to one "race"—a "shared root" which had led to "kindred traits" (*verwandte Züge*) of cultural manifestations[31]—the European "peoples" had, according to Hitler, developed their own cultures (*Kulturen*) and peculiarities (*Eigenarten*). They "could not be alienated of their nature [*Wesen*] just like that"—and they should not, as Europe was a peculiar continent "exactly in the polymorphy of its cultures."[32] According to Hitler, Europe was a "family of peoples," but "the individual members of this family are infinitely hardened [*unendlich gehärtet*] within themselves."[33] The boundaries between "peoples" were therefore "virtually unchangeable"; only state borders could be altered.[34]

It is important for the argument of this chapter that this essentialist understanding of culture, and the belief that "peoples" have their "peculiarities," is not necessary based on biological racism. It can be culture based, too. Ulrich von Hassell, for example, a contributor to the *Europa-Handbuch*, was not thinking in biological terms. He (who later on belonged to the conspirators of the 20 July plot in 1944) did not share the interpretation that Europe was bound together by "blood." Instead, he saw a "common ethic-Christian base" of the European cultures (*Kulturen*)—a much more traditional definition of Europe. What is remarkable is that this did not stop him from inscribing himself into the overall discourse insofar as he still insisted in the "*völkisch* peculiarity" of each of Europe's "peoples' individualities" (*Volksindividualitäten*).[35] These peculiarities had to be defended against Anglo-American "egalitarianism" (*Gleichmacherei*).[36] It appears that the Nazi discourse on Europe was flexible enough to integrate more conservative views like Hassell's. This then was a strength, which also helps to explain its attractiveness outside Germany.

"New Europe" in Other Countries

Four of the non-German contributors to the *Europa-Handbuch* came from Italy, and one from Bulgaria, Hungary, Romania, Vichy-France, Finland, and Spain, respectively. This distribution reflects political priorities and the strength of relations between Germany and other European countries. Italy played a special role. It is set apart from other countries in Ribbentrop's preface to the *Europa-Handbuch*, too.[37] The reason is obvious: as the first country with a fascist government, it held an exceptional position among European fascists.[38] Despite this, however, Nazi Germany had stronger academic and cultural ties to countries in Southeastern Europe than to Italy. These close relationships are reflected in the fact that three authors from that area—from Bulgaria, Hungary, and Romania—contributed to the *Europa-Handbuch*. There is probably no specific reason why Slovakia and Croatia, member states of the Tripartite and Anti-Comintern pacts, were not represented, unlike Germany's ally in Northern Europe, Finland, which was a member of the Anti-Comintern Pact too. Articles written by authors from officially neutral Vichy-France and Spain complemented the collection.

Remarkably, the *Europa-Handbuch* contains no contributions from Eastern or Northwestern Europe. The fact that authors from Eastern Europe (Poland and occupied Soviet territories) were missing can be explained relatively easily with reference to Nazi plans in this region. Even if it was regarded as Europe geographically, it would above all constitute a part of German *Lebensraum* ("living space"). Its ethnically non-German inhabitants were not allowed to participate in intellectual or cultural life within the Nazi "New Europe." It did not escape the attention of Nazi foreign policy makers, mainly around Joachim von Ribbentrop and Alfred Rosenberg, that this policy frustrated collaboration in these territories. Some of them even campaigned with memorandums for a better treatment of East Europeans as potential allies against the Soviet communist regime, and for an inclusion of this perspective in concepts of the European "New Order," but they did not achieve acceptance of their plans.[39] By contrast, it was generally possible to develop ideas for future Europe in Northwestern Europe. Robert Grunert has published about concepts of Europe of fascist movements in the Netherlands and in Belgium.[40] The "National Unity" Party (Nasjonal Samling) in Norway, led by Vidkun Quisling, also presented plans about the future of the continent to the public and to the German government.[41] But the Nazi regime ignored these concepts. Their long-term plans for the region envisaged the integration of Norway, Denmark, the Netherlands, and Belgium into a Greater Germanic Reich (*Großgermanisches Reich*).[42] For that reason, Germany's cultural diplomacy treated these countries differently from the rest of Europe.[43]

The majority of those who did publish in the *Europa-Handbuch* held a doctoral degree or were even professors. Many had been studying in Germany. Some were or had been holding high positions in the governments of their respective countries.[44] With Lázló Bárdossy there was even a former prime minister of Hungary among the authors. Bárdossy had started his political career soon after World War I. Since 1922, he had worked in the Hungarian Foreign Office in higher and higher positions until he became foreign minister in 1941. Shortly afterwards, he was appointed prime minister and served in this office during a crucial period between April 1941 and March 1942. First, he led his country into war against the Soviet Union and the Western Allies, on the side of Germany.[45] Second, an anti-Jewish law aimed at "racial purity of the Hungarian nation," banning marriage between Jews and non-Jews, passed during his term in office.[46] After his dismissal, Bárdossy presided over the anti-Semitic United Christian National League (Egyesült Kereszteny Nemzeti Liga, EKNL). The League and Bárdossy himself, who was elected to the Hungarian parliament in 1944, agitated for the continuation of Hungary's war on the German side.[47]

Bárdossy can be characterized as a *völkisch*, anti-Semitic, and anticommunist politician in favor of a German–Hungarian alliance. Neither his predecessor nor his successor as prime minister were proponents of such an alliance: Pál Teleki committed suicide when his "policy of armed neutrality" between the Axis powers, Great Britain, and the Soviet Union had failed.[48] Miklós Kállay, an "old-style gentry politician," cautiously contacted the Western Allies.[49] The German side regarded Bárdossy as a "serious, clever, and clear-sighted politician" who distinguished himself among other Hungarian politicians "by an honest and explicit commitment to the Führer and the axis."[50] He never was a member of a fascist organization, though. The EKNL was "carried by the traditional political class."[51]

Nevertheless, Bárdossy could integrate the envisaged Nazi "New Order" for Europe into his *völkisch*, anti-Semitic, and anticommunist worldview. The *Europa-Handbuch* contains an article that he had written in 1942 in which he equates "peoples" (*Völker*) to human beings. They had a "body," a "job," a "homeland;" they should live together harmonically, but they could—here Bárdossy transfers the social darwinist claim of the "survival of the fittest" to "peoples"— "cease to exist" (*die Schwachen müssen untergehen*) if they "relax and enjoy" (*Erschlaffen im Genuß bedeutet den sicheren Niedergang*).[52] Clearly, Bárdossy shared an essentialist view on "peoples" with German Nazis as well as with German *völkisch* conservatives like von Hassell.

Bárdossy's view was also identical to that of some other *völkisch* conservatives outside Europe, as the example of the second author from Southeastern Europe shows. Lüben Dikoff[53] had studied in Germany.[54] He was a professor of law and former Bulgarian minister of justice. Moreover, he had directed the University of Sofia in 1933/34. His article sketches a "new European order of peoples which lets every ethnos [*Volkstum*] achieve its indispensable right to have its own living space [*Lebensraum*], and by doing so saves the *völkisch*-racial sovereignty [of every ethnos]."[55]

In his essay, Bárdossy raises another central topic of many concepts of Europe at this time: that Europe had to stand united against "Bolshevism." The European "peoples" had a common destiny, Bárdossy argues (in accordance with an abundance of similar quotes from German Nazis), as World War II was a "fight for the protection of the endangered civilization [*Zivilisation*] and freedom of Europe." Hungary was taking part in that fight "with imperturbable dutifulness."[56] Bárdossy left no doubt where these dangers were coming from: from the "East."

That Europe had to defend itself against the common Soviet communist enemy was a claim that could even integrate individuals into the Nazi discourse about Europe who at first glance seem to have been ideologically far from any fascist and probably even from *völkisch* positions. Gheorghe N. Leon, the third author from Southeastern Europe, is such a special case.[57] Leon, a professor of finance at the University of Cluj since 1935 (and at the University of Bucharest until 1945, when he was brought to trial and imprisoned), had worked for the government in Romania—as Bárdossy had in Hungary—since 1934 as under-secretary of state in the Ministry of Industry and Trade, then in 1940 in the government of Ion Gigurtu as minister for economic affairs and as interim minister of finance, agriculture, and coordination and planning. For two months, he remained minister for economic affairs in the government of Ion Antonescu, but then resigned and returned to university. He subsequently served as auditor of the Romanian national bank. Leon was a member of the National Liberal Party and was elected to the Romanian parliament on this party's list. His doctoral advisor had been the German social liberal economist Lujo Brentano. His text does not contain any racist or anti-Semitic statements or *völkisch* stereotypes. He connected to the discourse about a Nazi "New Europe" through his anticommunism when he stated: "The Bolshevist threat has opened the eyes of the European states and caused them to unite in order to defend the common heritage of civilization and culture."[58]

All three authors from Southeastern Europe came out of the traditional elites carrying the authoritarian regimes in their countries. Hitler had a tendency to prefer alliances with authoritarian political systems based on the upper class, the army, and the executive branch, even though fascist movements existed in these countries.[59] The leaders of these regimes, most notably Miklós Horthy, suppressed fascist movements in their countries.[60] Carl Levy argues that "[i]n most cases … [Hitler] chose the more convenient traditionalist authoritarian conservatives because they served the interests of the German nation-state."[61] Even in occupied countries, Hitler installed fascist puppet governments "only as a last resort, when more legitimate or popular moderate political forces were not available."[62] When Croatia became nominally independent in 1941, Vladko Maček, head of the Croatian Peasant Party, was designated by the Germans as the leader of the new country. Only when he refused to act as a German puppet, Hitler gave power to Ante Pavelić and the Ustaša (which absorbed parts of the Peasant Party).[63]

Hitler's preference for traditional elites was first of all a pragmatic decision.[64] But as the analysis of the contributions of authors from Southeastern Europe in the *Europa-Handbuch* demonstrates, the relationships resulting from this decision had an ideological basis, because many conservatives in Southeastern Europe had integrated *völkisch* elements into their worldviews, and the vision of a *völkisch* Europe had become a consensus model of European fascists and *völkisch* conservatives. The anticommunist foundation of Nazi "New Europe" appealed to an even broader political spectrum.

Transnational Connections and Cooperations

How could a transnational discourse on Europe develop in the Nazi period? Which were the "places" where this discourse literally "took place"? One such "place" was of course the *Europa-Handbuch* itself. Publications as the *Handbuch*, newspapers, and journals triggered the exchange of ideas throughout Europe. Another non-institutionalized opportunity for the exchange of ideas across borders represented informal meetings of the protagonists of the discourse about Europe.

Gheorghe N. Leon, together with other colleagues, politicians, and business leaders, for example, joined a dinner in Bucharest organized in honor of Carl Schmitt when the latter gave lectures there in 1943.[65] Yet which of these non-institutionalized opportunities were actually used to talk about Europe cannot, of course, be determined.

More significant, therefore, are institutionalized forums, which existed precisely to fuel the discourse about Europe. The example of two other authors of contributions to the *Europa-Handbuch* illustrates this. The French writer Jacques Benoist-Méchin and his colleague from Finland, Veikko Antero Koskenniemi, were both members of the European Writers' Union (Europäische Schriftsteller-Vereinigung, ESV) founded on Joseph Goebbels' initiative as an "Anti-PEN-Club" in 1941.[66] Koskenniemi even became vice president of the organization.[67] The ESV was the framework for a number of meetings of writers from different European countries within the National Socialist sphere of influence that took place in Weimar. As Frank-Rutger Hausmann has observed, "German and foreign writers found actually closer to each other at the Weimar meetings" and, as one of the participants reported after the war, assured each other that they had "common literary ancestors" and a "cultural heritage connecting all."[68] According to Hausmann, it was at least the objective of the meetings to "commit the attendees to the fight against common enemies in the East and West."

Benoist-Méchin and Koskenniemi were indeed committed to this cause of European defense against its alleged common enemies. Benoist-Méchin warned in the *Europa-Handbuch* of the "unhuman methods of exploitation of the Anglo-Saxon capitalism and the Soviet communism" against which Europe was fighting.[69] Koskenniemi concentrated on the "danger which threatens from the East without interruption."[70] It has been shown and does not come as a surprise that it "was a belief generally held among the Finnish bourgeoisie and intelligentsia" that the Soviet Union posed the "gravest threat to European high culture."[71]

Nazi Germany established a number of "European" associations resembling the ESV: The European Youth Federation, the European Women's Federation, the International Film Chamber, the Union of National Journalists' Associations, the Permanent Council for International Cooperation among Composers, the International Law Chamber, and even a European Chess Federation (the attempt to establish a general European Sport Federation under Nazi leadership was not successful, though).[72] These organizations aimed at European-wide membership. In addition, networks that functioned on a bilateral basis have to be taken into account. The transnational discourse about Europe also took place in the network of German–foreign "friendship societies" (*zwischenstaatliche Gesellschaften*) and German Cultural Institutes (Deutsche Wissenschaftliche Institute) that had been established in European cities during the war.[73] Events organized by these institutions facilitated the development of Nazi "New Europe" as a concept. How German and non-German fascists and *völkisch* conservatives thought and spoke about Europe would not have developed in the same way without these transnational contacts. The Nazi "New Europe" was not static, but evolving over time.

On the one hand, ideas about a future Europe in the contact zone differed in many ways from one another. German fascists tended to believe in the existence of a common racial origin of the Europeans. According to their ideology, all European "peoples" belonged to the "Aryan" or "Indo-Germanic race."[74] By contrast, *völkisch* conservatives in and outside Germany often used culture-based arguments to define Europe. The idea of European unity could be based on the assumptions that Europe had had a common history since ancient or medieval times, or a common cultural tradition in the Christian faith. This difference reflects the importance of racism in the ideology of German fascists and the importance of tradition in the ideology of *völkisch* conservatives.

On the other hand, the participants in the discourse about Europe learned to combine these perspectives into one framework. This did not eliminate these differences, but rather acknowledged that they were not contradictory to one another. The conclusion from both perspectives could be that Europe had to stand united against those who were defined as the "other" (and as the enemy). What is more, fascists and *völkisch* conservatives both wanted to reorganize Europe along *völkisch* lines. In this respect, fascism and *völkisch* conservatism were overlapping ideologies.

Conclusion

Antonio de Luna, a Spanish Falangist and professor of law at the University of Madrid, wrote in the *Europa-Handbuch*: "A Spanish Falangist feels for the moment a certain consternation if he is asked to deal with the European idea with benevolence."[75] After some lines, though, he came to the conclusion: "But in our position lies no contradiction. ... Precisely because we were 'anti-European' until the end of the first quarter of the twentieth century, we must necessarily connect today with the pertinacious defenders of the new Europe."[76] Fascists like Luna had developed their own vision of Europe until 1943, when the *Europa-Handbuch* was published. Thomas Mann observed in the same year that everybody wanted European unification: "Hitler wants it, too, in his charming manner [*liebenswürdige Art*]. But this shows precisely that now it really just depends on the manner in which one wants it, just on the spirit [*Geist*] in which one says 'Europe'."[77]

The Nazis "wanted" Europe in a very special way. To them, Europe was a "family of peoples" (Hitler), which should be organized along *völkisch* lines with every "people" living according to "its" national culture and "its" *völkisch* way of life. Politically, Nazi Germany would dictate the fate of the continent. In cultural terms, it would dominate it, and only Germany's military might could defend it against its common enemies in the "West" and the "East". Losing the fight would lead to the "Bolshevization" and "Americanization" of Europe, which would be the end of the continent's history. "Europe will be united after this war—or it will be no more," the *Europa-Handbuch* knew.[78]

This concept of Europe was compatible with fascist ideology, but it also complied with the worldview of *völkisch* conservatives, and it made the prospect of a German-dominated Europe acceptable for them. In this regard, Nazi "New Europe" was a consensus model that fascists and *völkisch* conservatives could agree on.

Many details of this model were deliberately left vague. Hitler did not want to be tied by concrete conceptions of future Europe or even contractual obligations that would limit Germany's sovereignty— it should not promise anything to the neighboring countries, as he emphasized in his personal conversations as early as 1941.[79] So nobody knew which role European countries that were allied with Nazi Germany would exactly play in a German-dominated Europe after a German victory in the war. Those who thought that they knew it saw their plans contested by the visions of other participants in the Nazi discourse about Europe. What can be observed, though, is the formation of a clear-cut framework for all these plans and visions. It highlighted the limits of the concepts that could be proposed, endorsed, and even articulated. It could not be questioned that "peoples" as primordial entities played the central role in Europe, that Jews had to be excluded from the European community, and that Germany was the leader of the continent. Furthermore, regardless of the fact that the commonalities that were holding the different European "peoples" together were defined biologically by some, but culturally by others, all concepts accepted that there was something specifically "European" that had to be defended against the influence of Soviet communism and of Anglo-American democracy and "materialism"—or against the influence of them both.

By disassociating core ideological convictions like anticommunism, anti-Americanism, cultural essentialism, and anti-Semitism from a solely national rhetoric, the Nazis opened a discursive space that fascists and *völkisch* conservatives from other countries could enter, too. This lent them the potential to integrate non-German fascists and *völkisch* conservatives into the Nazi "New Europe." Similarly, the Nazis had integrated large strata of the population within Germany into the German *Volksgemeinschaft*. Concepts of transnational fascism should take this fluidity of borders between National Socialist, fascist, and *völkisch* conservative movements into account.

Until recently, historians tended to call the Nazis' talk about a "New Europe" "deceptive make-up,"[80] and the Nazi concepts of Europe an "anemic phantom."[81] "The inhuman war aims of Nazi Germany were hidden behind a *völkisch* ideology of Europe."[82] But did the Nazi concept of Europe really conceal something? And how can inhumanity hide behind *völkisch* reasoning? No, when the Nazis were telling the narrative about Europa and the bull their way—as a story about racial ideology, *völkisch* thinking, cultural essentialism, anti-Americanism, anticommunism, and German dominance—they did not tell a cock and bull story. They told a story about themselves.

JOHANNES DAFINGER, a predoctoral scientist at the Department for Contemporary History at the Alpen-Adria-Universität Klagenfurt, studied History at the LMU Munich and the European University at St. Petersburg, and as a research scholar at the University of Maryland, College Park. He is writing his dissertation about the role of German–foreign "friendship societies" in the Nazi "New Europe." Publication: *Wissenschaft im außenpolitischen Kalkül des "Dritten Reiches". Deutsch-sowjetische Wissenschaftsbeziehungen vor und nach Abschluss des Hitler-Stalin-Paktes* (Berlin, 2014).

Notes

1. *Illustrirte Zeitung Leipzig*, special edition *"Der europäische Mensch"* (1944). On this special edition, see Otto G. Oexle, "Leitbegriffe—Deutungsmuster—Paradigmenkämpfe. Über Vorstellungen vom 'Neuen Europa' in Deutschland 1944," in *Nationalsozialismus in den Kulturwissenschaften*, vol. 2: *Leitbegriffe—Deutungsmuster—Paradigmenkämpfe. Erfahrungen und Transformationen im Exil*, ed. Hartmut Lehmann and Otto G. Oexle (Göttingen, 2004), 13–40.

278 • *Johannes Dafinger*

2. *Illustrirte Zeitung Leipzig*, 10. A scan of the advertisement can be found on the homepage of Randall Bytwerk, URL: http://research.calvin.edu/german-propaganda-archive/ads.htm (accessed 11 March 2015), and in Oexle, "Leitbegriffe," 25.
3. *Illustrirte Zeitung Leipzig*, 8; Oexle, "Leitbegriffe", 24.
4. *Illustrirte Zeitung Leipzig*, 12.
5. Ibid., 3.
6. Ibid., 15.
7. Peter Longerich, *Propagandisten im Krieg. Die Presseabteilung des Auswärtigen Amtes unter Ribbentrop* (Munich, 1987), 52, n. 35.
8. It cannot have been published later than June 1943 because in mid June a review of the *Europa-Handbuch* came out. See BA Berlin, R 4902/9845, fol. 1, copy of Horst Seemann, "Das Europa-Handbuch (book review)," *Die Judenfrage* [in *Politik, Recht, Kultur und Wirtschaft*] [7], no. 12 (15 June 1943).
9. Ibid. Horst Seemann was the editor of the journal. See Werner Bergmann, "Antisemitische Aktion," in *Enzyklopädie des Nationalsozialismus*, ed. Wolfgang Benz, Hermann Graml, and Hermann Weiß, 4th ed. (Munich, 2001), 365.
10. Rainer Rutz, *Signal: Eine deutsche Auslandsillustrierte als Propagandainstrument im Zweiten Weltkrieg* (Essen, 2007), 253. Also see Martin Moll, "'Signal'. Die NS-Auslandsillustrierte und ihre Propaganda für Hitlers 'Neues Europa'," *Publizistik: Vierteljahreshefte für Kommunikationsforschung* 31 (1986).
11. Per Øhrgaard, "Die Zeitschrift *Junges Europa*: Ein Beispiel für die Europa-Propaganda der Nazis," in *Vielheit und Einheit der Germanistik weltweit*, vol. 5, ed. Franciszek Grucza (Frankfurt am Main, 2012), 127–31.
12. Aristotle A. Kallis, "'Fascism', 'Para-fascism' and 'Fascistization': On the Similarities of Three Conceptual Categories," *European History Quarterly* 33, no. 2 (2003); António Costa Pinto and Aristotle Kallis, "Introduction," in *Rethinking Fascism and Dictatorship in Europe*, ed. idem (Basingstoke and New York, 2014), 2.
13. Martin Broszat, "Die völkische Ideologie und der Nationalsozialismus," *Deutsche Rundschau* 84, no. 1 (1958): 61–62; Mark Bassin, "Blood or Soil? The *Völkisch* Movement, the Nazis, and the Legacy of Geopolitik," in *How Green Were the Nazis? Nature, Environment, and Nation in the Third Reich*, ed. Franz-Josef Brüggemeier, Mark Cioc, and Thomas Zeller (Athens, OH, 2005), 206ff.
14. Ulrich Prehn, "'Volk' und 'Raum' in zwei Nachkriegszeiten: Kontinuitäten und Wandlungen in der Arbeit des Volkstumsforschers Max Hildebert Boehm," in *Das Erbe der Provinz: Heimatkultur und Geschichtspolitik nach 1945*, ed. Habbo Knoch (Göttingen, 2001), 54–55.
15. On the *völkisch* movement in the German Empire, see Uwe Puschner, Walter Schmitz, and Justus H. Ulbricht, eds., *Handbuch zur "Völkischen Bewegung" 1871–1918* (Munich, New Providence, London and Paris, 1996).
16. George L. Mosse, *Die völkische Revolution: Über die geistigen Wurzeln des Nationalsozialismus* (Frankfurt am Main, 1991) (English original published in 1964 under the title *The Crisis of German Ideology: Intellectual Origins of the Third Reich*).
17. *Europa-Handbuch*, 239.

18. Birgit Kletzin, *Europa aus Rasse und Raum: Die nationalsozialistische Idee der Neuen Ordnung* (Münster, 2002), 95; and the following quote, ibid., 95ff.
19. Ibid., 98.
20. Ibid., 99.
21. "Erklärung der Reichsregierung—Rede des Reichskanzlers Adolf Hitler," 11 December 1941, in *Verhandlungen des Reichstags. 4. Wahlperiode 1939*, vol. 460: *Stenographische Berichte 1939–1942, Anlagen zu den Stenographischen Berichten. 1.–8. Sitzung* (n.p.), 93–106, 94–95, http://www.reichstagsprotokolle.de/Blatt2_n4_bsb00000613_00095.html and http://www.reichstagsprotokolle.de/Blatt2_n4_bsb00000613_00096.html (accessed 30 March 2015). Extract printed in *Europa-Handbuch*, 256–57.
22. "Erklärung der Reichsregierung—Rede des Reichskanzlers Adolf Hitler," 11 December 1941, 95.
23. *Illustrirte Zeitung Leipzig*, 28. The quote is from Adolf Hitler, *Mein Kampf: Zwei Bände in einem Band. Ungekürzte Ausgabe*, 102nd–106th ed. (Munich, 1934), 470; and quote in the following sentence ibid. The English translation follows Adolf Hitler, *Mein Kampf: Complete and Unabridged* (New York, 1939), 631; and quote in the following sentence ibid.
24. In the used translation: "races"; in the German original: "Völker."
25. For a succinct reformulation of these ideas, see Franz Alfred Six, "Das Reich und die Grundlegung Europas," *Jahrbuch der Weltpolitik* 2 (1942): 14; reprinted in idem, *Das Reich und Europa* (Berlin, 1943), 6: "Europe is the living space [*Lebensraum*] of the European races and peoples [*Völker*] formed by the creative power of the Arian race. The common racial origin is the uniting element of the European peoples, despite all separative political, governmental, and ideological differences."
26. Adolf Hitler, *Monologe im Führer-Hauptquartier 1941–1944: Die Aufzeichnungen Heinrich Heims*, ed. Werner Jochmann (Hamburg, 1980), entry of 23 September 1941, evening, 66.
27. Hermann Stein (pseudonym), "Europäisches Bewußtsein," in *Europa-Handbuch*, 15–19, 15, 17 (italics as in the original).
28. Hermann Giesecke, "Demokratie als Denk- und Lebensform: Ein Nachruf auf Theodor Wilhelm (1906–2005)," http://www.hermann-giesecke.de/wilhelm.htm (accessed 18 March 2015), first printed in *Das Gespräch aus der Ferne*. no. 375 (2005).
29. Theodor Wilhelm, "Europa als Kulturgemeinschaft," in *Europa-Handbuch*, 143–60, 154–55.
30. "Erklärung der Reichsregierung—Rede des Reichskanzlers Adolf Hitler," 17 May 1933, in *Verhandlungen des Reichstags. VIII. Wahlperiode 1933*, vol. 457: *Stenographische Berichte, Anlagen zu den Stenographischen Berichten, Sach- und Sprechregister* (Berlin, 1934), 47–54, 47; http://www.reichstagsprotokolle.de/Blatt2_w8_bsb00000141_00051.html (accessed 30 March 2015).
31. Adolf Hitler, *Reden des Führers am Parteitag der Ehre 1936* (Munich, 1936), 33.
32. "Erklärung der Reichsregierung—Rede des Reichskanzlers Adolf Hitler," 7 March 1936, in *Verhandlungen des Reichstags. IX. Wahlperiode 1933*, vol. 458: *Stenographische Berichte, Anlagen zu den Stenographischen Berichten* (Berlin, 1936), 63–75, 68; http://www.reichstagsprotokolle.de/Blatt2_w9_bsb00000142_00072.html (accessed 30 March 2015).

33. Hitler on 12 March 1936 in a speech in Karlsruhe, quoted after Max Domarus, *Hitler: Reden und Proklamationen 1932–1945. Kommentiert von einem deutschen Zeitgenossen*, vol. I: *Triumph. Zweiter Halbband 1935–1938* (Wiesbaden, 1973), 604.

34. Ibid.

35. Ulrich von Hassell, "Lebensraum oder Imperialismus?" in *Europa-Handbuch*, 27–33, 33; and the following quote from ibid., 32.

36. On Hassell's concept of Europe, see Manfred Asendorf, "Ulrich von Hassells Europakonzeption und der Mitteleuropäische Wirtschaftstag," *Jahrbuch des Instituts für deutsche Geschichte [Tel Aviv]* 7 (1978).

37. Joachim von Ribbentrop, "Geleitwort," in *Europa-Handbuch*, VII–VIII, VII.

38. Arnd Bauerkämper, *Der Faschismus in Europa 1918–1945* (Stuttgart, 2006), 166–82 and the introduction to this volume. As Monica Fioravanzo analyzes the Italian discourse about Europe in detail in this volume, I will concentrate on the contributions from other countries in the following.

39. Eckart Conze et al., *Das Amt und die Vergangenheit: Deutsche Diplomaten im Dritten Reich und in der Bundesrepublik* (Munich, 2010), 200–8; Mark Mazower, *Hitler's Empire: How the Nazis Ruled Europe* (New York, 2008), 144–57; Patrick Mulligan, "The Politics of Illusion and Empire: The Attempts to Reform German Occupation Policy in the U.S.S.R., Autumn 1942–Summer 1943," PhD dissertation, University of Maryland, 1985.

40. Robert Grunert, *Der Europagedanke westeuropäischer faschistischer Bewegungen 1940–1945* (Paderborn, Munich, Vienna, and Zurich, 2012).

41. Ibid., 104, n. 74.

42. Hans-Dietrich Loock, "Zur 'großgermanischen Politik' des Dritten Reiches," *Vierteljahrshefte für Zeitgeschichte* 8, no. 1 (1960); Jürgen Elvert, *Mitteleuropa! Deutsche Pläne zur europäischen Neuordnung (1918–1945)* (Stuttgart, 1999), 369–72.

43. Frank-Rutger Hausmann has the same explanation as to why no German Cultural Institutes (*Deutsche Wissenschaftliche Institute*) were established in either the Netherlands or Norway. Frank-Rutger Hausmann, *"Auch im Krieg schweigen die Musen nicht": Die Deutschen Wissenschaftlichen Institute im Zweiten Weltkrieg*, 2nd ed. (Göttingen, 2002), 15.

44. Information about the biographies of the authors is taken from the list of contributors in the *Europa-Handbuch* and, if not indicated otherwise, from common biographical handbooks.

45. Jörg K. Hoensch, *Geschichte Ungarns 1867–1983* (Stuttgart, Berlin, Cologne and Mainz, 1984), 146–47.

46. Christian Gerlach and Götz Aly, *Das letzte Kapitel: Realpolitik, Ideologie und der Mord an den ungarischen Juden 1944/1945* (Stuttgart and Munich, 2002), 48–50. Quote from the explanatory statement of a member of the government upon the session of the Hungarian parliament which passed the bill, cited in ibid., 49.

47. Pál Pritz, "War-Crimes Trial Hungarian Style: Prime Minister László Bárdossy before the People's Tribunal, 1945," *Hungarian Studies Review* XXII, no. 1 (1995): 62.

48. Karl P. Benziger, "The Trial of László Bárdossy: The Second World War and Factional Politics in Contemporary Hungary," *Journal of Contemporary History* 40, no. 3 (2005): 468. The quote is by the historian Thomas Sakmyster.

49. Margit Szöllösi-Janze, *Die Pfeilkreuzlerbewegung in Ungarn: Historischer Kontext, Entwicklung und Herrschaft* (Munich, 1989), 97.

50. Ibid., 280, n. 921. The quote is from a report by Edmund Veesenmayer.

51. Anikó Kocács-Bertrand, *Der ungarische Revisionismus nach dem Ersten Weltkrieg: Der publizistische Kampf gegen den Friedensvertrag von Trianon (1918–1931)* (Munich, 1997), 54. The following quote ibid.

52. László Bárdossy, "Ungarns europäische Sendung," in *Europa-Handbuch*, 63–65. Maybe because of translation issues, the terms "the Hungarian people" (*das ungarische Volk*) and "the Hungarian nation" (*die ungarische Nation*) are not separated clearly in Bárdossy's article. Therefore it is difficult to decide whether the "Hungarian people" or the "Hungarian nation" has the "body" ("bleeding" under Turkish attacks) and the "job." The other quotes clearly relate to the "Hungarian people."

53. This is the spelling used in the *Europa-Handbuch*; the scientific transliteration of his name from the kyrillic alphabet would be "Ljuben Dikov."

54. Dikoff was a student of the legal philosopher Julius Binder at the University of Göttingen. Ralf Dreier, "Julius Binder (1870–1939). Ein Rechtsphilosoph zwischen Kaiserreich und Nationalsozialismus," in *Rechtswissenschaft in Göttingen: Göttinger Juristen aus 250 Jahren*, ed. Fritz Loos (Göttingen, 1987), 436.

55. Lüben Dikoff, "Bulgariens Weg zum Dreimächtepakt," in *Europa-Handbuch*, 65–71, 70.

56. Bárdossy, "Ungarns europäische Sendung," 64.

57. On the following biographical details, see Paul Milata, *Zwischen Hitler, Stalin und Antonescu: Rumäniendeutsche in der Waffen-SS*, 2nd ed. (Cologne, Weimar, and Vienna, 2009), 339; Institute for the Investigation of Communist Crimes and the Memory of the Romanian Exile, "New Evidence Discovered by IICCMER in the Visinescu Case," 6 November 2013, http://www.iiccr.ro/index.html?lang=en&section=press/press_releases/new_evidence_discovered_by_iiccmer_in_the_visinescu_case (accessed 27 March 2015).

58. Gh[eorghe] N. Leon, "Der Südosten als europäischer Wirtschaftspartner," in *Europa-Handbuch*, 94–98, 95.

59. See chapter 6. Martin Broszat, "Deutschland–Ungarn–Rumänien: Entwicklung und Grundfaktoren nationalsozialistischer Hegemonial- und Bündnispolitik 1938–1941," *Historische Zeitschrift* 206 (1968): 90; Carl Levy, "Fascism, National Socialism and Conservatives in Europe, 1914–1945: Issues for Comparativists," *Contemporary European History* 8, no. 1 (1999): 113.

60. Levy, "Fascism, National Socialism and Conservatives in Europe," 114; Aristotle Kallis, "The 'Fascist Effect': On the Dynamics of Political Hybridization in Inter-War Europe," in *Rethinking Fascism and Dictatorship in Europe*, ed. António Costa Pinto and Aristotle Kallis (Basingstoke and New York, 2014), 30. Slovakia constitutes a special case in this regard as the Tiso government integrated both the "moderate patriots" around

Tiso, and the more "radical" circles leaning toward Italian Fascism and German National Socialism around Vojtech Tuka and Alexander Mach. See Tatjana Tönsmeyer, "Kollaboration als handlungsleitendes Motiv? Die slowakische Elite und das NS-Regime," in *Kooperation und Verbrechen: Formen der "Kollaboration" im östlichen Europa 1939–1945,* ed. Christoph Dieckmann, Babette Quinkert, and Tatjana Tönsmeyer (Göttingen, 2003), 25–54.

61. Levy, "Fascism, National Socialism and Conservatives in Europe," 114.
62. Stanley G. Payne, *A History of Fascism 1914–1945,* 2nd ed. (London, 1997), 404.
63. Ibid., 406–7; Levy, "Fascism, National Socialism and Conservatives in Europe," 113–14.
64. For means of comparison, influential Italian Fascists were open to cooperation with non-Fascists, too. Mussolini's foreign minister, Dino Grandi, for example, "emphasized the need to cooperate with Fascist and non-Fascist states and parties alike." Arnd Bauerkämper, "Interwar Fascism in Europe and Beyond: Toward a Transnational Radical Right," in *New Perspectives on the Transnational Right,* ed. Martin Durham and Margaret Power (New York, 2010), 46.
65. Frank-Rutger Hausmann, *"Vom Strudel der Ereignisse verschlungen": Deutsche Romanistik im "Dritten Reich"* (Frankfurt am Main, 2000), 597–98.
66. On the history of the ESV, see Frank-Rutger Hausmann, *"Dichte, Dichter, tage nicht!" Die Europäische Schriftsteller-Vereinigung in Weimar 1941–1948* (Frankfurt am Main, 2004), on its foundation especially 51ff. Also see Benjamin G. Martin, "'European Literature' in the Nazi New Order: The Cultural Politics of the European Writers' Union," *Journal of Contemporary History* 48, no. 3 (2013).
67. Hausmann, *"Dichte, Dichter, tage nicht!",* 66. Benoist-Méchin was probably a member of the French national body (*Landesgruppe*) of the European Writers' Union. Ibid., 179, n. 107.
68. Ibid., 42; and the following quote ibid.
69. J[acques] Benoist-Méchin, "Frankreich im neuen Europa," in *Europa-Handbuch,* 51–55, 54.
70. V[eikko] A[ntero] Koskenniemi, "Finnland und die europäische Zukunft," in *Europa-Handbuch,* 71–78, 71.
71. Mikko Salmela, "The Fight for European Culture: Finnish Philosopher's Perspectives on Totalitarianism during World War II," *Finnish Yearbook of Political Thought* 3 (1999): 150.
72. Overview: Martin, "European Literature," 490; Benjamin G. Martin, "A New Order for European Culture: The German–Italian Axis and the Reordering of International Cultural Exchange, 1936–1943," PhD dissertation, Columbia University, 2006, 233–39. A monograph by Benjamin G. Martin on this subject is forthcoming with Harvard University Press. Not all of these associations are well researched. On the European Youth Federation, see Christoph Kühberger, "Europa als 'Strahlenbündel nationaler Kräfte': Zur Konzeption und Legitimation einer europäischen Zusammenarbeit auf der Gründungsfeierlichkeit des 'Europäischen Jugendverbandes' 1942," *Journal of European Integration History* 15, no. 2 (2009); on the International

Film Chamber, see Benjamin G. Martin, "'European Cinema for Europe!' The International Film Chamber, 1935–42," in *Cinema and the Swastika: The International Expansion of Third Reich Cinema*, ed. Roel Vande Winkel and David Welch (Basingstoke and New York, 2007), 25–41; on the plans for a European Sport Federation, see Hans Joachim Teichler, *Internationale Sportpolitik im Dritten Reich* (Schorndorf, 1991), 356–66.

73. Hausmann, *"Auch im Krieg schweigen die Musen nicht"*. English summary: Frank-Rutger Hausmann, "The 'Third Front': German Cultural Policy in Occupied Europe, 1940–1945," in *German Scholars and Ethnic Cleansing 1919–1945*, ed. Ingo Haar and Michael Fahlbusch (New York and Oxford, 2005), 213–35.
74. Kletzin, *Europa aus Rasse und Raum*, 79–80.
75. Antonio de Luna, "Europa—von Spanien aus gesehen," in *Europa-Handbuch*, 55–62, 55.
76. Ibid., 56.
77. Letter of Thomas Mann to Richard Coudenhove-Kalergi, 24 February 1943, quoted after Marie-Louise von Plessen, ed., *Idee Europa: Entwürfe zum "Ewigen Frieden": Ordnungen und Utopien für die Gestaltung Europas von der pax romana zur Europäischen Union. Eine Ausstellung als historische Topographie* (Berlin, 2003), 291.
78. Friedrich Berber, "Europa als Erbe und Aufgabe," in *Europa-Handbuch*, 7–13, 12.
79. Note of Ernst von Weizsäcker (state secretary in the German Foreign Office), 2 May 1943, printed in Leonidas E. Hill, ed., *Die Weizsäcker-Papiere 1933–1950* (Frankfurt am Main, Berlin, and Vienna, 1974), 337. See Boris Schilmar, *Der Europadiskurs im deutschen Exil 1933–1945* (Munich, 2004), 138 (also on the following); Hans W. Neulen, "Einführung," in *Europa und das 3. Reich: Einigungsbestrebungen im deutschen Machtbereich 1933–45*, ed. Hans W. Neulen (Munich, 1987), 15–68, 40–41.
80. Klaus Hildebrand, *Das vergangene Reich: Deutsche Außenpolitik von Bismarck bis Hitler 1871–1945* (Stuttgart, 1995), 778.
81. Michael Salewski, "Europa: Idee und Wirklichkeit in der national-sozialistischen Weltanschauung und politischen Praxis," in *Europas Mitte*, ed. Otmar Franz (Göttingen and Zurich, 1987), 89.
82. Hausmann, *"Dichte, Dichter, tage nicht!"*, 11.

Bibliography

Asendorf, Manfred. "Ulrich von Hassells Europakonzeption und der Mitteleuropäische Wirtschaftstag." *Jahrbuch des Instituts für deutsche Geschichte [Tel Aviv]* 7 (1978): 387–419.
Bassin, Mark. "Blood or Soil? The *Völkisch* Movement, the Nazis, and the Legacy of Geopolitik." In *How Green Were the Nazis? Nature, Environment, and Nation in the Third Reich*, ed. Franz-Josef Brüggemeier, Mark Cioc, and Thomas Zeller, 204–42. Athens, OH, 2005.
Bauerkämper, Arnd. *Der Faschismus in Europa 1918–1945*. Stuttgart, 2006.

————. "Interwar Fascism in Europe and Beyond: Toward a Transnational Radical Right." In *New Perspectives on the Transnational Right*, ed. Martin Durham and Margaret Power, 39–66. New York, 2010.

Benziger, Karl P. "The Trial of László Bárdossy: The Second World War and Factional Politics in Contemporary Hungary." *Journal of Contemporary History* 40, no. 3 (2005): 465–81.

Bergmann, Werner. "Antisemitische Aktion," in *Enzyklopädie des Nationalsozialismus*, ed. Wolfgang Benz, Hermann Graml, and Hermann Weiß, 4th ed., 365. Munich, 2001.

Broszat, Martin. "Die völkische Ideologie und der Nationalsozialismus." *Deutsche Rundschau* 84, no. 1 (1958): 53–68.

————. "Deutschland–Ungarn–Rumänien: Entwicklung und Grundfaktoren nationalsozialistischer Hegemonial- und Bündnispolitik 1938–1941." *Historische Zeitschrift* 206 (1968): 45–96.

Conze, Eckart, et al. *Das Amt und die Vergangenheit: Deutsche Diplomaten im Dritten Reich und in der Bundesrepublik.* Munich, 2010.

Domarus, Max. *Hitler: Reden und Proklamationen 1932–1945: Kommentiert von einem deutschen Zeitgenossen*, vol. I: *Triumph. Zweiter Halbband 1935–1938.* Wiesbaden, 1973.

Dreier, Ralf. "Julius Binder (1870–1939): Ein Rechtsphilosoph zwischen Kaiserreich und Nationalsozialismus." In *Rechtswissenschaft in Göttingen: Göttinger Juristen aus 250 Jahren*, ed. Fritz Loos, 435–55. Göttingen, 1987.

Elvert, Jürgen. *Mitteleuropa! Deutsche Pläne zur europäischen Neuordnung (1918–1945).* Stuttgart, 1999.

Europa: Handbuch der politischen, wirtschaftlichen und kulturellen Entwicklung des neuen Europa, ed. by Deutsches Institut für Außenpolitische Forschung. Leipzig, 1943.

Gerlach, Christian, and Götz Aly. *Das letzte Kapitel: Realpolitik, Ideologie und der Mord an den ungarischen Juden 1944/1945.* Stuttgart and Munich, 2002.

Giesecke, Hermann. "Demokratie als Denk- und Lebensform: Ein Nachruf auf Theodor Wilhelm (1906–2005)." http://www.hermann-giesecke.de/wilhelm.htm (accessed 18 March 2015).

Grunert, Robert. *Der Europagedanke westeuropäischer faschistischer Bewegungen 1940–1945.* Paderborn, Munich, Vienna, and Zurich, 2012.

Hausmann, Frank-Rutger. *"Vom Strudel der Ereignisse verschlungen": Deutsche Romanistik im "Dritten Reich".* Frankfurt am Main, 2000.

————. *"Auch im Krieg schweigen die Musen nicht": Die Deutschen Wissenschaftlichen Institute im Zweiten Weltkrieg.* 2nd ed. Göttingen, 2002.

————. *"Dichte, Dichter, tage nicht!" Die Europäische Schriftsteller-Vereinigung in Weimar 1941–1948.* Frankfurt am Main, 2004.

————. "The 'Third Front': German Cultural Policy in Occupied Europe, 1940–1945." In *German Scholars and Ethnic Cleansing 1919–1945*, ed. Ingo Haar and Michael Fahlbusch, 213–35. New York and Oxford, 2005.

Hildebrand, Klaus. *Das vergangene Reich: Deutsche Außenpolitik von Bismarck bis Hitler 1871–1945.* Stuttgart, 1995.

Hill, Leonidas E., ed. *Die Weizsäcker-Papiere 1933–1950.* Frankfurt am Main, Berlin, and Vienna, 1974.

Hitler, Adolf. *Mein Kampf. Zwei Bände in einem Band. Ungekürzte Ausgabe.* 102nd–106th ed. Munich, 1934.

———. *Reden des Führers am Parteitag der Ehre 1936.* Munich, 1936.

———. *Mein Kampf. Complete and Unabridged.* New York, 1939.

Hoensch, Jörg K. *Geschichte Ungarns 1867–1983.* Stuttgart, Berlin, Cologne, and Mainz, 1984.

Illustrirte Zeitung Leipzig, special edition *"Der europäische Mensch"* (1944).

Jochmann, Werner, ed. *Adolf Hitler: Monologe im Führer-Hauptquartier 1941–1944. Die Aufzeichnungen Heinrich Heims.* Hamburg, 1980.

Kallis, Aristotle A. "'Fascism', 'Para-fascism' and 'Fascistization': On the Similarities of Three Conceptual Categories." *European History Quarterly* 33, no. 2 (2003): 219–49.

———. "The 'Fascist Effect': On the Dynamics of Political Hybridization in Inter-War Europe." In *Rethinking Fascism and Dictatorship in Europe*, ed. António Costa Pinto and Aristotle Kallis, 13–41. Basingstoke and New York, 2014.

Kletzin, Birgit. *Europa aus Rasse und Raum: Die nationalsozialistische Idee der Neuen Ordnung.* Münster, 2002.

Kocács-Bertrand, Anikó. *Der ungarische Revisionismus nach dem Ersten Weltkrieg: Der publizistische Kampf gegen den Friedensvertrag von Trianon (1918–1931).* Munich, 1997.

Kühberger, Christoph. "Europa als 'Strahlenbündel nationaler Kräfte': Zur Konzeption und Legitimation einer europäischen Zusammenarbeit auf der Gründungsfeierlichkeit des 'Europäischen Jugendverbandes' 1942." *Journal of European Integration History* 15, no. 2 (2009): 11–28.

Levy, Carl. "Fascism, National Socialism and Conservatives in Europe, 1914–1945: Issues for Comparativists." *Contemporary European History* 8, no. 1 (1999): 97–126.

Longerich, Peter. *Propagandisten im Krieg: Die Presseabteilung des Auswärtigen Amtes unter Ribbentrop.* Munich, 1987.

Loock, Hans-Dietrich. "Zur 'großgermanischen Politik' des Dritten Reiches." *Vierteljahrshefte für Zeitgeschichte* 8, no. 1 (1960): 37–63.

Martin, Benjamin G. "A New Order for European Culture: The German–Italian Axis and the Reordering of International Cultural Exchange, 1936–1943." PhD dissertation, Columbia University, 2006.

———. "'European Cinema for Europe!' The International Film Chamber, 1935–42." In *Cinema and the Swastika: The International Expansion of Third Reich Cinema*, ed. Roel Vande Winkel and David Welch, 25–41. Basingstoke and New York, 2007.

———. "'European Literature' in the Nazi New Order: The Cultural Politics of the European Writers' Union." *Journal of Contemporary History* 48, no. 3 (2013): 486–508.

Mazower, Mark. *Hitler's Empire: How the Nazis Ruled Europe.* New York, 2008.

Milata, Paul. *Zwischen Hitler, Stalin und Antonescu: Rumäniendeutsche in der Waffen-SS.* 2nd ed. Cologne, Weimar, and Vienna, 2009.

Moll, Martin. "'Signal': Die NS-Auslandsillustrierte und ihre Propaganda für Hitlers 'Neues Europa'." *Publizistik: Vierteljahreshefte für Kommunikationsforschung* 31 (1986): 357–400.

Mosse, George L. *Die völkische Revolution: Über die geistigen Wurzeln des Nationalsozialismus*. Frankfurt am Main, 1991.
Mulligan, Patrick. "The Politics of Illusion and Empire: The Attempts to Reform German Occupation Policy in the U.S.S.R., Autumn 1942–Summer 1943." PhD dissertation, University of Maryland, 1985.
Neulen, Hans W. "Einführung." In *Europa und das 3. Reich: Einigungsbestrebungen im deutschen Machtbereich 1933–45*, ed. Hans W. Neulen, 15–68. Munich, 1987.
Oexle, Otto G. "Leitbegriffe—Deutungsmuster—Paradigmenkämpfe. Über Vorstellungen vom 'Neuen Europa' in Deutschland 1944." In *Nationalsozialismus in den Kulturwissenschaften*, vol. 2: *Leitbegriffe— Deutungsmuster—Paradigmenkämpfe: Erfahrungen und Transformationen im Exil*, ed. Hartmut Lehmann and Otto G. Oexle, 13–40. Göttingen, 2004.
Øhrgaard, Per. "Die Zeitschrift *Junges Europa*: Ein Beispiel für die Europa-Propaganda der Nazis." In *Vielheit und Einheit der Germanistik weltweit* vol. 5, ed. Franciszek Grucza, 127–31. Frankfurt am Main, 2012.
Payne, Stanley G. *A History of Fascism 1914–1945*. 2nd ed. London, 1997.
Pinto, António Costa, and Aristotle Kallis. "Introduction." In *Rethinking Fascism and Dictatorship in Europe*, ed. idem, 1–10. Basingstoke and New York, 2014.
Plessen, Marie-Louise von, ed. *Idee Europa: Entwürfe zum „Ewigen Frieden". Ordnungen und Utopien für die Gestaltung Europas von der pax romana zur Europäischen Union. Eine Ausstellung als historische Topographie*. Berlin, 2003.
Prehn, Ulrich. "'Volk' und 'Raum' in zwei Nachkriegszeiten: Kontinuitäten und Wandlungen in der Arbeit des Volkstumsforschers Max Hildebert Boehm." In *Das Erbe der Provinz: Heimatkultur und Geschichtspolitik nach 1945*, ed. Habbo Knoch, 50–72. Göttingen, 2001.
Pritz, Pál. "War-Crimes Trial Hungarian Style: Prime Minister László Bárdossy before the People's Tribunal, 1945." *Hungarian Studies Review* XXII, no. 1 (1995): 47–70.
Puschner, Uwe, Walter Schmitz, and Justus H. Ulbricht, eds. *Handbuch zur "Völkischen Bewegung" 1871–1918*. Munich, New Providence, London and Paris, 1996.
Rutz, Rainer. *Signal: Eine deutsche Auslandsillustrierte als Propagandainstrument im Zweiten Weltkrieg*. Essen, 2007.
Salewski, Michael. "Europa: Idee und Wirklichkeit in der nationalsozialistischen Weltanschauung und politischen Praxis." In *Europas Mitte*, ed. Otmar Franz, 85–106. Göttingen and Zurich, 1987.
Salmela, Mikko. "The Fight for European Culture: Finnish Philosopher's Perspectives on Totalitarianism during World War II." *Finnish Yearbook of Political Thought* 3 (1999): 149–77.
Schilmar, Boris. *Der Europadiskurs im deutschen Exil 1933–1945*. Munich, 2004.
Six, Franz Alfred. "Das Reich und die Grundlegung Europas." *Jahrbuch der Weltpolitik* 2 (1942): 13–35.
Szöllösi-Janze, Margit. *Die Pfeilkreuzlerbewegung in Ungarn: Historischer Kontext, Entwicklung und Herrschaft*. Munich, 1989.
Teichler, Hans J. *Internationale Sportpolitik im Dritten Reich*. Schorndorf, 1991.
Tönsmeyer, Tatjana. "Kollaboration als handlungsleitendes Motiv? Die slowakische Elite und das NS-Regime." In *Kooperation und Verbrechen: Formen*

der "Kollaboration" im östlichen Europa 1939–1945, ed. Christoph Dieckmann, Babette Quinkert, and Tatjana Tönsmeyer, 25–54. Göttingen, 2003.

Verhandlungen des Reichstags. VIII. Wahlperiode 1933. vol. 457: *Stenographische Berichte, Anlagen zu den Stenographischen Berichten, Sach- und Sprechregister.* Berlin, 1934.

Verhandlungen des Reichstags. IX. Wahlperiode 1933. vol. 458: *Stenographische Berichte, Anlagen zu den Stenographischen Berichten.* Berlin, 1936.

Verhandlungen des Reichstags. 4. Wahlperiode 1939. vol. 460: *Stenographische Berichte 1939–1942, Anlagen zu den Stenographischen Berichten. 1.–8. Sitzung.* N.p.

✤ 11

COMMUNIST ANTIFASCISM AND TRANSNATIONAL FASCISM
Comparisons, Transfers, Entanglements

Kasper Braskén

The aim of this chapter[1] is to analyze the antifascist activities of the international communist movement, from 1922 to 1939/40, starting with Mussolini's "March on Rome" and concluding with the beginning of World War II. In particular, it will be demonstrated how antifascism was affected by the dynamics of international fascism and the transnational cooperation of fascist groups and parties. The antifascist movement perceived from the very outset in 1922 that fascism was an international movement that was not confined to Italy and Germany. The chapter will hence elaborate on how antifascist articulations of fascism as a transnational, entangled, and connected European movement empowered and animated cross-border cooperation between antifascists. Although communists were already engaged in forming an antifascist culture during the 1920s, the making of antifascism into a mass or popular culture was strongly dependent on a destructive and menacing fascist threat. Only when the atrocities of the Third Reich, the Italo-Abyssinian War and the brutality of the Spanish Civil War became reality, did antifascism emerge as a powerful culture of the global Left. The international fascist cooperation and the formation of the Anti-Comintern Pact with Germany and Japan in 1936 (with the inclusion of Italy in 1937) amplified the image of a new atrocious fascist world order that demanded a powerful response by the antifascist movement. Likewise, fascism in its various forms was fueled by the specter of a supposedly international communist conspiracy that through revolution and red terror threatened to destroy European culture and civilization.[2]

Communist antifascism was strongly dependent of the changing lines of the Third International—or, as it is more often known, the Communist International (Comintern)—and the often contradictory foreign policy needs of the Soviet Union. The analysis of communist antifascism must therefore take into account the changing circumstances and contexts during the period of united fronts (1922–1928), and the communist conception of social democracy as a form of "social fascism" during the so-called "third period" (1928–1934/35) that was characterized by its radical and aggressive class-against-class politics against social democracy. Two new departures were the popular front era (1934/35–1939) and communist antifascism after the Molotov–Ribbentrop Non-aggression Pact signed in August 1939, which stifled what was left of the communist antifascist movement. The final section of the chapter will include the often-overlooked antifascist groups of (oppositional) communists and socialists, which were united by their anti-Stalinism. It must be remembered that just as Italian and German fascism was in a constant transformation process throughout the interwar period, so was antifascism continually being redefined. The chapter will thus highlight the necessity to study in tandem the development of communist antifascism and transnational fascism.

Communist Antifascism between Transnational and International

The distinction between international and transnational is of crucial significance for the analysis of communist antifascism. Many scholars have interpreted the history of international communism and the Comintern as primarily a history of Soviet foreign policy and alas a subject for international relations—not transnational history. It is important not to disregard or abandon the meaning of international relations or governmental politics. Yet the very intersections and contestations between the international and the transnational are to be investigated. The analysis of transnational movements is a vital question, both in relation to the history of interwar fascism and communism, as both movements experienced a transformation from "pure" national and transnational movements to agents pursuing international relations as they became governmental actors. How did this change affect cross-border relations, interactions, and transfers?

Communist antifascism was actively made transnational especially through communist internationalism and transnational solidarity practices, the political and trade union internationals, and through special communist-led antifascist committees and organizations. These were internationally coordinated and followed the mission to establish national and local antifascist committees and organizations in Europe and beyond. Although the center of the Comintern was located in Moscow, it will be argued that it was in fact Berlin that constituted the main stage of the transnational organization of antifascist campaigns until 1933. Thereafter it moved to Paris and London.

Berlin was the base of such international organizations as the International Workers' Relief (Internationale Arbeiterhilfe, IAH, 1921–1933) and the Central European Bureau of the International Red Aid (Internationale Rote Hilfe, also known by its Russian acronym MOPR, 1924–1933). Special antifascist committees and organizations such as the International Action Committee against War Danger and Fascism (renamed the Anti-Fascist World League, 1923–1924) were also established in Berlin. The International Anti-Fascist Committee (1928–1929) had its headquarters in the German capital, and the first International Anti-Fascist Conference, held in March 1929, was also in Berlin.[3]

Yet the city of Berlin was deserted by the antifascist movement shortly after Hitler came to power and as a consequence of the full-blown Nazi persecution of communists and socialists launched after the Burning of the Reichstag in Berlin on 27 February 1933. Paris then became the new center for international communist-led antifascist organizations such as the World Committee against War and Fascism (Weltkomitee gegen Krieg und Faschismus), the International Relief Committee for the Victims of German Fascism (Welthilfskomitee für die Opfer des Hitlerfaschismus), and the International Committee for the Liberation of Dimitrov, Thälmann, and All Imprisoned Antifascists. Paris was also the main stage of the French Popular Front and the principal arena for the initiative to establish a German Popular Front (formed in the so-called Lutetia Circle). Moreover, the French capital was the location of the Library of the Burned Books (also known as the International Anti-Fascist Archive, or the Deutsche Freiheitsbibliothek). Not least, major European and international antifascist congresses and conferences were held in Paris during the 1930s.[4]

London was the site for antifascist campaigns such as the high-profile London Counter Trial organized parallel to the Reichstag trial in Leipzig, where among others the future leader of the Comintern, Georgi Dimitrov, was accused of involvement in the burning of the Reichstag. The central bureaus and branches of the Paris-based antifascist committees and organizations such as the Relief Committee for the Victims of German Fascism were also located in London. Moreover, the city became a central site of antifascist activities when London became a stage for street fighting between antifascists and British "Blackshirts," most famously resulting in the clashes at Olympia in 1934 and the

"Battle for Cable Street" in October 1936. Although the British fascist organizations remained marginal, recent scholarship has highlighted the wide spread of fascist ideas in interwar Britain. London also became a central location for the major antifascist campaigns against the Italian invasion of Abyssinia and the defense of Republican Spain during the Spanish Civil War.[5]

The spatial differentiation between Moscow on the one hand and Berlin, Paris, and London on the other leads to a necessary analysis of the relationship between the transnational and international. Can one even identify a difference between "Soviet antifascism" and "Communist antifascism"? For Soviet antifascism, the focal point of the analysis and activities was located in Moscow. From this perspective, understanding the relations between the Comintern and the Soviet government, especially that of Stalin and his henchmen, was essential. For communist antifascism, the main arena was Central and Western Europe. This shift in perspective allows us to analyze communist antifascism as part of a radical Western social movement in places and countries where communism was not in power and where fascism was a more tangible threat.[6] Obviously, the power, dependence, and control of the Russian Communist Party (Bolsheviks), RCP(B), remains crucial, but the differentiation opens up the analysis of the transnational connections. Communist internationalism was not only characterized by its relation between center and periphery, but constituted a translational network of multiple radiating points. As the German communist Willi Münzenberg (1889–1940), who was one of the most avid organizers of communist antifascism during the interwar period, bluntly stated in a letter to Moscow in 1937, he could never lead an antifascist propaganda bureau from Moscow. It had to be placed in the West in order to respond rapidly to the daily shifts in fascist propaganda. Only there was it possible to "constantly feel the pulse of the fascist rivals."[7] Moreover, antifascism as a political strategy was differently articulated in the democracies of Western Europe, compared to that of the totalitarian Soviet Union. In the history of democracy in Europe, the antifascist Popular Front of the mid-1930s signaled a major defensive regrouping of the Left. Due to the menacing rise of Nazi Germany, communists in the West could suddenly define themselves as the prime defenders of democratic rights in their efforts to hinder the further spread of fascism in Europe. However, in light of the connections and subordination of the Communist parties to the totalitarian Soviet state, this claim remained highly controversial.[8]

From the start, the Comintern constituted a hybrid international organization. The Comintern was "neither a transnational emanation of civil society nor an international organization of states."[9] Although it was not exactly an international non-governmental organization, the Comintern was founded on the basis of the idea of a radical transnational solidarity of the workers of the world. However, it is clear to anyone familiar with the history of the Comintern that during the late 1920s and 1930s it became all the more a vehicle for promoting Soviet foreign politics through the so-called Stalinization process. It could be interpreted as the development of a rising tension between the transnational and the international, where the transnational centers of communist antifascism were challenged and disrupted by the Soviet influence.

By refocusing the history of transnational antifascism to Western Europe, the main subject of interest is that of "sympathizing" international supra-party (or above-party) organizations and committees founded by the Comintern that were mentioned above. Contrary to Communist parties, these organizations had the Comintern's mandate to work on a global scale, whereas the Communist parties were to confine their activities to their national contexts. These new types of cultural and political organizations were at the forefront of a transnational revolution. It has been argued that the European culture of antifascism of the 1930s was a new mixture combining Soviet and foreign pro-Soviet contributions, sponsored and spread through various "front organizations" and cultural interactions.[10] However, antifascism was no Soviet or Russian conceptual innovation that was transferred or imposed upon the rest of Europe. Communist antifascism was by definition transnational, taking up influences from various directions from the very beginning. Perhaps a central point to be made is that the transformation of antifascism was as much caused by internal Soviet policy changes as by changes in the transnational and international fascist movement.

Antifascism and Fascism as Entangled Histories

In his study of "Soviet antifascism," Stanley Payne notes that the communists quickly understood the "great utility of the term 'fascist' as a political pejorative, and so they began to apply it to all manner of political forces of the bourgeoisie, the Right or 'reaction.'" As a result, communists saw "fascism" everywhere, which again resulted in an analysis so vague that by 1923/24 it had lost all meaning.[11] However, as Leonid Luks has demonstrated, the Comintern witnessed significant developments in its analysis of fascism between 1926 and 1928. These theoretical debates have largely been overlooked in overviews of communist antifascism. Instead, the lines are drawn straight between the debates in 1924, when the head of the Comintern, Georgi Zinoviev, and Stalin for the first time presented the idea of "social fascism," and the 1928 official endorsement of the doctrine. What happened in between to the analysis of fascism? Luks has differentiated between a pre-Stalinist phase of the communist analysis of fascism and a Stalinist phase after 1928.[12] Yet the major difference occurred not in the analysis of fascism, but in how the Soviet Union influenced the Comintern to use antifascism in its political work.

Already in the initial discussion in the organs of the Comintern in 1923, there was an understanding of fascism as a completely new form of "counterrevolution." Already then, Giulio Aquila, who later would be heavily involved in the Comintern's antifascist campaigns, warned of a generalization of the concept of fascism. Likewise, Clara Zetkin, the initial leader of the antifascist committee in Berlin, stated that one could not simply label all reactionary governments or authoritarian dictatorships, like the one established by Miklós Horthy in Hungary, as "fascist." Even the Polish communist and high-ranking Comintern official, Karl Radek, admitted that although the violence and suppression was ten times "wilder" in Horthy's Hungary than in Mussolini's Italy, it did not make Hungary a "fascist country." Rather, the country was ruled by an old-style feudalist-capitalist regime. By contrast, fascism was to be understood as a mass-based movement, primarily supported by the proletarianized petite bourgeoisie, who had been disillusioned by the developments after World War I.[13]

The basic idea of communist antifascist action formulated in 1923 was that as fascism was striking against the whole proletariat, irrespective of party affiliation, the whole "proletariat" was obliged to join forces in antifascist defense forces. However, the major objections to calls for a united front against fascism emanated from the Communist Party of Italy. In 1921, the left wing of the party had bitterly separated from the Socialist Party. As a consequence, the Comintern was urging the communists to collaborate with the socialists whom they had been calling "traitors of the working class." The left wing of the Communist Party refused to follow the Comintern's calls for "united front" politics, thereby practically paralyzing the whole party.[14]

In Germany, the rising threat of German fascism was identified in the context of the Ruhr Crisis. When the Ruhr area was occupied by primarily French troops in January 1923, it gave rise to nationalist fervor in Germany, where much of the nation was united in passive resistance to the occupying forces. In nationalist and right-wing circles, such as the various *völkisch* movements and the rising National Socialist Party, there was a deepening radicalization, just as the social crisis with hunger, unemployment, and deprivation resulted in rising support for the radical Left. In the context of the German crisis, the threat of fascism and war were strategically used by the communist movement in Germany and France to drum up support. Hence the Comintern's antifascist committee in Berlin was in practice essentially a German–French affair, at least in the beginning, although it had been envisaged as a worldwide endeavor. The two chair persons of the Internationale Aktionskomitee gegen Kriegsgefahr und Faschismus, which was officially launched in Frankfurt am Main in March 1923, were Clara Zetkin (Berlin) and Henri Barbusse (Paris).[15]

In one of the first publications of the new Action Committee, the role of Italian Fascism as a transnational movement was highlighted. The Action Committee claimed that Italian fascists had established national branches in Berlin and other German cities, supporting the German fascist forces. If fascism were to be allowed to grow stronger in Germany, the entire German working class would be doomed to the same fate as in Italy, it was proclaimed.[16] The idea of the Action Committee was to urge workers to organize "defense hundreds" in the workplaces to strike down the fascists at an early stage. Here, the antifascist identity was forged not only in the summoning of own defense forces against domestic fascism, but also in the solidarity shown to the victims of fascism in Italy and for the liberation of political prisoners.[17]

In its newspaper, *Chronik des Faschismus*, the Berlin-based antifascist Action Committee (in December 1923 renamed the Anti-Faschistische Weltliga) published numerous articles about the international networks and the influence of Italian Fascism. The authors emphasized that the Fascists were especially avid organizers in countries where there was a substantial Italian emigrant community such as France. It was clearly stated that the main goal of Fascist activities was to prevent the flow of antifascist propaganda among the Italians in exile. Against this background, the Fascist presence in France was already understood as a two-pronged phenomenon. On the one hand, it was a party and a propaganda organization, but on the other hand it was a government. The Italian embassy in Paris was therefore perceived not only as representing Italy, but much more as a branch of the Fascist Party. The antifascists claimed that the Italian fascists in France were only seemingly isolating themselves from French domestic politics, but in reality were sympathizing with the politics of Action Française. Furthermore, the *Chronik des Faschismus* pointed out that Action Française were boasting that they were imitating Italian Fascism. Already in this early analysis it was observed (with great satisfaction) that the transnational fascist cooperation clearly forced them to amend their ultranationalist propaganda. According to the report, Italian Fascists in France had, for example, handled the historic rivalry between Italy and France over Tunisia with great care and diplomacy, although everyone knew that it was a crucial and passionate issue for the nationalists in Italy.[18]

What seems to have animated the antifascist movement was exactly the perception of fascism as a mixture of a transnational movement and governmental power-pursuing politics on an international level. In many ways antifascism was made transnational through the active campaign of the antifascist organizations. Conversely, the actions of the fascist movement triggered and activated antifascist responses on a transnational scale. However, there were clear contradictions and paradoxes in the communists' antifascist activities. In the summer of 1924, for example, when Italy was shaken by the "Matteotti crisis" after the murder of the Italian socialist Giacomo Matteotti, the general outrage against Mussolini's regime gave its adversaries an unprecedented opportunity to mobilize a broad antifascist movement. However, in the midst of the crisis, the communist-led Anti-Fascist World League was disbanded by the Comintern, and the antifascist activities of the Comintern were played down.[19]

From the perspective of Soviet foreign policy, it was perhaps unsuitable to pursue a strong antifascist campaign against Mussolini's Italy, as the USSR had already signed a Soviet–Italian treaty in February 1924, just one week after Britain's *de jure* recognition of the Soviet Union. As another example for the contradictions between communist antifascism and Soviet politics (and a tension in fascist anticommunism), Mussolini had stated as early as 30 November 1923 that Italy was striving to be the first "victor state" to recognize the Soviet Union.[20] Conspicuously, Fascist Italy's foreign policy was at times relatively free from ideological considerations, although the fascist movement never swayed from its anti-bolshevism. Still, as Denis Mack Smith has demonstrated, some organs of the fascist press were remarkably sympathetic to the Soviet Union until the mid-1930s. Like the rulers of the USSR, Italy's Fascists were not prepared to sacrifice good relations for ideological constraints, much to the dismay of the European communist movement.[21]

The negative repercussions on the Italo-Soviet relations were clearly visible a decade later during the Italo-Abyssinian War, which was initially accompanied by a strong international communist-led antifascist campaign in Europe. According to Lorna Waddington, Mussolini reconsidered Italy's relationship with the Soviet Union as a result of the antifascist campaign. He, on his part, sent an envoy to discuss the formation of an anti-Soviet bloc of Germany, Italy, Hungary, and Poland with the German-led Anti-Comintern.[22]

When Willi Münzenberg (with the pseudonym "M. Willi") and Guilo Aquila wrote the official report on the fascist movement to the Comintern's Fifth World Congress in 1924, they focused on developments in Germany and Italy, but included short overviews of the movements in France, Britain, Spain, Hungary, and the United States. Important is the concluding remark of the report, which recommended that the communists should take into account the different methods of fighting fascism in specific situations. Like in Weimar Germany, it was, above all, crucial to influence and win over the souls of the supposedly disoriented peasants and petite bourgeoisie, but also, when necessary, to rise up and fight against the fascist paramilitary squadrons.[23] In other words, antifascism was not merely to be made a militant experience of convinced communists, but a worldview or even political identity accepted on a broader societal base.

The tensions between the Comintern in Moscow and the communist antifascist organizations in the West were a constant problem. After the establishment of the International Anti-Fascist Committee in 1929, Henri Barbusse wrote a sharp protest to the Comintern on how it was handling the question of antifascism. The first published appeal of the committee had apparently been penned in Moscow, but it had been signed with the signatures of Barbusse and other members of the committee. The problem, Barbusse explained, was that it had been written in the most rigid and polemic party jargon, to show everyone that the committee spoke exactly the same language as the Comintern. It identified a direct and fierce attack against the permanent enemy of communism, namely, social democracy. Barbusse tried to explain to the communist hardliners that if the committee wanted to distinguish itself from the Communist parties, it was impossible to pursue such a sectarian line. The point was to unite communists with socialists, party politically non-committed workers, and even the liberal bourgeoisie. The principal aim of the committee had to be the defeat of fascism, and not the victory of communism. This was the only way, Barbusse explained, to attract supporters who could never openly join the communists, but who were prepared to oppose fascism in a broad united front.[24]

Comparing Antifascist and Fascist Transnationalism

Throughout most of the twentieth century, the history of communism and fascism has been conceived as dichotomous in historiography. In sympathetic and pro-communist accounts, the communist movement has been glorified as the vanguard of the world antifascist movement. These publications have represented communism as the fiercest adversary to fascism. By contrast, critical studies have referred to the concept of totalitarianism, which has largely identified fascism and communism as two siblings of dictatorial rule that have been mistakenly perceived and conceived as radical opponents.[25] A third communist counternarrative that has also influenced Cold War historiography is the idea of "social fascism," which claims that it is not communism and fascism that are related, but rather that social democracy and fascism are twins.[26] The relations between communism and social democracy had, of course, since the split of the socialist movement during World War I, been highly strained. Especially in Germany, the Social Democratic Party (Sozialdemokratische Partei Deutschlands, SPD) was perceived from the perspective of the radical Left as betrayers of the German revolution and the German working class.[27]

This chapter does not embrace any of these interpretations, but aims at an analysis of the entanglements between the fascist and antifascist movements. These movements were highly heterogeneous, and just as recent research has highlighted the "varieties" of antifascism, so does the latest research on international fascism reveal the national characteristics, entanglements, and variations of fascist movements. Both movements were, furthermore, in a constant development both nationally and internationally, making them interesting themes for synchronic and diachronic comparison on the one hand, and significant themes for transnational and entangled history on the other.[28] As a corollary, the interpretation does not highlight difference or similarity, but entanglements, transfers of antifascist definitions and understandings of fascism as a movement and vice versa, and the spread of fascist understandings of "communist antifascism." Comparative studies have focused on the direct comparison of Nazi Germany and the Soviet Union to illuminate the differences and similarities between Nazism and Stalinism, or even fascism and communism. Recent entangled histories of interwar Germany and the USSR have opened a hitherto overlooked dimension, and focused on the exchanges and transfers of culture and ideas. Yet, these studies seem to neglect that they are in fact comparing and analyzing transnational phenomena that are not restricted to national units. One striking example is the role of emigrant and exile communities, and their impact on the image of their own countries. In this sense, the so-called Soviet image of Nazi Germany and fascism in Europe was to a large extent a product of a German and European antifascist intellectual milieu that resided in a West European exile.[29]

For the fascists, there was no communist antifascism, but only a Bolshevik/Soviet antifascism. For them, it was clear that antifascism, like communism, was being imported from Russia. It was seen as a tool to fool the German and European masses. The same strategy was used by the communists in their fight against fascism. The tangible transnational connections between European fascists and Fascist Italy were highlighted to delegitimize fascist movements in other countries, denouncing them as imitations and cheap imports superficially applied to domestic circumstances. In some other publications, such as the major left-wing illustrated newspaper *Arbeiter-Illustrierte-Zeitung* (AIZ) bought out by the *Internationale Arbeiterhilfe*, the connection between Italian Fascism and German National Socialism was emphasized in a much more devastating context, as it reported on how the violence and brutality exemplified by the Italian Fascist squadrons stood as an "inspiration" for the Nazis in Germany.[30] In a photomontage by John Heartfield, the connection between the two "brother" countries was made even more expressively clear in the work titled "Gleiche Brüder, gleiche Mörder." The caption of the image explained how a "blackshirt" said to a "brownshirt" while he handed over a dagger to the Nazi: "Dir gebührt der Dolch! Du hast uns im Meuchelmord übertroffen" (You deserve the dagger! You have surpassed us in treacherous murder).[31]

Although the transnational cooperation between fascist groups seems to contradict the movement's ultranationalism, they were clearly connected by their common enemy. They also shared the production and dissemination of anticommunist propaganda. As an example of transnational fascism directly aimed at discrediting communism and communist antifascism, the activities of the Anti-Comintern, which was founded under the supervision of the Reich Propaganda Ministry of Joseph Goebbels, are noteworthy. By 1935, it had established a Europe-wide network and pursued a German initiative to build "a world anti-Bolshevik movement." The Anti-Comintern stressed that the destruction of the Communist International is an objective of all the nations of the Christian and civilized world.[32] After coming to power, Italian Fascists had claimed that it had in fact saved the country from falling to bolshevism. The same applies to the Nazis, although as Goebbels stated at the Nürnberg party rally in 1935, the Nazis were not only going to save Germany from bolshevism, but the whole of Europe.

Anticommunism was surely not confined to the fascists, but supported by a variety of conservative, liberal, and social democratic parties. In their eyes, it justified the policies of fascism, at least partially.[33]

Italy's war efforts in Abyssinia left the country in a diplomatic isolation that only strengthened its collaboration with Nazi Germany. The advent of the Spanish Civil War enhanced Italo-German cooperation in their mutual support of the Spanish Nationalists. As the civil war inspired defenders of the republic to enroll in the International Brigades, there was a similar transnational movement in favor of the Spanish Nationalists. Fascist groups across Europe sent their volunteers to fight for Franco. In this case, the fascists' ultranationalist ideologies and policies were superseded by the common crusade against bolshevism.[34] Moreover, the Anti-Comintern itself strongly supported Nationalist Spain. It supplied the pro-Franco side with a wealth of anticommunist propaganda material and was successful in creating a permanent anticommunist center in Spain. The Spanish Civil War gave rise to the fascist doctrine that it had been the Bolsheviks who had caused this war. It also fueled Nationalist Spanish propaganda, not only in Spain, but across Europe and beyond. For example, the Anti-Comintern created networks that enabled it to disseminate its anticommunism to Latin American countries such as Argentina, Mexico, Brazil, and Bolivia.[35]

If the cultural mission of the Nazis was presented as a campaign to protect European civilization from barbaric bolshevism, the communist antifascism of the mid-1930s was also largely launched in the form of a cultural project. At least in Britain the popular front strived to form a new moral community based on the common fight against fascism. The role of artists and writers was especially important thanks to their ability to "stir the emotions, rouse the moral conscience and build antifascist awareness." Antifascist authors were invited to participate in the International Congress of Writers for the Defense of Culture. These kinds of venues and events, organized in Paris (1935), London (1936), and Madrid (1937), enabled the construction of transnational antifascist networks in Western Europe. Moreover, the significance of antifascist "blood sacrifice" in the Spanish Civil War forged the community of the popular front. In Britain, the war in Spain produced the first British antifascist martyrs who had fallen fighting on the republican side. These fallen "heroes" were then publicly revered, which gave the opportunity to involve all antifascists in public mourning.[36]

Fascism and communism became entangled on the level of collective and political identity during the 1930s. By the time the Spanish Civil War began in July 1936, the link between communism and antifascism had become so prominent that it formed the basis of a completely new identity. A communist was by necessity also antifascist, although antifascism was by no means restricted to communists, as Nigel Copsey and Andrzej Olechnowicz have demonstrated with regard to antifascism in interwar Britain.[37]

In previous research on Soviet antifascism, there has been a tendency to overestimate and exaggerate the role of the Comintern and the Soviet Union. The "myth" of antifascism is effectively put to rest by the studies of Bernhard H. Bayerlein, who has argued that a significant revision of the old antifascist legends is needed for the USSR and the Comintern. Firstly, the Soviet Union was much more concerned with maintaining good diplomatic relations with Germany, and effectively hindered any antifascist mass-propaganda by the German Communist Party (Kommunistische Partei Deutschlands, KPD), between 1930 and 1933. Moreover, it must be remembered that the Comintern's turn to popular fronts was not endorsed until 1935. Hence the main enemy was not National Socialism, but "social fascism" (i.e., social democracy) during the first two years after Hitler's rise to power. The idea of "social fascism" was part of Stalin's and the Comintern's endorsement of "ultra Left politics," which claimed that social democracy was in a process of fascist degeneration. The high ranking Soviet and Comintern official Dmitri Manuilsky stated in 1931 that social democracy constituted the "most active agent in implementing the Fascistization of the bourgeois state and thereby the main enemy in the camp of the working class."[38] This frigid ideological interpretation of fascism and social democracy largely hindered the Communist parties from actively engaging in campaigns against the Nazis between 1933 and 1935. The communist culture of antifascism was instead mainly created by the international communist-led "sympathizing" organizations and committees established in the West. They managed to reach out to a broad public, informing them about the atrocities of fascism and shaping their image of fascism through imaginative propaganda campaigns. Willi Münzenberg staged a number of model antifascist campaigns in Paris, which started a process of redefining the antifascist image of communism. These campaigns were transmitted globally in, for example, the *Brown Book of the Reichstag Fire and Hitler Terror* that spread an effective antifascist counternarrative to the National Socialist anticommunist narrative directed against the alleged Bolshevik infiltration of German society and culture.[39]

Although Stalin officially advocated the popular front line in December 1934, it was not until the Comintern's Seventh World Congress, held in Moscow from 25 July to 21 August 1935, that the Popular Front was made an official policy of Communist parties.[40]

Previous studies on the communist movement of the 1930s have insufficiently differentiated between the communists' policy of "united fronts" and "popular fronts." According to Gerd-Rainer Horn, the "late spring 1934 is generally regarded as the decisive turning point in the Comintern's sudden move away from open hostility toward other parties of the Left." Not even in France did the language of popular fronts emerge before the fall of 1934. May 1934 to May 1935 constitutes the most crucial period in the development of the popular front policy. During these months, the Comintern gave up advocating alliances restricted to the working class. Contrary to this traditional model of the united front, the Comintern and the Communist parties collaborated with social groups in popular fronts "from below." By contrast, they did not engage in popular fronts "from above" by actual collaboration with bourgeois parties. Until May 1935, the emphasis of communist policies was on "extra-parliamentary action by the ranks." The French Communist Party (Parti Communiste Français, PCF) was "politically and ideologically" unprepared to create an actual popular front as late as mid May 1935, despite its self-image as the vanguard of popular fronts. It is likewise notable that the social democratic Labour and Socialist International (LSI) never ratified a move toward united or popular fronts during the 1930s.[41]

Despite the popular front enthusiasm in the West, Stalin never gave any indication that antifascism was the mainstay of his politics. The turn to popular front politics in 1935 and Soviet support for the International Brigades in the Spanish Civil War might have deceived some observers about the nature of Stalinism. Although the Comintern launched a broad fight against fascism and war with the popular fronts after 1935, the Soviet Union still kept its options open to cooperate with Nazi Germany. For many activists, especially in Britain, the Soviet Union's favoring of good relations with Mussolini in 1935 instead of continuing a strong antifascist campaign, represented an unprecedented betrayal of the antifascist cause. However, the signing of the pact with Hitler ultimately evidenced that antifascism was never anything else than a tactical consideration for Stalin. It was endorsed at a time when ultra-radical politics and radicalism in international communism were to be checked. Antifascism had served the interests of the Soviet state, but once it was superfluous for these interests, it was discarded. After the Hitler–Stalin Pact had been signed in 1939, it was interdicted to openly criticize the German–Soviet friendship, both in the Soviet Union and within the international communist movement. It was only in June 1941, when Hitler launched Operation Barbarossa against the Soviet Union, that antifascism returned to the Soviet agenda. This time, however, it was not articulated in the context of international solidarity, but introduced as a state doctrine forwarding the symbols of Russian nationalism. From this perspective, the Hitler–Stalin Pact was not a sudden break in Soviet politics, but the conclusion of a longer process. Moreover, it was justified as a result of Stalin's unwillingness to explicitly close the door to a possible collaboration between the Soviet Union and the Third Reich directed against the "capitalist West."[42] Silvio Pons has argued along the same lines, that the Comintern's turn to popular fronts and antifascism never involved a fundamental innovation of the existing political culture. From this perspective, antifascism was never anything else but a "manipulative concept that did not redefine the original identity." It was "subordinate to the international communist hierarchy," meaning that it was a political tool of Stalins's personal dictatorship. The goal was not the formation of a new antifascist state or a new kind of democracy, but continued to be the defense of the Soviet Union and the realization of the "Soviet model."[43]

The ambiguity of Soviet antifascism became clear directly after the signing of the pact, as the international communist movement was utterly unprepared for the news. In most cases, the communists first heard (often in disbelief and shock) of the non-aggression pact in the newspapers, causing a major existential crisis for the movement that during the past decade had constructed its political identity on antifascism. Contrary to the period of popular front, the Comintern and its member parties were instructed to no longer distinguish between democratic and fascist states in their propaganda. The most extreme consequence was that Nazi Germany was not anymore perceived in the Soviet press as a fascist country, but a country moving toward socialism, or more specifically "national" socialism, which was not equated with fascism. The German–Soviet invasion of Poland was celebrated in communist circles as a liberation of Poland from a "fascist" and "parasitic" government. The most dramatic consequence of the pact was the global eradication of antifascism as a broad culture of the Left, halting the antifascist propaganda of the Comintern and the Communist parties. The "perverse" logic of the pact was that the German Communist Party, for example, could not agitate against Hitler anymore, as that would mean directly supporting an "imperialist" Britain that had declared war on Germany. To oppose Hitler was now identical to support for the capitalist West.[44]

For the German antifascist exile in France, the pact meant that they were placed in internment camps, resulting in the destruction of the transnational antifascist centers in Paris. The French Communist Party, which had been the most important symbol for the Popular Front era, totally lost its face; and the Spanish CP, which had been the leading light of the "antifascist republic," suffered the same fate and was thrown into a political and psychological shock. When the KPD's leadership again tried to release a resolution critical of Hitler's Third Reich, it was denounced and suppressed as a statement of "primitive antifascism" in Moscow, according to Anton Ackermann.[45] Among German Nazis as well, the news of the pact was not easily accepted. In a rare moment of Nazi dissent against the policies of Hitler, the morning after the announcement of the pact, the front garden of the Nazi headquarters in Munich was covered in party badges thrown there in protest and disgust. Just as antifascism had until then been constructed as a central pillar of communist identity, so anticommunism was deeply rooted in the Nazi ideology and identity.[46]

Although Soviet adulation among Western intellectuals peaked in the 1930s, there were already dark clouds on the horizon long before the revelation of the non-aggression pact. Stalin's show trials against leading communists starting in 1936, and the culmination of the Great Terror in 1937, as well as the intense international campaign against "Trotskyist infiltrators and spies" in the international communist movement caused significant dents in the image of the Soviet Union and the Comintern. Among the most devastating losses among the intellectual friends of the Soviet Union was the dramatic departure of André Gide. One of the most prominent communist politicians to part ways with the Comintern and the Soviet Union was Willi Münzenberg. His extended conflict with the KPD, and especially Walter Ulbricht and Stalin himself in 1936–38, led to the departure of the principal communist organizer of the antifascist campaigns in Western Europe. Münzenberg quickly formed his own political platform in Paris on the basis of both antifascism and anti-Stalinism. The main publication of this last attempt to forge an antifascist platform was called *Die Zukunft*. Edited by Arthur Koestler, Hans Siemens, and Werner Thormann, it included the most prominent lineup of internationally recognized intellectuals among its contributors, including Thomas, Klaus, and Erika Mann, Alfred Döblin, Lion Feuchtwanger, Manès Sperber, Stefan Zweig, Emil J. Gumbel, and Sigmund Freud. The *Zukunft* platform formed the last attempt to establish a broad antifascist alliance of the European Left. It represented a radical break with Stalinism and Soviet antifascism on the one hand, and a continuation of the united front and popular front articulations of antifascism on the other.[47]

The most spectacular article of the *Zukunft* was written by Münzenberg himself as a direct reaction on the Hitler–Stalin Non-aggression Pact. Many years earlier, he and some other communists had been ousted from the communist movement as traitors. After Stalin's "stab in the back," they declared, "the traitor, Stalin, is you." Yet the German invasion of France brought these activities to a sudden end in May–June 1940. Even Britain, where a substantial part of the German communist antifascists had sought refuge, was no longer open for antifascist activities, as all German political exiles (especially communists) were placed in internment camps. This was the inglorious end of the communist antifascist activities, only partially revived in the European resistance movements after the summer of 1941.[48]

Conclusion

It is hereby suggested that a new history of communist antifascism should be written in close relation to transnational fascism, and should deal with the interrelationships and entanglements between the two movements. This cannot be reduced to a comparison of Nazi Germany and the USSR, but must bring in the twofold method of first comparing transnational fascism with transnational communist antifascism in Europe, and second, analyzing the entanglements and transfers between them. The notion of a specific "communist" interpretation of antifascism has been delineated from the varieties of antifascism articulated during the interwar period. As has been demonstrated, however, the communist articulations were from the beginning perceived as a basis for a broad movement opposing and resisting the fascist threat. The chapter has argued that the transnational antifascist campaigns organized by the communists were strongly animated by the image of the existence of an international and transnational network of fascist parties and groups. Likewise the antifascist movement could use these connections and transfers of fascist culture and ideology to delegitimize fascist movements across Europe as crude imitations.

Conversely, the transnational cooperation between antifascists sparked and alleviated transnational cooperation between the various fascist parties, who united in a worldwide struggle against "bolshevism." The Fascist and Nazi rise to governmental power intensified the cross-border interaction, not only between these two but across Europe. The dual role of party and state representative in transnational and international cooperation enhanced the importance of common issues and the presence of a common enemy in bolshevism. The communist antifascist campaigns managed to involve a broad cultural front of authors, artists, and scientists standing against fascism. Communist antifascism was, however, in a constantly strained relationship with the Soviet Union and its foreign policy needs. Often the sectarian lines of the Comintern and the Soviet Union imposed a line on the European communist antifascist movement, highlighting the dichotomy between Soviet antifascism and "communist antifascism." This straightjacket was unsuitable for an antifascism that was conceived as a broad front by sympathizers. Clearly, it was repeatedly difficult for the communist antifascist movement to detect the difference between fighting "against fascism" and fighting "for communism." This severely hampered its ability and potential to construct a broad and lasting culture of antifascism in interwar Europe.

KASPER BRASKÉN is postdoctoral researcher at Åbo Akademi University in Turku, Finland. He is a historian specializing in German, transnational and social movement history. He is the co-editor of H-Socialisms and the author of several articles on international solidarity, communism, and antifascism. Braskén is currently engaged in a three-year postdoctoral project titled "The Origins of Anti-Fascism: Transnational Movements against Fascism, Nazism and the White Terror in Europe, 1923–1939" (2014–2016). Since 2008, he has done extensive archival research on the interwar international communist and socialist movement in Moscow and Berlin. His doctoral thesis was recently published by Palgrave Macmillan, titled *The International Workers' Relief, Communism, and Transnational Solidarity: Willi Münzenberg in Weimar Germany* (2015).

Notes

1. The chapter is written within the framework of the research project "The Origins of 'Anti-Fascism': Transnational Movements against Nazism, Fascism and the 'White Terror' in Europe, 1923–1939." The project is funded by the Kone Foundation in Finland.
2. Classic general studies on antifascism include the works of Larry Ceplair, *Under the Shadow of War: Fascism, Anti-Fascism, and Marxists, 1918–1939* (New York, 1987); Jacques Droz, *Histoire de l'antifascisme en Europe 1923–1939* (Paris, [1985] 2001). The first transnational study on European antifascism is the work by Gerd-Rainer Horn, *European Socialists Respond to Fascism: Ideology, Activism and Contingency in the 1930s* (New York, 1996). For the transnational history of antifascism, see *Rethinking Antifascism: History, Memory and Politics, 1922 to the Present*, ed. Hugo García, Mercedes Yusta, Xavier Tabet, and Cristina Clímaco, (Oxford and New York, 2016).

3. See, for example, International Antifascist Committee, "Faschismus: Bericht vom Internationalen Antifaschisten-Kongress, Berlin, 9. bis 10. März 1929" (Berlin, 1930).

4. On the German antifascist exile in Paris, see Dieter Schiller, *Der Traum von Hitlers Sturz: Studien zur deutschen Exilliteratur 1933–1945* (Frankfurt am Main, 2010).

5. On Britain, see Nigel Copsey, *Anti-Fascism in Britain* (Houndmills, 2000), 5–80; Martin Pugh, *"Hurrah for the Blackshirts": Fascists and Fascism in Britain between the Wars* (London, 2006); Dan Stone, *Responses to Nazism in Britain, 1933–1939: Before War and Holocaust* (Houndmills, [2003] 2012); Susan D. Pennybacker, *From Scottsboro to Munich: Race and Political Culture in 1930s Britain* (Princeton, NJ, 2009); and Hugo García, *The Truth about Spain! Mobilizing British Public Opinion, 1936–1939* (Brighton, 2010).

6. For the importance of differentiating between communism as a radical social movement in non-communist countries and in countries where communism was in power, see Hermann Weber, "Zur Rolle des Terrors im Kommunismus," in *Verbrechen im Namen der Idee: Terror im Kommunismus 1936–38*, ed. Hermann Weber and Ulrich Mählert (Berlin, 2007), 38–39.

7. Letter from Münzenberg to Dimitrov, late 1937, SAPMO–BArch, RY 5/I 6/10/68, 64–65. On Münzenberg as a political actor in the Weimar Republic, see Kasper Braskén, *The International Workers' Relief, Communism, and Transnational Solidarity: Willi Münzenberg in Weimar Germany* (Houndmills, 2015).

8. Geoff Eley, *Forging Democracy: The History of the Left in Europe, 1850–2000* (Oxford, 2002), 261–68.

9. Brigitte Studer, *The Transnational World of the Cominternians* (Houndmills, 2015), 5.

10. Michael David-Fox, *Showcasing the Great Experiment: Cultural Diplomacy and Western Visitors to the Soviet Union, 1921–1941* (Oxford, 2012), 90.

11. Stanley G. Payne, "Soviet Anti-Fascism: Theory and Practice, 1921–45," *Totalitarian Movements and Political Religions* 4, 2 (2003): 6.

12. Leonid Luks, *Entstehung der kommunistischen Faschismustheorie: Die Auseinandersetzung der Komintern mit Faschismus und Nationalsozialismus 1921–1935*, (Stuttgart, 1985), 14–15.

13. Ibid., 46. See also Karl Radek, "Die internationale Faschismus und die kommunistische Internationale," *Die Rote Fahne* 173 (29 July 1923).

14. Luks, *Entstehung der kommunistischen Faschismustheorie*, 32–33, 55.

15. See, for example, SAPMO–BArch, RY 1/I 2/3/226, 1.

16. Der Frankfurter Intern. Konferenz. Der Kampf gegen Ruhrbesetzung, Kriegsgefahr und Faschismus: Material für die Agitation (10 April 1923) Herausgegeben vom Internationalen Aktionsausschuß zum Kampf gegen Kriegsgefahr und Faschismus, RGASPI, 543/1/1, 57–72, here 66.

17. Ibid., 70–71.

18. "Die italienischen Faschisten in Frankreich," *Chronik des Faschismus* 10 (1 Dec. 1923).

19. On the Matteotti crisis, see Charles F. Delzell, *Mussolini's Enemies: The Italian Anti-Fascist Resistance* (Princeton, NJ, 1961), 12–15.

20. Zara Steiner, *The Lights that Failed: European International History 1919–1933* (Oxford, 2007), 172.
21. Denis Mack Smith, *Mussolini's Roman Empire* (London, 1976), 25.
22. Lorna L. Waddington, "The Anti-Komintern and Nazi Anti-Bolshevik Propaganda in the 1930s," *Journal of Contemporary History* 42(4) (2007), 578–79. On the campaign, see Joseph Fronczak, "Local People's Global Politics: A Transnational History of the Hands-Off Ethiopia Movement of 1935," *Diplomatic History* 39, 2 (2015): 245–74.
23. M. Willi and Giulio Aquila, *Bericht über die faschistische Bewegung: Frühjahr 1924. Unterbereitet dem Fünften Kongreß der Kommunistischen Internationale im Auftrage der Komintern-Kommission gegen den Faschismus* (Berlin, 1924).
24. Letter from Henri Barbusse to "Werter Genosse," 9 July 1929, RGASPI 543/1/10, 97.
25. On totalitarianism, see Richard Shorten, *Modernism and Totalitarianism: Rethinking the Intellectual Sources of Nazism and Stalinism, 1945 to the Present* (Basingstoke, 2012).
26. Siegfried Bahne, "'Sozialfaschismus' in Deutschland. Zur Geschichte eines politischen Begriffs," *International Review of Social History* X (1965): 211–45.
27. Eric D. Weitz, *Creating German Communism, 1890–1990: From Popular Protests to Socialist State* (Princeton, NJ, 1997), 263–70.
28. See, for example, Philip Morgan, *Fascism in Europe, 1919–1945* (London, 2003); Michael Mann, *Fascists* (Cambridge, 2004); and Arnd Bauerkämper, *Der Faschismus in Europa 1918–1945* (Stuttgart, 2006). On comparisons and entangled history, see Arnd Bauerkämper, "Transnationalism in Historiographical Practice: Historical Comparison and the Investigation of Entanglements in European History," in *Forgotten by History: New Research on Twentieth-Century Europe and America*, ed. Jaroslaw Suchoples and Katy Turton (Berlin, 2009), 12–20.
29. See Michael David-Fox, Peter Holquist, and Alexander M. Martin, eds., *Fascination and Enmity: Russia and Germany as Entangled Histories, 1914–1945* (Pittsburgh, 2012); and Katerina Clark and Karl Schlögel, "Mutual Perceptions and Projections: Stalin's Russia in Nazi Germany—Nazi Germany in the Soviet Union," in *Beyond Totalitarianism: Stalinism and Nazism Compared*, ed. Michael Geyer and Sheila Fitzpatrick (Cambridge, 2009), 396–441. On the role of exile communities in forging antifascist culture, see Volkmar Zühlsdorff, *Hitler's Exiles: The German Cultural Resistance in America and Europe* (London and New York, 2004); and Jean-Michel Palmier, *Weimar in Exile: The Antifascist Emigration in Europe and America* (London, 2006).
30. "Brauner Mord! Das italienische Vorbild des Naziterror," *Arbeiter-Illustrierte-Zeitung* 29 (17 July 1932).
31. John Heartfield, "Gleiche Brüder, Gleiche Mörder," *Arbeiter-Illustrierte-Zeitung* 43 (2 November 1933).
32. Quoted from Waddington, "The Anti-Komintern," 577.
33. Arnd Bauerkämper, "Interwar Fascism in Europe and Beyond: Toward a Transnational Radical Right," in *New Perspectives on the Transnational Right*, ed. Martin Durham and Margaret Power (New York, 2011), 42–44; and Jan C. Behrends, "Back from the USSR: The Anti-Comintern's Publications on

Soviet Russia in Nazi Germany, 1935–1941," in David-Fox et al., *Fascination and Enmity*, 83–84.

34. Bauerkämper, "Interwar Fascism in Europe and Beyond," 50–51.
35. Waddington, "The Anti-Komintern," 587–88.
36. Thomas Linehan, "Communist Culture and Anti-Fascism in Interwar Britain," in *Varieties of Anti-Fascism: Britain in the Inter-War Period*, ed. Nigel Copsey and Andrzej Olechnowicz (Houndmills, 2010), 39–49.
37. Nigel Copsey and Andrzej Olechnowicz, eds., *Varieties of Anti-Fascism: Britain in the Inter-War Period* (Houndmills, 2010); Silvio Pons, *The Global Revolution: A History of International Communism 1917–1991* (Oxford, 2014), 80.
38. Ben Fowkes, *Communism in Germany under the Weimar Republic* (London, 1984), 164.
39. On the Brown Book, see Anson Rabinbach, "Staging Antifascism: The Brown Book of the Reichstag Fire and Hitler Terror," *New German Critique* 35, 1 (2008): 97–126.
40. Linehan, "Communist Culture and Anti-Fascism," 37.
41. Horn, *European Socialists Respond*, 26–35.
42. Bernhard H. Bayerlein, "Abschied von einem Mythos. Die UdSSR, die Komintern und der Antifaschismus," *Osteuropa* 59, 7–8 (2009): 125–48; and Pons, *The Global Revolution*, 95–96.
43. Pons, *The Global Revolution*, 80–81.
44. Bernhard H. Bayerlein, *"Der Verräter, Stalin, bist Du!" Vom Ende der linken Solidarität. Komintern und kommunistische Parteien im Zweiten Weltkrieg 1939–1941* (Berlin, 2008), 65–67; and Payne, "Soviet Anti-Fascism," 44.
45. Private letter from Anton Ackermann to Franz Dahlem, Berlin, 5 March 1968, SAPMO–BArch, NY 4072/149, 4–7, here 5.
46. Richard J. Evans, *The Third Reich in Power 1933–1939* (London, 2006), 694–95.
47. See further in the ongoing research project "Die Exilzeitschrift 'Die Zukunft,' Organ der Deutsch-Französischen Union (1938–1940)" by Bernhard H. Bayerlein, Anne Hartmann, and Dieter Nelles <http://isb. rub.de/forschung/drittmittel/zukunft.html.de> (accessed 15 June 2016); see also Jacques Droz, "Die Zukunft: Wochenzeitung Willi Münzenbergs (Oktober 1938–Mai 1940)," in *Deutsche Exilpresse und Frankreich 1933–1940*, ed. Helene Roussel and Lutz Winckler (Bern, 1992), 117–21.
48. Charmain Brinson and Richard Dove, *A Matter of Intelligence: MI5 and the Surveillance of Anti-Nazi Refugees, 1933–50* (Manchester, 2014), 103–12.

Bibliography

Bahne, Siegfried. "'Sozialfaschismus' in Deutschland: Zur Geschichte eines politischen Begriffs." *International Review of Social History* X (1965): 211–45.
Bauerkämper, Arnd. "Interwar Fascism in Europe and Beyond: Toward a Transnational Radical Right." In *New Perspectives on the Transnational Right*, ed. Martin Durham and Margaret Power, 39–66. New York: Palgrave Macmillan, 2011.

―――. *Der Faschismus in Europa 1918–1945.* Stuttgart, 2006.

―――. "Transnationalism in Historiographical Practice: Historical Comparison and the Investigation of Entanglements in European History." In *Forgotten by History: New Research on Twentieth-Century Europe and America*, edited by Jaroslaw Suchoples and Katy Turton, 12–20. Berlin, 2009.

Bayerlein, Bernhard H. "Abschied von einem Mythos. Die UdSSR, die Komintern und der Antifaschismus." *Osteuropa* 59, 7–8 (2009): 125–48.

―――. *"Der Verräter, Stalin, bist Du!" Vom Ende der linken Solidarität. Komintern und kommunistische Parteien im Zweiten Weltkrieg 1939–1941.* Berlin, 2008.

Bernhard H. Bayerlein, Anne Hartmann, and Dieter Nelles <http://isb.rub.de/forschung/drittmittel/zukunft.html.de> (accessed 15 June 2016)

Braskén, Kasper. *The International Workers' Relief, Communism, and Transnational Solidarity. Willi Münzenberg in Weimar Germany.* Palgrave Studies in the History of Social Movements, edited by Stefan Berger and Holger Nehring. Houndmills: Palgrave Macmillan, 2015.

Brinson, Charmain and Richard Dove. *A Matter of Intelligence: MI5 and the Surveillance of Anti-Nazi Refugees, 1933–50.* Manchester, 2014.

Ceplair, Larry. *Under the Shadow of War: Fascism, Anti-Fascism, and Marxists, 1918–1939.* New York, 1987.

Clark, Katerina, and Karl Schlögel, "Mutual Perceptions and Projections: Stalin's Russia in Nazi Germany—Nazi Germany in the Soviet Union." In *Beyond Totalitarianism: Stalinism and Nazism Compared*, edited by Michael Geyer and Sheila Fitzpatrick (Cambridge, 2009).

Copsey, Nigel. *Anti-Fascism in Britain.* Houndmills, 2000.

Copsey, Nigel, and Andrzej Olechnowicz, eds. *Varieties of Anti-Fascism: Britain in the Inter-War Period.* Houndmills, 2010.

David-Fox, Michael. *Showcasing the Great Experiment: Cultural Diplomacy and Western Visitors to the Soviet Union, 1921–1941.* Oxford, 2012.

―――, Peter Holquist, and Alexander M. Martin, eds., *Fascination and Enmity: Russia and Germany as Entangled Histories, 1914–1945.* Pittsburgh, 2012.

Delzell, Charles F. *Mussolini's Enemies: The Italian Anti-Fascist Resistance.* Princeton, NJ, 1961.

Droz, Jacques. *Histoire de l'antifascisme en Europe 1923–1939.* Paris, [1985] 2001.

―――. "Die Zukunft: Wochenzeitung Willi Münzenbergs (Oktober 1938–Mai 1940)." In *Deutsche Exilpresse und Frankreich 1933–1940*, edited by Helene Roussel and Lutz Winckler. Bern, 1992.

Eley, Geoff. *Forging Democracy: The History of the Left in Europe, 1850–2000.* Oxford, 2002.

Evans, Richard J. *The Third Reich in Power 1933–1939.* London, 2006.

Fowkes, Ben. *Communism in Germany under the Weimar Republic.* London, 1984.

Fronczak, Joseph. "Local People's Global Politics: A Transnational History of the Hands-Off Ethiopia Movement of 1935." *Diplomatic History* 39, (2) (2015): 245–74.

García, Hugo, Mercedes Yusta, Xavier Tabet, and Cristina Clímaco, ed. *Rethinking Antifascism: History, Memory and Politics, 1922 to the Present.* Oxford and New York, 2016.

García, Hugo. *The Truth about Spain! Mobilizing British Public Opinion, 1936–1939.* Brighton, 2010.

310 • Kasper Braskén

Geyer, Michael, and Sheila Fitzpatrick, eds. *Beyond Totalitarianism: Stalinism and Nazism Compared*. Cambridge, 2009.
Horn, Gerd-Rainer. *European Socialists Respond to Fascism: Ideology, Activism and Contingency in the 1930s*. New York, 1996.
International Antifascist Committee. "Faschismus: Bericht vom Internationalen Antifaschisten-Kongress, Berlin, 9. bis 10. März 1929" [Fascism: Report from the World Antifascist Congress, Berlin, 9–10 March 1929]. Berlin, 1930.
Langkau-Alex, Ursula. "Die Zukunft der Vergangenheit oder die Zukunft der Zukunft? Zur Bündniskonzeptionen der Zeitschrift zwischen Oktober 1938 und August 1939." In *Deutsche Exilpresse und Frankreich 1933–1940*, edited by Helene Roussel and Lutz Winckler, 123–56. Bern, 1992.
Linehan, Thomas. "Communist Culture and Anti-Fascism in Interwar Britain." In *Varieties of Anti-Fascism: Britain in the Inter-War Period*, edited by Nigel Copsey and Andrzej Olechnowicz. Houndmills, 2010.
Luks, Leonid. *Entstehung der kommunistischen Faschismustheorie: Die Auseinandersetzung der Komintern mit Faschismus und Nationalsozialismus 1921–1935*. Studien zur Zeitgeschichte. Stuttgart, 1985.
Morgan, Philip. *Fascism in Europe, 1919–1945*. London, 2003.
Palmier, Jean-Michel. *Weimar in Exile: The Antifascist Emigration in Europe and America*. London, 2006.
Payne, Stanley G. "Soviet Anti-Fascism: Theory and Practice, 1921–45." *Totalitarian Movements and Political Religions* 4, 2 (2003): 1–62.
Pennybacker, Susan D. *From Scottsboro to Munich: Race and Political Culture in 1930s Britain*. Princeton, NJ, 2009.
Pons, Silvio. *The Global Revolution: A History of International Communism 1917–1991*, trans. Allan Cameron. Oxford, 2014.
Pugh, Martin. *"Hurrah for the Blackshirts": Fascists and Fascism in Britain between the Wars*. London, 2006.
Rabinbach, Anson. "Staging Antifascism: The Brown Book of the Reichstag Fire and Hitler Terror." *New German Critique* 35, 1 (2008): 97–126.
Smith, Denis Mack. *Mussolini's Roman Empire*. London, 1976.
Steiner, Zara. *The Lights that Failed: European International History 1919–1933*. Oxford, 2007.
Schiller, Dieter. *Der Traum von Hitlers Sturz: Studien zur deutschen Exilliteratur 1933–1945*. Frankfurt am Main, 2010.
Shorten, Richard. *Modernism and Totalitarianism: Rethinking the Intellectual Sources of Nazism and Stalinism, 1945 to the Present*. Basingstoke, 2012.
Stone, Dan. *Responses to Nazism in Britain, 1933–1939: Before War and Holocaust*. Houndmills, 2012 [2003].
Studer, Brigitte. *The Transnational World of the Cominternians*. Houndmills, 2015.
Waddington, Lorna L. "The Anti-Komintern and Nazi Anti-Bolshevik Propaganda in the 1930s." *Journal of Contemporary History* 42, 4 (2007): 573–94.
Weber, Hermann. "Zur Rolle des Terrors im Kommunismus." In *Verbrechen im Namen der Idee. Terror im Kommunismus 1936–38*, edited by Hermann Weber and Ulrich Mählert, 11–41. Berlin, 2007.
Weitz, Eric D. *Creating German Communism, 1890–1990: From Popular Protests to Socialist State*. Princeton, NJ, 1997.

Willi, M., and Giulio Aquila. *Bericht über die faschistische Bewegung: Frühjahr 1924. Unterbereitet dem Fünften Kongreß der Kommunistischen Internationale im Auftrage der Komintern-Kommission gegen den Faschismus.* Berlin, 1924.

Zühlsdorff, Volkmar. *Hitler's Exiles: The German Cultural Resistance in America and Europe.* London and New York, 2004.

ॐ 12

ANTIFASCISM IN EUROPE
Networks, Exchanges, and Influences. The Case of Silvio Trentin in Toulouse and in the Resistenza in Veneto (1926–1944)

Silvia Madotto

Antifascism in Europe in Transnational Perspective

The concept of antifascism in Europe is particularly difficult to grasp in all its complexity due to the heterogeneous ideologies, movements, and parties that coexisted in Europe between 1922 and 1945. However, this plurality of forces clearly constitutes its essence. In order to discuss this concept, it is essential to address some central issues. To which basic problem did antifascism aim at finding a response?[1] And in which dimension does it fall?

Antifascism in Europe originated and found its expression as a reaction to fascism, which had grown in an international environment. Responding to claims of supremacy in Europe by the elites of the Fascist regime in Italy and the National Socialist dictatorship in Germany, antifascist movements organized in different ways. However, looking at the European geographical and cultural dimension in which the movements developed, researchers increasingly recognized the importance to analyze and compare these movements in an international perspective of study.[2] As with studies of fascism, it seems important to extend the methodology and the perspectives of research about antifascism in a transnational way. This broader view enables scholars to trace the reactions of antifascist groups to transnational networks, actions, and ideologies of fascist regimes and movements throughout Europe. Moreover, this procedure allows researchers to identify the cross-border networks, cooperation, and communication of antifascist groups. Not least, this perspective highlights synergies and transfers among various national experiences. We will thereby be able to recognize coexisting ideas and purposes, which link different movements and experiences in Europe. Moreover, it will be possible to retrace the interactions among the antifascists groups, their exchanges of information, forms of transnational solidarity, and their strategy to eliminate fascism and establish peace in Europe. The effectiveness of this methodology has been highlighted by historians of antifascism and promoted in particular in recent years through international conferences, with the intent of supporting a discussion on this perspective of research.[3]

In order to understand the cultural and political dynamics of these various movements, it is essential to concentrate on their interconnections. This perspective, which focuses both on the national peculiarities and on the connections and transfers between different experiences, paves the way to investigations of the heterogeneous antifascist movements in Europe.

Antifascist resistance was pursued and supported by specific actors who occupied crucial positions at nodal points in networks. In this chapter, the focus will be on the case of an Italian academic, jurist, and antifascist, who lived in exile in France for almost twenty years: Silvio Trentin. Concentrating on his activities will allow us to analyze some central aspects of antifascism connected with academic resistance and intellectual exile in Europe.

From the 1920s until the end of World War II, the relationship between fascist dictatorships and universities in Europe, both in the occupied countries and in fascist states, were extremely complex. Cooperation and conflicts between the academic world and political powers within their respective countries differed between the nations. Academic resistance groups were dissimilar, as they reacted to different strategies of the dictatorships, both before 1939 and during the war. Besides strong national peculiarities, however, it is possible to trace types of international cooperation and exchange of ideas within the European resistance milieus. Transmission of information was possible thanks to international organizations, religious institutions that held meetings, and scientific conferences. Pre-existing friendships and contacts among academics, too, facilitated exchanges. Studies of the workings and impact of these connections as well as the aims and motives of their proponents will allow us to grasp the role and influence of these international dimensions on the national opposition movements.

Many intellectuals, among them university professors, left their countries and went into exile abroad as dissidents against fascism. The antifascist fighters in exile abroad were part of a complex network throughout Europe. They need to be analyzed not only with regard to their particular features, but also with respect to their roles in specific networks in a wider context. This will demonstrate how or allow us to determine in what way and dimension the fighters and their countries they exiled to were influenced by each other.[4]

This chapter traces the antifascist agenda and political activity of Silvio Trentin. It will analyze the evolution of Trentin's experiences starting from his exile in France in the 1920s, where he built a network of contacts, along with his engagement with the movement Libérer et Fédérer in Toulouse. Moreover, the contribution will focus on the key role Trentin played in the Resistenza in Veneto, Italy, after his return there in 1943. In particular, his connections with the antifascist leaders, who were active at the University of Padua, have to be dealt with. The aim is to highlight how the transnational contacts that Trentin was able to establish, as well as the exchange of information, contributed to his antifascist program and actions in a European context.

The focus will be on some recurring elements that characterized the antifascist experiences of Trentin, such as contacts with foreign dissidents, exchange and transfer of information, illegal antifascist propaganda, and political and social plans for a peaceful Europe free from fascism.

Silvio Trentin—Professor and Antifascist

Silvio Trentin was born in San Donà di Piave (Venice, Italy) on 11 November 1885. He studied law and began his academic career before taking part as a volunteer in World War I. From the 1920s onward, Trentin turned against Italian Fascism. He joined the political debate and served as a deputy of the Democrazia Sociale, a liberal party that had been founded in 1919. In 1924, he returned to academic activity at the University of Venice and linked with other antifascist personalities.[5] After the murder of Mussolini's opponent Giacomo Matteotti, Trentin's political positions became more intransigent; and in 1925 he decided to sign the "Manifesto degli intellettuali antifascisti" (Manifesto of the Antifascist Intellectuals) of Benedetto Croce.[6] He abandoned his academic career and fled to France in 1926. In his letter of resignation, Trentin explained that his choice was determined by the impossibility of conciliating his role as a legal expert with the authoritarian dispositions of Mussolini's Fascist dictatorship.[7]

Trentin first moved with his family to Auch, in southern France, where he worked as a farmer and printer. Immediately after his arrival, he got in contact with the antifascist milieu in the South of France, initially with Italian antifascists in exile.[8] In October 1926, he joined the Italian group of antifascists reunited by the initiative of the Italian antifascists Luigi Campolonghi and Alceste De Ambris, with the aim of founding a new united group of forces against fascism. This was the beginning of the Concentrazione Antifascista, a group officially formed in Paris in 1927.[9] Within the Concentrazione, a heated debate about the necessity of a unique centralized direction for all the antifascist exiled groups began. Trentin was always supportive of a comprehensive union, which would have enabled the forces to centralize and to cooperate with a common goal.

In 1929, Trentin participated in the Giustizia e Libertà (Justice and Freedom) movement.[10] He joined that organization with the aim of strengthening the front against fascism and encouraging the unity of action among all antifascist movements in exile. In 1934, Trentin and his family moved to Toulouse where he acquired a bookstore in Rue du Languedoc. He immediately got in touch with antifascist personalities in southern France and reinforced his contacts with Italian antifascists in Paris.[11] Trentin promoted the organization of a network between antifascists in order to encourage contacts and initiate a cultural and political debate.[12] The international bookstore became a center of political debates and was a meeting place for intellectuals and antifascists. Various professors of the University of Toulouse attended discussions there, and recommended the bookstore to their students.[13] It rapidly became a crossroads for French intellectuals, academics, Italian antifascists, political refugees, and Spanish politicians. Many professors and intellectuals were drawn into the activities—for instance, Camille Soula, Paul Guilhem, Jacques Maury, Henri Dupeyroux, André Hauriou, and philosopher Georges Canguilhelm, as well as Italian politicians Carlo Sforza and Pietro Nenni.[14]

In Paris, Carlo Rosselli, the founder of Giustizia e Libertà, supervised the mobilization in support of the Spanish antifascists for his group. Toulouse was a strategic place for the antifascists moving from France to Spain during the Spanish Civil War. This central location allowed Trentin to occupy a prominent role in the coordination of antifascists fighting in Spain, to establish a solid network of contacts, and to exchange ideas and experiences in an international context.[15] Emilio Lussu, antifascist a co-founder of the movement Giustizia e Libertà, wrote in his "Memory of Silvio Trentin" that the bookshop looked like an embassy.[16] Its central location enabled it to organize contacts and exchanges between France and Spain through the Pyrenees during the Spanish Civil War. The Italian Fascist political police soon recognized that Trentin had become both the most representative antifascist in the region of Toulouse and a reference person for exiled antifascists.[17] Trentin's central role in the network of antifascists extended and articulated across Europe, from Paris to Barcelona.

In Italy, the debate around the federalist theories was reinvigorated after the Fascist seizure of power. At the beginning, the discussions concentrated on domestic issues, and successively encompassed general reflections about the crisis of democracy in Europe. In particular during the 1930s, the Italian antifascists elaborated on fascism, antifascism, and strategies to build a pacified Europe. Several political personalities took part in those discussions, including Antonio Gramsci, Piero Gobetti, Gaetano Salvemini, and following Carlo Rosselli, Emilio Lussu, and Silvio Trentin.[18] Overturning the dictatorship and offering a programmatic basis for the future were the foci of that debate.[19] In his first treatise, Trentin concentrated on the critics of Italian fascism. After the National Socialists had seized power in Germany and expanded their influence in Europe, Trentin concentrated on the importance of an interrelated fight and supported the idea that only the federalist model could create a new political, social and cultural system in Europe.[20] In Trentin's view, a federation of European peoples would prevent totalitarian regimes from coming to power once more and prevent the outbreak of new wars in Europe.[21] The Italian jurist conceived this federation not strictly in a territorial or political sense, but more widely in a social, economic, cultural, and ethical meaning.[22] This federalist system did not aim at a decentralization of power, but a fundamental reconsideration of free effort and autonomy, which would form the basis of every political, economic, and cultural activity.[23] This would also influence the wider context, be it local, regional, national, or transnational. Trentin's starting point was the "defense of freedom of individuals and [the] autonomy of the groups that were threatened by the ultra-centralized state." Federalism was intended as a realization of the value of autonomy on a collective level, as a system. It was thought to be able to protect the autonomy of citizens and of the collective, defeating its own pluralities, which represented the essential basis of a democratic government.

Referring to the need for this revolution to embrace the whole European context, Trentin wrote that "if fascism is anti-Europe, then Europe must be antifascist."[24]

The 1940s—The Réseau Bertaux and the Beginning of Libérer et Fédérer

After the occupation of France by the National Socialists, Pierre Bertaux, professor of German studies at the University of Toulouse, became the leader of a *réseau* (network) of resistance in the region, which was formed by intellectuals and cosmopolites. Among the French intellectuals the most important protagonists were Jean Cassou, who was active in the "Groupe de Musée de l'Homme" in Paris,[25] socialists Achille Auban and Jean Maurice Hermann, syndicalist Marcel Vanhove, Letvian jurist Gilbert Zaksas, and sociologist Georges Friedmann.[26] Important personalities in the group were Silvio Trentin and Fausto Nitti, whose prestigious roles and status derived from their experience as antifascist organizers.

In this group, Trentin was to establish contacts among resistance fighters. His bookshop became a focal point in these networks once more. Intellectuals and political activists assembled in the bookstore, discussed politics, elaborated on strategies of actions, exchanged messages, and also linked with the Allies in London. Trentin exploited his contacts with resistance fighters and the experience he had acquired during the 1930s in order to promote this cooperation.

Contacts with the Allies in London were established in cooperation with the young lieutenant Henri Labit.[27] The group set up radio transmissions with London and France Libre's chiefs. The illegal conspiracy network included French and British special agents. They infiltrated France and partisan groups operating in the urban centers. In Toulouse, Trentin initiated one of the first connections with soldiers of the British Special Operations Executive (SOE), who were parachuted to its suburbs.

The police of Vichy discovered the *réseau* in December 1941. Several of the members were arrested, among them Bertaux, Cassou, and Nitti. After the dissolution of the *réseau*, the remaining members established the resistance movement Libérer et Fédérer, who published their underground journal beginning in July 1942.[28] Its core members were authors, university professors, scientists, and intellectuals. In the *Comité directeur*, Achille Auban, Adolphe Coll, Paul Descours, Maurice Fonvieille, Clément Laurent and Gilbert Zaksas were operative. Trentin's input proved decisive with regard to ideology, program, and political action. He thereby became a key protagonist. Trentin wrote the manifesto of the group and published it in the first issue of the journal. He also wrote a second programmatic text in 1942.[29]

Libérer et Fédérer was a specific resistance movement. Its programmatic reflections about autonomy and federalism have been considered original and unusually advanced. As historian Hans Werner Tobler has stressed, it is impossible to understand Libérer et Fédérer without considering the crucial influence that Trentin had on its program.[30]

The underground journal was published in fourteen issues, along with some other sporadic documents, from July 1942 until the liberation of Toulouse in August 1944. The journal had a clear political and social program and became a tool for political mobilization in the region.[31] *Libérer et Fédérer* supported a common fight against fascism and promoted the unity of all resistance forces, independent of their political views. At the same time, the group promulgated a program that aimed to transform French society under a socialist and federalist system. The members of Libérer et Fédérer called for a complete rupture with the past and for the formation of a new social order.

The main activities of the group included the production of falsified documents for persecuted people, supporting them to escape abroad—especially to Britain—and entertaining an information service for sabotage actions. The group lined up in the fight with *France Libre*, recognized the authority of the *Résistance* of Charles de Gaulle and the importance of unity in fighting, without abandoning its own strong independence.[32]

Libérer et Fédérer remained a movement with a limited number of members, compared to the major groups of the *Résistance*. However, Silvio Trentin's intellectual and cultural influence in Toulouse and its surrounding area is undeniable. Moreover, his role in the military fight is noteworthy.[33] The movement coordinated military armed forces, the *maquis*—farmers and workers were particularly active in them—and teams of saboteurs, who operated especially in the cities. The military coordination was organized in cooperation and under the support of British Major Anthony Brooks, "Alphonse".[34] After the Zone libre was occupied by Nazi Germany on 11 November 1942, Trentin tried to escape with the purpose of raising French forces in Algeria. On 25 July 1943, he and his family were able to return to Italy on legal terms.

1943—The University of Padua as a Center of Conspiracy, and Silvio Trentin as a Leader of the Resistenza in Veneto

During the 1920s and the 1930s Fascist ideology had strongly spread in the university of Padua, although it did not take over all the academic sector. The voice of the opposition could survive in some university's academic milieus, in particular among some professors.[35] 8 September

1943 represented the turning point for the organization of the patriotic fight in structured networks.

The experience of the University of Padua was an exceptional case of organized resistance in Italy. Following the collapse of Italian Fascism on 25 July 1943, Badoglio's government appointed Concetto Marchesi, a well-known communist professor in Padua, as the new dean. His academic position was confirmed by the new minister of national education of the Italian Social Republic (Repubblica Sociale Italiana RSI), Carlo Biggini. Marchesi and Biggini struck an agreement, which guaranteed the university an extraordinary independence. The old and strong tradition of university autonomy and academic freedom, celebrated in the academic motto *Universa Universis Patavina Libertas,* along with these concessions of autonomy and the presence of strong antifascist personalities inside the university, made it possible to organize and coordinate a well-structured resistance organization in the university within a short period.

Marchesi took advantage of the conciliatory approach promoted by Biggini to create a "state inside the state" at the university, which became a conspiratorial center.[36] Professors and students played an influential role as fighters in the Resistenza and from 1943 to 1945 they effectively coordinated the expansion and organization of the regional resistance network.

In 1943, Trentin resumed his Chair at the University of Venice Ca' Foscari. After his return, he started to attend the antifascist group formed around Concetto Marchesi and Egidio Meneghetti at the University of Padua under the name of Professor Ferrari.[37] He immediately enjoyed a strong reputation and was seen as one of the most prestigious antifascists in Veneto.[38] His authority derived from his recognition as promoter of the movement in France, from his role during the Spanish Civil War, as well as from the connections he had been able to build with antifascist European intellectuals.

The Resistance Central Committee in Veneto (Comitato di liberazione nazionale regionale Veneto, CLNRV) was coordinated by the three professors: Concetto Marchesi, the dean of the university and member of the Communist Party; the vice dean, Egidio Meneghetti; and Silvio Trentin, who represented the Partito d'Azione (Action Party). This illegal resistance committee was founded in September 1943 by the delegates of all the most important antifascist parties. The committee's mission was to become the coordination center of conspiratorial activities in Veneto, promoting unity and collaboration among the major antifascist parties in order to prevent internal conflicts and rivalries among the factions. The actions of the group concentrated on the resistance fight against the National Socialists and the Fascists.

The responsibilities of the committee were accurately divided among the members. Trentin was the only one who had any experience with guerrilla tactics, which he had acquired during the coordination of the French *maquis*.[39] At that time, one of his main ambitions was to establish a central authority, in charge of the coordination of all military forces.[40] Immediately, Silvio Trentin and Egidio Meneghetti perceived the danger that the conflicts between the political authority and the fragmented military forces represented. This discord could have led to a dangerous fragmentation. In November 1943, Trentin and Meneghetti reached an agreement and established a unique military executive group, coordinated by the political authority of the CLNRV. It was accepted as a legitimate government.

Trentin engaged in central activities of the resistance fight. He promoted sabotage of the railway transport in order to obstruct the National Socialist war effort. In these activities, he took advantage of his experience in the French *Résistance* and utilized his friendships and contacts in Veneto.

Illegal propaganda played a crucial role in the resistance fight. Printed in 1943–44, the journal *Fratelli d'Italia* was one of the most influential antifascist publications in Veneto. Its pages contained and spread the official positions and guidelines of the CLNRV.[41] Meneghetti was the principal coordinator of illegal propaganda and in collaboration with him, Trentin supported the need to circulate information to make sure the aim of the resistance fight was properly understood.

The influence of Trentin's political and cultural views emerged at several points. An article published in October 1943, entitled "European Italy," focused on the European dimension of the war. The author emphasized that the fighters in Padua, as in the rest of Italy, needed to become Europeans, because "there is a unity of destiny for the European populations. They have to feel like interdependent brothers. It is also the unity of free countries that make us believe in a renaissance."[42] In the Venetian journal *Giustizia e Libertà*, which was printed by the Partito d'Azione, Trentin published the "Appello ai Veneti" (Appeal to the Venetians) on 1 November 1943. In this text, he called upon citizens to join the fight against fascism, and he also explained to them the forms and the political aims of the *Resistenza*.[43]

Within a few months, Trentin had become intensely involved in the organization of the resistance fight and in the political coordination of the movement, lending the fragmented formations unity. He also contributed to make the CLNRV the central authority in Veneto. Trentin joined the Partito d'Azione immediately after his return to Italy, and his writings echoed throughout in the internal debate and program of the party.[44] A central contribution were his works *Libérer et Fédérer* and *Stato, Nazione, Federalismo*, written in France, translated by Antonio Giuriolo and Giovanni Perego, and disseminated within the group.[45]

On 23 October 1943, Trentin wrote a letter to his friend Emilio Lussu, who had become a leading antifascist in Rome. In this text, Trentin described the trembling actions that occurred in Veneto and affirmed that he was operating "with heart and soul" in the fight. He recognized that it had become a "success beyond his desires" and that he was directing "the whole Resistance in Veneto." He stressed that the young fighters, so enthusiastic and devoted to the fight, gave him new strength and faith for the "struggle for the antifascist mission."[46]

On 19 November 1943, Silvio Trentin was arrested in Padua by the Fascist police. However, they did not reveal how strong his involvement in the coordination of the *Resistenza* was, and they released him in December. His cardiac problems, which had already been serious in the previous years, aggravated. Trentin finally died on 12 March 1944. In March, Radio London broke the news with the title "Death of a Leader."[47]

Summary

Silvio Trentin was an independent intellectual and antifascist. Thanks to his strong morality, his ability in securing contacts, and his innovative plans for a federal political and social system, he became a crucial contact person for antifascists in Europe during the 1930s and until his death in 1944.

During the almost twenty years he spent in France, Trentin developed his political and social theories on fascism and antifascism, becoming a political writer. As Norberto Bobbio has pointed out, it is impossible to understand Trentin's works without acknowledging the French cultural and political tradition.[48] Trentin connected it to his Italian education and antifascist experiences, as well as to the various cultural influences that had resulted from his contacts with other European intellectuals. The reworking of all these elements and influences allowed him to develop his comprehensive political and social theories, and to become a central protagonist of the resistance fight.

Trentin can, indeed, be considered a European intellectual and antifascist. His activities and works concentrated on the importance of unity in the fight against fascism and on the necessity of establishing a new federalist order in Europe. The Italian jurist was able to establish contacts and collaborate with different resistance groups, whilst preserving his strong identity, distinct ideology, and specific political concepts. Aiming at consensus and unity in the antifascist movement, he strongly encouraged an alliance of socialists, Catholics, liberals, and communists, while recognizing the unavoidable influence of the Communist Party on the workers. This approach allowed Trentin to become a crucial element in the network of Italians in exile and the French fighters. His bookshop in Toulouse was a meeting place that promoted debate among dissidents. He also engaged in the coordination of this network. Different from many resistance organizations, and thanks to Trentin's contribution, Libérer et Fédérer had a clear political understanding of the resistance fight. Its program was focused on a fundamental political and social renewal.[49] After Trentin's return to Italy, Libérer et Fédérer combined with the insurgents in the Mouvement révolutionaire socialiste in March 1944. In the journal of the movement some key elements of Trentin's theories persisted, such as the concepts of international peace and United States of Europe. Gilbert Zaksas, an original member of Libérer et Fédérer, supported the ideas of the group in the Comité Français pour la Fédération européenne and in the secretariat of the Comité international pour la fédération européenne after the Congrès fédéraliste de Paris on March 1945.[50]

After his return to Italy, Trentin immediately engaged in illegal actions, becoming one of the leaders of the CLNRV. He achieved important aims in a short period of time. Due to his experience, Trentin was able to introduce changes and innovations, as well as to coordinate and encourage fighters. In particular, his experience was essential in arranging urban sabotage, establishing contacts with the allied powers, and promoting underground propaganda. As historian De Luna has pointed out, the discussions about the "Venetian model" in the resistance movement cannot be understood without consideration of Silvio Trentin's crucial political and military contribution.[51] Moreover, Trentin developed an innovative program for a new postwar political system in Europe. His writings contributed to the political and social debate on the need for solid cooperation and union on the continent.

The influence of the Italian jurist on antifascist and resistance networks in France and Italy is undeniable. Moreover, some of Trentin's political plans survived after the end of the war. The main body of his juridical and political production was written in France. When Trentin came back to Italy in 1943, the first translations started to be produced, along with the dissemination of some copies of his writings among the members of the Partito d'Azione. However, Trentin died at the beginning of 1944, when the resistance fight was still in progress. Bobbio has stressed that it happened "too early" to allow Trentin's French books to break into the political debate that was resumed after the end of the war in Italy.[52] Moreover, the Partito d'Azione—Trentin's party—dissolved in 1947. Therefore, Trentin did not participate in shaping the postwar order, and his heritage was not capitalized as a political or theoretical agenda by a political party.

However, Trentin's moral heritage was taken over by his companion in the fight in Veneto. Professor Egidio Meneghetti celebrated Trentin in an article published on *Fratelli d'Italia* in May 1944. The author honored Trentin's strong personality, his engagement in the resistance, and his political reflections. Trentin's heritage also survived in the academic opposition milieu. After his death the "Brigata Guastatori Silvio Trentin" was established. It reunited students and workers of different political views, and was led by engineer and academic Otello Pighin.

The resistance organization, which centered on the university and involved many professors and students, continued the fight. The group, which sustained arrests and deportations, arranged a transnational network in support of persecuted, coordinated partisan groups, and established contacts with the Allies in London until the liberation of Padua at the end of April 1945. After the end of the war, the University of Padua was the only academic center in Italy awarded with the Gold Medal for Military Value because, "first among the others, it became a center of conspiracy and war. Padua had in its university a temple of civil faith and a presidio of heroic resistance."

Trentin's juridical and political theories about federalism have been discussed and studied by academics, political scientists, and scholars since the end of the war until today. In 1974, the research center "Centro Studi e Ricerca Silvio Trentin" was created in Jesolo, with the aim of collecting documents, sources, and publications on Silvio Trentin, as well as promoting the research on his role and activities in the antifascist fight. In 2014, the seventieth anniversary of Trentin's death, a conference on his intellectual heritage was organized at the University of Venice.[53] The presentations and debate focused on Trentin's juridical and political elaborations, on his activities between France and Italy, and on the European perspective of his experience and reflections. The discussants highlighted the role of Trentin's works in the development of federalist theories, insisting on the need for interdisciplinary studies on his work.

The transnational perspective of this chapter has allowed a reconstruction of the interrelated actions of the various members of the network around Silvio Trentin in order to understand the exchanges and transfer of information among these intellectuals, politicians, and activists. Moreover, this approach has permitted us to grasp how and in what way these transfers of information among various protagonists influenced the various national resistance experiences in France and Italy.

Moreover, Trentin's example allows researchers to trace some aspects of intellectual and academic antifascist and resistance experiences between France and Italy. The significance of the academic milieu in Trentin's experience has clearly emerged, both in the structure of his network in Toulouse and in the resistance fight in Veneto. It is possible to detect forms of interactions and exchanges of experiences and information among academics and intellectuals in Europe. These exchanges in networks conditioned and influenced the political and social views and works of the individual fighters.

In order to reconstruct the complexity of the antifascist experiences in Europe, its results are essential to enhance both the national and international dimensions of the antifascist fight, focusing on the local peculiarities, transnational elements, influences, and exchanges.

SILVIA MADOTTO is currently a PhD candidate at the Freie Universität Berlin. She studied Ancient and Modern History at the universities of Udine, Padua, and Berlin. Madotto's PhD thesis explores antifascism and resistance at universities in Europe during World War II. Her research interests include transnational history, fascism and antifascism in Europe, the history of universities, and Italian history of the twentieth century. Selected publications: "Le capitali della Resistenza universitaria. Padova, Oslo e Praga" (2013), which is about academic resistance against fascisms.

Notes

1. Franco De Felice, "Introduzione," in *Antifascismi e resistenze*, ed. F. De Felice (Rome, 1997), 16.
2. Starting with the postwar period, discussions and studies on antifascism and resistance in various nation states in Europe increasingly developed. Approaching a comparative and international vision and methodology, researchers collided with the clear ideological, geopolitical, and existential divisions existing among the different movements and parties, i.e. Catholics, socialists, liberals, democrats and in particular the communists. However, comparative analyses and international conferences were promoted by historians in order to encourage debates on both the history

of antifascism and resistance, and the memory after 1945. In the last few years, in particular, researchers have insisted on the innovative contribution of the transnational methodology in the studies on antifascism. For a general historiography on antifascism in Europe, see the introduction to this volume. On communist antifascism, see Chapter 11 and "Introduction. Beyond Revisionism. Rethinking Antifascism in the Twenty-First", in *Rethinking Antifascism. History, Memory and Politics, 1922 to the Present*, eds. Hugo García, Mercedes Yusta, Xavier Tabet, and Cristina Clímaco (Oxford and New York, 2016): 1–19.

3. For example, the conferences in: Geneva 2012, "Antifascism as a Practice and as a Discourse"; Paris 2013, "L'antifascisme en question, 1922–1945"; and Saarbrücken 2014, "Antifascism as a Transnational Phenomenon: New Perspectives of Research." Also see Alexander de Grand, "'To Learn Nothing and To Forget Nothing': Italian Socialism and the Experience of Exile Politics, 1935–1945," *Contemporary European History* 14 (2005): 539–58; Glenda Sluga, "Fascism and Anti-Fascism," in *The Palgrave Dictionary of Transnational History*, ed. Akira Iriye (Basingstoke, 2009): 381–82; Nigel Copsey, "Communists and the Inter-War Anti-Fascist Struggle in the United States and Britain," *Labour History Review* 76 (2011): 184–206; Mercedes Yusta, Marie-Pierre Arrizabalaga, and Diana Burgos, *Femmes sans frontières: stratégies transnationales féminines face à la mondialisation, XIXe-XXIe siècles* (Bern, 2011); Isabelle Richet, "Marion Cave Roselli and the Transnational Women's Anti-fascist Networks," *Journal of Women's History* 24 (2012): 117–39; David Featherstone, "Black Internationalism, Subaltern Cosmopolitanism, and the Spatial Politics of Antifascism," *Annals of the Association of American Geographers* 103 (2013): 1406–20; Jens Späth, "Was heißt Antifaschismus nach 1945? Das Beispiel der italienischen Sozialisten in westeuropäischer Perspektive," *Archiv für Sozialgeschichte* no. 53 (2013): 269–304; Hugo García, Mercedes Yusta, Xavier Tabet, and Cristina Clímaco, ed. *Rethinking Antifascism History, Memory and Politics, 1922 to the Present* (New York, 2016). See the recent publication edited by Hugo García for a special issue of *Contemporary European History* 25/2016 in the theme "Transnational Antifascism," Kasper Braskén, postdoctoral project in progress, "The Origins of 'Anti-Fascism': Transnational Movements against Nazism, Fascism and the 'White Terror' in Europe, 1923–1939,'", Andrea Acle-Kreysing, postdoctoral project in progress, "Anti-fascist Exile in Mexico City and Buenos Aires: The Construction of a Transatlantic Political Culture (1930s–1940s)" and the forthcoming book of Michael Seidman, *Atlantic Antifascisms, 1936–1945*.

4. Dan Stone, "Anti-fascist Europe comes to Britain: Theorizing Fascism as a Contribution to Defeating It", in *Varieties of Anti-Fascism. Britain in the Inter-War Periods*, ed. Nigel Copsey and Andrzej Olechnowicz (Basingstoke, 2010), 183–201. See Werner Röder, "The Political Exiles: Their Policies and Their Contribution to Post-War Reconstruction," in *International Biographical Dictionary of Central European Emigrés 1933–1945*, vol. II, 1, ed. Herbert Strauss and Werner Röder (Munich, 1983): xxvii–xl; Enzo Traverso, "Intellectuals and Anti-Fascism: For a Critical Historization," *New Politics* IX(4) (2004), http://newpol.org/content/intellectuals-and-anti-fascism-

critical-historization (accessed 20 October 2015); Anson Rabinbach, "Paris, Capital of Anti-fascism", in *The Modernist Imagination: Intellectual History and Critical Theory*, ed. W. Breckman (New York, 2009): 183–209. On war, resistance and identity in Europe see Antoine Fleury and Robert Frank, eds. *Le rôle des guerres dans la mémoire des Européens: leur effet sur la conscience d'être européen* (Berne, 1997); Alberto De Bernardi and Paolo Ferrari, eds. *Antifascismo e identità europea.* (Rome, 2004). Also see Henri Michel, *Les Idées politiques et sociales de la Résistance* (Paris, 1954); Jacques Droz, *Histoire de l'antifascisme en Europe, 1923–1939* (Paris, 1985); Antoine Prost, ed. *Pour une histoire sociale de la Résistance* (Paris, 1997); Olivier Wieviorka, *Histoire de la Résistance 1940–1945* (Paris, 2013). Enzo Collotti, *L'Antifascismo in Italia e in Europa 1922–1939* (Turin, 1975); Claudio Pavone, *Una guerra civile: Saggio storico sulla moralità della Resistenza* (Turin, 1991); Santo Peli, *La Resistenza in Italia. Storia e critica* (Turin, 2004).

5. Silvio Trentin, *Diritto e democrazia: scritti sul fascismo 1928-1937*, ed. G. Paladini (Venice, 1988); Alba Lazzaretto, *Giulio Alessio e la crisi dello stato liberale* (Padua, 2012).
6. The "Manifesto degli intellettuali antifascisti" was the response against the "Manifesto degli intellettuali fascisti" of Giovanni Gentil. See Emilio. E. Papa, *Storia di due manifesti. Il fascismo e la cultura italiana* (Milan, 1958).
7. Centro Studi e Ricerca Silvio Trentin, doc. Silvio Trentin, Lettera di dimissioni dall'Università Ca' Foscari di Venezia. (Trentin's Resignation letter to the University Ca' Foscari of Venice)
8. On the Italian antifascists in exile, see Aldo Garosci, *Storia dei fuoriusciti* (Bari, 1953); Leonardo Rapone, "I fuoriusciti antifascisti, la Seconda Guerra Mondiale e la Francia," in *Les Italiens en France de 1914 à 1940*, ed. P. Milza (Rome, 1986), 343–84; Rom, Presidenza del Consiglio dei Ministri, ed., *L'Italia in esilio: l'emigrazione italiana in Francia tra le due guerre* (Rome, 1993); Pierre Milza and Denis Peschanski, *Exil et migrations. Italiens et Espagnols en France 1938–1946* (Paris, 1994); Stéfanie Prezioso, "Aujourd'hui en Espagne, demain en Italie: l'exil antifasciste italien et la prise d'armes révolutionnaire", *Vingtième siècle. Revue d'histoire* 93 (2007): 79–92.
9. Santi Fedele, *Storia della Concentrazione antifascista 1927–1934* (Milan, 1976); Paul Arrighi, *Silvio Trentin. Un Européen an résistance (1919–1943)* (Portet-sur-Garonne, 2007); Carlo Verri, "Il primo antifascismo in esilio in una lettera di Trentin a Turati," *Italia Contemporanea* 252–53 (2008): 529–38; Moreno Guerrato and Giannantonio Paladini, eds. *L'Antifascismo italiano tra le due guerre: alla ricerca di una nuova unità. Seminario di studi italo-francese Jesolo 2–3 aprile 2004* (Jesolo, 2005).
10. Gaetano Salvemini, *Memorie di un fuoriuscito* (Milan, 1960); Carlo Rosselli, *Opere scelte* (Turin, 1973–92); Nicola Tranfaglia, *Carlo Rosselli dall'interventismo all'antifascismo* (Bari, 1968); Simona Colarizi, *Classe operaia e ceti medi. Rosselli, Nenni, Morandi: il dibattito sulle alleanze negli anni trenta* (Venice, 1976).
11. Arrighi, *Silvio Trentin*, 115–26.
12. On the concept of network, see D. Nohlen, ed., *Lexikon der Politikwissenschaft: Theorien, Methoden, Begriffe*, 2 vols. (Munich, 2002), 571. Network is "a political and social concept," it describes "people or organizations," which

"hold or aim to build relations to other persons or organizations in order to achieve cooperation, support, exchanges." Bernd Marin and R. Mayntz, eds., *Policy Networks: Empirical Evidence and Theoretical Considerations* (Frankfurt/Main, 1991). On the analysis of the policy network concept, see Volker Schneider, "Die Analyse politischer Netzwerke. Konturen eines expandierten Forschungsfeldes," in *Politiknetzwerke. Modelle, Anwendungen, Visualisierungen*, ed. Volker Schneider (Wiesbaden, 2009), 2–27.

13. Frank Rosengarten, *Silvio Trentin dall'interventismo alla Resistenza* (Milan, 1980), 148–49; Arrighi, *Silvio Trentin*, 101–3; Hans W. Tobler, *Silvio Trentin und die Widerstandsbewegung Libérer et Fédérer* (Munich, 1967); Rémy Cazals and Michelle Perrot, *Lettres de réfugiées: le réseau de Boriblanque: des étrangères dans la France de Vichy* (Paris, 2004); Eric J. Hobsbawm, "Gli intellettuali e l'antifascismo", in *Storia del Marxismo*, vol. 3, II. (Turin, 1981), 448–459; André Gueslin, ed. *Les facs sous Vichy: étudiants, universitaires et universités de France pendant la Seconde guerre mondiale* (Clermont-Ferrand, 1994); Albrecht Betz and Stefan Martens, eds. *Les intellectuels et l'Occupation, 1940–1944. Collaborer, partir, résister* (Paris, 2004).

14. Arrighi, *Silvio Trentin*, 124–26; Fioravanti, in Giannantonio Paladini and Nicoletta Pannocchia, *Silvio Trentin e la Francia. Saggi e Testimonianze* (Venice, 1991), 67.

15. On Trentin's experience and network of contacts in Spain, see Carlo Verri, *Guerra e libertà. Silvio Trentin e l'antifascismo italiano (1936–1939)* (Rome, 2011).

16. Emilio Lussu, "Ricordo di Silvio Trentin," *Mondo Operaio* (1954): 10.

17. Arrighi, *Silvio Trentin*, 156; Fioravanti, in Paladini, *Silvio Trentin e la Francia*, 67.

18. On the concept of Federalism, see Iain McLean and A. McMillan, *The Concise Oxford Dictionary of Politics*, 3rd ed. (Oxford, 2009), 195–96. Nohlen, *Lexikon der Politikwissenschaft*; Klaus Schubert and Martina Klein, *Das Politiklexikon. Begriffe, Fakten, Zusammenhänge* (Bonn, 2011). See also Arthur Benz, *Föderalismus. Analysen in entwicklungsgeschichtlicher und vergleichender Perspektive* (Wiesbaden, 2002); Daniel Judah Elazar, *Federal Systems of the World: A Handbook of Federal, Confederal, and Autonomy Arrangements* (Harlow, 1991). On Italy, see Giovanna Angelini, Arturo Colombo, and Virgilio P. Gastaldi, *Poteri e libertà. Autonomia e federalismo nel pensiero democratico italiano* (Milan, 2001); Piero Graglia, *Unità europea e federalismo: da Giustizia e libertà ad Altiero Spinelli* (Bologna, 1996). See the plan for a federated Europe elaborated in the "Manifesto di Ventotene" by Ernesto Rossi, Eugenio Colorni, and Altiero Spinelli during the summer of 1941: Altiero Spinelli and Ernesto Rossi, *Il Manifesto di Ventotene*, ed. Sergio Pistone (Turin, 2001). These themes had a big resonance inside the Giustizia e Libertà movement. Carlo Rosselli discussed a European Federation in several articles. See Carlo Rosselli, "Contro lo stato," *Quaderni di Giustizia e Libertà* 21 (1934); Carlo Rosselli and C. Bernardi, "Discussione sul federalismo e l'autonomia," *Quaderni di Giustizia e Libertà* (1935); Corrado Malandrino, "Idea di Europa e federalismo in Carlo Rosselli," in *Republicanesimo, democrazia, socalismo delle libertà. Incroci per una rinnovata cultura politica*, ed. T. Casadei (Milan, 2004), 71–94.

19. Norberto Bobbio, "Il pensiero federalista di Silvio Trentin," in Paladini, *Silvio Trentin e la Francia*, 147–71. See Norberto Bobbio, *Ricordo di Silvio Trentin* (Venice, 1955).

20. Silvio Trentin, *Stato, Nazione, Federalismo* (Milan, 1945) and *Libérér et Féderer*, now in Trentin, *Scritti inediti. Testimonianze, studi*, ed. Paolo Gobetti (Parma, 1972); Silvio Trentin, "Federalismo e libertà," in *Scritti Teorici 1935–1943*, ed. Norberto Bobbio (Vicenza, 1986); Bobbio, in Paladini, *Silvio Trentin e la Francia*, 147–72; Hans W. Tobler, "Il pensiero politico di Silvio Trentin", in Trentin, *Scritti inediti*, 47–80; Corrado Malandrino, "Il contributo di Silvio Trentin alla causa dell'unità Europea", in *L'idea di Europa nel Movimento di liberazione 1940–1945*, ed. Gaetano Arfé (Rome,1986): 193–205; Fulvio Cortese, *Libertà individuale e organizzazione pubblica in Silvio Trentin* (Milan, 2008). Trentin wrote on a draft of a federalist constitution for France and Italy. See Trentin, "Ebauche de la figure constitutionnelle de la France à l'issue de la Révolution en cours de développement," and "Abbozzo di un piano tendente a delineare la figura costituzionale dell'Italia al termine della rivoluzione federalista in corso di sviluppo," now in Trentin, *Scritti inediti*, 279–94 and 295–318; Giovanni Focardi, *Storia dei progetti di riforma della pubblica amministrazione: Francia e Italia 1943-1948* (Bologna, 2004).

21. "Liberare la Francia e l'Europa dall'invasione fascista e nazista e federare i popoli europei per evitare il ritorno di nuove guerre." Cit. in Bobbio, in Paladini, *Silvio Trentin e la Francia*, 148.

22. Tobler in Trentin, *Scritti inediti*, 69–70.

23. On the concept of autonomy, see Nohlen, *Lexikon der Politikwissenschaft*; Schubert and Klein, *Das Politiklexikon*; McLean and McMillan, *Concise Oxford Dictionary of Politics*.

24. Silvio Trentin, *Antidémocratie* (Paris, 1930), now in *Opere scelte*. ed. Norberto Bobbio, Moreno Guerrato, Giannantonio Paladini, and Alessandro Pizzorusso. Venice, 1983–88, vol. III, *Antifascismo e Rivoluzione*, 52.

25. Anne Hogenhuis, *Des savants dans la Résistance: Boris Vildé et le réseau du musée de l'Homme* (Paris, 2009); Julien Blanc, *Au commencement de la Résistance: du côte du Musée de l'Homme, 1940–1941* (Paris, 2010).

26. Arrighi, *Silvio Trentin*, 257–62. The author highlighted the participation of those intellectuals and students who were leaving from Paris after the National Socialist occupation; cf. Jean Vidalenc, *L'exode de mai–juin 1940* (Paris, 1957); Archives Nationales Paris (AN), 72AJ/526, Papiers du Comité d'histoire de la Deuxième Guerre mondiale.

27. Michael R.D. Foot, *SOE in France: An Account of the Work of the British Special Operations Executive in France, 1940–1944*, (London, 1966), 151.

28. *Libérer et fédérer. Organe du Mouvement révolutionnaire pour la libération et la reconstruction de la France* (Toulouse, 1942–44); Bibliothèque nationale de France, RES G 1470 (218) n. 1 1942—n. 16 1944; AN AG 3(2)/378 Charles de Gaulle (Bureau Central de Renseignements et d'Action) and AN 72AJ/527 Papiers du Comité d'histoire de la Deuxième Guerre mondiale.

29. Silvio Trentin, "Liberare e federare," in Trentin, *Scritti inediti*, 187–278. See the reflections of Tobler, "Aspetti paramilitari e organizzativi del

movimento *Libérer et Fédérer*. Il giornale clandestino *Libérer et Fédérer* come strumento della Guerra psicologica," in Trentin, *Scritti inediti*, 96–102.

30. Hans W. Tobler, "Silvio Trentin et son influence idéologique sur les idées politiques et sociales de la Résistance française," in Paladini, *Silvio Trentin e la Francia*, 100; Arrighi, *Silvio Trentin*, 330–32.

31. Tobler in Paladini, *Silvio Trentin e la Francia*, 100.

32. "Sur le pian de la résistance, nous nous intégrons dans la France combattante. Pour libérer la France nous nous rangeons aux côtés de tous ceux qui luttent contre l'envahisseur et en tout premier lieu aux côtés de la France Libre et de son chef le général de Gaulle qui est le symbole vivant de la résistance française à l'envahisseur." *Libérer et fédérer*, 14 July 1942, n. 1, 3; see Tobler, *Silvio Trentin*, 75–78.

33. Rosengarten, *Silvio Trentin*, 198–99; Paul Arrighi, "Silvio Trentin et le mouvement de résistance *Libérer et Fédérer*: de la Résistance vers la révolution", *Guerres mondiales et conflicts contemporains* 2 (2007), 126; Fioravanti, in Paladini, *Silvio Trentin e la Francia*, 67; Pia C. Leonetti, *Gli italiani del maquis* (Milan, 1966), 193–94.

34. Rosengarten, *Silvio Trentin*, 182.

35. Angelo Ventura, "Padova nel regime fascista," in *Padova nel 1943: dalla crisi del regime fascista alla Resistenza*, ed. G. Lenci and G. Segato (Padua, 1996), 11–30; Chiara Saonara, *Una città nel regime fascista: Padova 1922–1943* (Venice, 2011); Giulia Simone, *Fascismo in cattedra: La Facoltà di Scienze politiche di Padova dalle origini alla Liberazione 1924–1945* (Padua, 2015).

36. Mario Isnenghi, "Rettori fascisti e rettori partigiani. Documenti di vita universitaria a Padova fra regime e dopoguerra," *Venetica* IV (1987): 94–161; Angelo Ventura, "L'Università di Padova nella Resistenza," *Quaderni per la storia dell'Università di Padova* 28 (1995): 157–72; Chiara Saonara, "Studenti in guerra e nella Resistenza," in *Studenti, università, città nella storia padovana. Atti del convegno Padova 6–8 febbraio 1998*, ed. F. Piovan and L. Sitran Rea (Trieste, 2001): 693–707 and *Egidio Meneghetti: scienziato e patriota combattente per la libertà* (Padua, 2003); Egidio Meneghetti, "Cronaca dell'Università di Padova," *Anche l'Italia ha vinto, Mercurio* 16 (1945): 179–80; Anonimus, *L'Università di Padova durante l'occupazione tedesca* (Padua, 1946); Concetto Marchesi, *Pagine all'ombra* (Padua, 1946); Egidio Meneghetti, *Scritti clandestini* (Milan, 1975); Adolfo Zamboni, *Il comitato di liberazione nazionale di Padova: durante il periodo cospirativo* (Padua, 1945). See Maria Cristina Giuntella, *Autonomia e nazionalizzazione dell'Università: il fascismo e l'inquadramento degli atenei* (Rome, 1992); Zunino, P.G., ed. "Università e accademie negli anni del fascismo e del nazismo". Proceedings of the International Conference, Turin, 11–13 May 2005 (Florence, 2008).

37. Egidio Meneghetti, "Breve relazione sul CLNRV dal settembre 1943 a tutto il 1944," in the archive of *Centro di Ateneo per la storia della Resistenza e dell'età contemporanea* (CASREC), sez. I. b. 13 fasc. Relazioni; Concetto Marchesi, "Appunti inediti," in Ezio Franceschini, *Uomini liberi. Scritti sulla Resistenza*, ed. Franca M. Peri (Casale Monferrato, 1993); Egidio Meneghetti, "Cronaca dell'Università di Padova," in *Anche l'Italia ha vinto*, special number of *Mercurio* 16 (1945): 178–79.

38. Meneghetti, "Breve Relazione."
39. On the military transfers among communist fighters cf. Santo Peli, *Storie di Gap: Terrorismo urbano e Resistenza* (Turin, 2014). For Giustizia e Libertà, see Giovanni de Luna ed., *Le formazioni di GL nella Resistenza: Documenti settembre 1943 – aprile 1945* (Milan, 1985), 17–33.
40. On the military organization of the *Resistenza* in Veneto, see Teodolfo Tessari, *Le origini della Resistenza militare nel Veneto* (Vicenza, 1959); Anna M. Preziosi, *Politica e organizzazione della Resistenza Armata I, Atti del Comando militare regionale veneto. Carteggio degli esponenti azionisti (1943–1944)* (Vicenza, 1992); Chiara Saonara, *Politica e organizzazione della Resistenza Armata II, Atti del Comando militare regionale Veneto 1945* (Vicenza, 1993).
41. CASREC, sez. I, b. 49, Stampa clandestina, fasc. CLNRV, Fratelli d'Italia. Bollettino del Comitato di liberazione nazionale, 1943–1945.
42. Ibid., *Fratelli d'Italia* 2 (13 October 1943).
43. Silvio Trentin, "Appello ai Veneti," in Silvio Trentin, *Opere scelte, Antifascismo Rivoluzione. Scritti e Discorsi 1927–1944*, ed. Paladini (Venice, 1985), 521–33.
44. Giovanni De Luna, "L'esperienza di Silvio Trentin nel Partito d'Azione," in Paladini, *Silvio Trentin e la Francia*, 29–44. On the Partito d'Azione, see Giovanni De Luna, *Storia del Partito d'Azione 1942–1947* (Milan, 1982).
45. Francesco Feltrin and Anna Maria Preziosi, *Nuovi documenti su Silvio Trentin. Il Clnrv e i problemi della scuola* (Padua, 2000), 25–26. Trentin's federalist theories differentiated from those of the members of Partito d'Azione; on this reflection, see Bobbio, in Paladini, *Silvio Trentin e la Francia*, 169.
46. "Qui io mi trovo immerso fino al collo nell'azione, fin dal 10 settembre." … "Mi sono buttato anima e corpo per raggruppare, raddrizzare, rafforzare le forze suscettibili di concorrere utilmente alla lotta. Non posso disconoscere di aver raggiunto dei risultati insperati. Da lunedì mi trovo praticamente investito della direzione della Resistenza di tutto il Veneto". Silvio Trentin, "Lettera a Emilio Lussu del 23 ottobre 1943," in Silvio Trentin, *Scritti inediti:* 25–28..
47. Maura Piccialuti Caprioli, *Radio Londra 1940–1945. Inventario delle trasmissioni per l'talia*, vol. II (Rome, 1976), 554.
48. Norberto Bobbio, "Introduzione," in Paladini, *Silvio Trentin e la Francia*, 15–18. On Bobbio's analysis on federalism and resistance see the several publications edited by Pietro Polito, "Federalismo ed europeismo nell'opera di Norberto Bobbio", in *Europeismo e federalismo in Piemonte tra le due guerre mondiali: La Resistenza e i Trattati di Roma*, eds. S. Pistone and C. Malandrino, (Florence, 1999): 153–173; *Eravamo ridiventati uomini. testimonianze e discorsi sulla Resistenza in Italia. 1955–1999* (Turin, 2015).
49. Tobler, in Paladini, *Silvio Trentin e la Francia*, 104.
50. Walter Lipgens, *Documents on the History of European Integration: Continental Plans for European Union: 1939–1945* (Berlin, 1985), 346–47. On the so far not clear reception of Trentin's works on fascism written in France, see Tobler in Paladini, *Silvio Trentin e la Francia*, 99–107 and Giorgio Vaccarino, "Libérer et Fédérer e le idee federaliste della Resistenza in Europa", in Paladini, *Silvio Trentin e la Francia*, 109–124.
51. Giovanni De Luna, in Paladini, *Silvio Trentin e la Francia*, 43.
52. Bobbio, "Introduzione", in Paladini, *Silvio Trentin e la Francia*, 18.

53. "Liberare e Federare. L'eredità intellettuale di Silvio Trentin," Venice, Aula Magna "Silvio Trentin," Ca' Dolfin-Ca' Foscari, 5 December 2014, organized by the Centro Documentazione e Ricerca Trentin, Venice.

Bibliography

Archives
Centro di Ateneo per la storia della Resistenza e dell'età contemporanea (CASREC). Padua, Italy.
Archives Nationales de Paris, Site de Pierrefitte-sur-Seine. Paris, France.

Journals
Fratelli d'Italia: Bollettino del Comitato di liberazione nazionale. Padua, 1943–44.
Libérer et fédérer: Organe du Mouvement révolutionnaire pour la libération et la reconstruction de la France. Toulouse, 1942–44.

Literature
Anonimus. *L'Università di Padova durante l'occupazione tedesca.* Padua, 1946.
Bobbio, Norberto. *Ricordo di Silvio Trentin.* Venice, 1955.
Lussu, Emilio. "Ricordo di Silvio Trentin," *Mondo Operaio* (1954): 9–10.
Marchesi, Concetto. *Pagine all'ombra.* Padua, 1946.
———. "Appunti inediti." In Ezio Franceschini *Uomini liberi. Scritti sulla Resistenza*, ed. F.M. Peri. Casale Monferrato, 1993.
Meneghetti, Egidio. "Breve relazione sul CLNRV dal settembre 1943 a tutto il 1944." Archive of *Centro di Ateneo per la storia della Resistenza e dell'età contemporanea* (CASREC), sez. I. b. 13 fasc. Relazioni.
———. "Cronaca dell'Università di Padova." *Anche l'Italia ha vinto, Mercurio* 16 (1945): 179–80.
———. *Scritti clandestini.* Milan, 1946.
Trentin, Silvio. *Antidémocratie.* Paris, 1930.
———. *Stato Nazione Federalismo.* Milan, 1945.
Scritti inediti: Testimonianze, studi, ed. Paolo Gobetti. Parma, 1972.
———. *Opere scelte.* 5 vols., ed. Norberto Bobbio, Moreno Guerrato, Giannantonio Paladini, and Alessandro Pizzorusso. Venice, 1983–88.
———. *Scritti teorici 1935–1943.* ed. Norberto Bobbio. Venice, 1987.
———. *Diritto e democrazia: scritti sul fascismo 1928–1937.* ed. Giannantonio Paladini. Venice, 1988.
Zamboni, Adolfo. *Il comitato di liberazione nazionale di padova durante il periodo cospirativo.* Padua 1945.

Arrighi, Paul. *Silvio Trentin. Un Européen en résistance (1919–1943).* Portet-sur-Garonne, 2007.
———. "Silvio Trentin et le mouvement de résistance *Libérer et Fédérer*: de la Résistance vers la révolution." *Guerres mondiales et conflicts contemporains* 2 (2007): 121–30.

Betz, Albrecht, and Stefan Martens, eds. *Les intellectuels et l'Occupation, 1940–1944: Collaborer, partir, résister*. Paris, 2004.

Blanc, Julien. *Au commencement de la Résistance: du côté du Musée de l'Homme, 1940–1941*. Paris, 2010.

Cazals, Rémy and Michelle Perrot. *Lettres de réfugiées. Le réseau de Boriblanque: des étrangères dans la France de Vichy*. Paris, 2004.

Colarizi, Simona. *Classe operaia e ceti medi. Rosselli, Nenni, Morandi: il dibattito sulle alleanze negli anni trenta*. Venice, 1976.

Collotti, Enzo. *L'Antifascismo in Italia e in Europa 1922–1939*. Turin, 1975.

Copsey, Nigel and Andrzej Olechnowicz, eds. *Varieties of Anti-Fascism: Britain in the Inter-War Period*. Basingstoke, 2010.

Cortese, Fulvio. *Libertà individuale e organizzazione pubblica in Silvio Trentin*. Milan, 2008.

De Bernardi, Alberto, and Paolo Ferrari, eds. *Antifascismo e identità europea*. Rome, 2004.

De Felice, Franco. ed. *Antifascismi e resistenze*. Rome, 1997.

De Grand, Alexander. "'To Learn Nothing and To Forget Nothing': Italian Socialism and the Experience of Exile Politics, 1935–1945," *Contemporary European History* 14 (2005): 539–58.

De Luna, Giovanni. *Storia del Partito d'Azione 1942–1947*. Milan, 1982.

———. ed., *Le formazioni di GL nella Resistenza: Documenti settembre 1943 — aprile 1945*. Milan, 1985.

Droz, Jacques. *Histoire de l'antifascisme en Europe, 1923–1939*. Paris, 1985.

Eismann, Gaël, and Stefan Martens. *Occupation et répression militaire allemandes: La politique de "maintien de l'ordre" en Europe occupée, 1939–1945*, Paris, 2007.

Fedele, Santi. *Storia della Concentrazione antifascista 1927–1934*. Milan, 1976.

Feltrin, Francesco, and Anna Maria Preziosi, eds. *Nuovi documenti su Silvio Trentin. Il Clnrv e i problemi della scuola*. Padua, 2000.

Fleury, Antoine and Robert Frank, eds. *Le rôle des guerres dans la mémoire des Européens: leur effet sur la conscience d'être européen*. Berne, 1997.

Focardi, Giovanni. *Storia dei progetti di riforma della pubblica amministrazione: Francia e Italia 1943–1948*. Bologna, 2004.

Foot, Michael R.D. *SOE in France: An Account of the Work of the British Special Operations Executive in France, 1940–1944*. London, 1966.

García, Hugo, Mercedes Yusta, Xavier Tabet, and Cristina Clímaco, eds. *Rethinking Antifascism. History, Memory and Politics, 1922 to the Present*. Oxford and New York, 2016.

Garosci, Aldo. *Storia dei fuorusciti*. Bari, 1953.

Giuntella, Maria Cristina. *Autonomia e nazionalizzazione dell'Università: il fascismo e l'inquadramento degli atenei*. Rome, 1992.

Graglia, Piero. *Unità europea e federalismo: da Giustizia e libertà ad Altiero Spinelli*. Bologna, 1996.

Guerrato, Moreno. *Silvio Trentin: un democratico all'opposizione*. Milan, 1981.

———. and Giannantonio Paladini, eds. *L'Antifascismo italiano tra le due guerre: alla ricerca di una nuova unità. Seminario di studi italo-francese Jesolo 2—3 aprile 2004*, Jesolo, 2005.

Gueslin, André, ed. *Les facs sous Vichy: étudiants, universitaires et universités de France pendant la Seconde guerre mondiale: actes du colloque des Universités de Clermont-Ferrand et de Strasbourg—Novembre 1993*. Clermont-Ferrand, 1994.

Hobsbawm, Eric J. "Gli intellettuali e l'antifascismo." In *Storia del Marxismo*, ed. E. Hobsbawm, vol. 3, II. Turin, 1981, 448–459.

Hogenhuis, Anne. *Des savants dans la Résistance: Boris Vildé et le réseau du musée de l'Homme*. Paris, 2009.

Isnenghi, Mario. "Rettori fascisti e rettori partigiani: Documenti di vita universitaria a Padova fra regime e dopoguerra," *Venetica* IV (1987): 94–161.

Lazzaretto, Alba. *Giulio Alessio e la crisi dello stato liberale*. Padua, 2012.

Lenci, Giuliano, and Giorgio Segato. *Padova nel 1943: dalla crisi del regime fascista alla Resistenza*. Padua, 1996.

Leonetti, Pia C. *Gli italiani del maquis*. Milan, 1966.

Lipgens, Walter. *Document on the History of European Integration: Continental Plans for European Union: 1939–1945*. vol. I, Berlin, 1985.

McLean, Iain and Alistair McMillan. *The Concise Oxford Dictionary of Politics*. 3rd ed. Oxford, 2009.

Malandrino, Corrado. "Il contributo di Silvio Trentin alla causa dell'unità Europea." In *L'idea di Europa nel Movimento di liberazione 1940–1945*, ed. G. Arfé. Rome, 1986, 193–205.

———. "Idea di Europa e federalismo in Carlo Rosselli." In *Republicanesimo, democrazia, socalismo delle libertà: Incroci per una rinnovata cultura politica*, ed. T. Casadei. Milan, 2004, 71–94.

———. *Silvio Trentin: Pensatore politico, antifascista, rivoluzionario, federalista. Studi trentiniani*. Bari and Rome, 2007.

Michel, Henri. *Histoire de la résistance (1940—1944)*. Paris, 1950.

———. *Les Idées politiques et sociales de la Résistance*. Paris, 1954.

Milza, Pierre, and Denis Peschanski. *Exil et migrations: Italiens et Espagnols en France 1938–1946*. Paris, 1994.

Nohlen, Dieter ed. *Lexikon der Politikwissenschaft: Theorien, Methoden, Begriffe*. Munich, 2002.

Papa, Emilio. E. *Storia di due manifesti: Il fascismo e la cultura italiana*. Milan, 1958.

Paladini, Giannantonio, and Nicoletta Pannocchia. *Silvio Trentin e la Francia. Saggi e Testimonianze*. Venice, 1991.

Pavone, Claudio. *Una guerra civile. Saggio storico sulla moralità della Resistenza*. Turin, 1991.

Peli, Santo. *La Resistenza in Italia: Storia e critica*. Turin, 2004.

———. *Storie di Gap: Terrorismo urbano e Resistenza*. Turin, 2014.

Piccialuti Caprioli, Maura. *Radio Londra 1940–1945: Inventario delle trasmissioni per l'Italia*. Rome, 1976.

Piovan, Francesco, and Luciana Sitran Rea, eds. *Studenti, università, città nella storia padovana. Atti del convegno Padova 6–8 febbraio 1998*. Trieste, 2001.

Polito, Pietro. "Federalismo ed europeismo nell'opera di Norberto Bobbio." In *Europeismo e federalismo in Piemonte tra le due guerre mondiali: La Resistenza e i Trattati di Roma*, eds. S. Pistone and C. Malandrino. Florence, 1999, 153–173.

———. *Eravamo ridiventati uomini: testimonianze e discorsi sulla Resistenza in Italia. 1955–1999*. Turin, 2015.

Preziosi, Anna M. *Politica e organizzazione della Resistenza Armata I, Atti del Comando militare regionale veneto: Carteggio degli esponenti azionisti (1943–1944)*. Vicenza, 1992.

Prezioso, Stéfanie. "Aujourd'hui en Espagne, demain en Italie: l'exil antifasciste italien et la prise d'armes révolutionnaire." *Vingtième siècle. Revue d'histoire* 93 (2007): 79–92.

Prost, Antoine ed. *Pour une histoire sociale de la Résistance*. Paris, 1997.

Rabinbach, Anson. "Paris, Capital of Anti-fascism." In *The Modernist Imagination: Intellectual History and Critical Theory*, ed. Warren Breckman. New York, 2009, 183–209

Rapone, Leonardo. "I fuoriusciti antifascisti, la Seconda Guerra Mondiale e la Francia." In *Les Italiens en France de 1914 à 1940*, ed. Pierre Milza. Rome, 1986, 343–84.

———. "Antifascismo e storia d'Italia.", *Italia contemporanea*, no. 212 (1998): 565–575.

Richet, Isabelle. "Marion Cave Roselli and the Transnational Women's Anti-fascist Networks." *Journal of Women's History*, no. 24 (2012): 117–39.

Rosengarten, Frank. *Silvio Trentin dall'interventismo alla Resistenza*. Milan, 1980.

Saonara, Chiara. *Politica e organizzazione della Resistenza Armata II, Atti del Comando militare regionale Veneto 1945*. Vicenza, 1993.

———. "Studenti in guerra e nella Resistenza." In *Studenti, università, città nella storia padovana: Atti del convegno Padova 6–8 febbraio 1998*, ed. F. Piovan and L. Sitran Rea. Trieste, 2001, 693–707.

———. *Egidio Meneghetti: scienziato e patriota combattente per la libertà*, Padua, 2003.

———. *Una città nel regime fascista: Padova 1922–1943*. Venice, 2011.

Simone, Giulia, *Fascismo in cattedra: La Facoltà di Scienze politiche di Padova dalle origini alla Liberazione 1924–1945*. Padua, 2015.

Sluga, Glenda. "Fascism and Anti-Fascism." In *The Palgrave Dictionary of Transnational History*, ed. Akira Iriye. Basingstoke, 2009, 381–82.

Späth, Jens. "Was heißt Antifaschismus nach 1945? Das Beispiel der italienischen Sozialisten in westeuropäischer Perspektive." *Archiv für Sozialgeschichte* 53 (2013): 269–304.

Tessari, Teodolfo. *Le origini della Resistenza militare nel Veneto*.Vicenza, 1959.

Tobler, Hans W. *Silvio Trentin und die Widerstandsbewegung Libérer et Fédérer*. Munich, 1967.

Traverso, Enzo. "Intellectuals and Anti-Fascism: For a Critical Historization." *New Politics* IX(4) (2004) online.

Ventura, Angelo. "L'Università di Padova nella Resistenza." *Quaderni per la storia dell'Università di Padova* 28 (1995): 157–72.

———. "Padova nel regime fascista." In *Padova nel 1943: dalla crisi del regime fascista alla Resistenza*, ed. G. Lenci and G. Segato. Padua 1996, 11–30.

Verri, Carlo. "Il primo antifascismo in esilio in una lettera di Trentin a Turati." *Italia Contemporanea* 252–53 (2008): 529–38.

———. *Guerra e libertà. Silvio Trentin e l'antifascismo italiano (1936–1939)*. Rome, 2011.

Vidalenc, Jean. *L'exode de mai–juin 1940*. Paris, 1957.

Wieviorka, Olivier. *Histoire de la Résistance 1940-1945*. Paris, 2013.

Yusta, Mercedes, Marie-Pierre Arrizabalaga, and Diana Burgos. *Femmes sans frontières: stratégies transnationales féminines face à la mondialisation, XIXe-XXIe siècles*. Bern, 2011.

Zunino, P.G., ed. "Università e accademie negli anni del fascismo e del nazismo." Proceedings of the International Conference, Turin, 11–13 May 2005, Florence, 2008.

13

GERMAN AND ITALIAN DEMOCRATIC SOCIALISTS IN EXILE

Interpretations of Fascism and Transnational Aspects of Resistance in the Sopade and Giustizia e Libertà

Francesco Di Palma

Introduction

This chapter offers a new perspective on international antifascism by conceptualizing the theoretical development and debate of the interwar Social Democratic Party in exile (Sozialdemokratische Partei Deutschlands, "Sopade") and the Giustizia e Libertà (Justice and Freedom, GL) movement, mostly during exile in Prague, Paris, and later in London, as the result of a combined effort to renew and re-educate the social democratic sector and its adherents. Since the parties' executive groups were literally dispersed after the press ban in the late 1930s, with the SPD having to leave Prague in early 1938, the chapter will mainly deal with the period of exile in Czechoslovakia and Paris. The focus is on the international and transnational character of the parties' policies between 1929 and 1945. The contribution will investigate their main representatives, who were responsible for a considerable shift in social democratic principles and their political alignment in that period, as well as for the reception of new ideological concepts.

As for the exile executive groups, the focus of this chapter will primarily be on those individuals who helped define the political as well as the cultural agenda of the Sopade and GL, and who significantly affected the postwar social democracy. Among these for Sopade were Rudolf Hilferding,[1] Friedrich Stampfer,[2] and Paul Hertz;[3] and for GL, Carlo Rosselli, Gaetano Salvemini, and Silvio Trentin, to name a few. In the following, I will focus on their contributions to the most defining ongoing debates within the social democratic and socialist antifascism of the time, by drawing the attention to their transnational, "pan-European" character.[4]

Fascism soon became the driving force to action for both parties. It metaphorically embodied "darkness" and "barbarism," which were to be fought by the inspiring values of resistance: righteousness and humanity. A pan-European basis would be most appropriate to successfully tackle the fascist menace, the more so as Nazi Germany was seemingly embarking on a military quest to conquer all of Europe, and Fascist Italy sought to restore at least partially the Old Roman Empire. Against this background, the leaders of the Sopade and GL emphasized the need for a firm transnational antifascism in socialist hands, and they fostered the myth of its specific role as the "elected savior" of Europe from the fascist infection. In sum, this chapter should be seen as a contribution to the current debate about the influence of interwar "social democracies" on their later offspring as well as about their interpretation of Nazism and Fascism.

Giustizia e Libertà and Sopade in Exile

Giustizia e Libertà was founded by a handful of dissidents in 1929. The heterogeneous group gathered in Paris in the mid-1920s and gave birth to a liberal socialist platform. It was inspired by the teachings of Giuseppe Mazzini and Piero Gobetti, who had been, besides their political commitment, editors of journals such as *L'Unità* and *Il Quarto Stato*.[5]

Between 1929 and 1931, GL pursued a wide range of so-called "educatory measures" for the masses, aimed at teaching them sheer democracy. GL also believed that the liberal tenets, dominating at the beginning of the twentieth century, should be fought with great determination. The main protagonists and interpreters of liberalism would have put the key foundation stones in place for fascism and corporatism in Italy. Propaganda was thus deemed to be fundamental in order to offset the looming erosion of democratic attitudes, which eventually paved the way to the seizure of power by Mussolini and his squads. In the summer of 1931, a pact of action was drafted and signed by both GL and the Italian Socialist Party (Partito socialista italiano, PSI), whose executives had first joined their mutual efforts in Paris as part of the "Concentrazione antifascista."[6] In this broad coalition, the GL immediately emerged as one of the guiding forces against Italian Fascism, and developed an ambivalent connection to established parties, notably to the PSI.

The executive power of the SPD during exile from 1933 to 1945 is commonly referred to as "Sopade."[7] Previously, on 23 June 1933, the SPD had been banned, along with all the remaining democratic parties. As a result of the rigid censorship established by the National Socialist German Workers' Party (Nationalsozialistische Deutsche Arbeiterpartei, NSDAP) soon after its rise to power in early 1933, the SPD was forced to make major adjustments. As the party's leaders met in the collapsing German parliament, the Reichstag, on 27 April 1933, to estimate the lingering problems and to discuss possible solutions, they could reach no agreement on what to do or how to react to such an acute menace for state and society. Two opposing attitudes emerged: one group, led by the chief-editor of the *Vorwärts*, Friedrich Stampfer, made the case for the immediate creation of new "headquarters" abroad to start an antifascist propaganda campaign; the second one, the "legalistic" group around the leader Paul Löbe, former president of the Reichstag, opposed Stampfer's strategy vehemently, which they called dangerous and highly disruptive. In their opinion, no impending ban should be feared, and all undemocratic measures by the regime should be considered as temporary.[8]

As a matter of fact, all fears proved to be well founded. On 4 May of the same year, the party's executive group gathered in an extraordinary session to informally set up a representative committee abroad, based in Prague. The members designated for this purpose were Hans Vogel (1881–1945), Siegmund Crummenerl (1892–1940), Friedrich Stampfer (1874–1957), Paul Hertz (1888–1961), Erich Ollenhauer (1901–1964), and Otto Wels (1873–1939) as chairman. Additional SPD politicians, who would exert a major influence on the intellectual and political development of the exile delegation, were Rudolf Hilferding (1877–1941) and Rudolf Breitscheid (1974–1944).[9]

Interpretations of Fascism and National Socialism: Comparative Remarks

As mentioned above, the formal rejection of the unrestrained liberalism of the early twentieth century set the course for the interpretation of Fascism by GL. Gaetano Salvemini believed that Fascism had deep roots in Italian culture and had to be regarded as a direct result of the highly corrupt liberal governments of the beginning of the century. By the same token, he criticized the Italian Socialist Party, of which Mussolini had been a fervid member in the 1920s. According to Salvemini, the PSI had fallen short of rebuilding both its ideology and its party structure, and so remained a prey to its inflexible centralism. Combined with a striking lack of autonomy and an excessive dogmatism, this had eventually proven to be no match for the rise of the Fascist Party.[10]

Carlo Rosselli articulated an even more radical interpretation of Italian Fascism. He suggested that it had flourished because of the "immobility" of the traditional political parties. Fascism could not therefore be resisted and fought by traditional means. In his vision, a broad front of peasants, workers, and the middle class should be established in order to tackle Fascism. In his opinion, this was the only way to counteract the radical degeneration of the "petty bourgeoisie," immobilized between the working class and the big companies, both pursuing their own interests. Against this background, the "bourgeois capitalism" had eventually embarked on Fascism, which seemed to be the only political system able to safeguard its position within the Italian society.[11]

According to GL, the confrontation between the bourgeoisie and the workers was the crucial problem of modernity. Fascism, and the opposition against it, provided nevertheless the possibility to surmount that conflict and give birth to a new, socialist-egalitarian and comprehensive kind of society. The leftist core around Silvio Trentin maintained that the working class should be leading the battle against the dictatorship of Mussolini. Long enough prey of social injustice, the workers represented the only class that had the potential and the determination to overthrow the regime. In this claim, Trentin blatantly differed from the rest of GL and its will to build up, by education of the masses, a broad inter-class front.[12]

The economic aspects of interwar Germany—which at that time was a much more industrialized country than Italy—assumed an important and relevant role in the interpretation of Nazism and Fascism by the Sopade. By contrast, the analysis of GL was to a large extent based on the political failures of previous governments and held out the prospect of a proletarian society. Still it did not indulge in any kind of naive conviction that this would quite naturally occur, as dogmatic Marxists believed. The liberal socialism it intended to promote was bound to a critical understanding of the pending tasks, as well as to the involvement of the working class, as being the only possible ways to stimulate active participation in politics, and pragmatism within all oppressed classes.

In this respect, the Sopade and GL differed the most throughout their exile years. The German Social Democrats always opted for a political solution to Nazism, the only exception being the initial revolutionary attempt. By contrast, GL never ceased to consider itself as a movement rather than a party, or to call for active resistance against Fascism.

There are several reasons for this difference. As Hitler came to power, the Weimar Republic still existed. Few Germans were able to predict just how quickly the Nazis would abolish all democratic institutions. A rather theoretical explanation should also be taken into account. In the eyes of the Sopade, the Nazis did not possess any political autonomy, let alone the ability to dominate an entire country. The lack of attention to the rising National Socialist Party in the last years of the Weimar Republic was striking. By highlighting the correlation between the political problems (i.e., the collapse of the Weimar Republic) and the economic difficulties Germany was facing, the SPD had in fact implicitly downplayed the propagandistic and cultural appeal the Nazis had been able to exert on the German population.

Major interpretative differences can also be observed with regard to the specific role played by the middle class as part of the Nazi and Fascist penetration in state and society. Theoreticians of the Sopade tended to ascribe the success of Nazism primarily to the German middle class, imbued with nationalist revanchism. On the other hand, GL denied that the Italian middle class had any autonomy. It deemed fascism as the passive result—with Rosselli's words "the autobiography of the nation"—of a massive centralization of power through big companies and bureaucracy.

Overall it can be argued that both organizations, even GL with its focus on activism until the outbreak of the Spanish Civil War, fell prey to an excessive ideological justification of their activity in exile. This eventually prevented them from having political success, becoming often entangled in theoretical disputes and disciplinary procedures that narrowed their scope of action increasingly over the years. With regard to the strategic establishment of a broad front against Fascism, both organizations showed similar approaches. They favored such a plan, yet at the same time none of their members would agree on producing compromises with the communist counterparts as to who and how they were to lead the front, or which common political goals should be defined beforehand. Between the end of the Concentrazione antifascista in Italy in 1934 and the onset of the Spanish Civil War (April 1939), both parties underwent a thorough ideological and political transition, from the initial revolutionary activism, be it apparent or intended, to a new democratic Marxism.[13]

Carlo Rosselli, who had been fighting in Spain for the international brigades, was eventually seized by OVRA (Organizzazione di Vigilanza e Repressione dell'Antifascismo), the Fascist secret police, and sentenced in 1937. This marked the beginning of a rapid decline of GL, whose members were scattered all over Europe. In 1936, the Sopade released its second manifesto in exile. It committed the group to liberal socialism. The party organ *Neuer Vorwärts* displayed the title "Break the Chains" (*Zerbrecht die Ketten*) on its cover on 25 June 1933. The workers in Germany received this message shortly after a ban was imposed on the democratic parties and showed signs of a revolutionary rebellion, which the Sopade claimed to have decisively sparked soon thereafter in its oncoming manifesto.

In January 1934, the SPD in exile released the so-called "Revolutionary Manifesto," which was published both in *Neuer Vorwärts* and the *Sozialistische Aktion*. The first draft had been outlined by Kurt Geyer, Erich Rinner and Friedrich Stampfer. Yet Rudolf Hilferding, still the group's leading theoretician, was the most influential figure behind it.[14] The radical left wing in exile, the so-called "old Left" (*alte Linke*), around Karl Böchel and Siegfried Aufhäuser, to which Paul Hertz to a certain extent contributed too, was also very influential. The pledge to organize a firm, subversive reaction to the National Socialist regime was partly a result of the theoretical debate promoted by the radical Left. As first editor-in-chief of *Sozialistische Aktion*, Paul Hertz was in a position to have a strong impact on the ideological development of the early Sopade, until he was forced to leave the party in 1938 for allegedly having initiated unauthorized contacts with other socialist and even communist groups.[15]

By the same token, Carlo Rosselli had published *Socialismo liberale e altri scritti* in 1929, a book which would soon become a manifesto for GL. Its revolutionary tone eventually turned out to have a broad appeal—just as much as it was for the Sopade[16]—even among the most radical members. At the same time, it gave the GL the chance to deal with past mistakes and devise effective solutions.

Whereas the Sopade indulged in self-criticism, the GL directed its disapproval mostly at the PSI, from which it wanted to create distance. The instrumental character of the German manifesto was immediately palpable. It aimed at cementing the leadership of the Social Democratic Party within the heterogeneous alliance of German socialist antifascism. Moreover, the document drew attention to different issues which would turn out to be of crucial importance for the development of the Sopade. Besides the criticism addressed to the SPD of the Weimar Republic, the exiled group advocated freedom and respect of human rights. As a matter of fact, the creation of a socialist society or even of a socialist state did not appear at all in the manifesto. Instead, it called for a "governance of people" (*Volksherrschaft*).[17]

As for Paul Hertz, the SPD had failed to analyze thoroughly the intrinsic undemocratic nature of Weimar society and had lost track of its development by insisting on a class-based interpretation of capitalism. The steady improvement of the economic and social status of the working class from the beginning of the century, which the SPD praised as a major advancement, had eventually led party members to lose sight of the undemocratic nature of the state in the Weimar Republic.[18] Hertz made a case for the need to overcome latent structural obstacles—such as a far too uncoordinated party base and the ideological adherence to reformism—and thus set the course for a major revision.[19] In this respect, fascism inspired and enforced major adjustments.

Mutual Perceptions and Transnational Connections between Antifascists

The executive committees of the two antifascist parties, GL and Sopade, reassembled in exile, at first in Prague, then in Paris. Apparently, they did not show noticeable similarities, especially as regards their ideologies. They had much in common though, as they shared a determination to conduct and represent the whole socialist antifascist opposition abroad and to be considered as the legitimate and only "heirs" of pre-fascist social democracy; this makes them comparable and worth being analyzed jointly. In truth a number of significant personalities from both groups knew each other personally or had experienced equivalent forms of education and political breeding.

Gaetano Salvemini, a professor of history at the University of Bari, was an expert on German social democracy. Carlo Rosselli[20] had studied for a long time in Germany and eventually assimilated the theories of Neo-Kantianism; in addition, he was a member of the Internationaler Sozialistischer Kampfbund (International Socialist Association, ISK), where he had the chance to meet many of the most influential socialist theoreticians of his time. He and his brother, Nello Rosselli, along with Silvio Trentin, had been introduced to Rudolf Hilferding, Julius Deutsch, Fritz Adler, and Otto Bauer, among others, during their regular stays in Berlin in the 1920s. They then kept in contact with these social democrats by correspondence.[21]

Mutual influences between the Sopade and Italian antifascism were numerous, and included in some cases personal connections. Hilferding's work *Das Finanzkapital* from 1910, which had marked a decisive moment in Marxist doctrines and indeed could exert great influence in Italy,[22] has to be mentioned here. Rudolf Hilferding himself was befriended by Giuseppe Emanuele Modigliani and temporarily found refuge at his house while hiding from the Gestapo in Paris.[23]

Through Modigliani's intercession, Hilferding also met Carlo Rosselli, one of the most authoritative social democratic Italian intellectuals and politicians as well as leader of the short-lived Italian antifascist socialist front.[24] The members of the Sopade shared with these Italian liberal socialists the libertarian interpretation of Marxism, corroborated by their strict rejection of an opportunistic alliance with communist forces.

The project of establishing a united socialist front against fascism would dominate the ideological debates of the Sopade and GL, as well as of the rest of socialist antifascism in Europe during the 1930s.[25] In his retrospective assessment of the exile-politics of the Sopade during their stay in Prague, Friedrich Stampfer praised the consistency of his party in rejecting any proposal of cooperation with radical socialist or communist organizations. The communists "are overtly trying to reach undemocratic objectives," and would only be able to appeal to a very narrow range of citizens, while social democracy endorsed political and social freedom, beyond any class barrier.[26]

Stampfer was very influential in that he was able to launch a strong message to his homeland, in 1939 still under Nazi rule. He emphasized that his party was not going to embrace any pragmatic measures with communists "and the like," but that it would rather engage in missions aimed at reaching a larger, "enlightened" opposition.[27] The consequences of this mindset proved to be disruptive for the entire left-wing antifascism, as is known today. Yet it meant an utmost commitment to a libertarian tradition, which had characterized the ideological development of the Sopade from the mid-1930s onward.

The executive group of the SPD in exile was mainly influenced by two factors. On the one hand, the Czechoslovakian government had prohibited their press in the winter of 1937, under strong pressure from the German authorities. On the other hand, the stance of West European countries such as England and France toward Germany was considered to be too cautious, and dangerously underestimated the Nazi threat in the eyes of the Sopade observers.[28]

Patriotism, combined with a pan-European liberal socialist ideal, was imbued with eclecticism and humanitarianism. Against this background, the executive group in exile saw itself as bearer of the highest mission: the awakening of the European masses facing the Nazi menace and the renovation of the traditional values of the European occident, such as freedom, equality, and justice. This led to the rejection of any cooperation with other socialist groups. In April 1939, for instance, the Austrian and German Communist parties unsuccessfully proposed an alliance for underground activities to the Sopade.[29] Their leaders in exile declared that from that point on they would focus their activity on the intellectual education of the working class by helping disclose the danger represented by the barbaric nature of the Nazi regime. Stampfer claimed that socialism should not strike compromises with radical positions, because in so doing it would eventually lose its identity and become easy prey for Nazism. Social democracy was to position itself between socialism and liberalism, which he called the two main pillars of modernity.[30]

After leaving Prague, the Sopade settled in Paris, where it stayed until 1940, before eventually moving to London until the end of the war. In those years, many members left the party or joined other resistance groups elsewhere in Europe; the core that stuck together was thereafter the object of debate on whether or not it could claim the legitimacy to represent the Social Democrats. The Sopade considered the Weimar SPD as its political and ideological point of reference, thus underlining the close ties to the former party and the right to speak on behalf of it. This right was also recognized by the majority of the antifascist underground organizations.[31]

Conclusion

As suggested in this chapter, German and Italian moderate Socialists and theoreticians in Prague, in Paris, and finally in London sought to find alternatives to orthodox Marxism, or even a "Marxism without Marx,"[32] and thus deeply influenced the German SPD and the Italian left wing after 1945. They strongly advocated a humanistic approach to socialism, in which autonomy and individual conscience would eventually combine and produce moral and practical justice.

As has been shown, the revolutionary attitude of the early manifestos vanished rapidly. GL focused its initial militant activity in the late 1920s on fighting the Fascist regime. Early plans of action even encompassed initiatives to murder Mussolini; one of these audacious schemes included the use of an airplane to launch a bomb on Piazza Venezia, where Mussolini used to sojourn.[33] Yet the harsh repression of antifascists seriously hurt GL to its core, so that it had to considerably reduce its operating radius. By 1931 it had joined the Concentrazione antifascista, and committed almost completely to a political and propagandistic form of resistance, pursuing the ultimate goal of a new social democracy and a solid democratic state, with no communist "contamination."

In 1936, some of the GL leaders, Carlo Rosselli and Camillo Berneri among others, organized an own volunteer military unit to join the International Brigades in fighting Falangist troops in the Spanish Civil

War. They aimed at reinvigorating the Italian antifascist resistance by adopting and promulgating the slogan *"Oggi in Spagna, domani in Italia"* (Today in Spain, tomorrow in Italy), yet their effort eventually turned out to be insufficient. Several GL representatives were killed in the war; Rosselli fell to an ambush by French fascists in June 1937, presumably commissioned by Mussolini personally. With his death and the end of the Spanish Republic in 1939, GL partisans were dispersed all over Europe. Those who had remained in Paris had no other choice but to go into hiding as soon as German military forces invaded France in 1940. The members who managed to return to Italy soon regrouped themselves as the Partito d'Azione (Action Party), which provided the first prime minister of post-Fascist Italy in the person of Ferruccio Parri.[34]

In an article published in 1933, Rudolf Hilferding characterized the singular role Germany had been bestowed with by naming it a "political destiny." He predicted that his home country would be "damned to become the bearer of revolution in all of Europe," thus liberating it from moral slavery,[35] and believed that social democracy should embark on this mission and pave the way for such a revolutionary breakthrough by concentrating on the "intellectual education" (*geistige Erziehung*) of the people to fight and govern in the future.[36]

Internally, the debate soon shifted to more practical topics, such as the intellectual and spiritual education of society in order to prepare it for new challenges. As Hilferding stressed, the experience of failure that Germany and, above all, her working class had gone through had to be regarded as a chance to reflect on the mistakes that had been committed, and to learn from them. The downfall of the Weimar Republic should be considered as the ultimate proof of the weakness of reformist strategies by the SPD and the remaining left-wing organizations. A "total remodeling" (*totale Umgestaltung*) of society, from one indulging in capitalistic attitudes to one aiming at political freedom and the establishment of democratic institutions, was urgently needed.[37] The working papers of the executive group provided a clear blueprint of the desired form of socialism: the party should move away from its role as "national-liberal representative," which it had been exercising during the Weimar Republic, and return to its original social democratic stance—namely, Marxism deprived of its axiomatic finality.[38]

Hilferding argued that reformism, as well as the radical, dogmatic, and in many ways undemocratic views of the Communist parties, had failed to grasp the human aspect of "libertarian" Marxism, which was eventually bound to set up a society without barriers, just like a sort of religion for all mankind.[39] What could Marxist doctrine revised along these lines offer against the barbarism of the Nazi regime? The short answer was freedom.[40]

This is yet no evidence at all for a return to Marxist positions, and quite the contrary eventually occurred. The most influential members of the Sopade recognized the intrinsic vagueness of Marx's doctrine and denounced its "immobility," represented among other factors by its expressed reliance on a natural, imminent dissolution of capitalism. A Marxist teaching centering on justice and freedom was surely attractive to them. Yet not all of them were enthusiastic about the envisaged "dictatorship of the proletariat." Theoreticians of the party essentially pleaded for a comprehensive revision of core beliefs of Marxism in order to meet the needs of an underground antifascist organization like the Sopade and to support the call for insurrectionary action.[41]

This had direct implications for calls for decentralization of the party structure, which went on to be one of the most discussed subjects during exile and resulted in a major transformation in the postwar SPD.[42] The representatives of the executive committee in exile truly set the tone as they reiterated the immediate correlation between freedom and socialism, however stressing that such a paradigm would not be effective without "rising to action." According to them, freedom was to be reconquered by any means necessary. But its understanding and preservation would only be guaranteed by an active education that emphasized its moral superiority.[43]

In addition to this, the concurrence with libertarian visions was mainly responsible for the rejection of a close alliance with the several communist or more radical socialist organizations in exile by the Sopade. This would eventually have invalidated the substantial connection between the party and its members. Moreover, it would have distracted them from the crucial goal of social democracy to secure freedom, not simply the acquisition of "total power" (*Totalität der Staatsmacht*), as the communists had contemplated.[44]

After the Battle of France in May–June 1940, the German military forces were quickly able to occupy most parts of northern France, Paris included. For all of the German expatriates it soon became clear that they could no longer stay. Rudolf Hilferding tried to escape persecution via Francoist Spain in order to reach Portugal. However, he was eventually caught by the Gestapo and tortured to death in 1941. Others managed to go abroad and settle in London or New York, like Friedrich Stampfer and Erich Rinner.[45] Hans Vogel and Erich Ollenhauer sought refuge in London, from where they demanded to officially represent the SPD and the transitory Sopade.[46] Their commitment to the ideological principles of the exile-SPD found confirmation throughout their manifold propagandistic activity, essentially on the radio, and this was reiterated in a comprehensive document in 1941, which offered significant reference points for social democracy in a German society after Nazism.

Together with the endorsement of a mixed economy, with a state-run and a private market-based sector, the authors highlighted the central objective of preparing a "revolution of society" by introducing forms of decentralized self-administration on both local and regional levels. This would stimulate economic growth and safeguard democratic stability, both nationally and in international politics.[47] The paper also strongly endorsed self-assertion and activism, intended as an encouragement to the still enslaved German population—it rebutted, though, the revolutionary attitude by all means.

The interaction of national and supranational elements within the political and ideological propaganda by the Sopade, and its all-European attempt to consolidate democracy, had a symbolic meaning to the former exiled opponents of National Socialism. They generally tended to romanticize "exile" and idealized it as a necessary lot that they had to endure in order for humanity to be fully restored after Fascism.[48] Reasoning about the future form of government along these lines meant revising a body of teachings they all owed much to, as socialists as well as Germans: Marxism. How could they possibly revitalize Marxism through its libertarian component? How, finally, could they promulgate Marxism, while expunging deceptive side effects such as "class struggle" and "dictatorship of the proletariat?"[49] In the eyes of German socialists, the rise of Nazism and Fascism had been a turning point in the history of Western civilization. Before anything else, the renewal was to start with a moral revolution, breaking with the deterministic theory and bringing Marxism back to liberalism.[50] The specific doctrine that the Sopade and the Giustizia e Libertà drew on was admittedly not new.[51] Yet they significantly helped it become a source of inspiration for subsequent political reorientation of the Left in the two countries.[52]

Among the members of the initial group of the Sopade in Prague, only Erich Rinner, Friedrich Stampfer, Hans Vogel, and Erich Ollenhauer survived the plight of the war. Several intellectual circles of immigrants who had hidden in Paris were suppressed right after the invasion of France by the German Wehrmacht. The executive group decided to encourage all partisans to flee, by any means necessary and according to their personal options, at an extraordinary party convention in Marseille in the summer of 1940. The Sopade branch in New York was able to collect a considerable amount of money and obtained visas for their German comrades.[53]

This chapter has demonstrated that both the Sopade and the GL committed to a thorough ideological overhaul of socialism, which had become even more compelling after the insurgence of fascism in Europe. The socialism they advocated avoided any dogmatic interpretation of society or state (in this they shared their condemnation of communism), and instead fostered humanity and justice. Fascist repression affected both groups very badly, both politically and physically, so much so that they were forced to systematically curb their activities in exile. Yet their ideas survived, and indeed went on to exert great influence on the reconstruction processes in (West) Germany and Italy after World War II.

FRANCESCO DI PALMA is a postdoctoral research fellow and lecturer at the Institute of History and Cultural Studies, Freie Universität Berlin. Selected publications: Monographs: *Liberaler Sozialismus in Deutschland und in Italien im Vergleich. Das Beispiel Sopade und Giustizia & Libertà* (Berlin: Metropol Verlag, 2010); *Die SED, die kommunistische Partei Frankreichs (PCF) und die kommunistische Partei Italiens (PCI) von 1968 bis 1989/90. Beziehungen, Verflechtungen, Policy-Making* (forthcoming, 2017); Edited books: *Bruderparteien jenseits des Eisernen Vorhangs. Die Beziehungen der SED zu den kommunistischen Parteien West- und Südeuropas (1968 bis 1989)* (Berlin: Ch. Links Verlag, 2011, with Arnd Bauerkämper); *Kommunismus und Europa. Europapolitik und -vorstellungen europäischer kommunistischer Parteien im Kalten Krieg* (Paderborn: Schöningh Verlag, 2016, with Wolfgang Mueller).

Notes

1. Rudolf Hilferding (1877–1941), Dr. med., born in Vienna, was a German politician and theoretician of the SPD. His work *Das Finanzkapital* (1910), in which he described the modern development stage of capitalism and its social consequences, was to exert major influence on the social democracy of the early twentieth century. He was minister of finance in 1923, and again from 1928 till 1929, finally in exile after 1933 as a member of the Sopade, at first in Zurich, then in Paris where he was eventually caught by the Gestapo and tortured to death in 1941.
2. Friedrich Stampfer (1874–1957), born in Brno, was a German politician and journalist. Having been the chief editor of the SPD organ, *Vorwärts*, from 1916, Stampfer was one of the most influential social democrats of his time and responsible for a major shift of his party toward more liberal positions. He was in exile in Prague as a member of the Sopade from 1933, then in Paris, and in 1940 he went to the United States.

3. Paul Hertz (1888–1961), born in Worms, was a social democratic politician and theoretician. He led the periodical *Sozialistische Aktion* and was, with Rudolf Hilferding, co-editor of the *Zeitschrift für Sozialismus*. He was in exile in Prague as member of the Sopade from 1933. After breaking with the Sopade in 1938, he went to the United States in 1939 and returned to Germany in 1949.

4. With regard to external impulses on both the Sopade and Giustizia e Libertà, originating for instance from England and the Labour Party as well as from France and francophone countries, see Francesco Di Palma, "Jews and the SPD: The Influence of Jewish Intelligence on German Exile Social-Democracy (1933–1945)," *Zeitgeschichte* 1 (2014): 4–19.

5. Among the founders of the party figured Carlo Rosselli (1899–1937), professor of economics and social liberal theorist, the historian Gaetano Salvemini (1873–1957), and the social republicans Emilio Lussu (1890–1975), Francesco Fausto Nitti (1899–1974), and Alberto Cianca (1884–1966). On this see, Gaetano Salvemini, *Memorie d'un fuoriuscito* (Milan, 1960); Francesco Di Palma, *Liberaler Sozialismus in Deutschland und in Italien im Vergleich: Das Beispiel Sopade und Giustizia e Libertà* (Berlin, 2010), esp. 152–65.

6. "Concentrazione antifascista" was an aggregation of Italian antifascist groups, mostly operating from France, which existed from 1927 until 1934. On this, see Ugo Mancini, *Il fascismo dallo Stato liberale al regime* (Soveria Mannelli, 2007).

7. The founding core took refuge at first in Prague, where it stayed until 1938; it moved then to Paris and from there finally to London in 1940, where it remained until the collapse of the Third Reich. Although no official agreement stipulated the Sopade's autonomy or its legitimacy as the representative of the German SPD in exile, it is arguably correct to maintain that it was so as late as 1934. In that year the Sopade released the Revolutionary Manifesto of the German Social Democratic Party, a symbolic action that conferred on it the control over the party and its main press organs, such as the *Vorwärts* and the *Neuer Vorwärts*, as well as the more theoretical *Deutschland-Berichte*, *Sozialistische Aktion* and *Zeitschrift für Sozialismus*. On the Sopade, its structrure and its press, see among others, Peter Grasmann, *Sozialdemokratie gegen Hitler 1933–1945* (Munich, 1976); Wolfgang Abendroth, *Aufstieg und Krise der deutschen Sozialdemokratie* (Frankfurt a.M., 1964). The sole monography on the Sopade constitutes the aged, yet not superseded, and much interesting study by Lewis J. Edinger, *Sozialdemokratie und Nationalsozialismus: Der Parteivorstand der SPD im Exil von 1933–1945*, trans. K.H. Tjaden (Hannover, 1960). On the Sopade and its international ties to other social democratic antifascist organizations, see, Di Palma, *Liberaler Sozialismus*.

8. On this aspect, see, Georg Fülberth and Jürgen Harrer, *Die deutsche Sozialdemokratie 1890–1933* (Darmstadt and Neuwied, 1974), 156–60.

9. On the "Löbe Group," see, Hans J.L. Adolph, *Otto Wels und die Politik der deutschen Sozialdemokraten: 1894–1939* (Berlin, 1971); and Paul Löbe, *Der Weg war lang: Erinnerungen* (Berlin, 1990). On the early exile-party, see, Edinger, *Sozialdemokratie und Nationalsozialismus*; Jutta v. Freyberg, *Sozialdemokraten*

und Kommunisten—Die Revolutionären Sozialisten Deutschlands vor dem Problem der Aktionseinheit 1934–1937 (Cologne, 1973); and Fülberth and Harrer, *Die deutsche Sozialdemokratie*.

10. Giorgio Galli, *Storia del socialismo italiano: da Turati al dopo Craxi* (Milan, 2007); Pietro Nenni, *La battaglia socialista contro il fascismo 1922–1944* (Milan, 1977).

11. Carlo Rosselli, *Dizionario delle idee* (Rome, 2000).

12. Fulvio Cortese, *Libertà individuale e organizzazione pubblica in Silvio Trentin* (Milan, 2008); Paul Arrighi, *Silvio Trentin: un Européen en résistance (1919–1943)* (Portet-sur-Garonne, 2007).

13. The term "democratic Marxism" refers to a political philosophy based on a libertarian interpretation of socialism, primarily rejecting the final goal of the dictatorship of the proletariat. On this, see among others, David Bates, ed., *Marxism, Intellectuals and Politics* (Basingstoke, 2007); Tibor C. Machan, *Revisiting Marxism: A Bourgeois Assessment* (Lanham, MD, 2006); and Mark Devenney, *Ethics and Politics in Contemporary Theory: Between Critical Theory and Post-Marxism* (London, 2004).

14. On the revolutionary manifesto of the Sopade, see Wolfgang Saggau, *Faschismustheorien und antifaschistische Strategien in der SPD* (Cologne, 1981), 244–47; Erich Matthias and Werner Link, eds., *Mit dem Gesicht nach Deutschland: Eine Dokumentation über die sozialdemokratische Emigration. Aus dem Nachlass von Friedrich Stampfer* (Düsseldorf, 1968), 215–25.

15. Boris Schilmar, *Der Europadiskurs im deutschen Exil, 1933–1945* (Munich, 2004), 123–30.

16. On this aspect, see Bärbel Hebel-Kunze, *SPD und Faschismus: Zur politischen und organisatorischen Entwicklung der SPD 1932–1935* (Frankfurt a.M., 1977), 202–10.

17. On this, see among others, Matthias and Link, *Mit dem Gesicht nach Deutschland*, 218–19. Di Palma, *Liberaler Sozialismus*, esp. 86–155.

18. Paul Hertz, "Unsere Aufgabe und ihre Erfüllung," *Zeitschrift für Sozialismus* (Jan. 1934): 424.

19. Ibid., 427.

20. Carlo Rosselli descended from a wealthy Tuscan Family with Jewish background. From 1925 he was professor of economics at the University of Genoa, and from 1926 until 1929 was co-editor, with Pietro Nenni, of the social democratic journal *Il Quarto Stato*. In 1929 he founded GL. On this, see Stanislao G. Pugliese, *Carlo Rosselli: Socialist Heretic and Antifascist Exile* (Cambridge, MA, 1999).

21. Salvo Mastellone, *Carlo Rosselli e "La Rivoluzione liberale del socialismo": con scritti e documenti inediti* (Florence, 1999), 58.

22. On Hilferding's influence on Marxist doctrines, see William Smaldone, *Rudolf Hilferding: The Tragedy of a Social Democrat* (Binghamton, NY, 1990).

23. Giuseppe Emanuele Modigliani (1872–1947), lawyer and politician, was one of the most influential social democrats in Italy and an Italian representative at the Socialist International; from 1926 he was in exile in Vienna, and later in Paris. On his tie to the German social democracy, see Pugliese, *Carlo Rosselli*, 230–40; and Anne Saint Sauveur-Henn, ed., *Fluchtziel Paris: Die deutschsprachige Emigration 1933–1940* (Berlin, 2002).

24. Carlo Rosselli (1899–1937), was born into a Jewish liberal upper-class Italian family with an English background. He studied economics in Florence and in London, where he assimilated the socialism of the Fabian Society. He dedicated his theoretical activity to a fusion of liberal socialism with Marxist doctrines, which he also tried to translate into practice in his role as leader of the underground movement Giustizia e Libertà in Paris. Chased by the Italian fascist secret police, OVRA, he escaped to Spain and was eventually caught at the Spanish–French border, on French territory, in 1937, where he was murdered. On his influence upon Italian and European antifascism, see Pugliese, *Carlo Rosselli*; Di Palma, *Liberaler Sozialismus*; as well as the standard reference, Esther Modena-Burkhardt, *Von "Giustizia e Libertà" zum "Partito d'Azione"* (Zurich, 1974).
25. See esp. Ursula Langkau-Alex, *Deutsche Volksfront 1932–1939: zwischen Berlin, Paris, Prag und Moskau*, vol. 3 (Berlin, 2005).
26. Friedrich Stampfer, "Volksfront im Wandel der Zeiten. Revolution und Koalition," *Neuer Vorwärts* (11 June 1939): 21–33.
27. Ibid., 28.
28. See esp. Rainer Behring, *Demokratische Außenpolitik für Deutschland: Die außenpolitischen Vorstellungen deutscher Sozialdemokraten im Exil 1933–1945* (Düsseldorf, 1999), 189–223.
29. Freyberg, *Sozialdemokraten und Kommunisten*, 189.
30. Friedrich Stampfer, "Sind wir liberal?" *Neuer Vorwärts* (6 Feb. 1938): 18.
31. See esp. Ulrich Cartarius, "Sozialdemokratisches Exil und innerdeutscher Widerstand," in *Autour du "Front populaire allemande": Einheitsfront-Volksfront*, ed. Michael Grunewald and Fritjof Trapp (Bern, 1990), 134–76; Grasmann, *Sozialdemokraten gegen Hitler* (Munich, 1976).
32. See on this, Alan Freeman, "Marxism without Marx: A Note towards a Critique," *Capital & Class 34* (Feb. 2010): 84–97.
33. See Pugliese, *Carlo Rosselli*, 51.
34. See, on this, Giovanni De Luna, *Storia del Partito d'Azione* (Turin, 2006).
35. Rudolf Hilferding, "Die Zeit und die Aufgabe," *Zeitschrift für Sozialismus* (Oct. 1933): 28.
36. Ibid., 29.
37. Rudolf Hilferding, "Marxismus und Gegenwart," *Sozialistische Aktion* (June 1936): 34.
38. Rudolf Hilferding, "Revolutionärer Sozialismus," *Zeitschrift für Sozialismus* (Feb. 1934): 146.
39. Ibid., 146–50. Moreover, on this aspect, see Petra Weber, *Sozialismus als Kulturbewegung. Frühsozialistische Arbeiterbewegung und das Entstehen zweier feindlicher Brüder: Marxismus und Anarchismus* (Bonn, 1989), 352–62.
40. Jan Greitens, *Finanzkapital und Finanzsysteme: "Das Finanzkapital" von Rudolf Hilferding* (Marburg, 2012).
41. See Hebel-Kunze, *SPD und Faschismus*, 176–93.
42. For the best account of the relationship between postwar SPD and Jewish Intelligence, see Hans Erler, *Judentum und Sozialdemokratie: Das antiautoritäre Fundament der SPD* (Würzburg, 2009). More generally on the postwar party, see Willy Albrecht, *Die SPD unter Kurt Schumacher und Erich Ollenhauer 1946 bis 1953* (Bonn, 2000).

43. Hebel-Kunze, *SPD und Faschismus*.
44. Saggau, *Faschismustheorien*, 370–79; Freyberg, *Sozialdemokraten und Kommunisten*, 33–47.
45. Smaldone, *Rudolf Hilferding*, 246–57.
46. Werner Röder, *Die deutschen sozialistischen Exilgruppen in Großbritannien 1940 bis 1945* (Hannover, 1968), 183–200.
47. Richtlinien auf dem Gebiet der Wirtschaftspolitik [1941], Archiv der sozialen Demokratie (AdsD), Bonn, Bestand PV-Emigration, Folder 179.
48. Matthias and Link, *Mit dem Gesicht nach Deutschland*.
49. Rudolf Hilferding, "Unter der Drohung des Faschismus," *Die Gesellschaft* 1 (1932): 2–11.
50. See, Stampfer, "Sind wir liberal?" 18–20; John Rosselli, ed., *Socialismo liberale e altri scritti* (Turin, 1979).
51. Leading theoreticians had been trying to complete a fusion of Marxism with libertarian doctrines since the end of the nineteenth century. Some of them believed they had found a practicable solution in mingling Marxism with aspects of neo-Kantianism. Leonard Nelson (1882–1927) was one of those. He had been born into an upper-class Prussian family with Jewish background, and was a philosophy professor in Göttingen and a most influential socialist theoretician. At first criticized by the SPD executive group, he would found the Internationaler Sozialistischer Kampfbund (ISK) in 1925, a political organization inspired by an ethically and humanistically grounded socialism. Famous intellectuals figured among its members, such as Albert Einstein, Käthe Kollwitz, and Erich Kästner. Nelson's positions would exert great influence on Rudolf Hilferding, and later on the postwar SPD in general. On his ties to Rudolf Hilferding and other European social democrats, like Carlo Rosselli, see, Willi Eichler, *Sozialisten* (Bonn-Bad Godesberg, 1972); Sabine Lemke-Müller, *Ethik des Widerstands: Der Kampf des Internationalen Sozialistischen Kampfbundes (ISK) gegen den Nationalsozialismus* (Bonn, 1996); and Ariane Landuyt, "Carlo Rosselli e la cultura europea di terza via," in *Carlo e Nello Rosselli e l'antifascismo europeo*, ed. Antonio Bechelloni (Milan, 2001), 127–40.
52. For instance, the long-lasting, crucial change, of course, in the history of the modern SPD: the official transformation from a working-class to a catch-all party in 1959. This decisive change was completed at the party convention in Bad-Godesberg in 1959. Willi Eichler (1896–1971), an assistant of Leonard Nelson and a member of the ISK (see previous note), was one of the main promoters of the SPD reorientation. On this aspect, see, Sabine Lemke-Müller, *Ethischer Sozialismus und soziale Demokratie: Der politische Weg Willi Eichlers vom ISK zur SPD* (Bonn, 1988); Willi Eichler, *Sozialismus als angewandte Ethik* (Bonn, 1954).
53. Mostly on account of the generous intercession of the American Jewish Labor Committee. On this, see Edinger, *Sozialdemokratie und Nationalsozialismus*, 196–200.

Bibliography

Abendroth, Wolfgang. *Aufstieg und Krise der deutschen Sozialdemokratie.* Frankfurt a.M., 1964.

Adolph, Hans J.L. *Otto Wels und die Politik der deutschen Sozialdemokraten, 1894–1939.* Berlin, 1971.

Albrecht, Willy. *Die SPD unter Kurt Schumacher und Erich Ollenhauer 1946 bis 1953.* Bonn, 2000.

Arrighi, Paul. *Silvio Trentin: un Européen en résistance (1919–1943).* Portet-sur-Garonne, 2007.

Bates, David, ed. *Marxism, Intellectuals and Politics.* Basingstoke, 2007.

Behring, Rainer. *Demokratische Außenpolitik für Deutschland. Die außenpolitischen Vorstellungen deutscher Sozialdemokraten im Exil 1933–1945.* Düsseldorf, 1999.

Cartarius, Ulrich. "Sozialdemokratisches Exil und innerdeutscher Widerstand," in *Autour du "Front populaire allemande": Einheitsfront-Volksfront,* ed. Michael Grunewald and Fritjof Trapp. Bern, 1990.

Cortese, Fulvio. *Libertà individuale e organizzazione pubblica in Silvio Trentin.* Milan, 2008.

De Luna, Giovanni. *Storia del Partito d'Azione.* Turin, 2006.

Devenney, Mark. *Ethics and Politics in Contemporary Theory: Between Critical Theory and Post-Marxism.* London, 2004.

Di Palma, Francesco. *Liberaler Sozialismus in Deutschland und in Italien im Vergleich: Das Beispiel Sopade und Giustizia e Libertà.* Berlin, 2010.

———. "Jews and the SPD: The Influence of Jewish Intelligence on German Exile Social-Democracy (1933–1945)." *Zeitgeschichte* 1 (2014): 4–19.

Edinger, Lewis J. *Sozialdemokratie und Nationalsozialismus: Der Parteivorstand der SPD im Exil von 1933–1945,* trans. K.H. Tjaden. Hannover, 1960.

Eichler, Willi. *Sozialismus als angewandte Ethik.* Bonn, 1954.

———. *Sozialisten.* Bonn-Bad Godesberg, 1972.

Erler, Hans. *Judentum und Sozialdemokratie: Das antiautoritäre Fundament der SPD.* Würzburg, 2009.

Freeman, Alan. "Marxism without Marx: A Note towards a Critique," *Capital & Class* 34 (Feb. 2010): 84–97.

Freyberg, Jutta v. *Sozialdemokraten und Kommunisten—Die Revolutionären Sozialisten Deutschlands vor dem Problem der Aktionseinheit 1934–1937.* Cologne, 1973.

Fülberth, Georg, and Jürgen Harrer. *Die deutsche Sozialdemokratie 1890–1933.* Darmstadt and Neuwied, 1974.

Galli, Giorgio. *Storia del socialismo italiano: da Turati al dopo Craxi.* Milan, 2007.

Grasmann, Peter. *Sozialdemokratie gegen Hitler 1933–1945.* Munich, 1976.

Greitens, Jan. *Finanzkapital und Finanzsysteme: "Das Finanzkapital" von Rudolf Hilferding.* Marburg, 2012.

Hebel-Kunze, Bärbel. *SPD und Faschismus: Zur politischen und organisatorischen Entwicklung der SPD 1932–1935.* Frankfurt a.M., 1977.

Hertz, Paul. "Unsere Aufgabe und ihre Erfüllung." *Zeitschrift für Sozialismus* (Jan. 1934): 422–32.

Hilferding, Rudolf. "Unter der Drohung des Faschismus." *Die Gesellschaft* 1 (1932): 2–11.

———. "Die Zeit und die Aufgabe." *Zeitschrift für Sozialismus* (Oct. 1933): 28.

———. "Revolutionärer Sozialismus." *Zeitschrift für Sozialismus* (Feb. 1934): 145–56.

———. "Marxismus und Gegenwart." *Sozialistische Aktion* (June 1936): 34.

Landuyt, Ariane. "Carlo Rosselli e la cultura europea di terza via," in *Carlo e Nello Rosselli e l'antifascismo europeo*, ed. Antonio Bechelloni. Milan, 2001.

Langkau-Alex, Ursula. *Deutsche Volksfront 1932–1939: Zwischen Berlin, Paris, Prag und Moskau*, vol. 3. Berlin, 2005.

Lemke-Müller, Sabine. *Ethischer Sozialismus und soziale Demokratie: Der politische Weg Willi Eichlers vom ISK zur SPD*. Bonn, 1988.

———. *Ethik des Widerstands. Der Kampf des Internationalen Sozialistischen Kampfbundes (ISK) gegen den Nationalsozialismus*. Bonn, 1996.

Löbe, Paul. *Der Weg war lang: Erinnerungen*. Berlin, 1990.

Machan, Tibor C. *Revisiting Marxism: A Bourgeois Assessment*. Lanham, MD, 2006.

Mancini, Ugo. *Il fascismo dallo Stato liberale al* regime. Soveria Mannelli, 2007.

Mastellone, Salvo. *Carlo Rosselli e "La Rivoluzione liberale del socialismo": con scritti e documenti inediti*. Florence, 1999.

Matthias, Erich, and Werner Link, eds. *Mit dem Gesicht nach Deutschland. Eine Dokumentation über die sozialdemokratische Emigration: Aus dem Nachlass von Friedrich Stampfer*. Düsseldorf, 1968.

Modena-Burkhardt, Esther. *Von "Giustizia e Libertà" zum "Partito d'Azione."* Zurich, 1974.

Nenni, Pietro. *La battaglia socialista contro il fascismo 1922–1944*. Milan, 1977.

Pugliese, Stanislao G. *Carlo Rosselli: Socialist Heretic and Antifascist Exile*. Cambridge, MA, 1999.

Röder, Werner. *Die deutschen sozialistischen Exilgruppen in Großbritannien 1940 bis 1945*. Hannover, 1968.

Rosselli, Carlo. *Dizionario delle idee*. Rome, 2000.

Rosselli, John, ed. *Socialismo liberale e altri scritti*. Turin, 1979.

Saggau, Wolfgang, *Faschismustheorien und antifaschistische Strategien in der SPD*. Cologne, 1981.

Saint Sauveur-Henn, Anne, ed. *Fluchtziel Paris: Die deutschsprachige Emigration 1933–1940*. Berlin, 2002.

Salvemini, Gaetano. *Memorie d'un fuoriuscito*. Milan, 1960.

Schilmar, Boris. *Der Europadiskurs im deutschen Exil, 1933–1945*. Munich, 2004.

Smaldone, William. *Rudolf Hilferding: The Tragedy of a Social Democrat*. Binghamton, NY, 1990.

Stampfer, Friedrich. "Sind wir liberal?" *Neuer Vorwärts* (6 Feb. 1938): 18.

———. "Volksfront im Wandel der Zeiten. Revolution und Koalition." *Neuer Vorwärts* (11 June 1939): 21–33.

Weber, Petra. *Sozialismus als Kulturbewegung: Frühsozialistische Arbeiterbewegung und das Entstehen zweier feindlicher Brüder: Marxismus und Anarchismus*. Bonn, 1989.

ᴄᑊᴇAfterword

BETWEEN COOPERATION AND CONFLICT
Perspectives of Historical Research on Transnational Fascism

Arnd Bauerkämper

As the contributions to this volume have demonstrated, relations between fascists were not restricted to representatives of states. In fact, most fascist movements never managed to seize power, nor entered coalition governments. Moreover, fascist ultranationalism did not exclude a sense of common mission or solidarity, giving rise to a wide scope of relations, from mere perceptions to contacts, interactions, transfers, and processes of learning. In some instances, fascists even became intertwined with each other; and, more generally, these entanglements also influenced their development. Thus, the rise of Italian Fascism dramatically brightened the prospects for their adherents in some other European states. Conversely, they sought—or intensified—relations to German National Socialism as soon as it became clear that Hitler's dictatorship was superior to Mussolini's regime. With the collapse of the Third Reich, European fascism was ultimately doomed. In both success and failure, fascists clearly depended on each other.

Yet these general entanglements as well as the more concrete mutual perceptions, interactions, and transfers by no means excluded sharp disagreements, conflicts, or mutual recriminations.[1] The antagonism resulted from a number of sources. Firstly, ideological differences separated fascists. Whereas they shared a strong nationalism, anticommunism, and the rejection of democracy, as well the vision of a new civilization directed against the Enlightenment and its version of modernity, the role of anti-Semitism remained particularly contested. Disagreements about attitudes and policies vis-à-vis the Jews surfaced as early as the Montreux conference of the Comitati d'Azione per l'Universalità di Roma in 1934. Even before Mussolini decided to adopt anti-Semitism (partly as a consequence of the preceding pronouncement on Fascist racism), he and his inferiors, as well as his admirers and adherents, had rejected anti-Semitism as the central pillar of fascist ideology. Similarly, Hitler's quest for "living space" in the East met serious reservations and objections among some other fascists.

Secondly, the different personalities of fascist leaders impeded cooperation and collaboration. Thus, the folklorist and clerical posture cultivated by the leaders of the Romanian "Iron Guard" was alien to Hitler. The German dictator also despised Mussolini's leniency toward the monarchy in Italy and his overtures to the Catholic Church. Not least, his frugal and ascetic lifestyle starkly contrasted to the Duce's lavish consumerism, and the German Führer did not share Mussolini's enthusiasm for sports.

Thirdly and most importantly, vested interests and particular aims nourished controversies and animosities. Hitler, for example, allowed Romanian marshal, prime minister and *conducător* (leader) Ion Antonescu to suppress the fascist "Iron Guard" in early 1941 because he prioritized a stable ally over ideological commitment to fascist "comrades." In a similar vein, the German leader detained the radically anti-Bolshevik, racist, and anti-Semitic Ukrainian nationalists in mid-1941 because they had proclaimed an independent state, which contradicted his geopolitical plans for the territories to be taken from the Soviet Union. As Grzegorz Rossoliński-Liebe demonstrates, this clash of interests even led Hitler to intern Stepan Bandera in Nazi Germany in July 1941. Later, the latter was imprisoned together with Horia Sima, the leader of the Iron Guard, in the same building of the Sachsenhausen concentration camp in which the last chancellor of the Austrian *Ständestaat*, Kurt Schuschnigg, also resided. Not least, Léon Degrelle's Walloon Rexists rejected the claims of Flemish fascists who aspired to a Germanic state encompassing the Third Reich, the Netherlands, and Belgium. Political expediency and the aim to secure economic resources rather than ideological commitment shaped transnational relations between fascists, especially in World War II.

These conflicts must be investigated in detailed studies of transnational fascism that should not exaggerate harmony between the national movements and groups. Disagreements between them restricted or even impeded exchange, cooperation, and collaboration. At the same time, opposing views and controversies did not exclude mutual perceptions or relations. In fact, they were inscribed in rejections. Even though Mussolini sought to prevent the war that Hitler actively promoted in the summer of 1939, he and his son-in-law, the Foreign Secretary Count Galeazzo Ciano, exchanged views with the German dictator and Joachim von Ribbentrop. This complex relationship was not restricted to fascist leaders. As Matteo Pasetti has emphasized in his chapter, corporatist conceptions diffused from Fascist Italy. At the same time, alternative and rival schemes emanated from Portugal and Austria. Ion Moţa, the leading member of the Romanian "Iron Guard," also insisted on particular features of Romanian fascism such as a militant Christianity. As Raul Cârstocea has evidenced, Moţa and many other members of the Iron Guard (which had been founded as the "Legion of the Archangel Michael" in 1927) believed in a common fascist mission to save civilization from the perceived grip of the Jews and Bolshevism. The complex interplay of national specifics and transnational influences also comes to the fore in Marleen Rensen's portrait of French fascist intellectual Robert Brasillach, who was attracted by Italian Fascism and German National Socialism, while pitting French "classical" culture against German "irrationalism." As these case studies demonstrate, disagreements and conflicts should not simply be juxtaposed with cooperation in historical studies of fascism. In fact, fascists related to each other even in rejection. Altogether, the very dialectics of conflicts and relations between them merits close attention in detailed studies of transnational fascism.

The same applies to the multiple asymmetries that characterized relations between fascists. First, the power of the two major dictators and their regimes was unequal. After Italy's conservative elites had vested Mussolini with power in October 1922, the Duce's regime became a model that fascists in some countries attempted to emulate. Mussolini's ardent followers included Adolf Hitler, who unsuccessfully waged a coup d'état against the democratic government of Germany's Weimar Republic in November 1923. When the Duce opened the spectacular exposition on the occasion of the tenth anniversary of the fascist "revolution" in October 1932, he could still count on many visitors from foreign countries. As late as May 1934, at their meeting in Venice, he still appeared to be Hitler's teacher. However, Mussolini became dependent on the Führer after the League of Nations imposed sanctions on Italy. The Fascist regime had decided to attack Ethiopia in October 1935 and thus take revenge for the humiliating defeat at Adwa in 1896. Italian warfare in Africa, too, also deprived Mussolini of the French and British backing that the Duce had secured with the agreement between the prime ministers of three states in Stresa in April 1935. By contrast, the Third Reich supported Italy's expansionist policy, and the two countries collaborated in the Spanish Civil War from July 1936 onward. Even though Mussolini proclaimed the new "Axis Rome–Berlin" and thereby claimed leadership in the alliance with Nazi Germany in November 1936, it was Berlin and Nuremberg (the sites of the yearly congresses of the Nazi Party) rather than Rome that became the most important destinations for fascists in the latter half of the 1930s. After Italy had suffered devastating and humiliating defeats in 1940–41, the power balance irrevocably tilted toward Germany. As a consequence, Italian Fascists unsuccessfully propagated the country's cultural mission in Europe. In her chapter, Monica Fioravanzo also provides evidence of the failure of last-minute Italian attempts to promise national independence to European nations as an antidote to German concepts and policies of full-scale domination. Nevertheless, Mussolini's faltering Fascist regime increasingly lost clout in Europe, not least because the Nazis camouflaged their claims to preeminence in Europe by ambivalent visions that Johannes Dafinger has exemplified in his chapter of this book.

Second, the fate of the minor fascist groups largely depended on the success of the two major regimes. The fiercely nationalist and Catholic Croatian Ustaša, for instance, was founded by Ante Pavelić in Italy after Yugolav King Alexander I had imposed his dictatorial regime in 1929. The new fascist movement was strongly supported by Italy, and by Hungary's authoritarian ruler Miklós Horthy and his pro-Fascist prime minister Gyula Gömbös (1932–36). After the Axis powers had invaded and portioned Yugoslavia in April 1941, Pavelić formed a government under German and Italian tutelage, and ordered atrocious crimes in the following years. The Organization of Ukrainian Nationalists, which had been founded in Vienna in 1929, hinged their fate on Nazi Germany's imperialism. Unlike the Ustaša in April 1941, however, the OUN was not granted a state although it yearned for collaboration with Germany, welcomed its extermination policies against the Jews, and stressed the place of a Ukrainian fascist state in a "New Europe" in letters addressed to Hitler, Mussolini, Franco, and Pavelić. The radical anti-Semitic and fascist groups and movements in occupied Norway, Western and Eastern Europe (such as Vidkun Quisling's Norwegian Nasjonal Samling, and Anton Mussert's Dutch Nationaal-Socialistische Beweging) were protected by the Third Reich. Hitler and his Propaganda Minister Joseph Goebbels also condescendingly advised the "Leader" of the British Union of Fascists, Oswald Mosley, when the fortunes of his movement flagged in the mid-1930s.[2] The relationship between the Italian Fascist Party, the Partito Nazionale Fascista, and the BUF, too, was asymmetrical, as Anna Lena Kocks has demonstrated in her contribution to the volume. More generally, the minor fascist parties selectively adopted concepts, organizations, and styles that had been successful in Italy and Germany. Although they fused these foreign imports with indigenous traditions of their specific countries, this process made the fascist supporters of Mussolini and Hitler vulnerable to attacks from their opponents, who charged them with aping foreign dictatorships.[3]

Not least, the asymmetries between the minor fascist groups and movements must be taken into account. The British Union of Fascists (BUF) rapidly sidelined the British Fascists (BF), which had been founded as "British Fascisti" in 1923 in the aftermath of Mussolini's much-acclaimed "March on Rome" in the previous year. In fact, some members, such as Neil Francis Hawkins, became influential functionaries in Oswald Mosley's BUF after its formation in October 1932.[4] Similarly, Quisling's Norwegian fascists felt superior to Frits Clausen's Danish National Socialists, not least because the German Nazis largely rejected them. Yet relations between fascist parties were by no means universally asymmetrical, as Goran Miljan's investigation of interaction between the youth organizations of the Croation Ustaša and the Slovakian Hlinka Guard highlights. All in all, asymmetrical relations between European fascists were the rule rather the exception. The degree and forms of this asymmetry, however, varied, and have to be investigated in detailed case studies.

Nevertheless, fascists perceived each other, interacted, and cooperated. The cross-border influence of fascism, however, was not restricted to like-minded groups. Undoubtedly, fascists were opposed to conservatives and authoritarian rulers. Whereas conservative parties sought to preserve the status quo and to protect a traditional nationalism in their countries, fascist movements and regimes believed in ultranationalist revolutions and proclaimed a new civilization that was to amend the perceived weaknesses of modern life and the degeneracy of liberal-cultural pluralism.[5] Thus, although both conservative authoritarians and fascists shared a hatred of liberal democracy, they were not similar in nature. Whereas fascists portrayed themselves a dynamic young force, conservatives and authoritarian organizations such as the Austrian Heimwehr and the veterans of the German Stahlhelm aimed to restore a premodern world that they romanticized. Yet some ideological overlap is conspicuous, and fascists tapped traditional values such as respect, and the conservative quest for order and discipline. Conversely, authoritarian regimes selectively appropriated fascist political conceptions, forms of representation, and organizational principles. As Cláudia Ninhos has demonstrated, however, they distinguished between Fascist Italy and Nazi Germany, adopting those elements that seemed most amenable to their needs. These processes resulted in a complex relationship of transnational borrowings between authoritarian and fascist regimes. The Austrian

Fatherland Front, for example, was influenced by the conservative *Ständestaat* and Fascist Italy.

Fascists even learnt from their democratic adversaries. For example, fascist dictators held elections. Contrary to authoritarian rulers, they sought plebiscitary, pseudo-democratic legitimacy. Conversely, democratic politicians and states adopted some policies pursued by fascist regimes. Winston Churchill, for instance, admired Mussolini's clout and steadfastness in the mid-1930s. Even the Nazi Reichsarbeitsdienst (RAD, State Labor Service) impressed numerous foreign observers and visitors from democratic states. The operation of the US Civilian Conservation Corps (CCC), which President Franklin D. Roosevelt had established in 1933, was partially influenced by the RAD, although the CCC was voluntary rather than obligatory. This also applies to the "National Fitness Campaign" that Chancellor of the Exchequer Neville Chamberlain announced on behalf of Prime Minister Stanley Baldwin in October 1936 under the impact of the performance of German athletes at the Summer Olympic Games in Berlin.[6]

Transnational relations between fascists also impinged on their unbending opponents. As fascist movements advanced and gained political power, antifascists sought to understand fascism in order to combat it. For this purpose, they also collaborated (at least partially and temporarily), and they formed alliances.[7] The consolidation of Mussolini's dictatorship in Italy and—even more challenging—Hitler's seizure of power in Germany led communists to collaborate with socialists and social democrats, who had been denounced as "social fascists" before 1933. By contrast, the World Congress of the Communist International embraced the concept of a broad "people's front" at their conference in July–August 1935. The German communists dutifully followed suit when they assembled in Kunzewo (close to Moscow) in October. As Kasper Braskén has stressed in his chapter, some communists, like publisher and intellectual Willi Münzenberg, had initiated efforts to establish a network of opponents to fascism as early as the 1920s. They had thereby rejected the official doctrine of Soviet communists. Transnational cooperation between fascists was a sting for socialist intellectuals like Italian publicist and scholar Carlo Rosselli, whose political initiatives have been reconstructed by Francesco Di Palma in this volume. Moreover, Silvia Madotto's contribution has testified to the cross-border appeal of antifascism in major European universities as a response to collaboration between fascisms, or at least to the perception of a united front of fascists.

Even though this understanding underrated the differences between their adversaries, collaboration between antifascists of various countries cannot be explained without considering the challenge of transnational cooperation between fascists. The collaboration of parties and groups in the two opposing camps differed, not least because antifascists assembled in exile or worked in the political underground. Yet the transnational activities of fascists and antifascists were interrelated, as Raul Cârstocea has demonstrated in his chapter. Although Ion Moţa stressed national particularities in the specifically Romanian brand of fascism, he called for a common fight of fascists against common enemies, especially the communists and the Jews. In fact, the belief in a "Judeo-Bolshevik" world conspiracy provided strong common ground between fascists, as the considerable contingents of foreign soldiers in the Waffen-SS in the last few years of the war evidenced.[8]

All in all, transnational fascism can be conceived of as an ensemble of selective cross-border perceptions, contacts, collaborative activities, transfers, appropriations and implementations of ideas, practices, styles, and institutions by fascists and non-fascists for specific ends, according to the prevailing conditions, needs, and demands. Cooperation between fascists was a bee-sting even to their opponents, who were frightened by a putatively united foe, although multiple differences and disagreements separated fascists from each other. Fascists, on their part, saw themselves confronted by a seemingly united enemy. These complex transnational relationships between fascists, as well as between them and non-fascist governments, parties, and groups, are to be investigated in further detailed studies. Nevertheless, the contributions to this book testify to the strong influence of fascism as a major radiating power in Europe, especially between 1918 and 1945.

Arnd Bauerkämper, Professor of Modern European History at the Freie Universität Berlin, studied History and English at the universities of Bielefeld, Oxford, and Göttingen. Selected publications: Der *Faschismus in Europa 1918–1945* (Stuttgart, 2006); *Das umstrittene Gedächtnis. Die Erinnerung an Nationalsozialismus, Faschismus und Krieg in Europa seit 1945* (Paderborn, 2012).

Notes

1. Arnd Bauerkämper, "The Denigration of British Fascism: Traditional Anti-British Stereotypes and Claims of Superiority in Nazi Germany," in *Britain as a Model of Modern Society? German Views*, ed. Arnd Bauerkämper and Christiane Eisenberg (Augsburg 2006): 147–67.

2. Salvatore Garau, *Fascism and Ideology: Italy, Britain, and Norway* (New York, 2015), 187, 190, 201, 216, 235, 242, 246, 252; David D. Roberts, *Fascist Interactions: Proposals for a New Approach to Fascism and Its Era, 1919-1945* (New York, 2016), 127, 145–148.
3. Martin Pugh, *'Hurrah for the Blackshirts': Fascists and Fascism in Britain between the Wars* (London, 2006), 129.
4. Roger Griffin, *Modernism and Fascism: The Sense of a Beginning under Mussolini and Hitler* (Basingstoke, 2007).
5. Norbert Götz and Kiran Klaus Patel, "Facing the Fascist Model: Discourse and the Construction of Labour Services in the USA and Sweden in the 1930s and 1940s," *Journal of Contemporary History* 41 (2006): 57–73; Kiran Klaus Patel, "'All of This Helps Us in Planning.' Der New Deal und die NS-Sozialpolitik," in *Vom Gegner lernen: Feindschaften und Kulturtransfers im Europa des 19. und 20. Jahrhunderts,* ed. Martin Aust and Daniel Schönpflug (Frankfurt/Main, 2007), 234–52; Anna Maria Lemcke, "'Providing the Superiority of Democracy.' Die 'National Fitness Campaign' der britischen Regierung (1937–1939) im transnationalen Zusammenhang," *Vierteljahrshefte für Zeitgeschichte* 57 (2009): 543–70, esp. 543–45, 563. For an overview, see Roberts, *Interactions,* 188–201.
6. Dan Stone, "Anti-Fascist Europe Comes to Britain: Theorising Fascism as a Contribution of Defeating It," in *Varieties of Anti-Fascism: Britain in the Inter-War Period,* ed. Andrzej Olechnowicz and Nigel Copsey (Basingstoke 2010), 183–201.
7. Randall L. Bytwerk, "Believing in 'Inner Truth': The Protocols of the Elders of Zion in Nazi Propaganda, 1933–1945," *Holocaust and Genocide Studies* (2015): 212–29; Lorna L. Waddington, *Hitler's Crusade: Bolshevism, the Jews and the Myth of Conspiracy* (London, 2007).

Bibliography

Bauerkämper, Arnd. "The Denigration of British Fascism: Traditional Anti-British Stereotypes and Claims of Superiority in Nazi Germany." In *Britain as a Model of Modern Society? German Views,* ed. Arnd Bauerkämper and Christiane Eisenberg, 147–67. Augsburg, 2006.

Bytwerk, Randall L. "Believing in 'Inner Truth': The Protocols of the Elders of Zion in Nazi Propaganda, 1933–1945." *Holocaust and Genocide Studies* (2015): 212–29.

Garau, Salvatore. *Fascism and Ideology: Italy, Britain, and Norway.* New York, 2015.

Götz, Norbert, and Kiran Klaus Patel. "Facing the Fascist Model: Discourse and the Construction of Labour Services in the USA and Sweden in the 1930s and 1940s." *Journal of Contemporary History* 41 (2006): 57–73.

Griffin, Roger. *Modernism and Fascism: The Sense of a Beginning under Mussolini and Hitler.* Basingstoke, 2007.

Lemcke, Anna Maria. "'Providing the Superiority of Democracy': Die 'National Fitness Campaign' der britischen Regierung (1937–1939) im transnationalen Zusammenhang." *Vierteljahrshefte für Zeitgeschichte* 57 (2009): 543–70.

Patel, Kiran Klaus. "'All of This Helps Us in Planning': Der New Deal und die NS-Sozialpolitik." In *Vom Gegner lernen: Feindschaften und Kulturtransfers im Europa des 19. und 20. Jahrhunderts,* ed. Martin Aust and Daniel Schönpflug, 234–52. Frankfurt/Main, 2007.

Pugh, Martin. *'Hurrah for the Blackshirts': Fascists and Fascism in Britain between the Wars.* London, 2006.

Roberts, David D. *Fascist Interactions:. Proposals for a New Approach to Fascism and Its Era, 1919–1945.* New York, 2016.

Stone, Dan. "Anti-Fascist Europe Comes to Britain: Theorising Fascism as a Contribution of Defeating It." In *Varieties of Anti-Fascism: Britain in the Inter-War Period,* ed. Andrzej Olechnowicz and Nigel Copsey, 183–201. Basingstoke, 2010.

Waddington, Lorna L. *Hitler's Crusade: Bolshevism, the Jews and the Myth of Conspiracy.* New York, 2007.

❧ Index

A

Ackermann, Anton, 303
Alexander I (king of Yugoslavia), 10, 136n33, 358
Almodôvar, António, 152, 153
Anti-Comintern Pact, 267, 270, 288, 296, 298–99
anticommunism, 16, 107, 142–43, 186, 207, 221, 271, 273, 277, 295, 298–99, 300, 303, 355
antifascism, 7, 16–17, 18, 21, 66, 288–89, 291–93, 295–305, 312–13, 316, 321, 324–25n2, 336–37, 341–43, 360
antiliberalism, 44, 47, 55, 69, 159, 169
anti-Semitism, 10, 11, 15, 18, 20, 23n6, 40, 42, 47–55, 107, 145, 169, 170, 171, 172, 176, 179–80, 185, 192, 207–8, 217, 219, 220, 221–24, 226–31, 233, 238n92, 265, 269, 271, 276–77, 355–56, 358. *See also* Jews
Antonescu, Ion, 169, 182–86, 272, 356. *See also* Romania
Aquila, Giulio, 293, 296
Argentina, 17, 39, 299
assassinations, 10, 177, 180, 181, 183, 220, 227, 234
Aunós Pérez, Eduardo, 72, 74–76
Austria, 4, 170–75, 185, 227–28, 247, 357
 Anschluss of, 12, 175, 248, 249
 Fatherland Front, 170–72, 174–75, 185, 186, 359–60
 Home Guard (Heimwehr), 10, 73, 170–72, 174, 186, 359
Austria-Hungary, 124, 219, 221, 222
Axmann, Arthur, 121, 122

B

Baldoli, Claudia, 108
Baligand, Albert von, 147–48

Bandera, Stepan, 177–79, 184, 185, 186, 356
Barbusse, Henri, 294, 296
Barcelona, 76, 316
Bárdossy, Lázló, 271–72
Barthou, Louis, 10
Bastianini, Giuseppe, 8, 253–54
Bauerkämper, Arnd, 21–22, 361
Bauman, Zygmunt, 47
Bayerlein, Bernhard, 300
Belgium, 12, 48–49, 71, 122, 193, 196, 198, 202, 208, 228–29, 271, 356
 Rexist Party, 4, 10, 49, 193, 196–98, 356
Belzer, Allison Scardino, 102
Benoist-Méchin, Jacques, 274, 282n67
Berlin, 2, 10, 11, 48, 147, 157, 176, 177, 178, 179, 181, 183, 219, 222, 247, 248, 249, 251, 253, 254, 265, 290, 291, 293, 294, 342, 357, 360
Berner, Wilhelm, 151
Bertaux, Pierre, 317
Biggini, Carlo, 319
Bloch, Marc, 5
Bobbio, Norberto, 321, 323
Bottai, Giuseppe, 75, 76, 250
Brasillach, Robert, 20, 192–209, 209n9, 210n20, 210n33, 214n91, 357
Braskén, Kasper, 18, 21, 305, 360
Britain, 11, 71, 77, 106–7, 110, 147, 149, 247, 291, 299
 British Union of Fascists (BUF), 9, 10, 11, 17, 19, 46, 49, 82, 95–97, 100, 107–114, 116n45, 193, 358–59. *See also* Mosley, Oswald
Brkljačić, Ante, 127
Bucharest, 184, 219, 222, 225, 234, 272, 274
Budapest, 124, 221, 223, 253
Bulgaria, 46, 79, 122, 129, 182, 270, 272

C

Caetano, Marcelo, 80, 157
capitalism, 19, 43, 70, 77–78, 143, 172,
    194, 254, 274, 339, 342, 346, 348n1
Carneiro Pacheco, António, 154, 155
Carol II (king of Romania), 180–82,
    234
Carroll, David, 203
Cârstocea, Raul, 18, 20, 234, 357, 361
Catholicism (Catholic Church;
    Catholics), 9, 16, 67, 68, 70, 77,
    78, 82, 101, 142, 152, 156, 158,
    199–200, 244, 246, 250, 322, 356
China, 9
Christianity (Christian tradition and
    values), 68, 152, 154, 180, 181,
    199, 200, 218, 221, 223–24, 229,
    231–33, 252, 255, 269, 275, 298,
    357
Churchill, Winston, 8, 360
Codreanu, Corneliu, 46, 179–80, 182,
    196, 198, 217–20, 222, 224–25,
    230–31, 233–34
Cole, George Douglas Howard,
    69–70
colonialism, 19
Comitati d'Azione per l'Universalità
    di Roma (CAUR), 1, 20, 23n6,
    78, 226, 228, 230, 245
communism, 3, 4, 14, 16, 43, 78, 143,
    144, 151, 164n89, 176, 180, 198,
    221, 231–33, 274, 276, 289, 291,
    296, 297–301, 305, 306n6, 348
Communist International
    (Comintern), 4, 45, 288, 289–96,
    300–303, 305
comparative history, 1, 2, 5–6, 43–44,
    75–76, 297
concentration camp, 12, 175–76,
    178–79, 183–86, 356
conflicts, 3, 8, 12, 15, 18, 20, 68, 70,
    71, 72, 73, 77, 81, 96, 108, 158,
    160, 168–71, 177, 182, 185, 186,
    198, 199, 200, 223, 224, 243, 244,
    250–53, 267, 303, 313, 319–20,
    339, 355–57
conservatism, 3, 8–9, 12, 16, 67,74,
    77, 94, 169, 171, 172, 181, 185–86,

233, 243, 246, 266–67, 270, 272–
    73, 275–77, 299, 357, 359–60
Coppola, Francesco, 245–46
Copsey, Nigel, 300
Cristo, Fernando Homem, 153
Croatia, 7, 19, 50, 53, 120, 124,
    129–30, 132, 136n32, 177–78, 179,
    270, 273
    Ustaša, 2–3, 10, 12, 14, 19, 53–54,
        120–33, 169, 176–77, 186, 273,
        358, 359
Cuza, Alexandru, 179–80, 219–22,
    225, 230
Czechoslovakia, 124, 177, 246, 336,
    343

D

Dafinger, Johannes, 18, 277, 358
De Grazia, Victoria, 100
Degrelle, Léon, 4, 10, 196–98, 199,
    200, 356
De Lucena, Manuel, 144, 161n13
De Luna, Antonio, 275
De Luna, Giovanni, 322
De Man, Henri, 77, 82
democracy, 3, 14, 16, 43, 46, 58n30,
    69, 81, 176, 180, 194, 227, 276,
    289, 291, 296, 297, 300, 302, 316,
    336, 337, 342, 343, 344, 345, 346,
    347, 355, 359
Denmark, 122, 228, 229, 271, 359
De Poterre, Georg, 221, 228, 229, 230
De Unamuno, Miguel, 143
Dikoff, Lüben, 272, 281nn53–54
Di Palma, Francesco, 16, 18, 21, 348,
    360
Dobry, Michel, 44
Dogliani, Patrizia, 119
Dollfuss, Engelbert, 79, 171–74, 227.
    See also Austria
Dontsov, Dmytro, 7, 10. *See also*
    Ukraine
Dundas, Ian Hope, 108

E

Eatwell, Roger, 40
economics, 19, 41, 43, 65, 67, 69,
    71–73, 77, 100, 103, 133, 143, 149,

159, 160, 224, 244, 250, 254, 265, 267, 339, 340, 347
entangled history, 2, 6–7, 14, 44, 55, 88n63, 216, 288, 297–98, 299–300, 304, 355
eugenics, 15, 21, 103

F
fascism
and corporatism, 19, 65–82, 84n23, 170, 172, 181, 337
against "decadence", 41, 46, 47, 55, 96, 119, 120, 194, 199, 200, 208
and "degeneration", 94, 103, 109, 169, 254, 339, 359
as generic concept, 22n1, 39–40, 43, 44, 56, 66, 169
interrelationship between antifascism and 5, 7, 16–17, 21, 66, 81, 288–91, 292–96, 297–305, 312–13, 316–20, 337–48, 360–61
in interwar years, 2, 3, 5, 16, 19, 39–41, 42, 44, 45, 55, 66, 67, 74, 79, 82, 145, 217, 289, 291, 297
and leisure, 19, 94–114, 181, 202
in national perspective, 1–2, 5–6
and semi-fascist movements, 169, 170, 171, 185, 266
and social Darwinism, 1, 272
symbolism and rituals of, 3, 15, 99, 100, 102, 105, 107, 112, 119, 125, 128, 151, 171, 180, 202
as transnational phenomenon, 1–7, 13–19, 39–43, 51, 55–56, 66–67, 216–17, 297, 361
and youth, 2, 14, 15, 19, 23n6, 95, 104–7, 109, 110, 112–13, 119–134, 135n1, 143, 146, 150–57, 181, 194, 195, 197, 198, 202, 203, 205, 220, 221, 222, 250, 274, 359
fascists
asymmetry between (dissents, disagreements), 15, 20, 23n6, 145, 152, 158–59, 168, 171, 172, 178, 182, 184, 185–86, 228, 251–55, 355–59, 361

and conservatives, 8, 9, 186, 266–67, 272–73, 275, 276, 277, 359–60
and their ideal of a "new man", 8, 40, 41, 104, 119–20, 128, 143, 159, 193, 197, 267
and their vision of a "new Europe", 19, 21, 41, 122, 123, 133, 168, 184, 204, 207, 243–46, 248–55, 264–77, 279n25, 358
and their vision of a "New Order", 17, 18, 21, 41–43, 45, 47, 48, 49, 53, 55–56, 126, 133–34, 143, 244, 246, 251–54, 264, 267, 270–71
Febvre, Lucien, 5
Finchelstein, Federico, 39
Finland, 122, 270, 274
Fioravanzo, Monica, 18, 20, 255, 358
France, 13, 50, 69, 71, 77, 148, 192, 193, 194, 195, 198, 200, 201, 205, 207, 222, 228, 251, 270, 294, 296, 301, 317
Action Française, 68, 70, 195, 220, 229, 294
and German Fascism (Fascist Germany), 7, 10, 12, 198, 202–3, 204, 206, 213n76, 304, 343
and Italian Fascism (Fascist Italy), 7, 12, 247, 248, 294, 295, 322, 323, 324
Franco, Francisco, 146, 149, 178, 299, 358. *See also* Spain; Spanish Civil War
Freytag, Hans, 145

G
gender. *See* women and gender
Germany (Nazi Germany), 3, 7, 10, 11–13, 41–42, 43, 45, 46–47, 81, 143, 146, 159, 169, 178, 185, 203, 216, 247, 253–55, 265–67, 274–77, 298, 358
Auswärtiges Amt (AA), 146–48, 155, 158
battle of Stalingrad (and its implications), 123, 132, 183, 252–53, 265

and Catholic Church, 152, 156, 172
Deutscher Akademischer
  Austauschdienst (DAAD),
  148, 159
Gestapo, 149, 175, 178, 342, 346
Hitlerjugend (HJ), 120, 121, 125,
  129, 133, 150, 151, 153–57, 159,
  202
and Italy (Fascist Italy), compared,
  10, 45, 46–47, 81, 203, 228, 298,
  357–58
and Italy (Fascist Italy), interaction
  with, 4, 11, 12, 173, 182, 183,
  246, 247–50, 251–55, 270, 294,
  299, 357
Kraft durch Freude (KdF), 148,
  150, 153, 159, 174, 181
as model (influence on others),
  10–12, 15, 17, 42–43, 47–50,
  51–55, 107, 130, 133, 144, 146,
  148, 151–53, 154, 159–60,
  161n20, 174, 181, 198, 201–3,
  205, 216–17, 224, 254, 266, 358,
  360
Nationalsozialistische Deutsche
  Arbeiterpartei (NSDAP), 9,
  10, 49, 148, 155, 170–71, 173,
  224, 225, 227, 228, 244, 246,
  338, 340
population policy (anti-Semitism,
  eugenics, racism), 21, 42,
  47–48, 49–50, 55, 268–69, 270,
  275, 276, 277, 279n25
Reichssicherheitshauptamt
  (RSHA), 178, 182, 183
and "special path" thesis
  (*Sonderweg*), 43
SS (Schutzstaffel), 6, 13, 54–55,
  161n20, 174, 175, 183, 184, 198,
  234, 361
Stahlhelm, 9, 73, 359
Volksgemeinschaft ideal in, 81, 277
See also Hitler, Adolf
Ginsborg, Paul, 101
Giustizia e Libertà (GL), 16, 21, 315,
  320, 327n18, 336–45, 347–48
Goebbels, Joseph, 11, 123, 182–83,
  227, 252, 265, 274, 298, 358

Göring, Hermann, 174
Gottlieb, Julie, 110
Gravelli, Asvero, 23n6
Great Depression, 67, 77
Greece, 3, 77, 79, 87n50, 229, 251,
  264, 268
Griffin, Roger, 40, 169, 194, 203, 217
Grunert, Robert, 270–71

H
Habicht, Theodor, 171, 172, 173
Habsburg Monarchy, 124, 170, 176
Halat, Luka, 120
Hassell, Ulrich von, 269–70, 272
Hausmann, Frank-Rutger, 274,
  280n43
Heinen, Armin, 221, 224, 225, 230,
  231,
Hertz, Paul, 336, 338, 341–42, 349n3
Hilferding, Rudolf, 336, 338, 341,
  342–43, 345, 346, 348n1, 349n3,
  352n51
histoire croisée, 75. *See also* entangled
  history
Hitler, Adolf, 3, 4, 7, 9, 10, 15, 45, 81,
  122, 171, 172, 173, 174, 178, 179,
  182–85, 193, 197, 198, 201, 204,
  207, 225, 244, 246, 247, 248, 249,
  255, 267, 268, 269, 273, 276, 301,
  303, 356, 357, 358
Hitler-Stalin Pact, 181, 289, 301–3
Holocaust (extermination of Jews),
  17–18. *See also* anti-Semitism;
  Jews
Horn, Gerd-Rainer, 301
Horthy, Miklós, 3, 52, 184, 273, 293,
  358. *See also* Hungary
Hoyningen-Huene, Oswald von,
  144, 145, 146, 148–50, 155, 156
Hungary, 3–4, 50, 52–53, 122–23, 124,
  179, 182, 184, 185, 221, 223, 253,
  270, 271, 272, 293, 296, 358. *See
  also* Austria-Hungary
hybrid (hybridization), 4, 39, 40, 45,
  51, 56, 69, 79, 80, 88n63, 169, 291

I
imperialism, 42, 107, 152, 250, 358

International Labour Organization
  (ILO), 7, 74, 76, 82
Iordachi, Constantin, 134
Italo-Abyssinian War (1935–36), 4,
  12, 100, 108, 174, 195, 248, 249,
  288, 291, 295, 299, 357
Italy, Fascist (Italian Fascism), 2–3,
  4, 7–12, 15, 16, 19–21, 22n1,
  44–45, 47, 65, 73, 87n49, 96, 103,
  143, 174, 203, 216, 228, 243–45,
  247–49, 251–55, 295, 337, 355,
  356–58, 360
  and Britain, 7–8, 9, 19, 46, 48–49,
    95–97, 107–8, 109–10, 113–14,
    247, 248, 357, 360
  dopolavoro, 96, 97–104, 174
  Fasci Italiani all'Estero, 8, 9, 20,
    77, 243
  and Germany (Nazi Germany),
    compared, 10, 13, 45, 46–47,
    81, 203, 228, 282n64, 298,
    355–56, 358
  and Germany (Nazi Germany),
    interaction with, 2–3, 4, 9,
    11, 12, 173, 182, 183, 244, 246,
    247–50, 251–55, 294, 299, 355,
    356, 357, 358
  Gioventù Italiana del Littorio
    (GIL), 105, 120, 121, 122, 125–
    26, 129, 133, 136–37n43
  "March on Rome", 2, 4, 45, 46, 179,
    288, 359
  as model (influence on others),
    2–3, 4, 7–9, 11–12, 15, 17, 19,
    46, 73–74, 77–81, 96–97, 100,
    107, 125–26, 130, 133, 144, 146,
    152, 170, 171–72, 179–80, 198,
    205, 216–17, 226, 245, 248, 266,
    357, 358, 360
  Partito Nazionale Fascista (PNF),
    73, 96, 105, 108, 121, 358
  See also Italo-Abyssinian War;
    Mussolini, Benito

J
Japan, 17, 121, 267, 288
Jews, 3, 7, 11, 13, 19, 20, 21, 42, 47–55,
  123, 133, 177, 179, 180, 181, 182,
  186, 207–8, 218, 220, 221–24, 226,
  228–30, 232–33, 254, 269, 271,
  276, 356, 357, 358, 361. *See also*
  anti-Semitism
  annihilation of, 13, 19, 20, 179, 186,
    358
  "Jewish question", 42, 48, 207, 229

K
Kallis, Aristotle, 18, 56
Kaplan, Alice, 206
Kiev, 176
Koch, Hannsjoachim Wolfgang, 123
Kocka, Jürgen, 75, 114n1
Kocks, Anna Lena, 18, 19, 114, 358
Konovalets, Ievhen, 177
Koskenniemi, Veikko Antero, 274

L
Leon, Gheorge N., 272–73, 274
Levy, Carl, 273
Lewis, David Stephen, 113
liberalism, 3, 6, 8, 9, 13, 14, 16, 41,
  43– 45, 47, 55, 68–71, 75–78, 82,
  94, 101, 143–44, 159, 169, 172,
  194, 225, 243, 246–47, 251, 272,
  296, 299, 314, 322, 324n2, 337–39,
  341, 343–45, 347, 359
Lisbon, 145, 147, 148, 149, 150, 151,
  152, 155, 156, 157
Lithuania, 3–4, 12, 176, 178, 228
Loewenstein, Karl, 5, 16
London, 11, 65, 69, 108, 157, 290, 291,
  299, 317, 321, 323, 336, 344, 346
Luks, Leonid, 292–93
Lussu, Emilio, 315, 316, 321, 349n5
Lviv, 12, 176, 177, 178

M
Macek, Alojz, 123, 125, 127, 128
Maček, Vladko, 124, 273
Madotto, Silvia, 16, 18, 21, 324, 360
Madrid, 123, 124, 186, 275, 299
Maier, Charles, 68n30
Malvić, Zvonimir, 128, 131
Mann, Thomas, 276, 303
Manuilsky, Dmitri, 300
Marchesi, Concetto, 319

Marxism, 58n30, 194, 226, 340, 343, 344, 345–46, 347, 350n13, 352n51. *See also* communism
Massis, Henri, 195, 199, 200, 201
Matteotti Giacomo, 295, 314
Matzenauer, Otto J., 127–28, 132
Maurras, Charles, 68–69, 195, 196, 200, 201–2, 204
Mel'nyk, Andrii, 177
Meneghetti, Egidio, 319–20, 323
militarism, 103, 104, 169
Miljan, Goran, 18, 19, 134–35, 359
Modigliani, Giuseppe Emanuele, 342–43, 350n23
Morgan, Philip, 223, 238n92
Moscow, 290, 291, 296, 300, 303, 360
Mosley, Maud, 111
Mosley, Oswald, 9, 10, 23n6, 46, 48–49, 96, 100, 106, 109–10, 358, 359
Mosse, George L., 40
Moṭa, Ion, 20, 180, 217–21, 223, 225–34, 235n10, 357, 361
Münzenberg, Willi, 291, 296, 300, 303–4, 360
Mussert, Anton, 11, 48, 193, 358
Mussolini, Benito, 3, 4, 7, 8, 9, 10, 12, 13, 20, 43, 45, 46, 79, 96, 102, 106, 108, 122, 152, 171, 173, 177, 178, 182, 183, 196, 198, 205, 225, 226, 228, 243, 244, 246, 248, 249, 252, 253, 254, 295, 337, 338, 344, 355, 356, 357, 358. *See also* Italy

N
nationalism, 15, 21, 40, 54, 55, 68, 69, 72, 75, 77, 103, 114, 169, 171, 176, 180, 186, 199, 203, 231, 232, 302, 355, 359
Nelson, Leonard, 352n51
neo-fascism, 17–18
Netherlands, 11, 228, 280n43
   and Germany, 10, 48, 271, 356
   Nationaal Socialistische Beweging (NSB), 11, 17, 48
"New Order", 17, 18, 21, 39, 41, 43, 45, 47, 48, 49, 53, 55, 56, 126, 134, 143, 244, 251, 252, 253, 254, 264, 267, 270, 271

New York, 9, 65, 347
Ninhos, Cláudia, 18, 19, 160, 359
Nitti, Fausto, 317, 349n5
Nobre Guedes, Francisco, 154, 155, 156, 157, 158, 164n81
Nolte, Ernst, 40, 235n2
Norway, 11, 12, 13, 123, 228, 271, 280n43, 358, 359

O
Olechnowicz, Andrzej, 300
Ollenhauer, Erich, 338, 346, 347
Orano, Paolo, 245, 248–49
Orestano, Francesco, 245, 246–47, 252, 259n43
Oršanić, Ivan, 120, 122, 123, 128, 133–34
Orwell, George, 5, 17

P
Padua, 21, 251, 314, 318, 319, 320, 321, 323
Paris, 4, 9, 195, 201, 205, 206, 219, 222, 290, 291, 294, 299, 300, 302, 303, 304, 315, 316, 317, 322, 336, 337, 342, 344, 345, 346, 347
Pasetti, Matteo, 18, 19, 82, 357
Pauley, Bruce, 174
Pavelić, Ante, 53, 124–25, 178, 273, 358
Paxton, Robert, 17
Payne, Stanley, 292
Pieracki, Bronisław, 10, 177
Piłsudski, Józef, 3–4
Pirenne, Henry, 5
Pius XI (pope), 78
Platon, Mircea, 230–31
Poland, 3–4, 12, 52, 54, 79, 176, 177, 223, 224, 270, 296, 302
Pons, Silvio, 302
populism, 169, 180
Portugal (Salazar regime), 3, 71, 77, 79, 80, 82, 142–59, 193, 200, 228, 357
   and Britain 144, 149, 155–56, 157, 158, 160
   and Catholic Church, 142, 152, 156, 157–58

and Germany, 19, 143–60
Prague, 132, 176, 224, 337, 338, 342, 343, 344, 347
Preto, Rolão, 80, 144
Primo de Rivera, Miguel, 72, 74, 198. *See also* Spain
propaganda, 3, 5, 9, 11, 14, 15, 17, 18, 19, 65, 66, 67, 76, 77, 80, 96–103, 106, 108, 109–10, 112, 123, 131, 132, 143, 148, 152, 159, 160, 172, 180, 207, 220, 225, 251, 266, 291, 294–95, 298–300, 302, 314, 320, 322, 337, 338, 347

Q

Quisling, Vidkun, 23n6, 121, 271, 358, 359

R

racism, 4, 8, 11, 15, 20, 21, 54, 168, 169, 176, 180, 186, 228, 229–30, 269, 275, 356. *See also* anti-Semitism
Radek, Karl, 293
religion, 15, 18, 20, 40, 52, 53, 54, 68, 69, 87n52, 124, 169, 180, 185, 193, 199, 229, 230–33, 237n59, 345. *See also* Catholicism
Rensen, Marleen, 18, 20, 209, 357
resistance, 16, 21, 114, 133, 186, 198, 204, 293, 304, 313, 317–24, 324–25n2, 337, 339, 344, 345. *See also* antifascism
Ribbentrop, Joachim von, 252, 253, 265, 270, 356
Ribbentrop-Molotov Pact. *See* Hitler-Stalin Pact
Richert, Gertrud, 150–51
Riding, Alan, 206
Rinner, Erich, 341, 346, 347
Rodgers, Daniel, 77
Romania, 20, 48, 179, 181, 183, 184, 219, 220, 222, 223, 224, 228, 232, 253, 361
    and Germany, 179, 183, 185, 225–226, 234, 356
    Legion of Archangel Michael (Iron Guard), 13, 14, 20, 46, 48, 82,
168, 169, 177, 180–86, 193, 217, 218, 220–34, 238n92, 356, 357
    See also Antonescu, Ion; Codreanu, Corneliu; Moța, Ion
Rome, 2, 4, 7, 8, 9, 11, 20, 45, 46, 48, 49, 74, 78, 96, 108, 179, 183, 197, 226–28, 245, 246, 247, 248, 249, 250, 251, 252, 254, 255, 289, 321, 357, 358, 359
Roosevelt, Franklin Delano, 82, 121–22, 360
Rosenberg, Alfred, 178–79, 246, 254–55, 270
Rosselli, Carlo, 16, 315, 316, 327n18, 336, 339, 340, 341, 342–43, 344–45, 349n5, 350n20, 351n24, 360
Rossoliński-Liebe, Grzegorz, 18, 20, 22, 187, 356
Russia, 176, 177, 199, 221, 290, 291, 292, 298, 302
    Russian Empire, 176
Rychlík, Jan, 124

S

Sachsenhausen, 175, 178, 179, 184, 356
    Zellenbau, 178
Salazar, António de Oliveira, 79, 80, 142, 143, 145, 149, 151, 152, 157, 158, 164n81, 164n89, 193, 196. *See also* Portugal
Salvemini, Gaetano, 65–66, 316, 336, 338–39, 342, 349n5
Schirach, Baldur von, 121, 122, 156
Schmitt, Carl, 274
Schuschnigg, Kurt, 172, 174–76, 185, 186, 356. *See also* Austria
Seipel, Ignaz, 68
Sima, Horia, 181–84, 185, 186, 235n10, 356
Skillen, Fiona, 111
Slovakia, 50, 52, 79, 120, 126, 127, 128, 129, 131, 133, 177, 178, 270, 281–82n60, 359
    Hlinka Party, 12, 19, 124, 169, 176, 177, 186
    Hlinka Youth (HM), 120, 123, 124, 125–33

Smith, Denis Mack, 295
social democracy. *See* democracy
Social Democratic Party of Germany
in exile (Sopade), 336–37, 338,
339, 340–41, 342–44, 346–47, 348,
349n7
Sofia, 272
Soviet Union, 3, 6, 12, 13, 20, 54,
164n89, 177, 181–82, 185, 204,
207, 271, 274, 289, 291–93, 295–
96, 297, 300–305, 356
Spain, 3, 13, 71, 74–77, 146, 149,
159, 198–200, 228, 231–32, 270,
291, 299, 315. *See also* Franco,
Francisco; Primo de Rivera,
Miguel; Spanish Civil War
Spanish Civil War, 47, 143, 149, 154,
159, 180, 195, 198–200, 204, 217,
231–32, 267, 288, 291, 299, 301,
315, 319, 340, 344–45, 357
Stalinism (Stalin, Joseph), 291–93,
297, 300–304
Stampfer, Friedrich, 336, 338, 341,
343, 344, 346, 347, 348n2
Starace, Achille, 96, 97
Steinmetz, George, 85n35
Sternhell, Zeev, 84n17, 193
Stets'ko, Iaroslav, 177–79, 186
Stone, Dan, 16, 55
Strachey, St. Leo, 8
Switzerland, 77, 177, 228, 251
Szálasi, Ferenc, 184, 189n63

T
Taylor, Matthew, 112
Tiso, Jozef, 79, 281–82n60
Tobler, Hans Werner, 318
transnational history, 6, 41, 51, 55,
66, 76, 80, 85n35, 87–88n54, 289
Trentin, Silvio, 21, 313, 314–24,
328n20, 330n45, 336, 339, 342
Tucker, William, 211n43

U
Ukraine, 4, 7, 11, 20, 52, 176, 177, 178,
179, 188n25
and Germany, 176–79, 185–86, 356,
358

Organization of Ukrainian
Nationalists (OUN), 10, 11, 12,
169, 176–79, 184, 186, 358
Ukrainian Insurgent Armee
(UPA), 179
ultranationalism, 2, 4, 40, 168, 169,
179–80, 185, 194, 217, 225, 226,
233, 294–95, 298, 299, 355, 359
Umani, Giorgio, 249, 258n29
United States of America, 8, 82,
121–22, 296
universities, 11, 21, 65, 105, 125, 132,
147, 148, 159, 179, 186, 219, 246,
249, 251, 272, 275, 313, 314, 315,
317, 318, 319, 323, 342, 360

V
Valois, Georges, 69, 195
Vatican, 16. *See also* Catholicism
Vienna, 121, 122, 124, 172, 173, 175,
176, 177, 179, 184, 224, 358
violence, 3, 15, 16, 17, 18, 21, 41–43,
47, 52–56, 103, 111, 112, 142–43,
168, 169, 176, 207, 220, 249, 293,
298
völkisch, 9, 21, 48, 170, 266–67, 269,
271–73, 275, 276, 277, 294
Vogel, Hans, 338, 346–47

W
Waddington, Lorna, 295–96
Warsaw, 10
Weimar Republic, 9, 81, 147, 148,
296, 340, 341–42, 345, 357
Wilhelm, Theodor, 269
Witt, Mary Ann Frese, 204
women and gender, 19, 94, 98, 100–
103, 105–7, 110–11, 112–13
working class, 45, 94, 97, 101, 103,
107, 112, 293, 294, 297, 300, 301,
339, 342, 344, 345, 352n52
World War I (and its immediate
aftermath), 9, 67–72, 82, 94, 101,
103, 170, 176, 179, 219, 243, 293,
297
World War II, 3, 4, 12–13, 17, 54, 56,
244, 264, 272, 356

Y

youth organizations. *See* fascism and
    youth
Yugoslavia, 10, 53, 54, 124, 136n33,
    358

Z

Zagreb, 127, 128, 129, 132
Zetkin, Clara, 293, 294
Zinoviev, Georgi, 293

www.ingramcontent.com/pod-product-compliance
Lightning Source LLC
Chambersburg PA
CBHW070901030426
42336CB00014BA/2280